FOURTH EDITION

THE
SOCIAL
DIMENSION
OF WESTERN CIVILIZATION
VOLUME 1

Readings to
THE SEVENTEENTH CENTURY

FOURTH EDITION

THE SOCIAL DIMENSION

OF WESTERN CIVILIZATION
VOLUME 1

Readings to
THE SEVENTEENTH CENTURY

RICHARD M. GOLDEN
University of North Texas

BEDFORD/ST. MARTIN'S
Boston/New York

For Bedford/St. Martin's

History Editor: Katherine E. Kurzman
Developmental Editor: Charisse Kiino
Associate Production Editor: Jessica Zorn
Production Supervisor: Dennis J. Conroy
Marketing Manager: Charles Cavaliere
Art Director: Lucy Krikorian
Text Design: Anna George and ErinBen Graphics
Copy Editor: Judith Green Voss
Cover Design: Ann Gallager
Cover Art: Camera Degli Sposi: The Meeting, by Andrea Mantegna. Palazzo Cucole, Mantua, Italy/Superstock
Composition: ComCom
Printing and Binding: Haddon Craftsmen, Inc.

President: Charles H. Christensen
Editorial Director: Joan E. Feinberg
Director of Editing, Design, and Production: Marcia Cohen
Managing Editor: Erica T. Appel

Library of Congress Catalog Card Number: 98-86770

4 3 2 1 0 9
f e d c b a

For information, write: Bedford/St. Martin's, 75 Arlington Street, Boston, MA 02116 (617-426-7440)

ISBN: 0-312-17880-8

Acknowledgments

Acknowledgments and copyrights are at the back of the book on pages 379–80, which constitute an extension of the copyright page.

PREFACE

The Social Dimension of Western Civilization, Fourth Edition (previously entitled *Social History of Western Civilization*), is a two-volume reader for Western Civilization courses. The essays in each volume deal with social history because I believe that the most original and significant work of the past three decades has been done in this area and because some Western Civilization textbooks tend to slight social history in favor of the more traditional political, intellectual, and cultural history, though this bias is changing.

Throughout the past twenty years in the classroom, I have used a number of anthologies, but the selections often assume a degree of background knowledge that the typical student does not possess. To make *The Social Dimension* better suited to students, I have sifted through hundreds of essays to find those that are both challenging and accessible, interesting and significant. To enhance the readability of the selected articles, I have included more than five hundred gloss notes that translate foreign words or identify individuals and terms that students might not recognize. All the footnotes are therefore my own unless otherwise indicated. Based on my classroom experience, gloss notes are invaluable to students using anthologies.

A Western Civilization anthology cannot be all things to all instructors and students, but I have consciously tried to make these two volumes flexible enough to work in a wide variety of Western Civilization courses. The fourth edition's broader range of themes and its expanded notion of Europe should meet more instructors' needs in that the coverage is now more tightly correlated to survey texts. Some historians argue that Western civilization began with the Greeks, but I have included in Volume One a section on Mesopotamia, Israel, and Egypt for the courses that begin there. In addition, both volumes contain material on the sixteenth and seventeenth centuries because instructors and institutions divide Western Civilization courses differently.

In this fourth edition, certain elements have been retained and strengthened, while new features have been added. It is my hope that instructors will find this edition not only more flexible but also more helpful in sparking class discussion and making thematic comparisons among the essays.

New Readings. In preparing this edition, there always seemed to be somewhere a more attractive article on every topic, as is the case every time I revise. While maintaining a balance between classical pieces in social history and those on the cutting edge of recent scholarship, I have changed fourteen of this volume's twenty-four essays. I have based the substitutions not only on my own searches but also on feedback from those who have used previous editions. The new readings, on subjects such as food, Gnosticism, warfare, table manners, ritual murder, sanitation, the body, Carnival, and weddings, reflect the active nature of historical scholarship today.

Thoroughly Revised Apparatus. In this fourth edition, I have extensively revised the part introductions as well as the selection headnotes, incorporating pertinent prereading questions to guide students through the essays and to encourage active reading about the problems and issues raised.

Social History Emphasis. Throughout the introductory and headnote material, I discuss the practice of social history — its growth and importance as well as its goals within the discipline. For each selection, I mention the types of sources the author used, in order to show students that social historians consult a variety of evidence.

Making Connections Questions. Three themes — in this volume, religion and ritual, sexuality and the body, and women and the family — have been singled out, with an article on each theme carried over from part to part. New Making Connections questions at the end of particular selections link these themes over historical periods, encouraging students to think about change over time while comparing various cultures and peoples.

Topical Table of Contents. This alternate table of contents groups all the selections under the topics they discuss, enabling instructors and students to compare articles according to theme.

Instructor's Manual. Prepared by Denis Paz, who has used this anthology in class since 1988, *Teaching Suggestions:* THE SOCIAL DIMENSION OF WESTERN CIVILIZATION includes discussion questions, topics for term papers, and student exercises. The manual also has useful handouts that show students how to underline and annotate a reading and a correlation chart that relates each essay to a relevant chapter in the major Western Civilization textbooks currently on the market.

Acknowledgments

Many people suggested essays to me, critiqued what I wrote, and helped in other ways as well. I thank Ove Anderson, Jay Crawford, Fara Driver, Patricia Easley, Phillip Garland, Laurie Glover, Tully Hunter, Christopher Koontz, John Leonard, Laurie McDowell, and James Sanchez. Especially generous with their time and comments on the first three editions were Philip Adler, Kathryn Babayan, William Beik, Robert Bireley, Richard Bulliet, Elizabeth D. Carney, Suzanne A. Desan, Lawrence Estaville, Hilda Golden, Leonard Greenspoon, Alan Grubb, Christopher

Guthrie, Sarah Hanley, George Huppert, Thomas Kuehn, Charles Lippy, Donald McKale, Steven Marks, Victor Matthews, John A. Mears, William Murnane, David Nicholas, Thomas F. X. Noble, James Sack, Carol Thomas, and Roy Vice. Steven D. Cooley, Charles T. Evans, Anita Guerrini, Benjamin Hudson, Jonathan Katz, Donna T. McCaffrey, Maureen Melody, Kathryn E. Meyer, Lohr E. Miller, Gerald M. Schnabel, Paul Teverow, Sara W. Tucker, and Lindsay Wilson reviewed the third edition or responded to questionnaires for preparing this edition. Edward Coomes, Henry Eaton, Lee Huddleston, Terje Leiren, Marilyn Morris, Laura Stern, and Harold Tanner provided generous assistance with the fourth edition.

The following historians gave helpful feedback via questionnaires or reviews for *The Social Dimension:* Ann T. Allen, University of Louisville; David Burns, Moraine Valley Community College; Leslie Derfler, Florida Atlantic University; John E. Dreifort, Wichita State University; Amanda Eurich, Western Washington University; William J. Events Jr., Champlain College; Marie T. Gingras, University of Colorado at Denver; Christopher E. Guthrie, Tarleton State University; Carla Hay, Marquette University; Daniel W. Hollis III, Jacksonville State University; John Hunt, Joseph College; Katharine D. Kennedy, Agnes Scott College; Thomas Kuehn, Clemson University; Joyce M. Mastboom, Cleveland State University; John McCole, University of Oregon; David Nicholas, Clemson University; Philip Otterness, Warren Wilson College; Catherine Patterson, University of Houston; Dolores Davidson Peterson, Foothill College; Lowell Satre, Youngstown State University; Stephanie Sherwell, Charles County Community College; Malcolm Smuts, University of Massachusetts at Boston; Larissa Taylor, Colby College; Michael C. Weber, Northern Essex Community College; Michael Wolfe, Pennsylvania State University at Altoona; Anne York, Youngstown State University; and Ronald Zupko, Marquette University.

I have been fortunate in working with publishers and editors who show wonderful empathy for history and for historians. My experiences have been completely positive, and I thank all of the good people at Bedford/St. Martin's: the publishers, Chuck Christensen and Joan Feinberg, who have a feeling and appreciation for both books and the book market; Becky Anderson, Molly Kalkstein, and Tom Pierce, Editorial Assistants, who have always been professional and efficient; Charisse Kiino, who as Developmental Editor did an absolutely superb job in helping me with a rather thorough revision; and Katherine Kurzman, Sponsoring Editor, who expertly and gently helped guide the project over a two-year period. Erica Appel, Jessica Zorn, and Judy Voss handled expertly production and copy editing, while Donna Dennison designed the new book covers and Fred Courtright handled permissions.

Denis Paz, an eminent social historian who is more familiar with this anthology than anyone else, has given me for all four editions his perspectives as a historian and a professor. His help has been invaluable.

Finally, I have been blessed with the support of my wife, Hilda, and my three children — Davina, Irene, and Jeremy. They have sharpened my perception of social life and have always given me their love. I dedicate this book to them.

CONTENTS

PREFACE   v

TOPICAL TABLE OF CONTENTS   xv

INTRODUCTION   xix

PART ONE

MESOPOTAMIA, ISRAEL, AND EGYPT

Vern L. Bullough, Brenda Shelton, and Sarah Slavin, FORMATION OF
WESTERN ATTITUDES TOWARD WOMEN   5

*"Women legally were property. They were neither to be seen nor
heard. Monogamy was the normal way of life, but monogamy meant
something different for the man than for the woman."*

Isaac Mendelsohn, SLAVERY IN THE ANCIENT NEAR EAST   17

*"Poverty or debt drove people to sell their children first and then
themselves into slavery. . . . For those driven from the soil by war,
famine, or economic misfortune, a man or woman had only one recourse to save himself from starvation, and that was self-sale into
slavery."*

Jean Soler, WHY THE HEBREWS KEPT KOSHER   27

*"There must be . . . a relationship between the idea [man] has formed
of specific items of food and the image he has of himself and his place*

in the universe. There is a link between a people's dietary habits and its perception of the world."

K. A. Kitchen, Workaday Life under Ramesses the Great   40

"A small group of men and their families lived apart, as a closed community, in their special village. . . . These men [worked] deep underground in a valley utterly barren of any sign of natural life — the Valley of the Kings."

PART TWO

CLASSICAL GREECE AND ROME

William J. Baker, Organized Greek Games   61

"The Olympics were the Super Bowl, the World Cup, the Heavyweight Championship of Greek athletics. By Olympic standards were the other festivals judged; at Olympia the sweet 'nectar of victory' filled athletes with self-esteem and accorded them public acclaim."

K. J. Dover, Classical Greek Attitudes to Sexual Behavior   70

"It seems to have been believed not only that women enjoyed sexual intercourse more intensely than men, but also that experience of intercourse put the woman more under the man's power than it put him under hers, and that if not segregated and guarded women would be insatiably promiscuous."

Suzanne Dixon, Roman Marriage   80

"The ideal of harmony was almost as strongly embedded in the Roman notion of marriage as was its reproductive purpose. . . . Marriage was viewed . . . as a partnership in which each side supported the other and which was ideally harmonious and long-lasting."

Paul Veyne, Pleasures and Excesses in the Roman Empire   101

"It is widely but mistakenly believed that antiquity was a Garden of Eden from which repression was banished, Christianity having yet to insinuate the worm of sin into the forbidden fruit. Actually, the pagans were paralyzed by prohibitions."

Alex Scobie, Slums, Sanitation, and Mortality in the Roman World   117

"Lavishly ornamented public baths, temples, and amphitheatres no doubt produced in the poor a momentary forgetfulness of fetid,

cramped, living quarters, but could hardly be considered as genuine substitutes for what must justifiably be called slums."

Elaine Pagels, GOD THE FATHER/GOD THE MOTHER: THE GNOSTIC GOSPELS AND THE SUPPRESSION OF EARLY CHRISTIAN FEMINISM   141

"Jewish, Christian, and Islamic theologians today are quick to point out that God is not to be considered in sexual terms at all. Yet . . . who, growing up with Jewish or Christian tradition, has escaped the distinct impression that God is masculine?"

PART THREE

THE MIDDLE AGES

Georges Duby, RURAL ECONOMY AND COUNTRY LIFE IN THE MEDIEVAL WEST   161

"One fact is outstanding: in the civilization of the ninth and tenth centuries the rural way of life was universal. Entire countries, like England and almost all the Germanic lands, were absolutely without towns."

David Herlihy, MEDIEVAL CHILDREN   169

"Paradoxically . . . the growing complexities of social life engendered not truly a discovery but an idealization of childhood: the affirmation of the sentimental belief that childhood is . . . a blessed time and the happiest moment of human existence."

Jacques Rossiaud, SEXUAL ORDER AND THE SUBVERSION OF YOUTH   184

"In most French cities . . . a male-oriented morality encouraged 'the boys' . . . to form aggressive bands that disturbed order. These gangs . . . roamed the city in the evening . . . taunting the night watch, chasing girls, and organizing a rape."

David Herlihy, THE FAMILY IN RENAISSANCE ITALY   194

"Frequent deaths undermined the durability and stability of the basic familial relations — between husband and wife, and parents and children. High mortalities threatened the very survival of numerous family lines."

John Keegan, THE FACE OF BATTLE: AGINCOURT, OCTOBER 25TH, 1415   207

"It is a victory of the weak over the strong, of the common soldier over the mounted knight, of resolution over bombast, of the desperate, cornered and far from home, over the proprietorial and cocksure."

Norbert Elias, THE DEVELOPMENT OF MANNERS   229

> *"To use the hand to wipe one's nose was a matter of course. Hand-kerchiefs did not yet exist. But at table certain care should be exercised; and one should on no account blow one's nose into the table-cloth. Avoid lip-smacking and snorting."*

R. Po-Chia Hsia, A RITUAL MURDER TRIAL OF JEWS IN GERMANY   237

> *"The crucial question concerns not a murder; at issue is the fabrication of the 'event' of a ritual murder out of diverse fragments of social reality: the discovery of the bodies, the long-standing suspicion of Jews, their incarceration and judicial torture, and their execution."*

PART FOUR

EARLY MODERN EUROPE

William H. McNeill, TRANSOCEANIC DISEASE EXCHANGES, 1500–1700   257

> *"A 90 per cent drop in population within 120 years . . . as happened in Mexico and Peru, carries with it drastic psychological and cultural consequences. Faith in established institutions and beliefs cannot easily withstand such disaster; skills and knowledge disappear."*

Edward Muir, CARNIVAL, CHARIVARI, AND RITES OF VIOLENCE   271

> *"The very battle between Carnival and Lent introduced the idea of a world in which the normal rules of social order and the pieties of Christian life were disputed and mocked."*

Merry Wiesner, NUNS, WIVES, AND MOTHERS: WOMEN AND
THE REFORMATION IN GERMANY   288

> *"Women's role in the Reformation . . . was largely determined by what might be termed 'personal' factors — a woman's status as a nun or laywoman, her marital status, her social and economic class, her occupation."*

Sara F. Matthews Grieco, THE BODY, APPEARANCE, AND SEXUALITY   308

> *"In Italy, France, Spain, Germany, and England the basic aesthetic was the same: white skin, blond hair, red lips and cheeks, black eyebrows. The neck and hands had to be long and slender, the feet small, the waist supple. Breasts were to be firm, round, and white, with rosy nipples."*

Robin Briggs, THE WITCH-FIGURE AND THE SABBAT 329

"Even when reading the actual documents, it can be hard to believe that such [witchcraft] trials really happened, that real people, flesh, blood and bone, were subjected to appalling cruelties in order to convict them of an impossible crime."

Natalie Z. Davis, THE RITES OF VIOLENCE: RELIGIOUS RIOT IN SIXTEENTH-CENTURY FRANCE 346

"A . . . frequent goal of these riots . . . is that of ridding the community of dreaded pollution. The word 'pollution' is often on the lips of the violent, and the concept serves well to sum up the dangers which rioters saw in the dirty and diabolic enemy."

David Cressy, WEDDING CELEBRATIONS IN TUDOR AND STUART ENGLAND 360

"Returned from church, the revellers tackled their feast of beef . . . , mince pies, and custard. . . . Now it was time for the serious business of promiscuous kissing and sexual jesting, with music, dancing, and 'mirth and merry glee.'"

TOPICAL TABLE OF CONTENTS

CHILDREN

David Herlihy, *Medieval Children*   169
Jacques Rossiaud, *Sexual Order and the Subversion of Youth*   184
David Herlihy, *The Family in Renaissance Italy*   194

CRIME

Jacques Rossiaud, *Sexual Order and the Subversion of Youth*   184
R. Po-Chia Hsia, *A Ritual Murder Trial of Jews in Germany*   237
Robin Briggs, *The Witch-Figure and the Sabbat*   329
Natalie Z. Davis, *The Rites of Violence: Religious Riot in Sixteenth-Century France*   346

DISEASE AND DEATH

Alex Scobie, *Slums, Sanitation, and Mortality in the Roman World*   117
John Keegan, *The Face of Battle: Agincourt, October 25th, 1415*   207
R. Po-Chia Hsia, *A Ritual Murder Trial of Jews in Germany*   237
William H. McNeill, *Transoceanic Disease Exchanges, 1500–1700*   257

ENTERTAINMENT AND SPORTS

William J. Baker, *Organized Greek Games*   61

Paul Veyne, *Pleasures and Excesses in the Roman Empire*   101

Edward Muir, *Carnival, Charivari, and Rites of Violence*   271

FAMILY

Vern L. Bullough, Brenda Shelton, and Sarah Slavin, *Formation of Western
Attitudes toward Women*   5

K. J. Dover, *Classical Greek Attitudes to Sexual Behavior*   70

Suzanne Dixon, *Roman Marriage*   80

David Herlihy, *Medieval Children*   169

David Herlihy, *The Family in Renaissance Italy*   194

Merry Wiesner, *Nuns, Wives, and Mothers: Women and the Reformation in Germany*   288

David Cressy, *Wedding Celebrations in Tudor and Stuart England*   360

POPULAR MENTALITIES AND COLLECTIVE ATTITUDES

Vern L. Bullough, Brenda Shelton, and Sarah Slavin, *Formation of Western
Attitudes toward Women*   5

K. J. Dover, *Classical Greek Attitudes to Sexual Behavior*   70

Paul Veyne, *Pleasures and Excesses in the Roman Empire*   101

Jacques Rossiaud, *Sexual Order and the Subversion of Youth*   184

Norbert Elias, *The Development of Manners*   229

Sara F. Matthews Grieco, *The Body, Appearance, and Sexuality*   308

RELIGION AND RITUAL

Jean Soler, *Why the Hebrews Kept Kosher*   27

Elaine Pagels, *God the Father/God the Mother: The Gnostic Gospels and the
Suppression of Early Christian Feminism*   141

R. Po-Chia Hsia, *A Ritual Murder Trial of Jews in Germany*   237

Edward Muir, *Carnival, Charivari, and Rites of Violence*   271

Merry Wiesner, *Nuns, Wives, and Mothers: Women and the Reformation in Germany*   288

Robin Briggs, *The Witch-Figure and the Sabbat* 329

Natalie Z. Davis, *The Rites of Violence: Religious Riot in Sixteenth-Century France* 346

David Cressy, *Wedding Celebrations in Tudor and Stuart England* 360

SEXUALITY AND THE BODY

K. J. Dover, *Classical Greek Attitudes to Sexual Behavior* 70

Paul Veyne, *Pleasures and Excesses in the Roman Empire* 101

Jacques Rossiaud, *Sexual Order and the Subversion of Youth* 184

Edward Muir, *Carnival, Charivari, and Rites of Violence* 271

Sara F. Matthews Grieco, *The Body, Appearance, and Sexuality* 308

SOCIAL CONDITIONS

Isaac Mendelsohn, *Slavery in the Ancient Near East* 17

K. A. Kitchen, *Workaday Life under Ramesses the Great* 40

Paul Veyne, *Pleasures and Excesses in the Roman Empire* 101

Alex Scobie, *Slums, Sanitation, and Mortality in the Roman World* 117

Georges Duby, *Rural Economy and Country Life in the Medieval West* 161

Norbert Elias, *The Development of Manners* 229

URBAN LIFE

Paul Veyne, *Pleasures and Excesses in the Roman Empire* 101

Alex Scobie, *Slums, Sanitation, and Mortality in the Roman World* 117

Jacques Rossiaud, *Sexual Order and the Subversion of Youth* 184

Norbert Elias, *The Development of Manners* 229

Edward Muir, *Carnival, Charivari, and Rites of Violence* 271

VIOLENCE AND WAR

Paul Veyne, *Pleasures and Excesses in the Roman Empire* 101

Jacques Rossiaud, *Sexual Order and the Subversion of Youth* 184

John Keegan, *The Face of Battle: Agincourt, October 25th, 1415* 207

R. Po-Chia Hsia, *A Ritual Murder Trial of Jews in Germany*   237

Natalie Z. Davis, *The Rites of Violence: Religious Riot in Sixteenth-Century France*   346

WOMEN

Vern L. Bullough, Brenda Shelton, and Sarah Slavin, *Formation of Western Attitudes toward Women*   5

K. J. Dover, *Classical Greek Attitudes to Sexual Behavior*   70

Suzanne Dixon, *Roman Marriage*   80

Paul Veyne, *Pleasures and Excesses in the Roman Empire*   101

Elaine Pagels, *God the Father/God the Mother: The Gnostic Gospels and the Suppression of Early Christian Feminism*   141

Jacques Rossiaud, *Sexual Order and the Subversion of Youth*   184

David Herlihy, *The Family in Renaissance Italy*   194

Merry Wiesner, *Nuns, Wives, and Mothers: Women and the Reformation in Germany* 288

Sara F. Matthews Grieco, *The Body, Appearance, and Sexuality*   308

Robin Briggs, *The Witch-Figure and the Sabbat*   329

David Cressy, *Wedding Celebrations in Tudor and Stuart England*   360

WORK AND ECONOMIC LIFE

Isaac Mendelsohn, *Slavery in the Ancient Near East*   17

K. A. Kitchen, *Workaday Life under Ramesses the Great*   40

Georges Duby, *Rural Economy and Country Life in the Medieval West*   161

INTRODUCTION

The selections in this volume deal with the social history of Western civilization from the ancient world to the seventeenth century. Social history encompasses the study of *groups* of people rather than focusing on prominent individuals, such as kings, intellectual giants, and military leaders. Over the last three decades, social historians have examined a host of topics, many of which are included here: the family, women, sex, disease, everyday life, death, social groups (such as the peasantry and nobility), entertainment, work, leisure, popular religion and politics, criminality, the experience of soldiers in war, economic conditions, and collective mentality (the attitudes, beliefs, and assumptions held by a population). Social history, then, sheds light both on previously neglected areas of human experience and on forgotten and nameless people, including minorities and those at the bottom of the social scale. Indeed, some recent historians, perhaps a bit too optimistically, endeavor to write "total history," to include all aspects of people's lives.

Social historians take an analytical approach instead of the narrative and chronological approach generally used by biographers and traditional political historians. Social historians do not attempt to celebrate the heroes and heroines of a nation's history, although that is precisely the type of "feel good" history that many in the public wish to read and to see taught in school systems. They do not glorify any Alamos. Instead, their goal is to re-create and make known the lives of ordinary people. In taking this approach, social historians have expanded their research beyond diaries, personal and government correspondence, and court documents to include such sources as police reports, tax rolls, census schedules, writings by nonelite people, conscription lists, parish registers, marriage contracts, wills, church records, government commissions, records of small businesses, newspapers and magazines, popular literature, oral histories, songs, and material artifacts. By using such a variety of sources, social historians are able to reveal the private and public lives of people in all social groups. The headnotes to the articles in this volume mention some of the types of sources historians have consulted as they strive to explain the social past. Some students may, of course, choose to seek out primary sources and other evidence to research some of the topics covered here, and they may indeed arrive at different conclusions from those of the historians.

Many of the articles treat similar themes, as shown in the Topical Table of Contents. For three of these themes (religion and ritual, sexuality and the body, and women and the family), I have developed Making Connections questions, which link readings to each other so students can begin to make comparisons among countries, cultures, and time periods. These questions will also help students make connections to material in their textbooks and in lectures. It is important to make such comparisons in order to place subjects in perspective and to discern causality and change over time.

Although contemporary problems should not be the sole criterion for a historian's choice of topics, many major issues of social history still exist today, but in different forms. For this reason, the social history of ancient civilizations or the Middle Ages is intrinsically of interest to us as citizens of the twentieth century. Often, an awareness of concerns in present society has led historians to investigate similar problems in the past.

Well-researched and well-written social history should convey excitement, for it makes us vividly aware of the daily lives, habits, and beliefs of our ancestors. In some ways, their patterns of behavior and thought will seem similar to ours, but in other ways our predecessors' actions and values may appear quite different, if not barbaric or alien. It is important to keep in mind that the living conditions and attitudes that exist in the present are not necessarily superior to those of the distant or recent past. Social history does not teach progress. Rather than drawing facile lessons from the daily lives of those who came before us, we might, as historians, attempt to immerse ourselves in their cultures and understand why they lived and acted as they did.

PART ONE

MESOPOTAMIA, ISRAEL, AND EGYPT

Vern L. Bullough, Brenda Shelton, and Sarah Slavin
Isaac Mendelsohn
Jean Soler
K. A. Kitchen

W here did Western civilization begin? Some argue that it began with the Greeks because they were so like us: They questioned all areas of life, they reflected on the human predicament, and they thought historically (that is, some had a sense of change over time and explained developments without recourse to the supernatural). The Greeks invented history, drama, and philosophy and so were the first to tackle in a systematic way the major questions basic to humanity: What are goodness, truth, beauty, justice, love? The Greeks were also the first to study nature as an autonomous and distinct entity, without considering outside, supernatural forces.

In history, science, and philosophy, then, the Greeks parted company with the earlier civilizations of Mesopotamia, Israel, and Egypt. But a cogent argument could be made to include those societies in Western civilization as well. The cultures in what is today known as the Middle East, extending from Egypt to Iran, contributed writing, the alphabet, iron, astronomy, elements of common mathematics, agriculture, monumental architecture, cities, codes of law, and, with the Hebrews, a religion of ethical monotheism. All of these contributions influenced Greco-Roman civilization and thus our own.

Filling the universe with exotic gods, early peoples often seem alien to us. In social life and personal relationships, however, they bear affinities with the Western cultures that followed them. Slavery, for example, was a feature of every ancient society, dying out in the modern West only in 1865 and in the Middle East in the 1970s. Isaac Mendelsohn examines the nature of slavery in Mesopotamia, Israel, and Egypt, noting its universal acceptance and practice.

Pervasive as well was the belief in the inferiority of women, although glimmerings of their relative equality could be found in these early civilizations. Vern L. Bullough, Brenda Shelton, and Sarah Slavin note the differences in the treatment of women in Mesopotamia and Egypt, but both societies oppressed women and maintained negative attitudes toward them. Rancorous debates in the twentieth century echo these convictions.

K. A. Kitchen also points up many similarities between contemporary Western civilization and that of ancient Egypt. He discusses the comfortable lives of the Egyptian workers who labored on the complex of tombs associated with Pharaoh Ramesses II and in so doing illuminates the near universality of certain human desires and actions.

Hebrew culture was similar to other cultures in its imperialism and in its unification of life around religion. The Hebrew religion, though, was unusual in that it is the only ancient religion from the Middle East to survive to the present. Aside from the theological reasons for the continuation of Judaism, its penetration into every aspect of life certainly contributed to its longevity. Slavery, child rearing, and diet all bore the imprint of Hebraic religion. Jean Soler explains how keeping kosher was part of the Hebrew religion's demand for purity.

The selections in Part One address fundamental topics in the social history of Western civilization. They identify common as well as dissimilar features among the civilizations of Mesopotamia, Israel, and Egypt. At the same time, they provide comparisons with conditions of life in later cultures.

FORMATION OF WESTERN ATTITUDES TOWARD WOMEN

Vern L. Bullough, Brenda Shelton, and Sarah Slavin

To better understand later attitudes toward women in Western civilization, Vern L. Bullough, Brenda Shelton, and Sarah Slavin investigate and compare the roles of women in Mesopotamia and ancient Egypt. Vern L. Bullough, professor emeritus at California State University at Northridge, has written widely on the history of human sexuality; Sarah Slavin, a specialist in judicial process and public law, has been interested in women's issues; and Brenda Shelton has written on United States social history. The authors affirm that male oppression of females and the belief in the inferiority of women date from antiquity.

For their sources, the authors rely for the most part on law codes, which have limitations: Males wrote them exclusively, and we do not know to what extent their provisions were actually enforced. Nevertheless, used with proper caution, law codes permit us to see how ancient societies treated and subordinated women. Likewise, religion, always a reflection of culture, preached female inferiority. The inhabitants of the Tigris-Euphrates River valley, whether Sumerians, Babylonians, or Assyrians, treated women as property rather than as persons. What implications did this have for marriage, the treatment of adultery, and the lives of female slaves? That we know the names of only a few Mesopotamian women suggests the tight grip of male dominance in this period; women were rarely able to distinguish themselves as individuals.

Women fared better in Egypt. There was certainly no pretense of equality, but at least Egyptian women had greater standing in law than their Mesopotamian counterparts. What legal rights did Egyptian women have? Do you agree with the authors' reasons for the comparatively higher status of women in Egypt? The most famous Egyptian woman, besides Cleopatra VII, was Hatshepsut, who reigned for approximately twenty years. How did her gender affect her rule?

Vern L. Bullough, Brenda Shelton, and Sarah Slavin, *The Subordinated Sex: A History of Attitudes toward Women* (Athens, GA: University of Georgia Press, 1988), 16–35.

Societies did not permit women to be warriors, for the military was a means to power. The only power attributed to women, other than motherhood, was the ability — or so men thought — to trap, delude, and steer men away from the right path. The Egyptians, for example, revered the faithful wife and doting mother. Why do you think the negative attitudes toward women predominated and became a legacy of ancient times?

The cradle of civilization, or at least of Western civilization, was the river valleys of the Near East (sometimes called the Middle East), particularly in the area extending from modern Egypt to modern Iraq. Attitudes formed in these areas were incorporated into Jewish, Greek, and later Western Roman and Christian attitudes. . . .

It has been said that man's vision of the gods reflects his own vision of himself and his activities. If there is any merit to this statement it seems clear that the inhabitants of the Tigris-Euphrates Valley quite early held man to be superior to woman, and in fact relegated her to being a kind of property. There are hints that in the beginning of Sumerian society women had a much higher status than in the heyday of Sumerian culture. Tiamat, a mother goddess, was a dominant figure, and it was her body that was used to form the earth and the heavens after she was killed by Enlil (called Marduk in the Babylonian versions and Asshur in the Assyrian ones). The blood of Tiamat's consort, Kingu, served to form individual humans. This death of a female goddess and her replacement by a dominant male figure is a common theme in the mythology of many peoples. The meanings of this matricide are unclear, and all we can say for certain is that by the time the Babylonian theology was organized into the form in which it has come down to us, the mother goddess was clearly subordinate to male gods.

The names and positions of the gods changed during different periods of Mesopotamian civilization as differing peoples achieved dominance. There were hundreds of deities but there were two major triads of gods: Anu, Enlil, and Ea; Sin, Shamash, and Ishtar. Over and above them was another god, Marduk or Asshur. The only female in the group was Ishtar, or in Sumerian, Inanna, goddess of war and of love. Like humans, the gods had wives and families, court servants, soldiers, and other retainers. Ishtar, however, remained unmarried. Her lovers were legion, but these unhappy men usually paid dearly for her sexual favors. She was identified with the planet Venus, the morning and evening star, and could arouse the amorous instinct in man, although she also had the power of causing brothers who were on good terms to quarrel among themselves and friends to forget friendship. If she perchance withdrew her influence, "The bull refuses to cover the cow, the ass no longer approaches the she-ass, in the street the man no longer approaches the maidservant." Part of her difficulty was that she did not really know her place. In the poem translated as *Enki and World Order* the god Enki (whose powers are similar to Ea's) assigned the gods various tasks. Ishtar, however, felt left out and complained to Enki. Her complaint applies to woman in general: "Me, the woman, why did you treat differently?/ Me, the holy Inanna, where are my powers?" She was given various tasks as a result, but because she was an unmarried and erotic figure it was no wonder that sacred prostitution formed part of her cult. When she descended to earth she was accompanied by courtesans and prostitutes. The implication might well be . . . that woman was to be either wife and mother or an unmarried professional, a prostitute.

The mere presence of Ishtar, or Inanna, in the heavenly triad is probably striking evidence of the great strength of the forces of nature, which were so deeply rooted in primitive society. She represented the blending of several different characters into one, most obviously the lady of love and the lady of battles, although these different aspects of her powers were worshiped at different places. If Ishtar chose to favor a mere mortal, he could gain fame and riches, and she was much sought after. Sargon, the Akkadian conquerer who lived toward the end of the third millennium B.C., felt himself to be under the protection of Ishtar and believed it was through her influence that he became king. . . .

If the place of women in official mythology was somewhat circumscribed, it was even more so in actual life. Our chief source of information about actual conditions is the various law codes. These might be regarded as the official male view of women since they are essentially male social constructs. . . . Formal law codes are known from Ur-Nammu of the third dynasty of Ur [c. 2050 B.C.] and Lipit Ishtar of Isin [c. 1870 B.C.]. Neither of these codes is preserved completely and their great importance to us lies in the influence they had on later laws. In the Semitic dialects the first law code was that of the town of Eshnunna, dating from about 1800 B.C. The best known, however, was that of Hammurabi (c. 1700 B.C.), which contained about 250 laws. Later from the Assyrian scribes there exists another legal corpus dating from 1100 B.C., which has a long section on women and marriage.

Women legally were property. They were neither to be seen nor heard. Monogamy was the normal way of life, but monogamy meant something different for the man than for the woman. A wife who slept with another man was an adulteress but a man could not only visit prostitutes but in practice also took secondary wives as concubines.[1] Rich men and royalty often had more than one legal wife. Women were always under the control of a male. Until the time of her marriage a girl remained under the protection of her father, who was free to settle her in marriage exactly as he thought fit. Once married she was under the control of her husband. During the marriage ceremony a free woman assumed the veil that she wore from then on outside her home. In fact the veil was the mark of a free woman, and anyone who met a slave or courtesan wearing a veil had the duty of denouncing her. A concubine could only wear a veil on those occasions when she accompanied the legal wife out of doors. It was an offense for a woman to have any dealings in business or to speak to a man who was not a near relation.

---

[1] A concubine is a woman who cohabits with a man to whom she is not married.

Some scholars have argued that the earliest form of marriage required the bridegroom to purchase his bride, emphasizing even further the woman as property. . . .

The economic dependence of the woman upon the male was reinforced by the various provisions allowing her to remarry. In cases where a woman's husband was taken captive and he had not left enough for her to eat, she could live with another man as his wife. If her husband returned, though, she was to go back to him. Any children by the temporary husband remained with him. If, however, the absence of her husband was malicious, motivated by a "hatred of king and country," he had no further claim upon his wife if she took a second husband. Women could also hold property. An unmarried daughter, for example, could be given either a dowry, a share of her father's property, or the usufruct, the right to the profits from the land. She was free to dispose of her dowry as she wished, but in other cases her property rights upon her death reverted to her brothers, except under special conditions.

The purpose of marriage was by law procreation, not companionship. The wife's first duty was to raise her children and a sterile marriage was grounds for divorce. The wife who gave birth to children, particularly to sons, was accorded special protection. The man who divorced the mother of his sons or took another wife was committing a culpable act. Her childbearing responsibilities were emphasized by penalties to anyone injuring a woman sufficiently to cause a miscarriage and also by statutes against abortion.

Adultery was not a sin against morality but a trespass against the husband's property. A husband had freedom to fornicate, while a wife could be put to death for doing the same thing. Free women were inviolable and guarded; a man who gave employment to a married woman not closely related to him was in difficulty. A man caught fornicating with an adulterous woman could be castrated or put to death, while the woman could be executed or have her nose cut off. Offenses with unmarried free women were treated differently from those with married women because there was no husband. If the offender had a wife, she was taken from him and given to her father for prostitution and the offender was compelled to marry the woman who was his victim. If he had no wife, he had to pay a sum of money to the woman's father as well as marry her, although the father might accept money and refuse to give him his daughter. In any case, the payment was for damaging property, lessening the value of the woman. If a man could prove by oath that an unmarried woman gave herself to him, he was not compelled to surrender his own wife, although he still had to pay a sum of money for the damage he had caused. If a married woman was seized by a man in a street or public place and, in spite of her efforts to defend herself, was violated, she was regarded as innocent. If, however, she was acting as a prostitute either in a temple brothel or in the street, the man could be convicted of engaging in an adulterous relationship only if he was shown to have had guilty knowledge.

These laws applied to freewomen. There were other women, particularly slaves. A slave had no human personality but instead was real property. If she was injured, it was her master and not she herself who was entitled to compensation.

A female slave was under obligation to give her purchaser not only her labor but also herself, without any counter obligation on his part. He could in fact turn her over to prostitution. Even when she became the purchaser's concubine and had children by him, she still remained a slave liable to be sold. At her owner's death, however, she and her children received liberty. If a female slave was bought by a married woman either as her servant or as a concubine for her husband (as in the case of a childless woman), she remained the property of the wife. A male slave could, with his master's consent, marry a freewoman, and even if she lacked a dowry, she and her children would still remain free. If she brought a dowry, she could keep it, but any increase from investment was split with her husband's master. There were also temple slaves who were not confined to the temple but worked in the towns and hired out to private employers. Their legal status was harsher than that of ordinary slaves since they had no hope of adoption, while their children automatically became the property of the gods. Children and wives of freemen were different from slaves, but the father still had almost total control. He could deposit his children with creditors, and apparently also his wife, although she could not be kept for more than four years. . . .

Specific laws dealt with women as tavernkeepers, priestesses, and prostitutes, occupations in which women could act outside conjugal or paternal authority. In general, however, the law failed to recognize women as persons. For example, a woman could be careless with animals just as a man could, but the law only refers to men. As far as priestesses and prostitutes were concerned, there were various kinds of both. At the head of the priestesses was the Entu, the wife of the gods, or the "lady [who is] a deity." They were of very high standing and the kings could make their daughters Entu of a god. They were expected to remain virgins, although they might eventually take husbands, perhaps after menopause. A second class of priestesses was the Naditu, who were lower in rank but who were also not expected to have children. The Hammurabic code had several provisions attempting to ensure the rights of a priestess to dowry and other shares of her father's goods. Apparently their conduct was rigidly circumscribed since any priestess who went to a tavern to drink could be put to death. Prostitutes seem to have been quite common and there was a considerable variety of harlots and hierodules.[2] . . .

With such a male-oriented society, few women emerged as real individuals in the history of the Mesopotamian civilizations. . . .

. . . It was only through their sons that women in the Mesopotamian civilizations seem to have had any influence at all. Even the wives of the king were not important enough to be regarded as queens since the use of the term was restricted to goddesses or to women who served in positions of power. The chief wife instead was usually called "she of the palace," and she lived along with the concubines and other wives in a harem guarded by eunuchs.[3] Their way of life was

---

[2] Temple slaves.

[3] Castrated men.

carefully regulated by royal edicts, although in the last period of the Assyrian kingdom the influence of the king's wife and mother was somewhat greater than before.

Other than a few exceptional royal wives, only a handful of women managed to break through into the pages of history. There is an isolated reference to a woman physician at the palace in an Old Babylonian text, and we can assume that women attended other women in childbirth, but there is no further reference. The professional physician was usually a male. Women were also generally illiterate if only because in this period reading and writing were restricted to a professional class of scribes who underwent long training. Poetry, however, is a preliterate form of literature, and one of the most remarkable poets, in fact one of the few we know by name, was a woman, Enheduanna. She was the daughter of Sargon, whose administration marked the fusion of Semitic and Sumerian culture. As part of this fusion the Sumerian Inanna and the Akkadian Ishtar came together, and in this process Enheduanna played an important role, at least if her identification is correct. She was a high priestess of the moon god, the first of a long line of royal holders of this office, and in this capacity she wrote a poem usually entitled "The Exaltation of Inanna." Her poetry served as a model for much subsequent hymnography and her influence was so great that she later seems to have been regarded as a god herself. . . . Most of the cuneiform[4] literature from the area is anonymous, or at best pseudonymous, so how many other women poets there were must remain unknown. The attitudes expressed about women in most of the poetry tend to indicate that they had male authors.

In one of the great classics of Mesopotamian literature, the Gilgamesh epic, it seems obvious that woman's duty was to keep man calm and peaceful. In the beginning of the account Gilgamesh was oppressing the city of Erech, taking the son from the father, the maiden from her lover. The people complained to the gods, who created a rival, Enkidu, from clay to deal with Gilgamesh. Enkidu was a wild man whose whole body was covered with hair, who knew neither people nor country. When the existence of Enkidu was reported to Gilgamesh he sent forth a temple harlot to ensnare the wild man: "Let her strip off her garment; let her lay open her comeliness;/He will see her, he will draw nigh to her. . . . " Then with his innocence lost he could be more effectively handled by Gilgamesh.

> *The prostitute untied her loin-cloth and opened her legs,*
> *and he took possession of her comeliness:*
> *She used no restraint but accepted his ardour,*
> *She put aside her robe and he lay upon her.*
> *She used on him, the savage, a woman's wiles,*
> *His passion responded to her.*
> *For six days and seven nights Enkidu approached and*
> *coupled with the prostitute.*
> *After he was sated with her charms,*

---

[4] Wedge-shaped writing system Mesopotamians developed by the third millennium B.C.

He set his face toward his game.
[But] when the gazelles saw him, Enkidu, they ran away;
The game of the steppe fled from his presence.
Enkidu tried to hasten [after them, but] his body was
    [as if it were] bound.
His knees failed him who tried to run after his game.
Enkidu had become weak, his speed was not as before.
But he had intelligence, wide was his understanding.

. . . The legend suggests that woman was designed to ensnare a man, to weaken him, to prevent him from realizing his full potentiality. In this forerunner of the stereotype of Eve, woman was both a source of pleasure and yet a delusion. . . .

Woman, nonetheless, was designed to be at the side of man, and as a proverb stated, "a house without an owner is like a woman without a husband." The ideal wife was both passionate and able to bear sons: "May [the goddess] Inanna cause a hot-limbed wife to lie down for you;/May she bestow upon you broad-armed sons;/May she seek out for you a place of happiness." Even a good wife was a burden and responsibility: "The man who does not support either a wife or a child,/His nose has not borne a leash." Or in a more hostile vein: "As the saying goes: 'Were not my wife in the cemetery, and were not also my mother in the river, I should die of hunger.'" Women, as well as men, enjoyed sex. "Conceiving is nice," but "being pregnant is irksome." It was also recognized that the "penis of the unfaithful husband" was no better "than the vulva of the unfaithful wife," but in most things a woman was discriminated against. "A rebellious male may be permitted a reconciliation;/A rebellious female will be dragged in the mud." Obviously women were regarded as a mixed blessing, and it was thought best that they be kept in their place.

Life in Mesopotamia was harsh and unpredictable. There were floods, famine, scorching heat, and cloudbursts, and always the danger of invasions. It might well be that in such a society the strong man was admired while the weak woman was regarded as a liability but necessary because of her childbearing abilities. Inevitably the male was forced to assert himself, to man the armies, to do the fighting, to keep his womenfolk in subordination. Is this an adequate explanation for male dominance? The difficulty with such a thesis is that these same attitudes are found in other cultures where environmental conditions are quite different. Nonetheless environment might have had some influence, since the place of women in Egyptian society seems to be quite different from that of Mesopotamian society.

. . . Most recent studies would not regard Egypt as a matriarchal society, but all would agree that the status of women was probably higher there than in Mesopotamia and that women had the right to own and transmit property. . . .

Part of the difficulty with reconstructing the real status of women in Egypt is that we lack the kind of comprehensive law codes present in ancient Mesopotamian society. We do, however, have numerous legal documents, particularly from the time of the Persians and the Greeks who occupied Egypt in the last half of the first millennium B.C. From these it would appear that women had the right to own property, to buy, sell, and testify in court. . . . [I]t is apparent that women not only enjoyed full equality to own property but also could go about their transactions in the same manner as men. Moreover, they were allowed to regain the property they brought with them as dowry if their marriage broke up. If, however, the woman had committed adultery, no such guarantee existed. Women were listed as taxpayers, and they could also sue. Apparently a woman did not need a guardian to be able to execute legal acts, nor did it matter whether she was married or not. A daughter, at least in the Ptolemaic period,[5] was entitled to equal succession in the estate of her father. Women could acquire wealth or property through their parents or husbands or purchase it. A wife was entitled to a third of her husband's possessions after his death, whereas the other two-thirds had to be divided among the children and sisters and brothers of the testator. If a husband desired his wife to receive more, he had the right to donate it to her before he died.

The comparative economic independence of women may have given them greater freedom than in Mesopotamia. . . . Such independence must have been limited to the upper levels of society. The ordinary peasant, whether male or female, lacked many possessions, and the slave was even lower on the scale. Nevertheless, women of all classes were recognized as important, as is evidenced by the numerous goddesses. Particularly important were the triads of gods composed of a man, woman, and child, almost always a son. . . .

Since goddesses were so important it would seem to follow that royal women would also be important, if only because the pharaoh's first wife was the consort of a god. Inevitably, too, she became the "mother of the god" who would be the successor to her husband. At all periods in Egyptian society the queens were the first ladies of the land, and originally the tombs of some were as big and as elaborate as those of the kings. . . .

. . . [I]t was not until the eighteenth dynasty (c. 1570–1305 B.C.) that the Egyptian queen achieved her highest prestige. The most influential of all was Hatshepsut (c. 1486–1468 B.C.), who stole the throne from her young nephew and stepson, Thutmose III, and wielded the scepter for about twenty years. Hatshepsut, however, ruled as a king and not as a queen, an indication of the difficulties women had in ruling. The reigning monarch of Egypt had to be male: the titles, laudatory inscriptions, and ceremonies were all designed for men and were so deeply rooted in tradition and dogma that it was easier for a woman to adapt herself to fit the titles than to change the titles to fit her sex. Inevitably her reign is somewhat confusing since she is shown both in a man's kilt (and body) wearing the king's crown and artificial beard, and as a woman with feminine dress and queen's crown. She also has two tombs, one in her capacity as queen and one as king, the latter being larger. When she died or was driven from the throne by her

---

[5] Named after Ptolemy, a general of Alexander the Great who became king in 304 B.C. The Ptolemaic dynasty ended in 30 B.C.

nephew, Thutmose III, he destroyed almost anything Hatshepsut had ever touched, and even tried to obliterate all inscriptions which referred to her. Though Hatshepsut must have been a strong-willed woman, one of her great difficulties seems to have been her inability to lead an army. She recorded no military conquests or campaigns; her great pride was in the internal development of Egypt. Some would say she lacked military exploits because she may have been a leader of a peace party opposed to expansion. Actually there is nothing in a woman's biological makeup that would prevent her from being a soldier or general, in fact; many women disguised themselves as males to serve in the American Civil War, but women almost without exception were not trained as soldiers. In the past, when kings had to lead their armies, this discrimination might have prevented more women from being rulers. Hatshepsut obviously was supported by the bureaucracy of the state, but civil powers can be diffused. In a military crisis, however, power must be centralized into the hands of one person, and though a woman might appoint a male to act as commander, there is little to stop him from turning against her, particularly if he has the loyalty of the troops. It might well be that Thutmose III used his military ability to regain the throne, since he either deliberately introduced military imperialism or was forced to expand in order to defend his country's borders.

Hatshepsut was not the only woman to sit on the throne. There were at least three others, although only as regents for their sons. . . . Women continued to exercise considerable influence down to the time of Cleopatra.[6] . . . Though Cleopatra was Greek rather than Egyptian, her importance emphasizes the continuing influence of women in Egyptian affairs, whether foreign or native.

The relative importance of the queen mother was no indication that the king was restricted to one wife. Concubines and harems were common, but such women seldom appeared in public. The size of the harem probably varied and at times reached remarkable numbers. Ramses II (1290–1224 B.C.), for example, had at least seventy-nine sons and fifty-nine daughters. The members of the royal harem lived apart from the rest of the court. Employees of the harem were not eunuchs, as in Mesopotamia, but included normal men, many of them married, as well as numerous women. In general the harem women were chosen by the pharaoh either for political reasons or for their great beauty. It was through this last procedure that many nonroyal women gained admission and some became queens. There were also a number of women of foreign birth. Inevitably there were conspiracies in the harem as various wives tried to maneuver their sons into key positions. When women were not in the harem for political reasons, their chief purpose was to amuse their lord. They were instructed in dancing and singing and other arts designed to arouse and delight the male. Some of the richer Egyptians also had harems and concubines, but as a general rule Egyptians practiced monogamy if only because economic factors worked against polygamy. The husband could dismiss his wife if he wished to remarry or if his wife ceased to

---

[6] 69–30 B.C.

please him, but he had to return her dowry and give other forms of settlement. Women had no such freedom.

Like most societies, Egypt practiced a double standard. Concubinage existed but not polyandry.[7] Maidservants belonged to their owner and adultery for the male was not considered a sin. Prostitution was widespread. . . . If a married woman committed adultery, however, she could be deprived of her property and be subject to punishment. We have two folktales from the Middle and New Kingdom of women committing adultery: in the first the woman was burned to death; in the second her husband killed her and threw her corpse to the hounds. In other folktales women appeared as very sexual creatures, willing to betray their husbands, use various kinds of tricks, and do other things in order to get the men who attracted them physically into bed. . . .

. . . Instead of evidence of female promiscuity, such tales might only be male-oriented pornography, designed to arouse the male. By emphasis on female sexual desire, however, female insubordination might also be encouraged. Thus to reassert their control men emphasized clitoridectomies, allowing unlimited pleasure for the male but only limited temptation for females to be insubordinate. We also know that before this time the Egyptian woman was seldom pictured in any negative way in the literature. She was always portrayed as the faithful caring wife, the princess with many suitors, or the mistress praised by songs and poems. Motherhood was her revered function. Not to have children was a terrible and lamentable situation, and mother and children were depicted at all times in Egyptian tombs and pictures.

Women seldom appeared in public life although some women did hold public offices. There are records of a woman director of a dining hall, a manageress of a wig workshop, a headmistress of singers, a female supervisor of a house of weavers, and numerous mistresses of royal harems or superintendents of houses. In later Egyptian history wives of eminent persons or members of old noble families also were allowed to use honorary official titles. We know of at least one woman scribe who belonged to the household of a thirteenth-dynasty queen, and it is possible some queens and princesses knew how to write. Most women, even of the upper classes, could not. Women could also serve in the temples, and priestesses were recruited not only from the royal house, the civil services, or clergy, but also from the working class. Generally women served as musicians or dancers in the temple, although some might have become high priestesses.

Egyptians also believed that males rather than females were the key to procreation, and the male phallus was often portrayed. The female sex organs were not usually depicted in ancient Egypt. There was, however, a widespread belief that a women might succumb to hysteria if the womb remained barren long after puberty. . . .

---

[7] A woman having more than one husband.

The extant literature seems to be from the hands of males, and it reflects the various attitudes of men toward women. Ptah Hotep, the semilegendary sage of the Old Kingdom who lived in the third millennium B.C., said: "If you are a man of note, found for yourself a household, and love your wife at home, as it beseems. Fill her belly, clothe her back; unguent is the remedy for her limbs. Gladden her heart, so long as she lives; she is a goodly field for her lord [that is, she will produce children if you cultivate her]. But hold her back from getting the mastery. [Remember that] her eye is her stormwind, and her vulva and mouth are her strength." Though wives were good if kept in their place, care should be exercised in their choice. . . . Women were also dangerous: "If you would prolong friendship in a house to which you have admittance, as master, or as brother, or as friend, into whatsoever place you enter, beware of approaching the women. It is not good in the place where this is done. Men are made fools by their gleaming limbs of carnelian. A trifle, a little, the likeness of a dream, and death comes as the end of knowing her." . . . Motherhood was especially revered. "Double the bread that thou givest to thy mother, and carry her as she carried [thee]. When thou wast born after thy months, she carried thee yet again about her neck, and for three years her breast was in thy mouth. She was not disgusted at thy dung, she was not disgusted and said not: 'What do I?' She put thee to school, when though hadst been taught to write, and daily she stood there [at the schoolhouse] . . . with bread and beer from her house." When a man married he should keep the example of his mother in front of him. "When thou art a young man and takest to thee a wife and art settled in thine house, keep before thee how thy mother gave birth to thee, and how she brought thee up further in all manner of ways. May she not do thee harm nor lift up her hands to the Gods and may he not hear her cry." . . .

Women, in general, however, were a snare and a delusion. "Go not after a woman, in order that she may not steal thine heart away." In particular beware "of a strange woman, one that is not known in her city. Wink not at her . . . have no carnal knowledge of her. She is a deep water whose twisting men know not. A woman that is far from her husband, 'I am fair,' she saith to thee every day, when she hath no witnesses."

Yet a woman could also be a delight.

Lovely are her eyes when she glances,
Sweet are her lips when she speaks,
*   and her words are never too many!*
Her neck is long, and her nipple is radiant,
*   and her hair is deep sapphire.*
Her arms surpass the brilliance of gold,
*   and her fingers are like lotus blossoms.*
Her buttocks curve down languidly from her trim belly,
*   and her thighs are her beauties.*
Her bearing is regal as she walks upon the earth —
*   she causes every male neck to turn and look at her.*

Yes, she has captivated my heart in her embrace!
In joy indeed is he who embraces all of her —
   he is the very prince of lusty youths!

In sum, the Egyptian woman had a relatively pleasant life and we do not need to resort to questionable generalizations like that of primitive matriarchy in order to explain it. Her somewhat higher status than that of the Mesopotamian woman still did not mean that she was considered equal to men. Women were clearly subordinate, and compared to men's, their lives were circumscribed. It might well be that the very passivity of living in Egypt, owing to the great fertility of the soil and to the regularity of life, lent less emphasis to war and to the making of war. Women worked in the fields along with the men in ancient times, as they do now, although their assigned functions differed. Even the fact that women appeared as rulers does not mean that they had equality, since all apparently exercised their power in the name of a son or took a male name. It is also worthy of comment that most of the women rulers appeared at the end of a dynasty, apparently striving to keep the family in power either because their sons were young or their husbands were enfeebled. Hatshepsut, of course, was an exception. Some Egyptian women worked outside of their homes, but the professions were not open to them nor were any of the crafts, except the traditionally feminine ones. They were not priests, nor were they carpenters, sculptors, or scribes. Woman's place was in the home, and it was as mothers that they had their greatest influence. If Egypt is the example of the power that women had under what some have called a matriarchy, their status in times past must never have been very high. . . .

MAKING CONNECTIONS:
WOMEN AND THE FAMILY

1. Vern Bullough, Brenda Shelton, and Sarah Slavin take us to the beginnings of Western civilization to help us understand the nature of male attitudes toward women. The authors' premise is that men have held negative attitudes toward women throughout the history of Western civilization but that those attitudes have differed among cultures. How did women fare in ancient Mesopotamia and in Egypt? Why do you think men in those societies believed women were evil, more carnal than men, and a detriment to society? How did men use religion to substantiate their biases? Compare the attitudes toward women in these early civilizations to male perceptions of women today. Which of these early views persist? In which realms of our culture are the negative attitudes most prevalent? Why do you think men, to varying degrees, have treated women badly and thought of them negatively through the centuries?

2. Women were central to family life in Mesopotamia and Egypt. Did husbands love their wives? Did society value women's roles in marriage and in child rearing? How did Mesopotamian and Egyptian laws treat wives and mothers? Compare our current laws regarding women and the family to ancient laws. How do ours differ? To what extent has the unequal treatment of women been a legacy of ancient laws?

SLAVERY IN THE ANCIENT NEAR EAST
Isaac Mendelsohn

For people in antiquity, a society without slaves was virtually inconceivable. Trading in slaves linked the cultures of the ancient world, as did the shared belief in the necessity and virtue of slavery. That belief was as widespread then as the conviction today that slavery is morally wrong. Isaac Mendelsohn, former lecturer in Semitic languages and curator of Near East collections at Columbia University, analyzes slavery's place in Mesopotamia and ancient Israel.

Mendelsohn first discusses the various ways — war, sale, and indebtedness — in which one could become a slave. War was endemic in Mesopotamia. As invading armies routinely crisscrossed the countryside from present-day Iraq to Israel, individuals and entire populations could suddenly lose their freedom. Poverty was omnipresent and the main cause of the sale of minors and oneself into slavery. Enormous disparities in wealth, poor weather, and erratic harvests all helped to plunge the destitute into slavery. How did slavery affect family relationships in these conditions?

Second, Mendelsohn analyzes the legal status of slaves — how they were treated by various law codes, particularly that of Hammurabi in Babylonia and the Bible. Were there significant differences between the Hebrew Bible and Hammurabi's Code concerning the regulation of slavery? Is there reason to believe that slaves were treated as the laws specified? How could a slave become free, if indeed slaves always desired liberty?

Third, in explaining the economic role of slavery, Mendelsohn shows the institution of slavery to be even more nuanced. Not only did slavery differ from culture to culture but also according to the economic functions of the slaves. Slaves worked for governments, temples, and private individuals, most often in agriculture or in industry.

Finally, Mendelsohn uses law codes as well as the Hebrew Bible to understand the attitude of religions toward slavery. We should not be surprised to learn that the religions of Mesopotamia and Israel accepted slavery as part of the natural order of things. But what remarks in the Hebrew Bible would later lead to moral outrage against one person owning another person?

Isaac Mendelsohn, "Slavery in the Ancient Near East," *Biblical Archaeologist* 9 (1946): 74–88.

The earliest Sumerian terms for male and female slaves are the composite signs *nita* + *kur* "male of a foreign country," and *nunus* + *kur* "female of a foreign country," indicating that the first humans to be enslaved in Ancient Babylonia were captive foreigners. That prisoners of war, spared on the battlefield, were reduced to slavery is amply attested in the annals of the long history of the Ancient Near East. The Hammurabi Code[1] took this universal practice of the enslavement of war captives for granted and decreed that (1) a captive state official should be ransomed, in case he had no resources of his own, by his city temple or by the state, and (2) that a woman whose husband was taken prisoner may re-marry in case she had no means to support herself and her children. The Late Assyrian annals repeatedly mention large numbers of war captives "from the four corners of the world" who were dragged to Assyria and were compelled to perform forced labor. The small city-states of Syria in the middle of the second millennium B.C. employed the same procedure with regard to their war prisoners. In a war between the cities of Carchemish and Ugarit in which the former was victorious, many prisoners were taken. The king of Ugarit then requested the king of Carchemish to free one of the captives, offering him one hundred shekels as ransom. In answer to this request the king of Carchemish pointed out that he had already sold many prisoners for forty shekels apiece and that he could not be expected to free a high ranking captive for the small sum offered. The Tell el-Amarna letters (14th century B.C.)[2] tell us of war captives being sent as "gifts" by Syrian and Palestinian princes to their Egyptian overlords. The Old Testament tells us that in their conquest of Palestine the Israelites enslaved many of their Canaanite enemies.

No sooner was this practice of enslaving foreigners established than it was carried over and applied to natives themselves. Man became a commodity and the total exploitation of his physical strength served as a new source of profit. Although captives of war and imported foreign slaves made up a substantial part of the slave population of the Ancient Near East, the bulk of the Babylonian, Assyrian, Canaanite, and Hebrew slaves originally came from the ranks of the free-born native population. The native-born slaves were recruited from the following three sources: sale of minors by their parents, voluntary self-sale by adults, and enslavement of defaulting debtors.

Poor parents who were either unable to support their children or were in need of money sold their offspring in the market. These sales were transacted in two ways: (1) unconditional sale; that is, the parent(s) handed the child over to the buyer and in return received the purchase price "in full," and (2) conditional sale or sale-adoption; that is, the parent(s) received the price and the sold minor was adopted by the purchaser. We have documentary evidence showing that the prac-

---

[1] Main collection of law in Mesopotamia, named after the Babylonian king of the eighteenth century B.C.

[2] Correspondence uncovered at Tell el-Amarna in Egypt between Egyptian pharaohs and Syro-Palestinian rulers.

tice of the sale of minors was in use throughout the history of Babylonia and Assyria. Our evidence from Syria and Palestine, however, is very inadequate. Still, there are enough references to prove that this practice was also prevalent there. The Tell el-Amarna letters tell us that some people were forced to sell their children in order to procure food. From the Old Testament we learn that parents sold their daughters into conditional slavery (Ex. 21:7–11); that creditors seized the children of their deceased debtors (II Kings 4:1); and that debt-ridden farmers were forced to hand over their sons and daughters as slaves (Nehemiah 5:5).

The evidence of the existence of the second method of sale, namely, the sale of young girls into conditional slavery, comes from Nuzi[3] and Palestine. Nuzian and Hebrew parents often sold their daughters with the condition that the purchaser give them into marriage when the girls will have reached puberty. In Nuzi this type of sale was drawn up in the form of a fictitious adoption. The general scheme of a Nuzian sale-adoption contract runs as follows: (1) Preamble: Contract of daughtership and daughter-in-lawship. A has given his daughter B "into daughtership and daughter-in-lawship" to C. (2) Conditions: After [B has] reached puberty C shall give B into marriage either to a free-born man or to a slave. (The free-born man may be the purchaser himself, one of his sons, or a stranger "in the gate." In case the girl is given into marriage to one of her purchaser's slaves, she must remain in her owner's house as long as she lives.) (3) Price: The sum paid by the purchaser to the girl's father. The condition that the girl be married was fundamental. Fathers took the precaution to safeguard for their daughters a continuous marital status by inserting in the sale document a special clause (in case the condition was that the girl be married to a slave) to the effect that should her first slave-husband die, her master would give her into marriage to another one of his slaves. In some documents provisions are made for four husbands and in one for as many as eleven: "If ten of her husbands have died, in that case to an eleventh into wife-hood she shall be given."

This Nuzian practice had its parallel in Palestine. A section of the earliest Old Testament slave legislation, that of Exodus 21:7–11 reads:

> If a man sells his daughter to be an *amah* ("handmaid, female slave"), she shall not leave as the slaves do (i.e., in the seventh year). If her master dislikes her, although he had appointed her (as wife) for himself, then shall he let her be redeemed; to sell her (as a wife) to a stranger he shall have no power for he has dealt deceitfully with her. But if he has appointed her for his son, he shall treat her in the manner of daughters. If he takes to himself another (wife), he shall not diminish her food, her clothing, and her conjugal rights. If he does not do these three (things) to her, then she shall go out free without compensation. . . .

In view of the Nuzian practice, this Biblical law represents a fragment of a series of enactments which originally dealt with all cases of conditional sales of young girls. The section before us deals, to use the Nuzian terminology, with a "daugh-

---

[3] A city in Assyria.

tership and daughter-in-lawship" sale. The conditions as set forth in this case are: (1) that the master himself marry the girl (hence the prohibition of treating her like a slave woman or selling her into marriage to a stranger); (2) in case he refuses, after she had reached puberty, to abide by the stipulation in the contract on the ground that the girl now does not find favor in his eyes, he may take recourse to one of the following alternatives: (a) he may let her be redeemed, (b) he may give her as wife to one of his sons, or (c) he may retain her as his concubine. Should he refuse, however, to comply with any of these alternatives open to him; then, as a penalty for breach of contract, "she shall go out free without compensation." . . .

Poverty or debt drove people to sell their children first and then themselves into slavery. In the absence of any state or community help for those driven from the soil by war, famine, or economic misfortune, a man or woman had only one recourse to save himself from starvation, and that was self-sale into slavery. Voluntary self-sale was a common phenomenon especially among strangers. From Nuzi we possess a number of documents relating to self-enslavement. These documents concern themselves mostly with the Habiru,[4] who not being able to find employment entered "of their own free will," singly or with their families, into the state of servitude. The term "servitude" is here used advisedly in preference to "slavery," because legally most of the Habiru self-sale cases in Nuzi differ fundamentally from the self-sale documents of Babylonia. In Babylonia the person who sold himself received his purchase price and as a result he became a slave, the property of another man. But in Nuzi no purchase price is paid to those who "sell themselves." The Habiru enter voluntarily into the state of servitude in exchange for food, clothing, and shelter. . . . These Habiru then, retain some kind of legal personality for in some documents it is expressly stated that only after desertion will they "be sold for a price," that is, be reduced to slavery.

Of all the ancient law codes, the Old Testament alone mentions the case of self-sale or voluntary slavery. Ex. 21:2–6 and Deut. 15:16–17 deal with the case of a Hebrew debtor-slave who refuses "to go out" after his six year term of service has been completed because he loves his master, his wife, and his children. The law provides that such a man (who prefers slavery with economic security to freedom with economic insecurity) shall have his ear bored through and shall remain a slave "forever." Leviticus 25:39–54 deals with a free Hebrew who, because of poverty, is forced to sell himself. In this case, the law provides that such a man, regardless of the fact that he had sold himself forever, shall be freed in the year of the jubilee.

Although slaves were recruited from various indigenous and foreign sources, the basic source of supply for the ever mounting number of slaves in the Ancient Near East was the native defaulting debtor. Insolvency could be the result of many causes, such as drought, war, etc., against which the individual was pow-

---

[4] Possible ancestors of the Hebrews.

erless to act, but one of the chief factors leading to the foreclosure of property and man was unquestionably the exorbitant interest rate charged on loans. The average rate of interest in Ancient Babylonia was 20–25% on silver and 33⅓% on grain. Assyria had no fixed or average rate. In Late Assyria the usurer had a free hand in determining the rate of interest. Interest on money varied from 20% to as high as 80% per annum. In addition to this general type there were two other kinds of loans current in Babylonia and Assyria. These were loans granted without interest by the temples and the landlords to their tenant-farmer and loans on which interest was charged only after the date of maturity. In the latter case the interest was enormous. In Babylonia the double of the principal, that is, 100% was charged; in Neo-Babylonia[5] we find 40% and also 100%; and in Late Assyria 100% and even 141% was charged. In Nuzi the average interest rate seems to have been 50% "till after the harvest." There is no information in the Old Testament as to the rate of interest charged in Palestine. From the injunction against the taking of interest from a fellow Hebrew we may infer that a higher interest rate was charged and that Palestine was no exception to the rule.

The fate of the defaulting debtor was slavery. The creditor had the right to seize him and sell him into slavery. It was at this unlimited power of the creditor, which tended to reduce large numbers of free-born people into slavery, that . . . laws . . . of the Hammurabi Code were aimed. These laws demand that the defaulting debtor or his free-born pledge shall be released after three years of compulsory service. The right of seizure of the defaulting debtor by his creditor was in like manner exercised in Palestine. In II Kings 4:1–2 the creditor seized the children of a deceased debtor and the widow appealed to Elisha for help: "The creditor has come to take unto him my children as slaves." This practice of seizure and the subsequent sale into slavery of the unsolvent debtor is reflected in the prophetic literature: "Because they have sold the righteous for a pair of sandals" (Amos 2:6), and "Which of my creditors is it to whom I have sold you?" (Isaiah 50:1). Nehemiah 5:1 ff. shows that creditors foreclosed the land of their defaulting debtors and reduced pledged children to slavery. Like the Hammurabi Code, the Old Testament codes (Ex. 21:2–3 and Dt. 15:12–18) sought to arrest the power of the creditor by demanding that the Hebrew defaulting debtor should be released after six years of compulsory labor.

Legally the slave was considered a chattel. He was a commodity that could be sold, bought, leased, or exchanged. In sharp contrast to the free man, his father's name was almost never mentioned; he had no genealogy, being a man without a name. . . . Family ties were disregarded in the disposal of slaves. Husbands were separated from their wives, wives were sold without their husbands, and even young children were not spared. The only exception made was in the case of infants "at the breast" who were sold with their mothers.

Babylonia had a class legislation but it was not a caste state. The inequality and discrimination before the law, displayed in the Hammurabi Code in regard to

---

[5] Period of the eleventh dynasty (626–539 B.C.), when Babylonia achieved its greatest power.

the three main classes which constituted Babylonian society, were based not on race or birth but primarily on wealth. To be sold or to sell oneself into slavery, because of poverty or indebtedness, was a misfortune that could befall any man. This new status, however, was not irrevocable. The fact that the slave could, theoretically at least, be freed, made him a member of a low, dependent class, but not a member of a caste. However, as long as he remained a slave, he was subject to the wearing of a visible property mark. . . . It may have been an incised mark upon the forehead, a tattooed sign upon some visible part of the body, or a small tablet of clay or metal hung on a chain around the neck, wrist, or ankle. In the Neo-Babylonian period the prevailing custom of marking slaves was to tattoo the name of the owner (and in case of a temple slave the symbol of the god) on the wrist of the slave. There is no evidence that the Assyrian slave was marked. . . .

The Biblical law prescribes that he who voluntarily submits to perpetual slavery shall have his ear pierced with an awl (Ex. 21:6; Dt. 15:17). . . . We may, therefore, conclude that just as in Babylonia, the Palestinian slaves were marked with a property sign either in the form of a suspended tag attached to the ear, or with a tattoo mark bearing the owner's name on the wrist.

While, legally, the slave was a mere chattel, classed with movable property, both law and society were forced to take into consideration the constantly self-asserting humanity of the slave. We thus have the highly contradictory situation in which on the one hand, the slave was considered as possessing the qualities of a human being while on the other hand, he was recognized as being void of the same and regarded as a mere "thing." The slave's status as a chattel, deprived of any human rights, was clearly and unmistakably emphasized in his relation to a third party. If injured, maimed, or killed by a third party, his owner was compensated for the loss, not the slave. The Biblical legislation mentions only the case of a slave who was killed by a goring ox and provides that the owner shall be compensated for his loss (Ex. 21:32).

. . . The slave's fate was in fact in his master's hand. Beatings and maltreatment of slaves seem to have been . . . common. . . . The Biblical legislation does not prohibit the maltreatment of a Hebrew slave by his master "for he is his money." It is only when the slave dies immediately (within three days) as a result of the beating that the master becomes liable to punishment (Ex. 21:20–21). In Ancient Babylonia a runaway slave was put in chains and had the words "A runaway, seize!" incised upon his face. The Hammurabi Code decrees the death penalty for those who entice a slave to flee from his master and also for those who harbor a fugitive slave. Furthermore, a reward of two shekels is promised to anyone who captures a fugitive slave and brings him back to his master.

The Old Testament slave legislations (Ex. 21, Dt. 15, Lev. 25) do not mention the case of the fugitive slave although the tendency to run away was prevalent in Palestine as it was in the adjacent countries. . . . Fugitive slaves were extradited when they fled into foreign countries (I Kings 2:39 ff.). In view of these facts how should the Deuteronomic ordinance (chap. 23:16) "You shall not deliver a slave unto his master who escapes to you from his master" be interpreted? It is a most extraordinary law for its application in life would have spelled the end of slavery in Palestine. Perhaps this ordinance should be explained from a national-economic point of view. It was most probably drawn up in favor of Hebrew slaves who had fled from foreign countries. If this interpretation be correct, then the Deuteronomic law would have its parallel in . . . the Hammurabi Code according to which a native Babylonian slave who had been sold into a foreign country and fled from there was set free by the state. . . .

The slave enjoyed certain privileges which neither law nor society could deny him. According to the Hammurabi Code a slave could marry a free-born woman and a female slave could become her master's concubine.[6] In both cases the children born of such unions were free. The slave could amass a peculium[7] and enjoy it during his life-time, though legally it belonged to his master. And finally the slave could be manumitted.[8] The Hammurabi Code recognizes four legal ways by which a slave received his freedom ipso facto: (1) wives and children sold, or handed over as pledges, are to be freed after three years of service . . . ; (2) a slave concubine and her children become free after the death of the master . . . ; (3) children born of a marriage between a slave and a free woman are free . . . ; and (4) a native Babylonian slave bought in a foreign country and brought back to Babylonia is unconditionally freed. . . . In addition to these laws which applied only to certain classes and to specific cases of slaves, there were two other ways of manumission: release by adoption and by purchase. Release by adoption was, like that by purchase, a business transaction. . . . The manumitted slave entered into a sonship (or daughtership) relation to his former master and took upon himself the obligation to support him as long as he lived. After the death of the manumitter, the fictitious relationship and the very real material support were terminated and the "son" became completely free. If the adopted slave failed to live up to his promise of support, that is, repudiated his "parents" by saying "you are not my father" or/and "you are not my mother," the adoption was annulled and the "son" reverted to his former slave status. The difference between release by adoption with the condition to support the manumitter (or release with the condition of support without adoption) and that of release by purchase is that in the former case the released slave still remains in a state of dependency to his former master and becomes completely free only after the death of his former master, while in the second case, the slave severs all connections with his master and becomes immediately and irrevocably free.

According to the Biblical law there were five ways by which a Hebrew slave obtained his freedom. These were: (1) a debtor-slave is freed after six years of service (Ex. 21:2, Dt. 15:12); (2) he who sold himself into slavery is to be freed in the year of the jubilee (Lev. 25); (3) a free-born girl who was sold by her father with the condition that her master or his son marry her, is to be freed if the mas-

---

[6] A woman who cohabits with a man to whom she is not married.

[7] Small savings.

[8] Freed.

ter refuses to abide by the conditions of the sale (Ex. 21:7–11); (4) by injury (Ex. 21:26–27); and (5) by purchase (Lev. 25:47 ff.). The six-years service limit of the defaulting debtor has its parallel in the Hammurabi Code . . . which demands the release of a debtor-slave in the fourth year. We have no evidence to prove that the Hammurabi law was ever enforced in Ancient Babylonia. We have hundreds of documents showing that this law was not enforced in Neo-Babylonia. Debtors were foreclosed and sold into slavery if the loans were not paid on the date of maturity. In view of the fact that we have no private documents from the Biblical period we cannot say whether the law of release of the debtor-slave was enforced in Palestine. . . . The law of the release of the Hebrew slave in the year of the jubilee is part of a great land reform utopia according to which all land, whether sold or given as security, must revert to its original owners in the year of the jubilee. . . . Was the law of the jubilee ever enforced in life? The sages of the Talmud[9] were very much in doubt about it. The law of release by injury presents considerable difficulties. The meaning of the law is, of course, quite clear. The loss of limb, as a result of beatings administered by the master, is considered sufficient ground for meriting release. . . . It seems . . . that the only plausible interpretation . . . would be to assume that the law . . . applies to the Hebrew defaulting debtor. From the point of view of the law, the Hebrew defaulting debtor is not a slave at all but merely a debtor temporarily in the service of his creditor. When such a debtor is permanently injured by his creditor, the loss of limb is considered to be the equivalent of the amount of the debt and hence he is to be released.

There were three main classes of slaves in the Ancient Near East, viz., state slaves, temple slaves, and privately owned slaves. Of these, the first group, recruited from war prisoners, was economically the most important. In Babylonia and Assyria the state slaves, with the assistance of corvee[10] gangs and hired laborers, constructed roads, dug canals, erected fortresses, built temples, tilled the crown lands, and worked in the royal factories connected with the palace. The small city-states of Syria and Palestine also had their state slaves. In the El-Amarna period (c. 1400 B.C.), Syrian and Palestinian "kings" sent large numbers of slaves and war captives . . . as gifts to their Egyptian overlords. . . . That this institution existed in Palestine from the days of David down to the period of Nehemiah and Ezra is attested by the numerous references to the state slaves in the Old Testament. Since this class of slaves (recruited from war captives and from the tribute paying Canaanites) was officially created by Solomon, they were appropriately called *abde Shelomo* ("Solomon's slaves"). Once formed, this class of state slaves remained in existence until the end of the Judaean kingdom.[11] . . . The end of independent statehood marked also the end of the institution of slavery.

---

[9] The authoritative body of postscriptural Jewish law and tradition.

[10] Forced labor.

[11] 586 B.C.

Already at the dawn of history the Babylonian temple with its vast wealth constituted the richest agricultural, industrial, and commercial single unit within the community. It was a well organized and efficiently run corporation controlling extensive tracts of land, enormous quantities of raw material, large flocks of cattle and sheep, sizeable amounts of precious metal, and a large number of slaves. This was also true, though to a lesser degree, of the Assyrian, Syrian, and Palestinian temples. . . .

Temple slaves were recruited from two sources: prisoners of war who were presented to the temples by victorious kings, and dedications of slaves by private individuals. The sanctuaries in Palestine recruited their slaves from the same sources. After the successful campaign against the Midianites,[12] Moses is reported to have taken one of every five hundred, or one of every fifty, prisoners, and presented them as a gift to Yahweh (Num. 31:25 ff.). Joshua made the Gibeonites[13] "hewers of wood and drawers of water in the sanctuary" (chap. 9:21 ff.). . . . We have no evidence to prove that privately owned slaves were dedicated to temples in Palestine. The case of young Samuel who was dedicated to the sanctuary of Shiloh, however, shows that this practice was known in Palestine. While the number of state and temple slaves was very large, their economic role must not be overestimated. The state . . . employed them in non-competitive enterprises and the temple used them primarily for menial work. In its two main branches of activity, agriculture and industry, the temple employed mostly free-born people and not slaves. The land was cultivated by free-born tenant-farmers, and free-born artisans worked in the shops.

Unlike Egypt, where the land belonged to the crown, private ownership of land was the rule in the Sumero-Semitic countries. The case of the Israelite farmer Naboth who chose death in preference to selling his ancestral plot to king Ahab was characteristic of the attitude of all peasantry in the Ancient Near East. With the exception of the large holdings of the crown and the temples, the land was owned by two classes of people: small farmers and large landowners. Since the land property of the average farmer was small and his family large there was no great need for outside help either in the form of hired laborers or of slaves. The labor situation was, of course, different in the second group. These large estates had to be worked with hired help. This help, however, was only to a very small degree drawn from the ranks of hired laborers and slaves. It was drawn primarily and overwhelmingly from the ranks of the dispossessed peasantry croppers. . . . Instead of buying, maintaining, and guarding considerable numbers of unwilling slaves, the large landowners (and to a degree even the kings and the temples) preferred to lease parcels of their land to free-born tenant-farmers. . . . Like the upper class in the cities, well-to-do farmers owned slaves and employed them on the

---

[12] Semitic people who invaded southern Palestine after 1200 B.C.

[13] Palestinian people who derived their name from the city Gibeon.

land, but slave labor was not a decisive factor in the agricultural life of the Ancient Near East.

The counterpart of the free-born tenant-farmer in agriculture was the free-born "hired laborer" in industry. There was, of course, great competition between free laborers and slaves in the field of unskilled labor, but the skilled fields were dominated by the free artisans. The reasons for this phenomenon, that is, the small number of slave artisans in the Ancient Near East, were: (1) the apprenticeship period lasted from two to six years, a period during which the slave not only did not bring in any profit, but the owner had to spend money for his upkeep; (2) the number of slaves in well-to-do families averaged from one to three and therefore only a few of them could be spared to be used as an investment with a view of future returns; and finally (3) the general unwillingness of the employer to hire slaves because they could not be trusted to operate expensive tools even when they possessed the skill to handle them. We thus come to the conclusion that the role played by slaves in the skilled industries was very insignificant indeed. Ancient Near Eastern craftsmanship was the product of free labor.

We have seen that economically the Ancient Near Eastern civilization was not based on slave labor. We have also seen that society was unable to maintain consistently the legal fiction that the slave was a mere chattel, and hence some freedom was accorded to him. There remains one more aspect to be considered and that is the attitude of religion toward slavery, the ownership of man by man. Nowhere in the vast religious literature of the Sumero-Accadian world is a protest raised against the institution of slavery, nor is there anywhere an expression of sympathy for the victims of this system. The Old Testament justifies perpetual slavery of the Canaanites, but demands the release of the Hebrew defaulting debtor in the seventh year and of those who sold themselves in the year of the jubilee. The first case — the release of the debtor-slave after a limited term of service — has a parallel in the earlier Hammurabi Code which also demands the release of the defaulting debtor. But in the second case where the release is demanded of even those who had sold themselves voluntarily into slavery, we have for the first time an open denial of the right of man to own man in perpetuity. This denial of the right of possession of man by man is as yet restricted to Hebrews only (cf. Nehemiah 5:8), but it is a step which no other religion had taken before. The first man in the Ancient Near East who raised his voice in a sweeping condemnation of slavery as a cruel and inhuman institution, irrespective of nationality and race, was the philosopher Job. His was a condemnation based on the moral concept of the inherent brotherhood of man, for

> "Did not He that made me in the womb make him (the slave) also? And did not One fashion us in the womb?" (31:15)

WHY THE HEBREWS KEPT KOSHER
Jean Soler

At one time nearly all Jews kept kosher, that is, lived according to specific dietary laws. And many Jews, though certainly not a majority, maintain kosher households today. Yet the reasons for these customs and laws have remained somewhat of a puzzle. In this bold piece, Jean Soler examines the Hebrew Bible not only to provide a coherent explanation for the Hebrews' dietary prohibitions but also to use this evidence about food to understand the ancient Hebrews' collective way of thinking.

Soler begins at the beginning, in paradise. What type of food was available there, according to the Hebrew Bible, and how did food mark the difference between man and god? What event was a turning point between the eating habits in paradise and those after the expulsion of Adam and Eve? What other developments refined the Hebrews' conception of proper food?

After describing the major changes in the evolution of the dietary prohibitions, Soler organizes the totality of customs around the themes of cleanness, purity, and order. He uses these concepts to describe what meats could be eaten, why some animals are forbidden, and what fish and birds are edible. Are his explanations satisfactory, and is he justified in expanding the discussion to the Hebrews' notion of the priesthood, homosexuality, incest, and even to what clothes Hebrews' were permitted to wear? Finally, what do the dietary laws of the Hebrews tell us about the nature of their god and why Mosaic logic was bound to reject the god-man, Jesus?

How can we explain the dietary prohibitions of the Hebrews? To this day these rules — with variations, but always guided by the Mosaic laws[1]—are followed by many orthodox Jews. Once a number of false leads, such as the explanation that they were hygienic measures, have been dismissed, the structural approach appears to be enlightening.

Jean Soler, "The Semiotics of Food in the Bible," in *Food and Drink in History*, ed. Robert Forster and Orest Ranum (Baltimore: Johns Hopkins University Press, 1979), 126–138.

[1] The 613 commandments contained in the Torah, the first five books of the Hebrew Bible.

Lévi-Strauss[2] has shown the importance of cooking, which is peculiar to man in the same manner as language. Better yet, cooking is a language through which a society expresses itself. For man knows that the food he ingests in order to live will become assimilated into his being, will become himself. There must be, therefore, a relationship between the idea he has formed of specific items of food and the image he has of himself and his place in the universe. There is a link between a people's dietary habits and its perception of the world.

Moreover, language and dietary habits also show an analogy of form. For just as the phonetic system of a language retains only a few of the sounds a human being is capable of producing, so a community adopts a dietary regime by making a choice among all the possible foods. By no means does any given individual eat everything; the mere fact that a thing is edible does not mean that it will be eaten. By bringing to light the logic that informs these choices and the interrelation among its constituent parts — in this case the various foods — we can outline the specific characteristics of a society, just as we can define those of a language.

. . . [T]he dietary laws of the Hebrews have been laid down in a book, the Book, and more precisely in the first five books of the Bible, which are known as the Torah to the Jews and the Pentateuch to the Christians. This set of writings is composed of texts from various eras over a wide span of time. But to the extent that they have been sewn together, have coexisted and still do coexist in the consciousness of a people, it is advisable to study them together. I shall therefore leave aside the historical dimension in order to search for the rules that give cohesion to the different laws constituting the Law. . . .

Man's food is mentioned in the very first chapter of the first book. It has its place in the plan of the Creation: "Behold, I have given you every plant yielding seed which is upon the face of all the earth, and every tree with seed in its fruit; you shall have them for your food" (Gen. 1:29), says Elohim. Paradise is vegetarian.

In order to understand why meat eating is implicitly but unequivocally excluded, it must be shown how both God and man are defined in the myth by their relationship to each other. Man has been made "in the image" of God (Gen. 1:26–67), but he is not, nor can he be, God. This concept is illustrated by the dietary tabu concerning the fruit of two trees. After Adam and Eve have broken this prohibition by eating the fruit of one of these trees, Elohim says: "Behold, the man has become like one of us, knowing good and evil; and now, lest he put forth his hand and take also of the tree of life, and eat, and live forever" (Gen. 3:22). This clearly marked distance between man and God, this fundamental difference, is implicitly understood in a threefold manner.

First, the immortality of the soul is unthinkable. All life belongs to God, and to him alone. God is Life, and man temporarily holds only a small part of it. We

---

[2] Twentieth-century anthropologist (b. 1908). He is the leading exponent of structuralism, which maintains that cultural elements have meaning only as part of an entire system of relationships.

know that the notion of the immortality of the soul did not appear in Judaism until the second century B.C. and that it was not an indigenous notion.

Secondly, killing is the major prohibition of the Bible. Only the God who gives life can take it away. If man freely uses it for his own ends, he encroaches upon God's domain and oversteps his limits. From this it follows that meat eating is impossible. For in order to eat an animal, one must first kill it. But animals, like man, belong to the category of beings that have within them "a living soul." To consume a living being, moreover, would be tantamount to absorbing the principle that would make man God's equal.

The fundamental difference between man and God is thus expressed by the difference in their foods. God's are the living beings, which in the form of sacrifices (either human victims, of which Abraham's sacrifice represents a relic, or sacrificial animals) serve as his "nourishment" according to the Bible; man's are the edible plants (for plants are not included among the "living things"). Given these fundamental assumptions, the origins of meat eating constitute a problem. Did men, then, at one point find a way to kill animals and eat them without prompting a cataclysm?

This cataclysm did indeed take place, and the Bible does speak of it. It was the Flood, which marks a breaking point in human history. God decided at first to do away with his Creation, and then he spared one family, Noah's, and one pair of each species of animal. A new era thus began after the Flood, a new Creation, which coincided with the appearance of a new dietary regime. "Every moving thing that lives shall be food for you; as I gave you the green plants, I give you everything" (Gen. 9:3).

Thus, it is not man who has taken it upon himself to eat meat; it is God who has given him the right to do so. And the cataclysm does not come after, but before the change, an inversion that is frequently found in myths. Nevertheless, it must be understood that meat eating is not presented as a reward granted to Noah. If God has wanted "to destroy all flesh in which is the breath of life from under heaven" (Gen. 6:17), it is because man has "corrupted" the entire earth: "and the earth was filled with violence" (Gen. 6:17), in other words, with murder. And while it is true that he spares Noah because Noah is "just" and even "perfect" (Gen. 6:9), the human race that will come from him will not escape the evil that had characterized the human race from which he issued. The Lord says, after the Flood: "I will never again curse the ground because of man, for the imagination of man's heart is evil from his youth; neither will I ever again destroy every living creature as I have done" (Gen. 8:21). In short, God takes note of the evil that is in man. A few verses later, he gives Noah permission to eat animals. Meat eating is given a negative connotation.

Yet even so, it is possible only at the price of a new distinction; for God adds the injunction: "Only you shall not eat flesh with its life, that is, its blood" (Gen. 9:4). Blood becomes the signifier of the vital principle, so that it becomes possible to maintain the distance between man and God by expressing it in a different way with respect to food. Instead of the initial opposition between the eating of meat and the eating of plants, a distinction is henceforth made between flesh and blood. Once the blood (which is God's) is set apart, meat becomes desacralized — and permissible. The structure remains the same, only the signifying elements have changed.

At this stage the distinction between clean and unclean animals is not yet present, even though three verses in the account of the Flood refer to it. Nothing is said that would permit Noah to recognize these two categories of animals, and this distinction is out of place here, since the power to eat animals he is given includes all of them: "Every moving thing that lives shall be food for you."

It is not until Moses appears that a third dietary regime comes into being, one that is based on the prohibition of certain animals. Here we find a second breaking point in human history. For the covenant God had concluded with Noah included all men to be born from the sole survivor of the Flood (the absence of differentiation among men corresponded to the absence of differentiation among the animals they could consume), and the sign of that covenant was a cosmic and hence universal sign, the rainbow (Gen. 9:12–17). The covenant concluded with Moses, however, concerns only one people, the Hebrews; to the new distinction between men corresponds the distinction of the animals they may eat: "I am the Lord your God, who have separated you from the peoples. You shall therefore make a distinction between the clean beasts and the unclean; and between the unclean bird and the clean; you shall not make yourselves abominable by beast or by bird or by anything with which the ground teems, which I have set apart for you to hold unclean" (Lev. 20:24–25). The signs of this new covenant can only be individual, since they will have to become the distinctive traits of the Hebrew people. In this manner the Mosaic dietary code fulfills the same function as circumcision or the institution of the Sabbath. These three signs all involve a cut (a cut on the male sex organ: a partial castration analogous to an offering, which in return will bring God's blessing upon the organ that ensures the transmission of life and thereby the survival of the Hebrew people; a cut in the regular course of the days: one day of every seven is set apart, so that the sacrificed day will desacralize the others and bring God's blessing on their work; a cut in the *continuum* of the created animals — added to the already accomplished cut, applying to every animal, between flesh and blood, and later to be strengthened by an additional cut within each species decreed to be clean between the first-born, which are God's, and the others which are thereby made more licit). The cut is at the origin of differentiation, and differentiation is the prerequisite of signification.

Dietary prohibitions are indeed a means of cutting a people off from others, as the Hebrews learned at their own expense. When Joseph's brothers journeyed to Egypt in order to buy wheat, he had a meal containing meat served to them: "They served him by himself, and them by themselves, for the Egyptians might not eat bread with the Hebrews, for that is an abomination to the Egyptians" (Gen. 43:32). It is likely that the nomadic Hebrews already had dietary prohibitions but, according to Biblical history, they began to include their dietary habits among the defining characteristics of their people only after the exodus, as if they were taking their model from the Egyptian civilization.

　　Dietary habits, in order to play their role, must be different; but different from what? From those, unquestionably, of the peoples with whom the Hebrews were in contact. Proof of this is the famous injunction: "You shall not boil a kid in its mother's milk," for here a custom practiced among the people of that region was forbidden. Yet the dietary regime of the Hebrews was not contrary to the regimes of other peoples in every point; had this been the case they would have had very few things to eat! Why, then, did they strictly condemn some food items and not others? The answer must not be sought in the nature of the food item. . . . A social sign — in this case a dietary prohibition — cannot be understood in isolation. It must be placed into the context of the signs in the same area of life, together with which it constitutes a system; and this system in turn must be seen in relation to the systems in other areas, for the interaction of all these systems constitutes the sociocultural system of a people. The constant features of this system should yield the fundamental structures of the Hebrew civilization or — and this may be the same thing — the underlying thought patterns of the Hebrew people.

　　One first constant feature naturally comes to mind in the notion of "cleanness," which is used to characterize the permissible foods. In order to shed light on this notion, it must first of all be seen as a conscious harking back to the Origins. To the extent that the exodus from Egypt and the revelation of Sinai represent a new departure in the history of the World, it can be assumed that Moses — or the authors of the system that bears his name — felt very strongly that this third Creation, lest it too fall into degradation, would have to be patterned after the myth of Genesis. . . . Man's food would therefore be purest of all if it were patterned as closely as possible upon the Creator's intentions. Now the myth tells us that the food originally given to man was purely vegetarian. Has there been, historically, an attempt to impose a vegetarian regime on the Hebrews? There is no evidence to support this hypothesis, but the Bible does contain traces of such an attempt or, at any rate, of such an ideal. One prime trace is the fact that manna, the only daily nourishment of the Hebrews during the exodus, is shown as a vegetable substance. . . . Moreover, the Hebrews had large flocks, which they did not touch. Twice, however, the men rebelled against Moses because they wanted to eat meat. The first time, this happened in the wilderness of Sin: "Would that we had died by the hand of the Lord in the land of Egypt, when we sat by the flesh-pots" (Exod. 16:3). God thereupon granted them the miracle of the quails. The second rebellion is reported in Numbers (11:4): "O that we had meat to eat," wail the Hebrews. God agrees to repeat the miracle of the quails, but does so only unwillingly and even in great wrath. . . . And a great number of the Hebrews who fall upon the quails and gorge themselves die on the spot. Here, as in the myth of the Flood, meat is given a negative connotation. It is a concession God makes to man's imperfection.

　　Meat eating, then, will be tolerated by Moses, but with two restrictions. The tabu against blood will be reinforced, and certain animals will be forbidden. The setting apart of the blood henceforth becomes the occasion of a ritual. Before the meat can be eaten, the animal must be presented to the priest, who will perform the "peace offering," in which he pours the blood upon the altar. This is not only a matter of separating God's share from man's share; it also means that the murder of the animal that is to be eaten is redeemed by an offering. Under the elementary logic of retribution, any murder requires in compensation the murder of the murderer; only thus can the balance be restored. Since animals, like men, are "living souls," the man who kills an animal should himself be killed. Under this basic assumption, meat eating is altogether impossible. The solution lies in performing a ritual in which the blood of the sacrificial animal takes the place of the man who makes the offering. "For the life of the flesh is in the blood, and I have given it for you upon the altar to make atonement for your souls; for it is the blood that makes atonement, by reason of the life" (Lev. 17:11). But if a man kills an animal himself in order to eat it, "bloodguilt shall be imputed to that man; he has shed blood; and that man shall be cut off from among his people" (Lev. 17:4); that is, he shall be killed. The importance of the blood tabu thus becomes very clear. It is not simply one prohibition among others; it is the *conditio sine qua non*[3] that makes meat eating possible. . . .

As for the prohibition of certain animals, we must now analyze two chapters (Lev. 11 and Deut. 14) devoted to the distinction between clean and unclean species. Neither of these texts, which are essentially identical, provides any explanation. The Bible only indicates the particular traits the clean animals must possess — though not always; for when dealing with the birds, it simply enumerates the unclean species.

The text first speaks of the animals living on land. They are "clean" if they have a "hoofed foot," a "cloven hoof," and if they "chew the cud." The first of those criteria is clearly meant to single out the herbivorous animals. The Hebrews had established a relationship between the foot of an animal and its feeding habits. . . .

But why are herbivorous animals clean and carnivorous animals unclean? Once again, the key to the answer must be sought in Genesis, if indeed the Mosaic laws intended to conform as much as possible to the original intentions of the Creator. And in fact, Paradise was vegetarian for the animals as well. The verse dealing with human food, "I have given you every plant yielding seed which is upon the face of all the earth, and every tree with seed in its fruit; you shall have them for your food," is followed by a verse about the animals (and here, incidentally, we note a secondary differentiation, serving to mark the distance between humankind and the various species of animals): "And to every beast of the earth, and to every bird of the air, and to everything that has the breath of life, I have given every green plant for food" (Gen. 1:29–30). Thus, carnivorous animals are not included in the plan of the Creation. Man's problem with meat eating is compounded when it involves eating an animal that has itself consumed meat and killed other animals in order to do so. Carnivorous animals are unclean. If man were to eat them, he would be doubly unclean. The "hoofed foot" is thus the dis-

---

[3] Essential condition.

tinctive trait that contrasts with the claws of carnivorous animals — dog, cat, felines, etc. — for these claws permit them to seize their prey. Once this point is made, the prohibition against eating most of the birds that are cited as unclean becomes comprehensible: they are carnivorous, especially such birds of prey as "the eagle," which is cited at the head of the list.

But to return to the beasts of the earth. Why is the criterion "hoofed foot" complemented by two other criteria? The reason is that it is not sufficient to classify the true herbivores, since it omits pigs. Pigs and boars have hoofed feet, and while it is true that they are herbivores, they are also carnivorous. In order to isolate the true herbivores it is therefore necessary to add a second criterion, "chewing the cud." One can be sure that ruminants[4] eat grass; in fact, they eat it twice. In theory, this characteristic should be sufficient to distinguish true herbivores. But in practice, it is difficult to ascertain, especially in wild animals, which can properly be studied only after they are dead. Proof of this is the fact that the hare is considered to be a ruminant by the Bible (Lev. 11:6 and Deut. 14:7), which is false; but the error arose from mistaking the mastication of the rodents for rumination. This physiological characteristic therefore had to be reinforced by an anatomical criterion, the hoof, which in turn was strengthened by using as a model the hoof of the ruminants known to everyone: cows and sheep. (In the myth of Creation, livestock constitutes a separate category, distinct from the category of wild animals. There is no trace of the domestication of animals; livestock was created tame). This is why clean wild animals must conform to the domestic animals that may be consumed; as it happens, cows and sheep tread the ground on two toes, each encased in a layer of horn. This explains the third criterion listed in the Bible: the "cloven hoof."

One important point must be made here: The presence of the criterion "cloven hoof" eliminates a certain number of animals, even though they are purely herbivorous (the horse, the ass, and especially the three animals expressly cited in the Bible as "unclean": the camel, the hare, and the rock badger). A purely herbivorous animal is therefore not automatically clean. This is a necessary, though not a sufficient condition. In addition, it must also have a foot analogous to the foot that sets the norm: that of domestic animals. Any foot shape deviating from this model is conceived as a blemish, and the animal is unclean.

This notion of the "blemish" and the value attributed to it is elucidated in several passages of the Bible. Leviticus prohibits the sacrificing of animals, even of a clean species, if the individual animal exhibits any anomaly in relation to the normal type of the species: "And when any one offers a sacrifice of peace offerings to the Lord, to fulfill a vow or as a freewill offering, from the herd or from the flock, to be accepted it must be perfect; there shall be no blemish in it. Animals blind or disabled or mutilated or having a discharge or an itch or scabs, you shall not offer to the Lord or make of them an offering by fire upon the altar to the Lord"

---

[4] Animals that chew the cud — the food returned from the first stomach to the mouth to be chewed a second time.

(Lev. 22:21). This prohibition is repeated in Deuteronomy. . . . The equation is stated explicitly: the blemish is an evil. A fundamental trait of the Hebrews' mental structures is uncovered here. There are societies in which impaired creatures are considered divine.

What is true for the animal is also true for man. The priest must be a wholesome man and must not have any physical defects. The Lord says to Aaron (Lev. 21:17–18): "None of your descendants throughout their generations who has a blemish may approach to offer the bread of his God. For no one who has a blemish shall draw near, a man blind or lame, or one who has a mutilated face or a limb too long, or one who has an injured foot or an injured hand, or a hunchback, or a dwarf, or a man with a defect in his sight or an itching disease or scabs or crushed testicles. . . ." The men who participate in cultic acts must be true men: "He whose testicles are crushed or whose male member is cut off shall not enter the assembly of the Lord" (Deut. 23:1). To be whole is one of the components of "cleanness"; eunuchs[5] and castrated animals are unclean.

To the blemish must be added alteration, which is a temporary blemish. Periodic losses of substance are unclean, whether they be a man's emission of semen or a woman's menstruation (Lev. 15). The most unclean thing of all will therefore be death, which is the definitive loss of the breath of life and the irreversible alteration of the organism. And indeed, death is the major uncleanness for the Hebrews. It is so strong that a high priest (Lev. 21:11) or a Nazirite[6] (Num. 6:6–7) may not go near a dead body, even if it is that of his father or his mother, notwithstanding the fact that the Ten Commandments order him to "honor" them.

The logical scheme that ties cleanness to the absence of blemish or alteration applies to things as well as to men or animals. It allows us to understand the status of ferments and fermented substances. I shall begin with the prohibition of leavened bread during the Passover. The explanation given in the Bible does not hold; it says that it is a matter of commemorating the exodus from Egypt when the Hebrews, in their haste, did not have time to let the dough rise (Exod. 12:34). If this were the reason, they would have been obliged to eat poorly leavened or half-baked bread; but why bread without leavening? In reality, even if the Passover is a celebration whose meaning may have changed in the course of the ages . . . it functions as a commemoration of the Origins, a celebration not only of the exodus from Egypt and the birth of a nation but also of the beginning of the religious year at the first full moon after the vernal equinox. The Passover feast is a sacrifice of renewal, in which the participants consume the food of the Origins. This ritual meal must include "bitter herbs," "roasted meat," and "unleavened bread" (Exod. 12:8). The bitter herbs must be understood, it would seem, as the opposite of vegetables, which are produced by agriculture. Roast meat is the opposite of boiled meat, which is explicitly proscribed in the text (Exod. 12:9): the boil-

---

[5] Castrated men.

[6] An ancient Hebrew who took certain religious vows.

ing of meat, which implies the use of receptacles obtained by an industry, albeit a rudimentary form of it, is a late stage in the preparation of food. As for the unleavened bread, it is the bread of the Patriarchs. Abraham served cakes made of fine meal to the three messengers of God on their way to Sodom (Gen. 18:6). . . . But unleavened bread is clean not only because it is the bread of the Origins. It is clean also and above all because the flour of which it is made is not changed by the ferment of the leavening: it is true to its natural state. This interpretation allows us to understand why fermented foods cannot be used as offerings by fire: "No cereal offering which you shall bring to the Lord shall be made with leaven; for you shall burn no leaven nor any honey as an offering by fire to the Lord" (Lev. 2:11). A fermented substance is an altered substance, one that has become other. Fermentation is the equivalent of a blemish. Proof *a contrario* is the fact that just as fermentation is forbidden, so salt is mandatory in all offerings (Lev. 2:13). Thus, there is a clear-cut opposition between fermentation, which alters a substance's being, and salt, which preserves it in its natural state. Leavened bread, honey, and wine all have the status of secondary food items; only the primary foods that have come from the hands of the Creator in their present form can be used in the sacred cuisine of the offering. It is true, of course, that wine is used in cultic libations. But the priest does not consume it; indeed he must abstain from all fermented liquids before officiating in order to "distinguish between the holy and the common, and between the clean and the unclean" (Lev. 10:10). Fermented liquids alter man's judgment because they are themselves altered substances. The libation of wine must be seen as the parallel of the libation of blood, which it accompanies in burnt offerings. Wine is poured upon the alter exactly like blood, for it is its equivalent in the plant; wine is the "blood of the grapes" (Gen. 49:11, etc.).

To return to my argument, then, the clean animals of the earth must conform to the plan of the Creation, that is, be vegetarian; they must also conform to their ideal models, that is, be without blemish. In order to explain the distinction between clean and unclean fish, we must once again refer to the first chapter of Genesis. In the beginning God created the three elements, the firmament, the water, and the earth; then he created three kinds of animals out of each of these elements: "Let the waters bring forth swarms of living creatures, and let birds fly above the earth across the firmament of the heavens" (Gen. 1:20); "Let the earth bring forth living creatures according to their kinds, cattle and creeping things and beasts of the earth according to their kinds" (Gen. 1:24). Each animal is thus tied to one element, and one only. It has issued from that element and must live there. Chapter 11 of Leviticus and Chapter 14 of Deuteronomy reiterate this classification into three groups: creatures of the earth, the water, and the air. Concerning the animals of the water, the two texts only say: "Everything in the waters that has fins and scales . . . you may eat." All other creatures are unclean. It must be understood that the fin is the proper organ of locomotion for animals living in the water. It is the equivalent of the leg in the animal living on land and of the wing in the animal that lives in the air. . . . [T]he animals of the earth must walk, fish must swim, and birds must fly. Those creatures of the sea that lack fins and do not move about (mollusks) are unclean. So are those that have legs and can walk (shellfish), for they live in the water yet have the organs of a beast of the earth and are thus at home in two elements.

In the same manner, scales are contrasted with the skin of the beasts of the land and with the feathers of the birds. As far as the latter are concerned, the Biblical expression "birds of the air" must be taken quite literally; it is not a poetic image but a definition. In the formulation "the likeness of any winged bird that flies in the air" (Deut. 4:17), the three distinctive traits of the clean bird are brought together: "winged," "which flies," and "in the air." If a bird has wings but does not fly, (the ostrich, for instance, that is cited in the text), it is unclean. If it has wings and can fly but spends most of its time in the water instead of living in the air, it is unclean (and the Bible mentions the swan, the pelican, the heron, and all the stilted birds). Insects pose a problem. "All winged animals that go upon all fours are an abomination to you," says Leviticus (11:20). This is not a discussion of four-legged insects, for the simple reason that all insects have six. The key expression is "go upon" [walk]. The insects that are meant here are those that "go upon all fours," like the normal beasts of the earth, the quadrupeds. Their uncleanness comes from the fact that they walk rather than fly, even though they are "winged." The exception mentioned in Leviticus (11:21) only confirms the rule: no uncleanness is imputed to insects that have "legs above their feet, with which to leap on the earth." Leaping is a mode of locomotion midway between walking and flying. Leviticus feels that it is closer to flying and therefore absolves these winged grasshoppers. Deuteronomy, however, is not convinced and prohibits all winged insects (14:19).

Leviticus also mentions, toward the end, some unclean species that cannot be fitted into the classification of three groups, and it is for this reason, no doubt, that Deuteronomy does not deal with them. The first of these are the reptiles. They belong to the earth, or so it seems, but have no legs to walk on. "Upon your belly you shall go," God had said to the serpent (Gen. 3:14). This is a curse. Everything that creeps and goes on its belly is condemned. These animals live more under the earth than on it. They were not really "brought forth" by the earth, according to the expression of Genesis 1:24. They are not altogether created. And like the serpent, the centipede is condemned (Lev. 11:30) in the expression "whatever has many feet" (Lev. 11:42). Having too many feet or none at all falls within the same category; the clean beast of the earth has four feet, and not just any kind of feet either, as we have seen.

All these unclean animals are marked with a blemish; they show an anomaly in their relation to the element that has "brought them forth" or to the organs characteristic of life, and especially locomotion, in that element. If they do not fit into any class, or if they fit into two classes at once, they are unclean. They are unclean because they are unthinkable. At this point, instead of stating once again that they do not fit into the plan of the Creation, I should like to advance the hypothesis that the dietary regime of the Hebrews, as well as their myth of the Creation, is based upon a taxonomy in which man, God, the animals, and the plants are strictly defined through their relationships with one another in a series of opposites. The Hebrews conceived of the order of the world as the order underlying the creation of the world. Uncleanness, then, is simply disorder, wherever it may occur.

Concerning the raising of livestock and agriculture, Leviticus 19:19 mentions the following prohibition: "You shall not let your cattle breed with a different kind." A variant is found in Deuteronomy 22:10: "You shall not plow with an ox and an ass together." The reason is that the animals have been created (or classified) "each according to its kind," an expression that is a very leitmotif of the Bible. Just as a clean animal must not belong to two different species (be a hybrid), so man is not allowed to unite two animals of different species. He must not mix that which God (or man) has separated, whether the union take place in a sexual act or only under the yoke. Consider what is said about cultivated plants: "You shall not sow your field with two kinds of seeds" (Lev. 19:19), an injunction that appears in Deuteronomy as: "You shall not sow your vineyard with two kinds of seed." The same prohibition applies to things: "nor shall there come upon you a garment of cloth made of two kinds of stuff" (Lev. 19:19). In Deuteronomy 22:11, this becomes: "You shall not wear a mingled stuff, wool and linen together." Here the part plant, part animal origin of the material further reinforces the distinction. In human terms, the same schema is found in the prohibition of mixed marriages — between Hebrews and foreigners — (Deut. 7:3), and also in the fact that a man of mixed blood (offspring of a mixed marriage) or, according to a different interpretation, a bastard (offspring of adultery) may not enter the assembly of the Lord (Deut. 23:3). This would seem to make it very understandable that the Hebrews did not accept the divine nature of Jesus. A God-man, or a God become man, was bound to offend their logic more than anything else. Christ is the absolute hybrid.

A man is a man, or he is God. He cannot be both at the same time. In the same manner, a human being is either a man or a woman, not both: homosexuality is outlawed (Lev. 18:22). The prohibition is extended even to clothes: "A woman shall not wear anything that pertains to a man, nor shall a man put on a woman's garment" (Deut. 22:4). Bestiality is also condemned (Lev. 18:20) and, above all, incest (Lev. 18:6 ff.): "She is your mother, you shall not uncover her nakedness." This tautological formulation shows the principle involved here: once a woman is defined as "mother" in relation to a boy, she cannot also be something else to him. The incest prohibition is a logical one. It thus becomes evident that the sexual and the dietary prohibitions of the Bible are coordinated. This no doubt explains the Bible's most mysterious prohibition: "You shall not boil a kid in its mother's milk" (Exod. 23:19 and 34:26; Deut. 14:21). These words must be taken quite literally. They concern a mother and her young. They can be translated as: you shall not put a mother and her son into the same pot, any more than into the same bed. Here as elsewhere, it is a matter of upholding the separation between two classes or two types of relationships. To abolish distinction by means of a sexual or culinary act is to subvert the order of the world. Everyone belongs to one species only, one people, one sex, one category. And in the same manner, everyone has only one God: "See now that I, even I, am he, and there is no God beside me" (Deut. 32:39). The keystone of this order is the principle of identity, instituted as the law of every being.

The Mosaic logic is remarkable for its rigor, indeed its rigidity. It is a "stiff-necked" logic, to use the expression applied by Yahveh to his people. It is self-evident that the very inflexibility of this order was a powerful factor for unification and conservation in a people that wanted to "dwell alone." On the other hand, however, the Mosaic religion, inseparable as it is from the sociocultural system of the Hebrews, could only lose in power of diffusion what it gained in power of concentration. Christianity could only be born by breaking with the structures that separated the Hebrews from the other peoples. It is not surprising that one of the decisive ruptures concerned the dietary prescriptions. Matthew quotes Jesus as saying: "Not what goes into the mouth defiles a man, but what comes out of the mouth, this defiles a man" (15:11). Similar words are reported by Mark, who comments: "Thus he declared all foods clean" (7:19). The meaning of this rejection becomes strikingly clear in the episode of Peter's vision at Jaffa (Acts 10): a great sheet descends from heaven with all kinds of clean and unclean animals in it, and God's voice speaks: "Rise, Peter; kill and eat." Peter resists the order twice, asserting that he is a good Jew and has never eaten anything unclean. But God repeats his order a third time. Peter's perplexity is dispelled by the arrival of three men sent by the Roman centurion Cornelius, who is garrisoned in Caesarea. Cornelius wants to hear Peter expound the new doctrine he is propagating. And Peter, who had hitherto been persuaded that Jesus' reform was meant only for the Jews, now understands that it is valid for the Gentiles as well. He goes to Caesarea, shares the meal of a non-Jew, speaks to Cornelius, and baptizes him. Cornelius becomes the first non-Jew to be converted to Christianity. The vision in which the distinction between clean and unclean foods was abolished had thus implied the abolition of the distinction between Jews and non-Jews.

From this starting point, Christianity could begin its expansion, grafting itself onto the Greco-Roman civilization, which, unlike the Hebrew civilization, was ready to welcome all blends, and most notably a God-man. A new system was to come into being, based on new structures. This is why the materials it took from the older system assumed a different value. Blood, for instance, is consumed by the priest in the sacrifice of the Mass in the form of its signifier: "the blood of the grape." This is because the fusion between man and God is henceforth possible, thanks to the intermediate term, which is Christ. Blood, which had acted as an isolator between two poles, now becomes a conductor. In this manner, everything that Christianity has borrowed from Judaism . . . , must in some way be "tinkered with," to use Lévi-Strauss's comparison.

By contrast, whatever variations the Mosaic system may have undergone in the course of history, they do not seem to have shaken its fundamental structures. This logic, which sets up its terms in contrasting pairs and lives by the rule of refusing all that is hybrid, mixed, or arrived at by synthesis and compromise, can be seen in action to this day in Israel, and not only in its cuisine.

MAKING CONNECTIONS:
RELIGION AND RITUAL

1. Until recently, religion was a matter of behavior more than of belief. As Jean Soler shows, ritual and correct behavior were central to the Hebrews' religion. In the ancient world and, indeed, down to the eighteenth century, nearly all Jews were recognizable by their religious behavior: their observance of the Sabbath, of the law of circumcision, and of a specific dietary regimen (eating kosher food exclusively). What religious rituals did other peoples in the ancient world observe? Although we sometimes think of the religion of the Hebrews as different from other religions, there are some similarities. In what ways were other religions similar to Judaism?

2. Do you think the 613 laws in the Hebrew Bible, many of them about keeping kosher, accurately reflect the daily life of Jews in biblical times? What do the laws reveal about the Hebrews' perceptions of themselves and of their neighbors? What were the Jews' reasons for keeping kosher? Why didn't other ancient peoples keep kosher?

WORKADAY LIFE UNDER
RAMESSES THE GREAT
K. A. Kitchen

Perhaps because of the fame of its archeological remains or because of the grandeur of its monuments, we tend to think of ancient Egypt as a wealthy and prosperous kingdom. The Nile's regular flooding, the temperate climate, and the geographic near-isolation that protected the country from frequent invasion likewise encourage historians to see Egypt as a self-assured and optimistic civilization. In this selection, K. A. Kitchen, a British Egyptologist (retired from the University of Liverpool), indeed finds that the lives of workers at the tombs of the pharaoh were relatively comfortable. Ramesses II, sometimes referred to as Ramesses the Great, reigned from 1292 to 1225 B.C. He extended Egypt's conquests in the Middle East and embarked on a massive building program as well. His prosperous reign marked the height of Egyptian imperial power.

Archeological excavations of the workers' village allow Kitchen to recreate their closed world. They had their own homes, rest-days, good food and beer, a laundry service, recreation, and time to build their own tombs. Rarely in the ancient world are historians able to know nonelites, but the existence of inscriptions and written records enable Kitchen to describe the personalities and lives of individual workers. Do the people Kitchen brings to life reflect the specific culture of ancient Egypt, or are their behaviors and quirks what one would expect of any human beings? How would you characterize the workers' religion? How do the lives of the workers at the royal tomb compare to those of Egyptian peasant farmers?

At the head of Egypt stood one man — the Pharaoh. Immediately below him came the two viziers[1] of South and North, then the other high officials of state. Then, department by department, province by province, the supporting cohorts of middle-rank scribes, local dignitaries, personnel of minor temples, all the way down to the village clerk. Alongside the middle and lower ranges of functionaries came the practical specialists of all kinds — artists, sculptors, jewellers, glaze-

---

K. A. Kitchen, *Pharaoh Triumphant: The Life and Times of Ramesses II, King of Egypt* (Warminster, England: Aris & Phillips Ltd., 1982), 183–190, 191–200, 202–203, 205.

[1] Chief ministers.

makers, metal-workers, carpenters, leatherworkers, weavers and potters, and many more whose efforts contributed to the life of all. Plus the armed forces from general to simple recruit, for defence or foreign adventures.

But the whole of this imposing social pyramid required a broad, strong, ample base to function at all — in a word, it had to *eat*. Real wealth in early Egypt consisted of land, but more especially of land flooded annually by the Nile and then cultivated by human effort, whether for crops or livestock. And, in fact, by far the greater part of Egypt's population under Ramesses II (as at other periods) worked as peasant farmers on the land, providing the physical basis of life for the whole community.

Work on the land was always hard and often thankless. A good inundation meant plenty for all, farmers included; but a bad year could mean the same taxes to pay, and no grain to meet tax-demands or hungry stomachs. The scribes never tired of rehearsing the ills of the farmer to their pupils to keep them at their studies, bidding them remember:

> the state of the peasant farmer faced with registry of the harvest-tax, when the snake has taken one half (of the crop), and the hippo has devoured the other half. The mice overrun the field, the locust descends, and the cattle eat up. The sparrows bring poverty upon the farmer. The remnants (of harvest) upon the threshing-floor (fall) to the thieves. . . . The tax-official has landed on the river-bank to register the harvest-tax, with the janitors carrying staves, and the Nubians[2] palm-rods. They (say), "Give up the grain!," although there is none. They beat him up . . . he is thrown headlong down a well. . . . So the grain disappears. . . .

During the flood-season (July–September) with no farm-work on hand, the peasantry could be recruited for corvée or forced labour on other projects — as manpower for quarrying stone, manhandling it on temple sites, or in brickyards, and so on. But as the Nile waters receded from the land, the land had to be ploughed, the lumps of fertile mud broken up, the seed sown and then trodden in (sometimes by pigs). Then, month by month, the care of the growing crops, and ceaseless irrigation through channels from basins of retained water and by simple water-lifts ("shaduf") from river or canal into channels and fields. Then in spring (March–April), the assessors measured-off the standing crops to determine the amounts of tax payable by the cultivators (and their employing institutions) to the state treasury, before the golden grain was cut. Then, after work on the threshing-floors, the grain could be shipped away to the granaries and stores of the land-holding institutions, and treasury, leaving the farmer with his balance. He, of course, had also his vegetable plot for lettuce, cucumbers, melons and the like, besides the grain, flax and cattle-fodder that was his from the fields. And very large quantities of fish were regularly landed by the Nile fishermen.

---

[2] Inhabitants of the Nile river valley south of the First Cataract, in what is now southern Egypt and the northern Sudan.

But if hard, the farming life was by no means all misery, and the shrewd peasant-farmers learned how to maintain themselves through most difficulties. In contrast to the propaganda by bookish scribes, the paintings in the tomb-chapels show the rosy side of the farming life: good Niles, abundant crops, fine cattle, an aura of prosperous contentment with landworker and supervisor alike. More significantly, Egyptians in other walks of life (like Sennudjem, a workman of the Royal Tomb) happily showed themselves as raising the wondrous crops of the Afterlife, an activity hallowed in Spell 110 of the Book of the Dead[3] (and in the "Coffin Texts"[4] still earlier); thus, farming was widely recognised as the real basis of the community's life. The *Tale of the Two Brothers* also reflects the modest but satisfying life of the successful peasant-farmer, and in picturesque ways the feeling of the ancient farmer for his beasts:

> Now once upon a time, there were two brothers. . . . Anup was the name of the elder, and Bata of the younger. Anup had a house and a wife, and his younger brother was with him like a son. He it was who made clothes for him, while he (Bata) followed his cattle to the fields as he had to do the ploughing. And he (Bata) it was who reaped (the harvest) for him and did all the work in the fields. . . . Every evening, he left work to return home, loaded with all the vegetables of the field, with milk, with wood, and every good field-product; and he would place them before his elder brother as the latter sat with his wife. And so he (Bata) ate and drank, and [went off to sleep] in the byre,[5] among his cattle. . . .
>
> Now . . . (day by day) . . . , he would drive his cattle, to pasture in the fields. . . . And they would tell him, "The grazing is good in this (or that) place!" And he heeded all that they said, and took them to the spot with good grazing that they wanted. The cattle in his care thus flourished marvellously, and they calved every so often.
>
> So, at the season for ploughing, his elder brother said to him, "Get ready for us the [ox]-team for ploughing, for the fields have emerged (from the flood-waters) and they're fine for ploughing now! And also, bring the seed to the field, for we'll start ploughing in the morning."

The Egyptians were very fond of their cows, and often gave them names — the "Buttercup" and "Daisy" of those times. In the Deir el Medina tomb-chapel . . . of the Scribe Ramose, in a ploughing scene, his servant Ptah-seankh says to him, "The fields are in really top condition; their grain will flourish, you being with us — you being well, along with me and 'Right-hander' and 'Good-Flood-Comes'!" At another time and place, stalled cows being given their fodder are cheerfully enjoined, "Lovely grass! Eat it up!"

Not all was idyllic, even in the rosy world of the tomb-paintings. In the

---

[3] Collections of prayers and magical formulae — mass produced on papyrus for the middle classes — that ensured the survival of the deceased in the afterlife.

[4] Early prayers and magical formulae that the elite used to ensure their survival in the afterlife.

[5] Cowshed.

chapel . . . of the Theban priest Panehsy, we suddenly find a "wild-cow strike." Of a team of two animals, one has suddenly tired of the whole weary job of walking up and down, up and down, endlessly ploughing, and so had flopped flat on the ground, refusing to budge! One man belabours it with a stick, while with one large, reproachful eye, the bored beast coyly steals a glance at the ploughman, Pre-hotep, who hollers "Get up, get moving, stop shamming dead, you [brute]!"

While the vast majority of their brethren spent sunlit days labouring modestly and obscurely in the black mud and vivid green growth of the broad, level fields, a small group of men and their families lived apart, as a closed community, in their special village behind a sandy hill in Western Thebes, a mile or so from the nearest green cultivation. In striking contrast to the peasant-farmers out on the plain, these men crossed the dry, sun-scorched cliffs behind this village to work deep underground in a valley utterly barren of any sign of natural life — the Valley of the Kings.

These men were the "Workmen of the Royal Tomb" (also, "Servants in the Place of Truth"), a community founded in the 16th century B.C. by Amenophis I,[6] still their patron saint 300 years later. His successor Tuthmosis I[7] had built the village that nestled close behind Gurnet Murrai hill near the south end of Western Thebes — the settlement simply called "the Village" by its inhabitants and known today as Deir el Medina. Already in the later Eighteenth Dynasty,[8] an extension had been built along the west side of the village. Then, probably in the first years of Sethos I,[9] a further "block" of 12 or 14 houses was added at the south end — the entire village being enclosed as within a long rectangle by its outer wall. The close-set "high-density" housing for these workpeople was a tradition in Egypt going back centuries.

. . . The houses in the village, all of mud-brick on rough masonry foundations, followed one basic layout with only minor variations. Being crowded into the minimum space, they were long and narrow from front to rear, in the terraces or rows — somewhat reminiscent of European "industrial housing" of the last century. Each house fronted onto the street or an alley. Through the front door, the visitor stepped down into the "front parlour" past the water-pots. Beyond the front parlour was the main living-room whose higher roof (supported by a column) allowed subdued light to filter in through a skylight between the roof-levels of parlour and living-room. From one of these two rooms descended a stairway to an underground cellar, sometimes from under (or close to) the low brick bench or "divan" where the master of the house might sleep on mats, when at home — he thus guarded the family valuables in the vault! From the living-room also, we

---

[6] Amenhotep I (d. ca. 1526 B.C.).

[7] Pharaoh (d. ca. 1512 B.C.) who initiated raids into Palestine and Syria.

[8] The fifteenth and fourteenth centuries B.C.

[9] Sety I (d. ca. 1279 B.C.).

gain access to a workroom-cum-bedroom, and to a back-kitchen open to the sky with mortar and pestle for grinding flour and oven for baking bread. A short steep stairway led up to the roof — a useful additional living-space in the dry, sunny climate of Upper Egypt.

In the whitewashed walls of the main room, niches were cut for images of the local gods of hearth and home. A special enclosed chamber in the front parlour was particularly dedicated to (and decorated for) Bes[10] and the household deities of womanhood; it may have been a confinement room, where children might be born under the domestic protection of Bes, Taweret,[11] Isis[12] and Hathor.[13] Furnishings throughout were simple: low stools, rush mats, an abundance of pottery (which the house-wives of the village seemed to break in large quantities!), sometimes low, wooden beds with rope "springing," and occasionally a wooden chair. Besides pottery, the family had the use of attractive basketware of woven rushwork. The family's possessions would include the workman's personal tools (like Sennudjem's plumb-line and set-square) as opposed to state-supplied tools, the family store of linen garments, perhaps a copper or bronze vessel or two, and minor jewellery of coloured glazeware. The niches for household gods or formal busts of dear departed relatives could be framed with strips of limestone, engraved with hieroglyphic inscriptions invoking the favour of the gods on the householder, and his wife and children. The main entrance to the house could have stone doorjambs and lintel with the figures, names and titles of the householder and family.

In its little valley, the village did not stand alone. Opposite its long western wall there rose up along the steepening hill-slope terrace upon terrace of the tomb-chapels of the workmen and their families — courts with low walls, whitewashed brick chapels with small pyramids upon them, rising up in impressive array, while deep below (hidden from sight) was a maze of passages and burial-chambers. Outside the north approach to the village, past the great water-cistern, there clustered a whole series of little mud-brick temples and chapels for the gods. These had open courts, outer halls, inner sanctuaries; benches for the worshipping workmen, and a clutter of votive objects presented to the gods, especially small stone stelae, often inscribed with thanksgiving for help or healing as we shall see. Finally, outside the north and south approaches to the whole area, a "police-post" stood at either end to check on visitors — after all, this community was set aside for the service of the royal valley and the secret tombs of the pharaohs; casual contacts and gossip on these matters were probably not encouraged.

. . . Of the nearly 70 houses inside the village, almost a dozen are known

---

[10] God associated with music and dance and with the protection of women in childbirth.

[11] Goddess of fertility and childbirth; associated with the nursing of infants.

[12] Goddess of rebirth and resurrection.

[13] Goddess of the sky, queen of heaven, patron of women and marriage, and bestower of fertility and beauty.

today (33 centuries afterwards) to have belonged to particular men and their families. Thus sauntering south along the main street or alley, past a dozen doors on our right and seven equally ordinary doors on the left (east), we reach on our left a distinctive doorway set back a little and having a red-painted stone frame. This is the entrance to a house . . . more spacious than most — within, it has not only a front parlour with closet, two columned sitting-rooms and three bed-rooms/workrooms with stairway-vault beyond, but also two side-rooms — kitchen (two ovens) and passage-room. The red-painted hieroglyphs on the front doorframe proudly announce this to be the residence of the Chief Workman, Qaha and his wife Tuy. The ample rooms were certainly needful, as they had eight children, including Anhur-khaw whom Qaha hoped would eventually succeed to his own job.

About three doors further down, over to the right (west), probably lived Qaha's contemporary the draughtsman-painter Maai-nakhtef, son of Pashed whose house . . . it was in Sethos I's time. A few doors along, back on the left side, we meet Khawy, "Guardian of the Royal Tomb" with a modest three-room abode. . . . A few more doors down on the right is the roomier residence . . . of the sculptor Neferronpet, from whose extra-broad parlour open two little suites of two rooms each. His tastes are unknown to us, but his sculptor-colleague Ipuy was perhaps an animal-lover — tomcat and kitten fawn on him in his tomb-chapel . . . , and on a statuette of his, both a cat and a monkey appear!

Next, the main village-alley bends sharply right then left, into the newest, southern quarter. Off to the left down a common corridor, there opened off two small three-roomed houses . . . , one belonging to the ordinary workman Har-nufer. Round the bend three doors along, lived Neb-amentet and his son Neb-amun in adjacent dwellings of five rooms each. . . . Opposite them lived more modestly the draughtsman-painter Prehotep . . . , in the same profession as his fa-ther Pay and brother Nebre. Finally the last two houses . . . next to his belonged to the workman Kha-bekhnet and probably his brother Khons (inheriting from their father Sennudjem of Sethos I's time).

These are only a few of the village characters, and already they include sev-eral workmen, a security-guard, a sculptor, two draughtsmen-painters, and above all a Chief Workman, all in the direct employ of "Pharaoh, their good lord" (Ramesses II) through the vizier, for the cutting and decorating of the royal tombs in the Valleys of the Kings and Queens. The organisation of the work-force was in two halves, "port" and "starboard" or right and left sides, corresponding per-haps to the right and left sides of the long corridor-tombs in which they worked. Containing perhaps up to 30 ordinary workmen under Ramesses II, each side was headed by a Chief Workman or Foreman; these two men each had a Deputy. Alongside these two bosses and deputies, there stood correspondingly two Scribes of the Royal Tomb — responsible directly to the Vizier for all the administration concerning the village and royal tombs, just as the foremen were for all the progress of actual work. To the two sets of workmen, chiefs, deputies and scribes, one must add the specialists: draughtsman-painters who drew the first outlines of scenes and inscriptions in the tombs, and later coloured-in the reliefs carved from their outlines by the sculptors. Then there were the guardians (like Khawy) who kept the stores of copper tools, lighting-equipment, clothing, etc. There were also "outside services" represented by water-carriers, a staff of "serfs" (bringing supplies of fish, vegetables, firewood, gypsum, etc.), launderers, slave-women to mill flour, and three doorkeepers used as messengers and bailiffs and to check on supplies as delivered. A small squad of police under an officer, and a physician and scorpion-curer complete the picture.

For a village thus secluded in a desert setting, all supplies had to come from outside, and efficient delivery was vital. Thus, all the water, food, etc., was brought in relays by the "outside staff." The water-carriers were constantly borrowing or hiring donkeys to save themselves carrying volumes of water over the mile or two between the river and canals and the village — a practice that often led to disputes. The working "week" lasted 10 days (three "weeks" or decades in each month). Each 10th day was a rest-day or "weekend," when the new supplies of food were paid out to the workmen; foremen got double the pay of ordinary workmen. In Ramesses II's day, the custom of the "long weekend" had already begun — the 9th and 10th days of each decade or "week" were not worked.

Even today, the huge sepulchres of the Theban kings compel admiration — vast, brilliantly-decorated halls and corridors that run deep into the mountain. How *were* they done? And by whom, precisely? The second question is already answered. For Ramesses II, it was on the right side the Foremen Neferhotep the Elder, Nebnufer, and Neferhotep the Younger, all father-to-son, and on the left side Qaha and his son Anhur-khaw, and the sixty men under their joint command who hewed out Ramesses' vast tomb. The sculptors and draughtsmen we met in the village; such scribes as Ramose and Qen-hir-khopshef, Amenemope and Huy, kept the accounts and records of this work. The same people also produced the superb tombs in the Queens' Valley for Nefertari,[14] Bint-Anath[15] and the others.

So much, then, for the "credits" — what of the methods? Once the high-powered committee of the Theban vizier Paser and other notables had finally decided (doubtless with royal approval) on the appropriate spot for the tomb, then the royal workmen took over. At the beginning of the "week," the shift for duty was issued with its tools. To prevent any of the metal being quietly filched, these were meticulously weighed out to the men. As was the grease or fat used for lamp-wicks — it was an edible fat much appreciated by the workmen, but candle-fat was not for eating! Duly supplied, the party wended its way down the west side of the village. Then they climbed steeply up to their right (the west) by a narrow path onto the flank of the mountain. Then they turned back north, leaving the village well below, and went on along a rocky path flanked on the west by the towering Peak, their goddess Meresger,[16] while off to their east (and right) there

---

[14] Chief wife of Ramesses II.

[15] Daughter and secondary wife of Ramesses II.

[16] The patron goddess of Deir el Medina, symbolized by the mountain peak.

opened a view right across the hills of the Tombs of the Nobles, the memorial-temples of the kings, and the green-clad plain as far as the Nile, with Eastern Thebes, its temples and plain, and the Arabian hill-chain on the horizon.

Directly below the sacred Peak was a stopping-point, the "col,"[17] with rough stone huts built by the workmen and little shrines to Meresger and the gods. From here, the workmen's path dropped swiftly down the barren slopes into the Valley of the Kings. During their eight or nine days' stint, the workmen did not return daily to the village, but slept overnight in the few small stone huts in the Valley itself, or in those up at the "col." Only at the "weekend" did the party return home.

Under their chiefs, the workmen hewed their way downward into the limestone rock with copper and bronze picks, the broken stone being carted out in basketloads by their mates. But, as corridor succeeded corridor, receding ever further from the strong sunlight outside, artificial lighting became necessary. For this, long greased wicks (twisted-up from old clothing) were used, set to burn in bowls filled with salted oil. From a "battery" of these simple lamps, a clear, non-smoky light was obtained, enough by which to quarry, plaster, draw, carve and paint in halls deep within the mountain. . . .

So soon as the first corridor or so was quarried out "in the rough," and while the quarrying-party pressed steadily onward, the newly created room was smoothed-down by chisellers and sculptors, the walls surfaced with gypsum-plaster and again smoothed-off. Upon these fine surfaces, draughtsmen such as Nebre and Prehotep could get to work squaring-off the wall and laying out in fine red line the complex scenes and hieroglyphic inscriptions of the royal "guide-books" to the Nether-world, the master-draughtsman touching up their work here and there in black. Then it was the turn of the sculptors — Qen, Nefer-ronpet, Ipuy, and others — to carve down these master-sketches and texts into scenes in delicate low relief, of exquisite quality. Then finally, the draughtsmen-painters returned to add vivid colour to the finished texts and scenes. So the work progressed, each group following another, hall by hall, day by day, decade by decade, month by month, year by year. The same processes obtained in the Valley of the Queens, reached by another path that struck out south then west from the village.

From the site of the village, its tombs, and especially a nearby pit, there has been recovered an enormous mass of several thousands of "scrap jottings" on slips of limestone and potsherds — "ostraca" (singular, "ostracon"), as today's scholars call them. These are the off-the-cuff record of every conceivable aspect of the life and work of the villagers — letters, receipts, journals of work done, lawsuits, oracles, laundry-lists, hymns, magical spells against illness, extracts from lit-

---

[17] An elevated mountain pass.

erature (classics and contemporary), artists' sketches, in fact documents of every kind, from most of the four centuries' history (1500–1100 B.C.) of the village, particularly the second half, from the reign of Ramesses II onwards, and with the greatest concentration of surviving material in the last years of Ramesses III and under his immediate successors. Quite a remarkable selection of documents can be attributed to the denizens of Deir el Medina of Ramesses II's time, as vivid as any of the more copious later records.

While the current shift of workmen was away on their eight or nine days' stint in the royal valley, some of its members would send messages back home over the hill to the village with their requests for this or that — usually more food! Thus, one young workman to his mother, back in the village:

> Nebneteru to his mother Henut-nofret:-
>
>   Have brought to me some bread, also whatever (else) you have by you, urgently, urgently! And may Amun[18] grant (it) to you, that you be in (his) favour. May you enjoy (his) favour and be given peace!

. . . Sometimes the people recruited to help the workmen turned out to be "duds," as one draughtsman had to report to his father:

> The scribe Pabaki to his father, the draughtsman Maani-nakhtef. Thus: I have heeded what you told me, (namely), "Let Ib work with you." And now see, he's spent the whole day (supposedly) fetching the waterpot, and no other job laid on him the whole day long. He has not heeded your advice which I told to him. (Now), what'll you do today? . . . See now, the sun's gone down, and he's (still) away (with) the waterpot!

That oaf Ib never reappears in the records of Deir el Medina, and doubtless his one long day of lazy malingering by the Nile bank with the waterpot (so needed by the draughtsmen up at the desert) speedily got him the sack.[19]

However, other "additions to staff" were in a different class entirely. It was in Year 5, 3rd month of Inundation, Day 10 (late September, 1275 B.C.), only a few months before Ramesses II set out on the fateful campaign that ended at Qadesh,[20] that a new Scribe was appointed to Deir el Medina: Ramose. Son of a messenger or "postman," he had been a promising young scribe attached to the treasury of the memorial-temple of the long-dead Eighteenth-Dynasty king Tuthmosis IV, down on the desert edge near the Ramesseum. Rising quickly in the administration of the older temple, he had caught the eye of the Theban vizier Paser, and so (when a new scribe was needed) Ramose joined the staff of the Royal Tomb, resident in Deir el Medina.

Perhaps retaining some of his old charges as well as sharing the Tomb ad-

---

[18] God of the sun and chief deity of the New Kingdom.

[19] Got him fired.

[20] Battle, ca. 1274 B.C., between the Egyptian and Hittite armies.

ministration with his colleague Huy, Ramose has been called "the richest man who ever lived in . . . Deir el Medina." No-one in all the four centuries of the village's existence left there so many memorials as Ramose did — stelae[21] inscribed for the gods, in profusion in their chapels; not one, but *three* tombs and chapels . . . and a whole series of miscellaneous mementos that still bear his name — statues, offering-tables, his own seat up at the "col," and various bric-à-brac. Nor was Ramose any less successful in his personal relationships. He eagerly associated his name with that of his benefactor and immediate boss, the vizier Paser, on many a monument, just as doubtless the two men got on well together on Paser's periodic visits of inspection to look over the village, check through the accounts, and to see how work was progressing in the royal valleys of tombs. In turn, both men were well liked and respected by the foremen and the main body of workmen, several of whom included one or both of the pair in the painted scenes that adorned their own tombs and tomb-chapels — a warm mark of respect shown to few others of their rank. The sculptor Qen and the workmen Penbuy and Kasa did this, while Ramose himself included a scene of the King, Paser, and himself in his chapel. . . . He got on well with his colleague Huy whom he is shown honouring in Huy's own chapel. . . . The guardian Khawy showed the King and Paser on one of his own stelae.

In fact, Ramose's life and career were darkened by just one shadow: he had no son of his own to succeed him as Scribe some day, despite all his devotion to Hathor — he and Paser had built her a new temple in the name of Ramesses II, and in Year 9 had established an endowment for the king's statue there. He had also addressed fervent prayers to her, Min,[22] and Taweret, but all in vain. Faced with no answer to his problem in the course of nature, Ramose sought another solution. He and his wife Mutemwia adopted a lad Qen-hir-khopshef son of Panakht, and he schooled him in the scribal art. Thus, on his own later monuments, Qen-hir-khopshef as often names Ramose his "father" as Panakht. By Year 40 of Ramesses' long reign, young Qen-hir-khopshef was deemed able to follow Ramose in office, and was duly appointed Scribe of the Tomb. He was an able enough scribe, but (as time passed) his ever more cursive handwriting is *not* the favourite reading of Egyptologists at a later day! He continued in service quite some time after Ramesses' death. But he did not have the clear, attractive and upright character of his kindly teacher. He got into the habit of unduly diverting workmen to spend time on his own private projects (his own tomb, etc.) from their time on the royal tombs. Some of this was always permitted quietly "on the side" — but not to the extent of gross abuse. He had literary interests, copying out for himself parts of the Battle of Qadesh poem, owning a manual for interpreting dreams, and writing out magical charms. He was probably a rather pushful person (even to the vizier Khay, he is barely polite), and was not too well liked in the

---

[21] Inscribed pillars; singular is *stela*.

[22] The deified Menes, first king of united Egypt, end of fourth millennium B.C.

village community. The draughtsman Prehotep, having been slighted by this Scribe, wrote him the following angry note:

> The draughtsman-painter Prehotep greets his chief, the Scribe of the Place of Truth, Qen-hir-khopshef:-
>
> Greetings. What's the meaning of this rotten way you've treated me? I am to you just like the donkey:-
>
> When there's work (to do), they fetch a donkey, when there's eating (to be had), they fetch an ox.
>
> When there's beer, you're not wanting (me), when there's work, you are seeking (me)!
>
> If concerning us, I am (considered as) a man of bad character because of beer, then seek (me) out no (more). Hear it well, in the Domain of Amen-re King of Gods (bless him!).
>
> (PS): I am a man in whose house is *no* beer; I seek to fill my belly only with my letter to you!

Perhaps Qen-hir-khopshef had been cutting Prehotep out of his "party list" and loudly remarking as excuse that Prehotep couldn't carry his drink — but was still very glad to avail himself of Prehotep's skills as outline-draughtsman and painter of reliefs. Prehotep would not stand for that. His beerless house, of course, we have visited already. . . .

But beer (like everything else) depended on the regularity of supplies reaching the desert village, a fact that applied also to the "dues" or special payments that the workmen looked for at certain times in the year when festivities might be afoot. Most times under Paser's crisply efficient regime, all had gone well. His successor the vizier Khay perhaps had greater difficulty here — during Years 29 to 46, he was much occupied with the proclamation and organising of the first six jubilees of Ramesses II in rapid succession, on top of all the usual duties of his office. So, from time to time, the harrassed Khay got polite reminders from the workpeople of Deir el Medina that their allowances were due, and he impatiently reassured them that they *were* coming! So do we find the draughtsman Siamun tactfully addressing many fulsome compliments to the vizier, before at last venturing to blurt out:

> ". . . a further greeting to my lord — may my lord attend to the gang and give them their rations!"

. . . Meantime, out on the job in the Valley of the Kings, the team worked day by day — but not always at full strength; one or another member of the gang might be absent from work for any of a multitude of reasons. Careful check of presence and absence was kept on "worksheets" by the scribes, almost like a factory "attendance sheet" or clocking-on.[23] One great document of Year 40 of Ramesses II illustrates this side of life vividly; to each workman's name it appends dates of absence and reasons:

---

[23] Punching the time clock; starting work.

Pendua: 1st month of Inundation, Day 14 — (out) drinking with Khons . . .

Haremwia: 3rd of Inundation, Days 21, 22 — with his boss (foreman); 2nd of Winter, Day 8 — brewing beer; 3rd of Summer, Days 17, 18, 21 — ill.

Wennufer: 1st of Winter, Day 14, 4th of Summer, Day 4 — making offering to his god.

Huynefer: 2nd of Winter, Days 7, 8 — ill; 3rd of Summer, Days 3, 5 — eye-trouble; Days 7, 8 — ill.

Amenemwia: 1st of Winter, Day 15 — mummifying Harmose; 2nd of Winter, Day 7 — absent; Day 8 — brewing beer; Day 16 — strengthening the door . . .

Seba: 4th of Inundation, Day 17 — a scorpion bit him; 1st of Winter, Day 25 — ill.

Khons: 4th of Inundation, Day 7, 3rd of Winter, Days 25–28 — ill; 4th of Winter, Day 8 — attending his god; . . . 1st of Inundation, Day 14 — his feast; Day 15, — his feast [= a birthday hangover?].

Anuy: 1st of Winter, Day 24 — fetching stone for Qen-hir-khopshef; 2nd of Winter, Day 7 — *ditto*; Day 17 — absent; Day 24 — absent with the Scribe . . .

Still other entries record someone "preparing medicaments" with Khons or Haremwia, also the illnesses of mothers, wives or daughters, and sundry religious observances (libations; "burial" of a god). But the entries already quoted show the variety of incidents. Time off was allowed for brewing-up for festivals or "weekends"; and for illness, needless to say. Especially piquant is poor Seba's being bitten by a scorpion — nearly 50 years later, there was almost a plague of these incidents in the first years of king Siptah. Specially noteworthy is the reference to mummifying Harmose — his death is actually recorded on another document, as we shall see. Likewise, Huynefer's eye-trouble . . . , as "seeing darkness by day" was considered a punishment from the gods, as will be seen presently. Making offering to a patron-god was allowable — and apparently, both one's birthday and a hangover! Noticeable, too, are many days spent absent "with his boss," when a workman was off helping a foreman with other tasks — including work on the boss's own tomb and chapel; the Scribe Qen-hir-khopshef is seen here, freely availing himself of this "perk."

While all this was going on, in and out of the royal Valleys, more domestic affairs concerned the "outside services" and the housewives of the community. There was a "laundry service," doing so many households per day — oddly reminiscent of the towel and linen suppliers to our own offices and hotels of today. But then, as today, outside laundering sometimes had its problems. Thus, one rather irritated Scribe of the Tomb (Ramose?) wrote a curt note to Amenemope, his opposite number attached to these outside services, to the following effect:

To the Scribe Amenemope:-

As to the 8 (households) you've done, (saying), "Assign 4 houses per washerman to the washerman," and not the [6] (households per man) that Pharaoh assigned to him.

Now see (here), he has been assigned 6 households as work for 2 days, making 3 households per day. . . . A (right) good thing you've done! As for Nakht-

Sobki, I found no natron (i.e., "soap") in his possession — you (shall) give him [some]. . . . When you know the [amount] that's short, they can seek out natron for the clothes, and you shall not (further) [allow] this failure to supply natron. For Pharaoh has assigned natron to you — it (just) cannot be that he has not allotted it! And they'll high(light) your deceit. Now you know one side (of the matter)!

Back in the village, the housewives sometimes sent notes to each other, or to and from their husbands out at work, and to and from other women living outside the village altogether. So, one lady sends a short, sharp missive to some "junior miss" in her employ:

Nub-hir-maat, sister of Nebt-Iunu says:-
    Greetings. Furthermore:- Please attend to giving me the garment. Run along, gather in the vegetables that are due from you!

Much more effusive is the lady Wernuro, seeking a second chance for Huynefer's brother Khay:

Wernuro to the scribe Huynefer:-
    Greetings. (Yours) be the favour of Amen-re, King of the Gods, thus — see, I ask of every god and goddess in the district of the West, that you may be hale, hearty, and (enjoying) the favour of Pharaoh your good lord every day.

Then she gets around to her request:

Further. Please consider your brother — don't abandon him! And (my) other message is to (your sister) Nefert-khay, too: consider Khay your brother, don't desert him!

Perhaps at a date a few decades after Ramesses II's reign, a very sad little document was penned by a man less fortunate than Khay (and less deserving?). He writes:

Now I have no wife at all. Is she indeed my wife? — she finished saying her piece, and went out, flinging open the door. . . . (Her father said): "I am not (usually) one who'd have you seized, saying, 'Look what you've done to your wife,' and saying, 'You are blind to the extent of your upsetting me, and to the extent of your being deaf to this crime (before) Horus![24] It's an abomination to Montu.'"[25] (Her mother said): "I'll make you see these adulteries that your [. . .] has done to you!"

Not all of life was work in the tombs and domestic ups and downs. Each "weekend" was time off, when the community received the new decade's supplies, worked for themselves or each other ("odd-jobbing" on their houses, and their own tombs and chapels, or on furnishings for both) — or celebrated the festivals of their gods and patron saint, besides settling their lawsuits in their own tribunal

---

[24] Son of Isis, god of the sky and heaven.

[25] Falcon-headed god of war; protector of the king in battle.

or before the oracle of one form or another of "Saint Amenophis I" their patron. Of those various forms (based on statue-cults of aspects of the king), their favourite was understandably "Amenophis I, Lord of the Village," *their* Amenophis, of *their* village. Several feasts a year were celebrated for Amenophis I, when the workmen themselves served as his priests, as "Servants in the Place of Truth," and those chosen carried his image in joyful procession. On those days, food and drink flowed freely, offerings were made in the god's chapel, and all made merry. On his "Great Feast" in 3rd month of Winter, Day 29 (February), a later ostracon records that:

> . . . the gang made merry before him for 4 full days, drinking with their wives and children — 60 people from inside (the village) and 60 people from outside.

On a column-base from his shrine, a dozen of our villagers recorded their names in the role of priests of "their" Amenophis I — the draughtsman Nebre served as Lector-priest, leading the rites; Apehty was fan-bearer; the sculptor Qen was "servant"; others were *wab*, simple priest.

On other great festivals, too, the workmen had their holidays, as on the opening day of the Feast of Opet[26] and on the Feast of the Valley (over at Deir el Bahri and the Ramesseum, nearby), both of Amun, besides others. On these joyful days, people sometimes sent presents to each other, in appreciation of kindnesses for example. One man writes to another:

> What I'm forwarding to you by the hand of the policeman Pasaro (is) 12 cakes, two lots of incense at 5 measures each, on the day of the offering which you've made for Amun at the Festival of the Valley. They are not given from the things you sent me.

By his last remark, the writer seems to be covering himself against any charge of meanness in the source of his present!

Moreover, the workmen of Deir el Medina were by no means the only ones to appeal to the oracles of Amenophis I in Western Thebes. . . . It was a feast-day, with booths set up, full of tempting food and drink — bread, cakes, grapes, vegetables, etc. — offerings for the saint, food to regale his worshippers. Two men, Heqanakht and the servant Ramesses-nakht, were locked in dispute, and so appeared before Amenophis I as his priests carried his glittering image in procession from his temple, attended by great feather-fans and Amenmose censing. A previous divine judgement had already found for Ramesses-nakht, but perhaps Amenophis I might judge differently? So, Amenmose, chief priest of Amenophis I, put the matter to his god: ". . . 'My good Lord, — the god actually did say that Ramesses-nakht is right and that Heqanakht is wrong.' This god (Amenophis I) approved heartily, saying, 'Ramesses-nakht is (indeed) right!'" Cheered by this second decision in his favour, Ramesses-nakht cried out exultedly, "Ah, my Lord who has seen into the hearts of his [subjects]!" Nearby stand the ladies, tinkling their

---

[26] A festival celebrating the trinity of Amun the Father, Mut the Mother, and Khonsu the Son.

sistra[27] and with castanets and flutes, plus a trumpeter, for the music of the festival. How did Amenophis's image say "Yes" (or, "No")? For "Yes," his bearers felt a movement forward; for "No," a movement backward, — indicating the god's agreement to, or rejection of, the question or proposition set before him, whether spoken or in writing.

Back at Deir el Medina, many a little stone stela was deposited in the village shrines of Amun, Amenophis I, Hathor, Thoth,[28] Meresger, and the other gods, little inscriptions that touchingly witness to the devotion that these Egyptian workmen and scribes felt for their gods, praising them for their benefits and imploring their aid. Fearful respect also — this or that misfortune was often interpreted as divine punishment for some misdeed, which the miscreant confessed, begging for mercy and healing from the offended deity. . . .

The draughtsman-painter Nebre had several sons. One, Nakhtamun, fell ill, and was thought to have offended Amun. So, his father Nebre and brother Khay interceded with Amun for healing. Their plea was heard, so they set up a remarkable stela as thank-offering, to the glory of Amun:

> *Giving praise to Amun:-*
> *I shall make hymns in his Name,*
> *I shall sing his praises as high as heaven, as wide as earth,*
> *I shall declare his might to whoever sails by, to north or south.*
>
> *Beware of him!*
> *Mention him to son and daughter, to great and small.*
> *Tell of him to generation upon generation, not yet born.*
> *Tell of him to the fishes in the stream, to the birds in the sky.*
> *Mention him to those who know him, and those who do not.*
>
> *Beware of Him!*
> *You are Amun, Lord of the silent man,*
> *One who comes at the voice of the poor man.*
> *I called out to you when I was in distress,*
> *When you came, you delivered me. . . .*

Many another besides Nebre shared his respect for the Theban gods. The workman Nefer-abu sang of their local goddess Meresger (the Peak, guarding village and royal Valleys alike). Chastised for his errors and also healed, he enjoins:

> *Giving praise to the Peak of the West:-*
> *(I was) an ignorant and foolish man,*
> *who knew not good from bad.*
> *I committed a fault against the Peak,*
> *and she taught me a lesson.*
>
> *Beware of the Peak!*
> *For a lion is within the Peak,*

---

[27] Rattles of metal discs; used by Egyptians and Ethiopians in pagan and Christian worship.

[28] God of wisdom and writing.

She strikes with the blow of a raging lion.

I called out to my Lady,
    I found she came to me with sweet breezes

She turned to me again in mercy. . . .

I am a man who swore falsely by Ptah, Lord of Truth.
    He caused me to see darkness by day. . . .

Was this an attack of blindness, or some eye-complaint like that attested for Huynefer and Nakhtamun on the great "work-sheet" of absences of the Year 40 of Ramesses II, quoted earlier? Or was it some darkness of the mind? We cannot now be quite sure.

Stelae and statues were by no means the only gifts that the workmen offered to their gods, besides the oblations on feast-days. But, in their little desert-valley, such people of limited means and time could not serve their gods on the lavish scale of the great state temples with rich offerings and bouquets of fresh flowers daily. The latter problem, at least, they overcame by presenting fine model bouquets, well carved in wood or thin limestone and painted to look like fresh flowers and greenery — these, on the gods' offering-stands would last indefinitely in the dry desert atmosphere, just like the use of artificial and plastic flowers today! . . .

The workmen of the Royal Tomb in Western Thebes had, of course, to think of their own eventual burial, besides preparing for that of the pharaoh. On the hill-flank rising up to the west of the village, they tunnelled their tomb-chambers below ground, and over these vaults built whitewashed chapels with bright paintings within, fronted by open courts and the chapels often surmounted by small pyramids with stelae. Tomb-sites were assigned to families by the vizier in the King's name. Ownership of a tomb (as of a house) was a vital matter, record of assignment of such properties being jealously remembered or preserved.

Sooner or later, like their royal patron, the workmen came to occupy their eternal abodes. Here, their beliefs were at one with other Egyptians of the day of all ranks. The mummified body provided a material "housing" for the soul (as did statuary), as did the tomb for both body and soul (the latter, overnight). Tomb-decoration included, besides worship of appropriate funerary gods, scenes of the family (as at banquet), that all the family might be united together and be provided for, in the afterlife. Spells from the Book of the Dead would give safety and provision in that afterlife. Magically, goods placed in the tomb would be of service then also.

In one fleeting document, we actually witness the passing of one of our workmen, and arrangements for his funeral:

The scribe Piay, and the youth of the Tomb, Mahuhy, to:-
    The Chief Workman Neferhotep and the workman Pennub.
    Greetings. And further.
    Now, what was it that you said? — "If anyone dies here, will you go and make enquiry about them?" Does it exclude your man?

This man died in the house of Haremhab who sent word to me, saying, "Harmose's dead!" I went with Mahuhy, and [we] saw (it was so). And we made arrangements for him, and we had the [undertaker] fetched, saying, "Take care of him really well — we are looking after [his affairs]." [We shall?] make shrill the cries, when you make [mourning]. . . .

Doubtless the embalmers did their best for Harmose, allowing for his (and his colleagues') modest means. That his death occurred in Year 40 of Ramesses II (winter of 1240/39 B.C.), we already know from the great "work-sheet" of absences cited above, in which Amenemwia was entrusted with the final wrapping of Harmose's mummy. We know little of Harmose's life except that he was perhaps grandfather of the workman Pennub mentioned in the letter from Piay.

Beyond any doubt, it was in the time of Ramesses II that the community at Deir el Medina enjoyed its heyday of greatest prosperity. Never again were its members able to afford new tombs and chapels such as were built in this reign. Later generations were content to be buried in the same tombs, used as family vaults, and merely to adapt the houses and chapels; fewer, too, were the stone stelae and statues. So, with the eventual failure of the Ramesside empire, Deir el Medina also fell on leaner days until, finally, under Ramesses XI,[29] the village was abandoned, and the remaining work-force was based on the precinct of Ramesses III's great memorial-temple at Medinet Habu, still the centre of West-Theban administration at the end of the Empire. Then, during the following century and half of decline, the little group eventually shrank to *nil* with the end of all major works in Western Thebes by about 950 B.C.

---

[29] Last pharaoh of the New Kingdom (d. ca. 1085 B.C.).

PART TWO

CLASSICAL GREECE AND ROME

William J. Baker
K. J. Dover
Alex Scobie
Suzanne Dixon
Paul Veyne
Elaine Pagels

In the eighteenth century, Voltaire, the French intellectual, wrote that true glory belonged only to "four happy ages" in the history of the world. The first was ancient Greece, specifically the fifth and fourth centuries B.C., and the second the Rome of Julius Caesar and Augustus, the first emperor. (The other two were Renaissance Italy and Louis XIV's France.) Voltaire praised classical Greece and Rome because he saw them as civilized, holding the arts, literature, and refined living in high regard. The social historian, aware of the underside of classical civilization, would not be quite so positive.

Nevertheless, there is much to admire in Greek civilization. The political competition of its many independent city-states promoted some freedom of experimentation, as revealed in art, literature, and the diversity of Greek philosophy. Greek social life, too, was more heterogeneous than that of some other cultures of this period, such as Egypt. The Olympics and other games show that the Greeks admired brawn as well as brains. William J. Baker asserts that organized Greek games were essentially religious events that served to emphasize the importance of athletes.

Yet Greek civilization rested on slavery and oppression; life was difficult for most Greeks, and warfare among the city-states was constant. In Athens, the cradle of democracy and the center of classical Greek civilization, well-to-do males virtually locked up their wives and daughters for life giving them no freedom to leave their homes, make important decisions, or converse with men who were not related. (The segregation of women continued even in athletic contests; women had their own games, and the Olympics barred them from competing.) Just as the family in Athens is distinctive historically, so also is Greek sexuality, which has long been the subject of speculation and myth. K. J. Dover illuminates the puritanical side of Greek sexuality and sheds some light on why the Greeks accepted homosexuality.

Law, engineering, architecture, and literature bear witness to the glories of Rome. Gladiatorial combats, mass murders in the Colosseum, and the persecution of Christians, however, remind us of the streak of cruelty that was as Roman as an aqueduct. The Roman historian Tacitus remarked about imperial conquest: "Where they make a desert, they call it peace." Slavery, infanticide, and other brutalities pervaded Roman civilization, as they did Greek society. Paul Veyne looks at Roman pleasures and excesses, their social values and habits, and finds the Romans a bundle of contradictions. They were urbane, highly civilized, gregarious, and treasured friendship. Yet they killed thousands in the arenas and frequented them specifically to see humans die. They venerated laziness while praising civic involvement. They treated their women with macho domination while disdaining libertinage and following strict rules regarding lovemaking. From another perspective, Suzanne Dixon offers a positive assessment of Roman marriage, finding care and devotion between husband and wife to have been common. Women in Rome appear to have fared better than those in Athens. At least elite wives in Rome did not have to remain virtual prisoners in their homes as did their counterparts in Athens.

Historians have written much about the legacy of Greece and Rome to Western civilization. The greatness of Rome has become a historical cliché. Alex Scobie tears the marble curtain from Roman cities, finding them to be awash with filth, stench, and disease. Although the Romans are known for their public baths, magnificent roads and buildings, and aqueducts, the reality is that urban life for all but the wealthy was decidedly unpleasant and dangerous. One particularly noteworthy development in classical Rome was the rise of Christianity, which has had a powerful impact on Western civilization down to the present. In subjecting the Gnostic gospels to a critical examination, Elaine Pagels highlights the conflicts that existed among various Christian sects. She also notes Christianity's lost opportunity to empower women and to assimilate them into church leadership.

Scholars have documented the classical heritage in the Middle Ages, seventeenth-century France, eighteenth-century Germany, Victorian Britain, and in American universities. And indeed, when we apply the term *renaissance* to a culture such as fifteenth-century Italy, we refer to a rebirth of classical art, literature, and style. It is important to remember, though, that the social structures, attitudes, and lifestyles of Greeks and Romans are as significant and as rich as the cultural developments historians have more commonly studied.

ORGANIZED GREEK GAMES
William J. Baker

The history of sports, like women's history and the history of children, has become a growing area of interest for scholars over the last three decades. No longer do historians view sports and leisure activities as peripheral to the mainstream of history. They now recognize that a culture's games and its perception of sports and athletes can tell us much about that society's priorities, values, and beliefs.

Virtually everyone knows that the modern Olympics are patterned on the Olympic Games of ancient Greece, yet few people have more than a hazy understanding of the original Olympics. William J. Baker, professor of history at the University of Maine at Orono, has written extensively on both modern British history and the history of sports in Western civilization. Here he describes the Greek games (our knowledge of which comes primarily from art, such as vase paintings, and literary works) and points out how they differ from the modern games (which date only from 1896).

Keep in mind that although the Olympics were the most famous athletic contests in ancient Greece, there were other games as well, including some limited to women. Through his study of Greek athletics, Baker raises larger questions about Greek culture. Why were women excluded from the Olympic Games? What was the relationship between religion and athletics in Greece? How did Greek philosophers perceive the role of athletics? Answers to such questions lead one to conclude that sports were not a mere sideshow but a basic component of Greek civilization.

If that is so, then the Greeks were violent, for their wrestling and boxing events were more brutal than any modern Olympic contest. On the other hand, some events, such as footraces, seem almost identical to those staged today. The professionalism of the athletes and the honor they derived from their victories resemble the culture of sports in our present society. On balance, were the an-

William J. Baker, *Sports in the Western World* (Lanham, MD: Rowman and Littlefield, 1982), 14–23, 25–26.

cient games vastly different from our Olympics? What does the role of games in ancient Greece suggest about the significance of sports in any society?

The story of organized athletics in the ancient world is primarily the story of Greece. A land of sunshine, mild climate, and rugged mountains rimmed by sparkling seas, Greece spawned philosophers and civic leaders who placed equal value on physical activity and mental cultivation. A vast array of gymnasiums and palaestras (wrestling schools) served as training centers for athletes to prepare themselves to compete in stadiums situated in every major city-state.

For more than a thousand years athletic festivals were an important part of Greek life. Originally mixtures of religious ceremony and athletic competition, hundreds of local festivals were held each year throughout the country and in Greek colonies in Egypt, Sicily, and on the banks of the Bosporus. By the fifth century B.C. four major festivals dominated the scene, forming a kind of circuit for ambitious athletes. The Pythian Games, held every fourth year at the sacred site of Apollo in Delphi, crowned victory with a laurel wreath. The Isthmian Games at Corinth in honor of Poseidon, the god of the sea, were conducted every other year, providing a victor's wreath of pine from a nearby sacred grove. The Nemean Games at Nemea, honoring Zeus every second year, awarded a sacred wreath of celery. The oldest and most prestigious of all the festivals, the Olympic Games, bestowed the olive wreath every four years in honor of Zeus.

The Olympics were the Super Bowl, the World Cup, the Heavyweight Championship of Greek athletics. By Olympic standards were the other festivals judged; at Olympia the sweet "nectar of victory" filled athletes with self-esteem and accorded them public acclaim. . . .

The Olympic Games originated in a most unlikely place. Far removed from Athens, Corinth, and Sparta, the teeming centers of Greek culture and power, Olympia was a little wooded valley in the remote district of Elis on the northwestern tip of Peloponnesus (the peninsula that makes up the southern half of Greece). . . . Mount Olympus, a site readily associated with the gods, lay far to the northeast. Yet according to ancient lore, little Olympia was the place where gods and heroes mingled to accomplish feats worthy of immortal praise.

The origins of the Olympic Games are shrouded in mystery and legend. According to one yarn, Hercules founded the games in celebration of his matchless feats. Some Greeks insisted that their two mightiest gods, Zeus and Cronus, contested for dominance on the hills above Olympia, and that the games and religious ceremonies held later in the valley were begun in commemoration of Zeus's victory. Others clung to the legend of Pelops, who won his bride in a daring chariot escape. The girl's father was an expert with the spear, and according to tradition, thirteen suitors had met death while attempting to steal the daughter away. But Pelops was shrewd. He loosened the axle of his adversary's chariot, took off with his prize, and breathed a sigh of relief when his lover's father broke his neck in the ensuing crash. . . . [S]upposedly on that hallowed ground Pelops instituted the games and religious sacrifices in celebration of his god-given victory.

Significantly, all these tales involve competition, physical aggressiveness, and triumph. . . . [L]ike most sporting activities in the ancient world, the competitive games associated with Olympia grew out of religious ceremonies and cultic practices. With all their emphasis on man and his achievements, the Greeks were extremely religious. Polytheists, they looked to particular gods for assistance and blessing in every sphere of life. . . . Most of all they feared the wrath and sought the favor of Zeus, the mightiest of the gods.

In prayers, processions, and sacrifices, the ancient Greeks sought diligently to appease their gods. Religious festivals, accompanied by feasts, music, dancing, and athletic contests, were scattered throughout the Greek world. About 1000 B.C. Olympia became a shrine to Zeus. In addition to their religious ceremonies, young Greeks competed athletically in honor of Zeus, himself reckoned to be a vigorous warrior god who cast his javelinlike thunderbolts from on high. Competitors at Olympia swore by Zeus that they would play fair and obey all the rules. When they broke their oaths, they were required to pay fines, which in turn were spent to erect statues to Zeus.

The actual date of the first competitive games at Olympia is unknown. But the year 776 B.C. stands as a milestone, for in that year the Greeks first recorded the name of the victor in a simple footrace. For a time the footrace — a sprint of about 200 meters — was the only event associated with the religious festival at Olympia. In 724 B.C., however, a "double race" (400 meters) was added, and in 720 B.C. a long-distance race of 4,800 meters became a fixture. Within the next hundred years other events were established: wrestling and the pentathlon in 708 B.C., boxing in 688 B.C., chariot races in 680 B.C., and boys' footraces, wrestling, and boxing between 632 and 616 B.C. Finally in 520 B.C. the Olympic program was completed with the introduction of a footrace in armor. For almost a thousand years the list of events remained essentially intact. Every four years, strong, young Greeks gathered to compete, to strive for the victory wreath of olive branches.

In the beginning, however, Olympia was a simple site unadorned with buildings. A few scattered stone altars to Zeus stood in the *altis*, the sacred grove. . . . Competitive events were held in randomly selected open spaces, as near to the *altis* as possible. Not until about 550 B.C. were buildings constructed. . . . Finally a hippodrome and stadium were constructed, the latter . . . providing space for about 40,000 spectators. A gymnasium and palaestra completed the athletic complex.

In the spring of every fourth year three heralds departed from Olympia to traverse the Greek world, announcing the forthcoming games and declaring a "sacred truce." By the authority of Zeus, competitors and spectators making their way to Olympia were allowed to pass safely through the countryside, even in times of war. The athletes and their trainers arrived in Olympia a month before the games. First they had to prove their eligibility — that they were Greek, freeborn (not slaves), and without criminal records. Then they had to swear by Zeus that they had been in training for the previous ten months. Participation in the Olympic

Games was no lighthearted matter. Strict judges supervised a grueling month-long training program in order to ensure the fitness of prospective competitors, and they arranged elimination heats for those events that had attracted an unusually large number of athletes. . . .

While the athletes sweated and grunted through their preparatory exercises, little Olympia and the surrounding countryside took on a carnival atmosphere. Spectators came from all directions, and official delegations from Greek city-states arrived with gifts for Zeus. Food and drink vendors did a brisk business, as did hawkers of souvenirs and pimps with their prostitutes. Jugglers, musicians, dancers, and magicians displayed their talents, and soothsayers dispensed their wisdom. Deafening noise and stifling dust added to the midsummer heat, making attendance at the Olympic Games something of an ordeal.

Until late in the history of the games, tiny Olympia was ill-prepared to cope with the crowds. A few springs and the nearby rivers provided water for drinking and bathing, but sanitation and planned water facilities were not available until the second century A.D. Flies were everywhere. As one first-century visitor complained, life at the Olympics would have been unbearably crude and unpleasant were it not for the excitement of the games themselves: "Do you not swelter? Are you not cramped and crowded? Do you not bathe badly? Are you not drenched whenever it rains? Do you not have your fill of tumult and shouting and other annoyances? But I fancy that you bear and endure it all by balancing it off against the memorable character of the spectacle."

The athletes fared little better. Although they ate well during their month's training, they, too, received scant provision for physical comfort. Housing, or the lack of it, was a main problem. Servants of wealthy spectators and official delegations pitched richly embroidered tents on the hillsides, but most athletes simply wrapped themselves in blankets, slept under the stars, and hoped it would not rain. Not until about 350 B.C. was housing provided for the athletes, and even then it was too spartan for comfort. Certainly nothing approximating a modern Olympic village was ever constructed. . . .

For three centuries after the first recorded Olympic victor in 776 B.C., the sequence and duration of the games fluctuated from Olympiad to Olympiad according to the whims of the judges. In 472 B.C., however, the games were reorganized and fixed into a pattern that remained virtually unchanged for the next eight hundred years. The duration of the entire festival was set at five days, with only two and a half days devoted to the games themselves. The first day was given to religious ceremony: oaths, prayers, sacrifices, and the singing of hymns. Some athletes presented gifts and offered prayers to the statues of past victors who had been deified, at the shrines of various patron gods, and especially to the several statues of Zeus.

On the second day the sports competition began. Spectators gathered at the hippodrome, a level, narrow field about 500 meters long, to witness the chariot race. Amid great fanfare, splendid two-wheeled chariots pulled by four horses lined up in staggered starting places. Here was the most costly and colorful of all the Olympic events, a signal to the world that the owners were men of great wealth. Their drivers, decked out in finely embroidered tunics, tensely awaited the start. They could scarcely afford to relax. Their course was not a rounded oval but rather around posts set at each end of the hippodrome about 400 meters apart, requiring 180-degree turns for twelve laps. Rules forbade swerving in front of an opponent, but bumps and crashes and even head-on collisions around the posts were inevitable. In one race only one of forty chariots finished intact.

As soon as the dust settled and battered chariots were removed from the hippodrome, single horses and their jockeys moved into starting positions. Riding without saddles or stirrups, the jockeys were nude. Even more than the charioteers, jockeys got little credit if they won. They were the hirelings of wealthy owners, whose names were recorded as the winners of the race. Even the olive crown was placed on the owner's head, not the jockey's.

The morning having been given to these equestrian events, the afternoon was devoted to an altogether different contest, the pentathlon. Spectators crowded onto the grassy slopes of the stadium. Except for a few marble slabs provided for the Olympic officials, no seats were ever built. Through a narrow passageway at one end of the stadium the competitors entered. Naked and bronzed by the sun, they more than any of the other contestants at Olympia represented the Greek ideal of physical beauty. Pentathletes had to be fast as well as strong, with muscles well-proportioned and supple but not overdeveloped. . . .

Like the modern decathlon, the pentathlon rewarded the versatile athlete. First he had to throw the discus, a round, flat object originally made of stone and later of bronze. Five throws were allowed, and only the longest counted. Next came the javelin throw. About six feet long, the javelin had a small leather loop attached near the center of gravity. The athlete inserted one or two fingers in the loop, wound the thong around the javelin, and thus obtained leverage to make the javelin spin in flight. In the third event, the standing broad jump, the athlete carried weights in his hands, swung them forward to shoulder height, and then down as he leaped. Made of stone or metal in the shape of small dumbbells, the weights both increased the distance and helped the jumper to keep his balance when landing. A 200-meter sprint and a wrestling contest were the last two events in the pentathlon, but they were often not held: The athlete who first won three of the five events was declared the victor without further contest.

As the sun set on that second day of the Olympic festival, attention turned from athletic competition to religious ceremony. In honor of the hero-god Pelops, a black ram was slain and offered as a burnt sacrifice — always as the midsummer full moon appeared above the *altis*. On the following morning were religious rites, followed by a magnificent procession of priests, Olympic judges, representatives from the Greek city-states, the athletes and their kinsmen, and trainers. All finally arrived at the altar of Zeus, where one hundred oxen were slain and their legs burned in homage to Zeus. The carcasses were cooked and eaten at the concluding banquet on the final day of the festival.

On the afternoon of the third day, the footraces were held: 200-meter sprints the length of the stadium, 400-meter dashes around a post and back, and long-distance runs of 4,800 meters (twelve laps). Marble slabs provided leverage for quick starts, and a trumpet blast served as the starting signal. . . .

The fourth day of the festival brought on the "heavy" events: wrestling, boxing, the pancration, and armored footraces. The first three were especially violent, brutal contests of strength and will. There were few rules, no time limit, and no ring. More important, there were no weight limits, thus restricting top-level competitors to the largest, best-muscled, and toughest men to be found throughout Greece. In the wrestling contests biting and gouging were prohibited, but not much else. A wrestler won when he scored three falls, making his opponent touch the ground with his knees. Wrestlers therefore concentrated on holds on the upper part of the body and tripped their opponents when possible. . . .

Yet wrestling was mild exercise compared to boxing. Boxers wound heavy strips of leather around their hands and wrists, leaving the fingers free. They aimed primarily for the opponent's head or neck, rather than the body. Slapping with the open hand was permissible, and it was often done to divert the attention, cut the face, or close the eyes of the opposition. The fight went on without a break until one of the competitors was either exhausted or knocked out, or until one raised his right hand as a sign of defeat. Blood flowed freely. Scarcely an Olympic boxer finished his career without broken teeth, cauliflower ears, a scarred face, and a smashed nose. He was lucky if he did not have more serious eye, ear, and skull injuries.

As if boxing and wrestling were not brutal enough, the Greeks threw them together, added some judo, and came up with the contest most favored by spectators at Olympia — the pancration. Pancratiasts wore no leather thongs on the fists, but they could use their heads, elbows, and knees in addition to hands and feet. They could trip, hack, break fingers, pull noses and ears, and even apply a stranglehold until tapped on the back, the sign that the opponent had given up. In 564 B.C. a pancratiast who had won in two previous Olympics found himself in both a leg scissors grip and a stranglehold. Literally in the process of being choked to death, he frantically reached for one of his opponent's toes and broke it. As he gasped his final breath, his opponent, suffering excruciating pain, gave the signal of capitulation. So the strangled pancratiast was posthumously awarded the crown of victory, and in the central square of his native village a statue was erected in his honor.

After the deadly serious business of wrestling, boxing, and the pancration, the final Olympic contest added a farcical touch to the festival. The 400-meter footrace in armor pitted naked men clad only in helmets, shin guards, and shields, a fitting though ludicrous reminder of the military origins of most of the games. Although the armored footrace remained on the Olympic program from its introduction in 520 B.C. until the end, it was never a prestigious event. Apparently it provided comic relief at the end of a gory day.

The fifth and final day of the festival was devoted to a prize-giving ceremony, a service of thanksgiving to Zeus, and a sumptuous banquet at which the sacrificial animals were consumed. . . .

. . . [S]ome of the limited features of the Olympic Games should be noted. In the first place, the athletic program was narrowly confined to two equestrian contests, six track-and-field events, three physical-contact sports, and the armored footrace. From a modern point of view, conspicuously absent were relay races, hurdles, pole vaults, high jumps, running broad jumps, weight lifting, and shot puts. Nothing approximating a modern marathon ever appeared on the ancient Olympic program. . . .

Given the fact that Greece is a peninsula and half of it virtually an island, it is surprising to find no water sports such as swimming, diving, sailing, or rowing in the ancient Olympic program. . . . Less apparent was the reason for the lack of competitive ball games. In fact, the Greeks played a number of individual and team games of ball. At Sparta "ball player" and "youth" were synonymous. . . . Without doubt the Greeks played a kind of field hockey game. . . . Most common of all competitive ball play in Greece, however, was the game of *episkyros,* a team sport in which opposing sides threw a ball back and forth "until one side drives the other back over their goal line."

Why, then, were no ball games ever played in the ancient Olympics? When the Olympics began in the eighth century B.C., most ball play was still mere exercise, keep-away games at most. . . . [T]hey were played by women, children, and old men, but not by serious athletes. Not yet rough mock forms of combat, ball games were considered child's play compared to the warrior sports of chariot racing, javelin throwing, wrestling, and the like. By the time competitive ball play became respectable for adult males, the Olympic program was already set on its traditional course. . . .

Another limitation of the Olympics that more tellingly reflected the mentality of ancient Greek society was the exclusion of women from the games. In that patriarchal world, matters of business, government, and warfare were reserved for men. A woman might attend the theater if accompanied by a man, but even in the home she lived in separate quarters. Except for the honorary presence of the priestess of Demeter, women were altogether excluded from the Olympic Games, as spectators as well as competitors. Apparently only one woman ever broke the taboo, and her ploy provoked a rule change. In 404 B.C. a mother who wanted to see her son box slipped into the stadium disguised as a trainer. But when the boy won his match, she leaped over the barrier to congratulate him and in so doing gave herself away. Horrified Olympic officials immediately laid down a new rule: trainers henceforward must appear in the stadium stark naked, like the athletes.

Barred from the Olympic Games, women held their own competitive contests at Olympia in honor of Hera, the sister-wife of Zeus. Their competition was largely in the form of footraces, wrestling, and chariot races. Apparently these Heraean Games even predated the Olympic Games as fertility rites representing an early matriarchal society. During the history of the Olympic Games, however, Olympic officials proved to be a highly conservative group of men committed primarily to maintaining a successful formula, thus inadvertently protecting traditional male interests. Their conservatism is best seen by comparison with the other major Panhellenic games. As Greek women increasingly became emancipated (primarily in the cities) toward the end of the pre-Christian era, short-distance races for girls were introduced as an integral part of the program in the Pythian, Isthmian, and Nemean Games.

Olympia's relation to the other festivals on the athletic "circuit" calls to mind another myth long entertained about athletes in the ancient world: Olympic victors received no cash prizes or other material rewards with their olive crowns; thus it would appear that they were purely amateur, competing for the honor of victory. The appearance was a mere shadow of reality. Throughout the history of the Olympics, only aristocrats could afford the horses and chariots for the equestrian events. For the first 300 years or so, the games were dominated by athletes from wealthy families who could afford trainers and coaches, a proper diet (plenty of meat), full-time training, and travel. Around 450 B.C., however, lower-class athletes began participating in the track-and-field and physical-contact sports. Financed by local patrons and public funds drawn from taxes on wealthy citizens, they ran and fought to bring honor to their city-states as well as to themselves. Their city-states, in turn, rewarded them with cash prizes, free food, and lodging. Therefore, although the Olympic Games paid no direct material rewards, they existed in a maze of commercial enterprise. A victory at Olympia dramatically raised an athlete's value as he went off to sell his talents and brawn for further competition at the Pythian, Isthmian, and Nemean Games. Whether or not he received money for his Olympic exploits is beside the point. Well paid for his full-time efforts, he was a professional athlete.

A sure sign of this professionalism was the emergence of athletic guilds in the second century B.C. Like today's unions or players' associations, the guilds originated on the principle of collective bargaining. And bargain they did: for the athletes' rights to have a say in the scheduling of games, travel arrangements, personal amenities, pensions, and old-age security in the form of serving as trainers and managers.

When Greek poets, philosophers, and playwrights turned a critical eye on the athletes of their day, they seldom attacked professionalism. . . . Yet athletics were scarcely beyond criticism. For well-born, highly cultured Greeks, athletics appeared to be a lamentably easy way for lower-class citizens to rise quickly to affluence, then to fall back into poverty once the strength of youth waned. . . .

Worse still, the successful athlete had to specialize to such an extent that he made a poor soldier. . . .

Yet of all the barbs directed against Greek athletics, the most common had to do with the glorification of physical strength to the detriment of mental and spiritual values. To the philosopher and satirist Xenophanes, it was "not right to honor strength above excellent wisdom." . . . Milo of Croton was the butt of numerous jokes and slurs on the mindlessness of the muscle-bound athlete. "What surpassing witlessness," declared a moralist when he heard that Milo carried the entire carcass of a bull around the stadium at Olympia before cutting it up and devouring it. Before it was slaughtered, the bull carried its own body with much less exertion than did Milo. "Yet the bull's mind was not worth anything — just about like Milo's." The image of the "dumb jock" is as old as athletics.

. . . "How very unlike an athlete you are in frame," Socrates once chided a young Athenian weakling. "But I am not an athlete," retorted the literal-minded youth. "You are not less of an athlete," shot back the wise Socrates, "than those who are going to contend at the Olympic Games. Does the struggle for life with the enemy, which the Athenians will demand of you when circumstances require, seem to you to be a trifling contest?" For Socrates, the key words were *contend, struggle,* and *contest.* Moreover, for Socrates the athlete provided the model for the principle that "the body must bear its part in whatever men do; and in all the services required from the body, it is of the utmost importance to have it in the best possible condition."

Socrates' prize pupil, Plato, agreed fully with his master. Plato, in fact, trained under the best wrestling teacher in Athens and reportedly competed in the Isthmian games. Originally his name was Aristocles, but his wrestling teacher changed it to Plato, meaning "broad shouldered." In *The Republic,* Plato set up a dialogue with Socrates to argue logically that gymnastic exercise was the "twin sister" of the arts for the "improvement of the soul." His ideal was the body and mind "duly harmonized."

This sense of balance between the physical and the mental prompted the third of the great Greek philosophers, Aristotle, to devote several sections of his *Politics* to the training of children to be good Greek citizens. "What is wanted," he insisted, "is not the bodily condition of an athlete nor on the other hand a weak and invalid condition, but one that lies between the two." Coming to manhood a hundred years or so after Socrates, Aristotle was more critical of "the brutal element" involved in organized athletics. Yet he, too, held the Olympic victors in awe. . . .

Critical as they were of overspecialized athletes, the great philosophers still did not reject athletics. For them, the association of body and mind was literally intimate: gymnasiums were places where men not only exercised, but gathered to hear the lectures of philosophers and itinerant orators. Plato's Academy and Aristotle's Lyceum in Athens were, in fact, gymnasiums, centers of training "for the body and the soul." Ironically, the terms "academy" and "lyceum" have come to refer solely to intellectual pursuits, wholly divorced from physical training. . . .

CLASSICAL GREEK ATTITUDES
TO SEXUAL BEHAVIOR
K. J. Dover

In this article, Sir K. J. Dover, a classicist and former professor, dean, and chancellor at the University of St. Andrews, Scotland, analyzes Greek standards of sexual morality. Male citizens had numerous opportunities for sexual activity because slaves and prostitutes were readily available. Yet society placed restrictions on the free indulgence of male sexual appetites. At an early age, males learned responsibility and moral values. How were Greek adolescents supposed to behave sexually, and how did the city and family influence adolescents' sexual activity? How did the Greeks view love and lovemaking?

Homosexuality (more properly, bisexuality) is a frequently noted feature of ancient Greece. Dover discusses the sexual relationship between men, or between men and boys, as well as the sexual roles that daughters, wives, slaves, and prostitutes played. How do you account for the Greeks' tolerance of homosexuality, and why were men so attracted to other men? To what extent did a double standard exist in regard to men's and women's sexual appetites?

Dover's sources for this essay include public speeches, the theater, art, and the works of philosophers. What various attitudes toward sex do these sources present? As Dover notes, the reality of sexual activity in Greece may have been somewhat different from the attitudes expressed in speech and in writing.

The Greeks regarded sexual enjoyment as the area of life in which the goddess Aphrodite[1] was interested, as Ares was interested in war and other deities in other activities. Sexual intercourse was *aphrodisia*, "the things of Aphrodite." Sexual desire could be denoted by general words for "desire," but the obsessive desire for a particular person was *eros*, "love" in the sense which it has in our expressions

K. J. Dover, "Classical Greek Attitudes to Sexual Behavior," in *Women in the Ancient World: The Arethusa Papers,* ed. John Peradotto and J. P. Sullivan (Albany: State University of New York Press, 1984), 143–154.

[1] Goddess of love and beauty.

"be in love with . . . and fall in love with." . . . Eros, like all powerful emotional forces, but more consistently than most, was personified and deified. . . .

Eros generates *philia*, "love"; the same word can denote milder degrees of affection, just as "my *philoi*" can mean my friends or my innermost family circle, according to context. For the important question "Do you love me?" the verb used is *philein,* whether the question is put by a youth to a girl as their kissing becomes more passionate or by a father to his son as an anxious preliminary to a test of filial obedience.

Our own culture has its myths about the remote past, and one myth that dies hard is that the "invention" of sexual guilt, shame and fear by the Christians destroyed a golden age of free, fearless, pagan sexuality. That most pagans were in many ways less inhibited than most Christians is undeniable. Not only had they a goddess specially concerned with sexual pleasure; their other deities were portrayed in legend as enjoying fornication, adultery and sodomy. A pillar surmounted by the head of Hermes[2] and adorned with an erect penis stood at every Athenian front-door; great models of the erect penis were borne in procession at festivals of Dionysus,[3] and it too was personified as the tirelessly lascivious Phales.[4] The vase-painters often depicted sexual intercourse, sometimes masturbation (male or female) and fellatio, and in respect of any kind of sexual behaviour Aristophanic[5] comedy appears to have had total license of word and act. . . .

There is, however, another side of the coin. Sexual intercourse was not permitted in the temples or sanctuaries of deities (not even of deities whose sexual enthusiasm was conspicuous in mythology), and regulations prescribing chastity or formal purification after intercourse played a part in many Greek cults. Homeric epic, for all its unquestioning acceptance of fornication as one of the good things of life, is circumspect in vocabulary, and more than once denotes the male genitals by *aidos*, "shame," "disgrace." . . . Poets (notably Homer) sometimes describe interesting and agreeable activities — cooking, mixing wine, stabbing an enemy through a chink in his armour — in meticulous detail, but nowhere is there a comparable description of the mechanisms of sexual activity. Prose literature, even on medical subjects, is euphemistic ("be with" . . . is a common way of saying "have sexual intercourse with"). . . .

Linguistic inhibition, then, was observably strengthened in the course of the classical period; and at least in some art-forms, inhibition extended also to content. These are data which do not fit the popular concept of a guilt-free or shame-free sexual morality, and require explanation. Why so many human cultures use derogatory words as synonyms of "sexual" and reproach sexual prowess while praising prowess in (e.g.) swimming and riding, is a question which would take

---

[2] Messenger of the gods.

[3] God of wine and fertility.

[4] Personification of the phallus, often said to accompany Dionysus.

[5] Aristophanes (ca. 448–ca. 380 B.C.) was an Athenian writer of comedy.

us to a remote level of speculation. Why the Greeks did so is a question which can at least be related intelligibly to the structure of Greek society and to Greek moral schemata which have no special bearing on sex.

As far as was practicable . . . , Greek girls were segregated from boys and brought up at home in ignorance of the world outside the home; one speaker in court seeks to impress the jury with the respectability of his family by saying that his sister and nieces are "so well brought up that they are embarrassed in the presence even of a man who is a member of the family." Married young, perhaps at fourteen (and perhaps to a man twenty-years or more her senior), a girl exchanged confinement in her father's house for confinement in her husband's. When he was invited out, his children might be invited with him, but not his wife; and when he had friends in, she did not join the company. Shopping seems to have been a man's job, to judge from references in comedy, and slaves could be sent on other errands outside the house. Upholders of the proprieties pronounced the front door to be the boundaries of a good woman's territory.

Consider now the situation of an adolescent boy growing up in such a society. Every obstacle is put in the way of his speaking to the girl next door; it may not be easy for him even to get a glimpse of her. Festivals, sacrifices and funerals, for which women and girls did come out in public, provided the occasion for seeing and being seen. They could hardly afford more than that, for there were too many people about, but from such an occasion (both in real life and in fiction) an intrigue could be set on foot, with a female slave of respectable age as the indispensable go-between.

In a society which practices segregation of the sexes, it is likely that boys and girls should devote a good deal of time and ingenuity to defeating society, and many slaves may have co-operated with enthusiasm. But Greek laws were not lenient towards adultery, and *moikheia,* for which we have no suitable translation except "adultery," denoted not only the seduction of another man's wife, but also the seduction of his widowed mother, unmarried daughter, sister, niece, or any other woman whose legal guardian he was. The adulterer could be prosecuted by the offended father, husband or guardian; alternatively, if caught in the act, he could be killed, maltreated, or imprisoned by force until he purchased his freedom by paying heavy compensation. A certain tendency to regard women as irresponsible and ever ready to yield to sexual temptation . . . relieved a cuckolded husband[6] of a sense of shame or inadequacy and made him willing to seek the co-operation of his friends in apprehending an adulterer, just as he would seek their co-operation to defend himself against fraud, encroachment, breach of contract, or any other threat to his property. The adulterer was open to reproach in the same way, and to the same extent, as any other violator of the laws protecting the individual citizen against arbitrary treatment by other citizens. To seduce a woman of

---

[6] A husband whose wife has been unfaithful.

citizen status was more culpable than to rape her, not only because rape was presumed to be unpremeditated but because seduction involved the capture of her affection and loyalty; it was the degree of offense against the man to whom she belonged, not her own feelings, which mattered.

It naturally follows from the state of the law and from the attitudes and values implied by segregation that an adolescent boy who showed an exceptional enthusiasm for the opposite sex could be regarded as a potential adulterer and his propensity discouraged just as one would discourage theft, lies and trickery, while an adolescent boy who blushed at the mere idea of proximity to a woman was praised as *sophron*, "right-minded," i.e. unlikely to do anything without reflecting first whether it might incur punishment, disapproval, dishonour or other undesirable consequences.

Greek society was a slave-owning society, and a female slave was not in a position to refuse the sexual demands of her owner or of anyone else to whom he granted the temporary use of her. Large cities, notably Athens, also had a big population of resident aliens, and these included women who made a living as prostitutes, on short-term relations with a succession of clients, or as *hetairai*, who endeavoured to establish long-term relations with wealthy and agreeable men. Both aliens and citizens could own brothels and stock them with slave-prostitutes. Slave-girls and alien girls who took part in men's parties as dancers or musicians could also be mauled and importuned in a manner which might cost a man his life if he attempted it with a woman of citizen status. . . .

It was therefore easy enough to purchase sexual satisfaction, and the richer a man was the better provision he could make for himself. But money spent on sex was money not spent on other things, and there seems to have been substantial agreement on what were proper or improper items of expenditure. Throughout the work of the Attic orators,[7] who offer us by far the best evidence on the moral standards which it was prudent to uphold in addressing large juries composed of ordinary citizens, it is regarded as virtuous to impoverish oneself by gifts and loans to friends in misfortune (for their daughters' dowries, their fathers' funerals, and the like), by ransoming Athenian citizens taken prisoner in war, and by paying out more than the required minimum in the performance of public duties (the upkeep of a warship, for example, or the dressing and training of a chorus at a festival). This kind of expenditure was boasted about and treated as a claim on the gratitude of the community. On the other hand, to "devour an inheritance" by expenditure on one's own consumption was treated as disgraceful. Hence gluttony, drunkenness and purchased sexual relations were classified together as "shameful pleasures." . . . When a young man fell in love, he might well fall in love with a hetaira or a slave, since his chances of falling in love with a girl of citizen status were so restricted, and to secure the object of his love he would need to purchase

---

[7] Athenians who wrote or gave speeches in law courts or in the assembly.

or ransom her. A close association between eros and extravagance therefore tends to be assumed, especially in comedy; a character in Menander[8] says, "No one is so parsimonious as not to make some sacrifice of his property to Eros." More than three centuries earlier, Archilochus[9] put the matter in characteristically violent form when he spoke of wealth accumulated by long labour "pouring down into a whore's guts." A fourth-century litigant venomously asserts that his adversary, whose tastes were predominantly homosexual, has "buggered away all his estate."

We have here another reason for the discouragement and disapproval of sexual enthusiasm in the adolescent; it was seen as presenting a threat that the family's wealth would be dissipated in ways other than those which earned honour and respect from the community. The idea that one has a right to spend one's own money as one wishes (or a right to do anything which detracts from one's health and physical fitness) is not Greek, and would have seemed absurd to a Greek. He had only the rights which the law of his city explicitly gave him; no right was inalienable, and no claim superior to the city's.

Living in a fragmented and predatory world, the inhabitants of a Greek city-state, who could never afford to take the survival of their community completely for granted, attached a great importance to the qualities required of a soldier: not only to strength and speed, in which men are normally superior to women, but also to the endurance of hunger, thirst, pain, fatigue, discomfort and disagreeably hot or cold weather. The ability to resist and master the body's demands for nourishment and rest was normally regarded as belonging to the same moral category as the ability to resist sexual desire. Xenophon[10] describes the chastity of King Agesilaus[11] together with his physical toughness, and elsewhere summarises "lack of self-control" as the inability to hold out against "hunger, thirst, sexual desire and long hours without sleep."

The reasons for this association are manifold: the treatment of sex — a treatment virtually inevitable in a slave-owning society — as a commodity, and therefore as something which the toughest and most frugal men will be able to cut down to a minimum; the need for a soldier to resist the blandishments of comfort (for if he does not resist, the enemy who does will win), to sacrifice himself as an individual entirely, to accept pain and death as the price to be paid for the attainment of a goal which is not easily quantified, the honour of victory; and the inveterate Greek tendency to conceive of strong desires and emotional states as forces which assail the soul from the outside. To resist is manly and "free"; to be distracted by immediate pleasure from the pursuit of honour through toil and suf-

---

[8] Greek writer of comedy (342?–291? B.C.).

[9] Greek poet of the mid-seventh century B.C.

[10] Greek general and historian (430?–355? B.C.).

[11] Spartan king (444–360 B.C.) who began his reign in 399.

fering is to be a "slave" to the forces which "defeat" and "worst" one's own personality.

Here is a third reason for praise of chastity in the young, the encouragement of the capacity to resist, to go without, to become the sort of man on whom the community depends for its defence. If the segregation and legal and administrative subordination of women received their original impetus from the fragmentation of the early Greek world into small, continuously warring states, they also gave an impetus to the formation of certain beliefs about women which served as a rationalization of segregation and no doubt affected behavior to the extent that people tend to behave in the ways expected of them. Just as it was thought masculine to resist and endure, it was thought feminine to yield to fear, desire and impulse. "Now you must be a *man*"; says Demeas[12] to himself as he tries to make up his mind to get rid of his concubine,[13] "Forget your desire, fall out of love." Women in comedy are notoriously unable to keep off the bottle, and in tragedy women are regarded as naturally more prone than men to panic, uncontrollable grief, jealousy and spite. It seems to have been believed not only that women enjoyed sexual intercourse more intensely than men, but also that experience of intercourse put the woman more under the man's power than it put him under hers, and that if not segregated and guarded women would be insatiably promiscuous.

It was taken for granted in the Classical period that a man was sexually attracted by a good-looking younger male, and no Greek who said that he was "in love" would have taken it amiss if his hearers assumed without further enquiry that he was in love with a boy and that he desired more than anything to ejaculate in or on the boy's body. I put the matter in these coarse and clinical terms to preclude any misapprehension arising from modern application of the expression "Platonic love" or from Greek euphemism (see below). . . . Aphrodite, despite her femininity, is not hostile to homosexual desire, and homosexual intercourse is denoted by the same term, *aphrodisia,* as heterosexual intercourse. Vase-painting was noticeably affected by the homosexual ethos; painters sometimes depicted a naked woman with a male waist and hips, as if a woman's body was nothing but a young man's body plus breasts and minus external genitals, and in many of their pictures of heterosexual intercourse from the rear position the penis appears (whatever the painter's intention) to be penetrating the anus, not the vagina.

Why homosexuality — or, to speak more precisely, "pseudo-homosexuality," since the Greeks saw nothing surprising in the coexistence of desire for boys and desire for girls in the same person — obtained so firm and widespread a hold on Greek society, is a difficult and speculative question. Segregation alone cannot be the answer, for comparable segregation has failed to engender a comparable degree of homosexuality in other cultures. Why the Greeks of the Classical period

---

[12] Character in a play by Menander.

[13] A woman who cohabits with a man to whom she is not married.

accepted homosexual desire as natural and normal is a much easier question: they did so because previous generations had accepted it, and segregation of the sexes in adolescence fortified and sustained the acceptance and the practice.

Money may have enabled the adolescent boy to have plenty of sexual intercourse with girls of alien or servile status, but it could not give him the satisfaction which can be pursued by his counterpart in a society which does not own slaves: the satisfaction of being welcomed *for his own sake* by a sexual partner of equal status. This is what the Greek boy was offered by homosexual relations. He was probably accustomed (as often happens with boys who do not have the company of girls) to a good deal of homosexual play at the time of puberty, and he never heard from his elders the suggestion that one was destined to become *either* "a homosexual" *or* "a heterosexual." As he grew older, he could seek among his juniors a partner of citizen status, who could certainly not be forced and who might be totally resistant to even the most disguised kind of purchase. If he was to succeed in seducing this boy (or if later, as a mature man, he was to seduce a youth), he could do so only by *earning* hero-worship.

This is why, when Greek writers "idealize" eros and treat the physical act as the "lowest" ingredient in a rich and complex relationship which comprises mutual devotion, reciprocal sacrifice, emulation, and the awakening of sensibility, imagination and intellect, they look not to what most of us understand by sexual love but to the desire of an older for a younger male and the admiration felt by the younger for the older. It is noticeable also that in art and literature inhibitions operate in much the same way as in the romantic treatment of heterosexual love in our own tradition. When physical gratification is directly referred to, the younger partner is said to "grant favours" or "render services"; but a great deal is written about homosexual eros from which the innocent reader would not easily gather that any physical contact at all was involved. Aeschines,[14] who follows Aeschylus[15] and Classical sentiment generally in treating the relation between Achilles and Patroclus in the *Iliad*[16] as homoerotic, commends Homer for leaving it to "the educated among his hearers" to perceive the nature of the relation from the extravagant grief expressed by Achilles at the death of Patroclus. The vase-painters very frequently depict the giving of presents by men to boys and the "courting" of boys (a mild term for an approach which includes putting a hand on the boy's genitals), but their pursuit of the subject to the stage of erection, let alone penetration, is very rare, whereas depiction of heterosexual intercourse, in a variety of positions, is commonplace.

We also observe in the field of homosexual relations the operation of the "dual standard of morality" which so often characterizes societies in which segregation of the sexes is minimal. If a Greek admitted that he was in love with a

[14] Athenian orator (397?–322? B.C.).

[15] Athenian tragic poet (525–456 B.C.).

[16] Achilles was the great hero and Patroclus his friend in the *Iliad*, Homer's epic poem.

boy, he could expect sympathy and encouragement from his friends, and if it was known that he had attained his goal, envy and admiration. The boy, on the other hand, was praised if he retained his chastity, and he could expect strong disapproval if he was thought in any way to have taken the initiative in attracting a lover. The probable implication is that neither partner would actually say anything about the physical aspect of their relationship to anyone else, nor would they expect any question about it to be put to them or any allusion to it made in their presence.

Once we have accepted the universality of homosexual relations in Greek society as a fact, it surprises us to learn that if a man had at any time in his life prostituted himself to another man for money he was debarred from exercising his political rights. If he was an alien, he had no political rights to exercise, and was in no way penalized for living as a male prostitute, so long as he paid the prostitution tax levied upon males and females alike. It was therefore not the physical act *per se* which incurred penalty, but the incorporation of the act in a certain deliberately chosen role which could only be fully defined with reference to the nationality and status of the participants.

This datum illustrates an attitude which was fundamental to Greek society. They tended to believe that one's moral character is formed in the main by the circumstances in which one lives: the wealthy man is tempted to arrogance and oppression, the poor man to robbery and fraud, the slave to cowardice and petty greed. A citizen compelled by great and sudden economic misfortune to do work of a kind normally done by slaves was shamed because his assumption of a role which so closely resembled a slave's role altered his relationship to his fellow-citizens. Since prostitutes were usually slaves or aliens, to play the role of a prostitute was, as it were, to remove oneself from the citizen-body, and the formal exclusion of a male prostitute from the rights of a citizen was a penalty for disloyalty to the community in his choice of role.

Prostitution is not easily defined — submission in gratitude for gifts, services or help is not so different in kind from submission in return for an agreed fee — nor was it easily proved in a Greek city, unless people were willing (as they were not) to come forward and testify that they had helped to cause a citizen's son to incur the penalty of disenfranchisement. A boy involved in a homosexual relationship absolutely untainted by mercenary considerations could still be called a prostitute by his family's enemies, just as the term can be recklessly applied today by unfriendly neighbours or indignant parents to a girl who sleeps with a lover. He could also be called effeminate; not always rightly, since athletic success seems to have been a powerful stimulus to his potential lovers, but it is possible (and the visual arts do not help us much here) that positively feminine characteristics in the appearance, movements and manner of boys and youths played a larger part in the ordinary run of homosexual activity than the idealization and romanticisation of the subject in literature indicate. There were certainly circumstances in which homosexuality could be treated as a substitute for heterosexuality; a comic poet says of the Greeks who besieged Troy for ten years, "they never saw a hetaira . . . and ended up with arseholes wider than the gates of Troy." . . . A sixth-century vase in which all of a group of men except one are penetrating women shows the odd man out grasping his erect penis and approaching, with a gesture of entreaty, a youth — who starts to run away. In so far as the "passive partner" in a homosexual act takes on himself the role of a woman, he was open to the suspicion, like the male prostitute, that he abjured his prescribed role as a future soldier and defender of the community.

The comic poets, like the orators, ridicule individuals for effeminacy, for participation in homosexual activity, or for both together; at the same time, the sturdy, wilful, roguish characters whom we meet in Aristophanes are not averse to handling and penetrating good-looking boys when the opportunity presents itself, as a supplement to their busy and enjoyable heterosexual programmes. . . . [T]here is one obvious factor which we should expect to determine different sexual attitudes in different classes. The thorough-going segregation of women of citizen status was possible only in households which owned enough slaves and could afford to confine its womenfolk to a leisure enlivened only by the exercise of domestic crafts such as weaving and spinning. This degree of segregation was simply not possible in poorer families; the women who sold bread and vegetables in the market — Athenian women, not resident aliens — were not segregated, and there must have been plenty of women . . . who took a hand in work on the land and drove animals to market. No doubt convention required that they should protect each other's virtue by staying in pairs or groups as much as they could, but clearly . . . the obstacles to love-affairs between citizens' sons and citizens' daughters lose their validity as one goes down the social scale. Where there are love-affairs, both boys and girls can have decided views . . . on whom they wish to marry. The girl in Aristophanes' *Ecclesiazusae*[17] who waits impatiently for her young man's arrival while her mother is out may be much nearer the norm of Athenian life than those cloistered ladies who were "embarrassed by the presence even of a male relative." It would not be discordant with modern experience to believe that speakers in an Athenian law-court professed, and were careful to attribute to the jury, standards of propriety higher than the average member of the jury actually set himself.

Much Classical Greek philosophy is characterized by contempt for sexual intercourse. . . . Xenophon's Socrates, although disposed to think it a gift of beneficent providence that humans, unlike other mammals, can enjoy sex all the year round, is wary of troubling the soul over what he regards as the minimum needs of the body. . . . One logical outcome of this attitude to sex is exemplified by Diogenes the Cynic, who was alleged to have masturbated in public when his penis erected itself, as if he were scratching a mosquito-bite. Another outcome was the doctrine (influential in Christianity, but not of Christian origin) that a wise and virtuous man will not have intercourse except for the purpose of procreating le-

---

[17] The play *The Assembly of Women*.

gitimate offspring, a doctrine which necessarily proscribes much heterosexual and all homosexual activity.

Although philosophical preoccupation with the contrast between "body" and "soul" had much to do with these developments, we can discern, as the ground from which these philosophical plants sprouted, Greek admiration for invulnerability, hostility towards the diversion of resources to the pursuit of pleasure, and disbelief in the possibility that dissimilar ways of feeling and behaving can be synthesised in the same person without detracting from his attainment of the virtues expected of a selfless defender of his city. It is also clear that the refusal of Greek law and society to treat a woman as a responsible person, while on the one hand it encouraged a complacent acceptance of prostitution and concubinage, on the other hand led to the classification of sexual activity as a male indulgence which could be reduced to a minimum by those who were not self-indulgent.

MAKING CONNECTIONS:
SEXUALITY AND THE BODY

1. Attitudes toward sexuality and the body can vary tremendously from culture to culture. K. J. Dover captures the classical Greek reticence over wanton sexuality, the toleration of homosexuality, and the male domination of women's sex lives. In what notable ways did the Greeks' view of proper adolescent sexual behavior differ from our contemporary ideas? Why do you think younger men are no longer so attracted to older men, as they were in ancient Greece? Compare modern ideas toward the sexual appetites of men and women to classical Greek beliefs. Do you think there is such a thing as normal sexual behavior?

2. Why did Greek men think they were entitled to control the bodies of women, whether wives, daughters, sisters, slaves, or prostitutes? How did attitudes toward adultery reflect male thinking about women? How was the double standard in Greece different from that in the West today? Compare love in classical Greece to our notions of love.

ROMAN MARRIAGE
Suzanne Dixon

Historians of Roman society all have access to the same sources — correspondence, legal documents and laws, paintings, sarcophagi (stone coffins bearing inscriptions), literary works — but they still disagree about the nature of marriage, the status of women in marriage, and whether spouses cared for one another. Suzanne Dixon (an Australian classicist at the University of Queensland who specializes in Roman legal, social, and economic history) discusses the many aspects of matrimony and firmly presents her view that Roman marriage could be harmonious, companionate, and virtuous as opposed to being part of Rome's supposed moral decay.

Why did Romans marry, and what constituted a valid marriage? Romans had strong ideas about family, and family members played significant roles in marriage plans. The dowry — the property a wife brought to the marriage — was an important institution and actually provided protection for wives. Did most husbands and wives love one another? Did Roman society even expect them to be in love?

Rome was also a slave society, in which female slaves had to submit to their owners' sexual demands, and prostitution was common. Thus, Roman males did not need to be married to derive sexual pleasure. How did society view adultery and divorce?

Dixon has the arduous task of dealing with many centuries of Roman history, with marriage evolving slowly over time. She states that the most significant change in marriage occurred when Rome went from a merged to a separate regime. What does she mean by that? Christianity influenced Roman marriage as well, though perhaps not as greatly as one might have expected. Dixon sometimes compares Roman marriage to marriage in the West today. Note the similarities and differences.

If two Roman citizens with the legal capacity to marry one another each had the consent of the *paterfamilias*[1] and lived together with the intention of being mar-

Suzanne Dixon, *The Roman Family* (Baltimore: Johns Hopkins University Press, 1992), 61–90, 95–97.

[1] Father of the family; head of the household.

ried, that was recognized as a valid marriage *(iustum conubium* or *iustae nuptiae)*, and children born of the union were Roman citizens in the power of their father. This gives us a basic definition of marriage and a notion of its purpose in Roman society. . . .

. . . [T]he state and the community at large tended to agree that marriage was above all an institution for the production of legitimate children, and Roman legal discussions of marriage commonly focus on this question of the status of children. Illegitimate children could still be Roman citizens and suffered few legal disadvantages, but marriage remained the chief means of determining status from one generation to the next.

Marriage performed a number of roles, many of them common to marriage in most societies. It linked different families both immediately on the marriage and in subsequent generations if children resulted from the union. Dowry and inheritance, the two major forms of property transmission in the ancient world, were both tied to marriage. It should be pointed out, however, that inheritance between husband and wife, though common, was not seen as an obvious or obligatory form of inheritance (as it was between parents and children). Within the political elite, marriage was an important means of forging alliances, and thus mentions of Roman marriages crept into the works of historians, who normally disdained domestic or economic detail. Senatorial men married earlier than men lower down the social scale precisely because they needed the support of two family networks to assist them in gaining political office. Pliny[2] commends a candidate for marriage to his friend's niece by pointing out that the potential groom has already achieved office, so that his in-laws would not be put to the usual expense and trouble expected of the bride's family as part of an electoral campaign. . . . Marriage extended the network of support available for routine family needs and for emergencies.

Roman marriage was clearly perceived as a family affair, not an individual decision based on personal attraction. The marriage of Cicero's[3] brother Quintus to Pomponia, sister of Cicero's great friend Atticus, was intended to cement the ties between the two friends. Delighted to be asked to suggest a husband for his friend's young niece, Pliny enthuses: "You could not entrust me with anything which I value or welcome so much, nor could there be any more befitting duty for me than to select a young man worthy to be the father of Arulenus Rusticus's grandchildren." . . . He is aware of the young woman's interests and for her benefit mentions the potential groom's good looks, but the matter is clearly seen as one for family discussion, since it will have an impact on the family for generations to come. Apart from the stress on generations past and future, the letter reads rather like a standard *commendatio*[4] for a political candidate or a young man suit-

---

[2] Pliny the Younger, statesman and civil servant (A.D. 61/62–113).

[3] Roman orator and politician (106–43 B.C.).

[4] Recommendation.

able for attachment to a governor's retinue. Romans saw it as quite reasonable that friends of the family would offer up such suggestions, arguing the credentials of the candidate, to be considered by the members of the other family.

This public and rather communal approach to the arrangement of marriage contrasts greatly with the modern Western norm, which is pervaded by the ideology of young romantic love, in which two people after courtship decide to marry and announce their decision to their families. It is usually at this stage that families become involved and, if the marriage transgresses the understood marriage groups (class, age, ethnic, or religious), it is borne upon the couple that the decision does have ramifications for families. If it is acceptable, the match is welcomed (though often with a certain ritual grumbling or conflict symbolically played out over wedding arrangements, timing, or gifts from the parents) and the families of the engaged couple accept that they are now linked in some way.

Roman matches were clearly arranged by the older generation. The partners probably had some say in them, depending on their own age and status within family and society. A young upper-class girl, married in her early or mid-teens, might barely be consulted, and someone like young Quintus, Cicero's nephew, would be pressured by his parents and the older generation generally to accept their choice. Widows and widowers and the divorced tended to be involved actively in the process, but it was still a communal one, a matter of discussing candidates with their supporters. One of Cato the elder's[5] lower-class *clientes* assured him that he would not dream of arranging his daughter's marriage without consulting Cato, and Cicero lists finding a husband for a daughter as one of the problems on which an orator's advice might be sought.

Legally, the *paterfamilias* arranged a match. His consent was essential for its validity. So, in theory, was the consent of the bride and groom, but jurists' quibbles make it clear that this was assumed, and even express refusal could be discounted, particularly in the case of the bride. . . . [T]he mother of the bride (or groom) assumed the right to be actively involved in the process, although she had no legal basis for this social assumption. The decision was usually celebrated by an engagement party, at which agreements . . . and gifts were exchanged. Unfortunately, we do not know whether the couple then courted in the style familiar in modern societies practicing arranged matches, in which the groom conventionally woos the bride in a romantic way. It is logical to assume that matches lower down the social scale were more amenable to individual decision making, but this is not certain.

We know a little more about the marriage ceremony and the dowry arrangements, although neither dowry nor a ceremony was a legal requisite of a valid marriage. Parties and general hilarity attended the wedding rites, which probably began in the home of the bride, who then processed, attended by torchbearers,

---

[5] Cato the Elder (234–149 B.C.), a statesman of the Roman Republic.

to the home of the groom. Small boys would dance around the procession making ribald jokes and grabbing at nuts thrown in their midst. The groom probably awaited the bride in his home, and on her arrival they joined in a religious rite to mark her entry into her new home. A small image representing her *Genius*[6] would be placed on the symbolic conjugal couch in the *atrium*.[7] . . . Some aspects of the ceremony would vary according to personal preference, wealth, and the age of the partners. Probably the first marriage of a young girl was more elaborate than that of a mature widow or divorcée. Many funeral sculptures show bride and groom at the wedding grasping right hands symbolically, with figures in the background bearing torches. It is indeed interesting that Roman men whose sarcophagi were decorated with scenes of their military and public achievements should also have chosen their wedding and in many cases the common domestic scene of husband and wife reclining to eat dinner as images to be passed on to posterity. . . .

. . . Rules gradually arose about the timing and mode of payment and return of dowry. It seems to have been generally assumed that after an initial transfer of real property — a piece of land or a house, for example — the cash component would be paid over in annual installments and that this basic arrangement would be followed by the husband in repaying the dowry at the end of the marriage.

Such rules constituted a kind of safety net for people who had not made specific arrangements or could not agree on the terms. It seems to have been usual to draw up contracts . . . stating the rules for payment and return. . . .

In the event of the husband's death, the dowry was normally returned to the widow fairly speedily. If the wife died, in the absence of special conditions the dowry was returnable only if it had been given by her father. If the marriage ended in divorce, the wife and her father had a right to sue jointly for its return, but they probably did not do this unless the usual mechanisms broke down. We have some information about the repayment of dowry on the divorce of Cicero from Terentia and on the divorce (and subsequent death) of his daughter Tullia. This information suggests that negotiations about the dowry were conducted through intermediaries and that there was some flexibility in adapting the original agreement. The legal sources, for example, imply that a wife who initiated a divorce without cause might forfeit the right to the return of dowry and that the husband's right to retain part of the dowry for the maintenance of children was dependent on the wife's misconduct. In practice, however, the notion of fault seems to have been of little significance in late republican divorce. The arrangements were determined by the social assumption that children were entitled to part of the mother's dowry for their maintenance (or a daughter's dowry, which perhaps amounted to the same thing) and that a divorced mother (like a widow) needed a dowry to remarry. The provision of dowry (and, by implication, marriage) is explicitly seen as a matter of public interest:

---

[6] Guardian spirit.

[7] Entrance room.

It is a matter of state concern that women should have secure dowries which enable them to marry. (*Dig.*[8] . . .)

A case involving dowry takes priority at any time and in any place for it is actually in the public interest that dowries be preserved for women, since it is of the utmost necessity that women are dowered for the purpose of bringing forth progeny and replenishing the state with [citizen] children. . . . (*Dig.* . . .)

The tablets or papyrus scroll in which the dotal agreement[9] was recorded did not constitute a marriage contract or a wedding certificate in the modern sense, but it could be used to demonstrate that a marriage had taken place, and it would be invoked in the reassignment of property and money on the dissolution of the match. This forethought again conflicts somewhat with modern romantic notions of marriage. It is not clear whether the Romans were more materialistic than moderns or simply more realistic and efficient about their materialism. The common law tradition encouraged the presumption that the property of husband and wife was held in common. Perhaps as a result of this tradition (or because the law reflected an entrenched social assumption), Anglophone married couples today, regardless of their legal claims, still tend to treat their property as joint for the duration of the marriage. Divorce or death then forces a decision on them at a time when they are least likely to be capable of rational decision making. The trauma of divorce is exacerbated by the modern perception that it constitutes a personal failure to measure up to society's ideal of a lifelong partnership. The Romans also had an ideal of marriage as a lifelong union, while in fact they practiced remarriage (on the death or divorce of spouses), very much as modern Western cultures do. They seem to have been more pragmatic about their solutions, and the custom of bargaining through intermediaries (a general feature of Roman social relations) apparently worked fairly well. In the modern world, negotiation tends to be carried out directly by the parties or through lawyers. Prenuptial agreements and that most recent innovation, mediation, are closer to the Roman system, except that Romans began the process of mediation before marriage, then renewed it at its end.

I stated at the outset that the purpose of Roman marriage was the production of legitimate citizen children. It is from this that so many other consequences flow for subsequent generations. The production of legitimate citizen children is perennially the basis of any state's concern with marriage. When the Roman census was held, it was traditional for the censors[10] to put to men of the equestrian[11] and senatorial orders the question, "Have you married for the purpose of creating chil-

---

[8] The *Digest*, statements of renowned jurisprudents, contained in the *Corpus iuris civilis* (the "body of civil law"), a collection of Roman laws, decrees, and imperial orders drawn up during the reign of Emperor Justinian (who ruled from A.D. 527 to 565).

[9] The agreement concerning the dowry.

[10] Two censors oversaw the census of Roman citizens and their property.

[11] Economic rank below senator. In the late Republic, a member of the equestrian order was usually a businessman.

dren?" . . . [A]necdotes and comments imply that the public and private ideology of Roman marriage was continually associated with the desire for progeny but that the concept of marriage included other elements, such as compatibility, partnership, and love. This is more obviously the case from the first century B.C. on, though perhaps it is merely a reflection of the greater quantity and variety of sources available to the historian from that period. It is, however, plausible that there was a change in sentiment, just as there was in marriage preference. For example, anecdotal stories about the earlier period tend to focus on the "external" aspects of married life — the wife's fertility, industry, and chastity — rather than the feelings husband and wife held for each other. It becomes clear that marriage, while still firmly associated with the hope of children, was also expected to produce other satisfactions.

It is interesting that the apparent change coincides with the greater incidence of divorce, which is no longer associated with the adultery of the wife. In his *Life* of the general Aemilius Paullus, Plutarch[12] mentions Paullus's divorce of his first wife Papiria, which seemed inexplicable to his contemporaries. Plutarch then cites a general anecdote about "a Roman" who divorced his wife in spite of his friend's remonstrances that she was fertile, discreet, and altogether a good wife. The man picked up his sandal and said that it looked sound to the onlooker, but only the wearer could tell where it hurt. Plutarch agrees that it is the little everyday irritations that make some marriages unbearable. The old idea that divorce was rare and shameful seems to have passed away by the second century B.C. Probably the husband had to initiate divorce if the wife were in his *manus*,[13] but an agreement could probably be reached in many cases, and gradually the separate marital regime, in which women could also initiate divorce, became dominant. In a society where so much was public, divorce now became a matter for speculation, because the reason for divorces was not known. Aemilius Paullus's divorce was the precursor of the new style.

Partnership becomes an automatic inclusion in discussions of marriage. Livy,[14] writing in the Augustan period[15] about early Rome, creates a portrait of a virtuous soldier symbolic of the simplicity of the past who enjoys a partnership with his wife in his fortunes, his estate, and his children. Such references — usually expressed from the husband's perspective — proliferate. The notion that a wife was a welcome partner in prosperity and adversity was invoked, for example, by the emperor Augustus in Dio's[16] representation of his attempt to persuade the men of the upper classes to marry and by senators arguing that provincial governors should be permitted to take their wives with them on tours of duty rather than

---

[12] Greek moralist and biographer (ca. A.D. 46–120).

[13] Legal control.

[14] Titus Livy, Roman historian (59 B.C.–A.D. 17).

[15] During the reign of Emperor Augustus, who ruled from 27 B.C. to A.D. 14.

[16] Dio Cassius, statesman and historian during the late second and early third centuries A.D.

be deprived of their companionship. The notion of marriage as partnership and companionship was so established, then, as to be part of the civic rhetoric and the public sphere. The many literary and epigraphic references to companionship, mutual loyalty and support, and the ideal of a happy and harmonious marriage show that this was part of a popular ideal as well as public and imperial ideology.

The notion of *concordia*, or harmony, in marriage was frequently mentioned in literature and in epitaphs boasting that marriages, especially long marriages, had been without discord. . . . Ovid[17] has the aged bucolic couple Baucis and Philemon speak of their harmony throughout their long marriage leading to their wish to die together. The elder Arria[18] defends her decision to commit suicide on her husband's condemnation by arguing that she and he had such a long and harmonious marriage. When this ideal was attached to the imperial family, it carried the implication that harmony ensured stable rule and succession. . . .

. . . [T]he point to note is that the *ideal* of harmony was almost as strongly embedded in the Roman notion of marriage as was its reproductive purpose. Like the association of marriage and children, it is reflected in public and private discourse. Marriage was viewed, therefore, as the proper vehicle for continuing the citizenship and serving the state into the next generation, for maintaining an individual family or a particular order. It was also viewed, both privately and officially, as a partnership in which each side supported the other and which was ideally harmonious and long-lasting.

At Rome, marriage was essentially a private arrangement, but it had legal implications, and the state occasionally intervened to remedy what were perceived as injustices or anomalies. . . . Legal aspects of marriage — the capacity to marry, the payment of dowry, its return on the dissolution of the marriage — are set in the context of marriage as a social phenomenon, an important element of Roman family relations embedded in Roman notions of status, sentiment, and economic exchange. It is important to test any legal principles against practice as far as it can be ascertained not only from individual decisions recorded in the *Codices*[19] but from literary evidence (particularly the law court speeches of Cicero and the letters of Cicero and Pliny) and from inscriptions and papyri. . . . Some scholars now are more inclined to speak of strategies than of legal rules and make a persistent attempt to plot change over time, relating developments in marriage to other trends in Roman society. This presents a contrast with the earlier tendency to theorize from the *Digest* as if it were timeless and perfectly reflected Roman society.

We have seen that the partners in a Roman marriage were Roman citizens or, more rarely, people with the *ius conubii*, the right to contract a valid Roman marriage with Roman citizens, and that they had to have the *affectio maritalis*, the in-

---

[17] Poet (43 B.C.–A.D. 18) known for his love poems, especially *The Art of Love,* and for his mythological work, *The Metamorphoses.*

[18] Arria the elder was the model of a dutiful wife because she accompanied her husband into exile and because she courageously committed suicide in order to show him that it was not difficult.

[19] Late imperial (third through early sixth centuries) orders.

tention of being married. The contract itself was legally drawn up between two families through the heads of the families. If neither bride nor groom had a living father, the groom would be a *paterfamilias,* and the bride would be a full party to her own contract, with her *tutor*[20] giving his assent to the dotal arrangements and, if applicable, to her transfer to the husband's power or *manus.* Marriage for the most part was governed by customary rules rather than formal law. The legal history of marriage at Rome could be seen as a slow tendency for the state to regulate aspects of an essentially private arrangement.

It is particularly difficult to determine the nature of marriage in early Rome. Later sources are understandably vague or confidently oblivious of the distinction between law and custom, and the picture is blurred by the tendency to mythologize the past. Indeed, reference to marriage in early Rome is almost always part of a moral argument deploring contemporary practice. The traditional extent of the husband's power is a popular theme. Dionysius of Halicarnassus,[21] writing in the time of Augustus, comments approvingly on regal Rome of the eighth century B.C.:

> By passing a single law, Romulus[22] reduced women to modesty. The law was as follows: that a proper wife, who had passed into the *manus* of her husband by a sacral marriage (by *confarreatio*), should have a partnership with him in all his goods and rites. . . . Four relatives would decide the following issues in conjunction with the husband: these included adultery and whether the wife proved to have drunk wine, for Romulus allowed that either of these offences could be punished by death.

This "law" is, then, an affirmation of the power of the family to hold a *consilium*[23] to determine vital issues, including the discipline of family members, and represents a limitation on the husband's power in that capital punishment had to be a group decision. In Livy's account of the traditional story of Lucretia, set at the close of the regal period (late sixth-century B.C.), Lucretia[24] summons a meeting of her husband, her father, and two of their friends to announce that she has been raped, intends to commit suicide, and expects them to avenge her. The presumption here is that the families of husband and wife would be represented at a *consilium.* Perhaps the most frequently quoted passage on the subject is the statement by Cato the elder in the second century B.C. that a husband had the right to sit in judgment on his wife, even for offenses such as drunkenness, but that she had no such right to judge him, even if she caught him in the act of adultery. Dionysius of Halicarnassus reinforces this picture with the statement that Romulus gave the Roman *paterfamilias* full powers over wife and child, and Plutarch,

---

[20] Guardian.

[21] Greek historian of Rome, first century B.C.

[22] One of the mythical founders of Rome.

[23] Council, usually of family and friends. (Author's note.)

[24] Legendary model of the perfect Roman wife, chaste and hard-working.

writing in the second century A.D. in Greece, continued the tradition with the comment that Romulus's laws one thousand years earlier had allowed the husband the right to divorce his wife but she had no such right.

It is very likely that the husband's powers were restricted by custom and the relative interest and power of the wife's relations. It is, however, plausible that divorce, insofar as it occurred in early Rome, was initiated only by the husband and implied a severe marital fault — almost necessarily adultery — on the part of the woman. It is also generally agreed that although there were in archaic Rome two distinct types of marriage, one marking the woman's full legal entry into the family of her husband and the other allowing her to retain her legal status as a member of the family of her birth, most marriages in the early period did involve the transfer of the woman to the husband's family and to his power. . . . This legal transfer could occur by *confarreatio, coemptio,*[25] or *usus.*[26] *Confarreatio* was an elaborate ceremony open only to patricians and included a joint sacral meal of prescribed foods. Divorce was not possible from this form of marriage, which became very rare.

The "imaginary sale" of *coemptio* remained a common way in which a woman passed into the husband's *manus.* The "sale" resembled other legal ceremonies, such as the emancipation of a child from *patria potestas,*[27] the manumission[28] of a slave, or a Roman will. A woman could also come into her husband's *manus* if she spent a full year under his roof (*usus*) but this consequence of marriage could be avoided if she spent three nights away from the conjugal home. This practice seems to have become obsolete or unusual by the late Republic and certainly by the early Empire. In fact, by the middle of the first century B.C. there seems to have been a general preference for the form of marriage in which the woman retained her natal status and separate property.

. . . A woman who had entered her husband's *manus* on marriage became one of his *sui heredes,* or direct heirs, and inherited equally with their children on his death. Any property she owned at the time of marriage or acquired afterwards became part of the joint family holding owned by the husband as *paterfamilias.* In practice, such property seems to have been treated as dowry, which she could recover separately on the husband's death by the second century B.C. . . .

. . . Cicero tells us that all property of a wife *in manu mariti*[29] was legally classified as dowry by the middle of the first century B.C. This must have been a response to the popularity of the "separate regime" form of marriage, because it virtually restored the widow who had been *in manu mariti* to full ownership of "her"

---

[25] A formal "sale" involving change of legal status, for example, by a woman before making a will. (Author's note.)

[26] Use.

[27] The father's power.

[28] Formal liberation.

[29] In the legal control of the husband.

property, which as dowry was now recoverable in its own right rather than being merged with the conjugal holding so that the whole could be evenly divided between herself and her children.

The most significant historical development in Roman marriage is surely this shift from a merged to a separate regime, that is, from the earlier form in which the woman normally entered the husband's *manus* to the later form in which the wife retained her status as *filiafamilias*[30] or, if her father were dead, *sui iuris*.[31] It is frustrating that nobody has been able fully to explain the shift or to plot it precisely. Authors have sometimes called the separate-regime style of marriage "free marriage" and have interpreted the shift as one to greater individual female power. . . .

Certainly, the wife was not in the husband's formal control and had greater freedom to manage her own property and to initiate divorce. The problem is in determining how the *ancients* viewed the different marriage styles and, therefore, what moved them to alter their preference over time. It was probably a corporate decision based on corporate interest. At first glance it seems to be in the interest of the bride's family to defer the final division of the patrimony in any generation until the father's death. The dowry seems to have represented a smaller share of the family holding than a daughter's intestate (or testamentary) portion. This must be offset against the likelihood that so many women would be *sui iuris* at the time of marriage or within a few years of it because of the death of the father. The shift might have conferred on the woman's brothers greater control of her fortune, but . . . the tendency was to view a woman's property as destined eventually for her children, and even brothers who were *tutores* must have given permission for their sisters to make wills in favor of the brothers' nephews and nieces. In time, the *tutela*[32] of male relations over women was abolished, surely because the men of the family had no particular interest in it and did not see it as a means of keeping property in the family or under their control.

The Roman sources do not discuss the shift explicitly. The change could well be linked with economic transformations in Roman society, for the attitude towards wealth, particularly landed wealth, altered significantly from the third century B.C. Without reverting to Roman myth about the simplicity of the past, we can still acknowledge that after the second Punic War[33] and the subsequent expansion into the eastern Mediterranean, Romans of the elite class became more involved in conspicuous consumption, such as the building of elaborate private homes and gardens and public buildings such as temples, and less tied to the concept of maintaining landed holdings within the same family. The preferred early system of marriage, like the ideal system of inheritance enshrined in the rules on

---

[30] Daughter of the family.

[31] Independent of the father's or the husband's power.

[32] A form of guardianship imposed on women and young children *sui iuris*. (Author's note.)

[33] 218–201 B.C.

intestate succession, seems to have been posited on a more static society in which a woman moved physically from the holding of her father to that of her husband and remained there for life, sinking her own property into her husband's and identifying with his family and therefore with the children of the marriage (who necessarily belonged to his family).

From the second century B.C., this scenario was no longer followed by an aristocracy that treated land as a commodity to be exploited in any way offered. In spite of legislation directed against the concentration of wealth in female hands, we hear increasingly of wealthy women such as Aemilia and her daughter Cornelia (mother of the Gracchi)[34] in the second century B.C. In the first century B.C. women such as Caecilia Metella, Servilia, Clodia, and Fulvia seem to be characteristic of the political elite, prominent for their wealth, their patronage, and, to an extent, their public activity and image. The establishment of an *actio rei uxoriae*[35] for the return of dowry to a woman after divorce or widowhood slightly precedes these other developments and suggests that divorce and the departure of the widow from her marital home had already become more common than in early Rome. Even allowing for the recurrent historical problem of the greater abundance and reliability of sources for the later Republic, it is difficult to avoid the conclusion that the changing character of upper-class wealth and spending, the greater public profile of upper-class women, and the change in marriage preference and frequency of divorce are all somehow linked.

The affiliation of married women seems also to have changed from the early stress on the *univira,* the woman with one husband who came to him as a young *filiafamilias* and died as his *materfamilias.*[36] The term was extended to the widow who declined remarriage out of loyalty to her husband's memory. From the time of the late Republic at least, widows were likely to remarry, and divorce became quite common and casual. The relative instability of marriage might have been tied to the volatility of elite political alliances in that period, but the tendency continued in times of political calm. Perhaps the earlier ideal, elaborated in ritual and sentimental ideology, was actually grounded in the assumption of a static property system in which women moved only once in a lifetime, taking with them their intestate portion, which remained with their conjugal family whether they died in the marriage or not. The presumption of the late Republic is that women will move into other marriages, taking their property with them but on the understanding that their children will eventually share it. Politically, married women of the elite promoted the interests of their brothers and sons rather than those of their husbands. Economically, they favored their children. Emotionally, they showed great affection and loyalty towards their husbands. All of these characteristics are

---

[34] Tiberius Sempronius Gracchus (163–133 B.C.) and Gaius Sempronius Gracchus (153–121 B.C.), brothers who were Roman statesmen and reformers.

[35] A legal action for the recovery of dowry on the dissolution of marriage. (Author's note.)

[36] Mother of the family.

not only displayed by the actions of the elite women best documented by the sources but lauded as the proper behavior of an ideal wife, mother, or sister.

In a general way, the history of marriage and the family seems to be characterized by a very slow erosion of the powers of the *paterfamilias,* both as father and as husband. . . . [S]tories about early Rome are typically examples of extreme husbandly harshness, but even they reveal the importance of the *consilium* as a possible check on his arbitrary exercise of power. . . . Even the shocking story of the husband who successfully defended his fatal assault on his wife with the excuse that she was a drunkard reveals that he was tried for the murder, however unsatisfactory we might find the outcome. By the early Empire, the *consilium* as a medium for passing judgment on wives seems to have become obsolete, presumably because wives were no longer seen as being in their husband's power and because divorce was a remedy readily available to both parties. . . .

. . . The Augustan legislation[37] on adultery transferred much of the power of adultery trials to the public sphere, and such powers as remained tended to lie with the father of the errant woman rather than with the husband, although he had a right to punish summarily a male adulterer caught in the act in his own home.

Approximately one century after the Augustan legislation on marriage and the family, Tacitus[38] wrote that in characterizing the act of adultery as a breach of the religious and legal code Augustus exceeded the more lenient attitude of the ancestors and even went further than his own laws. It is not quite clear what he meant by this, but the gist of his statement is that marriage and offenses against marriage had belonged traditionally to the private realm. Any problems that arose, including adultery committed by the wife, were dealt with by the families involved. The legislation sponsored or actually inspired by Augustus represents a strong and significant incursion by the state into this private sphere.

This statement needs some qualification. We have already seen that the censors regularly put to men the question whether they had married for the purpose of producing children. . . . There were also times when the aediles[39] had, as public officials, judged cases of adultery and other female sexual transgressions. There had, moreover, been rules limiting intermarriage even between citizens. Until the *Lex Canuleia,*[40] of ca. 445 B.C., marriage between patricians and plebeians could not produce legitimate issue and was in effect invalid. Yet at this time Latins and many Italians had *conubium* with Roman citizens; that is, they had the capacity to contract proper legal marriages with Romans which could produce legitimate

---

[37] Worried about the family life of the Roman elite, Emperor Augustus established laws that, in addition to making the state responsible for the punishment of female adultery, modified marriage and divorce procedures and rewarded couples that had more than three children.

[38] Roman historian (ca. A.D. 55–ca. 117).

[39] Elected officials who supervised the grain trade, public buildings, archives, public games, and the physical fabric of the city.

[40] Canulean Law, which allowed marriage between patricians and plebeians.

Roman citizen children. There is some suggestion that marriage between freed and freeborn Roman citizens was either illegal or subject to strong social sanctions, including condemnation by the censor. Such unions were not prevented or punished by the law in the modern sense, but the effect of the law was to invalidate the union, that is, to determine that any children of the union were not legitimate Roman citizens. . . .

In sum, the law had always had some relevance to issues of marriage and related questions, such as betrothal, dowry, divorce, and the status of children. Notwithstanding, the Augustan legislation passed in at least two blocks, in 18 B.C. as the *Lex Papia Poppaea*[41] and in A.D. 9 as the *Lex Iulia,*[42] did represent a new development. Augustus saw himself as a moral crusader, one who was bound to restore the pristine virtue of the Roman state. He perceived a failure, particularly in the upper class, to marry and have children, and his legislation was designed to provide incentives in the form of more rapid promotion through the political and administrative ranks and advantages in inheritance for those who married and produced children, with penalties for those who failed to conform to his requirements. In addition, his legislation attempted to formalize divorce by requiring a formal letter of divorce and witnesses and by compelling husbands to divorce adulterous wives. Men were also to be punished as criminals for committing adultery with married women or fornication . . . with single women.

The laws were not markedly successful in suppressing adultery or propagating the Roman population. Marriage was probably already popular with those who could afford it and had marriageable partners available; indeed, some made a career of marriage, like their modern equivalents. It is therefore not clear whether there genuinely was a serious demographic and moral problem in Augustus's day. Nor is it entirely clear whether he hoped that his legislation would affect all echelons of society, since the rewards and penalties were largely directed towards the upper class, with significant property to bequeath and with political ambitions to satisfy. The legislation aroused strong protests from men of the upper classes, and Augustus chose to respond to these in a variety of ways. He himself mounted a demonstration of sorts by appearing in public with his grandchildren, in effect presenting a counter-example to errant citizens. He also harangued recalcitrant upper-class bachelors and praised married men in speeches. . . .

The legislation itself has not been well preserved, so we must rely heavily on ancient summaries of the laws. The provisions on adultery were retained in the sixth century A.D. *Digest,* but Justinian finally eradicated many references to rewards for marriage and parenthood because of the new Christian regard for celibacy and theoretical dislike of the remarriage of widows. From what can be pieced together we get a sense of Augustus's moral purpose. He seems, in part, to have aimed at providing a eugenically sound ruling class for the empire, furnish-

---

[41] The Papia-Poppaean Law attempted to have Romans marry others in the same social class.

[42] With the intent of increasing the population, the Julian Law established marriage as a duty for Roman patricians.

ing Italian soldiers for the imperial army and ensuring the survival of the great estates of the aristocracy. His methods were not successful; overall, their greatest significance is for the violence and extent of his intrusion into the private sphere. Henceforth, adultery was a criminal offense which could, moreover, be prosecuted by anyone moved by moral outrage, malice, or the hope of gaining a percentage of the confiscated wealth of convicted miscreants. This ensured the persistence of accusations and trials, and the legislation, slightly modified from time to time, was maintained by subsequent emperors. . . .

Just as marriage continued to consist of two Romans with the capacity and desire to marry cohabiting, so divorce continued to be a matter of mutual agreement or unilateral repudiation, instantaneous in its effect in either case and requiring no recourse to state authorities unless the parties failed to agree on the restitution of dowry. In many respects, then, Roman marriage was more "private" than many of its modern equivalents. The theory and practice of marriage was monogamous, but there was no equivalent to the penalties of some modern states for bigamy as a crime.

It was to be expected that Christianity would have some impact on Roman marriage, but in fact the legal and social impact was less immediate and less strong than one might have imagined, given the early theological decision that marriage was a sacrament. Divorce by mutual consent remained straightforward even under Justinian's legislation, but it became more difficult for one partner — especially the wife — to institute divorce even in the face of clear hardship. Among themselves, Christians imposed social penalties on those who remarried or who married out of the proper groups, and in time they formulated many complicated prohibitions on marriage between quite distant relations or between people related only by marriage or betrothals (or even by relations of godparenthood).

In earlier Roman law, marriages between close kin had been subject to sanctions, but it is not clear that it was ever illegal in the sense that it was a crime. There was a tradition that cousin marriage had been illegal or discountenanced in archaic Rome, but it seems to have been acceptable from an early period. . . . Authors of the late Republic and early Empire certainly seem to find nothing worthy of comment in the marriage of cousins. Cousin marriage has some obvious advantages for the preservation of estates in families and is in many societies a favored mode (given the usual prohibition on marriage between siblings). . . .

New prohibitions were introduced from time to time in the imperial era. The prohibition against a provincial governor marrying somebody within his province, against a *tutor* or his son marrying a *pupilla* (ward), against senators marrying freedwomen or actresses, and so on, all show a certain tendency to intervene in the private sphere of marriage, which by modern standards is surprising only in the emphasis on status. In general, then, it can be said that marriage remained an essentially private affair on which the state intermittently intruded, particularly where there was some economic advantage to be gained from the imposition of penalties. In other cases, the state tended to impose as rules accepted community norms. It is, for example, improbable that a great number of senators were ever given to marriage with freed slaves, and such rules (like the earlier prohibition on marriage between patricians and plebeians in an era when the distinction was meaningful) reflected the actual marriage groups. Subsequent legislation prohibiting marriage between Jews and Christians reflected the ideology of the official religion. It is not clear how strictly such rules were applied at any stage. They could have been enforced by recourse to the Julian laws on adultery, since people living in such relationships were actually committing adultery or fornication in legal terms, but . . . there was considerable acceptance of certain types of *de facto* marriage, e.g., soldier marriage or unions between slave and free partners.

The ground was certainly laid in the classical period for the harder line eventually followed by Christian rulers, who saw marriage as a matter for public regulation. The earlier trend away from husbands' absolute rights was also undermined in late antiquity, and women, subject to public penalties for adultery, gradually lost their relative equality with the increasing Christian stress on wifely endurance and one-sided virtue in marriage and on the impropriety of widow remarriage.

> No Roman thinks it shameful to take his wife to a dinner party. At home the wife, as mistress of the household, takes first place in it and is the center of its entertaining. Things are very different in Greece, where the wife is never present at dinner, except for a family party, and spends all her time in the Women's Quarter, separated from the rest of the house — an area broached only by close male relatives.
>
> —*Cornelius Nepos*[43]

. . . We have seen that partnership and harmony were Roman marital ideals. The relative social visibility of Roman women and the fact that men such as Cicero and Pliny had women friends, their references to the literary interests of such women (e.g., Juvenal's[44] savage attacks in the Sixth Satire on women who talk incessantly about politics, literature, or philology) all suggest a society in which a married couple might have interests and activities in common that give some meaning to the ideal of partnership beyond a community of interest in their children and the family generally.

There are serious problems in attempting to analyze relationships and feelings even in a contemporary society, where taped interviews and questionnaires give a more solid base to speculation. The evidence of attitudes within Roman marriages is difficult to interpret. . . .

. . . We know that matches were commonly arranged by the older generation with an eye to material and political advantage, that divorce was easy and common, that many marriages ended fairly soon with the death of one partner and subsequent remarriage. Scholars have argued that Roman marriage, especially within the political elite, therefore engaged little of the partners' emotions and that

---

[43] Roman biographer (ca. 99–24 B.C.).

[44] Roman satirist (ca. A.D. 55–ca. 140).

there was scant likelihood that affectionate feelings would develop in such a milieu. Yet the four surviving letters from Cicero to his wife during his exile 58–57 B.C. reveal his dependence on her emotional and practical support. Consider, for example:

> If these misfortunes are permanent, I truly desire to see you, light of my life . . . as soon as possible and for you to remain in my embrace, since neither the gods whom you have cultivated so virtuously nor the men whom I assiduously served have rendered us our proper return.

He ends his letter with the following:

> Take good care of yourself, as far as you are able, and believe me when I say that I am more desperately perturbed by your wretched position than by my own. My Terentia, most faithful and best of wives, and my most beloved little daughter and our one remaining hope, Cicero — farewell.

Letters to Terentia are replete with expressions of longing for her and terms of endearment: "most faithful and best of wives," "light of my life, my longing," "my own life," "dearer to me than anything ever." Ovid, exiled to the Levant a generation later, uses the same or similar expressions to his wife: "dearest," "light of my life," "best of wives." . . .

. . . Arria the elder was famous for following her dissident Stoic husband into exile and taking the lead in showing him how to commit suicide heroically. Pliny noted that she had also committed other brave acts which were less well known. She had, at one stage, attended her husband and son, who were both critically ill. The boy died, but she kept the sad news from her husband until he recovered. Pliny preserved her deeds for posterity:

> Indeed, that was a glorious act of hers, to draw the blade, to plunge it into her breast and to pull out the dagger and offer it to her husband, to utter besides the immortal, almost divine words, "It does not hurt, Paetus." But fame and posterity were before her eyes when she did those deeds and said those words. How much more glorious it was for her, without the incentive of immortality and fame, to hold back her tears, to suppress her grief, to go on acting the part of a mother, when she had lost her son.

There was a *genre* of such inspirational tales. . . .

We have already seen the great popularity of the tombstone formulae celebrating marriages without discord. There was another, somewhat less common formula, used more by wives and typically following a statement of the length of the marriage, that the only unhappy day in that time was the day of the husband's death. Sometimes these briefer epitaphs also give sufficient detail to make it clear that the sentiments are no empty convention. Such is [the inscription] where the bereaved husband follows his recital of his wife's virtues with the statement that he has added these details so that people reading the epitaph would understand how much they loved each other. Consider, too, the woman whose husband had befriended her as a young slave girl, bought her out of slavery, and married her. This suggests that even the most conventional formulae, far from being "essentially loveless," might represent a shorthand for much stronger emotions which could not be spelled out for reasons of custom and economy.

It has also been claimed that Roman men did not expect to gain sexual satisfaction from their wives but sought this with mistresses. Certainly the tradition of passionate attachment is associated with mistresses of a lower social group, but the literary conventions are adopted by authors speaking of married love. This is the case with Sulpicia's[45] love poetry to her husband, with Ovid's yearning for his absent wife, with Statius's[46] claim that he had been struck as by a thunderbolt with love for his wife, and with Pliny's letter to his young wife lamenting her absence and stressing his longing for her:

> I am seized by unbelievable longing for you. The reason is above all my love, but secondarily the fact that we are not used to being apart. This is why I spend the greater part of the night haunted by your image; this is why from time to time my feet lead me (the right expression!) of their own accord to your room at the times I was accustomed to frequent you; this is why, in short, I retreat, morbid and disconsolate, like an excluded lover from an unwelcoming doorway. The only time free of these torments is time spent in the forum and in friends' law cases. Just imagine what my life is like — I, for whom you are the respite from toil, the solace of my wretchedness and anxieties. Farewell.

There are probably elements of literary conceit in all of these, but all see it as appropriate to adopt the language and imagery of passionate, romantic love when speaking of married love.

Cato the elder's famous punishment of the senator who embraced his wife passionately before their young daughter, Seneca's[47] insistence that men should not make love too ardently to their wives, Lucretius's[48] contrast between the modest immobility of a wife and the unseemly coital gyrations of a prostitute, and Plutarch's caution against the use by wives of aphrodisiacs on their husbands all imply a dominant ideology of moderation and decorum in married relations, particularly as displayed in public behavior. Yet the very fact that these warnings are seen as necessary is an indication that married couples did show the symptoms of sexual infatuation celebrated by the lyric poets. Plutarch's contrast between the heady, obsessive attachment of newlyweds and the stabler and more profound love between long-married partners is a modern commonplace. The references in Catullus[49] . . . to burning passion and jealousy between the bridal pair imply that such references are stock elements of wedding songs and other ritual. Tacitus's account of the murder of a woman by her husband after a stormy night of alternating reconciliation and quarreling and the references to the well-known passion of the

---

[45] Roman poetess, late first century B.C.

[46] Poet (ca. A.D. 45–96).

[47] Roman statesman and philosopher (ca. 4 B.C.–A.D. 65).

[48] Roman poet (ca. 99–55 B.C.).

[49] Roman lyric poet (ca. 84–ca. 54 B.C.).

Stoic Seneca himself for his young wife remind us that this decorous ideal was not always realized (and that we should not take philosophical generalization too seriously?). Consider Seneca's own words:

> This is what I said to my Paulina, who tells me to watch out for my health. Because I know that her life is inextricably bound with my own, I begin to be considerate of myself as a way of considering her. And although old age has made me brave in many respects, I am losing this advantage of my state of life. . . . Sometimes, however pressing the reasons are for ending it, life must be maintained for the sake of our loved ones even at the cost of extreme pain. . . . He who does not think enough of his wife or friend to hang on longer to life but is obstinate in choosing death, is effete.

In the end Nero[50] gave him no choice about the suicide.

There is no doubt that men did have extramarital sexual relationships with women of their own class — Augustus's laws against adultery did not, after all, stop the practice!—and with others who were not seen as marriageable. Such phenomena are hardly unknown in the modern world, where sexual satisfaction is a highly publicized expectation of the partners. A dual sexual standard certainly prevailed — again, this is hardly unique to Roman society, upper-class or otherwise. In the ancient world, sex outside marriage might even have been seen as a means of limiting the legitimate family, and gratification of male sexual whims was easy in a society with an abundance of slaves of both sexes lacking any rights. Many men probably did find casual and adulterous sex an exciting variation from sex with a respected and even beloved wife of many years' standing. I have no difficulty in believing that wives might have felt the same. Yet this scarcely justifies a firm statement that Romans saw sexual satisfaction as entirely distinct from marriage. There is enough contrary evidence to give us pause in making absolute pronouncements on the subject.

It will be apparent by now that most of the examples of legendary married love and heroic conjugal *fides*[51] concern women. It is also true that wives are overrepresented in epitaphs. This reflects the generally masculine orientation of the sources and probably the notion that men should be identified primarily by their jobs or public offices, and women by their position in the family. There are, to be sure, husbands known for their extraordinary love, such as Tiberius Sempronius Gracchus, who virtually chose to predecease his young wife Cornelia when faced with an omen in the form of two snakes, one male and one female, and husbands who killed themselves on the death of a wife. The usual trend, however, is to laud the courage and loyalty of wives. Given the historical tendency for women to retain their status after marriage as members of their own natal families and the acknowledged identification of elite women with their brothers' in-

---

[50] Emperor from A.D. 54 to 68.

[51] Faith, reliance, promise.

terests rather than their husbands', the ideal and reality of wifely loyalty in an age of frequent divorce is quite striking.

Another curiosity already noted above is the persistence of the ideal of the *univira,* the woman with only one husband. This soubriquet was applied originally to the woman who had come to her husband as a young virgin in her father's power, transferred to the husband's *manus,* and died before him. By the late Republic it came to be applied approvingly to widows who chose to remain single out of loyalty to their husband's memory and their children's interest. The ideal is celebrated in tombstones and literature against a background of frequent remarriage occasioned by divorce and spousal death. The law . . . acknowledged the right of widows and divorcées to the full or partial return of dowry so that they could marry but increasingly applied safeguards for the children of the earlier marriage against the designs of a stepfather. How did the ideal manage to persist, then? Because, like many ideals, it was sometimes met, and because people accepted it as part of their culture. This paradox (if it is a paradox) is perfectly paralleled in modern states, where people promise to marry until parted by death and plan their happy life together as if unaware of the statistics that give them such a high chance of divorce and widowhood. The ideal of romantic love — once only and for life — is active today, promoted by literature, the visual media, and pop songs, all produced by industries not distinguished by great individual adherence to the ideal. But hope springs eternal. Perhaps it is not so ironic that Augustus, himself scarcely chaste, should have promoted moral legislation and the ideals of marriage and family, for he and Livia[52] were known for their devotion to each other and, once they had contracted the "right" marriage, stuck with it.

It is worth repeating that feelings are very difficult to reconstruct historically. It is possible to argue both ways about Roman marriage. Evidence of cold-blooded political marriage and divorce abound, and it could be maintained that tombstones and tales of model marriages are empty conventions against a background of arranged matches and frequent remarriage. This is the sort of evidence that influences scholars . . . to characterize Roman marriage, especially within the elite, as emotionally unrewarding. Yet the references to the ideal of happiness or harmony, the relative trouble taken to comment on marriages and the dead spouse in tombstones, and the popularity of stories of overriding conjugal love all suggest that these matches, arranged by the older generation for reasons of material and political advantage, were expected to yield affectionate, companionable relationships and that this happened in numerous cases.

. . . Roman marriages, undertaken for the purpose of producing legitimate citizen children, performed legal and emotional functions. The legal aspects involved the status of the partners and the children of the union and, to an extent, their economic rights and obligations. Such considerations would have loomed large in people's lives, but marriage was also viewed ideally as a source

---

[52] (58 B.C.–A.D. 29), wife to Augustus, the first Roman emperor.

of comfort and happiness. Scholars have questioned whether these ideals could have been achieved against a background of arranged matches and casual divorce, but there is sufficient evidence to suggest not only that the political elite often formed loving and loyal conjugal partnerships but that slaves and soldiers, their lives subject to so much external disruption and control, also sought and sometimes fulfilled these ideals even when denied the full legal benefits of marriage.

Those studies of marriage (or concubinage) which were not entirely concerned with legal detail have often been dominated by the view that Roman marriage showed all the symptoms of the Roman moral decline so beloved of popular films and novels. This picture of decline probably owes much to the legislation of Augustus and the writings of the early church fathers and it has been fleshed out by the satirists' racy accounts of adultery and grossness. Augustus's assumption of resistance to marriage is difficult now to assess, and Christian distaste for concubinage and divorce have given an impression that is difficult to sustain in face of the evidence that Romans generally wished to marry and that they hoped for and often found harmony and comfort in marriage. Some also committed adultery, some divorced, and many remarried repeatedly on the death or divorce of spouses. The overall picture does not seem to be one of depravity or disregard for marriage. On the contrary, epitaphs proclaim the virtues of spouses (and, by implication, of the married state), and dramatic stories circulated of model spouses, especially wives, whose love and loyalty gave inspiration and sentimental gratification to a wide audience.

It is frustrating that we cannot adequately explain the changes which did take place in Roman marriage. These changes rest in the alteration of preference whereby women (or their fathers or families for them) chose to retain their status as a member of their own natal families after marriage. These women fully acknowledged their obligations to the children of the marriage and were encouraged to do so by the community, including their own relations, so it is not entirely explicable in terms of retention of family holdings. Husband and wife seem to have looked to each other more for emotional than for financial support; this is reflected in the inheritance laws giving low priority to succession between them and the custom limiting their gifts to one another. Yet there are so many exceptions to this tendency that it is difficult to make too much of it beyond the statement that a married woman owed great loyalty to her husband but that that relationship, which could be severed, was probably not perceived, if it came to the crunch, as being on quite the same level as duty to children and close natal kin.

. . . The close analysis of ideals and of texts and inscriptions describing actual marriages continues to yield important material which is changing our conception of Roman marriage and might eventually enable us to make sound statements about class and regional differences. In the meantime, it is clear that marriage, beset by the mortality patterns of the preindustrial world and the oppression of economic demands and a hierarchical social structure, yet provided comfort and some measure of material and emotional security for many and remained a desirable ideal for those whose circumstances excluded them from it.

MAKING CONNECTIONS:
WOMEN AND THE FAMILY

1. According to Suzanne Dixon, Roman husbands and wives often loved or cared for one another. What differences do you perceive between these marriages and those in ancient Mesopotamia and Egypt, which Bullough, Shelton, and Slavin describe in "Formation of Western Attitudes toward Women"? Did Roman men dominate their wives and families any less than did Mesopotamian and Egyptian men? To what extent would the expression "happily married" apply to couples in Roman society? What social groups does Dixon exclude from her discussion of Roman marriage and family life, and why? How did family life in Rome compare to that in Mesopotamia and Egypt?

2. In which society did men have the most positive attitudes toward women — Rome, Mesopotamia, or Egypt? Explain your conclusion. How did Roman law affect women's lives? Compare the condition of women in terms of law, the family, and male attitudes in Mesopotamian, Egyptian, and Roman civilizations. Where do you think most women were better off? Bear in mind that social conditions do not necessarily improve over time.

PLEASURES AND EXCESSES IN THE ROMAN EMPIRE
Paul Veyne

Professor of history at the Collège de France, Paul Veyne delights in describing the specific and the interesting in order to illuminate the otherness of past experiences and societies. Thoroughly acquainted with Roman art, literature, correspondence, and legal records, he portrays Roman culture as a "tissue of exceptions." Romans were not sadistic, although they reveled in watching men kill one another in the arena. Romans did not praise unchecked passion, although they approved of masculine domination in sexual relationships. Romans acclaimed civic involvement, but they admired private indolence.

Far from the blood-thirsty debauchees depicted in film and popular literature, Romans, as Veyne describes them, reveled in urbanity and the good breeding that marked a man's actions. Romans valued friendship rather than passion, loved city life, good manners, and pleasant banquets. Why were banquets so important to the Romans? The common people also valued others' company, as the appeal of groups such as confraternities attests. Furthermore, the Romans were religious people. How did their cults as well as their civic religion function? To what extent was Roman religion a pleasure or an excess?

Baths and public spectacles were important features of Roman urban life. What pleasures did baths offer? Why were the Romans so passionate about chariot races and gladiatorial combats? Christians criticized severely the races and the arena spectacles, as they did Roman sexuality. Overall, does Veyne offer a positive depiction of Roman character, behavior, and daily life?

"Bathing, wine, and Venus wear out the body but are the real stuff of life," a proverb warns. In Sparta[1] — yes, Sparta — the following epitaph commented on an erotic relief that graced one tombstone (such things were not unknown):

Paul Veyne, *A History of Private Life,* ed. Philippe Ariès and Georges Duby, vol. 1 of *From Pagan Rome to Byzantium* (Cambridge: Harvard University Press, 1987), 183–191, 193–194, 196–205.

[1] Greek city-state known for its spartan lifestyle.

This is what is called a temple.
This is where your mysteries lie.
This is what a mortal must do
When he sees where life ends up.

To everything there was a season, and pleasure was no less legitimate than virtue. One picture is worth a thousand words: the ancients liked to show Hercules[2] in moments of weakness, spinning at the feet of his mistress Omphale or drunk on wine, barely able to stand, his eyes distracted and face alight. Besides pleasures, there were marvels: spectacles, the grandeur of public buildings, the size of a city. People also marveled at the miracles of technology; in the theater scenic machinery enchanted spectators with its ingenuity. . . . Technology in this period did not pretend to dominate and revolutionize nature, as it does today, but in isolated areas the ancients were capable of amazing feats — miracles, as astonishing as the feats of nature. Among them were the siphon (which enabled aqueducts to span valleys) and the sundial. In the first century B.C. the sundial was all the rage; every city wanted one. Emperor Nero,[3] well aware of the value of amazement, contrived to reign as, much later, the princes of the Renaissance would do — as *artifex,* a word meaning both "artist who creates spectacles" and "engineer." He was unfortunately overthrown, because the notables and the nobility preferred urbanity, at least in an emperor.

Urbanity required savoir-vivre.[4] A well-bred man *(pepaideumenos)* exhibited neither baseness nor presumptuousness in the company of his peers, and every noble, every notable, was well-bred by definition. Respect for others was to be shown with liberal ease; the deference due a superior was to be offered with familiar simplicity, the mark of the free man's civic pride. Let "barbarians stand petrified before kings" and the superstitious tremble before the gods like slaves before their masters. In the eyes of the governing class "liberty" reigned, and the reigning sovereign was a "good emperor" so long as he adopted a liberal tone with citizens of the upper class, gave orders as though speaking to equals, avoided acting like a living god or barbarian potentate, and refused to take seriously his own divinization, a concession to the religious enthusiasms of the masses. The political style of the High Empire[5] was one of conviviality. Public men, it was felt, should be as free and easy with one another as the participants in Cicero's[6] philosophical dialogues, and religious life should be conducted in the same liberal atmosphere. Nothing could be farther removed from Christian relations with the divine, based as they were on the model of the family. Filial love for the Father must

---

[2] Greek demigod; son of the god Zeus and the human Alcmene.

[3] Emperor from A.D. 54 to 68.

[4] Literally, "knowing how to live"; to have good manners, be well bred.

[5] Roman society during the rule of the "Five Good Emperors," from A.D. 96 to 180.

[6] Roman orator and politician (106–43 B.C.).

have struck the pagans as distastefully intimate and servilely humble. It probably seemed plebeian.

Even in politics, the style of interpersonal relations between the emperor and his subjects was frequently much more important than actual political or economic decisions or the manner in which power was shared. Here again it is hard to differentiate between public and private life. Emperors were toppled because of private immorality or because of what they thought privately about the people they governed. The prince's private misconduct obviously did no harm to political or material interests, but it was humiliating to Roman notables to think that their emperor entertained megalomanic or immoral ideas, which offended their sense of honor.

Our impression of the ancient world prior to the "decadence" of the late imperial period[7] — an impression of classicism, humanism, clarity, reason, and liberty — comes from the thin veneer of style that graced private relations within the governing class. The style of private letters and prose generally, including epitaphs, reflects the same values. Our impression is also shaped by Roman art, with its taste for realism. . . . [T]he catacomb painters and medieval sculptors who recreated the "Bible in images" represented the elements and content of legend in a conventional montage. By contrast, classical pagan art consisted of momentary images — snapshots — of legends that presumably everyone knew: man and the real stood on a footing of equality. Portraits of the emperors from late antiquity depict the sovereign with the traits of a mystic or a Mussolinian[8] hierarch. But imperial portraits from the period of High Empire show the prince with the head of a handsome young man, an intellectual, or a respectable gentleman. His features are individualized; his head is that of a man like other men. There is nothing ideological or didactic about these busts.

For those who subscribed to the liberal ideal, friendship rather than passion epitomized the desirable qualities of reciprocity and inward freedom. Love is slavery, but friendship is freedom and equality. This despite the fact that in reality the word "friendship" often (though not always) meant "clientage."[9] Did people really have more friends then than they do now? I don't know. But friendship was talked about far more often than we talk about it today. Frequently, though, a culture speaks not of what really exists but of imaginary solutions to its real contradictions. (The Japanese do not commit suicide more often than Westerners, but they talk about it much more.)

In late antiquity everything changes. Rhetoric turns dark and expressionistic, and the style of politics becomes authoritarian and sublime. The exaggerated tone of the Late Empire, so extreme that it is almost a caricature, is responsible for the

---

[7] Period between the rise of Diocletian (A.D. 284) and the deposition of the last emperor in the West (A.D. 476).

[8] Relating to Benito Mussolini (1883–1945), Italian Fascist dictator.

[9] The Roman political and social system whereby commoners placed themselves under the protection of powerful families.

period's reputation as "decadent." For a long time historians, misled by this, believed that the population of the Empire, urban life, production, the monetary economy, and the authority of the government all suffered a serious decline. Such is the power of style to deceive.

The style of the first two or three centuries of the Empire was one of urbanity and urbanism. The notables, as we know, were a nobility of the cities, who visited their rural estates only during the heat of summer. As for nature, these city folk appreciated only its agreeable aspects (amoenitas). They explored its wild depths in cumbrous hunting parties only to prove their virtu, or courage. The nature they loved was "humanized" with parks and gardens; a landscape made a better composition if the site's possibilities were exploited by, say, placing a small sanctuary on a hilltop or at the end of a spit of land. Men were fully themselves only in the city, and a city was not so much a place of familiar streets and bustling, anonymous crowds as an array of material conveniences (commoda) such as public baths and buildings, which lifted the spirits of residents and travelers alike and made the city much more than just a place where numbers of people lived. Pausanias[10] asks: "Can one call 'city' a place that has neither public buildings nor gymnasium nor theater nor square nor water to supply a single fountain, and where the people live in huts, small shacks (kalybai) perched on the edge of a ravine?" Romans did not really feel at home in the country. To feel at home they needed a city, in particular a city surrounded by ramparts. This is a trait of the Roman psychology: walls were a city's finest ornament, defining the space of the communal home. Nowadays, even if we do not live in fear of thieves, most of us lock our doors at night. Similarly, walled cities locked their doors at nightfall, and nocturnal comings and goings were suspect. Would-be miscreants did not dare apply to the night watch for the keys to the city gates and were forced to enlist the aid of accomplices, who might lower them in baskets from atop some poorly guarded section of the city wall.

Walls were a sign of civility, banquets a ceremony of civility. The moment Horace[11] arrived at his beloved country retreat he invited a woman friend to join him for dinner, most likely a freedwoman, a well-known singer or actress. Banquets were occasions for the private man to savor his accomplishments and show off to his peers. The banquet was as important to the Romans as the salon to the eighteenth-century French aristocracy, as important even as the court of Versailles to the seventeenth-century nobility. The emperors kept no court. They lived in their "palace," on the Palatine Hill, much as the nobles of Rome lived in their private villas, with only slaves and freedmen for company (which of course meant that the palace housed the various ministries of government). When night came, however, the emperor dined with his guests, senators and others whose company he relished. The time of public "honors" and "government" of the patrimony was

---

[10] Geographer and travel writer, ca. A.D. 150.

[11] Roman poet (65–8 B.C.)

over. Now the private man could relax at table. Even the poor people (*hoi penetes*), nine-tenths of the population, had their nights of revelry. During a banquet the private man forgot everything but his "profession," if he had one. Those who had vowed to devote their lives to the pursuit of wisdom celebrated not as the profane did but as philosophers.

There was an art to banqueting. Roman table manners were apparently less elaborate and formalized than ours, however. People dined with clients and friends of all ranks, and protocol was strictly observed in the assignment of "dining couches" around the pedestal table that held the platters of different dishes. Without couches there could be no real feast, even among the poor. Romans sat up to eat only at ordinary meals (with simple folk, the mother stood and served the father seated at table). Roman cooking strikes us as a mixture of oriental and medieval. The food was quite spicy and covered with complicated sauces. Meat was boiled more often than it was braised or roasted, so that it was bloodless, and served sugared. Romans preferred their food in the sweet-and-sour range. As for drink, there was a choice between wine with a flavor something like marsala[12] and a resiny wine such as one might drink in Greece today, both diluted with water. "Make it stronger!" the suffering erotic poet orders his cupbearer. The trickiest part of the evening, and the longest, was that set aside for drinking. Early in the dinner people ate without drinking. Later they drank without eating: this was the banquet in the strict sense of the word (*comissatio*). More than a feast, the banquet was a festival, and each man was expected to hold his own. As a token of festivity guests wore hats with flowers, or "wreaths," and were perfumed, that is, anointed with fragrant oil (alcohol was unknown, so oil was used as a solvent for perfumes). Banquets were unctuous and brilliant, as were nights of love.

The banquet was more than just a meal. Guests were expected to express their views on general topics and noble subjects or to give summaries of their lives. If the host had a domestic philosopher or tutor on his staff, he would be asked to speak. Between dishes there might be music (with dancing and singing), by professional musicians hired for the occasion. At least as much a social manifestation as an occasion for eating and drinking, the classical banquet gave rise to a literary genre, the "symposium," in which men of culture, philosophers, and scholars (*grammatici*) held elevated discussions. Ideally the banquet hall was supposed to resemble not a dining room but a literary salon; when this happened, confusion with popular merrymaking was no longer possible. "Drinking," then, meant the pleasures of good company, culture, and in some cases the charms of friendship. Thinkers and poets found it perfectly possible to philosophize about wine.

Ordinary folk enjoyed one another's company in less ostentatious ways. They had taverns and "colleges," or confraternities. As in Moslem countries today, men met friends at the barber, the baths, or the tavern. In Pompeii taverns (*cauponae*) were numerous. There one met travelers, had food warmed (not all the poor had

---

[12] A strong wine produced in Sicily.

ovens at home), and flirted with bejeweled waitresses. Amorous taunts are recorded on the walls. These popular customs were considered bad form by the nobility, and a notable seen lunching in a tavern risked tarnishing his reputation. Street life was disreputable. One old philosopher was so immoderate in his desires that he never went out without money, people said, so that he could buy any pleasure that he happened upon. The imperial government waged war for four centuries against the taverns to keep them from serving as restaurants (*thermopolium*), for it was considered morally healthier to eat at home.

As for the *collegia,* or confraternities, the emperors were suspicious of them, since they were places where numbers of men gathered for purposes that were hard to define. Rightly or wrongly, government feared their potential power. In principle, the collegia were free, private associations, whose members were free men and slaves who practiced a common trade or worshiped a common god. Nearly every city boasted one or more. In one town, for example, there was a weavers' association and a college of worshipers of Hercules. A neighboring town was home to a blacksmith's confraternity and an association of clothing merchants who worshiped Mercury.[13] Each confraternity was confined to a single city. Members lived in the town and knew one another. All were men; no women were admitted. Finally, all the collegia, whether religious or professional, were organized along the same lines as the city itself. Each had a council, magistrates who held office for a year at a time, and benefactors, who were honored with handsome declarations patterned after the honorary edicts issued by the city council. In sum, the collegia were make-believe cities. They served religious and professional purposes, and their members were common people from a particular city or town.

Why did people join such groups? Why did the carpenters in one town or the worshipers of Hercules in another feel the need to band together? One thing is certain: the colleges were nothing like modern trade unions, nor were they workers' mutual aid societies. They offered men a place to meet and to enjoy one another's company, away from women. If a college was religious in character, honoring its god provided a pretext for staging a banquet. If professional, it brought together men working in similar trades; cobblers liked to talk to other cobblers, carpenters to other carpenters. Each new member paid an entry fee. Coupled with gifts from benefactors, these dues enabled college members to stage joyous banquets and buy members decent burials (which were also followed by banquets). Slaves joined colleges to ensure that they would not be buried like dogs. . . . The two things that interest the collegia, Saint Cyprian[14] wrote, are banquets and burials. In a few cases the zeal for banqueting required no pretext; at Fano on the Adriatic there was a confraternity of *"bons vivants*[15] who dine together."

---

[13] Messenger of the gods in Greco-Roman mythology.

[14] Lived ca. A.D. 200–258; Bishop of Carthage in North Africa.

[15] Gourmets; lovers of good living.

Collegia proliferated to the point where they became the center of plebeian private life. Not surprisingly, the imperial government viewed them with suspicion. And not without reason, for any association tends to acquire purposes beyond its officially stated aims, beyond even its unconscious desire. When men come together for whatever reason, their conversation will quite naturally range over matters of common interest. At the end of the Republic, candidates for election sought the support of colleges as well as cities. Later, in the politically troubled city of Alexandria, religious colleges met and, "under the guise of taking part in some sacrifice, people drank and in their drunkenness talked nonsense about the political situation." After "talking nonsense" long enough they took to the streets, egged on by a notable who defended the privileges of the city's Greeks against the Roman governor and who, by means of generous donations, had secured for himself the position of president of these religious groups, the ancient equivalent of our political clubs.

More numerous, however, were the clubs where people went merely to drink with friends. The need for association was so great that groups formed even within households and, under the guise of piety, in the finest society. The slaves and freedmen of one household, or the sharecroppers and slaves of an estate, might band together in a college, pay dues to cover members' burial costs, and show devotion to the master's family by erecting a small domestic sanctuary in honor of the protective deities of the household or estate. These colleges also mimicked the political organization of the cities.

In the cities themselves, . . . wealthy benefactors paid for public feasts. Banquets were important occasions, rituals of conviviality and drink. Some were held at fixed intervals, others on special occasions; eagerly anticipated, they added solemnity to pleasure. Funerals, too, were important occasions for which people prepared diligently. The worship of Bacchus[16] symbolized and glorified Roman attitudes toward both feasting and death. "Worship" may be too strong a word. Even if people naively believed in the existence of Bacchus, they never worshiped this god, who was famous mainly from his legends. Certain mystical sects held that he was a truly great god, but most Romans, when they felt the need of divine protection, worshiped deities considered more authentic than Bacchus, to whom no shrines were erected. Yet the legend of Bacchus was more than a legend. Bacchic imagery was ubiquitous, and its meaning was obvious. Images of Bacchus are found in mosaics, in paintings that hung on the walls of houses and taverns, on dishes, and on household objects of all sorts, to say nothing of sarcophagi.[17] No other image was as widely disseminated, not even that of Venus.[18] Bacchic imagery was appropriate anywhere because it evoked only pleasant associations. The god of pleasure and sociability, Bacchus was always accompanied by a train of tipsy

---

[16] God of wine; symbol of ecstatic spirituality, pleasure, and sociability.

[17] Stone coffins bearing inscriptions.

[18] Goddess of sexual love.

friends and ecstatic female admirers; pleasant excesses of all sorts lay in store for them. A benevolent, civilizing god who soothed the mind, Bacchus won peaceful victories in every corner of the world. He was clever enough to calm the fiercest tigers, who hitched themselves like lambs to his chariot. His admirers were as beautiful, and as lightly clad, as his lovely mistress, Ariadne. Bacchic imagery certainly had no religious or mystical significance, but it was not merely decorative, either. It affirmed the importance of sociability and pleasure, on which it bestowed the blessings of the supernatural. It was an ideology, an affirmation of principle. Against this was set the image of Hercules, symbol of civic and philosophical "virtue."

Bacchus, emblematic of a principle, was one god the people did not doubt. His worshipers banded together in popular confraternities, whose chief concern (proved by their regulations) was to drink toasts in honor of this amiable diety. . . . To the cultivated, the Bacchus legend was a pleasant fancy; the god might exist, or he might be one of the many names of the godhead, or he might be a superhuman individual who had lived in the distant past and whose legend was based on authentic exploits. These beliefs were enough to encourage speculation about the god, and a few sects formed for the purpose of worshiping him: small, isolated groups in which exalted piety and authentic religious fervor coexisted with more worldly attitudes. . . . [T]he Bacchic sects had secret rites, initiation rituals (or "mysteries"), and a hierarchy from which women were not excluded. . . . [S]ects, popular and otherwise, were a feature of the age, and religious fervor was no less important than the need for sociability. The speculations of these mystery sects contributed to the spiritual revolution of late antiquity.

Feasting and piety could coexist in sects and confraternities because festival was an integral part of pagan religion. A cult was nothing more than a festival, which pleased the gods as much as it pleased the men and women who took part. All religions are likely to confound spiritual emotion with formal ritual; untroubled by the confusion, the faithful find sustenance in both. Was wearing a wreath in antiquity a sign of feasting or religious ceremony? How can we tell? Piety meant honoring the gods as they deserved. Religious festivals yielded a twofold pleasure: besides enjoying oneself, one did one's duty. The pagans never asked the faithful how they "really" felt; hence we have no way of knowing. Paying homage to the gods was a solemn way of enjoying yourself. Fortunate were those who, more than others, felt the presence of divinity and whose souls were moved.

The principal rite of every cult was of course the rite of sacrifice, which people attended in a contemplative mood. It is important to bear in mind, however, that in a Greek or Latin text the word "sacrifice" always implies "feast." Every sacrifice was followed by a dinner in which the immolated victim was cooked on the altar and eaten. (Great temples had kitchens and offered the services of their cooks to worshipers who came to sacrifice.) The flesh of the victim went to the participants in the ritual, the smoke to the gods. Scraps from the meal were left on the altar, and beggars (bomolochoi) spirited them away. When sacrifice was made not on a household altar but at a temple, the custom was to pay for the priests' services by leaving them a set portion of the sacrificial animal; temples earned money by selling this meat to butchers. (When Pliny the Younger[19] wishes to inform the emperor that he has eradicated Christianity in the province of which he is governor, he writes: "The meat of sacrificial animals is on sale once more," proving that sacrifices have resumed.) Which was it: Did people eat sacrificial victims or did they sacrifice animals they wanted to eat? That depends. The word for a man who made frequent sacrifice (*philothytes*) came to mean not a devout person but a host who gave good dinners, an Amphitryon.[20]

The religious calendar, which varied from city to city, was filled with festivals, days when no one was required to work. These occurred at irregular intervals throughout the year. (Incidentally, the week, a period of astrological rather than Judeo-Christian origin, did not come into common use until the end of antiquity.) On feast days people invited their friends to sacrifices in their homes; such invitations were considered a greater honor than mere dinner invitations. Vapors of incense spewed forth from many houses on these great occasions, according to Tertullian.[21] Among the important holidays were the national feasts of the emperors, the festivals of certain gods, New Year's Day, and the first day of each month. A custom cherished by Romans wealthy enough to practice it was that of sacrificing a piglet on the first of the month in honor of the household gods, the Lares or Penates. Once a year the birthday of the paterfamilias[22] was celebrated with genuine fervor. On that day the family feasted in honor of its protective deity, or *genius*. (Each individual had, as it were, a divine double, or genius, whose existence had little consequence other than to allow people to say "May my genius protect me!" or "I swear by your genius that I have carried out your orders.") The poor sacrificed less costly animals. If Aesculapius[23] cured them of some malady, they sacrificed a chicken at his temple, and then returned home to eat it. Or they might place a simple wheat cake on the family altar (*far pium*).

A simpler means of sanctifying a meal was what Artemidorus,[24] I think, called "theoxenies"; one invited the gods (*inpitare deos*) to dinner by removing their statuettes from the house's sacred niche and placing them in the dining room during the meal, as platters of food were heaped in front of them. After dinner the slaves feasted on these untouched dishes. This custom probably explains the following lines from Horace: "O nights, O dinners of the gods at which my friends and I ate before the household genius, and I gave my excited slaves consecrated dishes to eat." If the slaves were excited, it was the feast that excited them, and this was as

---

[19] Statesman and civil servant (A.D. 61/62–113).

[20] Husband of the beautiful Alcmene. In Greek mythology, Zeus assumed this man's form to seduce Alcmene; the product of their union was the hero Hercules.

[21] Christian theologian (ca. A.D. 160–ca. 225).

[22] Father of the family; head of the household.

[23] Greek god of medicine.

[24] Greek geographer and travel writer, ca. 100 B.C.

it should be. Peasants, too, celebrated seasonal festivals according to a rustic calendar. With gifts formally offered by sharecroppers, the great landlord of a district used to sacrifice a tithe of the soil's produce to the gods of the fields, after which everyone ate, drank, and danced. Then, at nightfall, as Horace states explicitly and Tibullus[25] implies, people had the right, even the duty, to make love as a fitting end to a day in which they had enjoyed themselves while honoring the gods. Someone once reproached Aristippus,[26] a philosopher and theoretician of pleasure, for leading a life of indolence. "If it is wrong to live like this," he replied, "why do people do it for the gods' feasts?"

In addition to the enthusiasms and delights of the religious calendar, there were other pleasures with nothing sacred about them that could be had only in the cities. These were among the benefits *(commoda)* of urban life, the product of public benefaction, . . . and included public baths, theaters, chariot races at the Circus, and fights between gladiators or hunters and wild animals in the arena of the amphitheater (or theater in Greek areas). Baths and public spectacles cost money, in Rome at any rate (we know little about the subject, and it seems likely that generosity of benefactors had some influence on the price of admission), but the cost was in any case modest. Free seats were reserved at every show, and lines began forming the night before. Free men, slaves, women, children — everyone had access to the baths, even foreigners. When gladiators were on display, people flocked to the cities from great distances. The better part of private life was spent in public establishments of one kind or another.

The baths were not for cleanliness. They offered an array of pleasures, rather like our beaches. Christians and philosophers denied themselves these pleasures. Not so soft as to lust after cleanliness, they bathed only once or twice a month. A philosopher's dirty beard was proof of the austerity on which he prided himself. No rich man's house *(domus)* was without a bath, which occupied several specially prepared rooms, with heating under the floor. And no city was without at least one public bath, supplied, if necessary, by an aqueduct, which also carried water to the public fountains. (Door-to-door water delivery was still a corrupt business monopolized by criminals.) The gong *(discus)* that announced the opening of the public baths each day was a sweeter sound, Cicero says, than the voices of the philosophers in their school.

For a few coins the poor people could spend several hours a day in a luxurious setting provided by the authorities, the emperor, or the city notables. Along with complex installations, including hot and cold baths, there were promenades and fields for sports and games. (The Greco-Roman bath was also a gymnasium and in Greek regions was still called by that name.) The two sexes were separated, at least as a general rule. Excavations at Olympia allow us to follow the revolution of the baths over more than seven centuries. Originally modest, functional

---

[25] Roman poet (ca. 55–19 B.C.).

[26] Greek philosopher of hedonism (ca. 435–360 B.C.).

buildings, with a cold pool, hot slipper baths,[27] and a steam bath, the "therms" eventually developed into pleasure palaces. A well-known quip calls them, along with the amphitheaters, "cathedrals of paganism." Beginning in the Hellenistic era,[28] their role expanded from one of facilitating cleanliness to one of making life as pleasant as possible. The great novelty (which dates from around 100 B.C. in Olympia and earlier still at Gortys in Arcadia) was the heating of the basement and even the walls of the building. Large numbers of people were offered an enclosed place that was always warm. At a time when, no matter how cold it became, people had no source of heat at home other than braziers and wore overcoats in the house as well as in the street, the baths were a place to keep warm. Ultimately in the baths of Caracalla the Romans introduced "climate control" throughout the building by means of convection. There was another kind of evolution in the baths: from functional edifice to dream palace, with sculptures, mosaics, painted decor, and sumptuous architecture making the splendor of a royal residence accessible to all. Life at the baths was like life at the beach in summertime; the greatest pleasure was to mix with the crowd, to shout, to meet people, to listen to conversations, to spot and tell stories about odd characters, and to show off.

Passion for the races at the Circus and the fights at the arena, Tacitus[29] complained, rivaled the study of eloquence among young men of good family. These spectacles were of interest to everyone, including senators and philosophers. Gladiators and chariots were not pleasures for the plebs[30] alone. Criticism of them, usually by Platonic philosophers,[31] smacked of that conventional utopian wisdom that we have learned to recognize. In the theater the plays known as pantomimes (a kind of opera; the word has since changed its meaning) were attacked for encouraging "softness" and occasionally prohibited. The gladiator shows were different. Infamous as they were, they at least had the merit of fortifying their spectators' courage by inuring them to the sight of blood. But even gladiator fights and chariot races had critics, who charged that such spectacles typified the human tendency to complicate life unnecessarily and waste time with frivolities. In Greek parts of the Empire intellectuals condemned athletic competitions for the same reason; to which other intellectuals responded that athletes offered lessons in endurance, moral strength, and beauty.

Intellectuals, along with everyone else, attended these spectacles. Cicero, who liked to say that he spent show days writing books, was one of the crowd and reported the events to his noble correspondents. When Seneca[32] felt the shadow

---

[27] Partially covered, slipper-shaped bathtubs.

[28] Greek, western Asian, and Egyptian history from the death of Alexander the Great (323 B.C.) to the Roman conquest (31 B.C.).

[29] Roman historian (ca. A.D. 55–ca. 117).

[30] Plebeians, the ordinary citizens of the Roman Republic.

[31] Followers of the Greek philosopher Plato (ca. 420–347 B.C.).

[32] Roman statesman and philosopher (ca. 4 B.C.–A.D. 65).

of melancholy steal across his soul, he headed for the amphitheater to cheer him-self up. Maecenas,[33] a sophisticated Epicurean noble, inquired of his client Horace about the program of the fights. But Marcus Aurelius,[34] good philosopher that he was, found one fight pretty much like another and went to see the gladiators only to fulfill his duty as emperor. The passions of the public were engaged, how-ever, and wealthy youths and honest yeomen divided into rival factions backing one actor or racing team or group of gladiators against another. The enthusiasm sometimes spilled over, but the ensuing riots concealed no ulterior political mo-tives or class divisions. Occasionally it was necessary to exile an actor or chariot racer who had stirred the passions of the crowd for or against him.

In Rome and other Italian cities spectacles were the great drawing card. In Greek areas, by contrast, athletic competitions were. Greeks flocked not only to great games (isolympicoi, periodicoi) and lesser games (stephanitai), which were as-sociated with fairs, but also to minor games (themides). The Greeks enthusiastically borrowed gladiatorial combats from the Romans. Athletes, actors, racers, and gladiators were stars. The theater set fashion, and many popular songs were first heard on the stage.

The role of spectacles and competition in ancient life at first seems surpris-ing. The most distinguished individuals, even public officials, confess a passion-ate interest in these events without the slightest embarrassment. Rather than build dams or docks, cities and their benefactors ruined themselves building aqueducts (to supply water to the public baths), theaters, and gigantic amphitheaters. This passion can be understood. Public spectacles were not dependent on individual tastes (as opposed to policy), nor were they leisure activities (as opposed to the more serious and laborious parts of life). Hence it is wrong to draw a parallel with our Olympic Games or World Cup Soccer or World Series. The ancients did not distinguish between popular and elite sports, and spectacles were public institu-tions, organized (and sometimes financed) by government authorities. In a period in which idleness was an ideal, no contrast was drawn between pleasure and work; nobles and plebeians alike took public spectacles seriously.

Philosophers charged that the passions aroused by these spectacles were ex-cessive, and Christians agreed: "The theater is lasciviousness, the Circus, sus-pense, and the arena, cruelty." As critics saw it, the cruelty belonged to the glad-iators themselves, who volunteered to commit murder and suicide. All were volunteers; otherwise they would have put on a poor show. The criticism that oc-curs to us — that the spectators must have been sadists — never occurred to any Roman, philosopher or not. The gladiators brought Rome a strong dose of sadis-tic pleasure of which people fully approved: pleasure at the sight of bodies and at the sight of men dying. Gladiator fights were not mere fencing matches with ac-tual risks. The whole point was to witness the death of one of the combatants or,

---

[33] Wealthy politician and patron of literary figures (ca. 74–8 B.C.).

[34] Emperor from A.D. 161 to 180.

better still, the decision whether to slit the throat or spare the life of a fallen gladiator who, exhausted and frightened for his life, was reduced to begging for quarter. The best fights were those that ended in exhaustion, with the life-or-death decision made by the patron who had paid for the show, in conjunction with the public. Innumerable images on lamps, plates, and household objects reproduced this great moment. And the patron boasted of having decided a man's fate: the cutting of the gladiator's throat was depicted in mosaic, painting, or sculpture and placed in his antechamber or on his tomb. If the patron had purchased from the imperial treasury men sentenced to death in order to have them executed during the intermissions in the fights, he also had the artists show these prisoners being thrown to wild beasts. After all, he had paid for them. In Greek regions the death of a boxer during a match was not a "sports accident." It was a glory for the athlete to die in the arena, just as if he had died on the field of battle. The public praised his courage, his steadfastness, his will to win.

It would be wrong to conclude that Greco-Roman culture was sadistic. People were not convinced that watching suffering was pleasurable; they were critical of those, such as Emperor Claudius,[35] who took obvious delight in viewing the slaughter, rather than adopting an objective attitude as if witnessing an exhibition of courage. Greek and Roman literature and imagery are not generally sadistic. In fact the contrary is true, and when the Romans colonized a barbarian nation their first concern was to prohibit human sacrifice. A culture is a tissue of exceptions, whose incoherence goes unnoticed by those involved in it, and in Rome spectacles were such exceptions. Images of victims occur in Roman art only because the victims died in spectacles that were sacred institutions. In our own time sadistic images, justified on patriotic grounds, occur in war films but are condemned elsewhere. Our pleasure in such things must be unwitting. The Christians were more critical of the pleasure than of the atrocity of the institution.

Similar incoherences and baffling limitations are found in every century. In Greco-Roman culture we find them associated with another pleasure: love. If any aspect of ancient life has been distorted by legend, this is it. It is widely but mistakenly believed that antiquity was a Garden of Eden from which repression was banished, Christianity having yet to insinuate the worm of sin into the forbidden fruit. Actually, the pagans were paralyzed by prohibitions. The legend of pagan sensuality stems from a number of traditional misinterpretations. The famous tale of the debauches of Emperor Heliogabalus[36] is nothing but a hoax perpetrated by the literati who authored that late forgery, the *Historia Augusta*.[37] The legend also stems from the crudeness of the interdictions: "Latin words are an affront to decency," people used to say. For such naive souls, merely uttering a "bad word"

---

[35] Emperor from A.D. 41 to 54.

[36] Emperor from A.D. 218 to 222.

[37] A collection of lives of the emperors, full of salacious stories, written by a fourth-century forger.

provoked a shiver of perverse imagination or a gale of embarrassed laughter. Schoolboy daring.

What were the marks of the true libertine? A libertine was a man who violated three taboos: he made love before nightfall (daytime lovemaking was a privilege accorded to newlyweds on the day after the wedding); he made love without first darkening the room (the erotic poets called to witness the lamp that had shone on their pleasures); and he made love to a woman from whom he had removed every stitch of clothing (only fallen women made love without their brassieres, and paintings in Pompeii's bordellos showed even prostitutes wearing this ultimate veil). Libertines permitted themselves to touch rather than caress, though with the left hand only. The one chance a decent man had of seeing a little of his beloved's naked skin was if the moon happened to fall upon the open window at just the right moment. About libertine tyrants such as Heliogabalus, Nero, Caligula,[38] and Domitian[39] it was whispered that they had violated other taboos and made love with married women, well-bred maidens, freeborn adolescents, vestal virgins, or even their own sisters.

This puritanism went hand in hand with an attitude of superiority toward the love object, who was often treated like a slave. The attitude emblematic of the Roman lover was not holding his beloved by the hand or around the waist or, as in the Middle Ages, putting his arm around her neck; the woman was a servant, and the lover sprawled on top of her as though she were a sofa. The Roman way was the way of the seraglio.[40] A small amount of sadism was permissible: a slave, for example, could be beaten in her bed, on the pretext of making her obey. The woman served her lord's pleasure and, if necessary, did all the work herself. If she straddled her passive lover, it was to serve him.

Machismo was a factor. Young men challenged one another in a macho fashion. To be active was to be a male, regardless of the sex of the passive partner. Hence there were two supreme forms of infamy: to use one's mouth to give a woman pleasure was considered servile and weak, and to allow oneself to be buggered[41] was, for a free man, the height of passivity (*impudicitia*) and lack of self-respect. Pederasty[42] was a minor sin so long as it involved relations between a free man and a slave or person of no account. Jokes about it were common among the people and in the theater, and people boasted of it in good society. Nearly anyone can enjoy sensual pleasure with a member of the same sex, and pederasty was not at all uncommon in tolerant antiquity. Many men of basically heterosexual bent used boys for sexual purposes. It was proverbially held that sex with boys

---

[38] Emperor from A.D. 37 to 41.

[39] Emperor from A.D. 81 to 96.

[40] Harem, the part of a Muslim house or palace reserved for women.

[41] British slang for anal intercourse.

[42] Anal intercourse between an adult male and a boy.

procures a tranquil pleasure unruffling to the soul, whereas passion for a woman plunges a free man into unendurable slavery.

Thus, Roman love was defined by macho domination and refusal to become a slave of passion. The amorous excesses attributed to various tyrants were excesses of domination, described with misleading Sadian[43] boldness. Nero, a tyrant who was weak more than cruel, kept a harem to serve his passive needs. Tiberius[44] arranged for young slave boys to indulge his whims, and Messalina[45] staged a pantomime of her own servility, usurping the male privilege of equating strength with frequency of intercourse. These acts were not so much violations as distortions of the taboos. They reflect a dreadful weakness, a need for planned pleasure. Like alcohol, lust is dangerous to virility and must not be abused. But gastronomy scarcely encourages moderation at table.

Amorous passion, the Romans believed, was particularly to be feared because it could make a free man the slave of a woman. He will call her "mistress" and, like a servant, hold her mirror or her parasol. Love was not the playground of individualists, the would-be refuge from society that it is today. Rome rejected the Greek tradition of "courtly love" of ephebes,[46] which Romans saw as an exaltation of pure passion (in both senses of "pure," for the Greeks pretended to believe that a man's love for a freeborn ephebe was Platonic). When a Roman fell madly in love, his friends and he himself believed either that he had lost his head from overindulgence in sensuality or that he had fallen into a state of moral slavery. The lover, like a good slave, docilely offered to die if his mistress wished it. Such excesses bore the dark magnificence of shame, and even erotic poets did not dare to glorify them openly. They chose the roundabout means of describing such behavior as an amusing reversal of the normal state of affairs, a humorous paradox.

Petrarch's[47] praise of passion would have scandalized the ancients or made them smile. The Romans were strangers to the medieval exaltation of the beloved, an object so sublime that it remained inaccessible. They were strangers, too, to modern subjectivism, to our thirst for experience. Standing apart from the world, we choose to experience something in order to see what effect it has, not because it is intrinsically valuable or required by duty. Finally, the Romans were strangers to the real paganism, the at times graceful and beautiful paganism of the Renaissance. Tender indulgence in pleasures of the senses that became, also, delights of the soul was not the way of the ancients. The most Bacchic scenes of the Romans

---

[43] Relating to the Marquis de Sade (1740–1814), French writer who extolled the pleasures of sexual cruelty.

[44] Emperor from A.D. 14 to 37.

[45] Wife of the emperor Claudius; executed in A.D. 48.

[46] Young men, taken as lovers by older men as part of their training for citizenship in Greek city-states.

[47] Italian poet and humanist (1304–1374).

have nothing of the audacity of some modern writers. The Romans knew but one variety of individualism, which confirmed the rule by seeming to contradict it: energetic indolence. With secret delight they discussed senators such as Scipio,[48] Sulla,[49] Caesar,[50] Petronius,[51] and even Catiline,[52] men scandalously indolent in private yet extraordinarily energetic in public. It was an open secret among insiders that these men were privately lazy, and such knowledge gave the senatorial elite an air of royalty and of being above the common law while confirming its authentic spirit. Although the charge of energetic indolence was a reproach, it was also somehow a compliment. Romans found this compliment reassuring. Their brand of individualism sought not real experience, self-indulgence, or private devotion, but tranquilization.

---

[48] Publius Cornelius Aemilianus the Younger (ca. 185–129 B.C.), adopted grandson of Scipio the Elder; general and politician.

[49] Lucius Cornelius Sulla (ca. 138–78 B.C.), general, leader of the supporters of the Roman Senate, and temporary dictator.

[50] Julius Caesar (100–44 B.C.), Roman general, conqueror of Gaul, and dictator of Rome from 48 to 44 B.C.

[51] Petronius Arbiter (d. A.D. 66), author of the *Satyricon,* a satire on Roman decadence.

[52] Lucius Sergius Catilina (ca. 108–62 B.C.), politician who led a conspiracy against the Republic in 63 B.C.

SLUMS, SANITATION, AND MORTALITY IN THE ROMAN WORLD
Alex Scobie

Rome was long the envy of the ancient world, glorious in its empire, armies, government, and laws. A model of urban culture, Rome — the "Eternal City" — boasted of aqueducts, temples, forums, the Coliseum, the circus, and public baths. Yet, behind this facade of marble the city wallowed in stench, refuse, and high mortality. Alex Scobie, a classicist at the University of Victoria, demonstrates that life in Rome and her sister cities was not as pleasant as textbooks would have us imagine. Scobie relies on archeological excavations and written sources to explore urban living conditions and sanitation. Although he finds circumstances squalid for all save the wealthy, Roman towns were still the most hygienic in the ancient world and should be credited for their baths and public latrines.

Housing for ordinary folk was deplorable: Shelter was often haphazard; buildings poorly constructed; and sanitary facilities inadequate. Overcrowding commonly led to violence and allowed for little privacy. (But could the Romans find privacy anywhere, and did they want or expect it?) Why didn't city governments, able to build magnificent public buildings, concern themselves very much with the horrible housing and sanitation of ordinary people? No wonder the poor flocked to public spectacles — the chariot races and gladiatorial combats!

How did Romans discard their waste in their homes, from their homes, and out of their cities? The presence of vultures, dogs, corpses, and flies conjures up appalling urban images. Such an environment led to widespread diseases. What diseases especially racked Roman cities, and which Romans were hardest hit by the unsanitary conditions and the prevalence of diseases? To what extent was the water supply contaminated, and why were the public baths not especially sanitary?

Alex Scobie, "Slums, Sanitation, and Mortality in the Roman World," *Klio* 68 (1986): 399–433.

Social conflict was common throughout Roman history. Given Scobie's analysis, we can begin to understand how the living conditions of the poor affected their relations with wealthy Romans.

In recent years a great deal has been written about life expectancy and mortality in the Roman empire, but very little has been said about the possible or probable causes of what by contemporary western standards must be regarded as a very low average life expectancy at birth of c. 25 years, an estimate which now appears to be generally accepted by many classicists. It is true that some writers hint that low levels of sanitation and poor standards of public health at Rome and in other large cities in the Roman empire are in some way to blame for a high mortality rate. . . . [One writer], for example, refers in passing to "fetid metropolises," but leaves his readers to imagine the details for themselves.

The aim of this paper, then, is to try to estimate, as accurately as available evidence permits, how sanitary or insanitary Roman towns were. Particular attention will be paid to fundamental inadequacies in various types of Roman housing, deficiencies in the disposal of human and animal wastes, and legal shortcomings which virtually ensured that large numbers of destitute and near-destitute inhabitants of Rome lived in squalid conditions which were well known to high-status Romans, but which were ignored by successive imperial administrations.

Despite the shortcomings of Roman urban hygiene which emerge when comparisons are made with standards of public health in modern western industrialized societies, it must be said that the Romans achieved a remarkable level of standardization in the provision of certain basic facilities such as public latrines and baths. These, as will be seen, had some serious deficiencies, but credit should be given to the Romans for some degree of progress in the sphere of public hygiene. References to hygiene-criteria established by modern authorities have been included in this paper mainly because of a lack of critical Roman evidence in this field. The modern criteria referred to in this paper serve primarily to provide the discussion with a structural framework. They are not intended to give a negative aspect to Roman achievement, though negative inferences will sometimes inevitably arise.

The difficulties involved in such an undertaking are not to be underestimated. Archaeologists rarely concern themselves with either latrines or sewers. Hence the extent of the underground sewer-networks of Pompeii,[1] Ostia,[2] and Rome are still very imperfectly known. Nor is the current lack of archaeological

---

[1] City near Naples; an eruption of the volcano Vesuvius in A.D. 79 preserved much of its structure.

[2] Major seaport at the mouth of the Tiber River.

reporting in this area counterbalanced by a sufficiency of evidence in ancient literary sources. Vitruvius[3] has much to say about such subjects as salubrious sites for villas[4] and the purity of domestic water supplies, but he has virtually nothing to say about the disposal of human and other wastes in houses or cities. Perhaps decorum precluded discussion of such topics, and it is possible that presumed knowledge of normal practice made such a discussion unnecessary. It is to be remembered that Vitruvius was writing for aristocratic patrons, and not for public health engineers. . . .

The enormous gulf which separated advantaged from disadvantaged in the Roman empire with respect to access to the legal system, medical care, and education, is also very evident in the case of housing which was taken to be an index of a person's social status. At the top of the Roman housing scale were the conspicuously lavish imperial palaces such as the short-lived *Domus Aurea*[5] and the longlived "Palatium" of Domitian[6] which provided this and all subsequent emperors in the Western empire with 40,000 m^2 [430,336 sq. ft.] of secure, comfortable, living space, and which virtually monopolized Rome's most prestigious hill. Next came senatorial[7] residences . . . , the charms of which Martial[8] contrasts with the disadvantages of his noisy city apartment. . . . But not all senators, equites,[9] and wealthy freedmen[10] lived in houses which could offer their occupants the delights of *rus in urbe*.[11] . . . [M]any members of these classes rented *cenacula*[12] in *insulae*[13] on long term leases. The apartments, subdivided into rooms with individual specific functions, would be situated on the lower floors of *insulae*. By contrast the upper floors of these buildings housed lower-status Romans in subdivided, undifferentiated *cellae*[14] rented probably on a daily basis. The poor also lived in *tabernae*[15] which in design ranged from single roomed shop/dwellings to larger complexes consisting of a shop with one or two living rooms at the rear with

---

[3] Roman engineer and author of *On Architecture,* he lived during the late first century B.C. and early first century A.D. He was a major influence on Renaissance architects.

[4] Country estates.

[5] The Golden House, an ostentatious palace built by Emperor Nero.

[6] Emperor from A.D. 81 to 96.

[7] Having to do with members of the Roman Senate.

[8] Roman poet (ca. A.D. 40–104).

[9] Wealthy landowners and merchants of the later Roman Republic.

[10] Slaves who had been freed by the imperial household or by wealthy families were often rich themselves.

[11] Literally, "the country in town."

[12] Attics.

[13] Apartment buildings.

[14] Rooms.

[15] Shops with attached living areas.

or without mezzanines. The very poor might also hire rooms in cheap boarding houses where rent was probably paid daily. The destitute (egeni) suffered the rigours of a wide range of improvised shelter: shanties pieced together from the detritus of the more fortunate . . . which must have been similar to the improvised shacks in slums which skirt the capitals of many developing countries. Several ancient sources refer to huts erected against or on top of public buildings, or between the columns of porticoes in front of shops. Such structures were likely to be demolished from time to time by city officials. The destitute also found refuge in tombs which also served on occasion as improvised brothels and lavatories. Others slept in spaces under the stairs of insulae (subscalaria), in underground cellars (crypta), vaults (fornices), or in the open air. To what extent public baths were used by the poor for shelter is impossible to estimate. The very low admission fee at Rome of ¼ as[16] would admit all but the poorest, but since so little is known about the administration of the baths at night, it is difficult to estimate how many people might have tried to sleep in them at night, especially during wintertime. This brief list of types of urban accommodation may be concluded by mentioning unicellular barrack-room units which were standard for legionaries, vigiles,[17] gladiators, and low-status prostitutes.

It is not unusual for classicists to claim that Rome's urban poor lived in "slums," but those who use this term do not define the word or specify its implications. It might be useful, therefore, to consider modern criteria and definitions of sub-standard accommodation and then apply these to the ancient evidence. P. Townsend in his massive study of poverty in the U.K.[18] isolates the following traditionally accepted indices of "poor," "unfit," or "slum" housing:

1. Structural defects (leaking roofs, damp walls, brickwork, ill-fitting doors and windows, etc.)
2. Inadequate housing facilities (lack of piped water, toilets, washing facilities, etc.)
3. Inadequate space, overcrowding (no more than two people to one room).

The structural shortcomings of Rome's insular which . . . outnumbered domus[19] by a ratio of c. 26:1, are widely attested in late Republican and imperial literature. Poor building materials, inadequate preparation of foundations, and inexpert or careless workmanship seem often to have resulted in structural collapse, a fate which was also feared though probably not so frequently experienced by the occupants of domus. As in other large cities in the Roman world, such as Carthage and Antioch, the rich at Rome tended to site their houses on the ridges or slopes of hills which were well ventilated, drained, and sunny, whereas the poor lived in the valleys between the hills, or in the areas close to the Tiber. When the

---

[16] A Roman coin of small value.

[17] Watchmen who served as firefighters and police.

[18] A major sociological study of poverty in Britain, published in 1979.

[19] A large single-family dwelling, usually occupied by a wealthy family.

river overflowed, as it frequently did, swirling flood-water might scour out and undermine foundations, or mud brick walls might become saturated and collapse.

Vitruvius . . . explicitly refers to *leges publicae*[20] . . . which prohibited the building of party walls[21] more than 1½' thick, and observes that other walls (*ceteri parietes*) were kept to the same breadth to maximize internal living space. This passage is instructive, since it not only explains one possible cause of structural collapse due to the inadequacy of load-bearing walls on the lower floors of apartment blocks, but also reveals the somewhat lackadaisical attitude of Roman officialdom towards the establishment of responsible and effective building codes. A law which lays down the maximum width of party walls, but which ignores the minimum thickness of freestanding, load-bearing external walls, is clearly likely to be open to abuse by speculators keen to save money on materials and increase rental revenues by letting the greatest available floor space to the largest possible number of tenants. Under such conditions overcrowding might become a contributing cause of structural failure.

Other Roman building laws give the impression of evincing some concern for the structural safety of *insulae*. The most important is the height restriction of 70 Roman feet established by Augustus.[22] Yet subsequent reiteration of this and the few other laws affecting the maintenance of dwellings suggests that they were largely ignored by property owners. The state lacked the machinery to enforce the observance of its rudimentary building regulations, and poverty-stricken *inquilini*[23] would be reluctant to prosecute delinquent landlords who regarded the collapse of rental properties with complete indifference for the fates of their tenants. Lacking both the financial and political resources requisite for redress, the *plebs urbana*[24] must have considered the risk of *ruina*[25] as much a part of life in the capital as the dangers of fire and flood. All available evidence about accommodation at Rome reveals a massive degree of indifference on the part of the state towards the housing needs of its indigent masses. A reflection of this indifference comes from the statement . . . in the *Digest*[26] . . . that subsistence was thought to refer only to food, though others considered it also comprised clothing and straw. . . . From this it is clear that shelter was not considered an essential part of the legal concept of subsistence in the Roman world.

However, it must not be assumed that all *insulae* at Rome were structurally unsound. Such an assumption would be as false as a belief based on Vitruvius'

---

[20] Public laws.

[21] Walls shared by two houses.

[22] First Roman emperor; ruled from 27 B.C. to A.D. 14.

[23] Tenants, lodgers.

[24] Ordinary townsfolk.

[25] The collapse of a building.

[26] The *Digest*, statements of renowned jurisprudents, contained in the *Corpus iuris civilis* (the "body of civil law"), a collection of Roman laws, decrees, and imperial orders drawn up during the reign of Emperor Justinian (who ruled from A.D. 527 to 565).

claim that *insularii* were comfortably housed and had agreeable views of the city, a reflection surely of the architect's will to flatter Augustus rather than a statement of his personal views of residential tower blocks at Rome.

. . . [T]he only "almost intact" *insula* at Rome, the Casa di via Giulio Romano, suggests that all the inhabitants of this Trajanic building,[27] from its ground floor shops to its fourth floor cubicles, must have experienced a wide range of discomforts and anxieties frequently alluded to by Martial and Juvenal;[28] but a fear of *ruina* is not likely to have been one of them, since this *insula* was built of brick-faced concrete, and concrete vaults are in evidence on all of its surviving floors. . . .

The Ostian evidence shows that *insulae* there were generally of an adequate structural soundness, but it is also acknowledged that conclusions made about housing at Ostia should not be uncritically applied to Rome which was larger, more congested, and even after the fire of A.D. 64, did not undergo the type of radical redevelopment experienced at Ostia in the reigns of Claudius,[29] Trajan, and Hadrian.[30] Despite the structural soundness of the via Giulio Romano *insula,* the persistence of an unfavourable literary tradition about Roman *insulae* from Cicero[31] to the end of the empire,[32] strongly suggests that jerry-built multiple dwellings were the norm at Rome, even though they appear to have been the exception at Ostia. It must be remembered, however, that because Roman architects were incapable of exactly calculating the strains and stresses in any given structure (just as Roman engineers could not measure velocity) structural soundness could not be guaranteed even for the most expensive and prestigious buildings. Thus the *basilica*[33] of Domitian's palace required considerable buttressing not long after its construction. . . .

Townsend's second broad indicator of substandard accommodation ("inadequate housing facilities") will be examined in relation to evidence for sanitation and hygiene in Roman houses and cities. To help in distinguishing adequate from inadequate sanitation (i.e., the disposal of human and other wastes), it would be helpful to refer to some basic modern criteria. . . . [such as those given by one writer].

"The improper disposal of human excreta and sewage is one of the major factors threatening the health and comfort of individuals in areas where satisfactory sewage systems are not available. This is so because very large numbers of different disease producing organisms can be found in the fecal discharges of ill and apparently healthy persons. . . . Sewage is satisfactorily disposed of when 1) It will not be accessible to children or household pets, pollute the surface of the ground,

---

[27] Built during the reign of the Roman emperor Trajan, which lasted from A.D. 98 to 117.

[28] Roman satirist (ca. A.D. 55–ca. 140).

[29] Emperor from A.D. 41 to 54.

[30] Emperor from A.D. 117 to 138.

[31] Roman orator and politician (106–43 B.C.).

[32] The end of the fifth century A.D.

[33] A public building having a central nave, side aisles, and apse; used as a courtroom or assembly.

or be exposed to the atmosphere when inadequately treated. 2) It will not contaminate any drinking water supply. 3) It will not give rise to a public health hazard by being accessible to insects, rodents, pets, or other possible mechanical carriers that may come in contact with food or drinking water. 4) It will not give rise to a nuisance due to odor or unsightly appearance. 5) It will not pollute or contaminate the waters of any bathing beach, shell-fish breeding ground, or stream used for public, domestic water supply, or recreational purposes. 6) It will not violate laws or regulations governing water pollution or sewage disposal."

Literary evidence concerning sewers and latrines in the Roman world is extremely meagre. Vitruvius, as already noted, . . . maintains a discreet silence. Frontinus[34] merely observes that the overflow . . . of Rome's fountains . . . and public basins (lacus) flushed the city's sewers. Agricultural writers make brief references to the use of human excrement as a supplement to animal fertilizers. There are a few other references to the cleansing of sewers by convict labour, and to those who profited from running public latrines (foricae), to the fullers'[35] terracotta jars placed in the streets for the public to use as urinals, and to Vespasian's[36] tax on urine. However, though some of these brief allusions are useful, there is nowhere extant a description of either a public or private Roman latrine, and no account of their administration.

Legal texts are also exiguous. The lex Julia municipalis[37] . . . states that [carts to remove excrement] were permitted to enter Rome during the daytime when most wheeled traffic was prohibited. Ulpian[38] . . . reports a praetor's[39] edict which states that sewers were to be kept clean and in a good state of repair. . . . While it is easy to understand that clogged sewers will create a fetid atmosphere, it is not immediately evident why they would be likely to cause the collapse of buildings. However, a major blockage in a large collector such as the Cloaca Maxima[40] which in winter must have conducted large volumes of marsh and storm water into the Tiber, could have caused floods with consequent scouring out of foundations and the dissolving of mud-brick structures.

The edict also distinguishes between public sewers maintained by the state, and private sewers the upkeep of which was the responsibility of individual property owners who . . . had the right to connect a private to a public sewer without hindrance, on receiving permission. . . .

It seems, then, that there was no legal obligation for a home-owner to connect his dwelling to a public street sewer. Such a connection was optional, and it

---

[34] Sextus Julius Frontinus (ca. A.D. 35–104), writer on warfare, surveying, and the city of Rome's water supply.

[35] Textile workers who prepare cloth for retail sale.

[36] Emperor from A.D. 69 to 79.

[37] The Julian law of municipal regulations, issued by Emperor Augustus.

[38] Roman jurist and author (d. A.D. 228).

[39] The second-ranking official in Roman municipal government.

[40] The main sewer of the city of Rome.

seems that the owner had to meet all the expenses resulting from such an operation. Extant Roman law is silent on the question of where domestic latrines were
to be situated and how they were to be constructed. The Romans were legally
more concerned about the intramural burial of the dead than they were about the
disposal of human and animal wastes within the city, though, as will be seen,
corpses seem to have been dumped within the city.

Currently available archaeological evidence from Pompeii, Ostia, and Rome
indicates that very few dwellings were directly connected to street drains. . . . At
Pompeii almost every house had a drain which conducted excess water from the
impluvium[41] or peristyle to the surface of the street; less frequently these drains also
conducted dirty water from kitchens on to the streets. With one exception . . . ,
drains leading directly from a latrine into the street were not found . . . , and only
exceptionally . . . in private houses latrines connected to sewers. In some cases the
connections were crudely improvised as . . . where a large hole in the floor of the
shop leads directly into the *cloaca* of the via dell'Abbondanza.

On the other hand, almost every house at Pompeii had a latrine situated either in or partly separated from the kitchen, or in a separate, very small, doorless
room, usually unlit and lacking adequate ventilation through an outside window.
None of these latrines, with the possible exception of a large latrine in the House
of the Silver Wedding, was flushed by water. All consisted of pits . . . of varying
depths dug into the porous lava-mass directly beneath or not far from the latrine
itself. The porous rock allowed fluids to drain away, but solids would periodically
have to be excavated from the cesspit, if the latrine was to remain in use. . . .

It hardly requires emphasis that such practices were extremely unhygienic. Internal cesspits even when emptied at regular intervals, would be constant sources
of major infections and offensive smells. To site a cesspit in a kitchen would have
the practical advantage of enabling cooks to dispose of kitchen fluids and garbage
without physical inconvenience, but the risk of food contamination in such combined kitchen/latrine areas must have been very high indeed. . . .

Latrines at Pompeii are for the most part not provided with running water or
washing facilities of any kind. Toilet paper was not apparently a standard item in
Roman latrines. . . . For the Romans a sponge on the end of a stick performed the
function of modern toilet paper. . . . The hygienic implications of using such an
implement are again at best dubious. In many public latrines (*foricae*) a continuous shallow gutter is often found at the base of the seats. It has been assumed that
this gutter was filled with water in which people rinsed out soiled sponges. However, this explanation can be regarded as nothing but conjecture, since these gut-
ters might have served to collect urine which failed to enter the aperture in the
face of each latrine seat.

The cesspit/latrine typical of Pompeian houses is also found in houses at
Cosa, established as a Roman settlement in B.C. 273. The town was provided with
an underground "sewage system," to which it seems domestic latrines were not

---

[41] A large tank to catch rainwater, located under an opening in the roof of the atrium (entrance
room) in a Roman house; also the opening itself.

connected. The usual arrangement at Cosa was for houses to have an underground cistern for water storage at one end of the house and a cesspit dug in unplastered fissured limestone at the other. The plastered cistern is often above the level of the cesspit thus avoiding, or minimizing the risk of water contamination through cesspit seepage. Many of the cesspits were at the rear of houses on plots which sloped towards gardens. In these cases seeping cesspit fluids would have escaped into gardens. . . . At Cosa, as at Pompeii, cisterns are often provided with overflow pipes to conduct excess water directly into the streets, and kitchen/latrines are situated directly above, or very close to cesspits.

The evidence of Cosa and Pompeii shows that from the third century B.C. to A.D. 79 the Romans adopted standard measures for the disposal of human and kitchen wastes within atrium-type dwellings. In both towns the same solutions were adopted for channelling excess cistern water on to city streets. In both towns there is very little evidence for the discharge of wastes into sewers beneath the streets.

At this point it would be useful to try to determine why, when . . . it was legally permitted, so few property-owners connected their dwellings to public *cloacae*. The expense of installing drains would seem at first sight to have been well worth the consequent improvement in hygiene within a property. Yet current archaeological evidence shows very clearly that the inhabitants of Roman towns preferred internal cesspits to sewer connections. Why? There are several possible explanations. Firstly, Roman drains lacked traps to prevent gases such as hydrogen sulphide (H_2S) and methane (CH_4) escaping from sewers and thus causing not only an odor nuisance, but also the danger of explosions. Gravity sewers, the only type known to the Romans, are especially subject to the formation of slime and sludge which generates H_2S. On contact with air this gas forms sulphuric acid which, if unchecked, can lead to the corrosion of concrete. However, these conditions are most frequently associated with sanitary sewers designed to carry off only sewage and domestic waste water. Again, there is no evidence that the Romans built separate sanitary and storm water drains. They knew only combined sewers intended to carry away excess water from public water basins which flowed night and day, the overflow of domestic rain water cisterns, rain water which fell directly on to the streets, and lastly sewage which entered the drainage network through *foricae* connected to *cloacae*, as, for example, was the case with the latrine at the Stabian baths at Pompeii. It might be argued that the constant flow of *aqua caduca* through a combined drainage system built with an effective fall from origin to exit point would keep it relatively clean and therefore free from noxious gases. On the other hand, it is known from several sources that Roman *cloacae* needed to be cleaned manually from time to time, a sure indication that by no means all Roman sewers were self-cleansing. . . .

It is also impossible to estimate the quantity of sewage which entered a Roman sewer daily. Health engineers today estimate that an individual generates c. 70–80 grammes of solid wastes per day. Since this figure is made up of food as well as body wastes, an estimate of c. 50 grammes p.d. might represent more closely the amount of body waste generated by an inhabitant of a Roman city, this lower figure being preferable, since food wastes were unlikely to enter a Roman *cloaca*. Thus a city the size of Rome with a population of c. 800,000–1,000,000 inhabitants in early imperial times would have produced c. 40–50,000 kgs. of body wastes per day. What proportion of this estimated total entered the sewerage network cannot even be guessed. . . . [There were] *foricae* for Rome in the fourth century, but this figure is of little value, since it is not known how many seats each *forica* contained, nor do we know what proportion of the population used public latrines. The situation is rendered more complicated by the fact that it is not known how many of Rome's *foricae* were connected to the sewage network. So far only two *foricae* have been discovered at Rome, one of Hadrianic date above shops in the Forum Julium, the other in the area sacra del largo argentina, and the drainage systems of both appear not to have been reported. It can only be assumed that at Rome and Ostia where *insulae* greatly outnumbered *domus*, *foricae* would have been more heavily patronised than at Pompeii where even the smallest *tabernae* have latrines.

If the absence of traps might lead to unpleasant odors as well as to creating risks of explosions inside houses, there were at least two other potentially disagreeable consequences. Firstly, in low lying areas of Rome sewers could back up when the level of the Tiber rose. Thus sewage and waste water which normally flowed into the river via the Cloaca Maxima (and other sewers) would be forced back into the network and up any house connections attached to the main collectors. Secondly, vermin in the sewers would be able to enter houses via any sewer connections. An anecdote . . . illustrates the danger in a somewhat spectacular manner.[42]

All these reasons singly or collectively would tend to discourage domestic sewer connections. There is, however, a further reason which might have outweighed those already discussed. Inhabitants of western industrialized societies tend to overlook the fact that flush toilets, while being conducive to high levels of hygiene, are extremely wasteful both of fresh water and of substances which are useful as fertilizers. In many pre-industrial societies without access to artificial fertilizers, human excrement is frequently used as a supplement to animal manures. That the Romans used human feces for agricultural purposes is well attested. It is probable that those who emptied cesspits (*stercorarii*) sold their contents to farmers on city outskirts. At Pompeii in cases where cesspits are only deep enough to house a large amphora or *dolium,* the vessel when full would probably have been removed by a *stercorarius* and replaced with an empty jar. . . . A few houses at Pompeii have a drain leading from the latrine directly into a garden, but such an arrangement is rare and must have created a permanent stench in the gardens of the houses concerned.

Thus the domestic cesspit without sewer connections not only benefitted Roman agriculture but also provided a group of unskilled workers in the towns with work which was a source of regular pay, even though the work must have involved a high health risk. . . .

The collection and use of urine by fullers for mordanting[43] certain dyestuffs reveals another area of private enterprise in the disposal and commercial ex-

---

[42] In this case an octopus swims up a house drain each night from the sea to eat pickled fish stored in the house by Iberian merchants. (Author's note.)

[43] Cleaning textiles with a weak acid bath.

ploitation of human wastes in Roman cities. However, the system of collecting urine was not hygienic since the terracotta jars placed in streets and alleyways were unglazed and porous, and sometimes cracked jars burst, spilling their malodorous contents into the streets. Other methods of collection were both less public and more hygienic; for example, at the Baths of Mithras at Ostia a lead pipe from a urinal ducted fluids directly into a *fullonica*[44] situated in the basement of the baths. However, this arrangement does not seem to have been attested elsewhere. . . .

Ostia seems to have lacked Pompeii's generous distribution of private latrines. A reason for this is the preponderance of *insulae* at Ostia which are not all provided with latrines. It is possible also that Ostia's higher water table would have made cesspits of any great depth impracticable. Further research on the drainage systems of the latrines . . . is essential before any certainty on the subject can be attained. It must also be assumed . . . that the lack of private latrines led to high usage of Ostia's 3 *foricae* as well as of those attached to *thermae*[45] which were accessible to all members of the public, not merely to bathers. As yet 3 *foricae* along with the latrines of the town's 3 *thermae* can hardly be regarded as a "very generous supply of public accommodation" . . . for a population of c. 20,000 inhabitants. Two dungheaps, one next to the E[ast] gate, the other in the city centre, discovered during the excavations of 1910 and 1920, suggest other solutions to the shortage of public latrines.

Evidence for the existence of private latrines at Rome is all but non-existent. There is no trace of latrines in the Casa di via Giulio Romano, but it would be hazardous to suppose from this that all Roman *insulae* lacked latrines. The Domus Transitoria had a very large latrine (60-seater), once thought to be "the machinery chamber of a hydraulic lift", but very obviously a latrine of the usual "keyhole" design; yet, again, the archaeological literature says nothing about drainage arrangements. . . .

A passage in the *Digest* . . . not only prohibits the digging of holes in the streets, . . . but also outlaws the throwing of excrement, corpses, and (animal) skins on to the streets. . . . It was likewise an offence to contaminate the public water supply or cover anyone with dung or filth. . . . An inscription found above a public water basin at Pompeii prohibiting the pollution of the water with excrement, shows that officials found it necessary to warn would-be delinquents. . . .

That many *inquilini* in Roman *insulae* flouted some or all of these laws is clear from other passages in the *Digest* where the question of damages is discussed in relation to those injured by debris and wastes thrown from the windows of multiple dwellings. On the other hand, the mere creation of a bad smell in the vicinity of a public road did not render the creator of the smell liable to prosecution . . . , a law which presumably allowed cesspit latrines in houses to be situated close to street fronts.

---

[44] Fulling shop, where cloth is treated with water and heat.

[45] Warm baths.

. . . [L]arge perforated manhole covers in some of the streets of Rome, not only admitted storm-water to the sewers, but also emitted "poisonous effluvia." Some of these *foramina* must have been quite large and not always well-protected, since the *grammaticus*[46] Crates Malleotes, credited by Suetonius[47] with the introduction of secondary education to Rome, fell down one in the Palatine region and broke his leg. Also the much hated Heliogabalus,[48] if his biographer is to be believed, was unceremoniously pushed down a sewer after being assassinated in a latrine.

Insularii who did not have a ground-floor latrine in their block, could resort to *foricae*, or use a variety of portable vessels in their own apartments. There were other possibilities. At Pompeii and elsewhere there is abundant evidence showing that many people relieved themselves in streets, doorways, tombs, and even behind statues. The occupants of rooms in the upper storeys of *insulae* would find it more convenient to tip the contents of *matellae*[49] and *lasana*[50] out of windows at night when no one could identify the culprits, than to descend several flights of stairs to the communal latrine (if one existed), or to walk in the unlit streets to the nearest *forica* and risk being mugged or murdered. . . .

The general impression gained from the admittedly very limited archaeological and literary evidence discussed above is that the inhabitants of Rome lived in an extremely insanitary environment which was in many respects similar to that in large European cities till shortly after 1842 when Edwin Chadwick's "Sanitary Report" was published in London and drew wide attention for the first time to the appalling consequences of inadequate waste disposal in large cities.[51] . . .

So far attention has been given to the nature of Roman public and private latrines. It would be appropriate at this point to ask how (and by whom) the human and animal wastes, which clearly must have fouled Rome's streets, were removed. The cleanliness of the city's streets was the responsibility of the aediles[52] as part of their *cura urbis*.[53] However, there was no official street cleaning service at Rome. Those who occupied properties with adjoining street fronts were responsible for keeping them clean. The overflow from public basins would have flushed only some of the filth from the streets, since there were not enough basins . . . to pro-

---

[46] A teacher of writing and composition.

[47] Gaius Suetonius Tranquillus (ca. A.D. 69–140), Roman historian and author of *Lives of the First Twelve Caesars*.

[48] Emperor from A.D. 218 to 222.

[49] Small pots.

[50] Chamber pots.

[51] Chadwick (1800–1890) was a British reformer whose report influenced the building of London's modern sewer system.

[52] Roman officials responsible for public works, firefighting, weights and measures, public markets, and policing.

[53] Administration of the city.

vide sufficient water to wash down all road surfaces in the city. Dogs and carrion birds such as vultures must also have played a significant part in the disposal of assorted street refuse. Dogs were to be found in many Roman houses where they disposed of food scraps in dining rooms; they also consumed human excrement as Martial twice points out, as well as corpses which, despite legal prohibitions, seem to have been dumped in the streets of Rome as they were at Antioch. Suetonius records that while Vespasian was lunching . . . a dog from the street . . . brought a human hand into the dining room and deposited it beneath the table. A portentous event, since it concerned an emperor, but such happenings were probably not rare at Rome or in other large cities in the Roman empire. . . . Before the pestilential Esquiline cemetery became the gardens of Maecenas,[54] dogs must have been a common sight there fossicking[55] among the many shallow or open mass-burial pits from which fragments of corpses could be conveyed to various parts of the city. Evidence that dogs (and other animals) gnawed improperly buried corpses has recently been reported from a Romano-British cemetery. . . .

At least some of the corpses in Rome's streets would be those of unwanted infants deposited on dung heaps, a custom attested in Greek cities also. It is impossible to determine how many infants exposed in this manner would have survived. Some were undoubtedly saved by slave dealers to be trained and sold off at a later date. . . . Many exposed infants also died as a result of cold, starvation, or the attack of dogs and other predators. It also seems that the corpses of gladiators of servile status were thrown on garbage heaps, though evidence for this is so far confined to Sassina.

Sick, dying, and dead slaves were also to be found in the streets of Rome, though the Tiber island was the traditional centre for depositing such slaves who had not been killed by their owners when they had become either incurably sick or debilitated by old age to the point where the slave was considered useless. . . .

Though these animals helped to eliminate organic matter from houses and streets, they would also have been carriers of a wide variety of diseases ranging from rabies to skin diseases such as ring-worm. Their feces would also have fouled the streets and in some cases have contaminated the water in public basins, and even the carcasses of the dogs themselves might find their way into the water supply.

Vultures, also necrophagous scavengers, were familiar enough to Romans for Seneca[56] . . . to compare a *captator*[57] sitting at the bedside of a patient to this predator. . . . As potential spreaders of diseases vultures were less of a threat than dogs, since there would be less possibility of direct human contact with them. But, as

---

[54] Wealthy politician and patron of literary figures (ca. 74–8 B.C.).

[55] Rummaging around.

[56] Roman statesman and philosopher (ca. 4 B.C.–A.D. 65).

[57] A hound; here, someone who attempts to wrest a legacy from a sick or dying person.

happens today in Bombay where the Parsis[58] expose their dead for ritual consumption by vultures, a nuisance could be created when the airborne birds dropped corpse fragments onto and around houses.

Another common nuisance resulting from the exposure of filth and carrion in the streets was the fly. . . . Human and animal manures also provide ideal breeding grounds for blow flies which can transmit many diseases to humans. The Romans knew of some fly-repellents such as a mixture of coriander seed and olive oil which was smeared on house walls, yet such remedies would not have been available to the poor, and even the rich could not have found them effective, especially in summer *triclinia*[59] which were often open on three sides. Thus it was sometimes felt necessary to employ a slave to keep flies from settling on guests and food in dining rooms. Roman food shops, unprotected by windows or screens and bordering on dirty streets, would also have been infested by flies. This would be especially likely in the case of butchers' shops where it seems animals were slaughtered before being cut up for sale. Rome did not have a centralized slaughterhouse from which meat was distributed to retail outlets. The animals were . . . driven live through the streets to butchers' shops where they were slaughtered, disembowelled, and dismembered. Sheep, pigs, and cattle en route to city markets or shops were a hindrance to pedestrians and no doubt contributed to the general fouling of the streets with excrement. The above mentioned . . . prohibition in the *Digest* against throwing skins into the streets suggests that . . . butchers used the streets as a dumping ground for blood and abattoir[60]-wastes which could not be sold. The average ox contains c. two gallons of blood, and though some of this might be used in preparing blood sausages, a great deal would remain to be disposed of.

It is clear that in Rome there was a very high risk of food and water contamination through direct or indirect contact with human or animal fecal matter which was inadequately dealt with by city authorities. Open cesspits in kitchens, a general lack of washing facilities in latrines, defecation and urination in the streets, the pollution of water basins with carrion and filth, lack of efficient fly control, and inadequate street cleaning, do not provide a basis for health in an urban community, but do help to explain a very high mortality rate.

What diseases in particular are associated with the above environmental conditions? The most common are cholera, dysentery, gastroenteritis, infectious hepatitis, leptospirosis, and typhoid. Potential pathogens such as salmonella, a species of which causes typhoid fever in man, and pseudomonas are often found in human and animal feces and wastewaters. Salmonellae are commonly carried by blow flies, dogs, cattle, pigs, and poultry. Leptospirosis, a species of which can cause a type of jaundice ("Weil's disease") to which sewer workers are prone, is

---

[58] Adherents of the ancient Iranian religion, Zoroastrianism.

[59] Dining rooms in Roman domae.

[60] Slaughterhouse.

found in the urine of infected pigs, dogs, and rats, and is potentially fatal. Other common *genera* of pathogenic organisms which can be found in water contaminated by infected feces are vibrio (cholera), shigella (dysentery), mycobacterium (tuberculosis, leprosy), pasteurella (classical plague). Tapeworms which if left untreated in humans, can cause hydatid cysts[61] on the liver, live in dogs' intestines. Humans can be infected by ingesting eggs from a dog's excrement. Other parasitic worms which can cause intestinal infestations, round worms and thread worms, are commonly transmitted through fecal contamination. The tetanus anaerobe is also passed in feces and may be present on roads and in the soil of gardens.

Since human excrement was used to manure gardens and fields, there was a risk that vegetables so fertilized would be contaminated with some of the above mentioned viruses, bacteria, and worm-eggs. Romans were also exposed to diseases transmitted by fish which fed on sewage. Several literary authorities refer to fish caught in the Tiber, usually identified as bass, which fed on sewage.

Babies and young infants, as well as undernourished adults, would be particularly susceptible to these infections and infestations. A dangerous stage for infants would occur at the time breast feeding ceased, since at that point they would be exposed to infections from unclean containers and contaminated food. The result must often have been gastroenteritis, dysentery and death through dehydration. . . .

Before condemning inadequate sanitation as being the most likely single cause of low life expectancy in large Roman cities, something must be said about hygiene in Roman public baths which are often thought to have compensated for the lack of washing facilities in most Roman dwellings. Some comment on Roman urban water supply is also necessary to complete the picture of Roman sanitation.

As Frontinus points out, prior to the building of the *aqua Appia*[62] in B.C. 312, Romans depended on wells, springs, and the Tiber for their water supply. As the population of the city grew, the demand for water also increased. In the time of Augustus, Agrippa[63] more than doubled the previous supply, one reason for this being that extra water was needed for Agrippa's baths in the Campus Martius which set a precedent for public munificence followed by many later emperors.

In the times of Frontinus a total of nine aqueducts provided the city with c. 992,000 m³ [262,433,862 gallons] of water a day. Most of this water was potable with the exceptions of Tepula (tepid water) and Alsietina built in B.C. 2 to supply the Naumachia[64] in Regio[65] 14. Unfortunately almost nothing is known about the

---

[61] Baglike structures containing water and tapeworm larvae.

[62] The first piped-in drinking water for the city of Rome.

[63] Marcus Vipsanius Agrippa (ca. 63–12 B.C.), soldier, statesman, and the son-in-law of Emperor Augustus.

[64] A facility for the enactment of mock naval battles.

[65] District, neighborhood.

distribution of water within the city of Rome. Frontinus . . . says there was a total of 591 open water basins (lacus) within the city from which most Romans would have collected their daily supplies. The positions of Pompeii's 40 lacus are precisely known. . . . [T]hey were very evenly distributed throughout the town, with the exception of Regio 6, a poor quarter, which has fewer basins than other regions so far excavated. At Rome even the approximate location of most of the basins is not known. One of the few to have been excavated and identified, the lacus Servilius, was situated in the Forum, fed by a branch of the highly prized aqua Marcia, and drained directly into the Cloaca Maxima which as Pliny says sometimes flooded the Forum with its backwash. Even without the complication of backwash, a direct untrapped drain connection between this basin and a sewer-main has a potential for contamination. The central position of this basin probably explains why it was chosen during the Sullan proscriptions[66] for the exhibition of senators' heads which were fixed above and round the water tank, thus creating an additional, if temporary, risk of pollution. Pompeian basins do not appear to have direct sewer connections. They are mostly tanks constructed of monolithic stone slabs placed at the edge of roads into which they overflowed. The Servilian basin is a paved depression in the ground and was presumably linked to the Cloaca Maxima because it passed conveniently below the Forum. The continuous flow of water into and out of these basins would retard the growth of weed and algae in the tanks, but not prevent it, so the tanks must have required periodic draining and cleaning to remove accumulations of slime and other extraneous rubbish.

There can be little doubt that those who drew their drinking water from such tanks were more at risk than the few who had water piped directly into their homes from covered distribution tanks (castella). Yet because of its relative cheapness and malleability, lead was frequently used for domestic water supply, despite Vitruvius' warning against its use. However, . . . it is impossible to gauge the likely toxicity of lead-conducted water, when it is not known whether the water in question is soft or hard. Hard water will quickly insulate the inside surface of a lead pipe with a harmless deposit of lime, whereas soft water is plumbosolvent and consequently a potential hazard to a consumer, who is at risk . . . when lead intake exceeds 0. 6 mg p.d. . . .

Quantitatively the inhabitants of Rome were provided with a more than adequate supply of water, at least from the time of Augustus, but the quality and purity of this water once it reached . . . the city's apartment buildings could hardly be vouched for, since there were pollution risks not only at open public basins (sewer connections, casual refuse disposal), but also from contaminated containers used by inquilini and aquarii. It might be argued that in smaller Roman towns inhabitants relied on rainwater collected in domestic cisterns, if a town was not

---

[66] Executions ordered by the Roman dictator Lucius Cornelius Sulla (ca. 138–78 B.C.).

supplied by an aqueduct or, if it was, repairs necessitated the temporary suspension of such a supply. . . . This generalization appears to be applicable to towns in Roman Africa, but hardly applies to post-Augustan Rome where the bulk of the population lived in *insulae* which lacked the internal water cisterns commonly found in atrium-houses. The very history of aqueduct construction at Rome shows that the earliest ducts were built in response to the need of an expanding population for more water. A passage in the *Digest* states quite clearly aqueduct repairs were thought more important than the repair of roads since, if the former were neglected, people would die of thirst.

. . . [The] statement that "it was in the public baths that the Romans kept clean" . . . reflects a generally held belief that a lack of domestic bathrooms in all but the houses of the very rich, was compensated for by the ample provision of public bathing facilities. There is clearly some truth in this belief, but the generalization requires some qualification.

That the ancients themselves associated the baths with health is evident from the fact that the deities most frequently represented in *thermae* were Aesculapius and his daughter Hygieia. This association had a particular significance for the sick and infirm who . . . were advised to go to baths to facilitate cures for various diseases. Hadrian's biographer says this emperor ordained that only the sick should use the baths before the eighth hour. Presumably prior to this ruling the sick and the healthy bathed together. . . .

Hadrian's measure to give the sick the exclusive use of the baths till the eighth hour was perhaps motivated by a wish to protect the healthy from the unhealthy rather than from a desire to spare the sick the embarrassment of exposing their ailments to the gaze of the curious and the derisive. Yet it is not clear that the Romans were aware that diseases such as cholera and dysentery could be transmitted by water as well as by direct contact.

There is no evidence that the Romans used disinfectants in the *solia*,[67] *alvei*,[68] and *natationes*[69] of their public baths. Today public swimming pools are usually equipped with filtering systems and water is chlorinated to minimize viral and bacterial contamination deriving from bathers. On the other hand, water probably flowed in and out of the pools in Roman public baths, as was the case with public water basins. However, as yet the water systems of Roman baths are not sufficiently known to support generalizations of this kind. The *natatio*[70] of the Stabian baths at Pompeii has in its S.E. corner a drain which ducted the overflow of the pool into the main collector in the via dell'Abbondanza. Exit pipes also con-

[67] Hot pools (tubs).

[68] Steam baths.

[69] Cold pools (tubs).

[70] Cool pool.

nect the cold pool of the *frigidarium*[71] and the *labra*[72] in the men's (and women's!) *caldaria*[73] to the same drainage network. However, no such outflow pipes are attached to the *alvei* of the men's *tepidarium*[74] and *caldarium*. How often were all these basins and pools drained and cleaned? At present there is no evidence on which to base an answer, but it must be assumed that such pools were periodically cleaned to remove slime and sediment. Seneca . . . says it was the responsibility of the aediles to supervise the general cleanliness (*munditiae*) of public baths. He also mentions as a sign of contemporary over-refinement in bathing habits the use of filtered water . . . , but such a luxury is likely to have been confined to baths in the houses of the rich.

It is conceivable that some of the sick who could afford the higher entry fee would for the sake of greater privacy prefer to go to private commercially run baths for therapeutic purposes, though as Martial shows, some of these establishments had unsavoury reputations.

Could a bathkeeper (*balneator*) exclude clients if he considered them undesirable for some reason? It seems from Martial . . . that he could. In . . . [Martial's example] a bathkeeper admits a diseased old woman only after extinguishing the lights, and then only in company with the lowest type of prostitutes (*bustuariae moechae*). That some Romans found the sight and smell of some bathers offensive, is clear enough from Martial . . . and Juvenal . . . where there are also racial overtones. The sight of diseased people at the baths would be the more obvious, since it seems to have been normal for both sexes to bathe unclothed. Though Artemidorus[75] says the sick entered the baths clothed, it is difficult to imagine how they could remain clothed when sitting in the various pools and basins in the public baths. Ausonius[76] suggests that the sick were unclothed when they entered plunge pools.

It seems probable, then, that Roman public baths might not have been as sanitary as is commonly assumed, and that the risks of becoming infected with a wide range of contagious and infectious diseases in such establishments would have been great.

In the sixth and seventh centuries public baths in the Eastern Roman empire continued to attract the sick. Plentiful evidence from this later period also shows that the ill preferred to visit the baths at midday or at night when the general public did not frequent them. In the West public baths lingered on till the sixteenth century when a combination of church preaching and syphilis led to their demise.

---

[71] A room containing a cold bath.

[72] Tubs.

[73] Rooms containing hot baths.

[74] A room having a lukewarm bath.

[75] Artemidorus of Tarsus, ca. first century B.C., grammarian and writer of pastoral poems.

[76] Decimus Magnus Ausonius (ca. A.D. 310–ca. 395), poet and teacher of rhetoric.

The third and last point in Townsend's index of substandard housing is overcrowding which also has implications for health and sanitation. The question of determining what levels of room/building occupancy are or are not acceptable in any given society is extremely complex. The bureaucratic maximum quoted by Townsend, two persons per room, is a quick, but arbitrary way of establishing a national norm. More satisfactory, because it tries to account for the views of the people concerned, is the approach of Wikan[77] who points out that "in some places, people *wish* to be close together and to carry on all sorts of activities in the same room. Therefore I find it more adequate to measure overcrowding in terms of the degree to which the tenants themselves feel that they fail to fulfil some of their cherished values because of lack of space."

Since there is no reliable evidence in literary sources about the occupancy levels of either *insulae* or *domus* assumptions based on archaeological remains have been made by several authorities. For example, . . . [one writer] considers that the fourth and fifth floors of the Casa di via Giulio Romano were overcrowded and squalid, not only because the rooms were dark and damp, but because according to his estimate, these floors with c. 48 tenants to c. 138 m^2 were more densely occupied than floors one to three. The three parallel rows of cubicles on the fourth floor "are very small (c. 10 m^2), but it is still entirely probable that a small family could have occupied such humble quarters." This conjecture . . . is possible since the smallest one-roomed shops at Ostia measure 10–12 m^2, but whether families lived in such cubicles in *insulae* is more doubtful than in the case of *tabernae* where child labour would make limited child rearing more profitable for a manufacturer/shopkeeper. At Pompeii some of the *cellae* at the gladiatorial barracks are larger (c. 10–15 m^2) and only one or two gladiators slept in each room. At Rome in the *ludus magnus* the rooms for gladiators were larger still at c. 20 m^2, twice the size of cubicles in the Capitoline *insula,* and with a much lower probable occupancy level. The *vigiles* at Ostia occupied rooms of c. 36 m^2 (at least on the ground floor) with approx. ten men to a room. This level of density (1 man to 3 + m^2) might seem intolerable but for the fact that these rooms were dormitories for men who had washing facilities in the courtyard of their building . . . , a latrine room for all the occupants of the building, and food shops at the main entrances to the barracks. These conditions, though certainly not luxurious, were certainly much better than those suffered by the tenants of the upper floors of the Capitoline *insula.*

A close modern equivalent to the *cellae* of this building is provided by the concrete seven-storey resettlement blocks hurriedly erected in Hong Kong between 1955–1961. These buildings provided 64 rooms per floor, each floor consisting of two rows of 32 rooms placed back to back. Each room is c. 10 × 12 feet (c. 13 m^2) and was designed by the colonial authorities to house 5 adults (a child counting as ½ adult). Flush latrines and communal washing facilities were pro-

---

[77] Unni Wikan, author of a major study of life among the poor of Cairo, published in 1980.

vided on each floor as well as standpipes providing mains water. Each floor was designed to accommodate 320 adults making a total of 2240 adults for an entire block. Such densities would clearly be unacceptable in the United Kingdom with its official maximum density of two people per room cited by Townsend. Such densities seem not to have been approached in any known Ostian *insula* complex such as the four-storey *Case a Giardino* . . . which perhaps housed a total of c. 946 occupants. The relatively large number of small shops with only one room and the existence in *insulae* of small rooms "subdivided by flimsy partitions into two or three tiny apartments," suggest that even at Ostia crowding above the level of 2 people to one room was not infrequent in lower class dwellings.

One literary source remarks that sixteen members of the Aelian family lived in one *domuncula,* a term which might mean either a small *domus,* in which case there need not have been excessive crowding, or a home in a figurative sense in a *taberna* or even in an improvised shelter such as a tomb which Ulpian calls a *domuncula,* where crowding would have been more certain. At Rome high rents would have tended to encourage crowding on the upper floors of *insulae* since the financial burden might only become tolerable, if shared between a plurality of co-tenants. An unskilled worker who paid rent on a daily basis, might not be able to find employment for every day of the year, a circumstance which could cause eviction through default if he rented a room by himself. However, this consequence of temporary unemployment would not be so likely to occur when a room was shared, and a degree of privacy afforded through subdivision by means of wooden partitions.

All the well known passages from Martial and Juvenal which are often cited to attest the discomforts of poor *insularii* contain no comment on crowding or lack of privacy. This is probably because these two poets never lived in the poorest type of accommodation, rather than because the Romans had low space expectations and consequently were less concerned with individual privacy. Privacy was prized by high status Romans who often had isolated, quiet rooms built in their *villae* or *domus* where they could meditate, read, or sleep, undisturbed by the rest of the household. Seneca . . . vividly evokes the assorted noises he heard when living in rooms over baths, and assures his reader that such noises will not be bothersome if inner peace and tranquillity has been achieved. . . . However, . . . he makes it clear that the best way to deal with such noise problems is simply to leave the building and go elsewhere. Seneca was merely testing his individual tolerance of noise, and . . . could afford to move to quieter surroundings.

Yet Roman sensitivity to privacy is not easy to assess. Members of all socio-economic levels, from emperor to beggar congregated in the public baths where there was virtually no individual privacy. Changing rooms (*apodyteria*), massage rooms (*destrictoria*) as well as all the main bathing rooms, were totally devoid of facilities such as partitioned cubicles which are normal in the changing rooms of modern public swimming pools. At the Stabian baths at Pompeii there was a small number of individual bathrooms, but these belong to the earliest (Greek) phase of the site, and later fell into disuse after the building of the Roman baths. The general lack of privacy at the baths gave rise to annoyances such as voyeurism and worse. The infamous Hostius Quadra[78] who enjoyed distorting mirror images of himself being debauched, is reported to have scoured the baths for men with large genitals. That this was not an isolated case is shown by several other sources. Also the sick and the deformed might be ridiculed at the baths for their physical defects. Martial, for example, pillories a man who derided hernia patients at the baths, till he suffered from the same complaint himself. . . .

Privacy is also felt to be a normal necessity in modern Western societies, both for defecation and sexual intercourse ("sex/elimination amalgam"). No extant Roman author gives his impression of a Roman *forica* where as many as sixty or more people, men and women, sitting on stone or wooden seats, relieved themselves in full view of each other. One surviving piece of evidence from Suetonius depicts the poet Lucan[79] reciting a verse by Nero while relieving himself in a public latrine. The other occupants fled the latrine in consternation, presumably in fear of being implicated in a possible charge of *maiestas*.[80] The passage is interesting in that it suggests that high status Romans used public latrines.

The contrast between Roman practice and contemporary Western views on bathroom privacy may be seen from . . . [a] summation of modern expectations: "Our cultural norms strongly encourage an association of embarrassment and shame with such functions and privacy for these becomes essential. It is fairly common . . . for people in a public lavatory to retain their feces within their rectum if other people come within earshot — even though visual privacy is assured — so that the splash as the stool hits the water will not be heard by others, and will not thereby cause embarrassment." It seems reasonably clear that Romans did not feel embarrassment or shame in *foricae;* otherwise different design features such as cubicles with doors would have been standard in these facilities. Some concern for privacy is evident in one aspect of *forica*-design: a small vestibule often separates the latrine chamber from the street, and the door in the street wall is in several such structures not aligned with the door in the inner wall which gave entrance to the latrine room itself. Thus if someone entered the outer door at the same time as another person left the latrine room, it would be impossible for the person entering and for pedestrians passing while the door was open to see the people sitting on the latrine. This design can be seen both in the public latrine in the N.E. corner of the Forum at Pompeii, and a similar design is evident in the *forica* at the entrance to the Roman Agora at Athens. The public latrine at Ostia . . . made by converting two shops was less satisfactory in providing customers with protection from the public gaze, since entrance was gained by two revolving doors which opened directly into the latrine room. Consequently every time a client entered, a *sessor*[81] would be briefly revealed to any passerby who looked in. However, Ovid says it

---

[78] A member of Emperor Nero's circle of friends.

[79] Poet and friend of Emperor Nero (A.D. 39–65).

[80] Treason.

[81] Sitter.

was contrary to custom to watch such activities, and Seneca shows that even a prisoner of war was thought to be entitled to privacy in a latrine, a paradoxical concession when Roman citizens were denied privacy in similar circumstances.

Though the Romans appear not to have objected to a lack of privacy in baths and latrines, they seem to have expected it for sexual activities. Martial jeers at an adulteress . . . for conducting her affairs with the doors of her room open and unguarded to enable the curious to see her at work, and contrasts her behaviour with normal practice in the lowest brothels where curtains and doors were the norm to ensure customer privacy.

To return to the *cellae* of the upper floors of Roman *insulae* as exemplified by the Casa di via Giulio Romano. There are no sure means of calculating the occupation densities of such rooms, but a combination of uncontrolled rents, which might have caused malnutrition as a byproduct, and the total lack of legislation enforcing minimum occupation densities in multiple dwellings, are likely to have created congested living conditions. A further lack of enforceable regulations to ensure adequate light, ventilation, water supply, and waste disposal, in combination with unsatisfactory street cleaning would also have created an extremely unhealthy environment for those who had no choice but to live in the concrete cubicles of the Capitoline *insula*. To what extent cohesive family units could survive under such circumstances is difficult to estimate. Adults and children would lack separate rooms and probably even separate beds, a situation which in Hong Kong causes hotels and motels to rent rooms by the hour "not for illicit liaisons, but so that married couples can briefly share a bed away from their teenage children." Children who survived childbirth, and were not exposed,[82] would have no recreation space on the fourth floor of this building except for the damp, totally unlit rear corridor. Roman children used to play at being gladiators. In these circumstances they would only be able to play at being *andabatae*[83] who fought each other while wearing visors with no eyeholes. So children would probably play in the streets, especially as they would not spend any time at schools which their parents could not afford.

To suggest . . . that such atrocious conditions at home were "made tolerable by the attractive spaciousness of public facilities" would probably strike a Roman on an erratic daily wage . . . with a dependent family, as a cynical acceptance of the state's indifference to the lot of the urban poor. If an unskilled worker was by the very nature of his housing denied privacy for the most fundamental life functions, if he could never be sure of adequate food and clothing, and if he lacked resources to gain access to formal education and the protection of the law, what compensation would he be likely to derive from costly public buildings which re-

---

[82] Left on public refuse dumps to die.

[83] Blindfolded gladiators.

flected the *maiestas imperii*,[84] or from a few public parks? The condition of the urban poor and indigent in the Roman world must have been aggravated by a consciousness of their own hopelessness made all too obvious by the wealth of high status Romans who in the most conspicuous manner displayed their riches which the state did not try to redistribute to minimize the disequilibrium between rich and poor. Lavishly ornamented public baths, temples, and amphitheatres no doubt produced in the poor a momentary forgetfulness of fetid, cramped, living quarters, but could hardly be considered as genuine substitutes for what must justifiably be called slums.

Life for the poor in Rome's high rise tenements was dangerous not merely because of the constant risks of fire, collapse, and the rapid spread of communicable diseases in overcrowded badly ventilated rooms, but also because such conditions frequently produce a high level of violence and crime. The *atrium*-type house provided the wealthy with a very private environment which was also relatively secure from burglary. Windows in outer walls on ground floors were usually small, placed high above the road, and frequently protected by spiked iron grilles *(fenestrae clatraiae)*. Close to the vestibule a doorman *(ostiarius)*, sometimes chained to the wall of his *cella,* kept an eye on those who entered, and guard-dogs, also sometimes chained, were regularly on the premises. *Impluria* were also sometimes protected by iron grilles to prevent burglars from entering the *atrium* via the roof. In the interior of the building was a strongroom *(herreum)* where the owner's valuables were safeguarded. In addition, the rich hired their own private security guards. . . . Though the rich would be the most desirable targets of burglars, the defences of their inward looking fortress-like residences would be difficult to penetrate. It seems from passages in the *Digest* that in towns burglary was more frequent in *insulae* and public *horrea.* The public baths were also frequented by thieves who were sometimes the very people hired by bathers to guard their clothes.

Low status *insularii* were exposed to official and unofficial violence in their dwellings. If they lit a brazier in their home to heat themselves or cook food, they risked being clubbed or flogged on the authority of the *praefectus vigilum.*[85] Also high levels of violence are commonly associated with high density living. . . . These risks in addition to the non-human threats in their environment such as poor plumbing (in the case of *insularii*, non-existent) and the consequential smells, combine to give such tenants a sense of being moral outcasts.

The *insularius* who tried to escape the anxieties created by his living conditions by going into the streets would find little relief. The casual statement made by Suetonius that Augustus derived special pleasure from watching groups of people brawling in narrow city streets reveals a great deal not only about the em-

---

[84] Grandeur and dignity of the empire.

[85] Superintendent of watchmen.

peror's personal tastes in entertainment, but also about the official tolerance of disorder in the streets which were in any case very congested. . . . At night the streets were less congested, but dangers of a different kind lay in store for the solitary pedestrian, including mugging, and being struck by rubbish and wastes thrown from the windows of *insulae*. The *Digest* sometimes provides pictures of lower class Roman life as vivid, and perhaps more trustworthy, as any given by Juvenal. One such vignette is of a Roman street scene at night. A *tabernarius*[86] puts his lantern on the pavement. A passerby makes off with the light with the shopkeeper in pursuit. The thief strikes him with a lash *(flagellum)* and a brawl ensues which ends when the shopkeeper knocks out one of the thief's eyes. Such street violence was probably commonplace at Rome, but is only reported by historians where it takes place on a scale large enough to have serious political implications.

High density living in insanitary urban dwellings and surroundings can have only one major consequence in a preindustrial society which lacks effective and cheap medical care: a short, often violent, life. That this was the common lot of the millions of people in the Roman world who lived on or below subsistence level, can hardly be doubted, given the conditions discussed above.

---

[86] Shopkeeper.

GOD THE FATHER/GOD THE MOTHER: THE GNOSTIC GOSPELS AND THE SUPPRESSION OF EARLY CHRISTIAN FEMINISM

Elaine Pagels

Sixteenth-century church reformers such as Martin Luther and John Calvin urged Christians to return to the beliefs and practices of early Christianity. During the first centuries after the death of Jesus, the reformers argued, Christians had been united. Only afterward did corruption and false beliefs set in. The reformers' interpretation is pure myth, for Christianity has always been rent by dissension. In this provocative essay, Elaine Pagels, Harrington Spear Paine Professor of Religion at Princeton University, examines the Gnostic gospels and shows how the Gnostics' faith differed from that of other Christians.

In 1945, Egyptian peasants discovered scrolls of holy books at Nag Hammadi, approximately three hundred miles south of Cairo. Gnostic Christians, who believed in Jesus' secret teachings (those he had not spoken of publicly) and who also looked for knowledge ("gnosis") within themselves, had hidden these gospels because they feared that so-called orthodox Christians (those who eventually established an institutional church in the West) would burn them. Gnostic Christians, along with many others (such as Donatists and Nestorians) from the first centuries A.D., do not exist today, but in the second through fourth centuries they challenged the orthodox church that ultimately succeeded in suppressing rival Christian confessions during the Roman Empire.

According to Pagels, theology reflects social and political concerns. Why did orthodox Christians reject out of hand the Gnostic gospels' use of feminine imagery to describe their god? Why did the orthodox exclude all of the Gnostic holy books from the New Testament? Women held important roles during the formation of early Christianity, but orthodox Christians insisted that women remain subordinate to men in the emerging church and in other areas of social and political life. Why did the orthodox Christians fear women and oppose the more

Elaine Pagels, *The Gnostic Gospels* (New York: Random House, 1979), 48–69.

open attitude toward females that the Gnostics and their gospels advocated? How did other religions of the time — such as Judaism and the cult of the Egyptian goddess Isis — treat women? How did different Christian descriptions of their god mirror conflicting ideas of the place of women in Christianity?

Unlike many of his contemporaries among the deities of the ancient Near East, the God of Israel shared his power with no female divinity, nor was he the divine Husband or Lover of any. He can scarcely be characterized in any but masculine epithets: king, lord, master, judge, and father. Indeed, the absence of feminine symbolism for God marks Judaism, Christianity, and Islam in striking contrast to the world's other religious traditions, whether in Egypt, Babylonia, Greece, and Rome, or in Africa, India, and North America, which abound in feminine symbolism. Jewish, Christian, and Islamic theologians today are quick to point out that God is not to be considered in sexual terms at all. Yet the actual language they use daily in worship and prayer conveys a different message: who, growing up with Jewish or Christian tradition, has escaped the distinct impression that God is *masculine?* And while Catholics revere Mary as the mother of Jesus, they never identify her as divine in her own right: if she is "mother of God," she is not "God the Mother" on an equal footing with God the Father!

Christianity, of course, added the trinitarian terms to the Jewish description of God. Yet of the three divine "Persons," two — the Father and the Son — are described in masculine terms, and the third — the Spirit — suggests the sexlessness of the Greek neuter term for spirit, *pneuma.* Whoever investigates the early history of Christianity (the field called "patristics" — that is, study of "the fathers of the church") will be prepared for the passage that concludes the *Gospel of Thomas:*[1]

> Simon Peter said to them [the disciples]: "Let Mary leave us, for women are not worthy of Life." Jesus said, "I myself shall lead her, in order to make her male, so that she too may become a living spirit, resembling you males. For every woman who will make herself male will enter the Kingdom of Heaven."

Strange as it sounds, this simply states what religious rhetoric assumes: that the men form the legitimate body of the community, while women are allowed to participate only when they assimilate themselves to men. Other texts discovered at Nag Hammadi[2] demonstrate one striking difference between these "heretical"[3]

---

[1] A Christian gospel, purportedly by the Apostle Thomas, probably written ca. A.D. 140, containing sayings attributed to Jesus.

[2] An Egyptian village where, in 1945, thirteen leather-bound Christian holy books were found buried in a storage jar.

[3] Relating to religious opinions that are contrary to the established teachings of church authorities.

sources and orthodox[4] ones: gnostic sources continually use sexual symbolism to describe God. One might expect that these texts would show the influence of archaic pagan traditions of the Mother Goddess, but for the most part, their language is specifically Christian, unmistakably related to a Jewish heritage. Yet instead of describing a monistic[5] and masculine God, many of these texts speak of God as a dyad[6] who embraces both masculine and feminine elements.

One group of gnostic sources claims to have received a secret tradition from Jesus through James[7] and through Mary Magdalene.[8] Members of this group prayed to both the divine Father and Mother: "From Thee, Father, and through Thee, Mother, the two immortal names, Parents of the divine being, and thou, dweller in heaven, humanity, of the mighty name. . . ." Other texts indicate that their authors had wondered to whom a single, masculine God proposed, "Let us make man [*adam*] in our image, after our likeness" (Genesis 1:26). Since the Genesis account goes on to say that humanity was created "male and female" (1:27), some concluded that the God in whose image we are made must also be both masculine and feminine — both Father and Mother.

How do these texts characterize the divine Mother? I find no simple answer, since the texts themselves are extremely diverse. Yet we may sketch out three primary characterizations. In the first place, several gnostic groups describe the divine Mother as part of an original couple. Valentinus,[9] the teacher and poet, begins with the premise that God is essentially indescribable. But he suggests that the divine can be imagined as a dyad; consisting, in one part, of the Ineffable, the Depth, the Primal Father; and, in the other, of Grace, Silence, the Womb and "Mother of the All." Valentinus reasons that Silence is the appropriate complement of the Father, designating the former as feminine and the latter as masculine because of the grammatical gender of the Greek words. He goes on to describe how Silence receives, as in a womb, the seed of the Ineffable Source; from this she brings forth all the emanations of divine being, ranged in harmonious pairs of masculine and feminine energies.

Followers of Valentinus prayed to her for protection as the Mother, and as "the mystical, eternal Silence." For example, Marcus the magician invokes her as Grace . . .: "May She who is before all things, the incomprehensible and indescribable Grace, fill you within, and increase in you her own knowledge." In his secret celebration of the mass, Marcus teaches that the wine symbolizes her blood. As the cup of wine is offered, he prays that "Grace may flow" into all who drink of

---

[4] Conforming to doctrines or practices that church authorities hold as right or true.

[5] Relating to the metaphysical view that there is only one kind of substance or ultimate reality.

[6] Two units treated as one; a couple or pair.

[7] The Apostle James, son of Zebedee and brother of the Apostle John.

[8] A follower of Jesus and his disciples who, according to the gospel stories, was the first person to see the empty tomb and the resurrected Jesus.

[9] A prominent Gnostic leader, founder of a widespread sect in second-century Rome.

it. A prophet and visionary, Marcus calls himself the *"womb and recipient* of Silence" (as she is of the Father). The visions he received of the divine being appeared, he reports, in female form.

Another gnostic writing, called the *Great Announcement*, . . . explains the origin of the universe as follows: From the power of Silence appeared "a great power, the Mind of the Universe, which manages all things, and is a male . . . the other . . . a great Intelligence . . . is a female which produces all things." Following the gender of the Greek words for "mind" (*nous* — masculine) and "intelligence" (*epinoia* — feminine), this author explains that these powers, joined in union, "are discovered to be duality. . . . This is Mind in Intelligence, and these are separable from one another, and yet are one, found in a state of duality." This means, the gnostic teacher explains, that

> there is in everyone [divine power] existing in a latent condition. . . . This is one power divided above and below; generating itself, making itself grow, seeking itself, finding itself, being mother of itself, father of itself, sister of itself, spouse of itself, daughter of itself, son of itself — mother, father, unity, being a source of the entire circle of existence.

How did these gnostics intend their meaning to be understood? Different teachers disagreed. Some insisted that the divine is to be considered masculofeminine — the "great male-female power." Others claimed that the terms were meant only as metaphors, since, in reality, the divine is neither male nor female. A third group suggested that one can describe the primal Source in either masculine or feminine terms, depending on which aspect one intends to stress. Proponents of these diverse views agreed that the divine is to be understood in terms of a harmonious, dynamic relationship of opposites — a concept that may be akin to the Eastern view of *yin* and *yang*,[10] but remains alien to orthodox Judaism and Christianity.

A second characterization of the divine Mother describes her as Holy Spirit. The *Apocryphon of John* relates how John[11] went out after the crucifixion with "great grief" and had a mystical vision of the Trinity. As John was grieving, he says that

> the [heavens were opened and the whole] creation [which is] under heaven shone and [the world] trembled. [And I was afraid, and I] saw in the light . . . a likeness with multiple forms . . . and the likeness had three forms.

To John's question the vision answers: "He said to me, 'John, Jo[h]n, why do you doubt, and why are you afraid? . . . I am the one who [is with you] always. I [am the Father]; I am the Mother; I am the Son." This gnostic description of God — as Father, Mother and Son — may startle us at first, but on reflection, we can recognize it as another version of the Trinity. The Greek terminology for the Trinity, which includes the neuter term for spirit (*pneuma*) virtually requires that the third

---

[10] The idea that male and female opposites are simultaneously a unity.

[11] An apostle, son of Alphaeus and relative of Jesus.

"Person" of the Trinity be asexual. But the author of the *Secret Book* has in mind the Hebrew term for spirit, *ruah*, a feminine word; and so concludes that the feminine "Person" conjoined with the Father and Son must be the Mother. The *Secret Book* goes on to describe the divine Mother:

> . . . (She is) . . . the image of the invisible, virginal, perfect spirit. . . . She became the Mother of everything, for she existed before them all, the mother-father [*matropater*]. . . .

The *Gospel to the Hebrews* likewise has Jesus speak of "my Mother, the Spirit." In the *Gospel of Thomas,* Jesus contrasts his earthly parents, Mary and Joseph, with his divine Father — the Father of Truth — and his divine Mother, the Holy Spirit. The author interprets a puzzling saying of Jesus' from the New Testament ("Whoever does not hate his father and his mother cannot be my disciple") by adding that "my (earthly) mother [gave me death], but [my] true [Mother] gave me life." So, according to the *Gospel of Philip,* whoever becomes a Christian gains "both father and mother" for the Spirit *(ruah)* is "Mother of many." . . .

If some gnostic sources suggest that the Spirit constitutes the maternal element of the Trinity, the *Gospel of Philip* makes an equally radical suggestion about the doctrine that later developed as the virgin birth. Here again, the Spirit is both Mother and Virgin, the counterpart — and consort — of the Heavenly Father: "Is it permitted to utter a mystery? The Father of everything united with the virgin who came down" — that is, with the Holy Spirit descending into the world. But because this process is to be understood symbolically, not literally, the Spirit remains a virgin. The author goes on to explain that as "Adam came into being from two virgins, from the Spirit and from the virgin earth" so "Christ, therefore, was born from a virgin" (that is, from the Spirit). But the author ridicules those literal-minded Christians who mistakenly refer the virgin birth to Mary, Jesus' mother, as though she conceived apart from Joseph: "They do not know what they are saying. When did a woman ever conceive by a woman?" Instead, he argues, virgin birth refers to that mysterious union of the two divine powers, the Father of All and the Holy Spirit.

In addition to the eternal, mystical Silence and the Holy Spirit, certain gnostics suggest a third characterization of the divine Mother: as Wisdom. Here the Greek feminine term for "wisdom," *sophia,* translates a Hebrew feminine term, *hokhmah.* Early interpreters had pondered the meaning of certain Biblical passages — for example, the saying in Proverbs that "God made the world in Wisdom." Could Wisdom be the feminine power in which God's creation was "conceived"? According to one teacher, the double meaning of the term conception — physical and intellectual — suggests this possibility: "The image of thought [*ennoia*] is feminine, since . . . [it] is a power of conception." The *Apocalypse of Adam,* discovered at Nag Hammadi, tells of a feminine power who wanted to conceive by herself:

> . . . from the nine Muses, one separated away. She came to a high mountain and spent time seated there, so that she desired herself alone in order to be-

come androgynous. She fulfilled her desire, and became pregnant from her desire. . . .

The poet Valentinus uses this theme to tell a famous myth about Wisdom: Desiring to conceive by herself, apart from her masculine counterpart, she succeeded, and became the "great creative power from whom all things originate," often called Eve, "Mother of all living." But since her desire violated the harmonious union of opposites intrinsic in the nature of created being, what she produced was aborted and defective; from this, says Valentinus, originated the terror and grief that mar human existence. To shape and manage her creation, Wisdom brought forth the demiurge, the creator-God of Israel, as her agent.

Wisdom, then, bears several connotations in gnostic sources. Besides being the "first universal creator," who brings forth all creatures, she also enlightens human beings and makes them wise. Followers of Valentinus and Marcus therefore prayed to the Mother as the "mystical, eternal Silence" and to "Grace, She who is before all things," and as "incorruptible Wisdom" for insight (*gnosis*). Other gnostics attributed to her the benefits that Adam and Eve received in Paradise. First, she taught them self-awareness; second, she guided them to find food; third, she assisted in the conception of their third and fourth children, who were, according to this account, their third son, Seth, and their first daughter, Norea. Even more: when the creator became angry with the human race

> because they did not worship or honor him as Father and God, he sent forth a flood upon them, that he might destroy them all. But Wisdom opposed him . . . and Noah and his family were saved in the ark by means of the sprinkling of the light that proceeded from her, and through it the world was again filled with humankind.

Another newly discovered text from Nag Hammadi, *Trimorphic Protennoia* (literally, the "Triple-formed Primal Thought"), celebrates the feminine powers of Thought, Intelligence, and Foresight. The text opens as a divine figure speaks:

> [I] am [Protennoia the] Thought that [dwells] in [the Light]. . . . [she who exists] before the All . . . I move in every creature. . . . I am the Invisible One within the All.

She continues: "I am perception and knowledge, uttering a Voice by means of Thought. [I] am the real Voice. I cry out in everyone, and they know that a seed dwells within." The second section, spoken by a second divine figure, . . . explains:

> I am androgynous. [I am both Mother and] Father, since [I copulate] with myself . . . [and with those who love] me. . . . I am the Womb [that gives shape] to the All. . . . I am . . . the glory of the Mother.

Even more remarkable is the gnostic poem called the *Thunder, Perfect Mind.* This text contains a revelation spoken by a feminine power:

I am the first and the last. I am the honored one and the scorned one. I am the whore, and the holy one. I am the wife and the virgin. I am (the mother) and the daughter. . . . I am she whose wedding is great, and I have not taken a husband. . . . I am knowledge, and ignorance. . . . I am shameless; I am ashamed. I am strength, and I am fear. . . . I am foolish, and I am wise. . . . I am godless, and I am one whose God is great.

What does the use of such symbolism imply for the understanding of human nature? One text, having previously described the divine Source as a "bisexual Power," goes on to say that "what came into being from that Power — that is, humanity, being one — is discovered to be two: a male-female being that bears the female within it." This refers to the story of Eve's "birth" out of Adam's side (so that Adam, being one, is "discovered to be two," an androgyne who "bears the female within him"). Yet this reference to the creation story of Genesis 2 (an account which inverts the biological birth process, and so attributes to the male the creative function of the female) is unusual in gnostic sources. More often, gnostic writers refer to the first creation account in Genesis 1:26–27 ("Then God said, Let us make man [*adam*] in our image, after our likeness . . . in the image of God he created him; male and female he created them"). Rabbis in Talmudic times[12] knew a Greek version of the passage that suggested . . . that

> when the Holy one . . . first created mankind, he created him with two faces, two sets of genitals, four arms and legs, back to back. Then he split Adam in two, and made two backs, one on each side.

Some gnostics adopted this idea, teaching that Genesis 1:26–27 narrates an androgynous creation. Marcus . . . not only concludes from this account that God is dyadic ("Let *us* make humanity") but also that "humanity, which was formed according to the image and likeness of God (Father and Mother) was masculofeminine." His contemporary, the gnostic Theodotus (c. 160), explains that the saying "according to the image of God he made them, male and female he made them," means that "the male and female elements together constitute the finest production of the Mother, Wisdom." Gnostic sources which describe God as a dyad whose nature includes both masculine and feminine elements often give a similar description of human nature.

Yet all the sources cited so far — secret gospels, revelations, mystical teachings — are among those not included in the select list that constitutes the New Testament collection. Every one of the secret texts which gnostic groups revered was omitted from the canonical collection, and branded as heretical by those who called themselves orthodox Christians. By the time the process of sorting the various writings ended — probably as late as the year 200 — virtually all the feminine imagery for God had disappeared from orthodox Christian tradition.

---

[12] Relating to the period in which rabbis compiled the Talmud (the authoritative body of postscriptural Jewish law and tradition), ca. the first to fifth centuries A.D.

What is the reason for this total rejection? The gnostics themselves asked this question of their orthodox opponents and pondered it among themselves. Some concluded that the God of Israel himself initiated the polemics which his followers carried out in his name. For, they argued, this creator was a derivative, merely instrumental power whom the Mother had created to administer the universe, but his own self-conception was far more grandiose. They say that he believed that he had made everything by himself, but that, in reality, he had created the world because Wisdom, his Mother, "infused him with energy" and implanted into him her own ideas. But he was foolish, and acted unconsciously, unaware that the ideas he used came from her; "he was even ignorant of his own Mother." Followers of Valentinus suggested that the Mother Herself had encouraged the God of Israel to think that he was acting autonomously, but, as they explain, "It was because he was foolish and ignorant of his Mother that he said, 'I am God; there is none beside me.'" According to another account, the creator caused his Mother to grieve by creating inferior beings, so she left him alone and withdrew into the upper regions of the heavens. "Since she had departed, he imagined that he was the only being in existence; and therefore he declared, 'I am a jealous God, and besides me there is no one.'" . . .

Yet all of these are mythical explanations. Can we find any actual, historical reasons why these gnostic writings were suppressed? This raises a much larger question: By what means, and for what reasons, did certain ideas come to be classified as heretical, and others as orthodox, by the beginning of the third century? We may find one clue to the answer if we ask whether gnostic Christians derive any practical, social consequences from their conception of God — and of humanity — in terms that included the feminine element. Here, clearly, the answer is *yes*.

Bishop Irenaeus[13] notes with dismay that women especially are attracted to heretical groups. "Even in our own district of the Rhône valley," he admits, the gnostic teacher Marcus had attracted "many foolish women" from his own congregation, including the wife of one of Irenaeus' own deacons. Professing himself to be at a loss to account for the attraction that Marcus' group held, he offers only one explanation: that Marcus himself was a diabolically clever seducer, a magician who compounded special aphrodisiacs to "deceive, victimize, and defile" his prey. Whether his accusations have any factual basis no one knows. But when he describes Marcus' techniques of seduction, Irenaeus indicates that he is speaking metaphorically. For, he says, Marcus "addresses them in such seductive words" as his prayers to Grace, "She who is before all things," and to Wisdom and Silence, the feminine element of the divine being. Second, he says, Marcus seduced women "by telling them to prophesy" — which they were strictly forbidden to do in the orthodox church. When he initiated a woman, Marcus concluded the initiation prayer with the words "Behold, Grace has come upon you; open your

---

[13] Saint and theologian (ca. A.D. 140–ca. 202).

mouth, and prophesy." Then, as the bishop indignantly describes it, Marcus' "deluded victim . . . impudently utters some nonsense," and "henceforth considers herself to be a prophet!" Worst of all, from Irenaeus' viewpoint, Marcus invited women to act as priests in celebrating the eucharist with him: he "hands the cups to women" to offer up the eucharistic prayer, and to pronounce the words of consecration.

Tertullian[14] expresses similar outrage at such acts of gnostic Christians:

> These heretical women — how audacious they are! They have no modesty; they are bold enough to teach, to engage in argument, to enact exorcisms, to undertake cures, and, it may be, even to baptize!

Tertullian directed another attack against "that viper" — a woman teacher who led a congregation in North Africa. He himself agreed with what he called the "precepts of ecclesiastical discipline concerning women," which specified:

> It is not permitted for a woman to speak in the church, nor is it permitted for her to teach, nor to baptize, nor to offer [the eucharist], nor to claim for herself a share in any *masculine* function — not to mention any priestly office.

One of Tertullian's prime targets, the heretic Marcion,[15] had, in fact, scandalized his orthodox contemporaries by appointing women on an equal basis with men as priests and bishops. The gnostic teacher Marcellina traveled to Rome to represent the Carpocratian group,[16] which claimed to have received secret teaching from Mary, Salome, and Martha. The Montanists,[17] a radical prophetic circle, honored two women, Prisca and Maximilla, as founders of the movement.

Our evidence, then, clearly indicates a correlation between religious theory and social practice. Among such gnostic groups as the Valentinians, women were considered equal to men; some were revered as prophets; others acted as teachers, traveling evangelists, healers, priests, perhaps even bishops. This general observation is not, however, universally applicable. At least three heretical circles that retained a masculine image of God included women who took positions of leadership — the Marcionites, the Montanists, and the Carpocratians. But from the year 200, we have no evidence for women taking prophetic, priestly, and episcopal roles among orthodox churches.

This is an extraordinary development, considering that in its earliest years the Christian movement showed a remarkable openness toward women. Jesus himself violated Jewish convention by talking openly with women, and he included them among his companions. Even the gospel of Luke in the New Testament tells his reply when Martha, his hostess, complains to him that she is doing house-

---

[14] Christian theologian (ca. A.D. 160–ca. 225).

[15] Second-century Gnostic founder of the Marcionite sect.

[16] Followers of Carpocrates, who taught that humans can reach a higher degree of illumination than that of Jesus.

[17] Followers of Montanus, who claimed that the Holy Spirit dwelt within true believers.

work alone while her sister Mary sits listening to him: "Do you not care that my sister has left me to serve alone? Tell her, then, to help me." But instead of supporting her, Jesus chides Martha for taking upon herself so many anxieties, declaring that "one thing is needful: Mary has chosen the good portion, which shall not be taken away from her." Some ten to twenty years after Jesus' death, certain women held positions of leadership in local Christian groups; women acted as prophets, teachers, and evangelists. . . . [A]t Christian initiation, the person presiding ritually announced that "in Christ . . . there is neither male nor female." Paul quotes this saying, and endorses the work of women he recognizes as deacons and fellow workers; he even greets one, apparently, as an outstanding apostle, senior to himself in the movement.

Yet Paul also expresses ambivalence concerning the practical implications of human equality. Discussing the public activity of women in the churches, he argues from his own — traditionally Jewish — conception of a monistic, masculine God for a divinely ordained hierarchy of social subordination: as God has authority over Christ, he declares, citing Genesis 2–3, so man has authority over woman:

> . . . a man . . . is the image and glory of God; but woman is the glory of man. (For man was not made from woman, but woman from man. Neither was man created for woman, but woman for man.)

While Paul acknowledged women as his equals "in Christ," and allowed for them a wider range of activity than did traditional Jewish congregations, he could not bring himself to advocate their equality in social and political terms. Such ambivalence opened the way for the statements found in I Corinthians 14, 34 f., whether written by Paul or inserted by someone else: ". . . the women should keep silence in the churches. For they are not permitted to speak, but they should be subordinate . . . it is shameful for a woman to speak in church."

Such contradictory attitudes toward women reflect a time of social transition, as well as the diversity of cultural influences on churches scattered throughout the known world. In Greece and Asia Minor, women participated with men in religious cults, especially the cults of the Great Mother[18] and of the Egyptian goddess Isis.[19] While the leading roles were reserved for men, women took part in the services and professions. Some women took up education, the arts, and professions such as medicine. In Egypt, women had attained, by the first century A.D., a relatively advanced state of emancipation, socially, politically, and legally. In Rome, forms of education had changed, around 200 B.C., to offer to some children from the aristocracy the same curriculum for girls as for boys. Two hundred years later, at the beginning of the Christian era, the archaic, patriarchal forms of Roman mar-

---

[18] Originating in Syria, this cult worshiped a maternal figure who represented fertility, creation, and new life.

[19] The Egyptian goddess of rebirth and resurrection, who became the focus of one of the largest religions in the Roman Empire.

riage were increasingly giving way to a new legal form in which the man and woman bound themselves to each other with voluntary and mutual vows. . . . [B]y the second century A.D., upper-class women often insisted upon "living their own life." Male satirists complained of their aggressiveness in discussions of literature, mathematics, and philosophy, and ridiculed their enthusiasm for writing poems, plays, and music. Under the Empire,

> women were everywhere involved in business, social life, such as theaters, sports events, concerts, parties, travelling — with or without their husbands. They took part in a whole range of athletics, even bore arms and went to battle . . . and made major inroads into professional life. Women of the Jewish communities, on the other hand, were excluded from actively participating in public worship, in education, and in social and political life outside the family.

Yet despite all of this, and despite the previous public activity of Christian women, the majority of Christian churches in the second century went with the majority of the middle class in opposing the move toward equality, which found its support primarily in rich or what we would call bohemian circles. By the year 200, the majority of Christian communities endorsed as canonical the pseudo-Pauline letter of Timothy, which stresses (and exaggerates) the antifeminist element in Paul's views: "Let a woman learn in silence with all submissiveness. I permit no woman to teach or to have authority over men; she is to keep silent." Orthodox Christians also accepted as Pauline the letters to the Colossians and to the Ephesians, which order that women "be subject in everything to their husbands."

Clement, Bishop of Rome,[20] writes in his letter to the unruly church in Corinth that women are to "remain in the rule of subjection" to their husbands. While in earlier times Christian men and women sat together for worship, in the middle of the second century — precisely at the time of struggle with gnostic Christians — orthodox communities began to adopt the synagogue custom, segregating women from men. By the end of the second century, women's participation in worship was explicitly condemned: groups in which women continued on to leadership were branded as heretical.

What was the reason for these changes? . . . [T]he influx of many Hellenized Jews into the movement may have influenced the church in the direction of Jewish traditions. . . . [T]he change may have resulted from Christianity's move up in social scale from lower to middle class. . . . [I]n the lower class, where all labor was needed, women had been allowed to perform any services they could (so today, in the Near East, only middle-class women are veiled).

Both orthodox and gnostic texts suggest that this question proved to be explosively controversial. Antagonists on both sides resorted to the polemical tech-

---

[20] Pope from ca. A.D. 92 to 101.

nique of writing literature that allegedly derived from apostolic times, professing to give the original apostles' views on the subject. As noted before, the *Gospel of Philip* tells of rivalry between the male disciples and Mary Magdalene, here described as Jesus' most intimate companion, the symbol of divine Wisdom:

> . . . the companion of the [Savior is] Mary Magdalene. [But Christ loved] her more than [all] the disciples and used to kiss her [often] on her [mouth]. The rest of [the disciples were offended by it . . .]. They said to him, "Why do you love her more than all of us?" The Savior answered and said to them, "Why do I not love you as [I love] her?"

The *Dialogue of the Savior* not only includes Mary Magdalene as one of three disciples chosen to receive special teaching but also praises her above the other two, Thomas and Matthew: ". . . she spoke as a woman who knew the All."

Other secret texts use the figure of Mary Magdalene to suggest that women's activity challenged the leaders of the orthodox community, who regarded Peter as their spokesman. The *Gospel of Mary* relates that when the disciples, disheartened and terrified after the crucifixion, asked Mary to encourage them by telling them what the Lord had told her secretly, she agrees, and teaches them until Peter, furious, asks, "Did he really speak privately with a woman, (and) not openly to us? Are we to turn about and all listen to her? Did he prefer her to us?" Distressed at his rage, Mary replies, "My brother Peter, what do you think? Do you think that I thought this up myself in my heart, or that I am lying about the Savior?" Levi breaks in at this point to mediate the dispute: "Peter, you have always been hot-tempered. Now I see you contending against the woman like the adversaries. But if the Savior made her worthy, who are you, indeed, to reject her? Surely the Lord knew her very well. That is why he loved her more than us." Then the others agree to accept Mary's teaching, and, encouraged by her words, go out to preach. Another argument between Peter and Mary occurs in *Pistis Sophia* ("Faith Wisdom"). Peter complains that Mary is dominating the conversation with Jesus and displacing the rightful priority of Peter and his brother apostles. He urges Jesus to silence her and is quickly rebuked. Later, however, Mary admits to Jesus that she hardly dares speak to him freely because, in her words, "Peter makes me hesitate; I am afraid of him, because he hates the female race." Jesus replies that whoever the Spirit inspires is divinely ordained to speak, whether man or woman.

Orthodox Christians retaliated with alleged "apostolic" letters and dialogues that make the opposite point. The most famous examples are, of course, the pseudo-Pauline letters cited above. In I and II Timothy, Colossians, and Ephesians, "Paul" insists that women be subordinate to men. The letter of Titus, in Paul's name, directs the selection of bishops in terms that entirely exclude women from consideration. Literally and figuratively, the bishop is to be a father figure to the congregation. He must be a man whose wife and children are "submissive [to him] in every way"; this proves his ability to keep "God's church" in order, and its members properly subordinated. Before the end of the second century, the *Apostolic*

Church Order appeared in orthodox communities. Here the apostles are depicted discussing controversial questions. With Mary and Martha present, John says,

> When the Master blessed the bread and the cup and signed them with the words, "This is my body and blood," he did not offer it to the women who are with us. Martha said, "He did not offer it to Mary, because he saw her laugh." Mary said, "I no longer laugh; he said to us before, as he taught, 'Your weakness is redeemed through strength.'"

But her argument fails; the male disciples agree that, for this reason, no woman shall be allowed to become a priest.

We can see, then, two very different patterns of sexual attitudes emerging in orthodox and gnostic circles. In simplest form, many gnostic Christians correlate their description of God in both masculine and feminine terms with a complementary description of human nature. Most often they refer to the creation account of Genesis I, which suggests an equal or androgynous human creation. Gnostic Christians often take the principle of equality between men and women into the social and political structures of their communities. The orthodox pattern is strikingly different: it describes God in exclusively masculine terms, and typically refers to Genesis 2 to describe how Eve was created from Adam, and for his fulfillment. Like the gnostic view, this translates into social practice: by the late second century, the orthodox community came to accept the domination of men over women as the divinely ordained order, not only for social and family life, but also for the Christian churches.

Yet exceptions to these patterns do occur. Gnostics were not unanimous in affirming women — nor were the orthodox unanimous in denigrating them. Certain gnostic texts undeniably speak of the feminine in terms of contempt. The *Book of Thomas the Contender* addresses men with the warning "Woe to you who love intimacy with womankind, and polluted intercourse with it!" The *Paraphrase of Shem,* also from Nag Hammadi, describes the horror of Nature, who "turned her dark vagina and cast from her the power of fire, which was in her from the beginning, through the practice of darkness." According to the *Dialogue of the Savior,* Jesus warns his disciples to "pray in the place where there is no woman," and to "destroy the works of femaleness. . . ."

Yet in each of these cases the target is not woman, but the power of sexuality. In the *Dialogue of the Savior,* for example, Mary Magdalene, praised as "the woman who knew the All," stands among the three disciples who receive Jesus' commands: she, along with Judas and Matthew, rejects the "works of femaleness" — that is, apparently, the activities of intercourse and procreation. These sources show that some extremists in the gnostic movement agreed with certain radical feminists who today insist that only those who renounce sexual activity can achieve human equality and spiritual greatness.

Other gnostic sources reflect the assumption that the status of a man is superior to that of a woman. Nor need this surprise us; as language comes from social experience, any of these writers, whether man or woman, Roman, Greek,

Egyptian, or Jewish, would have learned this elementary lesson from his or her social experience. Some gnostics, reasoning that as *man* surpasses *woman* in ordinary existence, so the *divine* surpasses the *human*, transform the terms into metaphor. The puzzling saying attributed to Jesus in the *Gospel of Thomas* — that Mary must become male in order to become a "living spirit, resembling you males. For every woman who will make herself male will enter the Kingdom of Heaven" — may be taken symbolically: what is merely human (therefore *female*) must be transformed into what is divine (the "living spirit" the *male*). So, according to other passages in the *Gospel of Thomas*, Salome and Mary become Jesus' disciples when they transcend their human nature, and so "become male." In the *Gospel of Mary*, Mary herself urges the other disciples to "praise his greatness, for he has prepared us, and made us into *men*."

Conversely, we find a striking exception to the orthodox pattern in the writings of one revered father of the church, Clement of Alexandria. Clement, writing in Egypt c. 180, identifies himself as orthodox, although he knows members of gnostic groups and their writings well: some even suggest that he was himself a gnostic initiate. Yet his own works demonstrate how all three elements of what we have called the gnostic pattern could be worked into fully orthodox teaching. First, Clement characterizes God in feminine as well as masculine terms:

> The Word is everything to the child, both father and mother, teacher and nurse. . . . The nutriment is the milk of the Father . . . and the Word alone supplies us children with the milk of love, and only those who suck at this breast are truly happy. For this reason, seeking is called sucking; to those infants who seek the Word, the Father's loving breasts supply milk.

Second, in describing human nature, he insists that

> men and women share equally in perfection, and are to receive the same instruction and the same discipline. For the name "humanity" is common to both men and women; and for us "in Christ there is neither male nor female."

As he urges women to participate with men in the community, Clement offers a list — unique in orthodox tradition — of women whose achievements he admires. They range from ancient examples, like Judith, the assassin who destroyed Israel's enemy, to Queen Esther, who rescued her people from genocide, as well as others who took radical political stands. He mentions Arignote the writer, Themisto the Epicurean philosopher, and many other women philosophers, including two who studied with Plato, and one trained by Socrates. Indeed, he cannot contain his praise:

> What shall I say? Did not Theano the Pythagorean make such progress in philosophy that when a man, staring at her, said, "Your arm is beautiful," she replied, "Yes, but it is not on public display."

Clement concludes his list with famous women poets and painters.

But Clement's demonstration that even orthodox Christians could affirm the feminine element — and the active participation of women — found little following. His perspective, formed in the cosmopolitan atmosphere of Alexandria and articulated among wealthy and educated members of Egyptian society, may have proved too alien for the majority of Western Christian communities which were scattered from Asia Minor to Greece, Rome, and provincial Africa and Gaul. The majority adopted instead the position of Clement's severe and provincial contemporary, Tertullian:

> It is not permitted for a woman to speak in the church, nor is it permitted for her to teach, nor to baptize, nor to offer [the eucharist], nor to claim for herself a share in any masculine function — least of all, in priestly office.

Their consensus, which ruled out Clement's position, has continued to dominate the majority of Christian churches: nearly 2,000 years later, in 1977, Pope Paul VI, Bishop of Rome, declared that a woman cannot be a priest "because our Lord was a man"! The Nag Hammadi sources, discovered at a time of contemporary social crises concerning sexual roles, challenge us to reinterpret history — and to reevaluate the present situation.

MAKING CONNECTIONS: RELIGION AND RITUAL

1. Jean Soler's interpretation of Jewish dietary laws portrays a unified people (who, in fact, have always had their disagreements and factions). By contrast, Elaine Pagels focuses on fundamental disagreements between Christian groups, namely the Gnostics and those who successfully established an institutional church in western Europe. Both Soler and Pagels explore the relationship of religion to social concerns. Soler associates dietary customs with ideas of sexuality and clothing, for example, whereas Pagels sees differing interpretations of Jesus' tenets in light of notions of power and the place and status of women. Describe the extent to which Hebrew society and culture affected Jewish religion and the degree to which various social values conditioned both Gnostic and orthodox Christianity. What similarities existed between Judaism and Christianity in the ancient world?

2. Why did Christians disagree so vehemently about the role of women in religion? Did Jews likewise debate the participation of women in religious rituals? Do you think Christianity shaped gender roles? Or did the legal and social relationships between Christian men and women define their roles? Explain. To what extent do Christians and Jews today still debate the issues that Soler and Pagel discuss?

PART THREE

THE MIDDLE AGES

Georges Duby
David Herlihy
Jacques Rossiaud
John Keegan
Norbert Elias
R. Po-Chia Hsia

Covering the years roughly from 500 to 1500, the Middle Ages included a variety of cultures and territories. Western civilization during this epoch was increasingly confined to western Europe, leaving the eastern Mediterranean to the expanding Islamic world. Beginning with Germanic invasions of the western Roman Empire, the Middle Ages concluded with European invasions of exotic and distant lands as Europeans crossed the oceans in the fifteenth and sixteenth centuries to discover, fight, and convert indigenous peoples.

Some historians further subdivide the medieval epoch into the early (500–1000), high (1000–1300), and late (1300–1500) Middle Ages. The early Middle Ages, often misnamed the Dark Ages, witnessed Germanic invasions, political fragmentation, a rural economy, small population, little international trade, and a decline in education, urbanization, and commercialization. During this time, Christianity spread throughout western Europe, and some historians label the entire Middle Ages as the Age of Faith or the Christian centuries. Other historians stress that Christianity formed only a veneer grafted onto existing belief systems. Following Charlemagne's reign (768–814), which saw administrative innovations and a small cultural advance, invasions by the Vikings, Hungarians, and Saracens plunged Europe back into the chaotic conditions that recalled the collapse of Roman rule in the fifth and sixth centuries. The ninth and tenth centuries also provided the final elements that defined manorialism, the economic system, and feudalism, the method of governance. Nearly all Europeans were peasant farmers whose lives, as Georges Duby shows, consisted of unremitting toil and a poor diet. Wars, crop failures, and recurrent disease contributed to a precarious existence, alleviated somewhat by notable agricultural improvements.

The high Middle Ages was an era of relative prosperity that saw medieval civilization approach its zenith, marked by the prodigiously tall cathedrals built according to a new architectural and artistic style, the Gothic. Population expanded because of the surplus provided by improved agricultural techniques; towns and commerce grew; education (though highly limited in social scope) blossomed, first in cathedral schools and later in universities; and the slow accumulation of power in fewer hands offered a greater measure of political stability. In discussing medieval children, David Herlihy points to the greater social and psychological investment that Europeans now placed in their offspring in part because of the positive developments of the twelfth and thirteenth centuries.

Religion infused the economy, social order, politics, art, and mentality of the Middle Ages. The Crusades exemplified the brash exuberance and confidence of this period. It took the unprecedented disasters of the fourteenth and fifteenth centuries to end this vibrant civilization, though there was certainly much continuity with succeeding centuries. A worsening climate, famines, economic depression, international warfare, peasant revolts, and the worst scourge in history — the Plague — made the late Middle Ages a bleak era in many ways. John Keegan explores the horrors of warfare from the vantage point of the ordinary soldiers in an analysis of the battle of Agincourt in 1415. The violence of late medieval society is apparent as well in Jacques Rossiaud's account of ritualized gang rape by youths in fifteenth-century Dijon. Youths passed through a masculine rite of passage but in so doing devastated the lives of their female victims.

The late Middle Ages in Italy was the age of the Renaissance, an elite cultural flowering that coincided with economic depression and severe population loss. Humanism (the major intellectual movement of the Renaissance), artistic innovation, and political experimentation made Italy arguably the most dynamic area in Europe at the end of the Middle Ages. In studying the Italian Renaissance family, David Herlihy underscores the significance of the maternal education of sons for the development of the new Renaissance culture. He emphasizes also that the age of marriage indirectly led to the appearance of novel cultural values. While a new courtly ethos and artistic style appeared in southern Europe, fifteenth-century Germany maintained closer links to medieval patterns of thought and action. R. Po-Chia Hsia tells the story of a ritual murder of Jews in a German town, uncovering the persistence of venomous anti-Semitism, stereotyping, religious zealotry, and cruelty. Norbert Elias demonstrates the possibility of change as he explores the development of manners that led some Europeans to acquire a sense of shame. According to Elias, Europe, as its civilizing process attests, became a more mature society.

The Middle Ages possessed an energetic culture, difficult to categorize because of the substantial gap between people's ideals and the harsh reality of their daily lives. The essays in this section, then, show medieval societies to have been violent, intense, severe, patriarchal, and devoted to professed values and traditional modes of conduct from which they sometimes managed to break away.

RURAL ECONOMY AND COUNTRY LIFE IN THE MEDIEVAL WEST
Georges Duby

Europe of the ninth and tenth centuries was a rural civilization in which seasonal rhythms and patterns of cultivation determined the lifestyles of all, even the few who lived in small towns. In contrast, today less than 20 percent of the population of the Western world live in rural areas, large-scale mechanized agriculture is the norm, and television, automobiles, and the computer link farmers to the outside world.

Georges Duby (1919–1996) was a distinguished medieval historian at the Collège de France. Using estate records, manorial documents, and tax rolls, he recreates the economic lives of the peasantry. He begins his study of medieval agricultural communities by describing peasant settlements. What did a village comprise? Beyond the living area and the fields were forests. How did medieval people use the forests? What type of food did peasants consume? How effectively did the agricultural technology of the time exploit the land? Put another way, what factors limited the production of more food?

For most of history, people have stood helpless before the inadequacies of their land, the unpredictability of the weather, and their own inability to influence their environment in a stable, effective way. Medieval peasants were no exception. Their constant battle against the soil and climate, not to mention the parasitic aristocracy and clergy, yielded little food and much insecurity. In theory at least, the lords and clergy provided certain forms of security, but the reality was that the peasantry faced an epic struggle, with few material rewards.

One fact is outstanding: in the civilization of the ninth and tenth centuries the rural way of life was universal. Entire countries, like England and almost all the Germanic lands, were absolutely without towns. Elsewhere some towns existed: such as the few ancient Roman cities in the south which had not suffered com-

Georges Duby, *Rural Economy and Country Life in the Medieval West*, trans. Cynthia Postan (Columbia: University of South Carolina Press, 1968), 5–11, 15, 21–25, 27.

plete dilapidation, or the new townships on trade routes which were making their appearance along the rivers leading to the northern seas. But except for some in Lombardy, these "towns" appear as minute centres of population, each numbering at most a few hundred permanent inhabitants and deeply immersed in the life of the surrounding countryside. Indeed they could hardly be distinguished from it. Vineyards encircled them; fields penetrated their walls; they were full of cattle, barns and farm labourers. All their inhabitants from the very richest, bishops and even the king himself, to the few specialists, Jewish or Christian, who conducted long-distance trade, remained first and foremost countrymen whose whole life was dominated by the rhythm of the agricultural seasons, who depended for their existence on the produce of the soil, and who drew directly from it their entire worldly wealth. . . .

Another thing is also certain. It was a countryside created by man around a few fixed points of settlement. Western Europe was peopled by a stable peasantry rooted in its environment. Not that we should picture it as totally immobile. There was still room in rural life for nomadic movements. In high summer cartage and pastoral activities took many peasants to distant places, while others were occupied in gathering the wild products of the woodland, in hunting, in raiding their neighbours, and in some other activities that were necessary to acquire vital food supplies for survival. Other members of the rural population regularly participated in warlike adventures. However, most of these were only seasonal or part-time nomads. They spent most of their days on land which housed their families and formed part of organized village territories. They give the impression of belonging to villages.

Indeed the countryman's life was very rarely conducted in solitude. Dwelling houses appear to have been close together and very seldom isolated. Clusters of houses were usual. . . . [T]he village, whatever its size or shape, provided the normal background of human existence. In Saxon England, for instance, the village served as the basis for the levying and collection of taxes. Around these fixed points was laid out the pattern of the cultivated land, and particularly the network of trackways and paths, which appear in the landscape of today as the most tenacious relic of our ancient heritage, the reality which provides the starting point for archeological study of the village territory.

In western Europe, pioneer excavations are under way which will one day help us to know better what medieval rural dwellings were like. Already evidence exists which leads us to believe that, except in the Mediterranean coastal lands where building was in stone, men's habitations in the early, and even the not-so-early, Middle Ages were huts of wattle and daub,[1] short-lived and destructible; even at the beginning of the thirteenth century an English peasant was found guilty of having destroyed the house of his neighbour by merely sawing through the central beam.

---

[1] Wattle is a fabrication of stakes interwoven with twigs or tree branches to make walls and a roof; daub refers to interior materials, such as mud, used to cover or coat the walls.

. . . [T]he land on which the village stood was subject to a particular legal status, different from that of the surrounding land, and enjoying customary privileges which made its boundaries unalterable. Legal historians have shown that the village was made up of contiguous parcels of land which most Carolingian documents describe by the word *mansus,* and which the peasant dialects of the earliest Middle Age called variously *meix, Hof, masure, toft.* . . . We understand by this an enclosure, solidly rooted to its site by a permanent barrier such as a palisade or a living hedge, carefully maintained, a protected asylum to which the entry was forbidden and the violation of which was punished by severe penalties: an island of refuge where the occupant was assumed to be the master and at whose threshold communal servitude and the demands of chiefs and lords stopped short. These enclosures provided a haven for possessions, cattle, stocks of food, and sleeping men, protected them against natural and supernatural dangers, and taken together, constituted the kernel of the village, and expressed in terms of land and territory the essence of a society of which the family was the nucleus. Furthermore, it is probable that occupation of such a *manse* carried with it a place in the village community with collective rights over the surrounding fields. By the same token newcomers remained dwellers in a secondary zone of habitations outside the enclosures. . . .

. . . The soil which lay nearest to the house and to the stable was especially rich and fertile. By proximity alone the site of peasant settlement fertilized itself: household waste and the domestic animals were sufficient to establish around the dwelling, precisely because it was immovable, a permanent condition of fertility. Moreover, this land, because it was so conveniently placed, could be repeatedly dug over. In no other spot could the natural state of the earth be so profoundly modified to meet the needs of man; the constant manuring and digging created there an artificial soil and raised on it a specialized and particular plant life. Thus each domestic fence enclosed and protected a vegetable garden, . . . in other words a continually cultivated plot, where the ground was never left to rest, and where in carefully protected conditions grew tender plants, the herbs and roots of the daily diet, hemp and the vine. These plots were undoubtedly most productive and the atmosphere of garden care which they cast over their surroundings did much to anchor the village to its site.

Beyond the encircling hedges, nature was also subject to a certain, even if a not very rigorous, discipline. Without the need to tame her, men could win from nature a large part of their subsistence. River, marsh, forest and thicket offered to whoever could take advantage of them, fish, game, honey and many other edible substances in generous measure. . . . We are encouraged to believe that [the countryman] was as skilled in the use of the hunting spear, the net and the warrener's stick as he was with the plough. In 1180 when Alexander Neckham, an English teacher in the schools of Paris, wrote his treatise *Du Nom des Outils,*[2] he listed nets,

---

[2] *The Names of Tools.*

lines, and snares for trapping hares and deer amongst the ordinary tools of the peasant household. It is certain that the thinly growing forest of the early Middle Ages, with its numerous clearings, and its varied vegetation ranging from thick woodland to grassy glades, formed an essential background to the domestic economy. Apart from the livelihood that it bestowed generously on foodgatherer and hunter, it furnished the larger domestic animals with their chief sources of nourishment. Sheep and cows grazed there and war- and farm-horses were let loose in it. But above all else the woods were the domain of pigs. . . . Indeed over vast stretches of northern Europe in the ninth century bacon was an essential ingredient in the household economy. Herds of swine yielding both meat and lard formed everywhere the mainstay of every farming system, large and small. . . . In fact agrarian archeology leads us to suppose that many villages and especially those in the north-west and north-east, in England, Frisia and Saxony, possessed no cultivated lands, apart from the "tofts."[3] And in the eleventh century we know of communities in the English fenlands, on the Wash and in the flooded valley of the Saône which lived solely by fishing.

However, because of man's customary eating habits the cultivation of the small plots around the dwelling houses and the quest for the gifts of nature were nearly everywhere allied to the efforts to farm more extensively. We know very little about the food of early medieval man in western Europe outside the monastic communities. . . . It is clear that at this period not only were men unable to feed themselves on what they found by chance, but they were driven to grow what custom decreed they should consume. . . . [T]he expansion of winegrowing in Gaul was a direct consequence of the social habits of the nobles, with whom it was a point of honour to drink and to offer their guests none but the best wine. But on a much humbler level also the whole system of agricultural production was organized to fulfil the social requirements which determined eating habits.

References in documents . . . reveal the universal acceptance of bread as a basic foodstuff, even in the least civilized regions of the Christian world. . . . Indeed, all the documents indicate that peas, vetches, beans — the leguminous plants — together with "herbs" and "roots," the ancestors of our garden vegetables (the hermits were praised for restricting their diet to these) and of course meat, a most desirable item of consumption from which the clergy ostentatiously abstained, comprised only the *companaticum,* the accompaniment to bread. It was the latter that was the mainstay of existence.

It is reasonably clear that bread was not baked solely from wheat, rye or spelt, but also from other, lesser, cereals, such as barley and even oats, which [were] eaten as much by humans as by animals. What is less easy to distinguish is in what measure these food grains were consumed in the form of porridge . . . or brewed into ale, the commonest beverage throughout north-western Europe. Ale had often the consistency of thick soup and so could be counted perhaps more

---

[3] House sites and their adjacent arable lands.

as a food than a drink. Eleventh-century peasants had to grow cereals even when climatic conditions were not favourable. As arable fields had to be laid out around the villages, the least exposed and most easily worked sites had to be cleared for the purpose, in close proximity to habitations and in the midst of woods and pastures.

Here and there, in places where the climate allowed grapes to ripen, a few vines were planted for the masters on the most suitable and permanently enclosed plots. Meadows were confined to damper ground, and the hay, together with the grass and rushes which could be gathered in the marshes, provided winter fodder for the cattle. Nevertheless neither vines nor meadows covered more than a very limited part of the cultivated area since the cereal crop was the really important one, and almost the whole of the area given over to agricultural activity was reserved for its culture. These fields had also to be protected against the depredations of animals, both domestic and wild. They can thus be visualized as separated from the uncultivated lands, which were open to pasture, by enclosures which in the country of the Franks seemed generally to have been temporary. In spring as soon as the new grass began to push up and the corn to sprout these mobile barriers made of wooden stakes . . . were erected and signs were put up forbidding shepherds to let their animals stray there. For a season therefore these strips seemed, like the cultivated "tofts" of the village, to be the territory of individual owners. But after the harvest, signs and fences were removed, and the strips returned for a time to pastoral use, and were reincorporated into the larger areas where access to animals was free. To a greater or lesser extent then, according to the quantity of bread men were used to eating, the arable appeared as a limited and temporary extension of the cultivated "toft" area and thus private property, at the expense of the wild area which was left to collective use.

Can we ever hope, even in the best documented regions, to plot the portion of village lands occupied by the arable fields? . . . What we know now suggests that this area was small everywhere and that a large space was being left to natural vegetation, the forest and pasture, whose presence "had helped to form this combination of agriculture and animal husbandry which was the principal feature" of rural economy in the west. . . . This union indeed appears constant and fundamental throughout the Middle Ages. What we might describe as three concentric zones formed the picture . . . — the village enclosures, the *coûtures,* that is the arable, and finally surrounding all, a broad uncultivated belt. These were the three zones in which the effects of man's labour became less and less visible as the distance from the inhabited centre grew greater, but which were of equal importance to him as a means of subsistence.

Village communities thus found themselves hemmed in with no way of absorbing the increase in their birth rate. Periodic waves of mortality, such as those caused by military activity and, increasingly in the second half of the ninth and in the tenth centuries, raids of invaders, rather than any systematic clearing of the wastes and the resulting hiving off of colonists, relieved demographic pressure at intervals. Such a situation suggests a peasantry poorly equipped with efficient tools and incapable for this reason of taming the encircling wilderness.

Was the undoubted technical progress to which the diffusion of the water mill bears witness accompanied in Europe of the ninth and tenth centuries by the spread of ploughs with wheeled foreparts, by improvements in harness, and by the adoption of a more efficient ploughshare? This important problem of technique cannot be resolved, but it is reasonable to assume that even in the most favoured sectors of rural life, those of the great farming complexes described by inventories, men used feeble wooden implements. They found themselves ill-equipped to come to grips with nature and worked with their bare hands for a great part of the time. The primitive technical equipment obviously restricted narrowly the individual's productive capacity. And this observation agrees completely with the impression gained from land settlement. Villages teemed with people whose efforts were needed to work the soil on the home fields, but they were situated in clearings separated by stretches of wild country because agricultural tools were not robust enough to overcome the obstacles of heavy, wet and thickly wooded land. Areas of natural vegetation adjoining the villages were of course actually necessary because the cultivation of cereals was so demanding of manpower that each rural community had to supplement its means of livelihood by making the most of the products of the wastelands — animal husbandry, hunting and foodgathering.

These limited portions of the village lands suitable for grain growing and therefore providing the village's main food supply . . . , or "furlongs" to use the English term, were not given over wholly to food production every year. Unlike the cultivated "tofts" whose soil, manured by the household waste and stable dung, could be cultivated without interruption, the fields demanded a periodic rest if fertility was not to be lost. Every spring a section of the arable was not sown; it remained open, unenclosed, available for pasture, in the same way as the wild area of wastes and commons. For an understanding of the productivity of the land and the manner in which it was able to support human life, we need to know the rhythm of the resting periods. What was the place of the fallow and what the place of spring-sown corn, oats and leguminous crops? How much land was devoted to autumn-sown corn, that is the bread grains — wheat, rye and spelt (the most widely grown grain in the Rhineland and north-west France), and lastly barley, which was in those days often a winter-sown crop? . . .

1. The description of harvest and sowing and, more often, that of dues in the form of grain exacted from peasant tenants proved that the fields of peasants as well as lords very frequently produced spring as well as winter corn and especially oats.
2. The arrangement of the ploughing services exacted from manorial dependants in the agricultural calendar shows that the cycle of ploughing was often divided into two sowing "seasons," one in the winter . . . , and the other in the summer or the spring. . . .
3. Ploughing units on the great properties appear often in groups of three. . . . This arrangement leads us to think that cultivation was organized on a ternary rhythm. . . . By this arrangement, a third portion was prepared in May by a

preliminary ploughing, and was turned over again by the plough in November before sowing; the following year after harvest the same fields were left throughout autumn and winter for the animals to graze on, and were then ploughed in Lent and sown with spring grain, after which they rested for a year. Thus at least a third of the agricultural area produced nothing, while another third produced bread grains and the last third the ingredients of porridge and soup.

I do not consider, however, that these indications are sufficient for us to conclude without further consideration that a regular three-year rotation was general, or even widespread. What argues against any such conclusion is that none of our examples is in southern Europe where climatic conditions, and above all early spring droughts, made March sowings somewhat hazardous, and also that our documents describe none but the great monastic or royal farms which were run in an unusually rational and even scientific manner. . . .

. . . It is therefore safest to conjecture that there was considerable variation in the crop rotation in use. Man was forced to bow to the natural capacity of the soil because he was poorly prepared to alter it. We can imagine an infinite variety of systems in use ranging all the way from the strict three-course rotation to temporary cultivation based on burning where bits and pieces of land on the outer fringes of the village enclave would be tilled after the undergrowth had been burned, and continued to be cropped for years until fertility was exhausted. It is also probable that oats and other spring grains were often a supplementary crop taken from the fallow, and that such a system, even when the regular ploughings in winter and early spring . . . were adhered to, frequently lasted more than one year on the largest part of the available arable. It must be added that seed corn was sown very thinly. . . . The agricultural practice of those early days demanded not only plentiful manpower, but wide open spaces.

The insistent demands for long fallow periods, and the need to scatter the seed thinly arose at least partly because of mediocre ploughing implements which could not turn the ground over properly, but they were also due to the virtual absence of manure. It is true that animal husbandry was always complementary to agriculture and the draught oxen whose task was to plough the fields could also fertilize them with their dung. In reality the combination of arable with pasture was not close enough to enable animal manure to make much impression. Men who were so inadequately equipped with tools were forced to devote all their energies to producing their own food, and cattle had to take second place. A little fodder was harvested, but barely enough to keep those few beasts which had not been slaughtered in the autumn alive during the lean winter months when nature's offerings failed. But for the rest of the year the herds grazed alone in the open air on the land which was not enclosed. They must also have ranged over the fallow fields and in doing so deposited their manure on them; but the deposit was quite insufficient to maintain fertility. Scarce fodder meant restricted periods of stall-feeding, and the limited quantities of stable manure thus available were almost wholly devoured by the cultivated "tofts" in the inner fertile belt of the village territory. No wonder areas of fallow had to be huge. And we can appreciate afresh the need of each family to dispose of as large a space for subsistence as possible which had to cover, besides pasture, an arable area much more extensive than the portion actually in use each year. Even so, despite the long resting periods, output remained extremely low.

. . . These elusive details allow at any rate one firm conclusion. Carried out with rudimentary equipment and in a generally unfavourable climate, the cultivation of cereal crops was at the mercy of the caprices of the weather. Even on the best equipped farms an excessively wet spring or summer could render the heavy toil in the fields totally unproductive. Despite an enormous expenditure of manpower and the disproportionate size of the village lands country folk could be racked with hunger. Obviously their main preoccupation was to survive through spring and early summer, that period of backbreaking toil. When the scraps of food remaining to them after the demands of their masters had been exhausted, the yearly nightmare of hand-to-mouth existence began, and the pangs of hunger had to be stilled by devouring garden herbs and forest berries and by begging bread at the gates of the rich. At such moments the threat of starvation overshadowed the whole village world.

MEDIEVAL CHILDREN
David Herlihy

David Herlihy (1930–1991) was an eminent medieval historian who specialized in the history of the family and of women. In this survey, he emphasizes the complexity of the subject of children in the Middle Ages. Adequate documentation is a problem. Children did not write about themselves, and adults usually did not specifically detail their attitudes and behavior toward children. Herlihy thus had to consult many different types of source materials, including literary works, art, theological writings, pedagogical literature, monastic rules, correspondence, diaries, and contemporary histories and chronicles. The sources available about medieval children can lead the historian to quite opposite conclusions — the people of the Middle Ages either maltreated offspring or took pleasure in their spirituality and goodness. Which conclusion does Herlihy adopt? How does the evidence support his interpretation?

What explains the different treatment of children in classical, Germanic, and medieval cultures? Instead of looking within the family for the causes of these differences, Herlihy usually points to external influences, such as Christianity and socioeconomic developments. Christian theologians disagreed on the basic nature of children, stressing their ties to original sin or their holy innocence. In the eleventh and twelfth centuries, increasing commercialization and urbanization led to a new concern for children, one that was both practical and psychological. The establishment of schools and orphanages also suggests that children received more attention and care. Educators of this era, both religious and lay, worried about children's schooling, health, and spiritual well-being. To what extent do you think medieval children led happy and satisfying lives, free from fear of parental neglect or brutality?

Many, perhaps most, children in most traditional societies did no more than come and go. And most never acquired, or were given, a voice which might have recorded and preserved their impressions concerning themselves, their parents,

David Herlihy, "Medieval Children," in *Essays on Medieval Civilization,* ed. Bede Karl Lackner and Kenneth Roy Philip (Austin: University of Texas Press, 1978), 109–130.

and the world they had recently discovered. Of all social groups which formed the societies of the past, children, seldom seen and rarely heard in the documents, remain for historians the most elusive, the most obscure.

The difficulties of interviewing the mute have doubtlessly obstructed and delayed a systematic investigation of the history of childhood. But today, at least, historians are aware of the commonplace assumption of psychologists, that childhood plays a critical role in the formation of the adult personality. Perhaps they are awakening to an even older wisdom, the recognition that society, in the way it rears its children, shapes itself. . . .

Today, the literature devoted to the history of children in various places and epochs may be described, rather like children themselves, as small but growing daily. It remains, however, difficult to discern within that literature a clear consensus, an acceptable hypothesis, concerning the broad trends of children's history, even within Western societies. To be sure, there is frequent allusion within these recent publications to a particular interpretation which, for want of a better name, we shall call the "theory of discovered childhood." The principal formulator of this interpretation, at least in its most recent form, has been the French social historian Philippe Ariès. In a book published in 1960, called in its English translation *Centuries of Childhood,* Ariès entitled the second chapter "the discovery of childhood." In it he affirmed that the Middle Ages of Western history did not recognize childhood as a distinct phase in life. Medieval people allegedly viewed and treated their children as imperfectly formed adults. Once the infant was weaned, medieval parents supposedly made no concessions to its special and changing psychological needs and took little satisfaction in the distinctive traits of the young personality. The corollary to this assumption is that, at some point in the development of Western society and civilization, the young years of life were at last discovered: childhood needed a Columbus.

Proclamations of the alleged discovery of childhood have become commonplace in the growing literature, but wide differences in interpretation still separate the authors. When, for example, was childhood first recognized? On this important question, Ariès himself is indefinite, even evasive, and seems to place the discovery over three or four hundred years, from the fifteenth to the eighteenth centuries. . . .

If historians of the modern world do not agree concerning the date of childhood's discovery, their colleagues, working in more remote periods, show signs of restiveness with Ariès' postulate, that medieval people did not distinguish children from adults. A number of scholars . . . have noted among the pedagogues, humanists, and even artists of fifteenth-century Italy a new orientation toward children, a new awareness of their problems, and an appreciation of their qualities. The fat and frolicksome babies, the *putti,* who cavort through many solemn paintings of the Italian Renaissance, leave little doubt that the artists of the epoch knew how to depict, and they or their patrons liked to contemplate, children. A still more radical departure from Ariès' views was proposed, in 1968, by the French medievalist Pierre Riché. Riché accepted Ariès' phrase, the "discovery of childhood," but radically changed his chronology. The initial explorers of childhood were, for Riché, the monastic pedagogues active in Western Europe between the sixth and eighth centuries. Their sensitivity toward the psychology of children allegedly transformed the harsh educational methods of classical antiquity and developed a new pedagogy which was finely attuned to the personality of the child-monk. Thus, over an extended period of time, from the early Middle Ages until the present, one or another author would have us believe that a consciousness of childhood was at last emerging.

The lessons that I would draw from this confusion of learned opinions are the following. Historians would be well advised to avoid such categoric and dubious claims, that people in certain periods failed to distinguish children from adults, that childhood really did lie beyond the pale of collective consciousness. Attitudes toward children have certainly shifted, as has the willingness on the part of society to invest substantially in their welfare or education. But to describe these changes, we need terms more refined than metaphors of ignorance and discovery. I would propose that we seek to evaluate, and on occasion even to measure, the psychological and economic investment which families and societies in the past were willing to make in their children. However, we ought also to recognize that alternative and even competitive sets of child-related values can coexist in the same society, perhaps even in the same household. Different social groups and classes expect different things from their children; so do different epochs, in accordance with prevailing economic, social, and demographic conditions. In examining the ways in which children were regarded and reared in the past, we should not expect either rigorous consistency across society or lineal progress over time.

In the current, lively efforts to reconstruct the history of children in Western civilization, the long period of the Middle Ages has a special importance. The medieval child represents a kind of primordial form, an "eo-pais," a "dawn child" as it were, against whom Western children of subsequent epochs must be measured if we are to appreciate the changes they have experienced. To be sure, the difficulties of observing medieval children cannot be discounted. Medieval documentation is usually sparse, often inconsistent, and always difficult. . . . We can hope to catch only fleeting glimpses of medieval children in their rush through, or out of, life. On the other hand, even glimpses may be enough to dispel some large misconceptions concerning medieval children and to aid us toward a sound reconstruction of the history of children in the Western world.

In surveying medieval children, it is first necessary to consider the two prior traditions which largely shaped the medieval appraisal of the very young — the classical and the barbarian. It is important also to reflect upon the influence exerted upon child rearing by a special component of the ancient Mediterranean heritage: the Christian church.

Classical society, or at least the elites within it, cultivated an impressive array of intellectual traditions, which were founded upon literacy and preserved over time through intensive, and expensive, educational methods. Classical civilization would be inconceivable in the absence of professional teachers, formal instruction, and numerous schools and academies. But as social historians of antiquity now emphasize, the resources that supported ancient society were in truth scant. "The classical Mediterranean has always been a world on the edge of starvation," one historian has recently written, with much justice if perhaps some exaggeration. Scarce resources and the high costs of rearing children helped form certain distinctive policies regarding the young. The nations which comprised the Roman Empire, with the exception only of the Jews, refused to support deformed, unpromising, or supernumerary babies. In Roman practice, for example, the newborn baby was at once laid before the feet of him who held the *patria potestas*[1] over it, usually the natural father. Through a ritual gesture called *susceptio*, the holder of paternal authority might raise up the infant and receive it into his family and household. But he could also reject the baby and order its exposure. Infanticide, or the exposure of infants, was a common and accepted social practice in classical society, shocking perhaps to modern sensibilities but rational for these ancient peoples who were seeking to achieve goals with limited means.

Here however is a paradox. Widespread infanticide in ancient society does not imply disinterest in or neglect of those children elected for survival. On the contrary, to assure a good return on the precious means invested in them, they were subject to close and often cruel attention and to frequent beatings. St. Augustine[2] in his *Confessions* tells how his father, Patricius, and even his pious mother, Monica, urged him to high performance at school, "that I might get on in the world and excel in the handling of words, to gain honor among men and deceitful riches." "If I proved idle in learning," he says of his teachers, "I was soundly beaten. For this procedure seemed wise to our ancestors; and many, passing the same way in the days past, had built a sorrowful road, by which we too must go, with multiplication of grief and toil upon the sons of Adam." The memories which the men of antiquity preserved of their childhood were understandably bleak. "Who would not shudder," Augustine exclaims in the *City of God,* "if he were given the choice of eternal death or life again as a child? Who would not choose to die?"

The barbarian child grew up under quite different circumstances. Moreover, barbarian practices of child rearing seem to have been particularly influential in the society of early medieval Europe, between the fifth and eleventh centuries. This is not surprising. Early in the Middle Ages, the cities which had dominated society and culture in antiquity lost importance, the literate social elites of classical society all but disappeared, and their educational institutions and ideals went down amid the debacle of the Western empire. On the other hand, barbarian practices were easily preserved within, and congenial to, the semibarbarized society of the early medieval West.

In a tract called *Germania,* written in A.D. 98, the Roman historian Tacitus has described for us the customs of the barbarian Germans, including their treatment of children. Tacitus, to be sure, likes to contrast barbarian virtues with

---

[1] Paternal authority.

[2] Christian theologian (354–430) and Bishop of Hippo in North Africa.

Roman vices and doubtlessly exaggerates in his depictions of both, but his words are nonetheless worth our attention. The Germans, he claims, did not, like the Romans, kill their supernumerary children. Rather, the barbarians rejoiced in a numerous progeny. Moreover, the barbarian mother, unlike her Roman counterpart, nursed her own baby and did not hand it over for feeding to servants or a hired nurse. On the other hand, Tacitus notes, the barbarian parents paid little attention to their growing children. "In every household," he writes, "the children grow up naked and unkempt. . . . " "The lord and slave," he continues, "are in no way to be distinguished by the delicacy of their bringing up. They live among the same flocks, they lie on the same ground. . . . " Barbarian culture did not depend for its survival on the costly instruction of the young in complex skills and learned traditions; barbarian parents had no need to invest heavily in their children, either psychologically or materially. The cheap costs of child rearing precluded the adoption of infanticide as standard social policy but also reduced the attention which the growing child received from its parents. Only on the threshold of adulthood did the free German male re-establish close contacts with adult society. He typically joined the following of a mature warrior, accompanied him into battle, observed him, and gained some instruction in the arts of war, which, like the arts of rhetoric in the classical world, were the key to his social advance.

A casual attitude toward children seems embodied in the laws of the barbarian peoples — Franks, Lombards, Visigoths, Anglo-Saxons, and others — which were redacted into Latin largely between the sixth and the ninth centuries. The barbarian laws typically assigned to each member of society a sum of money — a fine, or wergeld — which would have to be paid to the relatives if he or she was injured or killed. The size of the wergeld thus provides a crude measure of social status or importance. One of the barbarian codes, the Visigothic, dating from the middle seventh century, gives a particularly detailed and instructive table of values which shows how the worth of a person varied according to age, sex, and status. A free male baby, in the first year of life, was assigned a wergeld of 60 solidi. Between age 1 and age 9, his social worth increased at an average rate of only 3.75 solidi per year, thus attaining the value of 90 solidi in the tenth year of life. Between ages 10 and 15, the rate of increase accelerated to 10 solidi per year; and between ages 15 and 20 it grew still more, to 30 solidi per year. In other words, the social worth of the free Visigothic male increased very slowly in the early years of childhood, accelerated in early adolescence, and grew most substantially in the years preceding full maturity. Considered mature at age 20, he enjoyed a wergeld of 300 solidi — five times the worth of the newborn male infant — and this he retained until age 50. In old age, his social worth declined, to 200 solidi between ages 50 and 65 and to 100 solidi from age 65 to death. The old man, beyond age 65, was worth the same as a child of ten years.

The contrast between the worth of the child and the worth of the adult is particularly striking in regard to women. Among the Visigoths, a female under age 15 was assigned only one-half the wergeld enjoyed by males — only 30 solidi during her first year of life. Her social worth, however, increased enormously when she entered the years of childbearing, between ages 15 and 40 in the Visigothic codes. Her wergeld then leaped to 250 solidi, nearly equal to the 300 solidi assigned to the male and eight times the value of the newborn baby girl. The sterile years of old age brought a reduction of the fine, first to 200 solidi, which she retained to age 60, and then to 100 solidi. In old age, she was assigned the same worth as the male. . . .

The low values assigned to children in these barbarian codes is puzzling. Did the lawgivers not realize that the supply of adults, including the especially valued childbearing women, was critically dependent on the protection of children? This obvious truth seemingly escaped the notice of the barbarian lawgivers; children, and their relation to society, did not loom large in their consciousness.

Apart from laws, one other source offers some insight into the treatment of children in the early Middle Ages: surveys of the population settled on particular estates and manors. These sporadic surveys have survived from the Carolingian period of medieval history, the late eighth and ninth centuries. The largest of them, redacted in the first quarter of the ninth century, lists nearly 2,000 families settled on the lands of the abbey of Saint-Germain-des-Prés near Paris. The survey gives no exact ages, but of 8,457 persons included in it, 3,327 are explicitly identified as *infantes,* or children. . . .

The proportion of known children within the population is very low — only 85 children for every 100 adults. Even if all those of uncertain age are considered *infantes,* the ratio then becomes 116 children for every 100 adults. This peasant population was either singularly barren or it was not bothering to report all its children. Moreover, the sexual composition of the population across these age categories is perplexing. Among the known adults, men and women appear in nearly equal numbers. But among the known children, there are 143 boys for every 100 girls — a male-to-female ratio of nearly three to two. Among those of uncertain age, the sex ratio is even higher. The high sex ratio among the known children may indicate widespread female infanticide, but if this were so, we should expect to find a similarly skewed ratio among the known adults. The death of numerous baby girls inevitably would affect over time the proportions of adult women in this presumably closed population. But the proportions of males and females among the known adults are reasonably balanced. The more likely explanation is that the monastic surveyors, or the peasants who reported to them, were negligent in counting children and were particularly deficient in reporting the presence of little girls in the households. As the barbarian legal codes suggest, children, and especially girls, became of substantial interest to society, and presumably to their families, only as they aged.

The low monetary worth assigned to the very young, and the shadowy presence of children in the statistical documents of the early Middle Ages, should not, however, imply that parents did not love their children. Tacitus notes that the barbarian mother usually nursed her own babies. Kinship ties were strongly emphasized in barbarian society, and these were surely cemented by affection. The German epic fragment the *Song of Hildebrand* takes as its principal theme the love which should unite father and son. The warrior Hildebrand flees into exile to live among the Huns, leaving "a babe at the breast in the bower of the bride." Then, after sixty years of wandering, he confronts his son as his enemy on the field of battle. He recognizes his offspring and tries to avoid combat; he offers the young warrior gold and, as the poet tells us, his love besides. . . . If classical methods of child rearing can be called cruel but closely attentive, the barbarian child grew up within an atmosphere of affectionate neglect.

The Christian church also powerfully influenced the treatment of children in many complex ways. Christianity, like Judaism before it, unequivocally condemned infanticide or the exposure of infants. To be sure, infanticide and exposure remained common social practices in Western Europe across the entire length of the Middle Ages. Church councils, penitentials, sermons, and secular legal codes yield abundant and repeated references to those crimes. As late as the fifteenth century, if we are to believe the great popular preachers of the period, the streams and cesspools of Europe echoed with the cries of abandoned babies. But medieval infanticide still shows one great difference from the comparable practice in the ancient world. Our sources consistently attribute the practice to two motivations: the shame of seduced and abandoned women, who wished to conceal illegitimate births, and poverty — the inability of the mother, and often of both parents, to support an additional mouth. The killing or abandonment of babies in medieval society was the characteristic resort of the fallen, the poor, the desperate. In the ancient world, infanticide had been accepted practice, even among the social elites.

Christian teachings also informed and softened attitudes toward children. Christian scriptures held out several examples of children who enjoyed or earned God's special favor: in the Old Testament, the young Samuel and the young Daniel; in the New, the Holy Innocents and the Christ child himself. According to the evangelists, Jesus himself welcomed the company of children, and he instructed his disciples in the famous words: "Unless you become as little children, you will never enter the Kingdom of Heaven."

This partiality toward children evoked many echoes among patristic[3] and medieval writers. In a poem attributed to St. Clement of Alexandria,[4] Christ is called the "king of children." Pope Leo the Great[5] writes . . . "Christ loves childhood, for it is the teacher of humility, the rule of innocence, the model of sweetness." . . .

A favorable appraisal of childhood is also apparent in the monastic culture of the early Middle Ages. Western monasteries, from the sixth century, accepted as oblates to the monastic life children who were hardly more than toddlers, and the leaders of the monastic movement gave much attention to the proper methods of

---

[3] Referring to the fathers, or theologians, of the early Christian Church.

[4] Greek Christian theologian (ca. 150–ca. 215).

[5] Pope from 440 to 461.

rearing and instructing these miniature monks. In his famous rule, St. Benedict of Nursia[6] insisted that the advice of the children be sought in important matters, "for often the Lord reveals to the young what should be done." St. Columban[7] in the seventh century, and the Venerable Bede[8] in the eighth, praised four qualities of the monastic child: he does not persist in anger; he does not bear a grudge; he takes no delight in the beauty of women; and he expresses what he truly believes.

But alongside this positive assessment of the very young, Christian tradition supported a much harsher appraisal of the nature of the child. In Christian belief, the dire results of Adam's fall were visited upon all his descendants. All persons, when they entered the world, bore the stain of original sin and with it concupiscence, an irrepressible appetite for evil. Moreover, if God had predestined some persons to salvation and some to damnation, his judgments touched even the very young, even those who died before they knew their eternal options. The father of the Church who most forcefully and effectively explored the implications of predestination for children was again St. Augustine. Voluminous in his writings, clear in his logic, and ruthless in his conclusions, Augustine finally decided, after some early doubts, that the baby who died without baptism was damned to eternal fires. There were heaven and hell and no place in-between. "If you admit that the little one cannot enter heaven," he argued, "then you concede that he will be in everlasting fire."

This cruel judgment of the great African theologian contrasts with the milder views of the Eastern fathers, who affirmed that unbaptized children suffer only the loss of the vision of God. The behavior of Augustine's God seems to mimic the posture of the Roman paterfamilias, who was similarly arbitrary and ruthless in the judgment of his own babies, who elected some for life and cast out others into the exterior darkness. And no one in his family dared question his decisions. . . .

Augustine was, moreover, impressed by the early dominion which evil establishes over the growing child. The suckling infant cries unreasonably for nourishment, wails and throws tantrums, and strikes with feeble but malicious blows those who care for him. "The innocence of children," Augustine concludes, "is in the helplessness of their bodies, rather than any quality of soul." . . .

The suppression of concupiscence thus becomes a central goal of Augustine's educational philosophy and justifies hard and frequent punishments inflicted on the child. While rejecting the values of pagan antiquity, he adheres to the classical methods of education. Augustine prepared the way for retaining under Christian auspices that "sorrowful road" of schooling which he, as a child at school, had so much hated.

---

[6] Italian monk (ca. 480–ca. 547) and founder of Western monasticism.

[7] Irish monk and missionary (ca. 543–615).

[8] English monk, historian, and saint (ca. 673–735).

Medieval society thus inherited and sustained a mix of sometimes inconsistent attitudes toward children. The social historian, by playing upon one or another of these attitudes, by judiciously screening his sources, could easily color as he pleases the history of medieval children. He could compile a list of the atrocities committed against them, dwell upon their neglect, or celebrate medieval views of the child's innocence and holiness. One must, however, strive to paint a more balanced picture, and for this we obviously need some means of testing the experiences of the medieval child. The tests we shall use here are two: the social investment, the wealth and resources which medieval society was apparently willing to invest in children; and the psychological investment, the attention they claimed and received from their elders. The thesis of this essay, simply stated, is that both the social and psychological investments in children were growing substantially from approximately the eleventh and twelfth centuries, through to the end of the Middle Ages, and doubtlessly beyond.

The basic economic and social changes which affected medieval society during this period seem to have required a heightened investment in children. From about the year 1000, the medieval community was growing in numbers and complexity. Commercial exchange intensified, and a vigorous urban life was reborn in the West. Even the shocking reduction in population size, coming with the plagues, famines, and wars of the fourteenth century, did not undo the importance of the commercial economy or of the towns and the urban classes dependent upon it. Medieval society, once a simple association of warriors, priests, and peasants, came to include such numerous and varied social types as merchants, lawyers, notaries, accountants, clerks, and artisans. A new world was born, based on the cultivation and preservation of specialized, sophisticated skills.

The emergence of specialized roles within society required in turn a social commitment to the training of children in the corresponding skills. Earlier educational reforms — notably those achieved under Charlemagne[9] — had largely affected monks and, in less measure, clerics; they had little impact on the lay world. One novelty of the new medieval pedagogy, as it is developed from the twelfth century, is the attention now given to the training of laymen. Many writers now comment on the need and value of mastering a trade from early youth. Boys . . . should be taught a trade "as soon as possible." . . . "Men from childhood," Thomas Aquinas[10] observes, "apply themselves to those offices and skills in which they will spend their lives. . . . This is altogether necessary. To the extent that something is difficult, so much the more must a man grow accustomed to it from childhood."

Later in the thirteenth century, Raymond Lull,[11] one of the most learned men of the epoch, compares society to a wheel upon which men ride ceaselessly, up and down, gaining and losing status; the force which drives the wheel is educa-

---

[9] Carolingian emperor from 768 to 814.

[10] Saint and theologian (ca. 1225–1274).

[11] Missionary and philosopher (ca. 1223–ca. 1315).

tion, in particular the mastery of a marketable skill. Through the exercise of a trade, a man earns money, gains status, and ultimately enters the ranks of the rich. Frequently, however, he becomes arrogant in his new status, and he neglects to train his children in a trade. His unskilled offspring inevitably ride the wheel on its downward swing. And so the world turns. A marketable skill offers the only certain riches and the only security. . . .

One hundred and fifty years later, the Florentine Dominican Giovanni Dominici voices exactly the same sentiments. Neither wealth nor inherited status offers security. Only a marketable skill can assure that children "will not be forced, as are many, to beg, to steal, to enter household service, or to do demeaning things." . . .

Although statistics largely elude us, there can be little doubt that medieval society was making substantial investments in education from the twelfth century. . . . The chronicler Giovanni Villani[12] gives us some rare figures on the schools functioning at Florence in the 1330s. The children, both boys and girls, who were attending the grammar schools of the city, presumably between 6 and 12 years of age, numbered between eight and ten thousand. From what we know of the population of the city, better than one out of two school-aged children were receiving formal instruction in reading. Florentine girls received no more formal instruction after grammar school, but of the boys, between 1,000 and 1,200 went on to six secondary schools, where they learned how to calculate on the abacus, in evident preparation for a business career. Another 550 to 600 attended four "large schools" where they studied "Latin and logic," the necessary preparation for entry into the universities and, eventually, for a career in law, medicine, or the Church. Florence, it might be argued, was hardly a typical medieval community. Still, the social investment that Florentines were making in the training of their children was substantial.

Another indicator of social investment in children is the number of orphanages or hospitals devoted to their care, and here the change across the Middle Ages is particularly impressive. The care of the abandoned or orphaned child was a traditional obligation of Christian charity, but it did not lead to the foundation and support of specialized orphanages until late in the Middle Ages. The oldest European orphanage of which we have notice was founded at Milan in 787, but we know nothing at all concerning its subsequent history or that of other orphanages sporadically mentioned in the early sources. The great hospital orders of the medieval Church, which sprang up from the twelfth century, cared for orphans and foundlings, but none initially chose that charity as its special mission.

The history of hospitals in the city of Florence gives striking illustration of a new concern for abandoned babies which emerged in Europe during the last two centuries of the Middle Ages. In his detailed description of his native city, written in the 1330s, Villani boasts that Florence contained thirty hospitals with more

---

[12] Florentine (d. 1348).

than a thousand beds. But the beds were intended for the "poor and infrm," and he mentions no special hospital for foundlings. A century later, probably in the 1420s, another chronicler, Gregorio Dati,[13] . . . composed another description of the marvels of Florence. By then the city contained no fewer than three hospitals which received foundlings and supported them until an age when the girls could marry and the boys could be instructed in a trade. . . .

Even a rapid survey of the foundling hospitals of Europe shows a similar pattern. Bologna seems not to have had an orphanage until 1459, and Pavia not until 1449. At Paris, the first specialized hospital for children, Saint-Esprit en Grèves, was founded in 1363, but according to its charter it was supposed to receive only orphans of legitimate birth. Care of foundlings, it was feared, might encourage sexual license among adults. But the hospital in practice seems to have accepted abandoned babies, and several similar institutions were established in French cities in the fifteenth century.

This new concern for the survival of children, even foundlings, seems readily explicable. Amid the ravages of epidemics, the sheer numbers of orphans must have multiplied in society. Moreover, the plagues carried off the very young in disproportionate numbers. Parents feared for the survival of their lineages and their communities. . . . The frequent creation of foundling hospitals and orphanages indicates that society as a whole shared this concern and was willing to invest in the survival of its young, even orphans and foundlings.

The medieval social investment in children thus seems to have grown from the twelfth century and to have passed through two phases: the first one, beginning from the twelfth century, largely involved a commitment, on the part of the urban communities, to the child's education and training; the second, from the late fourteenth century, reflected a concern for the child's survival and health under difficult hygienic conditions.

This social investment also presumes an equivalent psychological investment, as well as a heightened attention paid to the child and his development. This is evident, for example, in the rich tradition of pedagogical literature intended for a lay audience, which again dates from the twelfth century. One of the earliest authors to provide a comprehensive regimen of child care was Vincent of Beauvais, who died in 1264. . . . [H]e gives advice on the delivery of the baby; its care in the first hours, days, and months of life; nursing and weaning; the care of older children; and their formal education. Later in the century, Raymond Lull . . . is similarly comprehensive, including passages not only on formal schooling but also on the care and nourishment of the child. "For every man," he explains, "must hold his child dear." . . . The learning of the scholars seems to have spread widely, even among the humble social classes.

These medieval pedagogues also developed a rudimentary but real psychology of children. Vincent of Beauvais recommends that the child who does not

---

[13] Florentine writer, businessman, and statesman (1362–1435).

readily learn must be beaten, but he warns against the psychological damage which excessive severity may cause. "Children's minds," he explains, "break down under excessive severity of correction; they despair, and worry, and finally they hate. And this is the most injurious; where everything is feared, nothing is attempted." A few teachers . . . wanted to prohibit all corporal punishment at school. For them physical discipline was "contrary to nature"; it "induced servility and sowed resentment, which in later years might make the student hate the teacher and forget his lesson."

The teacher — and on this all writers agree — should be temperate in the use of force, and he should also observe the child, in order to identify his talents and capacities. For not all children are alike, and natural differences must be recognized and developed. Raymond Lull affirms that nature is more capable of rearing the child than the child's mother. The Florentine Giovanni Dominici stresses the necessity of choosing the proper profession for the child. Society, he notes, requires all sorts of occupations and skills, ranging from farmers to carpenters, to bankers, merchants, priests, and "a thousand others." . . .

To read these writers is inevitably to form the impression that medieval people, or some of them at least, were deeply concerned about children. Indeed, Jean Gerson[14] expressly condemns his contemporaries, who, in his opinion, were excessively involved with their children's survival and success. In order to gain for them "the honors and pomp of this world," parents, he alleges, were expending "all their care and attention; they sleep neither day nor night and often become very miserly." In investing in their children, they neglected charitable works and the good of their own souls. . . .

Medieval society, increasingly dependent upon the cultivation of sophisticated skills, had to invest in a supporting pedagogy; when later threatened by child-killing plagues, it had to show concern for the survival of the very young. But the medieval involvement with children cannot be totally described in these functional terms. Even as they were developing an effective pedagogy, medieval people were re-evaluating the place of childhood among the periods of life.

One indication of a new sympathy toward childhood is the revision in theological opinion concerning the salvation of the babies who died without baptism. Up until the twelfth century, the leading theologians of the Western church . . . reiterated the weighty opinion of St. Augustine, that such infants were surely damned. In the twelfth century, Peter Abelard and Peter Lombard, perhaps the two most influential theologians of the epoch, reversed the condemnation of unbaptized babies to eternal fires. A thorough examination of the question, however, awaited the work of Thomas Aquinas, the first to use in a technical theological sense the term *limbus puerorum*, the "limbo of children." The unbaptized baby, he taught, suffered only the deprivation of the Beatific Vision.[15] . . .

---

[14] French theologian (1363–1429).

[15] The immediate vision of god in heaven.

Aquinas' mild judgment on babies dead without baptism became the accepted teaching of the medieval Church. Only one prominent theologian in the late Middle Ages, Gregory of Rimini,[16] resisted it, and he came to be known as the *tortor puerorum,* the "torturer of children."

No less remarkable is the emergence, from the twelfth century, of a widespread devotion to the Child Jesus. The texts from the early Middle Ages which treat of the Christ Child . . . present Christ as a miniature wonder worker, who miraculously corrects Joseph's mistakes in carpentry, tames lions, divides rivers, and even strikes dead a teacher who dared reprimand him in class. All-knowing and all-powerful, he is the negation of the helpless, charming child. A new picture of the Child Jesus emerges, initially under Cistercian auspices, in the twelfth century. For example, between 1153 and 1157 the English Cistercian Aelred of Rievaulx composed a meditation, "Jesus at the Age of Twelve." Aelred expatriates on the joy which the presence of the young Christ brought to his elders and companions: " . . . the grace of heaven shone from that most beautiful face with such charm as to make everyone look at it, listen to him, and be moved to affection. . . . Old men kiss him, young men embrace him, boys wait upon him. . . . Each of them, I think, declares in his inmost heart: 'Let him kiss me with the kiss of his mouth.'" . . .

Doubtlessly, the special characteristics of Cistercian monasticism were influential here. Like other reformed orders of the twelfth century, the Cistercians no longer admitted oblates, the boys placed in the monastery at tender ages, who grew up in the cloister with no experience of secular life. The typical Cistercians . . . were raised within a natural family, and many were familiar with the emotions of family life. Grown men when they entered the monastery, they carried with them a distinct mentality — a mentality formed in the secular world and open to secular values. Many doubtlessly had considered and some had pursued other careers before electing the monastic life; they presumably had reflected upon the emotional and spiritual rewards of the married state and the state of parenthood. While fleeing from the world, they still sought in their religious experiences analogues to secular and familial emotions. . . . In celebrating the joys of contemplating a perfect child, they find in their religious experience an analogue to the love and satisfaction which parents feel in observing their growing children. The Cistercian cult of the Child Jesus suggests, in other words, that lay persons, too, were finding the contemplation of children emotionally rewarding.

In the thirteenth century, devotion to the Child Jesus spread well beyond the restricted circle of Cistercian monasticism. St. Francis of Assisi,[17] according to the *Legenda Gregorii*[18] set up for the first time a Christmas crèche, so that the faithful might more easily envision the tenderness and humility of the new-born Jesus. St.

---

[16] d. 1358.

[17] Founder of the Franciscans (ca. 1182–1226).

[18] *Legends by Gregory.*

Francis, the most popular saint of the late Middle Ages, was thus responsible, at least in legend, for one of the most popular devotional practices still associated with Christmas. . . .

This cult of the Christ Child implies an idealization of childhood itself. "O sweet and sacred childhood," another Cistercian . . . writes of the early years of Christ, "which brought back man's true innocence, by which men of every age can return to blessed childhood and be conformed to you, not in physical weakness but in humility of heart and holiness of life."

How are we to explain this celebration of "sweet and sacred childhood"? It closely resembles other religious movements which acquire extraordinary appeal from the twelfth century — the cults of poverty, of Christian simplicity, and of the apostolic life. These "movements of cultural primitivism" . . . point to a deepening psychological discontent with the demands of the new commercial economy. The inhabitants of towns in particular, living by trade, were forced into careers of getting and spending, in constant pursuit of what Augustine had called "deceitful riches." The psychological tensions inherent in the urban professions and the dubious value of the proferred material rewards seem to have generated a nostalgic longing for alternate systems of existence, for freedom from material concerns, for the simple Christian life as it was supposedly lived in the apostolic age. Another model for an alternate existence, the exact opposite of the tension-ridden urban experience, was the real or imagined life of the child, who was at once humble and content, poor and pure, joyous and giving joy.

The simple piety of childhood remained an ideal of religious reformers for the duration of the Middle Ages. At their close, both Girolamo Savonarola[19] in the south of Europe and Desiderius Erasmus[20] in the north urged their readers to look to pious children if they would find true models of the Christian life. . . .

Moreover, the medieval cult of childhood extends beyond religious movements and informs secular attitudes as well. . . . Later in the Middle Ages, a Florentine citizen and merchant . . . , reflecting on his own life, calls childhood "nature's most pleasant age." In his *Praise of Folly,* Erasmus avers that the simplicity and unpretentiousness of childhood make it the happiest time of life. "Who does not know," Folly asks her audience, "that childhood is the happiest age and the most pleasant for all? What is there about children that makes us kiss and hug them and cuddle them as we do, so that even an enemy would help them, unless it is this charm of folly?" Clearly, we have come far from Augustine's opinion, that men would prefer eternal death to life again as a child.

The history of medieval children is as complex as the history of any social group, and even more elusive. This essay has attempted to describe in broad outline the cultural attitudes which influenced the experiences of medieval children, as well as the large social trends which touched their lives. The central movements

---

[19] Dominican reformer who ruled Florence from 1494 to 1498.

[20] Dutch humanist (ca. 1466–1536).

which, in this reconstruction, affected their fate were the social and economic changes widely evident across Europe from the twelfth century, most especially the rise of a commercialized economy and the proliferation of special skills within society; and the worsening health conditions of the late Middle Ages, from the second half of the fourteenth century. The growth of a commercialized economy made essential an attentive pedagogy which could provide society with adequately trained adults. And the deteriorating conditions of hygiene across the late Middle Ages heightened the concern for, and investment in, the health and survival of the very young. Paradoxically, too, the growing complexities of social life engendered not truly a discovery but an idealization of childhood: the affirmation of the sentimental belief that childhood is, as Erasmus maintains, a blessed time and the happiest moment of human existence. . . .

SEXUAL ORDER AND THE SUBVERSION OF YOUTH

Jacques Rossiaud

The French medievalist Jacques Rossiaud, who teaches at the University of Lyons, uses records of criminal investigations and trials to examine the phenomenon of gang rape in fifteenth-century Dijon, in southeastern France. Young men's organizations initiated youths into manhood, with the gang rape as a rite of passage. Who joined the youth groups, and which women did they target? What happened to the women after they had been raped? Rossiaud says that both the marriage market and the prevailing culture of violence contributed to the prevalence of gang rape. How did the ages when people married affect the selection of the youths' victims? How did city officials view youth solidarity and gang rape?

Rossiaud's essay tells us much about fifteenth-century urban life, sexual violence and morality, male attitudes toward women, and ideas of masculinity. He questions those who idealize and mythologize the popular culture of the French past, because ritualized violence against women was brutal and had lasting consequences for the victims.

Criminal records and the reports of the courts' preliminary investigations and the trials instituted by the city's procureurs-syndics[1] help us to sketch the general outlines of urban sexual economy in Dijon. One image stands out in the vast, truculent and sordid chronicle of the ordinary people in this series of legal documents: it is that of sexual violence.

These inquiries, together with civil sentences and the decisions rendered by the mayor in the city council, give us information on 125 cases of rape between 1436 and 1486. This figure does not include rapes committed on prostitutes taken, perhaps against their will, into places of prostitution, nor does it represent

Jacques Rossiaud, *Medieval Prostitution,* trans. Lydia G. Cochrane (New York: Basil Blackwell, 1988), 11–26.

[1] City attorneys.

anything like the true total for such assaults. We know from victimization studies conducted by socio-criminologists that in societies in which the forces of law and order are stronger than they were in fifteenth-century France and in which taboos have weakened or disappeared, the "dark figure" for rape, both in middle-sized cities and in larger metropolitan centres, is of the order of seventy-five to eighty.[2] This means that judicial archives reflect only from one-fifth to one-quarter of sexual crimes. Here our series is discontinuous: the documents are stored in bundles, not in register books, and we have hardly any information on eighteen of the fifty years. Furthermore, either out of shame, fear of reprisals, or because the families sought a monetary settlement with the attackers and had no interest in going to court, most of the victims did not press charges (and of course there is no record of proceedings when there is no "plaintiff"). We can thus reasonably estimate that an absolute minimum of twenty "public" rapes were committed annually in Dijon.

Eighty per cent of these, however, were gang rapes committed by groups of from two to fifteen individuals. After making their preparations, they would force the woman's door at night. They made no attempt to disguise themselves, and interjecting brutal remarks with lewd invitations, threats and insults, they either raped their prey on the spot, often in the presence of one or more terrorized witnesses, or else they dragged her through the streets into the house of an accomplice and had their pleasure of her all night long. Four times out of five, out of fear, the neighbours did not intervene.

Were the perpetrators of these acts outlaws or outsiders? The admirably conscientious reports of the city procureur-syndic, Jean Rabustel, tells us of 400 men involved as protagonists or accomplices in a total of ninety fully documented cases. Only thirty outsiders take part in these assaults. Most of the others — townspeople or their sons or servants — are identified. They come from all levels of society, but the overwhelming majority of them are artisans and day labourers, not pimps or protectors. Only one-tenth of the attacks can be put down to thugs operating under the leadership of a chief. But 85 per cent of the assailants are *jeunes fils* (sons of burghers[3]) and unmarried journeymen, one-half of them between the ages of eighteen and twenty-four. Assaults are not strictly connected with holidays, nor with heavy summertime drinking, nor with times of intensive agricultural labour, but are spread throughout the year.

It would be inaccurate to conclude, however, that all young women in Dijon lived in terror after nightfall. Many women and girls had no reason to fear rape. Attacks occurred perhaps once or twice a month, maintaining an atmosphere of insecurity only among certain groups in the female population. Dijon was a middle-sized city, and public security was no less there than in other towns. Brief

---

[2] On the "dark figure" *(numerus obscurus)*, the ratio of crimes actually committed to those appearing in the statistics, studies carried out in England, the United States, Germany and France on rural areas and large cities all lead to relatively concordant conclusions. . . . (Author's note.)

[3] Members of the urban middle class; especially, prosperous solid citizens.

episodes of civic turmoil . . . were not reflected in a higher incidence of rape. The city was relatively prosperous: ducal officials, men of law and churchmen lent support to commerce and the crafts, and this was the period of the full expansion of Burgundian power.[4] Furthermore, Dijon was not a princely capital: professional soldiers and bands of young pages were not involved and had little to do with setting the tone of social relations.

Although the *échevins*[5] of the city council kept careful minutes of their deliberations (conserved in their entirety), they give not the least hint of such disturbances. The viscount-mayor certainly reported to his city council on the sentences meted out for crimes and kidnappings, but the *échevins* never discussed or denounced these aggressive gangs. Only once or twice in fifty years is there mention of "nocturnal disorders," but such events are immediately put down to vagabonds and foreigners, not to the city's own rowdies who appear in Rabustel's charges. The apparent complacency of the city council's deliberations should not mislead us, however, especially since the magistrates did not have jurisdiction over such cases and seldom discussed matters outside their competence. Brief allusions in similar documents in Lyons, Valence and Tarascon to the "insolences" committed *campana pulsata* (after the evening curfew) and the rare mentions of scandals or of armed "gallants" probably refer to acts similar to those described. We can conclude, then, that sexual violence was an everyday dimension of city life. There was probably less of it, proportionally speaking, in smaller towns, but it was an even more serious problem in the largest cities. . . . The first place to seek the cause of this sort of behaviour is in demographic and matrimonial structures.

When a serious offence had been committed and a complaint registered, the procureur and his clerks went without delay to the scene of the crime and interrogated the victim's neighbours. Thus we have available an impressive series of depositions taken (unlike those in civil investigations) from the humbler levels of society. We see men and women, adolescents and the elderly, the married and the unmarried who, under oath, report their "quality" and their age to the courts. After 1500, we also have a number of interrogations of the suspects themselves, for the most part "youths," which give us information on dates of marriage, among other things, thus permitting an estimate of age at marriage and of the gap between spouses. . . . The documentation at hand is too sketchy to permit precise conclusions concerning age at marriage, but we can discern some long-term trends.

These sources provide information between 1500 and 1550 on only 84 individuals, 52 men and 32 women, all from the lower end of the social scale. The average age at first marriage is 24.5 years for men and 21.9 years for women. Although the sampling is perhaps ridiculously small, these data are confirmed by two other series that are based on larger samplings. The average age difference be-

---

[4] The high point of the Duchy of Burgundy, during the fourteenth and fifteenth centuries, when that state maintained a precarious independence between France and Germany.

[5] City officials; aldermen.

tween husbands under thirty years of age and their wives (150 couples) is less than three years; on the other hand, we can see an abrupt decline in the number of marriageable girls between the ages of sixteen and twenty-five: at age twenty-two, 75 per cent of women are married.

We have no direct standard of comparison for the fifteenth century, but it is legitimate to compare the average age of husbands between twenty and thirty years of age (the age decade during which the overwhelming majority of men married) and wives between fifteen and twenty-five years of age (for whom the same remark applies). Out of 350 cases documented between 1500 and 1550, the average age for men is 26.8 years and for women 22.5. These figures, admittedly, have no absolute value. Nevertheless, if we subject two identical series of couples (300 cases), between 1440 and 1550, to the same calculations we can see that the average age for married men is stable at 26.8 years, but the average age for women drops to 21.5. This corroborates the average age difference between husbands and wives among "young couples." . . .

. . . [W]e can fairly safely conclude that the average age at marriage remained stable for men during the century of demographic growth between 1450 and 1550, at twenty-four to twenty-five years of age. It was thus moderately high (and may be slightly underestimated, since I have omitted men over thirty from my calculations). In the same period, average age at marriage increased from twenty/twenty-one years to twenty-one/twenty-two years for women. Why should the age at marriage remain stable among males at a time of economic and demographic change? Let us try to explain.

The age gap between spouses can be reckoned directly and precisely from the data given in these investigations. . . . Three structural elements clearly emerge:

(1) Age inversion is rare. In 14.5 per cent of couples the husband is younger than his wife . . . , but only in 11.7 per cent of the cases is the difference significant (greater than two years). Such an inversion is exceptional both at first marriages and with couples in which the husband is elderly. Naturally, it is among couples in their thirties that it is most frequent. I would thus be willing to suggest that marriage with an "old woman" (a widow, for the most part) is characteristic of a late marriage for the man. The infrequency of this inversion probably signifies that in Dijon in the fifteenth century, as in other cities of France under the *ancien régime*,[6] in general young men rejected the social promotion by marriage with an "old woman."

(2) In 85.5 per cent of these couples, the husband is older than his wife, the average age gap being 7.9 years. But if husbands under thirty years of age are on the average 4.2 years older than their wives (the largest difference is eight years), couples in their thirties show an average age gap of six years (the greatest difference being sixteen years), and husbands in their forties and fifties are almost eleven years older than their tender young wives (the largest gap is thirty-four

---

[6] Old Régime, the two centuries before the French Revolution of 1789.

years). There is nothing remarkable in this, since what we see here are the effects of second or third marriages, which always accentuate differences in age. This situation remained largely unchanged during the first half of the sixteenth century, with only a slight tendency toward the equalization of ages among young couples.

. . . Other cities probably followed the same pattern; matrimonial order in the fifteenth century presented mature husbands and younger wives. Hence in the business negotiations that marriage represented, although the terms of the exchange were multiple and included ethnic origin, profession, social status and wealth, we can assume that the "freshness" of the woman was an asset sought by a man of established position, even in the minor trades.

(3) A closer view of the realities of the marriage market shows that 30 per cent of men from thirty to thirty-nine years of age had a wife who was from eight to sixteen years their junior (from ten to sixteen years in 20 per cent of the cases), and 15 per cent of the forty- and fifty-year-old husbands had a wife who was from twenty to thirty-four years younger than they. This means that these men chose their companion from an age group in which they competed with younger men. I am not so naive as to deduce from this that there was a shortage of wives for young men; still, we should note that nearly one-third of the marriageable girls and "remarriageable" women under thirty years of age were claimed by men who were "established," if not elderly. This syphoning off of young wives was considerable enough to be clearly felt by the young in sixteenth-century cities, as it had been in the fifteenth century. Without entering into the familial or affective consequences that they brought to couples, such age gaps seem to me to have caused both a certain amount of social tension between penniless and wifeless young men and more fortunate men who had both; and, even more, a rivalry between marriageable young men and married men or widowers of over thirty years of age. This rivalry may have contributed to age-based solidarities and collective behaviour patterns unique to young men.

When we apply concepts such as age groups, collective rites, and mediating institutions to traditional societies, we may very easily fail to get a satisfactory answer. Some historians go so far as to apply to the fifteenth or the sixteenth century a too removed "ethnographic model" or a "sociological model" that leads to anachronisms. . . .

I believe, to the contrary, that urban societies of the waning Middle Ages, like those of the Renaissance, tended to maintain and above all to develop the importance of age groups. . . . [A]pprenticeship, far from integrating the child into the adult world, frequently had the effect of keeping him out of it, at least temporarily. . . . Apprenticeship could certainly transmit a *savoir-faire*,[7] but not a *savoir-vivre*.[8] [Immigration had a] fundamental role . . . in youth solidarity, as the

---

[7] Sense of tact, knowing just what to do in every situation.

[8] Knowledge of the customs of polite society; good breeding.

rootless sons of newcomers were encouraged to band together with others of their ilk, and . . . the populations of Rhône valley cities were largely composed of recent immigrants. Finally, the conditions of family life encouraged adolescents to seek the company of their peers. Many of them lacked the presence in the home of a father capable of providing an adult role model, since the head of family was entering old age just as they were reaching their twenties. Above all, the conditions of communal life in the city encouraged the young to search out a suitable role model outside of the home.

It may well be true . . . that in more evolved cultural areas and in wealthy milieux in which the woman held an enviable position, maternal education profoundly influenced the sensitivities and the social attitudes of the young. In most French cities, however, . . . a male-oriented morality encouraged "the boys," unless they were born into patrician families, to form aggressive bands that disturbed order.

These gangs of young males that troubled the Dijon night have some quite distinguishing characteristics. First, they were all more or less of the same age. In eleven of the fifteen groups that form the basis of this analysis, more than one-half of the participants are of the same age cohort, and the presence among them of one or two older bachelors — experienced hands — does nothing to negate this homogeneity. Two-thirds of the groups have a strong socio-professional orientation: they are made up of journeymen and craftsmen's sons from the same or closely related trades, or of young men of the same social status. In similar proportions, these were also streetcorner gangs, comprising only from three to five individuals who knew each other well. Finally, and this is an essential trait, in more than 80 per cent of cases, the young men had never before faced charges of group delinquency. In other words, the *juvenes*[9] of these walled cities, victims of boredom, roamed the city in the evening, quite spontaneously on the lookout for adventure or for a good brawl, taunting the night watch, chasing girls, and organizing a rape.

Is it fair to call these assaults gang rape? This is a "crossroads of ambiguities," the socio-criminologists tell us, and with good reason. Any explanation of it must include the particular gang's motivations, the imprudence of a specific girl, vengeance, private or collective, the seizing of an offered opportunity, and the demands of clan rivalries. In this society in which images of violence were a daily experience and the sexual impulses of adults met with few constraints, the aggression of the night gangs quite naturally translated into sexual violence. It seems to me that there are two principal reasons for this:

(1) To acquire the privilege of masculinity. Masculinity is a social role, an acquired behaviour. One recurrent image, the cock and the hen, accurately reflects the relative place of man and woman in the fifteenth-century French city. By her

---

[9] Youth, especially young men.

very nature, the hen needed to be mastered and dominated. Add to that an extremely Manichaean[10] vision of young women, who could only be pure or public. This is what lent legitimacy to the actions of these young cocks: their attacks were always accompanied by degrading insults, humiliation of the victim, and blows. Well before they passed on to the act itself, the aggressors exculpated themselves, and from the outset the woman they chose was treated as guilty and viewed as a mere object and as obliged to submit.

Every year in Dijon a hundred or so individuals were implicated in rapes. If we exclude the outsiders, the repeat offenders and the adult instigators, there remains a minimum of fifty to sixty young men aged between eighteen to twenty-four years. This means that half the city youths had participated at least once in this sort of attack. It is, in my opinion, quite possible that this type of aggression constituted a rite of passage to manhood and of admission to neighbourhood gangs.

(2) Although the participants made full use of this opportunity to satisfy their sexual desires (the women were raped repeatedly), for many of them — poor journeymen, domestic servants and penniless sons of established families — collective rape expressed much deeper impulses or frustrations: it was a denial of social order. When they raped her, they marked the young widow or the marriageable girl by destroying her social standing. They attacked the serving girl rumoured to be "kept" by her master, the servant-mistress of a better-off journeyman, the priest's concubine, or the wife who had been "left" temporarily and who, they take care to add, should by rights "provide" pleasure to the "companions."

City notables and heads of large households had a stake in quelling this turbulence. They offered their sons, their domestics and their workingmen liberal opportunities for municipally-sponsored fornication (and they took advantage of it themselves). They may perhaps also have compromised with unmarried men by accepting some of the ways they expressed their solidarity and not objecting to the rowdy public behaviour of their "joyous brotherhoods."

Now that we have a firmer understanding of the complementary nature of matrimonial order and the subversion of the young, we need to return to the question of the place and the significance of "youth abbeys" in urban society.

It is well known that young men's organizations could be found under a wide variety of names in both towns and villages. Natalie Zemon Davis[11] has given us an excellent analysis of them, emphasizing the role that they played in rural communities in the socialization of the young, the control of their impulses, and the

---

[10] Relating to the belief that a cosmic conflict exists between a good realm of light and an evil realm of darkness, that matter and flesh are in the realm of darkness, and that humanity's duty is to aid the forces of good by practicing asceticism, especially by avoiding sex and meat.

[11] Historian of early modern France and former president of the American Historical Association.

defence of the community and its traditions. Nevertheless, when she bases her conclusion on the example of Lyons (in reality an exceptional metropolis), she is led to make too great a distinction between rural youth abbeys and their urban counterparts and to oppose the *maugouverts* — the organizations of "misrule" — of the sixteenth century to the *bachelleries* — unmarried men's societies — of the previous centuries. Davis claims that the conditions particular to the larger cities of the Renaissance, new elements in the apprenticeship system and the diffusion of a new culture restricted the social range of recruitment of these brotherhoods, which now welcomed both married and unmarried men and became associations dedicated to good neighbourly relations, adding to their supervision of matrimonial mores social, political and religious criticism. Without going into all the problems raised by Davis's arguments, I shall limit my remarks to the continuity that I see in the structure and the objectives of these groups in the urban milieu from the end of the fourteenth to the mid-sixteenth century.

(1) In all the cities of south-east France the abbeys of *jovens* or the joyous brotherhoods were institutions recognized by and integrated into the city's body politic. The abbot, his treasurer and his priors were often elected in the presence of city council members; the association's internal quarrels were arbitrated by the city council, which also controlled its finances, granted or refused permission for its public activities and set the limits of its jurisdiction. This was true from Dijon to Arles, in the sixteenth century as it was in the fifteenth. The few traces of conflict between the abbeys and the urban authorities should not mislead us: almost never was an abbey formed spontaneously; they were instigated or controlled by the urban collectivity.

(2) Youths exercised a jurisdiction over the unmarried and the married alike. This fundamental notion remained true throughout the sixteenth century. We should note, however, that the abbey's "rights" were negligible in the first marriage of a young couple (amounting to a few pennies or a share in the wedding party). They were relatively high when the union was seen as a threat to the young or when matrimonial customs were transgressed. In that case, the organization could levy fines that went into the group's coffers and were used, in part, to organize banquets. The groups' jurisdiction amounted to coercion only when the couple refused to submit to such customs. Then a charivari[12] or a forced ride on ass-back, with no physical violence, but which ended up in a drinking bout, helped youths put up with a situation that in their hearts they found intolerable.

When they performed these activities, however, the "kings," "prince abbots" and their henchmen compromised with matrimonial order by coming to terms with the situation. As for the new bridegrooms, they had good reason to accept the abbey's rights: by compromising with the young they wiped out their "error" and protected themselves against possible violence. Furthermore, husbands con-

---

[12] A ceremony, especially in peasant societies, in which a community attempts to impose its values on deviant members by means of raucous music, public humiliation, and crowd intimidation.

trolled these youthful demonstrations: their representatives sat on the city council that held authority over the "abbeys," and some of them were members of
youth brotherhoods themselves.

(3) Youth solidarity did not extend to both sexes: the troops ranged behind
their leader dancing a noisy saraband[13] around the dwelling of the "guilty couple"
or following mockingly after the ass did not work for the protection of the woman
as they did the man. Although men were on occasion the victims of these rites,
responsibility for the scandal denounced by the young was almost always laid to
the woman. She was seen as dominating, unfaithful, perfidious when she snared
a man younger than herself, and imbecilic (which was her nature) when she accepted marriage with a greybeard or, if she did so willingly, guilty of treachery toward eligible younger men. Youth groups punished the husband who beat his
wife, to be sure, but only in the month of May, and only if he was particularly
quarrelsome or was an outsider to the community. It was these same young men,
who had gained the esteem of their peers by well-publicized fornication, who in
May directed public scorn at young girls whose virtue they chose to suspect (and
girls had no solidarity structure to back them up), reserving the right to target
them for collective violence at a later date.

Contemporary vocabulary is profoundly indicative: every young male living
in the town above the poverty level owed it to himself to join the great band of
the *gars* ("the boys") who gave chase to *la garce* (one of many terms for a whore).
That was how one became known as an *homme joyeux* (a real man, "one of the
boys") whereas a *fille joyeuse* meant a prostitute. The *abbé* of a youth group held
a position of influence and prestige (their "queens," the *reinagières,* played an insignificant and purely accompanying role), whereas the term *abbesse* referred to
the manager of a bawdy house. In my view, then, until the beginning of the sixteenth century and possibly a good deal later, the youth abbeys (with the exception of the so-called *abbayes bourgeoises*[14]) were institutions for conserving and
passing on the most traditional sort of misogyny. They contributed to keeping
women subservient, at least in the middle and lower levels of society.

The "companions" who roamed the city at night in search of prey — those
ephèbes noirs (black adolescents) of the medieval city — underwent their apprenticeship in adulthood among their peers and under cover of night. Anonymously and through violence, they embodied a true counter-force controlling
marriage. When these same young men and their wealthier peers forced their victims to parade on ass-back through the city, or when they taunted couples at
their second marriages, they were not merely carrying on rites whose meaning
they no longer understood, nor were they simply actors in a collective psy-
chodrama in which the roles and the situations had remained fixed from time im-

---

[13] A quick Spanish dance of Middle Eastern origin, which evolved into a stately court dance of
the seventeenth and eighteenth centuries.

[14] Youth organizations for the sons of the city elites.

memorial. The kings, abbots and Mad Mothers who led them — in broad daylight — only rarely and in mitigated form expressed the frustrations of youth. The abbey was simply the opposition to "his lordship the State of Marriage." Above all, it was somewhat like the municipal brothels, an institution for harmony between age groups and social groups, and between newcomers and native townspeople and city dwellers. It integrated; it socialized; it amused. However, in the last analysis, both in their more aggressive behaviour and in the organized mockery of the *chahut*,[15] young people also proved themselves faithful followers of an order of which they expected to be a part one day.

Literature, legend and popular mythology have retained only the more benevolent aspects of these youth solidarities. The champions of a popular culture largely defined by laughter and what is called the Gallic tradition would do well to look twice, for these groups of grotesque maskers who resemble the comic characters of farces and *sotties*[16] lead us to forget the victims, most of whom were "abandoned" to a life of vagabondage or prostitution.

MAKING CONNECTIONS:
SEXUALITY AND THE BODY

1. Jacques Rossiaud depicts a culture that, for the most part, accepted sexual brutality against certain women. Why do you think fifteenth-century Dijon condoned gang rape? Do you know of other societies that have endorsed gang rape as a rite of passage in certain situations? How common has sexual violence toward women been in Western civilization?

2. In fifteenth-century Dijon, was gang rape primarily a sexual outlet or a means for youths to mark and control women? Do most female victims of rape in the West today belong to the same social and occupational groups as did the victims in Dijon? Explain.

3. Compare the attitudes of the classical Greeks to the attitudes of the late medieval residents of Dijon in regard to women and sexuality. What instances of empathy toward women do you perceive? Did men in both societies believe they "owned" women's bodies?

---

[15] To make a racket or kick up a rumpus.

[16] Short comic plays whose characters are sots ("fools").

THE FAMILY IN RENAISSANCE ITALY
David Herlihy

During the fourteenth and fifteenth centuries, a cultural flowering known as the Renaissance took place in Italy. David Herlihy (1930–1991) was an eminent medieval and Renaissance historian who specialized in the history of the family and of women. Here he focuses primarily on Florence, the center of the Renaissance and a leading city in Europe, in order to understand the nature of the family. Relying extensively on census data, he finds that three factors — demography, environment, and wealth — propelled the family's long-term development.

During this period, population trends shifted several times, especially after the Black Death. How did these changes influence the size of households and the number of servants? Herlihy makes many comparisons between urban and rural families. In other words, he shows how environment influenced the family. Urban families differed from their counterparts in the countryside not only in size but also in the establishment of new families, remarriage, and the functions the family performed. Wealth likewise affected the choice of a marriage partner, household size, and age at marriage. How effective is Herlihy's argument that demography, environment, and wealth led to a crisis of the Renaissance family?

Herlihy next discusses the composition of the Italian household, especially regarding marriage and children. Age at marriage provides much information about family structure. Why was there such a disparity in Florence between the age of first marriage for women and for men, and how did the situation differ in rural areas? Why did some men and women remain unmarried, and what was their fate? How did marriage patterns inspire the prevalence of prostitution and homosexuality?

Children were important to the Renaissance family, though the relationship between mother and child was unlike that between father and child. The fathers cared for their children's future, especially their sons', often leaving posthumous instructions specifying their upbringing. Mothers, closer in age to their offspring and tending to survive their husbands, influenced their children in areas of special concern to women. In this way, Herlihy believes that the female education of the young had a significant impact on the character of the Renaissance. Overall, he accords singular importance to the family and holds its peculiar

David Herlihy, *The Family in Renaissance Italy* (Wheeling, IL: Forum Press, 1974), 4–12.

structure responsible in large part for the cultural awakening of the Renaissance.

Sociologists and historians once assumed that the typical family in traditional Europe (that is, in Europe before the Industrial Revolution) was large, stable and extended, in the sense that it included other relatives besides the direct descendants and ascendants of the head and his wife. The sources of Renaissance Italy rather show that there is no such thing as a traditional family, or, in different terms, a family with unchanging characteristics. The family in ca. 1400 was perceptibly different from what it had been in ca. 1300, and was to be different again in the sixteenth century. Moreover, the rural family varied in marked respects from the city household, and the poor — can this be surprising? — lived differently from the rich. How precisely did the times, location and wealth affect the Renaissance household?

In Italy as everywhere in Europe, the population between the thirteenth and the sixteenth centuries experienced powerful, even violent, fluctuations. These directly affected the households in their average size and internal structure. The history of population movements in late medieval and Renaissance Italy may be divided into four periods, with distinctive characteristics: (1) stability in numbers at very high levels, from some point in the thirteenth century until ca. 1340; (2) violent contraction, from ca. 1340 to ca. 1410, to which the terrible Black Death of 1348 made a major but not exclusive contribution; (3) stability at very low levels, from approximately 1410 to 1460; (4) renewed expansion, which brought the Italian population to another peak in the middle sixteenth century.

To judge from Tuscan evidence, the population in our second period (ca. 1340 to ca. 1410) fell by approximately two-thirds. A city of probably 120,000 persons in 1338, Florence itself counted less than 40,000 in 1427. In some remote areas of Tuscany, such as the countryside of San Gimignano, losses over the same period surpassed 70 percent. The region of San Gimignano was in fact more densely settled in the thirteenth century than it is today.

It is difficult for a modern reader even to grasp the dimensions of these losses; for every three persons living in ca. 1300, there was only one to be found alive in ca. 1410, in many if not most Italian regions. And the population, stable at low levels from approximately 1410, shows no signs of vigorous growth until after 1460. The subsequent expansion of the late fifteenth and early sixteenth centuries was particularly notable on the fertile plain of the Po river in Northern Italy and in the Veneto (the region of Venice). Verona, near Venice, for example, had fewer than 15,000 inhabitants in 1425, but reached 42,000 by 1502, nearly tripling in size. Venice itself reached approximately 170,000 persons by 1563; it was not to reach that size again until the twentieth century. Rome and Naples were also gaining rapidly in population. Florence too was growing, but at a moderate rate. In 1562 Florence counted slightly fewer than 60,000 inhabitants, which made the city only a third larger than it had been in 1427. Florence, in sum, even in this period of growth, was losing relative position among the major cities of Italy.

Inevitably, the collapse in population, subsequent stability, then growth affected the average size of the households. At Prato, for example, a small region and city 20 miles west of Florence, the average size of the rural household was 5.6 persons in 1298, and only 5 in 1427. Within the city of Prato, average household size similarly fell from 4.1 persons in 1298 to only 3.7 in 1427. By the late fourteenth and fifteenth centuries, the urban household widely across northern Italy was extremely small: 3.8 persons per household at Florence in 1427; 3.6 at Pistoia in the same year; 3.5 at Bologna in 1395; and 3.7 at Verona in 1425.

The acute population fall and the ensuing period of demographic stability at low levels (to ca. 1460) also affected the internal structure of the households. The demographic catastrophes, especially the plagues and famines, left within the community large numbers of incomplete or truncated households — those which lacked a married couple and included only widowers, widows, bachelors or orphaned children. At Florence in 1427, the most common of all household types found within the city counted only a single person; these one-member households, represented some 20 percent of all urban households. The numerous, small, severely truncated and biologically inactive families (in the sense that they could produce no children) may be regarded as the social debris, which the devastating plagues and famines of the epoch left in their wake.

The renewed demographic expansion from about 1460 in turn affected average size and the internal structure of the household. Average household size at Verona, only 3.7 persons in 1425, reached 5.2 persons only thirty years later, in 1456, and was 5.9 persons in 1502. Within the city of Florence, average household size gained from 3.8 persons in 1427 to 4.8 persons in 1458 to 5.2 persons in 1480, and reached 5.7 members in 1552. Within the Florentine countryside, average household size similarly grew from 4.8 persons in 1427, to 5.3 in 1470, to 5.8 in 1552.

Several factors explain this increase in average household size in both city and countryside during this period of demographic growth after 1460. As the plague and famine lost their virulence, the numbers of very small, highly truncated and biologically inactive families diminished within the community. Families were also producing larger numbers of children (perhaps we should say, of surviving children). Paradoxically, however, the large households of the late fifteenth and sixteenth centuries also indicate an effort to slow the rate of population growth. In a rapidly growing community, average household size tends to remain relatively low, as sons and daughters leave the paternal home at an early age to marry, and the community contains many young, hence small, families. But no community can allow its population to grow without limit, and in traditional society the principal means of slowing or stopping growth was to prevent young persons from marrying, or marrying young. These young persons remained in their parents' house for long periods, thus increasing average household size. Many of them, especially males, remained unmarried even after the death of their parents, living as bachelors in households headed by an older, married brother. Within the city of Florence, for example, in 1427 some 17.1 percent of the households included a brother or sister of the household head, but 26.1 percent did so in 1480. We have no exact figures from the sixteenth century, but the percentage was doubtlessly even larger. The Florentine household, in other words, was much more laterally extended in the sixteenth century than it had been in 1427. The effort to slow or stop population growth, more than the growth itself, accounts for the larger size and more complex structure of the Italian household in the late fifteenth and sixteenth centuries.

Another factor which contributed to these shifts in average household size was the changing servant population. The drastic fall in the population in the late fourteenth century made labor scarce and forced wages upward, and this meant that households before 1460 could afford to support comparatively few servants. At Verona in 1425, for example, some 7 percent of the urban population were employed as household servants. After 1460, as the population once more was growing, wages tended to decline, and households could afford to support larger numbers of retainers. By 1502 at Verona, servants constituted 12.3 percent of the urban population. The numbers of servants grew especially large in the city of Florence, where, by 1552, 16.7 percent of the urban population were employed in household service; nearly half the urban households (42 percent) had at least one domestic, and one Florentine citizen employed no fewer than 57 servants. This growth in the number of servants has great social and cultural importance. It meant that the Italian urban family of some means could live with considerably greater comfort and elegance in ca. 1500 — during the height of the Renaissance — than had been possible a hundred years before.

By the sixteenth century, the typical Italian household was large in size and complex in structure; it included numerous children, servants, and lateral relatives of the head. Sociologists and historians used to consider this extended household characteristic of traditional European society. Today, we can discern that this type of household was characteristic only of particular periods and circumstances in the varied history of the Italian family.

The location of the household, its surroundings or environment, also exerted a powerful influence upon its internal structure. Unlike the long-term demographic trend, this factor exerted a largely uniform influence over time. In most periods and places, the rural household was larger than its urban counterpart. At Prato in 1298, the average household size was 5.6 in rural areas and 4.1 in the city; at Florence in 1427, the comparable figures are 4.8 in the countryside and 3.8 in the city. However, the changes we have already considered — particularly the great growth in the number of servants, which was more characteristic of the cities than of rural areas — tended to reduce these contrasts in the sixteenth century. In 1552, the average size of the urban household at Florence was 5.7 persons; it was 5.8 in the countryside.

Average household size, however, reveals very little about the internal character of the family. No matter what their relative size, the households of the countryside remained fundamentally different from those of the city. Perhaps the most evident contrast was this: almost invariably, the rural household contained at least one married couple; households headed by a bachelor, widow, widower or orphans were rarely found in rural areas. In the cities, on the other hand, bachelors and widows frequently appeared at the head of households at all periods. Households which lacked sexually active partners were therefore common in the city, but rare in the countryside. So also, the number of children supported in urban households tended to be below the number found in rural homes. . . .

These contrasts point to fundamental differences in the functions of the family in the countryside and the city. In the countryside, the family fulfilled both biological and economic functions: the procreation and rearing of children, and the maintenance of a productive enterprise, the family farm. In Italy, as everywhere in medieval Europe, a peasant economy dominated the countryside. In the peasant economy, the basic unit of labor was not so much the individual but the family. A single man or woman did not have the capacity to work an entire farm, but needed the help of a spouse and eventually children. The young peasant who wished to secure his own economic independence consequently had to marry. For the same reason, if a peasant or his wife were widowed, he or she tended to remarry quickly, unless a young married couple was already present in the household, for the farm could be successfully worked only through family labor. In rural areas there were consequently very few truncated households, that is, those which did not contain at least one married couple. The rural environment encouraged marriage, not only for biological but for economic reasons. Conversely, those residents of the countryside who did not wish to marry or remarry were strongly drawn to the cities.

Within the cities, the family of course continued to perform its biological functions of rearing children, but its economic functions were very different. The young man seeking to make his fortune in most urban trades or professions often found a wife more of a burden than a help. He frequently had to serve long years at low pay as an apprentice. He had to accumulate diligently his earnings and profits; capital alone permitted him one day to pursue his trade in his own right and name. Such a man could not usually contemplate marriage until his mature years, when he was economically established; even then, the urban family was not cemented, as was the rural household, by close participation in a common economic enterprise.

The urban environment, in other words, tended to be hostile to the formation of new households, and added little to their inner strength. Moreover, at the death of a spouse, his or her partner was not under the same pressures to remarry, as was the rural widower or widow who needed help in farming. Urban communities consequently contained far greater numbers of adult bachelors and widows than could be found in the rural villages. The urban environment was often hostile to the very survival of lineages. Both inside and outside of Italy, the city frequently proved to be the graveyard of family lines. . . .

The third factor which strongly influenced the character of the household was wealth or social position, but this influence was exerted in complex ways. In some respects, wealth reinforced the environmental influences reviewed above. Thus, in the cities, rich young men tended to approach marriage even more cautiously than their poorer neighbors. Marriage among the wealthy involved the conveyance of substantial sums of money through the dowry. Marriage also called for the sealing of family alliances, which affected the political and social position of all parties involved. The high stakes associated with marriage frequently led the wealthy young man (or his family) to search long for a suitable bride, and to protract the negotiations when she was found. Marriage, in other words, was not lightly regarded, or hastily contracted, among the rich. Moreover, if death should dissolve the marriage, the surviving partner, particularly the widow, usually controlled enough wealth in her own name to resist pressures to remarry. Bachelors and widows were therefore especially numerous among the wealthy. The poorer families of the city, in approaching marriage, had less reason for caution and restraint.

In the countryside, on the other hand, the wealthy peasant usually owned a large farm, which could only be worked with the aid of a wife and family. The rich inhabitant of the city looked upon marriage in the light of future advantages — the dowry and the family connections it would bring him; the substantial peasant needed family labor to make himself rich in harvests as well as land. Among the rural rich there were consequently few families headed by a bachelor or widow. Poorer inhabitants of the countryside — peasants who possessed less than an entire farm and who worked primarily as agricultural laborers — were less eager to take a wife, who, with children, might excessively tax already scant resources. Wealth, in sum, facilitated marriage in rural areas, while obstructing it within the city.

We must note, however, that there are important exceptions to the rule we have just enounced. In Tuscany, and widely in central Italy, there existed large numbers of sharecroppers, called *mezzadri,* who leased and worked entire farms in return for half the harvest. The owner of the farm provided his *mezzadro* with most of the capital he needed — cattle, tools, seed, fertilizer and the like. With few possessions of his own, the sharecropper usually appeared in the tax rolls as very poor, but he still required a wife and family to help him in his labors. In other words, the need to recruit a family of workers, rather than wealth itself, was the critical factor in encouraging marriages among the peasants.

Besides reinforcing environmental influences, wealth had another effect upon households, which was common to both cities and countryside. In both environments, almost invariably, rich households tended to be larger than poor households. And they were more abundantly supplied with all types of members: they supported relatively more children, more servants and more lateral relatives of the head. For example, if we consider only those households in the city of Florence in 1427 with a male head between age 43 and 47, the average size for the richer half of the urban households was 6.16 persons; it was 4.57 among the poorer half. In rural areas too, and in other periods, wealth exerted a similar, strong influence upon the size and complexity of households. It was as if the family head of the Renaissance, in both city and countryside, equipped himself with as large a household as his resources could reasonably support.

The marked influence of wealth upon household size had some paradoxical effects. Considerations of property . . . prompted rich young men in the city to marry late, and some did not marry at all; but once married, the rich were prolific in producing children. . . . The urban poor were far less hesitant in entering marriage, but the poor urban family was also far less successful than the rich in rearing children. Probably the children of the deprived fell victim, in greater relative numbers than the children of the privileged, to the rampant diseases of the age. Poor parents certainly had strong reasons for exercising restraint in procreating children, and they probably limited the number of their offspring in other ways — through primitive methods of birth control and through the abandonment of babies they could not support. In the countryside, on the other hand, wealth tended to encourage both early marriage and high fertility among those who married.

Our consideration of these three factors — the long-term demographic trend, environment and wealth — which strongly influenced the Renaissance family brings us to the following conclusion. The huge losses and slow recovery in the population in the late Middle Ages precipitated a major crisis within the Italian household, as it did in many other social institutions. Frequent deaths undermined the durability and stability of the basic familial relations — between husband and wife, and parents and children. High mortalities threatened the very survival of numerous family lines. The crisis was especially acute within the city, the environment of which was already basically hostile to the formation of households and to their cohesiveness. . . .

This grave crisis did, however, increase awareness of the family and its problems. Writers of the age were led to examine, and at times to idealize, familial relationships and the roles which father, mother and children played within the household. They sought to determine when young men should marry, how brides should be chosen, and how children should be trained, in order to assure the happiness and especially the survival of the family. . . .

Against this background, we can now look in more detail at the Renaissance household. Specifically, we shall examine what sociologists call the "developmental cycle" of the household — how it was formed through marriage, grew primarily through births, and was dissolved or transformed through deaths.

Perhaps the most distinctive feature of the Renaissance marriage was the great age difference which separated the groom from his bride. At Florence in 1427–28, in 55 marriages reported in the *Catasto*,[1] the average age difference between the bride and groom was 13.6 years. Demographers can also estimate age of first marriage from the proportions of the population remaining single at the various age levels, through somewhat complicated calculations we need not rehearse here. By this method, the average age of first marriage for women in the city of Florence in 1427 can be estimated at 17.9 years; for men it is 29.9 years.

In this, the city of Florence presents an extreme example of a common pattern. In the Florentine countryside in 1427, the estimated age of first marriage for

---

[1] 1427 census in Florence.

women, based on the proportions remaining single, was 18.3 years, and for men 25.6 years. The age difference between the spouses, 7.3 years, was less than in the city, but still considerable. In the city of Verona in 1425, the age difference was also smaller — 7 years — but still extended.

The three factors of environment, wealth and long-term demographic trend affected the formation of new households and inevitably therefore the age of first marriage. However, the age of first marriage for men was far more sensitive to all these influences than the marriage age for women. The typical bride was never much older than 20 years, and was usually much younger. The age of first marriage for men varied over a much wider range of years, from 25 to 35 and at times perhaps to 40. According to a Florentine domestic chronicler writing in the early 1400's, Giovanni Morelli, his male ancestors in the thirteenth century were prone to postpone their first marriage until age 40. . . . In the period before the devastating plagues,[2] when the mean duration of life was relatively extended, men would be forced to wait long before they would be allowed to marry. The medieval community had already reached extraordinary size in the thirteenth century and could ill support continued, rapid growth.

It is at all events certain that the great plagues and famines of the fourteenth century lowered the average age at which men first entered marriage. Thus, in 1427 in the city of Florence, the average age of first marriage for men was approximately 30 years, which compared to Morelli's estimate of 40 years for the thirteenth century. Subsequently, as the plagues grew less virulent, and lives became longer, the age of first marriage for men again moved upward. In 1458, for example, the estimated age of first marriage for Florentine men was 30.5 years, and it was 31.4 years in 1480.

The age of first marriage for women moved upward and downward in the same direction as that of men, but, as we have mentioned, over a shorter range of years. (The estimated age of first marriage for Florentine women was 17.9 years in 1427, 19.5 in 1458 and 20.8 in 1480.) The reasons for this relative inelasticity in marriage age for women seem to have been preeminently cultural: Italian grooms of the Renaissance, under almost all circumstances, no matter what their own age, preferred brides no older than 20.

So also, between city and countryside, the differences in age of first marriage for men (29.9 and 25.6 years respectively in 1427) were much greater than the differences in age of first marriage for women (17.9 and 18.3 years respectively). Women were slightly older at first marriage in rural areas, perhaps because the agricultural labors they were to perform required physical maturity. Again within the city, the richest Florentine males in 1427, from households with an assessment of over 400 florins, entered marriage for the first time at an estimated age of 31.2 years; their poorest neighbors, from households with no taxable assets, were considerably younger at first marriage — only 27.8 years. But rich girls and poor girls

---

[2] That is, before 1348.

married for the first time at nearly the same ages — 17.9 and 18.4 years respectively. Rich girls tended to be slightly younger, perhaps because their worried fathers wanted to settle their fate as quickly as possible. But almost all Florentine brides, in every corner of society, were remarkably young, at least by modern standards.

We should further note that in those segments of society where men married late (that is, in the towns, and particularly among the wealthy) many men, perhaps 10 percent, did not marry at all, but remained as bachelors, usually in the households of married relatives. On the other hand, girls who did not marry either entered domestic service — an option not open to girls from well-to-do households — or joined a religious order. There were almost no lay spinsters in urban society, apart from servants.

How does this pattern of marriage compare with modern practices? Sociologists now identify what they call a "west European marriage pattern," which is apparently found in no other, non-Western society. This pattern is distinguished by late marriages for both men and women, and by the presence in the population of many adult men and women who do not marry at all. How "modern" were the men and women of the Renaissance? Clearly, within the cities, male behavior already corresponded closely to this modern pattern; men married late and some did not marry at all, especially among the wealthy. The women of the Renaissance, on the other hand, even within the cities, were far from modern in their marital behavior; they married young and those who did not marry rarely remained in the lay world. Renaissance Italy, in other words, was not the birthplace of the modern marriage pattern, at least not for women.

The long span of years, which separated the groom from his bride, had distinctive effects upon both the character of the Renaissance household and upon the larger society. The young girl had little voice in selecting her mate, and usually no competence to choose. The first weeks of marriage must have been traumatic for these child brides. . . . But the position and status of these young matrons thereafter improved, for several reasons. The husbands were older, occupied men; many were already past the prime of their years. The brides, themselves only reaching maturity, rapidly assumed chief responsibility for the management of their households. . . . For many women, ultimate liberation would come with the deaths of their much older husbands. At the death of the husband, the dowry returned to the widow; the large sum of money which had taxed her family's resources at her marriage now could make her a woman of means, independent enough to resist a second marriage if she did not want it. As a widow with some property, she was free from male domination in a way she had never been as a child and a wife. The years of childhood, of service as a wife, were hard but often abbreviated for the lady of the Renaissance; and time worked in her favor.

Within the larger society, especially within the cities, the tendency for males to postpone marriage meant that the community would contain large numbers of unattached young men, who were denied legitimate sexual outlets for as long as two decades after puberty. Erotic tensions thus ran high within the city, and the situation inevitably promoted both prostitution and sodomy, for which the Renaissance cities enjoyed a merited reputation. The typical triad of many contemporary stories and dramas — the aged husband, beautiful young wife, and clever young man intent on seducing her — reflects a common domestic situation. These restless young men, uninhibited by responsibilities for a wife and family, were also quick to participate in the factional and family feuds and battles which were frequent occurrences in Renaissance social history. . . .

Delayed marriage for men inevitably affected the treatment and the fate of girls. Because of high mortalities and the inevitable shrinking of the age pyramid, there were fewer eligible and willing grooms, at approximately age 30, than prospective brides, girls between 15 and 20. The girls, or rather their families, had to enter a desperate competition for grooms, and this drove up the value of dowries to ruinous levels. . . . Since prospective brides outnumbered available grooms, many girls had no statistical chance of finding a husband. For most of them, there would be no alternative but the convent. A great saint of the fifteenth century, Bernardino of Siena, once described these unhappy girls, placed in convents because they were too poor, too homely, or too unhealthy to be married, as the "scum and vomit of the world."

The acts by which the marriage was contracted were several. The formal engagement usually involved the redaction of a notarial contract, which stipulated when the marriage should occur and how the dowry should be paid. The promise of marriage would often be repeated solemnly in church. On the wedding day, the bride and groom would often attend a special Mass, at which they received the Church's blessing. But that blessing, or even the presence of a priest, was not required for a legitimate marriage until the Council of Trent[3] in the sixteenth century made it obligatory for Catholics. The central act in the wedding ceremony was a procession, in which the groom led his bride from her father's house to his own. Through this public display, society recognized that this man and this woman would henceforth live together as husband and wife. The groom then usually gave as lavish a feast as his resources would allow, which sometimes lasted for days.

. . . Given the character of the marriage, the typical baby was received by a very young mother and a much older father. Within the city of Florence in 1427, the mean age of motherhood was approximately 26.5 years . . . ; the mean age of fatherhood was 39.8 years. The age differences between mothers and fathers were again, less extreme in the countryside or in other Italian towns, but still must be considered extended.

The great differences in the average ages of fathers and mothers affected the atmosphere of the home and the training of children. The mature, if not aged, fathers would have difficulty communicating with their children, and many would

---

[3] Church council (1545–1563) that clarified doctrines and reformed the Roman Catholic Church.

not live to see their children reach adulthood. One reason the male heads of family placed moral exhortations in their *ricordi*[4] is that they feared that they would
not survive long enough to give much advice . . . to the younger generation.

This distinctive situation placed the wife and mother in a critical position between the old generation of fathers and the children. Much younger and more vigorous than her husband, usually destined for longer and more intimate contact
with her children, she became a prime mediator in passing on social values from
old to young. Understandably, many of the educational tracts, which proliferate
in Italy from the early fifteenth century, are directed at women. One of the first of
them, Dominici's *Governance and Care of the Family*, . . . beautifully describes both
what Florentine mothers did, and what the author, a Dominican friar, wished
them to do. Mothers, according to the friar, spent the days pampering and playing with their young children, fondling and licking them, spoiling them with
beautiful toys, dressing them in elegant clothes, and teaching them how to sing
and dance. An effeminizing influence seems evident here, which was not balanced
by a strong masculine presence within the home. The friar recommends that the
mothers rather impart spiritual values to their children; in telling them how to do
this, he shows the new fifteenth-century awareness of the psychology of children. The home should contain a play altar, at which the young could act out the
liturgy, and pictures of Christ and St. John represented as playful children, to
whom real children will feel immediate rapport. Clearly, Dominici did not regard
the child simply as a miniature adult, without a mind and psychology of his own.

Two conclusions seem appropriate here. The Renaissance household, with an
aged, occupied and often absent husband and a young wife, was not ideally
equipped to give balanced training to its children. But this deficiency seems to
have increased the concern for the proper education of children. . . . [W]omen
continued to dominate the training of young children, and inevitably they incul-
cated in them qualities which they admired — a taste for refined manners and elegant dress, and a high esthetic sensibility. In the sixteenth century, a character in
the *Book of the Courtier,* by Baldassare Castiglione, then the most popular handbook of good manners, attributes all gracious exercises — music, dancing and poetry — to the influence of women. The gentleman of the Renaissance was fash-
ioned to the tastes of women; so also was much of the culture of the age.

Births also helped shape the total society. Here, an important factor was the
differences in relative fertility among the various segments of the community. The
rural population, as we have mentioned, tended to be more prolific than the
urban, and the rich, while slow to marry, still reproduced themselves more successfully than the poor. Differences in fertility rates inevitably generated flows of
people from some parts of society to others. Thus, differential fertility between city
and countryside assured that there would be constant immigration from rural
areas into the towns. . . . This immigration had important social effects. It appears

---

[4] Diaries.

to have been selective, as the city especially attracted the skilled and the highly motivated. At Florence, many of the cultural leaders of the Renaissance . . . were of rural or small-town origins. The urban need for people promoted the careers of these gifted men. On the other hand, by introducing them into a milieu which made their own reproduction difficult, immigration also tended over the long run to extirpate the lines of creative individuals. It was not an unmixed blessing.

Within the cities, the wealthier families, in spite of the male reluctance to enter marriage, still tended to produce more children than the poor. Many of these children would be placed in convents or enter careers in the Church, but some would face a difficult decision. Either they would have to accept a social position lower than their parents, or they would have to seek to make their fortunes outside of their native city, even outside of Italy. . . . Many were forced therefore to wander through the world in search of fortune. Demographic pressures, in other words, required that even the sons of the wealthy adopt an entrepreneurial stance. This helps explain the ambitions and high energy of the Florentines and other Italians, and the prominence they achieved all over Europe, in many fields, in the Renaissance period.

The final event in the history of a marriage was death, and we can deal with death more briefly, as we have already referred to its central role in the social history of the epoch. Death was everywhere present during the Renaissance, and the ravages it perpetrated were at the root of the crisis of the family, which was most severe in the late fourteenth and early fifteenth centuries. Here, we shall note only the distinctive reactions of the surviving partner in a marriage to the death of a spouse. For reasons already discussed, in the countryside it was typical for both widows and widowers quickly to remarry, if they were of suitable age. But in the city, the behavior of widowed men and women was quite different. The urban widower, who as a young man had usually waited long before entering his first marriage, quickly sought out a new wife. The widow, on the other hand, who as a young girl had been rushed into wedlock, delayed remarriage, and many widows did not remarry at all. The cities of the Renaissance consequently contained numerous male bachelors and widows, but very few spinsters and widowers. The mature male, who once had married, found it difficult to live without the continuing companionship of a woman. But the woman, after she had lost a husband, felt little compulsion to remarry.

MAKING CONNECTIONS:
WOMEN AND THE FAMILY

1.   When one compares David Herlihy's description of the Renaissance family to the analyses of the previous historians — Bullough, Shelton, and Slavin on Mesopotamia and Egypt and Dixon on Rome — it is clear that similar issues endure. Did love between husband and wife figure more prominently in Renaissance marriages than in marriages in Mesopotamia, Egypt, and Rome? Did people marry for the same reasons in Italy as they had in Mesopotamia, Egypt, and Rome? How did wealth affect mar-

riages and family life in these different civilizations? What roles did kin play in arranging marriages or in influencing families in these four cultures? What were parents' attitudes toward their children in these cultures?

2. To what extent were negative attitudes toward women, so prevalent in the ancient world, also common in Renaissance Italy? What could women in Italy do to improve their conditions, to empower themselves? Did Italian women have more opportunities to influence society in meaningful ways than did Mesopotamian, Egyptian, or Roman women? Explain.

3. Overall, Herlihy's and Dixon's articles are more optimistic about women and the family than is the article by Bullough, Shelton, and Slavin. Why do you think this is so? Do you think the articles effectively support the authors' conclusions? Did you arrive at any different conclusions? Explain.

THE FACE OF BATTLE:
AGINCOURT, OCTOBER 25th, 1415
John Keegan

Arguably the foremost military historian alive today, John Keegan taught at the English Royal Military Academy, Sandhurst, for more than a quarter century. Contemporary chroniclers (three of whom were present at the fray) left good accounts of the battle of Agincourt. Based on their documentation, Keegan seeks to understand combat from the ordinary soldier's point of view.

In the battle of Agincourt, one of the most famous battles of Western civilization, the underdog English soundly thrashed the larger French army during the Hundred Years' War. What drove the soldiers to fight? What did the battle sound like? How and in what situations did men — so many men — die? How did the social origins of different soldiers affect their motivations and methods of fighting? To what extent did the habitual violence of medieval society prepare the soldiers for the face-to-face carnage at Agincourt? Keegan engrosses us in each of the battle's stages, the soldiers' actions and perspectives, and the clash of cultures and bodies in the "fog of war."

Agincourt is one of the most instantly and vividly visualized of all epic passages in English history, and one of the most satisfactory to contemplate. It is a victory of the weak over the strong, of the common soldier over the mounted knight, of resolution over bombast, of the desperate, cornered and far from home, over the proprietorial and cocksure. . . . [I]t is an episode to quicken the interest of any schoolboy ever bored by a history lesson, a set-piece demonstration of English moral superiority and a cherished ingredient of a fading national myth. It is also a story of slaughter-yard behaviour and of outright atrocity.

John Keegan, *The Face of Battle* (New York: Random House, 1977), 79–91, 93–116.

THE CAMPAIGN

. . . In the late summer of 1415 Henry V,[1] twenty-seven years old and two years King of England, embarked on an invasion of France. He came to renew by force the claims of his house to the lands it had both won and lost during the previous century in the course of what we now call the Hundred Years War.[2] . . .

What military strategy he had in mind for the campaign can only be reconstructed by conjecture. . . . He would embark on mobile operations only after he secured a firm base, and he would seek to establish that base at the end of the shortest possible sea-route. This decision limited his choice of disembarkment place to the coasts of Normandy, Picardy, Artois or Flanders. Much the same set of considerations would cause the British and American planners of the D-Day landings[3] to plump in their case for Normandy. Henry chose the Bay of the Seine and the port of Harfleur.

The army embarked in the second week of August at Portsmouth and set sail on August 11th. It had been gathering since April, while Henry conducted deliberately inconclusive negotiations with Charles VI,[4] and now numbered about ten thousand in all, eight thousand archers and two thousand men-at-arms,[5] exclusive of camp followers. A good deal of the space in the ships, of which there were about 1,500, was given over to impedimenta[6] and a great deal to the expedition's horses: at least one for each man-at-arms, and others for the baggage train and wagon teams. The crossing took a little over two days and on the morning of August 14th the army began to disembark, unopposed by the French, on a beach three miles west of Harfleur. Three days were taken to pitch camp and on August 18th the investment[7] of the town began. . . . It lasted for nearly a month, until the collapse of an important gate-defence, the repulse of a succession of sorties and the failure of a French relieving army to appear, convinced the garrison that they must surrender. After parleys,[8] the town opened its gates to Henry on Sunday, September 22nd.

He now had his base, but was left with neither time nor force enough to develop much of a campaign that year; at least a third of his army was dead or disabled, chiefly through disease, and the autumnal rains were due. . . . At a long

---

[1] King of England from 1413 to 1422.

[2] A war (1337–1453) between the English and French kings over which ruler was the rightful king of France.

[3] The Allied invasion of German-occupied France on 6 June 1944, during World War II.

[4] King of France from 1380 to 1422.

[5] Heavily armed soldiers; sometimes mounted, but not knights.

[6] The baggage and supplies an army carries.

[7] Siege.

[8] Informal meetings to discuss the terms of surrender.

Council of War, held on October 5th, he convinced his followers that they could both appear to seek battle with the French armies which were known to be gathering and yet safely out-distance them by a march to the haven of Calais. On October 8th he led the army out.

His direct route was about 120 miles and lay across a succession of rivers, of which only the Somme formed a major obstacle. He began following the coast . . . and on October 13th swung inland to cross the Somme above its estuary. On approaching, however, he got his first news of the enemy and it was grave; the nearest crossing was blocked and defended by a force of six thousand. . . . For the next five days, while his army grew hungrier, the French kept pace with him on the northern bank until on the sixth . . . he got ahead of them. . . . On October 21st they marched eighteen miles, crossing the tracks of a major French army and, during the three following days, another fifty-three. They were now within two, at most three, marches of safety. All were aware, however, that the French had caught up and were keeping pace on their right flank. And late in the day of October 24th

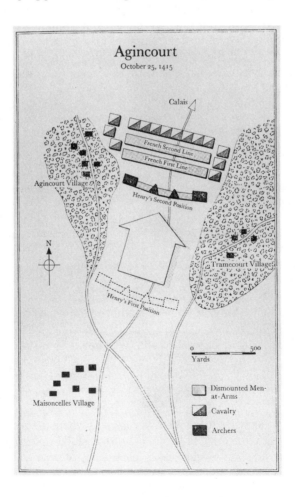

Agincourt
October 25, 1415

scouts came back with word that the enemy had crossed their path and were deploying for battle ahead of them. . . .

The English army found what shelter it could for the night in and around the village of Maisoncelles, ate its skimpy rations, confessed its sins, heard Mass and armed for battle. At first light knights and archers marched out and took up their positions between two woods. The French army, composed almost exclusively of mounted and dismounted men-at-arms, had deployed to meet them and was in similar positions about a thousand yards distant. For four hours both armies held their ground. Henry apparently hoped that the French would attack him; they, who knew that sooner or later he would have to move — either to the attack, which suited their book, or to retreat, which suited them even better — stood or sat idle, eating their breakfasts and calling about cheerfully to each other. Eventually Henry decided to up sticks (literally: his archers had been carrying pointed stakes to defend their lines for the last week) and advance on the French line. Arrived within three hundred yards — extreme bowshot — of the army, the English archers replanted their stakes and loosed off their first flights of arrows. The French, provoked by these arrow strikes, as Henry intended, into attacking, launched charges by the mounted men-at-arms from the wings of the main body. Before they had crossed the intervening space they were followed by the dismounted men-at-arms who, like them, were wearing full armour. The cavalry failed to break the English line, suffered losses from the fire of the archers and turned about. Heading back for their own lines, many riders and loose horses crashed into the advancing line of dismounted men-at-arms. They, though shaken, continued to crowd forward and to mass their attack against the English men-at-arms, who were drawn up in three groups, with archers between them and on the right and left flank. Apparently disdaining battle with the archers, although they were suffering losses from their fire, the French quickened their steps over the last few yards and crashed into the middle of the English line. For a moment it gave way. But the French were so tightly bunched that they could not use their weapons to widen the breach they had made. The English men-at-arms recovered their balance, struck back and were now joined by numbers of the archers who, dropping their bows, ran against the French with axes, mallets and swords, or with weapons abandoned by the French they picked up from the ground. There followed a short but very bloody episode of hand-to-hand combat, in which freedom of action lay almost wholly with the English. Many of the French armoured infantrymen lost their footing and were killed as they lay sprawling; others who remained upright could not defend themselves and were killed by thrusts between their armour-joints or stunned by hammer-blows. The French second line which came up, got embroiled in this fighting without being able to turn the advantage to their side, despite the addition they brought to the very great superiority of numbers the French already enjoyed. Eventually, those Frenchmen who could disentangle themselves from the mêlée made their way back to where the rest of their army, composed of a third line of mounted men-at-arms, stood watching. The English who faced them did so in several places, over heaps of dead, dying or disabled French men-at-arms, heaps said by one chronicler to be taller than a man's height.

Others were rounding up disarmed or lightly wounded Frenchmen and leading them to the rear, where they were collected under guard.

. . . [T]he English line . . . was still drawn up. Henry had prudently kept it under arms because the French third line — of mounted men — had not dispersed and he must presumably have feared that it would ride down on them if the whole English army gave itself up to taking and looting prisoners. At some time in the afternoon, there were detected signs that the French were nerving themselves to charge anyhow; and more or less simultaneously, a body of armed peasants, led by three mounted knights, suddenly appeared at the baggage park, inflicted some loss of life and stole some objects of value, including one of the King's crowns, before being driven off.

Either that incident or the continued menace of the French third line now prompted Henry to order that all the prisoners instantly be killed. The order was not at once obeyed, and for comprehensible reasons. Even discounting any moral or physical repugnance on the part of their captors, or a misunderstanding of the reason behind the order — that the prisoners might attack the English from the rear with weapons retrieved from the ground if the French cavalry were suddenly to attack their front — the poorer English soldiers, and perhaps not only the poorer, would have been very reluctant to pass up the prospects of ransom which killing the prisoners would entail. Henry was nevertheless adamant; he detailed an esquire[9] and two hundred archers to set about the execution, and stopped them only when it became clear that the French third line was packing up and withdrawing from the field. Meantime very many of the French had been killed; some of the English apparently even incinerated wounded prisoners in cottages where they had been taken for shelter.

The noblest and richest of the prisoners were, nevertheless, spared and dined that evening with the King at Maisoncelles, his base of the previous evening, to which he now returned. En route he summoned the heralds[10] of the two armies who had watched the battle together from a vantage point, and settled with the principal French herald a name for the battle: Agincourt, after the nearest fortified place. Next morning, after collecting the army, marshalling the prisoners and distributing the wounded and the loads of loot among the transport, he marched the army off across the battlefield towards Calais. Numbers of the French wounded had made their way or been helped from the field during the night; those still living, unless thought ransomable, were now killed. On October 29th, the English, with two thousand prisoners, reached Calais. The King left for England at once, to be escorted into London by an enormous party of rejoicing citizens.

These are the bare outlines of the battle, as recorded by seven or eight chroniclers, who do not materially disagree over the sequence, character or significance of events. . . .

---

[9] A minor officer of the king.

[10] Officers responsible for publicizing state proclamations, conveying messages between rulers, conducting state ceremonies, and regulating claims to titles and coats of arms.

THE BATTLE

What we almost completely lack, though, is the sort of picture and understanding of the practicalities of the fighting and of the mood, outlook and skills of the fighters which were themselves part of the eye-witness chroniclers' vision. We simply cannot visualize, as they were able to do, what the Agincourt arrow-cloud can have looked, or sounded, like; what the armoured men-at-arms sought to do to each other at the moment of the first clash; at what speed and in what density the French cavalry charged down; how the mêlée — the densely packed mass of men in hand-to-hand combat — can have appeared to a detached onlooker, say to men in the French third line; what level the noise of the battle can have reached and how the leaders made themselves heard — if they did so — above it. These questions lead on to less tangible inquiries: how did leadership operate once the fighting had been joined — by exhortation or by example? Or did concerted action depend upon previously rehearsed tactics and corporate feeling alone? Or was there, in fact, no leadership, merely every man — or every brave man — for himself? Less tangible still, what did "bravery" mean in the context of a medieval fight? How did men mentally order the risks which they faced, as we know it is human to do? Were the foot[11] more likely to be frightened of the horses, or of the men on them? Were the armoured men-at-arms more or less frightened of the arrows than of meeting their similarly clad opponents at a weapon's length? Did it seem safer to go on fighting once hard pressed than to surrender? Was running away more hazardous than staying within the press of the fighting?

The answers to some of these questions must be highly conjectural, interesting though the conjectures may be. But to others, we can certainly offer answers which fall within a fairly narrow bracket of probability, because the parameters of the questions are technical. Where speed of movement, density of formations, effect of weapons, for example, are concerned, we can test our suppositions against the known defensive qualities of armour plate, penetrative power of arrows, dimensions and capacities of the human body, carrying power and speed of the horse. And from reasonable probabilities about these military mechanics, we may be able to leap towards an understanding of the dynamics of the battle itself and the spirit of the armies which fought it.

Let us, to begin with, and however artificially, break the battle down into a sequence of separate events. It opened, as we know, with the armies forming up in the light of early morning. . . .

The two armies initially formed up at a distance of some thousand yards from each other; at either end of a long, open and almost flat expanse of ploughland, bordered on each side by woodland. . . .

The English men-at-arms, most of whom were on foot, took station in three blocks. . . . The archers were disposed between them and also on the flanks; the

---

[11] Foot soldiers.

whole line was about four or five deep. . . . Opposite them, the French were drawn up in three lines, of which the third was mounted, as were two groups, each about five hundred strong, on the flanks. The two forward lines, with a filling of crossbowmen between and some ineffectual cannon on the flanks were each, perhaps, eight thousand strong, and so ranked some eight deep. . . .

Deployed, the armies were ready for the battle, which, as we have seen, resolved itself into twelve main episodes: a period of waiting; an English advance; an English arrow strike; a French cavalry charge; a French infantry advance; a mêlée between the French and English men-at-arms; an intervention in the mêlée by the English archers; the flight of the French survivors from the scene of the mêlée; a second period of waiting, during which the French third line threatened, and a small party delivered, another charge; a French raid on the baggage park; a massacre of the French prisoners; finally, mutual departure from the battlefield. What was each of these episodes like, and what impetus did it give to the course of events?

The period of waiting — three or four hours long, and so lasting probably from about seven to eleven o'clock — must have been very trying. Two chroniclers mention that the soldiers in the front ranks sat down and ate and drank and that there was a good deal of shouting, chaffing and noisy reconciliation of old quarrels among the French. But that was after they had settled, by pushing and shoving, who was to stand in the forward rank; not a real argument, one may surmise, but a process which put the grander and the braver in front of the more humble and timid. There is no mention of the English imitating them, but given their very real predicament, and their much thinner line of battle, they can have felt little need to dispute the place of honour among themselves. It is also improbable that they did much eating or drinking, for the army had been short of food for nine days and the archers are said to have been subsisting on nuts and berries on the last marches. Waiting, certainly for the English, must then have been a cold, miserable and squalid business. It had been raining, the ground was recently ploughed, air temperature was probably in the forties or low fifties Fahrenheit and many in the army were suffering from diarrhoea. Since none would presumably have been allowed to leave the ranks while the army was deployed for action, sufferers would have had to relieve themselves where they stood. For any afflicted man-at-arms wearing mail[12] leggings laced to his plate armour, even that may not have been possible.

The King's order to advance, which he gave after the veterans had endorsed his guess that the French would not be drawn, may therefore have been generally and genuinely welcome. Movement at least meant an opportunity to generate body heat, of which the metal-clad men-at-arms would have dissipated an unnatural amount during the morning. . . .

The army had about seven hundred yards of rain-soaked ploughland to cover. At a slow walk (no medieval army marched in step, and no modern army would

---

[12] Flexible armor.

have done so over such ground — the "cadenced pace" followed from the hardening and smoothing of the surface of roads), with halts to correct dressing,[13] it would have reached its new position in ten minutes or so. . . . "Extreme bowshot," which is the distance at which Henry presumably planned to take ground, is traditionally calculated at three hundred yards. That is a tremendous carry for a bow, however, and two hundred and fifty yards would be a more realistic judgment of the distance at which he finally halted his line from the French. . . .

. . . [T]he archers, who had each been carrying a stout double-pointed wooden stake since the tenth day of the march, had now to hammer these into the ground, at an angle calculated to catch a warhorse in the chest. . . .

ARCHERS VERSUS INFANTRY AND CAVALRY

The archers were now in position to open fire (an inappropriate expression, belonging to the gunpowder age, which was barely beginning). Each man disposed his arrows as convenient. He would have had a sheaf, perhaps two, of twenty-four arrows and probably struck them point down into the ground by his feet. The men in the front two ranks would have a clear view of the enemy, those behind only sporadic glimpses: there must therefore have been some sort of ranging order passed by word of mouth. For the archers' task at this opening moment of the battle was to provoke the French into attacking, and it was therefore essential that their arrows should "group" as closely as possible on the target. To translate their purpose into modern artillery language, they had to achieve a very narrow 100° zone (i.e. that belt of territory into which *all* missiles fell) and a Time on Target effect (i.e. all their missiles had to arrive simultaneously).

To speculate about their feelings at this moment is otiose. They were experienced soldiers in a desperate spot; and their fire, moreover, was to be "indirect," in that their arrows would not depart straight into the enemy's faces but at a fairly steeply angled trajectory. They need have had no sense of initiating an act of killing, therefore; it was probably their technical and professional sense which was most actively engaged in an activity which was still preliminary to any "real" fighting that might come.

They must have received at least two orders: the first to draw their bows, the second to loose their strings. How the orders were synchronized between different groups of archers is an unanswerable question, but when the shout went up or the banner down, four clouds of arrows would have streaked out of the English line to reach a height of a hundred feet before turning in flight to plunge at a steeper angle on and among the French men-at-arms opposite. These arrows cannot, however, given their terminal velocity and angle of impact, have done a great deal of harm, at least to the men-at-arms. For armour, by the early fifteenth century, was composed almost completely of steel sheet, in place of the iron mail

---

[13] The proper alignment of soldiers in formation.

which had been worn on the body until fifty years before but now only covered the awkward points of movement around the shoulder and groin. It was deliberately designed, moreover, to offer a glancing surface, and the contemporary helmet, a wide-brimmed "bascinet," was particularly adapted to deflect blows away from the head and the shoulders. We can suppose that the armour served its purpose effectively in this, the opening moment of Agincourt. But one should not dismiss the moral effect of the arrow strike. The singing of the arrows would not have moved ahead of their flight, but the sound of their impact must have been extraordinarily cacophonous, a weird clanking and banging on the bowed heads and backs of the French men-at-arms. If any of the horses in the flanking squadrons were hit, they were likely to have been hurt, however, even at this extreme range, for they were armoured only on their faces and chests, and the chisel-pointed head of the clothyard arrow would have penetrated the padded cloth hangings which covered the rest of their bodies. Animal cries of pain and fear would have risen above the metallic clatter.

CAVALRY VERSUS INFANTRY

We can also imagine oaths and shouted threats from the French. For the arrow strike achieved its object. How quickly, the chroniclers do not tell us; but as a trained archer could loose a shaft every ten seconds we can guess that it took at most a few minutes to trigger the French attack. The French, as we know, were certain of victory. What they had been waiting for was a tactical pretext: either that of the Englishmen showing them their backs or, on the contrary, cocking a snook.[14] One or two volleys would have been insult enough. On the arrival of the first arrows the two large squadrons of horse on either flank mounted — or had they mounted when the English line advanced? — walked their horses clear of the line and broke into a charge.

A charge at what? The two chroniclers who are specific about this point make it clear that the two groups of cavalry, each five or six hundred strong, of which that on the left hand was led by Clignet de Brébant[15] and Guillaume de Saveuse,[16] made the English archer flanks their target. Their aim, doubtless, was to clear these, the largest blocks of the enemy which immediately threatened them, off the field, leaving the numerically much inferior centre of English men-at-arms, with the smaller groups of their attendant archers, to be overwhelmed by the French infantry. It was nevertheless a strange and dangerous decision, unless, that is, we work on the supposition that the archers had planted their stakes among their own ranks, so concealing that array of obstacles from the French. We may then

---

[14] Making an insulting gesture with thumb to nose and fingers spread out and wiggled.

[15] French admiral (d. ca. 1430).

[16] French knight and royal officer.

visualize the French bearing down on the archers in ignorance of the hedgehog[17] their ranks concealed; and of the English giving ground just before the moment of impact, to reveal it.

For "the moment of impact" otherwise begs an important, indeed a vital question. It is not difficult to picture the beginning of the charge: the horsemen booting their mounts to form line, probably two or three rows deep, so that, riding knee to knee, they would have presented a front of two or three hundred lances, more or less equalling in width the line of the archers opposite, say three hundred yards. We can imagine them setting off, sitting (really standing) "long" in their high-backed, padded saddles, legs straight and thrust forward, toes down in the heavy stirrups, lance under right arm, left free to manage the reins (wearing plate armour obviated the need to carry a shield); and we can see them in motion, riding at a pace which took them across all but the last fifty of the two or three hundred yards they had to cover in forty seconds or so and then spurring their horses to ride down on the archers at the best speed they could manage — twelve or fifteen miles an hour.

So far so good. The distance between horses and archers narrows. The archers, who have delivered three or four volleys at the bowed heads and shoulders of their attackers, get off one more flight. More horses — some have already gone down or broken back with screams of pain — stumble and fall, tripping their neighbours, but the mass drive on and . . . and what? It is at this moment that we have to make a judgment about the difference between what happens in a battle and what happens in a violent accident. A horse, in the normal course of events, will not gallop at an obstacle it cannot jump or see a way through, and it cannot jump or see a way through a solid line of men. Even less will it go at the sort of obviously dangerous obstacle which the archers' stakes presented. Equally, a man will not stand in the path of a running horse: he will run himself, or seek shelter, and only if exceptionally strong-nerved and knowing in its ways, stand his ground. Nevertheless, accidents happen. Men, miscalculating or slow-footed, and horses, confused or maddened, do collide, with results almost exclusively unpleasant for the man. We cannot therefore say, however unnatural and exceptional we recognize collisions between man and horse to be, that nothing of that nature occurred between the archers and the French cavalry at Agincourt. For the archers were trained to "receive cavalry," the horses trained to charge home, while it was the principal function of the *riders* to insist on the horses doing that against which their nature rebelled. . . .

The two opposed "weapon principles" which military theorists recognize had, in short, both failed: the "missile" principle, personified by the archers, had failed to stop or drive off the cavalry; they, embodying the "shock" principle, had failed to crush the infantry — or, more particularly, to make them run away, for the "shock" which cavalry seek to inflict is really moral, not physical in charac-

---

[17] The obstructive devices — the pointed wooden stakes the archers had driven into the ground.

ter. It was the stakes which must have effected the compromise. The French, coming on fast, and in great numbers over a short distance, had escaped the deaths and falls which should have toppled their charge over on itself; the English, emboldened by the physical security the hedgehog of stakes lent their formation, had given ground only a little before the onset; the horses had then found themselves on top of the stakes too late to refuse the obstacle; and a short, violent and noisy collision had resulted.

Some of the men-at-arms' horses "ran out" round the flanks of the archers and into the woods. Those in the rear ranks turned their horses, or were turned by them, and rode back. But three at least, including Guillaume de Saveuse, had their horses impaled on the stakes, thumped to the ground and were killed where they lay, either by mallet blows or by stabs between their armour-joints. The charge, momentarily terrifying for the English, from many of whom French men-at-arms, twice their height from the ground, and moving at ten or fifteen miles an hour on steel-shod and grotesquely caparisoned[18] war-horses, had stopped only a few feet distant, had been a disaster for the enemy. And as they rode off, the archers, with all the violent anger that comes with release from sudden danger, bent their bows and sent fresh flights of arrows after them, bringing down more horses and maddening others into uncontrolled flight.

INFANTRY VERSUS INFANTRY

But the results of the rout went beyond the demoralization of the survivors. For, as their horses galloped back, they met the first division of dismounted men-at-arms marching out to attack the English centre. Perhaps eight thousand strong, and filling the space between the woods eight or ten deep, they could not easily or quickly open their ranks to let the fugitives through. . . . As in that which had just failed against the archers, many of the horses would have shied off at the moment of impact. But those that barged in, an occurrence to which the chroniclers testify, broke up the rhythm of the advance and knocked some men to the ground, an unpleasant experience when the soil is wet and trampled and one is wearing sixty or seventy pounds of sheet metal on the body.

This interruption in an advance which should have brought the French first division to within weapon's length of the English in three or four minutes at most gave Henry's men-at-arms ample time to brace themselves for the encounter. It also gave the archers, both those in the large groups on the wings and the two smaller groups in the central wedges, the chance to prolong their volleying of arrows into the French ranks. The range was progressively shortened by the advance, and the arrows, coming in on a flat trajectory in sheets of five thousand at ten-second intervals, must have begun to cause casualties among the French foot. For though they bowed their heads and hunched their shoulders, presenting a

---

[18] Decoratively covered.

continuous front of deflecting surface (bascinet top, breastplate, "taces" — the overlapping bands across the stomach and genitals — and leg-pieces) to the storm, some of the arrows must have found the weak spots in the visor and at the shoulders and, as the range dropped right down, might even have penetrated armour itself. The "bodkin-point" was designed to do so, and its terminal velocity, sufficient to drive it through an inch of oak from a short distance, could also, at the right angle of impact, make a hole in sheet steel.

The archers failed nevertheless to halt the French advance. But they succeeded in channelling it — or helping to channel it — on to a narrower front of attack. . . . The leading ranks bunched into three assaulting columns and drove into . . . the English line, where the men-at-arms were massed a little in rear of the archers' staked-out enclosures.

Their charge won an initial success, for before it the English men-at-arms fell back "a spear's length." What distance the chronicler means by that traditional phrase we cannot judge, and all the less because the French had cut down their lances in anticipation of fighting on foot. It probably implies "just enough to take the impetus out of the onset of the French," for we must imagine them, although puffed by the effort of a jostling tramp across three hundred yards of wet plough-land, accelerating over the last few feet into a run calculated to drive the points of their spears hard on to the enemy's chests and stomachs. The object would have been to knock over as many of them as possible, and so to open gaps in the ranks and isolate individuals who could then be killed or forced back on to the weapons of their own comrades; "sowing disorder" is a short-hand description of the aim. To avoid its achievement, the English, had they been more numerous, might have started forward to meet the French before they developed impulsion; since they were so outnumbered, it was individually prudent and tactically sound for the men most exposed to trot backwards before the French spearpoints, thus "wrong-footing" their opponents (a spearman times his thrust to coincide with the forward step of his left foot) and setting up those surges and undulations along the face of the French mass which momentarily rob a crowd's onrush of its full impact. The English, at the same time, would have been thrusting their spears at the French and, as movement died out of the two hosts, we can visualize them divided, at a distance of ten or fifteen feet, by a horizontal fence of waving and stabbing spear shafts, the noise of their clattering like that of a bully-off[19] at hockey magnified several hundred times.

In this fashion the clash of the men-at-arms might have petered out, as it did on so many medieval battlefields, without a great deal more hurt to either side — though the French would have continued to suffer casualties from the fire of the archers, as long as they remained within range and the English had arrows to shoot at them (the evidence implies they must now have been running short). We can guess that three factors deterred the antagonists from drawing off from each

---

[19] The bunching up of several players from both teams, clacking their sticks together as they vie for possession of the puck.

other. One was the English fear of quitting their solid position between the woods and behind the archers' stakes for the greater dangers of the open field; the second was the French certainty of victory; the third was their enormous press of numbers. For if we accept that they had now divided into three *ad hoc* columns and that the head of each matched in width that of the English opposite — say eighty yards — with intervals between of about the same distance, we are compelled to visualize, taking a bird's-eye viewpoint, a roughly trident-shaped formation, the Frenchmen in the prongs ranking twenty deep and numbering some five thousand in all, those in the base a shapeless and unordered mass amounting to, perhaps, another three thousand — and all of them, except for the seven or eight hundred in the leading ranks, unable to see or hear what was happening, yet certain that the English were done for, and anxious to take a hand in finishing them off.

No one, moreover, had overall authority in this press, nor a chain of command through which to impose it. The consequence was inevitable: the development of an unrelenting pressure from the rear on the backs of those in the line of battle, driving them steadily into the weapon-strokes of the English, or at least denying them that margin of room for individual manœuvre which is essential if men are to defend themselves — or attack — effectively. This was disastrous, for it is vital to recognize, if we are to understand Agincourt, that all infantry actions, even those fought in the closest of close order, are not, in the last resort, combats of mass against mass, but the sum of many combats of individuals — one against one, one against two, three against five. This must be so, for the very simple reason that the weapons which individuals wield are of very limited range and effect, as they remain even since missile weapons have become the universal equipment of the infantryman. At Agincourt, where the man-at-arms bore lance, sword, dagger, mace or battleaxe, his ability to kill or wound was restricted to the circle centered on his own body, within which his reach allowed him to club, slash or stab. Prevented by the throng at their backs from dodging, side-stepping or retreating from the blows and thrusts directed at them by their English opponents, the individual French men-at-arms must shortly have begun to lose their man-to-man fights, collecting blows on the head or limbs which, even through armour, were sufficiently bruising or stunning to make them drop their weapons or lose their balance or footing. Within minutes, perhaps seconds, of hand-to-hand fighting being joined, some of them would have fallen, their bodies lying at the feet of their comrades, further impeding the movement of individuals and thus offering an obstacle to the advance of the whole column.

This was the crucial factor in the development of the battle. Had most of the French first line kept their feet, the crowd pressure of their vastly superior numbers, transmitted through their levelled lances, would shortly have forced the English back. Once men began to go down, however — and perhaps also because the French had shortened their lances, while the English had apparently not — those in the next rank would have found that they could get within reach of the English only by stepping over or on to the bodies of the fallen. Supposing continuing pressure from the rear, moreover, they would have had no choice but to do so; yet in so doing, would have rendered themselves even more vulnerable to a tumble than those already felled, a human body making either an unstable fighting platform or a very effective stumbling block to the heels of a man trying to defend himself from a savage attack to his front. In short, once the French column had become stationary, its front impeded by fallen bodies and its ranks animated by heavy pressure from the rear, the "tumbling effect" along its forward edge would have become cumulative.

Cumulative, but sudden and of short duration: for pressure of numbers and desperation must eventually have caused the French to spill out from their columns and lumber down upon the archers who, it appears, were now beginning to run short of arrows. They could almost certainly not have withstood a charge by armoured men-at-arms, would have broken and, running, have left their own men-at-arms to be surrounded and hacked down. That did not happen. The chroniclers are specific that, on the contrary, it was the archers who moved to the attack. Seeing the French falling at the heads of the columns, while those on the flanks still flinched away from the final flights of arrows, the archers seized the chance that confusion and irresolution offered. Drawing swords, swinging heavier weapons — axes, bills[20] or the mallets they used to hammer in their stakes — they left their staked-out positions and ran down to assault the men in armour. . . .

. . . [W]hile an archer swung or lunged at a man-at-arms' front, another dodged his sword-arm to land him a mallet-blow on the back of the head or an axe-stroke behind the knee. Either would have toppled him and, once sprawling, he would have been helpless; a thrust into his face, if he were wearing a bascinet, into the slits of his visor, if he were wearing a closed helmet, or through the mail of his armpit or groin, would have killed him outright or left him to bleed to death. Each act of execution need have taken only a few seconds; time enough for a flurry of thrusts clumsily parried, a fall, two or three figures to kneel over another on the ground, a few butcher's blows, a cry *in extremis*.[21] . . . Little scenes of this sort must have been happening all over the two narrow tracts between the woods and the fringes of the French main body within the first minutes of the main battle being joined. The only way for stranded Frenchmen to avoid such a death at the hands of the archers was to ask for quarter, which at this early stage they may not have been willing to grant, despite prospects of ransom. A surrendered enemy, to be put *hors de combat*,[22] had to be escorted off the field, a waste of time and manpower the English could not afford when still at such an apparent disadvantage.

But the check in the front line and the butchery on the flanks appear fairly quickly to have swung the advantage in their favour. The "return charge" of the French cavalry had . . . caused some of the French to retreat in panic, and it is pos-

---

[20] Shafted weapons with hook-like cutting blades.

[21] At the point of death.

[22] Out of action.

sible that panic now broke out again along the flanks and at the front. If that were so — and it is difficult otherwise to make sense of subsequent events — we must imagine a new tide of movement within the French mass: continued forward pressure from those at the back who could not see, a rearward drift along the flanks of the columns by those who had seen all too clearly what work the archers were at, and a reverse pressure by men-at-arms in the front line seeking, if not escape, at least room to fight without fear of falling, or being pushed, over the bodies of those who had already gone down. These movements would have altered the shape of the French mass, widening the gaps between its flanks and the woods, and so offering the archers room to make an "enveloping" attack. Emboldened by the easy killings achieved by some of their number, we must now imagine the rest, perhaps at the King's command, perhaps by spontaneous decision, massing outside their stakes and then running down in formation to attack the French flanks. . . .

Given the horror of their situation, the sense of which must now have been transmitted to the whole mass, the French ought at this point to have broken and run. That they did not was the consequence, once again, of their own superiority of numbers. For heretofore it had only been the first division of their army which had been engaged. The second and the third had stood passive, but as the first began to give way, its collapse heralded by the return of fugitives from the flanks, the second walked forward across the wet and trampled ground to lend it support. This was exactly *not* the help needed at that moment. Had the cavalry, in third line, been brought forward to make a second charge against the archers, now that they were outside the protection of their stakes and without their bows, they might well have achieved a rescue. But they were left where they were, for reasons impossible to reconstruct. Instead, the second division of infantrymen arrived and, thrusting against the backs of their tired and desperate compatriots, held them firmly in place to suffer further butchery.

From what the chroniclers say, we can suppose most of those in the French first line now to be either dead, wounded, prisoner or ready to surrender, if they could not escape. Many had made their surrender . . . ; some had not had it accepted: the Duke of Alençon,[23] finding himself cut off and surrounded in a dash to attack the Duke of Gloucester,[24] shouted his submission over the heads of his attackers to the King, who was coming to his brother's rescue, but was killed before Henry could extricate him. Nevertheless, very large numbers of Frenchmen had, on promise of ransom, been taken captive, presumably from the moment when the English sensed that the battle was going their way. Their removal from the field, the deaths of others, and the moral and by now no doubt incipient physical collapse of those left had opened up sufficient space for the English to abandon their close order and penetrate their enemy's ranks.

---

[23] John the Wise, duke from 1404 to 1415.

[24] Humphrey (1390–1447), brother of Henry V and lover of the wife of the Duke of Brabant.

This advance brought them eventually — we are talking of an elapsed time of perhaps only half an hour since the first blows were exchanged — into contact with the second line. They must themselves have been tiring by this time. For the excitement, fear and physical exertion of fighting hand-to-hand with heavy weapons in plate armour quickly drained the body of its energy, despite the surge of energy released under stress by glandular activity. Even so, they were not repulsed by the onset of the second line. Indeed, its intervention seems to have made no appreciable impact on the fighting. There is a modern military cliché, "Never reinforce failure," which means broadly that to thrust reinforcements in among soldiers who have failed in an attack, feel themselves beaten and are trying to run away is merely to waste the newcomers' energies in a struggle against the thrust of the crowd and to risk infecting them with its despair. And it was indeed in congestion and desperation that the second line appear to have met the English. . . .

What facts the chroniclers do provide about this, the culmination of the hand-to-hand phase, are difficult to reconcile. The English appear to have had considerable freedom of movement, for they were taking hundreds prisoner and the King and his entourage are reported to have cut their way into the second line (it may have been then that he took the blow which dented the helmet which is still to be seen above his tomb in Westminster Abbey). And yet in at least three places, suggested by the priest's narrative to have been where the enemy columns initially charged the English men-at-arms, the bodies of the French lay piled "higher than a man." Indeed the English are said to have climbed these heaps "and butchered the adversaries below with swords, axes and other weapons."

This "building of the wall of dead" is perhaps the best known incident of the battle. If it had occurred, however, we cannot accept that the King and his armoured followers were able to range freely about the field in the latter stages, since the heaps would have confined them within their own positions. Brief reflection will, moreover, demonstrate that the "heap higher than a man" is a chronicler's exaggeration. Human bodies, even when pushed about by bulldozers, do not, as one can observe if able to keep one's eyes open during film of the mass-burials at Belsen,[25] pile into walls, but lie in shapeless sprawling hummocks. When stiffened by rigor mortis, they can be laid in stacks, as one can see in film of the burial parties of a French regiment carting its dead from the field after an attack in the Second Battle of Champagne[26] (September 1915). But men falling to weapon-strokes in the front line, or tripping over those already down, will lie at most two or three deep. For the heaps to rise higher, they must be climbed by the next victims: and the "six-foot heaps" of Agincourt could have been topped-out only if men on either side had been ready and able to duel together while balancing on the corpses of twenty or thirty others. The notion is ludicrous rather than grisly.

---

[25] Site of a German extermination camp during World War II.

[26] A battle during World War I.

The dead undoubtedly lay thick at Agincourt, and quite probably, at the three places where fighting had been heaviest, in piles. But what probably happened at those spots, as we have seen, is that men-at-arms and archers achieved an envelopment of the heads of the French columns, hemmed in and perhaps completely surrounded groups of the enemy, toppled them over on top of each other with lance thrusts and killed them on the ground. The mounds thus raised were big and hideous enough to justify some priestly rhetoric — but not to deny the English entry into the French positions.

THE KILLING OF THE PRISONERS

Indeed, soon after midday, the English men were "in possession of the field" — by which soldiers would understand that they were able to move freely over the ground earlier occupied by the French, of whom only dead, wounded and fugitives were now to be seen. Fugitives too slow-footed to reach hiding in the woods, or sanctuary among the cavalry of the still uncommitted third division, were chased and tackled by bounty-hunters; others, greedy for ransom, were sorting through the recumbent bodies and pulling "down the heaps . . . to separate the living from the dead, proposing to keep the living as slaves, to be ransomed." At the back of the battlefield the most valuable prisoners were massed together under guard. They were still wearing their armour but had surrendered their right gauntlets to their captors, as a token of submission (and subsequent re-identification), and taken off their helmets, without which they could not fight.

Henry could not allow each captor individually to sequester his prisoners because of the need to keep the army together as long as the French third division threatened a charge. So while small parties, acting both on their own behalf and that of others still in the ranks, reaped the rewards of the fight, the main bodies of men-at-arms and archers stood their ground — now about two or three hundred yards forward of the line on which they had received the French charge. Henry's caution was justified. Soon after midday, the Duke of Brabant,[27] arriving late, half-equipped, and with a tiny following, charged into these ranks. He was overpowered and led to the rear. But this gallant intervention inspired at least two French noblemen in the third division . . . to marshal some six hundred of their followers for a concerted charge. They could clearly be seen massing, two or three hundred yards from the English line, and their intentions were obvious. At about the same time, moreover, shouting from the rear informed the English of a raid by the enemy on the baggage park, which had been left almost unguarded.

It was these events which precipitated Henry's notorious order to kill the prisoners. As it turned out, the charge was not delivered and the raid was later revealed to have been a mere rampage by the local peasantry. . . . The signs were enough, however, to convince Henry that his victory, in which he can scarcely

---

[27] Youngest son of John the Fearless, Duke of Burgundy.

have yet believed, was about to be snatched from him. For if the French third division attacked the English where they stood, the archers without arrows or stakes, the men-at-arms weary after a morning of hacking and banging in full armour, all of them hungry, cold and depressed by the reaction from the intense fears and elations of combat, they might easily have been swept from the field. They could certainly not have withstood the simultaneous assault on their rear, to which, with so many inadequately guarded French prisoners standing about behind them on ground littered with discarded weapons, they were likely also to have been subjected. In these circumstances, his order is comprehensible. . . .

His subordinates nevertheless refused to obey. Was this because they felt a more tender conscience? The notion is usually dismissed by medieval specialists, who insist that, at best, the captors objected to the King's interference in what was a personal relationship, the prisoners being not the King's or the army's but the vassals of those who had accepted their surrender; that, at worst, they refused to forgo the prospect of so much ransom money (there being almost no way for a man of the times to make a quick fortune except on the battlefield). But it is significant that the King eventually got his order obeyed only by detailing two hundred *archers,* under the command of an esquire, to carry out the task. This may suggest that, among the captors, the men-at-arms at any rate felt something more than a financially motivated reluctance. There is, after all, an important difference between fighting with lethal weapons, even if it ends in killing, and mere butchery, and we may expect it to have been all the stronger when the act of fighting was as glorified as it was in the Middle Ages. To meet a similarly equipped opponent was the occasion for which the armoured soldier trained perhaps every day of his life from the onset of manhood. To meet and beat him was a triumph, the highest form which self-expression could take in the medieval nobleman's way of life. The events of the late morning at Agincourt, when men had leapt and grunted and hacked at each other's bodies, behaving in a way which seems grotesque and horrifying to us, was for them, therefore, a sort of apotheosis, giving point to their existence, and perhaps assuring them of commemoration after death (since most chroniclers were principally concerned to celebrate individual feats of arms). But there was certainly no honour to be won in killing one's social equal after he had surrendered and been disarmed. On the contrary, there was a considerable risk of incurring dishonour, which may alone have been strong enough to deter the men-at-arms from obeying Henry's order.

Archers stood outside the chivalric system; nor is there much to the idea that they personified the yeoman[28] virtues. The bowmen of Henry's army were not only tough professional soldiers. There is also evidence that many had enlisted in the first place to avoid punishment for civil acts of violence, including murder. The chroniclers also make clear that, in the heat of combat, and during the more leisurely taking of prisoners after the rout of the French second division, there had

---

[28] A small landowner who worked his own fields.

been a good deal of killing, principally by the archers, of those too poor or too badly hurt to be worth keeping captive. The question of how more or less reluctant they were to carry out the King's command need not therefore delay us. . . .

. . . Henry's order, rather than bring about the prisoners' massacre, was intended by its threat to terrorize them into abject inactivity. . . . [T]he captors loudly announcing their refusal to obey the proclamation and perhaps assuring their prisoners that they would see them come to no harm; argument and even scuffling between them and members of the execution squad; and then a noisy and bloody cattle-drive to the rear, the archers harrying round the flanks of the crowd of armoured Frenchmen as they stumbled away from the scene of fighting and its dangerous debris to a spot nearer the baggage park, whence they could offer no serious threat at all. Some would have been killed in the process, and quite deliberately, but we need not reckon their number in thousands, perhaps not even in hundreds.

The killing, moreover, had a definite term, for Henry ordered it to end when he saw the French third division abandon their attack formation and begin to leave the battlefield. The time was about three o'clock in the afternoon, leaving some two hours more of daylight. The English began at once to spread out over the field looking for prisoners and spoil in places not yet visited. The King made a circuit and, on turning back for his quarters at Maisoncelles, summoned to him the French and English heralds.

THE WOUNDED

The heralds had watched the battle in a group together and, though the French army had left, the French heralds had not yet followed them. For the heralds belonged not to the armies but to the international corporation of experts who regulated civilized warfare. Henry was anxious to hear their verdict on the day's fighting and to fix a name for the battle, so that its outcome and the army's exploits could be readily identified when chroniclers came to record it. . . . [T]he principal French herald confirmed that the English were the victors and provided Henry with the name of the nearest castle — Agincourt — to serve as eponym.

That decision ended the battle as a military and historical episode. The English drove their prisoners and carried their own wounded back to Maisoncelles for the night, where the twenty surgeons of the army set to work. English casualties had been few: the Duke of York,[29] who was pulled from under a heap of corpses, dead either from suffocation or a heart-attack, and the Earl of Suffolk[30] were the only notable fatalities. The wounded numbered only some hundreds. What were their prospects? In the main, probably quite good. The English had not undergone

---

[29] Edward (ca. 1373–1415), politician known for his conniving.

[30] Michael de la Pole (1394–1415), earl for thirty-eight days, between his father's death at the siege of Harfleur and his own at Agincourt.

an arrow attack, so most of the wounds would have been lacerations rather than penetrations, clean even if deep cuts which, if bound up and left, would heal quickly. There would also have been some fractures; depressed fractures of the skull could not be treated — the secret of trepanning[31] awaited rediscovery — but breaks of the arm and lower leg could have been successfully set and splinted. The French wounded enjoyed a much graver prognosis. Many would have suffered penetrating wounds, either from arrows or from thrusts through the weak spots of their armour. Those which had pierced the intestines, emptying its contents into the abdomen, were fatal: peritonitis was inevitable. Penetrations of the chest cavity, which had probably carried in fragments of dirty clothing, were almost as certain to lead to sepsis. Many of the French would have suffered depressed fractures of the skull, and there would have been broken backs caused by falls from horses in armour at speed. Almost all of these injuries we may regard as fatal, the contemporary surgeons being unable to treat them. Many of the French, of course, had not been collected from the battlefield and, if they did not bleed to death, would have succumbed to the combined effects of exposure and shock during the night, when temperatures might have descended into the middle-30s Fahrenheit. It was, therefore, not arbitrary brutality when, in crossing the battlefield next morning, the English killed those whom they found alive. They were almost certain to have died, in any case, when their bodies would have gone to join those which the local peasants, under the supervision of the Bishop of Arras, dug into pits on the site. They are said to have buried about six thousand altogether.

THE WILL TO COMBAT

What sustained men in a combat like Agincourt, when the penalty of defeat, or of one's own lack of skill or nimbleness was so final and unpleasant? Some factors, either general to battle — as will appear — or more or less particular to this one are relatively easy to isolate. Of the general factors, drink is the most obvious to mention. The English, who were on short rations, presumably had less to drink than the French, but there was drinking in the ranks on both sides during the period of waiting and it is quite probable that many soldiers in both armies went into the mêlée less than sober, if not indeed fighting drunk. For the English, the presence of the King would also have provided what present-day soldiers call a "moral factor" of great importance. The personal bond between leader and follower lies at the root of all explanations of what does and does not happen in battle; and that bond is always strongest in martial societies, of which fifteenth-century England is one type and the warrior states of India, which the British harnessed so successfully to their imperial purpose, are another. The nature of the bond is more complex, and certainly more materialistic than modern ethologists would like to have us believe. But its importance must not be underestimated. And though the

---

[31] Cutting a hole in the skull to relieve brain injuries.

late-medieval soldier's immediate loyalty lay towards his captain, the presence on the field of his own and his captain's anointed king, visible to all and ostentatiously risking his life in the heart of the mêlée, must have greatly strengthened his resolve.

Serving to strengthen it further was the endorsement of religion. The morality of killing is not something with which the professional soldier is usually thought to trouble himself, but the Christian knight, whether we mean by that the ideal type as seen by the chroniclers or some at least of the historical figures of whom we have knowledge, was nevertheless exercised by it. What constituted unlawful killing in time of war was well-defined, and carried penalties under civil, military and religious law. Lawful killing, on the other hand, was an act which religious precept specifically endorsed, within the circumscription of the just war; and however dimly or marginally religious doctrine impinged on the consciousness of the simple soldier or more unthinking knight, the religious preparations which all in the English army underwent before Agincourt must be counted among the most important factors affecting its mood. Henry himself heard Mass three times in succession before the battle, and took Communion, as presumably did most of his followers; there was a small army of priests in the expedition. The soldiers ritually entreated blessing before entering the ranks, going down on their knees, making the sign of the cross and taking earth into their mouths as a symbolic gesture of the death and burial they were thereby accepting.

Drink and prayer must be seen, however, as last-minute and short-term reinforcements of the medieval soldier's (though, as we shall see, not only his) will to combat. Far more important, and, given the disparity of their stations, more important still for the common soldier than the man-at-arms, was the prospect of enrichment. Medieval warfare, like all warfare, was about many things, but medieval battle, at the personal level, was about only three: victory first, of course, because the personal consequences of defeat could be so disagreeable; personal distinction in single combat — something of which the man-at-arms would think a great deal more than the bowman; but, ultimately and most important, ransom and loot. Agincourt was untypical of medieval battle in yielding, and then snatching back from the victors the bonanza of wealth that it did; but it is the gold-strike and gold-fever character of medieval battle which we should keep foremost in mind when seeking to understand it.

We should balance it, at the same time, against two other factors. The first of these is the pressure of compulsion. The role which physical coercion or force of unavoidable circumstance plays in bringing men into, and often through, the ordeal of battle is one which almost all military historians consistently underplay, or ignore. Yet we can clearly see that the force of unavoidable circumstances was among the most powerful of the drives to combat at work on the field of Agincourt. The English had sought by every means to avoid battle throughout their long march from Harfleur and, though accepting it on October 25th as a necessary alternative to capitulation and perhaps lifelong captivity, were finally driven to attack by the pains of hunger and cold. The French had also hoped to avoid bringing their confrontation with the English to a fight; and we may convincingly surmise that many of those who went down under the swords or mallet-blows of the English had been drawn into the battle with all the free-will of a man who finds himself going the wrong way on a moving-staircase.

The second factor confounds the former just examined. It concerns the commonplace character of violence in medieval life. What went on at Agincourt appals and horrifies the modern imagination which, vicariously accustomed though it is to the idea of violence, rarely encounters it in actuality and is outraged when it does. The sense of outrage was no doubt as keenly felt by the individual victim of violence five hundred years ago. But the victim of assault, in a world where the rights of lordship were imposed and the quarrels of neighbours settled by sword or knife as a matter of course, was likely to have been a good deal less surprised by it when it occurred. As the language of English law, which we owe to the Middle Ages, reveals, through its references to "putting in fear," "making an affray" and "keeping the Queen's peace," the medieval world was one in which the distinction between private, civil and foreign war, though recognized, could only be irregularly enforced. Thus battle, though an extreme on the spectrum of experience, was not something unimaginable, something wholly beyond the peace-loving individual's ken. It offered the soldier risk in a particularly concentrated form; but it was a treatment to which his upbringing and experience would already have partially inured him.

THE DEVELOPMENT OF MANNERS
Norbert Elias

Norbert Elias (1897–1990) was a sociologist who fled Hitler's Germany and spent his academic career in England. He gained fame with his work *The Civilizing Process*, from which this selection on the development of manners is taken. Elias's starting point is the 1530 treatise by the Christian humanist Erasmus of Rotterdam, *On Civility in Children* (though Elias also consulted other contemporary books about social behavior). Erasmus instructs Europeans on proper table manners and on the control of bodily functions in public. What does Elias mean by the idea of civilité and the term *civilizing process?* Why is Erasmus's treatise so important, and what does his investigation of human conduct say about the notion of shame in the Middle Ages and in the sixteenth century?

A stark contrast existed between the behavior of medieval people at table and the conduct Erasmus advocates, yet a person today might still feel embarrassed by the discussion of the proverbial "three winds": burping, sneezing, and farting. Why does Erasmus stress outward bodily propriety? In the Middle Ages, what was socially acceptable behavior when eating, and what was the "threshold of delicacy"? Of course, proper behavior was different for the nobility than for the peasantry, as writers attempted to define manners according to social rank. Part of the difference was due to the abundance of the aristocratic table. For example, changes in utensils affected table manners. How did these changes relate to other changes for the aristocracy in education, economic and political activities, and literary and artistic tastes?

The concept of *civilité* acquired its meaning for Western society at a time when chivalrous society and the unity of the Catholic church were disintegrating. It is the incarnation of a society which, as a specific stage in the formation of Western manners or "civilization," was no less important than the feudal society before it. The concept of *civilité*, too, is an expression and symbol of a social formation embracing the most diverse nationalities, in which, as in the Church, a common lan-

Norbert Elias, *The Civilizing Process,* trans. Edmund Jephcott (New York: Urizen Books, 1978), 53–60, 62–65, 67, 69–70.

guage is spoken, first Italian and then increasingly French. These languages take over the function earlier performed by Latin. They manifest the unity of Europe, and at the same time the new social formation which forms its backbone, court society. The situation, the self-image, and the characteristics of this society find expression in the concept of *civilité*.

The concept of *civilité* received the specific stamp and function under discussion here in the second quarter of the sixteenth century. Its individual starting point can be exactly determined. It owes the specific meaning adopted by society to a short treatise by Erasmus of Rotterdam, *De civilitate morum puerilium* (On civility in children), which appeared in 1530. This work clearly treated a theme that was ripe for discussion. It immediately achieved an enormous circulation, going through edition after edition. Even within Erasmus's lifetime — that is, in the first six years after its publication — it was reprinted more than thirty times. In all, more than 130 editions may be counted, 13 of them as late as the eighteenth century. The multitude of translations, imitations, and sequels is almost without limit. . . .

. . . And a whole genre of books, directly or indirectly influenced by Erasmus's treatise, appeared under the title *Civilité* or *Civilité puérile*.[1] . . .

Here, as so often in the history of words, and as was to happen later in the evolution of the concept *civilité* into *civilisation,* an individual was the instigator. By his treatise, Erasmus gave new sharpness and impetus to the long-established and commonplace word *civilitas*.[2] Wittingly or not, he obviously expressed in it something that met a social need of the time. The concept *civilitas* was henceforth fixed in the consciousness of people with the special sense it received from his treatise. And corresponding words were developed in the various popular languages: the French *civilité,* the English "civility," the Italian *civilità,* and the German *Zivilität*. . . .

Erasmus's book is about something very simple: the behavior of people in society — above all, but not solely, "outward bodily propriety." It is dedicated to a noble boy, a prince's son, and written for the instruction of boys. . . . [T]he treatise points to attitudes that we have lost, that some among us would perhaps call "barbaric" or "uncivilized." It speaks of many things that have in the meantime become unspeakable, and of many others that are now taken for granted. . . .

Bodily carriage, gestures, dress, facial expressions — this "outward" behavior with which the treatise concerns itself is the expression of the inner, the whole man. Erasmus knows this and on occasion states it explicitly: "Although this outward bodily propriety proceeds from a well-composed mind, nevertheless we sometimes find that, for want of instruction, such grace is lacking in excellent and learned men."

---

[1] Childish civility.

[2] Civility.

There should be no snot on the nostrils, he says somewhat later. A peasant wipes his nose on his cap and coat, a sausage maker on his arm and elbow. It does not show much more propriety to use one's hand and then wipe it on one's clothing. It is more decent to take up the snot in a cloth, preferably while turning away. If when blowing the nose with two fingers something falls to the ground, it must be immediately trodden away with the foot. The same applies to spittle.

With the same infinite care and matter-of-factness with which these things are said — the mere mention of which shocks the "civilized" man of a later stage with a different affective molding — we are told how one ought to sit or greet. Gestures are described that have become strange to us, e.g., standing on one leg. . . .

The more one immerses oneself in the little treatise, the clearer becomes this picture of a society with modes of behavior in some respects related to ours, and in many ways remote. We see people seated at table. . . . The goblet and the well-cleaned knife on the right, on the left the bread. That is how the table is laid. Most people carry a knife, hence the precept to keep it clean. Forks scarcely exist, or at most for taking meat from the dish. Knives and spoons are very often used communally. There is not always a special implement for everyone: if you are offered something liquid, says Erasmus, taste it and return the spoon after you have wiped it.

When dishes of meat are brought in, usually everyone cuts himself a piece, takes it in his hand, and puts it on his plate if there are plates, otherwise on a thick slice of bread. . . .

. . . Some put their hands into the dishes when they are scarcely seated, says Erasmus. Wolves or gluttons do that. Do not be the first to take from a dish that is brought in. Leave dipping your fingers into the broth to the peasants. Do not poke around in the dish but take the first piece that presents itself. And just as it shows a want of forbearance to search the whole dish with one's hand . . . neither is it very polite to turn the dish round so that a better piece comes to you. What you cannot take with your hands, take on your *quadra.*[3] . . .

. . . Paintings of table scenes from this or earlier times always offer the same spectacle, unfamiliar to us, that is indicated by Erasmus's treatise. The table is sometimes covered with rich cloths, sometimes not, but always there is little on it: drinking vessels, saltcellar, knives, spoons, that is all. Sometimes we see the slices of bread, the *quadrae,* that in French are called *tranchoir* or *tailloir.* Everyone, from the king and queen to the peasant and his wife, eats with the hands. In the upper class there are more refined forms of this. One ought to wash one's hands before a meal, says Erasmus. But there is as yet no soap for this purpose. Usually the guest holds out his hands, and a page pours water over them. The water is sometimes slightly scented with chamomile or rosemary. In good society

---

[3] Plate or slice of bread.

one does not put both hands into the dish. It is most refined to use only three fingers of the hand. This is one of the marks of distinction between the upper and lower classes.

The fingers become greasy. . . . It is not polite to lick them or wipe them on one's coat. Often you offer others your glass, or all drink from a communal tankard. Erasmus admonishes: "Wipe your mouth beforehand." You may want to offer someone you like some of the meat you are eating. "Refrain from that," says Erasmus, "it is not very decorous to offer something half-eaten to another." And he says further: "To dip bread you have bitten into the sauce is to behave like a peasant, and it shows little elegance to remove chewed food from the mouth and put it back on the *quadra*. If you cannot swallow a piece of food, turn round discreetly and throw it somewhere."

Then he says again: "It is good if conversation interrupts the meal from time to time. Some people eat and drink without stopping, not because they are hungry or thirsty, but because they can control their movements in no other way. They have to scratch their heads, poke their teeth, gesticulate with their hands, or play with a knife, or they can't help coughing, snorting, and spitting. All this really comes from a rustic embarrassment and looks like a form of madness."

But it is also necessary, and possible, for Erasmus to say: Do not expose without necessity "the parts to which Nature has attached modesty." Some prescribe, he says, that boys should "retain the wind by compressing the belly." But you can contract an illness that way. And in another place: . . . (Fools who value civility more than health repress natural sounds.) Do not be afraid of vomiting if you must; "for it is not vomiting but holding the vomit in your throat that is foul."

With great care Erasmus marks out in his treatise the whole range of human conduct, the chief situations of social and convivial life. He speaks with the same matter-of-factness of the most elementary as of the subtlest questions of human intercourse. In the first chapter he treats "the seemly and unseemly condition of the whole body," in the second "bodily culture," in the third "manners at holy places," in the fourth banquets, in the fifth meetings, in the sixth amusement, and in the seventh the bedchamber. This is the range of questions in the discussion of which Erasmus gave new impetus to the concept of *civilitas*.

. . . The unconcerned frankness with which Erasmus and his time could discuss all areas of human conduct is lost to us. Much of what he says oversteps our threshold of delicacy.

But precisely this is one of the problems to be considered here. In tracing the transformation of the concepts by which different societies have tried to express themselves, in following back the concept of civilization to its ancestor *civilité,* one finds oneself suddenly on the track of the civilizing process itself, of the actual change in behavior that took place in the West. That it is embarrassing for us to speak or even hear of much that Erasmus discusses is one of the symptoms of this civilizing process. The greater or lesser discomfort we feel toward people who discuss or mention their bodily functions more openly, who conceal and restrain these functions less than we do, is one of the dominant feelings expressed in the judgment "barbaric" or "uncivilized." Such, then, is the nature of "barbarism and its discontents" or, in more precise and less evaluative terms, the discontent with the different structure of affects, the different standard of repugnance which is still to be found today in many societies which we term "uncivilized," the standard of repugnance which preceded our own and is its precondition. The question arises as to how and why Western society actually moved from one standard to the other, how it was "civilized." In considering this process of civilization, we cannot avoid arousing feelings of discomfort and embarrassment. It is valuable to be aware of them. It is necessary, at least while considering this process, to attempt to suspend all the feelings of embarrassment and superiority, all the value judgments and criticism associated with the concepts "civilization" or "uncivilized." Our kind of behavior has grown out of that which we call uncivilized. But these concepts grasp the actual change too statically and coarsely. In reality, our terms "civilized" and "uncivilized" do not constitute an antithesis of the kind that exists between "good" and "bad," but represent stages in a development which, moreover, is still continuing. It might well happen that our stage of civilization, our behavior, will arouse in our descendants feelings of embarrassment similar to those we sometimes feel concerning the behavior of our ancestors. Social behavior and the expression of emotions passed from a form and a standard which was not a beginning, which could not in any absolute and undifferentiated sense be designated "uncivilized," to our own, which we denote by the word "civilized." And to understand the latter we must go back in time to that from which it emerged. The "civilization" which we are accustomed to regard as a possession that comes to us apparently ready-made, without our asking how we actually came to possess it, is a process or part of a process in which we are ourselves involved. . . .

. . . What came before Erasmus? Was he the first to concern himself with such matters?

By no means. Similar questions occupied the men of the Middle Ages, of Greco-Roman antiquity, and doubtless also of the related, preceding "civilizations." . . .

The Middle Ages have left us an abundance of information on what was considered socially acceptable behavior. Here, too, precepts on conduct while eating had a special importance. Eating and drinking then occupied a far more central position in social life than today, when they provide — frequently, not always — rather the framework and introduction for conversation and conviviality. . . .

The standard of "good behavior" in the Middle Ages is, like all later standards, represented by a quite definite concept. Through it the secular upper class of the Middle Ages, or at least some of its leading groups, gave expression to their self-image, to what, in their own estimation, made them exceptional. The concept epitomizing aristocratic self-consciousness and socially acceptable behavior appeared in French as *courtoisie*, in English "courtesy," in Italian *cortezia*, along with other related terms, often in divergent forms. . . . All these concepts refer quite directly (and far more overtly than later ones with the same function) to a particular place in society. They say: That is how people behave at court. . . .

. . . What emerges as typical behavior, as the pervasive character of its precepts?

Something, in the first place, that in comparison to later times might be called its simplicity, its naïvté. There are, as in all societies where the emotions are expressed more violently and directly, fewer psychological nuances and complexities in the general stock of ideas. There are friend and foe, desire and aversion, good and bad people.

> You should follow honorable men and vent your wrath on the wicked.

. . .

> When your companions anger you, my son, see that you are not so hot-tempered that you regret it afterward.

In eating, too, everything is simpler, impulses and inclinations are less restrained:

> A man of refinement should not slurp with his spoon when in company; this is the way people at court behave who often indulge in unrefined conduct.

. . . Noble, courteous behavior is constantly contrasted to "coarse manners," the conduct of peasants.

> Some people bite a slice and then dunk it in the dish in a coarse way; refined people reject such bad manners.

If you have taken a bite from the bread, do not dip it in the common dish again. Peasants may do that, not "fine people."

> A number of people gnaw a bone and then put it back in the dish — this is a serious offense.

Do not throw gnawed bones back into the communal dish. From other accounts we know that it was customary to drop them on the floor. Another precept reads:

> A man who clears his throat when he eats and one who blows his nose in the tablecloth are both ill-bred, I assure you.

Here is another:

> If a man wipes his nose on his hand at table because he knows no better, then he is a fool, believe me.

To use the hand to wipe one's nose was a matter of course. Handkerchiefs did not yet exist. But at table certain care should be exercised; and one should on no account blow one's nose into the tablecloth. Avoid lip-smacking and snorting, eaters are further instructed:

> If a man snorts like a seal when he eats, as some people do, and smacks his chops like a Bavarian yokel, he has given up all good breeding.

If you have to scratch yourself, do not do so with your bare hand but use your coat:

> Do not scrape your throat with your bare hand while eating; but if you have to, do it politely with your coat.

Everyone used his hands to take food from the common dish. For this reason one was not to touch one's ears, nose, or eyes:

> It is not decent to poke your fingers into your ears or eyes, as some people do, or to pick your nose while eating. These three habits are bad.

Hands must be washed before meals:

> I hear that some eat unwashed (if it is true, it is a bad sign). May their fingers be palsied!

. . . If you have no towel, . . . do not wipe your hands on your coat but let the air dry them. Or:

> Take care that, whatever your need, you do not flush with embarrassment.

Nor is it good manners to loosen one's belt at table.

All this is said to adults, not only to children. To our minds these are very elementary precepts to be given to upper-class people, more elementary in many respects than what, at the present stage of behavior, is generally accepted as the norm in rural-peasant strata. . . .

This is, if it may so be called, the standard eating technique during the Middle Ages, which corresponds to a very particular standard of human relationships and structure of feeling. Within this standard there is . . . an abundance of modifications and nuances. If people of different rank are eating at the same time, the person of higher rank is given precedence when washing hands, for example, or when taking from the dish. The forms of utensils vary considerably in the course of centuries. There are fashions, but also a very definite trend that persists through the fluctuations of fashion. The secular upper class, for example, indulges in extraordinary luxury at table. It is not a poverty of utensils that maintains the standard, it is quite simply that nothing else is needed. To eat in this fashion is taken for granted. It suits these people. But it also suits them to make visible their wealth and rank by the opulence of their utensils and table decoration. At the rich tables of the thirteenth century the spoons are of gold, crystal, coral, ophite. It is occasionally mentioned that during Lent knives with ebony handles are used, at Easter knives with ivory handles, and inlaid knives at Whitsun. The soupspoons are round and rather flat to begin with, so that one is forced when using them to open one's mouth wide. From the fourteenth century onward, soupspoons take on an oval form. . . .

. . . From the sixteenth century on, at least among the upper classes, the fork comes into use as an eating instrument, arriving by way of Italy first in France and then in England and Germany, after having served for a time only for taking solid foods from the dish. Henri III[4] brought it to France, probably from Venice. His courtiers were not a little derided for this "affected" manner of eating, and at first they were not very adept in the use of the instrument: at least it was said that half

---

[4] King of France from 1574 to 1589.

the food fell off the fork as it traveled from plate to mouth. As late as the seventeenth century the fork was still essentially a luxury article of the upper class, usually made of gold or silver. What we take entirely for granted, because we have been adapted and conditioned to this social standard from earliest childhood, had first to be slowly and laboriously acquired and developed by society as a whole. . . .

However, the attitude that has just been described toward the "innovation" of the fork shows one thing with special clarity. People who ate together in the way customary in the Middle Ages, taking meat with their fingers from the same dish, wine from the same goblet, soup from the same pot or the same plate, with all the other peculiarities of which examples have been . . . given — such people stood in a different relationship to one another than we do. . . . Their affects were conditioned to forms of relationship and conduct which, by today's standard of conditioning, are embarrassing or at least unattractive. What was lacking in this *courtois* world, or at least had not been developed to the same degree, was the invisible wall of affects which seems now to rise between one human body and another, repelling and separating, the wall which is often perceptible today at the mere approach of something that has been in contact with the mouth or hands of someone else, and which manifests itself as embarrassment at the mere sight of many bodily functions of others, and often at their mere mention, or as a feeling of shame when one's own functions are exposed to the gaze of others, and by no means only then.

A RITUAL MURDER TRIAL OF JEWS IN GERMANY

R. Po-Chia Hsia

R. Po-Chia Hsia, professor of history at New York University, investigates the ritual murder trial of Jews in the fifteenth-century German town of Endingen. Hsia's sources include trial records, legal codes, literature, and art. Christians had long used Jews as scapegoats, and organized attacks on Jews occurred often in medieval Europe, especially at the time of the First Crusade and after the Black Death. In late medieval Germany, Christians charged Jews with ritual murder. According to the Christians, Jews were magicians who murdered because they needed Christian blood — especially the blood of children — to perform magic, to replace the blood Jewish males lost at circumcision, or to achieve a human appearance.

The Jews at Endingen confessed to the crime of ritual murder under torture or the threat of torture. Why do you think the magistrates and populace accepted the validity and accuracy of such confessions, and why did they fabricate the charge of ritual murder? What explains the methods of execution the court used after it had found the Jews guilty? Why did Germans link Jews to the devil? Why did Christians so hate Jews, and how did they link their execution of Jews to the death of Jesus?

Situated between the Black Forest and the Rhine, the Breisgau is a lush, fertile region irrigated by the Rhine and its tributaries with narrow, long, agricultural valleys extending from the elongated river plain gently upward onto the slopes of the Black Forest. The Breisgau occupies the heartland of the Upper Rhine valley and is today that part of Germany which borders on France and Switzerland. . . . With the elevation of the terrain the rich agricultural valleys give way to vineyards; in the later Middle Ages, viticulture was of great importance both to Alsace and to the Breisgau. The rich pastures also supported a flourishing animal husbandry:

R. Po-Chia Hsia, *The Myth of Ritual Murder: Jews and Magic in Reformation Germany* (New Haven: Yale University Press, 1988), 14–41.

horse and cattle markets could be found in the second half of the fifteenth century in Strasbourg, Freiburg, and Basel. A wide variety of handicraft and mercantile trades grew up on the basis of a fertile agrarian economy; cities like Strasbourg, Colmar, Freiburg, and Basel became centers for the wine trade, for food and leather processing, and for the many other occupations that characterized the guild economy of the later Middle Ages. . . .

The geographical, cultural, and economic unity of the Upper Rhine, however, belied its political division in the late fifteenth century: the territorial presence of the imperial Hapsburg dynasty, both in the Franche-Comté and in the Breisgau, posed a constant threat to the autonomous, republican aspirations of the Alsatian free cities and the Swiss Confederation. Politically, the Rhine formed a dividing line between the quasi-city republics of Alsace — Strasbourg, Rosheim, Obernai, Sélestat, Kaysersberg, Colmar, Münster, and Mulhouse — and the Hapsburg Further Austria (Vorderösterreich), formed around the core of Breisgau, the Black Forest, and parts of Alsace and Switzerland, with Ensisheim in Alsace as the provincial capital and Freiburg in Breisgau as its intellectual and economic center. An added dimension of tension was represented by the emergence of the Swiss Confederation after the original revolt of the peasant communities of Uri, Unterwalden, and Schwyz against the Austrian Hapsburg authorities and the subsequent incorporation of other urban and rural communities into the antinoble confederation of "the common men." The fifteenth century witnessed the growing political influence of the mountainous cantons and the emergence of a "free" communal Swiss political model, whose influence extended well into South Germany, as exemplified by the urban alliance linking Zurich with Strasbourg by means of the Rhine. Proud of their civic traditions and weary of the territorial ambitions of the Hapsburgs, the citizens of the imperial and free cities and the Swiss cantons harbored suspicions of the territorial ambitions of the imperial dynasty. But free citizens could determine their body politic without having to bend to the will of noble lords; civic freedom emboldened the magistrates and townsfolk of the Alsatian and Swiss cities to expel their Jews in the wake of the Black Death of 1348–50, despite the imperial protection accorded to this religious minority. Communal revolts, by which patrician regimes were overthrown or forced to share power with the guilds, often accompanied the pogroms.[1] Where the principle of communalism triumphed, even if Jews were permitted to return, their legal and social status became severely restricted; but for a few cases, Jews were forbidden to acquire citizenship. In contrast, where the authority of the nobility remained strong, Jews were granted the right of residence, often against the wishes of the common men. In their dynastic territories, the Hapsburgs encouraged Jewish settlement in order to benefit financially from the protection fees and taxes levied from the Jews. In 1446, the Hapsburg territorial government issued a decree in Further Austria threatening prompt prosecution of anyone who injured or

---

[1] Organized attacks on or massacres of Jews.

killed Jews. The free citizens were, so to speak, *"Judenfrei,"*[2] whereas the subjects of the Austrian regime in Breisgau, with the exception of the powerful city of Freiburg, had to tolerate the Jews of their lord.

Located on the road between Breisach and Riegel, the little town of Endingen in Breisgau perches on the north slope of the Kaiserstuhl, a high point of 557 meters overlooking the surrounding flat river valley. With a population of about two hundred households, or roughly one thousand souls, in 1470, Endingen was a small market town for the surrounding countryside. Corn and wine represented the chief commodities; most Endingers cultivated a patch of land, either as their major source of income or as an important secondary occupation. Grain, wine making, and barrel making were the three leading trades. The first handicraft guild, the shoemakers, did not appear until 1415, and the first guild ordinance dates back to 1447.

The Endingers enjoyed limited political rights. Around 1470 Endingen became a member of the third estate in the Provincial Estates (*die Landstände*), which collectively represented the towns and the peasant communities of Further Austria. In 1467, the community of Endingen consisted of a *Bürgermeister,*[3] a town council, and citizens; a civic court of ten members served as the lower court for civic and minor criminal cases. But as a territorial town the political autonomy of Endingen had clear limits. The administration of criminal justice had been pawned by the Austrian archdukes in order to raise cash for the perennial financial needs of the Hapsburgs. For most of the fourteenth and fifteenth centuries, the lords of Üsenberg, local noblemen, administered justice for the Hapsburg authorities; in 1467, the town's justice was administered by the nobleman Martin von Staufen. One of the hallmarks of subjection to feudal lordship was the need to tolerate Jews: in 1331, some Jews lived in Endingen under the protection of the lord of Üsenberg; and in 1427, Duke Friedrich of Austria promised the townsfolk that he would not force them to accept Jews, a promise the Hapsburg did not keep.

At Easter 1470, the charnel[4] of Saint Peter's Parish Church in Endingen caved in and had to be demolished. Removing bones from the charnel for reburial, workers came across the remains of a man, a woman, and what looked like two small, headless corpses. Someone remembered that eight years ago, in 1462, many Jews had gathered in the house of Elias to celebrate Passover and a poor beggar family had been given refuge by Elias. Suspicion of murder soon fell on the Jews of Endingen. It is not clear exactly who brought up the charges in 1470: oral legend and the subsequently composed *Judenspiel*[5] have the Bürgermeister and the town council of Endingen writing to Archduke Sigismund in Innsbruck, who

---

[2] Literally "Jew-free"; a term used by the Nazis to describe their goal for Europe.

[3] Mayor.

[4] A place to keep bones and corpses.

[5] "The Play of the Jews"; a morality play written about this episode.

had inherited the Hapsburg lands on the Upper Rhine; another account has Ludwig, the lord of Lichtenberg, as the initiator of the inquiry. In any event, the matter came to the attention of Archduke Sigismund, who then instructed Karl, margrave of Baden, his governor, or *Statthalter,* to take charge of the investigation. Karl of Baden ordered the arrest of the Endingen Jews.

On 24 March the magistrates arrested Elias of Endingen and his brothers, Eberlin and Mercklin. Thus began the notorious Endingen ritual murder trial, which resulted in the execution of the three brothers and the expulsion of the rest of the Jewish families. Five major sources of very different degrees of reliability document the Endingen ritual murder trial: the first is a record of the interrogation of the three Endingen Jews, Elias, Eberlin, and Mercklin, deposited in the city archive of Freiburg; the second, a copy of the confessions of Elias, Eberlin, and Mercklin and those of three Jews subsequently arrested in Pforzheim, deposited in the city archive of Strasbourg; the third, again a copy of the confessions of Elias and Mercklin of Endingen and of four Pfrozheim Jews, in addition to two imperial mandates, deposited in the city archive of Frankfurt; the fourth, a ballad, "The Song of the Parents and Innocent Children"; and the last, a play commemorating the occasion, the *Judenspiel* of Endingen.

The Freiburg copy of the confessions is probably the earliest account we have of the alleged murder — the arrest and confessions of the Pforzheim Jews came later — and any reconstruction of the real event has to begin here. We must, however, approach this document with extreme caution because the guilt of the Jews had already been assumed, as the opening sentence of the record clearly indicates. It is worth quoting the confessions at length:

> On the Saturday before Easter Sunday [24 March] in the year of Our Lord [14]70, Elias, Jew at Endingen, was held and questioned as to what he knew of the murder committed some years ago in Endingen by the Jews, because one knows well, that nobody else but the Jews had committed the murder. . . . First, he should answer whether he knew that some years ago several poor people had used his shearing shed as lodging. To this, Elias the Jew answered without any torture or pain that some time back, perhaps eight years ago, some poor people were resting on his lane and would have liked to have some lodging — they were a man, a woman, with two children and a small horse. Whereupon his wife Serlin invited these poor people into the shed, where they could find plenty of straw for their beds. The poor people then went into the shed with their two children. After that Elias was asked . . . as to who had murdered them and who else were present. To this Elias the Jew answered: the murder was committed in the same night in his shed by Mennlin the Jew, Mercklin the Jew, Leoman the Jew, Hesman the Younger, a Jew, Matthew the Jew, and an alien vagabond Jew. They helped one another to commit the murder and in the same night they carried the four murdered persons out the back door of the shed into the lane, passing by the house of Cunlin Binder on the way to the charnel. Elias was then asked whether he was in the shed at the same time and what he had done. To this he answered: he was not inside the shed but kept watch by the house. . . . He was told by the other Jews to wait there; he did their bidding, but went to the shed anyway to find out what the other Jews were doing with the poor folks, and

through a crack in the door, he saw how each of them took one person and murdered them with sickles and then carried the very same murdered persons out the back door to the charnel. He also said that his brother Eberlin was waiting in the street near the bridge. Elias the Jew said that the Jews then carried the blood of the young children in a glass and their heads into his room.

In confessing to being a witness of the gruesome murders, instead of being a killer himself, Elias was trying to gain some respite and a lighter sentence. Except for the first question, which he answered voluntarily, torture was undoubtedly applied during the rest of the interrogation. Eventually, enough pain produced the desired answers. Elias confessed further to the magistrates that Mennlin and Hesman wanted to buy his silence but that he did not take any money from them. They then threatened his life and warned him not to go before the Jewish elders; if he should denounce them, they would implicate him in the murder as well. Later Mercklin gave his wife, Serlin, money to buy her silence. Elias found out that the bodies were buried in the charnel house in the Christian cemetery. In the subsequent counsel to cover up the "crime," during which Elias was present, the Jews agreed to the pretense of praying so that people would not become suspicious of any cries of the poor folks they might have heard. It was the time, after all, when the Jews of Endingen were celebrating the Feast of the Tabernacle.[6] Later, Mennlin told Elias that he sold the blood to Leo, a rich Jew in Pforzheim, and that the foreign vagabond Jew rode away with the horse. When asked by the magistrates about the heads of the parents, Elias said he only saw the heads of the children. Finally, at the end of a lengthy interrogation, Elias described the children as a boy and a girl.

Eberlin's ordeal came next. According to the interrogation record, he confessed without torture. Probably the sight of the instruments of pain was enough to secure his cooperation. A new element emerged in Eberlin's testimony. He told of a counsel in Elias's house in which the decision was taken to murder the Christian family; his own task in the plot was to keep watch by the bridge. He repeated the information given by Elias that six men — Mennlin, Hesman, Mercklin, Leoman, Matthew, and a foreign Jew — had committed the murder. More gory details came out. The Jews who carried the blood of the children and their heads into Elias's room, where several old and young Jews were waiting, were bloody and had to wash the blood off their arms. According to Elias, the bodies of the victims were buried in the charnel so that if they were discovered, people would suspect Christians and not Jews of the crime. But when the magistrates questioned him about the blood, Eberlin seemed to have trouble satisfying his inquisitors:

> After that Eberlin the Jew was asked what the Jews did with the Christian blood and to say why the Jews needed it. In reply he answered badly . . . , that the Jews need Christian blood for their circumcision.

---

[6] A harvest festival also called Sukkot.

Furthermore, Eberlin also said he saw the heads of the two children; that Leoman gave him ten guldens[7] to buy his silence; that Mennlin and the foreign Jew went away with the blood and the two heads; that they murdered first the adults and then the children; and that the Jews back in the house conspired to make a loud cry while the others were slaughtering the Christians in the shed in order to drown out their death cries. Moreover, Eberlin stated that Serlin, his sister-in-law, had given the poor Christians some milk earlier in the evening to make them sleep more soundly. At the end of his interrogation, the clerk recorded:

> Thus all that is written down has been confessed to by Eberlin without torture, and he begged to be allowed to become a Christian, that he wanted to be and remain a good Christian until his end, and that he wanted to do all that a pious Christian would do.

While fear might have overwhelmed Eberlin and broken his spirit even without torture, the third brother, Mercklin, tried to be courageous. Two days later, on Monday, 26 March, the magistrates interrogated a more defiant Mercklin:

> He was asked what he knew of the murder in Endingen, which his two brothers, Elias and Eberlin, had each on their own confessed as to who had committed the murder and how it was done. To this Mercklin the Jew replied: if his brothers had said so, you should know well enough. Why do I need to say anything?

The magistrates rebuked him and told him that it did not matter what his brothers had said, they also wanted to hear about it from him. He was tortured and admitted "with many enforced words" to the crime, including his own role in killing the woman by slitting her throat, that the foreign Jew killed the husband, and that the parents were awake but the children were asleep when they were killed. After they had murdered the parents, they then slaughtered the children and collected their blood. Since he was the strongest, he carried the body of the man to the cemetery, while the other Jews carried the woman and the headless children. At the cemetery, Mennlin climbed up the bone hill, dug a hole, and threw the bodies into it, covering them up with bones.

The magistrates then asked Mercklin whether the Jews had used the blood of the adults:

> To that he answered no; they did not collect the blood of the adults, only the children's. Mercklin was then asked why they had killed off the adults if they did not use their blood. To that he answered: they did it because they wanted to have the children. Afterwards, Mercklin was asked as to why Jews need Christian blood. To that he answered in many words, saying at first that Jews need Christian blood because it has great healing power. . . . We would not be satisfied with this answer and told him he was lying, that we knew why they need it because his brother Eberlin had told us already. To this Mercklin said that Jews need Chris-

---

[7] Gold or silver coins of Germany, the Netherlands, and Austria.

tian blood for curing epilepsy. But we replied: Why then is your son an epileptic? And we would not be satisfied with the answer. Mercklin then said further that Jews need Christian blood for its taste because they themselves stink. But we would not be satisfied with the answer and told him he was lying, and must tell us the truth, because his brother Eberlin told us a different story; now he must also tell us the truth. To this he answered badly that he wanted to tell us the truth, that he saw it cannot be otherwise . . . but that Jews need Christian blood for circumcision. Mercklin was then asked once more about the aforementioned things and [we] reproached him: if you Jews all know so well that Christian blood is good and salutary . . . , why don't you make your own blood salutary and accept baptism? To that he answered, it is the devil's work.

Even a proud, defiant man like Mercklin could not stand up to repeated torture. It is clear from the testimony on the alleged Jewish use of Christian blood that the poor man was utterly confused. He obviously had some ideas of Christian blood superstitions and seemed to have been desperately seeking the correct answer that would satisfy the magistrates and end his torture. Eventually, he came upon the expected "truth." "Justice" came swiftly. The end of the interrogation protocol recorded the Jews' execution by burning on 4 April.

What can we make of this judicial record of confessions to a heinous crime? It would be tempting to dismiss it as propaganda, a document of hatred reflective of anti-Jewish prejudices and Christian superstitions and practically worthless as a historical record. Certainly it is useless as a documentation of an event, the alleged crime, because, in all probability, even if these were violent deaths, the Jews did not commit them. In other words, the crucial question concerns not a murder; at issue is the fabrication of the "event" of a ritual murder out of diverse fragments of social reality: the discovery of the bodies, the long-standing suspicion of Jews, their incarceration and judicial torture, and their execution. The interrogation record represents an attempt to create coherence out of troubling disparate facts; it is itself less a documentation of a historical event than a testimony to the process of cultural representation that blamed Jews for child murders and sent them to their deaths.

The unreliability of the interrogation record as a judicial document is borne out by a comparison with the confessions from the city archives of Frankfurt and Strasbourg, which contain some telling variations. Aside from the three main characters — the brothers Elias, Eberlin, and Mercklin — there is a coterie of accomplices whose identities remain shadowy in spite of zealous official investigation. The Freiburg copy of the interrogation record, on which the traditional tale of the Endingen trial is based, names Elias, Eberlin, Mercklin, Mennlin, Leoman, Hesman, Matthew, an unnamed foreign Jew, Serlin (Elias's wife), and Leo of Pforzheim. The Frankfurt manuscript contains, in addition to the condensed versions of the confessions of Elias and Mercklin, long confession by Smolle, the son of Mennlin, and shorter ones by Berman, Leo of Pforzheim, and Leo the Young Jew. These men were arrested in Pforzheim and interrogated by Karl of Baden after the three brothers had been executed. While Berman might have been the Hesman named by Elias, the two sets of confessions vary significantly, especially regarding the confusion of roles. In one set of confessions, Mennlin sold the children's blood to Leo of Pforzheim; in the other, it was his son, Smolle. In one, Mennlin climbed the bone hill to dig a hole in order to dispose of the bodies; in the other, it was again Smolle. In one confession, Mercklin suffered repeated tortures and gave many answers before he admitted, to the satisfaction of his interrogators, that Jews needed Christian blood for circumcision; in the other, he confessed right away to the alleged secret purpose behind the Jewish use of Christian blood. The Frankfurt version omits Eberlin's confession altogether, while the Strasbourg manuscript records the confessions of the three brothers but only three of the four Pforzheim Jews' testimonies; Leo the Younger's confession is missing. Evidently, the three copies amount to three variants of the same ritual murder confessions. According to any principle of jurisprudence, serious questions must be raised as to the accuracy of the confessions, especially if they contain contradictory information on roles in a murder case.

If these confessions are opaque as text of a judicial inquest, they are, however, richly revealing of the context in which they were generated, and by "decoding" this text in its political and religious context we can begin to reconstruct the historical process behind the so-called Endingen ritual murder.

Compared to the Frankfurt and Strasbourg manuscripts, which seem unstructured in legal format, lacking the exact dates of interrogation and the precise questions asked, the Freiburg copy is a model of procedural clarity. The Freiburg copy recorded the confessions according to the guidelines for judicial clerks specified in the 1507 Bamberg Criminal Code, which served as a model to the 1532 criminal code of Emperor Charles V,[8] the *Carolina*: the clerks were to record carefully the times and places of each interrogation, the questions asked, and the answers given by the suspects. By contrast, the six confessions in the Frankfurt manuscript lack details and structure. And why should Eberlin's confession be missing? A bad transcription of the original interrogation records might have produced the discrepancy, but it suggests that the lucid narrative structure of the Freiburg copy is the result of a synopsis, a redaction of the contradictory notes taken during the interrogations; it represents a "clean" copy, its clear chronology and sequence of events superimposed on the confused and spontaneous utterings of the men under torture. Moreover, internal evidence also suggests that the confessions were highly dubious as judicial records; contradictions and tensions in the confessions are clearly evident from a close reading of the text. First, the guilt of the Jews was already assumed in the opening sentence: "One knows well that nobody else but the Jews had committed these crimes." In addition, the interrogation record minimized the application of torture: Elias confessed "without any torture and pain" . . . , according to the Freiburg manuscript; in the Frankfurt manuscript, he confessed "out of free will and uncoerced" . . . ; Eberlin also confessed "without torture." . . . But there is evidence to contradict this. After Karl of

---

[8] Holy Roman Emperor from 1519 to 1556, and king of Spain.

Baden executed the three brothers, Emperor Friedrich III[9] wrote a stern letter, rebuking the margrave because he had, without imperial approval, "on account of the alleged murder of some Christians at Endingen in Breisgau imprisoned several Jews, condemned some of them to death, and held others in prison under severe torture and pain."

The terror and confusion faced by the three brothers and the other Jews arrested by Karl of Baden is easily imagined. Thrown into cold, damp, dark cells, often without ventilation, dragged before the rack and the pulley, iron fetters around their legs, necks, and arms, and forced to confess to a spurious murder eight years past, the Jews would have to muster superhuman strength to maintain their innocence. The ubiquitous instrument of torture in Europe before the French Revolution was the *strappada,* by which the suspect's hands were tied together behind his back with a rope, which was then thrown over a beam. Hoisted in midair, the poor fellow was left to hang for some time; often weights were added to his feet to increase the strain on the arms and back muscles. . . . A few jolts usually sufficed to loosen joints as well as tongues, and only the hardiest did not break down and confess. Apparently Eberlin broke down without actually undergoing torture, and the stronger Mercklin was also eventually reduced to confess. Both Elias and Eberlin tried to save their lives by confessing to acting as accomplices, hoping, perhaps, if not for pardon, then for imprisonment, mutilation, or a relatively quick death by the sword. Other ways of execution, as prescribed by the *Carolina* and the Bamberg Criminal Code, were much more painful: death by fire, by quartering, by the gallows, or by drowning, by having one's limbs broken on the wheel or by being buried alive, or by being tortured with red hot pincers before execution.

The brothers' confessions did not save them. Karl of Baden condemned all three to death. As the Endingen *Judenspiel* commemorated, the three brothers were stripped, wrapped in dry cowhide, tied to horsetails, dragged to their execution ground, and burnt. . . . The dragging of condemned criminals to execution sites was a customary practice at the time; it signified the denigration of the murderers to the level of beasts, men who had lost their human reason. For Jews, this kind of humiliation was not unusual. When Michael the Jew was executed for theft in Dortmund in 1486, he was hung at the gallows between two dogs, a particularly degrading mode of execution for Jewish criminals that gradually disappeared during the sixteenth century. . . . Death by burning for a murder was exceptional: men who committed premeditated murders were normally broken on the wheel and left to die; murders mitigated by anger or other circumstances deserved death by the sword; and women who killed infants were drowned. Only heretics and black magicians were burnt. To Christians of the late fifteenth century, the Jews of Endingen embodied a despicable cross of both.

Let us return for a moment to the interrogation record. Having examined its reliability as a judicial document, we conclude that it contains inaccuracies of tes-

---

[9] Holy Roman Emperor from 1440 to 1493.

timony and prior assumption of guilt. If it appears highly ambivalent as a historical and legal document, upon which the Jews were sent to their deaths, how is it to be interpreted? One strategy would be to examine it as a social text, a discourse, in which various social voices made use of the ensemble of religious, political, legal, and magical vocabularies to contest and define the nature of social reality; perhaps then can we begin to understand the multiplicity of meaning the language of accusation had for the participants.

Three structural levels to this ritual murder discourse can be distinguished. The first, or fundamental, level was also chronologically the earliest phase: the initial rumor and gossip when the bodies of the murdered Christians were discovered in the bone hill of the charnel. People immediately suspected the Jews. This initial process can be described as the appropriation of an immemorial legend — one transmitted by village gossip, chronicles, folk songs, tales, pictorial depictions, sculptures, pilgrimages, and shrines — namely, that Jews had murdered Christian children in the past and that blood played a central role in Jewish magic. The first phase of the ritual murder discourse thus activated a tradition about Jews and applied this "knowledge" toward explaining and resolving an immediate problem in daily life. In Endingen, a murder needed to be solved. The dialogue during this initial phase took place between an impersonal discourse and a particular actor: the impersonal discourse of ritual murder was articulated in part by historical events (ritual murder trials in the past), transmitted by the various media of popular culture, sanctioned by some ecclesiastical authorities, confirmed by the judicial actions of lords and magistrates, and authenticated and recorded in chronicles; the particular actor could be a peasant, a burgher, a nobleman, a prince, a town council, or a community. In the case of Endingen, the trial record refers to an impersonal, unspecified source — rumors, gossip, or popular discourse — which has come to take the place of truth "because one knows well that nobody else committed the murder but the Jews." As we shall see later, however, this was not exactly how suspicion first befell the Jews.

The second level or phase of a ritual murder discourse moved from accusation to official investigation. Now the murmurs and whispers of popular gossip became submerged in the official voice of the judicial apparatus and the protestations of the suspects. The interlocution took place between officers of the law in the Holy Roman Empire — princes, magistrates, and bailiffs, who acted both on the discourse of ritual murder and the common laws of the empire — and the accused Jews, who were interrogated under judicial torture to confess to the crimes. Naturally, the dialogue was uneven, since the magistrates called in witnesses, weighed the evidence, and applied torture, while the Jews tried steadfastly to maintain their innocence or broke down and confessed under fear and pain in this unequal power play. Legends of Jewish magic, which helped to trigger the initial accusation, were thus further reinforced by the confessions of the imprisoned. In the Endingen trial, Leo of Pforzheim, who was supposed to have purchased the children's blood from the Endingen Jews, confessed that some eighteen or twenty years back, he and his father had attended a circumcision. He saw red liquid in a cup and asked his father what it was. His father answered that it was Christian blood necessary for circumcision. The moment of "truth" extracted under torture in 1470 in fact retroactively validated ritual murder trials in the past; in ritual murder discourse, past and present engaged in a self-affirming historical dialectic, through which social knowledge produced eternal truths, and experience and interpretation formed a seamless whole.

At this stage the discourse turned political: city councils exchanged queries and warnings about other possible ritual murders, and jurisdictions were often contested, as when Emperor Friedrich III reproached Karl of Baden for summarily executing imperial Jews. Read as a social text, the Endingen confessions resemble the write-up of an originally unspoken and unarticulated dialogue, one that already existed in the minds of the magistrates and was finally written as text when the Jews were forced to utter their lines. The scenario of the "murder" was a confused montage of legends about Jews and biblical and parabiblical narratives woven into a meaningful whole by the central "fact" of a murder-sacrifice. No one would have missed the identification between the poor murdered Christian family and the Holy Family: the description of the husband and wife, their two young children, and their small horse in the shed, spending their night on straw, must have represented to the Endingers the image of Joseph and a pregnant Mary sojourning with their donkey in a stable in Bethlehem. The Christians were slaughtered in Elias's shearing shed like innocent lambs, like Jesus victims of the bloodthirsty Jews with their butcher knives.

The religious subtext and the social context of the Endingen trial record are manifest in the third and final level of this ritual murder discourse. After three gruesome days of torture, the climax of the investigation was not the admission of murder by Mercklin but the confession of motive: that Jews killed the children for the healing and salutary power of Christian blood. Without Christian blood, there would be no circumcision; without the even greater power of Christian sacrifice, Jewish magic was impotent. Christianity triumphed. Eberlin wanted to convert and live out the rest of his life as a good Christian; Mercklin admitted to the greater efficacy of Christian blood and confessed that the Devil was preventing the Jews from conversion. Only the sentencing and the public executions of the Jews remained. Banished were the discordant voices of unequal contestation during the interrogation: the "crime" had been confessed, the cries of the evildoers muted. Replacing the sound and fury of angry accusation, stern interrogation, and tormented protestations was the calm voice of unison between Jews and Christians; both parties now swore to the "truth" of the ritual murder and its inevitable detection and punishment. During this final phase, the discourse resounded in the voice of a vindicated and triumphant Christian community. The public execution itself served as a dramatic representation of the evil of Jews and the triumph of Christianity: the convicted were burnt as minions of the Devil, as black sorcerers, and, only incidentally, as murderers. The narrative structure of the interrogation record reflected the tripartite structure of the ritual murder discourse; crucial was not the actual deaths of the Christians but the meaningful representation of otherwise unknowable reality. . . .

In 1467, on the death of his brother and cousin, Martin von Staufen inherited the lordship of Üsenberg. Following custom, the citizens of Endingen swore allegiance to Martin, but with the new proviso that if they could have recourse to

better justice, Martin would not stand in their way of redeeming the judicial autonomy of the town, which had been pawned by the Hapsburg archdukes to the
lords of Üsenberg. Two years later, the townsfolk sold a municipal bond to a
Strasbourg citizen and raised five hundred guldens to buy back the town's independence. Martin, however, refused to return justice to the town council because
this right was pledged to his relatives by the Hapsburgs in exchange for a loan of
more than one thousand guldens. The dispute was eventually settled by arbitra-
tion; in November 1470, the city council of Freiburg suggested a compromise:
eight hundred guldens, plus restitution by Endingen to the nobleman for damages to his interests — namely, the execution of the Jews and the confiscation of
their properties. In other words, the Endingen ritual murder trial took place in the
middle of a confrontation between the townsfolk and their noble lord, who was
also the protector of the Jews. The crux of the conflict was, as we have just seen,
the power of jurisdiction: Who should pronounce justice, the lord and his bailiff
or the town council elected by the citizens? In the battle to assert communal solidarity and autonomy, the Jews were tempting scapegoats. A sensational murder
trial would bring the matter before higher authorities; a conviction of the Jews
would vindicate the townsfolk and humiliate the lord.

Once the three brothers were arrested, interrogated, and executed, the trial
took on a life of its own. Names of other Jews mentioned in the confessions led
to other arrests and interrogations. Elias, Eberlin, and Mercklin were arrested on
24 March; they died on 4 April. In less than two weeks, Karl of Baden and the territorial government in the Breisgau had gathered enough information from forced
confessions to suspect a widespread Jewish conspiracy. Named in Elias's confession, Leo of Pforzheim was arrested with three other Jews in his house. Leo was
a prominent Jew in Baden who had been granted protection in 1463 by Friedrich,
elector of the Palatine. Perhaps his arrest also reflected underlying political tensions about which the documents are silent. From the confessions of these four
Jews, extracted under torture, Endingen seemed to be the tip of an iceberg.
Smolle, Mennlin's son, confessed to knowledge of another child murder. In 1465,
according to Smolle, a five-year-old Christian shepherd boy from Wörde was kid-
napped and sold for twenty-two guldens to a rich Nuremberg Jew by the name
of Moses of Freyberg. He, Smolle, and another man, Abraham, hired themselves
out to kill the boy. Further, Smolle admitted that some ten or eleven years back
(1459/60), he had talked a poor woman in Speyer into selling her own child for
thirty guldens; he then resold the child to the rich Jew Lazar of Worms. The
Worms Jews then killed the child for its blood and buried its body near the Jewish cemetery. The confessions of Leo and Berman implicated the Jews of Worms,
Frankfurt, Nuremberg, Sélestat, and Pforzheim. In other words, the Endingen trial
could have served as the basis for the persecution of almost all the major Jewish
communities of the Holy Roman Empire. The Frankfurt Jews tried to save themselves the only way they could; they offered a generous monetary contribution to
the coffers of the emperor to buy his good graces.

Reminded of the usefulness and the compliant loyalty of the Jews, Emperor
Friedrich III intervened forcefully to stop the escalation of persecutions. On 5 May

Friedrich wrote a stern letter to Karl of Baden declaring that Karl had imprisoned, tortured, and executed Jews solely on his own will and without imperial sanction. Moreover, Karl was about to confiscate the properties of all the Jews in his territory. Friedrich commanded Karl to desist immediately:

> By Our Roman Imperial Might We recommend earnestly and firmly ask that you leave the Jews unharmed in regard to the aforementioned matter, and also to free all the Jews which you have imprisoned, without compensation and upon the receipt of this letter, and further by the authority of Our Imperial Mandate and order . . . not to undertake anymore violence against a single Jew or Jewess so as to avoid Imperial and Our great displeasure.

Finally, Emperor Friedrich admonished Karl of Baden that if he had any complaints against the Jews, he should raise them with the emperor according to law; what he was doing with the Jews was both arbitrary and without imperial permission. On the same day, an imperial mandate went out to "princes, both spiritual and secular, counts, free lords, city councils, servants, headmen, officeholders, curators and overseers, Bürgermeisters, judges, councillors, citizens, and communes, and all imperial subjects" condemning the arbitrary imprisonment, judicial torture, and execution of the Endingen Jews by Karl of Baden. The emperor informed his subjects that he had commanded Karl to free the Jews without bail and to refrain from confiscating their property or harming their persons, and he further enjoined the imperial estates to insure that the Jews come to no harm.

The four Jews of Pforzheim had already died at the stake; but apparently Karl of Baden complied with Friedrich's wishes, and no more Jews were arrested. For the burghers of Endingen, the trial represented a triumph for their communal Christian politic: by destroying the Jews in the town, the Endingers not only did away with an alien cultural and religious minority but also freed themselves from the intrusion of noble power, under which the Jews had previously been protected; moreover, they gained a privilege from Emperor Friedrich III, renewed by Emperor Maximilian[10] in 1517, not to tolerate Jews in the future. The ritual murder trial was the cause célèbre of the community; it occurred simultaneously as the town redeemed its juridical autonomy from Martin von Staufen. The process represented nothing less than the victory of a Christian civic community over the Jews and, by implication, over their noble protector as well. . . .

But had there been a murder in the first place? Perhaps Elias was right, and the vagabond family had simply moved on. No crime existed after all. The only murders that took place were in the townsfolk's fantasies, conjured by vivid imaginations of horror, inspired by a belief in Jewish magic, and excited by a haunting rumor spread by a Jew hater.

Ritual murder discourse transformed an unsolved murder or fantasy into material for its own reproduction: it expressed itself in the confessions, in the inter-

---

[10] Holy Roman Emperor from 1493 to 1519.

rogation record, in a ballad, in oral legends, and in a morality play. Two central themes ran through this discourse: murder-sacrifice and judgment. The representations of the Endingen "murders" provided a discursive outlet for the unspeakable crimes committed against the family, especially the children, who were cruelly beheaded. The discourse created a more meaningful, coherent, alternative explanative model, that argued for the dialectical opposition between the two binary opposites of Jew/murderer/magician and Christian/victim/believer, between black, demonic magic and life-giving, godly religion. At a deeper level, ritual murder discourse produced the powerful experience of sacrifice so central to the self-expression of late medieval piety in a century of the imitation of Christ and the many moving and gruesome depictions of the Crucifixion. A ritual murder discourse involved two sacrifices: by murdering the Christian family, Jews reenacted the Crucifixion, giving a historical event a salvific immediacy and power that the commemorative mass could not rival; by exposing the "crimes" of the Jews and avenging the "murders," sacrificing the evildoers to the offended deity, the townsfolk celebrated the triumph of Christianity and avenged and vindicated the historical Crucifixion of Jesus. A ritual murder discourse functioned as a form of *imitatio Christi*.[11] Just as the Christian community dispensed justice, so, too, could pious Christians expect divine justice at the end of the world. . . . To German Christians of the late fifteenth century, who understood their religion from various ecclesiastical sacraments and rituals, iconographical motifs, and biblical narratives, the twin themes of murder-sacrifice and judgment must have represented the essence of the salvific message.

Poignantly, sacrifice and judgment also reinforced the salvific message for the Jews. Their fate was to suffer, survive, and remember. Elias, Eberlin, and Mercklin were great-uncles of Josel of Rosheim, who became an energetic spokesman and leader for the Jewish communities in the Holy Roman Empire during the reign of Charles V. His own father, who was just a boy at the time of the trial, fled Endingen and escaped death. Josel remembered the bitter fate of his relatives and of the other Jews in his memoirs.

Endingen was also remembered in Freiburg. The confessions of the Jews were transcribed in the *Kopialbuch* of the city of Freiburg. The Kopialbuch was a compilation of the most important legal documents of the city: it served as a record of the civic privileges, laws and customs, and more important business transactions, and was, in sum, a duplicate of the original diplomatics (*Urkunden*), which may be damaged or lost through time. It served as both a legal compendium and a historical reference for the practice of government. When the confessions of the Endingen Jews passed into the Kopialbuch, the trial of 1470 became uncontestable history, the ritual murder a fact. In the words of the play's prologue, "the many rogish tricks [of the Jews] against pious Christians are proven by history and evidenced by chronicles." A story became history.

---

[11] Literally "imitation of Christ," from a fifteenth-century devotional book of the same title.

MAKING CONNECTIONS: RELIGION AND RITUAL

1. From the time of the Crusades, Europe became what one historian has called a "persecuting society." Increasing intolerance toward homosexuals, heretics, lepers, and Jews became characteristic of late medieval and early modern Europe. Only after approximately the year 1700 did persecutions dissipate. The respite was temporary, because the twentieth century has witnessed oppression on a monumental scale for secular or ethnic, rather than for religious reasons. Anti-Semitism (hatred of Jews) took on more virulent forms of mistreatment in the late eleventh century, and Christians continued to discriminate against and kill Jews even into our own century. R. Po-Chia Hsia's examination of a ritual murder trial and the execution of Jews in fifteenth-century Germany illustrates well the entrenched hatred of Jews. Why have Christians persecuted Jews for so long? Why did Christians fear Jews in the fifteenth century? Did the belief in ritual murder become almost a Christian ritual? How did the Christian religion condition Christians to hate the Jews? Why did Christians hate Jews above all other groups? Is there anything the Jews could have done to save themselves from brutal treatment? How did the orthodox hounding of Gnostics, which Pagels discusses, differ from the late medieval treatment of Jews, as described by Hsia? Reflect upon whether Christianity has been, overall, a force for good or for evil in Western civilization.

2. Compare anti-Semitism in fifteenth-century Germany to anti-Semitism in the twentieth century. What other groups have western societies persecuted both in medieval and in contemporary times?

PART FOUR

EARLY MODERN EUROPE

William H. McNeill
Edward Muir
Merry Wiesner
Sara F. Matthews Grieco
Robin Briggs
Natalie Z. Davis
David Cressy

In one sense, history is the solving of problems. Two classic problems for historians have been the difficulty of defining *modern* and, following from that, the difficulty of determining when the modern world began. Wrangling over these issues persists, with little agreement. The Italians of the Renaissance considered themselves, with little modesty, the first modern people, more closely akin to the ancient world than to their immediate ancestors, whom they called Gothic and barbaric. Renaissance Italy saw the centuries after the fall of Roman civilization as the Middle Ages, a period between the classical world of Greece and Rome and fourteenth- and fifteenth-century Italy. In the nineteenth century, historians began to debate whether or not Renaissance Italy was indeed modern, or rather gave rise to the protomodern world, or was even medieval in fundamental ways. This debate continues today and is part of the larger problem of historic periodization. Are there actual periods in history? Or do historians arbitrarily classify certain centuries as periods, labeling them as distinct when in fact they are not?

As a way out of the dilemma, many favor the term *early modern Europe,* partly because its chronological boundaries are so vague that historians can use it when discussing very different cultures. Sometimes the early modern period in Europe refers to the years from 1400 to 1789, thus encompassing Renaissance Italy, or the years 1500 to 1789, omitting both the Renaissance and the French Revolution. In either case, early modern Europe always includes the sixteenth and seventeenth centuries, the period that the following selections describe.

These were the centuries when Italian humanism spread beyond the Alps, becoming northern or Christian humanism. This is the era of the Protestant Reformation and Catholic Counter-Reformation. Merry Wiesner explains the varied impact of the Reformation on German women, and Natalie Z. Davis portrays the intensity of religious feeling in the sixteenth-century in her analysis of religious riots in France. During this time, Europeans also explored, colonized, and conquered overseas. The results of European invasions of other continents could be disastrous, as William H. McNeill shows in his account of transatlantic disease exchanges between 1500 and 1700. The age of Michelangelo, Cervantes, Shakespeare, and Milton had an unappealing underside to its cultural and artistic achievements.

This was a premodern society as well, characterized by tradition, relative immobility, and privilege. In discussing women's bodies, cleanliness, beauty, and prudery, Sarah F. Matthews Grieco illuminates changes that occurred in the midst of feverish efforts to preserve traditional ideas of male domination and of marriage. We come to understand the centrality of marriage and its importance as a rite of passage in David Cressy's lively discussion of English wedding celebrations and customs.

During the sixteenth and seventeenth centuries, society was still predominantly rural, though urban centers increased in size. Capitalism also expanded, but this was surely not its heyday. Monarchy remained the political ideal and reality, even though there were some calls for socialist or republican governments. The religion was Christian, but Christianity changed dramatically. In sum, the early modern era in Europe combined the old and the new. It was a period of rapid change in some areas, but unlike the current Western world, it was not a period in which people expected or wanted ongoing change.

Some historians refer to this era as an age of crisis, because so much was called into question and so many institutions, beliefs, and conventions were shaken. Edward Muir invokes the experience of Carnival, where raucous demonstrations and festivities could mock the social, political, and religious elite, leading at times to violence. The fear that gripped Europeans can be seen in the persecution of witches, which Robin Briggs reveals to have been endemic in the rural world. Community conflicts sometimes led to accusations of witchcraft and to charges of consorting with Satan. Witches, Europeans believed, worked to destroy Christian society.

The following selections show dramatically a life that could be described in the words of the English philosopher Thomas Hobbes as "poor, nasty, brutish, and short." Condemned to hunger and cold, wracked by disease, intensely religious if not fanatical, often violent, and subject to increasing supervision by church and state, sixteenth- and seventeenth-century Europeans could, moreover, expect a lifespan less than half that of ours today.

TRANSOCEANIC DISEASE
EXCHANGES, 1500–1700
William H. McNeill

One can hardly exaggerate the historical importance of disease. William H. Mc-
Neill, former professor of history at the University of Chicago and past president
of the American Historical Association, relies on contemporary firsthand accounts and on works by anthropologists, medical historians, and demographers
to examine the disease exchanges between the New and Old Worlds following
Columbus's voyage. The Europeans brought smallpox, measles, diptheria, and
mumps to the native populations of North and South America, causing a catastrophe, a virtual demographic collapse. Why did these diseases have such disastrous effects on Indians but not on Europeans? How did the new diseases affect Indian society and religion?

Along with the subsequent importation of African slaves to the New World
came malaria and yellow fever. How did these African diseases affect Indians and
Europeans? The Old World did not escape the consequences of disease exchanges either. How did syphilis, typhus, and the "English sweats" alter European society?

McNeill explains how new contacts between disease-experienced peoples
and previously isolated communities favored Eurasia. According to McNeill,
what have been the long-term results of the geographic and demographic disease
exchanges of late medieval and early modern times?

In view of what happened after the Spaniards inaugurated free exchange of infections between the Old World and the New, it seems certain that Amerindian encounters with disease before Columbus had been unimportant from an epidemiological[1] point of view. The inhabitants of the New World were bearers of no
serious new infection transferable to the European and African populations that

---

William H. McNeill, *Plagues and Peoples* (Garden City, NY: Anchor Press/Doubleday, 1976), 199–224.

[1] Referring to the incidence and prevalence of disease in large populations.

intruded upon their territory — unless, as some still think, syphilis was of ·
Amerindian origin — whereas the abrupt confrontation with the long array of infections that European and African populations had encountered piecemeal across
some four thousand years of civilized history provoked massive demographic
disaster among Amerindians.

Reasons for this disbalance are not far to seek. The New World was, by comparison with the mass and ecological complexity of the Old, no more than an
enormous island. Forms of life were, in general, more highly evolved in Eurasia
and Africa, having responded to a wider range of variability arising in the larger
land mass. Consequently, plants and animals from the Old World introduced by
Europeans to the Americas often displaced native American species, and disturbed pre-existing ecological balances in explosive and, at least initially, highly
unstable ways. . . . American food plants had far-reaching importance for the
peoples of Europe, Asia, and Africa after 1500, but few organisms of American
provenance were successful in competing in the wild with Old World life-
forms — though some examples do exist, e.g., the spread of the plant louse,
phyllox-era, that nearly destroyed European vineyards in the 1880s.

The undeveloped level of Amerindian disease was, therefore, only one aspect
of a more general biological vulnerability, but one that had peculiarly drastic consequences for human life. Precise information about disease in the Americas before Columbus is difficult to come by. Bone lesions can be found on pre-
Columbian skeletons indicating some sort of infection. These have sometimes
been interpreted as syphilitic by doctors seeking to confirm the American origins
of that disease. But such identifications are controversial, since the way one mi-
croorganism attacks a bone is very similar to the way another is likely to do so;
and tissue reactions to such invasions are also similar, no matter what the infectious agent may be. . . .

Indication of disease and epidemic death have been found in Aztec codices;[2]
but these seem related to famine and crop failure and may not have been the result of the sort of human-to-human infectious chain that existed in the Old World.
Moreover, disasters came far apart in time, only three being discernible in surviving texts. After the Spanish conquest, old men even denied that disease had existed in any form in the days of their youth. It looks, therefore, as though
Amerindian communities suffered little from disease, even though in both Mexico and Peru, the size and density of settlement had reached far beyond the critical threshold at which contagious disease organisms could sustain a simple
human-to-human chain of infection indefinitely. In this, as in some other respects, the Amerindian civilizations seem comparable to ancient Sumer and Egypt,
rather than to the epidemiologically scarred and toughened communities of
sixteenth-century Spain and Africa.

---

[2] Volumes of manuscript pages sewn together at the left edge; similar in appearance to the modern printed book.

Several centuries — perhaps more than a thousand years — had passed since favored regions of Mexico and Peru had begun to carry human populations dense enough to sustain human-to-human disease chains indefinitely. Yet such infections do not seem to have established themselves. Presumably the reason was that the domesticable animals available to the Amerindians did not themselves carry herd infections of a sort that could transfer their parasitism to human populations when those populations became sufficiently large. This sort of transfer is what must have happened in the Old World, where massive herds of wild cattle and horses, dispersed across the steppe and forest lands of Eurasia, were sufficiently numerous and made close enough contact with one another in a wild state to be able to sustain infections that passed from animal to animal without any sort of intermediate host. By comparison, wild llamas and alpacas lived high in the Andes in small and dispersed groups. These were too few and too isolated to sustain such infections in the wild. There seems to be no plausible reconstruction of the style of life of the wild ancestors of the guinea pig — the other distinctive Amerindian domesticated animal. And as for dogs, mankind's oldest domesticated animal, though they today share many infections with humans, it is clear enough that in their wild state they, too, must have existed in relatively small and isolated packs. Thus with the possible exception of the guinea pig, the Amerindians' domesticated species, like the human hunting bands that had initially penetrated the Americas, were incapable of supporting infectious chains of the sort characteristic of civilized diseases. No wonder, then, that once contact had been established, Amerindian populations of Mexico and Peru became the victims, on a mass scale, of the common childhood diseases of Europe and Africa.

The scope of the resultant disaster reflected the fact that both central Mexico and the heartlands of the Inca empire were very densely settled at the time of the European discovery of America. The two most important American food crops, maize[3] and potatoes, were more productive of calories per acre than any Old World crops except rice. This allowed denser populations per square mile of cultivated ground in the Americas than was attainable anywhere in the Old World outside of the East Asian rice paddy region. . . .

Ecological adjustment in Mexico and Peru showed signs of strain, even before the Spaniards arrived and upset everything so radically. In Mexico, erosion was already a serious problem; and in some irrigated coastal areas of Peru, salting of the soil seems to have led to population collapse not long before Pizzaro appeared. Everything points to the conclusion that Amerindian populations were pressing hard against the limits set by available cultivable land in both Mexico and Peru when the Spaniards arrived. Moreover, the absence of any considerable number of domesticated animals meant that there was a smaller margin between the sum of agricultural productivity in the Americas and direct human consumption than was commonly the case in the Old World. In time of crop failure

---

[3] Sweet or Indian corn.

or other kind of food crisis, Eurasian flocks and herds constituted a sort of food bank. They could be slaughtered and eaten; and in times and places when over-population started to be felt, human beings always displace herds by turning pas-tureland into cropland — at least for a while. No such cushion existed in the Americas, where domesticated animals played a merely marginal part in human food patterns.

All these factors therefore conspired to make Amerindian populations radi-cally vulnerable to the disease organisms Spaniards and, before long, also Africans, brought with them across the ocean. The magnitude of the resultant disaster has only recently become clear. Learned opinion before World War II systematically underestimated Amerindian populations, putting the total somewhere between eight and fourteen million at the time Columbus landed in Hispaniola.[4] Recent es-timates, however, based on sampling of tribute lists, missionary reports and elab-orate statistical arguments, have multiplied such earlier estimates tenfold and more, putting Amerindian population on the eve of the conquest at about one hundred million, with twenty-five to thirty million of this total assignable to the Mexican and an approximately equal number to the Andean civilizations. Rela-tively dense populations also apparently existed in the connecting Central Amer-ican lands.

Starting from such levels, population decay was catastrophic. By 1568, less than fifty years from the time Cortez[5] inaugurated epidemiological as well as other exchanges between Amerindian and European populations, the population of central Mexico had shrunk to about three million, i.e., to about one tenth of what had been there when Cortez landed. Decay continued, though at a reduced rate, for another fifty years, reaching a low point of about 1.6 million by 1620. Re-covery did not definitely set in for another thirty years or so and remained very slow until the eighteenth century. . . .

In an age of almost world-wide population growth, it is hard for us to imag-ine such catastrophes. . . . [A] 90 per cent drop in population within 120 years (i.e., across five to six human generations), as happened in Mexico and Peru, car-ries with it drastic psychological and cultural consequences. Faith in established institutions and beliefs cannot easily withstand such disaster; skills and knowledge disappear. This, indeed, was what allowed the Spaniards to go as far as they did in transferring their culture and language to the New World, making it normative even in regions where millions of Indians had previously lived according to stan-dards and customs of their own.

Labor shortage and economic retrogression was another obvious concomi-tant. The development of forms of compulsory labor and dispersal from cities (where disease losses concentrate) to rural estates are necessary responses if so-cial hierarchies are to survive at all. Late Roman institutions and those of

---

[4] An island in the West Indies, today comprised of Haiti and the Dominican Republic.

[5] Hernán Cortez (1485–1547), Spanish soldier and conqueror of Mexico.

seventeenth-century Mexico have an uncanny likeness in this respect, which Spain's heritage of the Roman law only partially explains. Landlords and tax collectors, facing a radically decaying population from which to derive support, can be counted on to react in parallel fashion; and this seems to be what happened in both the late Roman and the seventeenth-century Spanish empires. . . .

Wholesale demoralization and simple surrender of will to live certainly played a large part in the destruction of Amerindian communities. Numerous recorded instances of failure to tend newborn babies so that they died unnecessarily, as well as outright suicide, attest the intensity of Amerindian bewilderment and despair. European military action and harsh treatment of laborers gathered forcibly for some large-scale undertaking also had a role in uprooting and destroying old social structures. But human violence and disregard, however brutal, was not the major factor causing Amerindian populations to melt away as they did. After all, it was not in the interest of the Spaniards and other Europeans to allow potential taxpayers and the Indian work force to diminish. The main destructive role was certainly played by epidemic disease.

The first encounter came in 1518 when smallpox reached Hispaniola and attacked the Indian population so virulently that Bartoleme de Las Casas[6] believed only a thousand survived. From Hispaniola, smallpox traveled to Mexico, arriving with the relief expedition that joined Cortez in 1520. As a result, at the very crisis of the conquest, when Montezuma[7] had been killed and the Aztecs were girding themselves for an attack on the Spaniards, smallpox raged in Tenochtitlán. The leader of the assault, along with innumerable followers, died within hours of compelling the Spaniards to retreat from their city. Instead of following up on the initial success and harrying the tiny band of Spaniards from the land, therefore, as might have been expected had the smallpox not paralyzed effective action, the Aztecs lapsed into a stunned inactivity. Cortez thus was able to rally his forces, gather allies from among the Aztecs' subject peoples, and return for the final siege and destruction of the capital.

Clearly, if smallpox had not come when it did, the Spanish victory could not have been achieved in Mexico. The same was true of Pizarro's[8] filibuster[9] into Peru. For the smallpox epidemic in Mexico did not confine its ravages to Aztec territory. Instead, it spread to Guatemala, where it appeared in 1520, and continued southward, penetrating the Inca domain in 1525 or 1526. Consequences there were just as drastic as among the Aztecs. The reigning Inca died of the disease while away from his capital on campaign in the North. His designated heir also died, leaving no legitimate successor. Civil war ensued, and it was amid this wreckage of the

---

[6] Bartolomé de Las Casas, early Spanish Roman Catholic missionary in America (1474–1566) who protested against the enslavement of the Indians.

[7] Montezuma II (1466–1520), the last Aztec emperor.

[8] Francisco Pizarro (ca. 1470–1541), Spanish soldier and conqueror of Peru.

[9] To engage in unauthorized warfare against a country with which one's own country is at peace.

Inca political structure that Pizarro and his crew of roughnecks made their way to Cuzco and plundered its treasures. He met no serious military resistance at all.

Two points seem particularly worth emphasizing here. First, Spaniards and Indians readily agreed that epidemic disease was a particularly dreadful and unambiguous form of divine punishment. Interpretation of pestilence as a sign of God's displeasure was a part of the Spanish inheritance, enshrined in the Old Testament and in the whole Christian tradition. The Amerindians, lacking all experience of anything remotely like the initial series of lethal epidemics, concurred. Their religious doctrines recognized that superhuman power lodged in deities whose behavior toward men was often angry. It was natural, therefore, for them to assign an unexampled effect to a supernatural cause, quite apart from the Spanish missionary efforts that urged the same interpretation of the catastrophe upon dazed and demoralized converts.

Secondly, the Spaniards were nearly immune from the terrible disease that raged so mercilessly among the Indians. They had almost always been exposed in childhood and so developed effective immunity. Given the interpretation of the cause of pestilence accepted by both parties, such a manifestation of divine partiality for the invaders was conclusive. The gods of the Aztecs as much as the God of the Christians seemed to agree that the white newcomers had divine approval for all they did. And while God thus seemed to favor the whites, regardless of their mortality and piety or lack thereof, his wrath was visited upon the Indians with an unrelenting harshness that often puzzled and distressed the Christian missionaries who soon took charge of the moral and religious life of their converts along the frontiers of Spain's American dominions.

From the Amerindian point of view, stunned acquiescence in Spanish superiority was the only possible response. No matter how few their numbers or how brutal and squalid their behavior, the Spaniards prevailed. Native authority structures crumbled; the old gods seemed to have abdicated. The situation was ripe for the mass conversions recorded so proudly by Christian missionaries. Docility to the commands of priests, viceroys, landowners, mining entrepreneurs, tax collectors, and anyone else who spoke with a loud voice and had a white skin was another inevitable consequence. When the divine and natural orders were both unambiguous in declaring against native tradition and belief, what ground for resistance remained? The extraordinary ease of Spanish conquests and the success a few hundred men had in securing control of vast areas and millions of persons is unintelligible on any other basis.

Even after the initial ravages of smallpox had passed, having killed something like one third of the total population, nothing approaching epidemiological stability prevailed. Measles followed hard upon the heels of smallpox, spreading through Mexico and Peru in 1530–31. Deaths were frequent, as is to be expected when such a disease encounters a virgin population dense enough to keep the chain of infection going. Still another epidemic came fifteen years later, in 1546, whose character is unclear. Perhaps it was typhus. Probably typhus was a new disease among Europeans, too; at least the medical men who first described it clearly enough to make diagnosis possible thought it was new when it broke out among troops fighting in Spain, in 1490.

Hence if the pestilence of 1546 in the Americas was in fact typhus, the Amerindians were beginning to participate in epidemic diseases that also affected the populations of the Old World. This becomes unambiguous in course of the next American disease disaster: an influenza epidemic that raged in 1558–59. This epidemic, which broke out in Europe in 1556 and lasted on and off till 1560, had serious demographic consequences on both sides of the Atlantic. One estimate places die-off in England from the influenza at no less than 20 per cent of the entire population, for instance; and comparable losses occurred elsewhere in Europe. Whether the influenza outbreak of the 1550s was a genuinely global phenomenon, like its more recent parallel, 1918–19, cannot be said for sure, but Japanese records also mention an outbreak of "coughing violence" in 1556 from which "very many died."

The incorporation of Amerindian populations into the circle of epidemic disease that happened to be current in Eurasia in the sixteenth century did not relieve them of special exposure to still other infections coming across the ocean. Relatively trifling endemic afflictions of the Old World regularly became death-dealing epidemics among New World populations that were totally lacking in acquired resistances. Thus diphtheria, mumps, and recurrent outbreaks of the first two great killers, smallpox and measles, appeared at intervals throughout the sixteenth and seventeenth centuries. Whenever a new region or hitherto isolated Amerindian population came into regular contact with the outside world, the cycle of repeated infections picked up renewed force, mowing down the helpless inhabitants. The peninsula of Lower California, for instance, began to experience drastic depopulation at the very end of the seventeenth century, when a first recorded epidemic broke out there. Eighty years later the population had been reduced by more than 90 per cent, despite well-intentioned efforts by Spanish missionaries to protect and cherish the Indians assigned to their charge. . . .

The long and lethal series of European diseases was not all that Amerindians had to face. For in tropical regions of the New World climatic conditions were suitable for the establishment of at least some of the African infections that made that continent so dangerous to the health of strangers. The two most significant African diseases to establish themselves in the New World were malaria and yellow fever. Both of them became important in determining human patterns of settlement and survival in tropical and subtropical parts of the New World.

Fevers, leading to heavy die-off, often afflicted early European settlements in the New World. Columbus, for example, had to shift his headquarters in Hispaniola to a more healthful location in 1496. This and other disasters met by early expeditions of explorers and colonists have been adduced as proof that malarial fevers and/or yellow fever existed in the New World before European ships began crossing the ocean. But extremes of malnutrition arising from inadequate provisioning of expeditions that counted on somehow living off the land explain most such cases; and there are a number of contrary evidences that make it practically certain that neither malaria nor yellow fever existed in the Americas before Columbus.

As far as malaria is concerned, the most telling argument rests on studies of the distribution of human genetic traits associated with tolerance of malarial infection. These appear to have been entirely absent from Amerindian populations. Similarly, malarial parasites that infect wild monkeys of the New World appear to be identical with those of the Old — transfers, in fact, from human bloodstreams. Nothing like the extraordinary specialization of malarial parasites that occurs in Africa, whereby different forms of the plasmodium[10] infect different host species and prefer different mosquitoes as alternate hosts, can be found in the Americas. Such facts make it almost certain that malaria is a newcomer to the American scene, and that neither man nor monkey harbored the parasites in pre-Columbian times. . . .

The establishment of malaria was not so long delayed in other, more traversed regions of the New World, although no clear time and place for the debut of the plasmodium in the New World can be discovered. Almost certainly, the infection was introduced many times, since Europeans as well as Africans suffered chronically from malaria. . . . Yet malaria appears to have completed the destruction of Amerindians in the tropical lowlands, so as to empty formerly well-populated regions almost completely.

Yellow fever announced its successful transfer from West Africa to the Caribbean for the first time in 1648, when epidemics broke out in both Yucatán and Havana. What delayed its establishment until this comparatively late date was probably the fact that before it could become epidemic in the New World, a specialized species of mosquito, known as *Aedes aegypti,* had to find and occupy a niche in the New World environment. This mosquito, in fact, is highly domesticated, preferring as its breeding places small bodies of still water. Indeed, it is said never to breed in water with a natural bottom of mud or sand, but to require a manufactured container — water cask, cistern, calabash, or the like, for laying its eggs.

Until this specialized mosquito crossed the ocean aboard ship (riding, no doubt, in water casks) and established itself ashore in places where the temperature always stayed above 72 degrees Fahrenheit, yellow fever could not propagate itself in the New World. But when these conditions had been met, the situation became ripe for yellow fever to assume epidemic proportions among men and monkeys alike. Europeans were as vulnerable as Amerindians to this infection; and its sudden onset and frequently lethal outcome made it more feared among whites than malaria. Nonetheless, malaria was far more widespread and undoubtedly accounted for a larger number of deaths than its dreaded African cousin, whom English sailors nicknamed "Yellow Jack." . . .

---

[10] A unicellular parasite found in the blood.

In regions of the New World where tropical infections from Africa could establish themselves freely — coming as they did on top of crushing exposure to European infections — the result was almost total destruction of the pre-existing Amerindian population. On the other hand, in regions where tropical infections could not penetrate, like the Mexican interior plateau and the Peruvian *altiplano*,[11] the destruction of pre-Columbian populations was less complete, though drastic enough even there.

African slaves took the place of the vanished Amerindians along the Caribbean coast and in most of the islands of the Caribbean where plantation enterprises called for heavy input of human labor. Since many Africans were already attuned to survival in the presence of malaria and yellow fever, losses from these diseases were relatively small, although other unfamiliar infections — gastrointestinal in particular — led to a high mortality among the slaves. In addition, a heavy preponderance of males, unfavorable conditions for raising infants, and continual disturbance of local disease patterns as a result of the arrival of new human cargoes from Africa meant that the black population of the Caribbean area did not grow very rapidly until the nineteenth century. Then, when the flow of newcomers was cut off, and the noisome slave ships that for two and a half centuries had propagated disease on both sides of the ocean, ceased to ply the seas, black numbers began to surge upward in most of the Caribbean islands, whereas whites diminished proportionately and sometimes absolutely. Economic and social changes — the end of slavery and exhaustion of soils devoted single-mindedly to sugar cane — contributed to this result; but black epidemiological advantages in resisting malaria also helped.

Overall, the disaster to Amerindian populations assumed a scale that is hard for us to imagine, living as we do in an age when epidemic disease hardly matters. Ratios of 20:1 or even 25:1 between pre-Columbian populations and the bottoming-out point in Amerindian population curves seem more or less correct, despite wide local variations. Behind such chill statistics lurks enormous and repeated human anguish, as whole societies fell apart, values crumbled, and old ways of life lost all shred of meaning. A few voices recorded what it was like:

> Great was the stench of death. After our fathers and grandfathers succumbed, half the people fled to the fields. The dogs and vultures devoured the bodies. The mortality was terrible. Your grandfathers died, and with them died the son of the king and his brothers and kinsmen. So it was that we became orphans, oh, my sons! So we became when we were young. All of us were thus. We were born to die!

Though Amerindians were certainly the main victims of the new disease regime, other populations also had to react to the changed patterns of disease dissemination arising from transoceanic shipping, and the altered patterns of inte-

---

[11] The high plateau of the Andes Mountains in modern Bolivia, Peru, and Argentina.

rior trade routes that the rise of such shipping involved. Details are for the most part irrecoverable, yet an over-all pattern is quite clearly discernible.

First of all, previously isolated populations like the Amerindians, when brought into contact with European and other seafarers, regularly experienced a series of drastic die-offs, like that which so massively altered American history. Which civilized diseases wreaked the greatest damage differed from case to case, depending partly on climate, partly on the mere chance of what infection arrived when. But the vulnerability of isolated populations to such diseases was an epidemiological fact of life — and death. Locally disastrous die-offs therefore became recurrent phenomena of all the centuries after 1500.

Among civilized populations, however, the effect was just the opposite. More frequent contacts across ocean distances tended to homogenize infectious disease. As this took place, sporadic and potentially lethal epidemics gave way to endemic patterns of infection. To be sure, in the first centuries after ships began to ply the oceans of the earth and united all the coastlines of the world into a single intercommunicating network, the process of homogenization of disease distribution involved expansion of some diseases onto new ground. Such arrivals, at more and more frequent intervals, could and did produce locally destructive epidemics. Cities like London and Lisbon became notorious in Europe as seats of disease, and deservedly so. By about 1700, however, sailing ships had done what they could to spread new diseases to new lands. Thereafter, the demographic significance of epidemic outbreaks began to drop off. Where other factors did not supervene to mask the phenomenon, the result was to open the way for our modern experience of persistent, pervasive growth among the disease-exposed and disease-experienced populations of all the earth.

Such a contrast between radical decay of previously isolated communities on the one hand and a globally enhanced potential for population growth among disease-experienced peoples on the other, acted to tip the world balance sharply in favor of the civilized communities of Eurasia. The cultural and biological variety of humankind was reduced correspondingly, as the age-old process of epidemiological disruption and absorption of survivors into the expanding circle of civilized society accelerated everywhere on earth. . . .

As usual, we are far better informed about disease events in Europe. Three new infections assumed spectacular forms during the age of the oceanic explorations, 1450–1550; and each of them came to European attention as a byproduct of wars. One, the so-called "English sweats," disappeared after a brief career; the other two, syphilis and typhus, have lasted to our time.

Both syphilis and typhus appeared in Europe during the long series of Italian wars, 1494–1559. The first of them broke out in epidemic fashion in the army that the French king, Charles VIII,[12] led against Naples in 1494. When the French withdrew, King Charles discharged his soldiers, who thereupon spread the

---

[12] King of France from 1483 to 1498.

disease far and wide to all adjacent lands. Syphilis was regarded as a new disease not merely in Europe, but in India, where it appeared in 1498 with Da Gama's[13] sailors, and in China and Japan as well, where it arrived in 1505, a full fifteen years before the first Portuguese reached Canton. Symptoms were often peculiarly horrible so that the disease attracted a great deal of attention wherever it appeared.

Contemporary evidence therefore amply attests that syphilis was new in the Old World, at least in the sense that the veneral mode of transmission and the symptoms that resulted therefrom were new. But . . . this may have arisen independently of contacts with America, if a strain of the spirochete causing yaws[14] found a means of short-circuiting the increasingly ineffective path of skin-to-skin infection by instead moving from host to host via the mucous membranes of the sex organs.

Yet medical opinion is not unanimous. Some competent experts continue to believe that syphilis came to Europe from America, and was therefore exactly what contemporaries thought it was — a new disease against which Eurasian populations had no established immunities. The timing of the first outbreak of syphilis in Europe and the place where it occurred certainly seems to fit what one would expect if the disease had been imported from America by Columbus' returning sailors. This theory, once it had been promulgated in 1539, became almost universally accepted among Europe's learned until very recently, when the inability to distinguish between the spirochete causing yaws and that of syphilis in laboratory tests led a school of medical historians to reject the Columbian theory entirely. Proof, one way or the other, awaits the development of precise and reliable methods whereby the organisms causing lesions in ancient bones can be identified. If this proves permanently beyond the reach of biochemical techniques, it seems unlikely that any adequate basis for choice between the rival theories as to the origin of syphilis will be attainable.

However conspicuous and distressful syphilis may have been for those who contracted it, its demographic impact does not seem to have been very great. Royal houses often suffered and the political decline of Valois France (1559–1589) and of Ottoman Turkey (after 1566) may have been related to the prevalence of syphilis in the respective reigning families of the two states. Many aristocrats suffered similarly. But the inability of royal and aristocratic families to give birth to healthy children merely accelerated social mobility, making more room at the top of society than there would otherwise have been. Lower down the social scale syphilis had less devastating effects, for the fact seems to be that European populations continued to increase throughout the sixteenth century when the disease was at its height. By the end of the century, syphilis began to recede. The more fulminant forms of infection were dying out, as the normal sorts of adjustment between host and parasite asserted themselves, i.e., as milder strains of the spiro-

---

[13] Vasco Da Gama (ca. 1469–1524), Portuguese navigator who discovered the sea route around Africa.

[14] An infectious, nonvenereal tropical disease.

chete displaced those that killed off their hosts too rapidly, and as the resistance of European populations to the organism increased. Even though data seem lacking, the same pattern of relatively speedy adjustment without significant demographic loss along the way presumably also prevailed in the other parts of the Old World.

The same must also be said of typhus. As a recognizable and distinct disease, typhus made its debut on European soil in 1490, when it was brought to Spain by soldiers who had been fighting in Cyprus. Thence it came into Italy with the wars between Spaniards and French for dominion over that peninsula. Typhus achieved a new notoriety in 1526 when a French army besieging Naples was compelled to withdraw in disarray due to the ravages of the disease. Thereafter, outbreaks of typhus continued to be sporadically important in disrupting armies and depopulating jails, poorhouses, and other — in the literal sense — lousy institutions, down to World War I, when two or three million died of this infection.

Yet the occasional military and political importance of typhus fever was not matched by any notable demographic significance for the peoples of Europe or anywhere else, so far, at least, as the very sketchy indications of population trends allow one to judge. Typhus was, after all, a disease of crowding and of poverty. For most of the poor who died of typhus, statistical probability assures us that if infected lice had not assisted their demise, some other disease would soon have carried them off. Particularly in urban slums, or anywhere else that undernourished people huddled miserably together, there were plenty of other infections — tuberculosis, dysentery, pneumonia — competing for victims. The fact that typhus brought death quicker than most of the other infections therefore perhaps made less difference demographically than the number of typhus deaths might suggest at first glance.

The third new, or apparently new, infection, the "English sweats," is of interest on two counts. It exhibited an opposite social impact from typhus, preferring to attack the upper classes much as poliomyelitis did in more recent times. Secondly, it disappeared after 1551 as mysteriously as it had come in 1485. The disease broke out first in England as the name implies, soon after Henry VII[15] had won his crown at the battle of Bosworth Field. Then it spread to the Continent and created considerable furor because of the high mortality it caused among upper classes. Symptoms resembled scarlet fever, but such an identification has not won general acceptance among medical historians. The fact that it was believed to be a new disease does not prove that it had not existed in some endemic form as a modest childhood affliction elsewhere, perhaps in France whence Henry VII recruited some of the soldiers who won him his crown. But even more clearly than in the cases of syphilis and typhus, the sweats did not affect enough people to have any noticeable over-all demographic effect.

---

[15] King of England from 1485 to 1509.

On the other hand, it is the case that an outbreak of the dreaded "sweats" in 1529 led Luther[16] and Zwingli[17] to break off their colloquy in Marburg,[18] without achieving agreement on a definition of the eucharist. Whether a longer conference would have led to agreement between these two headstrong paladins of ecclesiastical reformation may well be doubted. Nevertheless, the fact remains that it was their precipitate flight from risk of infection that sealed the split between Lutheran and Swiss (soon to become Calvinist) reform along lines that deeply affected subsequent European history, and have endured to the present. . . .

. . . [P]opulation in Europe, or those parts of it where reasonable estimates can be made, seems to have increased uninterruptedly and relatively rapidly from the mid-fifteenth century (when recovery from plague losses set in) until about 1600. Yet it was during these decades that the oceanic discoveries took place, and European sailors had the opportunity to import new infections into their homelands from the ports of all the earth. Even so, the new disease risks such transport patterns permitted did not prove very serious for European populations, presumably because most infections that could flourish in the European climate and under the conditions then prevailing in European cities and villages had already penetrated the Continent as a result of older circulation of infections within the Old World.

For Europe, as for other civilized lands, infections by familiar epidemic disease surely became more frequent, at least in the major ports and at other foci of communication; but infections that returned at more and more frequent intervals became, by necessity, childhood diseases. Older persons would have acquired suitably high and repeatedly reinforced levels of immunity through prior exposures. Thus by a paradox that is only apparent, the more diseased a community, the less destructive its epidemics become. Even very high rates of infant mortality were relatively easily borne. The costs of giving birth and rearing another child to replace one that had died were slight compared to the losses involved in massive adult mortality of the sort that epidemics attacking a population at infrequent intervals inevitably produce.

Consequently, the tighter the communications net binding each part of Europe to the rest of the world, the smaller became the likelihood of really devastating disease encounter. Only genetic mutation of a disease-causing organism, or a new transfer of parasites from some other host to human beings offered the possibility of devastating epidemic when world transport and communications had attained a sufficient intimacy to assure frequent circulation of all established human diseases among the civilized populations of the world. Between 1500 and about 1700 this is what seems in fact to have occurred. Devastating epidemics of

---

[16] Martin Luther (1483–1546), initiator of the Protestant Reformation in Germany.

[17] Huldrych Zwingli (1484–1531), Swiss Protestant reformer.

[18] A conference between German and Swiss Protestant reformers in October 1529, which failed to settle theological disagreements, especially over whether Jesus was present physically or spiritually in the bread and wine of the Mass.

the sort that had raged so dramatically in Europe's cities between 1346 and the mid-seventeenth century tapered off toward the status of childhood diseases, or else, as in the case of both plague and malaria, notably reduced the geographic range of their incidence.

The result of such systematic lightening of the microparasitic drain upon European populations (especially in northwestern Europe where both plague and malaria had about disappeared by the close of the seventeenth century) was, of course, to unleash the possibility of systematic growth. This was, however, only a possibility, since any substantial local growth quickly brought on new problems: in particular, problems of food supply, water supply, and intensification of other infections in cities that had outgrown older systems of waste disposal. After 1600 these factors began to affect European populations significantly, and their effective solution did not come before the eighteenth century — or later.

All the same, the changing pattern of epidemic infection was and remains a fundamental landmark in human ecology that deserves more attention than it has ordinarily received. On the time scale of world history, indeed we should view the "domestication" of epidemic disease that occurred between 1300 and 1700 as a fundamental breakthrough, directly resulting from the two great transportation revolutions of that age — one by land, initiated by the Mongols,[19] and one by sea, initiated by Europeans.

---

[19] A nomadic people of central Asia who established an empire that included China, eastern Europe, and the Middle East during the thirteenth century.

CARNIVAL, CHARIVARI, AND RITES OF VIOLENCE
Edward Muir

When we see the word *carnival,* we often think of the famous carnivals of New Orleans and Rio de Janeiro. These carnivals are, in fact, similar to earlier festivities in European history. Edward Muir, professor of history at Northwestern University, studies ritual in early modern Europe. In this essay, he explores Carnival, the season or festival of merrymaking before Lent (in the Christian calendar, forty days of fasting before Easter); *charivari,* ceremonies that involved raucous music and public humiliation; and rites of violence. Muir relies on folklore, theater, literature, art, contemporary descriptions of ritualized behavior, laws and legal records, and other historians' studies to evoke what he calls the rituals of the lower body.

What was the purpose of the various Carnival rites, and how did Carnivals — such as the disturbances at Romans, France, in 1580, or the famous annual event at Venice — differ from one another? What symbolic imagery appeared at Carnival, and what does the battle between Carnival and Lent signify? According to historians, what purposes did Carnivals serve?

The *charivari* was another ritual used throughout Europe. What functions did it serve, and what victims did it target? How did feuding function as a ritual?

Until the explosion of social history in the last three decades, historians tended to think of rituals in relation to those who walked the corridors of power, whether religious or secular. King, queens, presidents, and church leaders invoked rituals. Historians, aided by anthropologists' work, know now that rituals existed at all levels of European society and helped to give order and meaning to disparate events and community practices. Carnival evokes the richness of early modern European social life.

In 1580 in Romans, France, a peculiar event took place. During Carnival,[1] . . . the lively festivities degenerated into a confrontation between members of the

---

Edward Muir, *Ritual in Early Modern Europe* (Cambridge: Cambridge University Press, 1997), 85–93, 96–99, 101–108, 114.

[1] Traditionally, the period of celebration before the Christian fast of Lent.

popular faction of craftsmen and the local notables. On Candlemas,[2] which fell during the Carnival season that year, the leader of the artisans showed up to a meeting of the town council dressed as a bear and proceeded to take a seat above his station, a mocking action typical of Carnival season. The judge who led the opposing elite faction, however, chose to interpret this gesture as a threatening demand for power. On the following day, 600 working men from the cloth trades marched through the streets fully armed in a demonstration, which heightened the climate of suspicion that a popular rebellion was at hand. For several days there were dances in the streets, including some involving the swinging of naked swords or the carrying of rakes, brooms, and flails for threshing wheat, all emblems of violence. The flail bearers wore death shrouds, which had traditionally signified their role in beating grain to death, that is acting out the death of the old growing season so that the new one could flourish.

On this occasion the flail bearers introduced an ominous new chant to their usual dance. As they marched through the streets swinging their flails, they called out that within three days the flesh of Christians would be on sale for six *deniers*[3] a pound, and with a macabre sense of humor the marchers offered what they said was the flesh of corpses for the bystanders to eat. Although this cannibalistic offering could have been interpreted as a traditional reference to how the living were nourished by the dead, the notables of the town took it as an act of intimidation, which it probably was. By *mardi gras*[4] proper the elite, organized in their Partridge Club,[5] ambushed members of the popular faction, who were masquerading as sheep and capons. Several of the artisans were killed or imprisoned.

To modern eyes the events that took place in Romans during Carnival in 1580 look quite bizarre. Why should an episode of violent civil strife take place during the most fun-filled holiday of the year? Why would threats and even political ambitions be encoded in festive images? The episode looks even stranger when one discovers that the Carnival ambush was part of the struggle between Catholics and Protestants that comprises the French Wars of Religion,[6] even though on the surface there hardly seems to be any religious content at all to the event.

When observed in the context of time, however, the Carnival in Romans appears rather typical of the ways in which people represented their hopes and desires through festive performances. Festivity, Carnival in particular, provided the occasion for public gatherings and supplied a ritual vocabulary and syntax for

---

[2] The Christian holiday commemorating Mary's purification ceremony after giving birth to Jesus and his presentation in the temple.

[3] French copper coins of small value.

[4] Fat Tuesday or Shrove Tuesday; in the Christian calendar, a festival the day before Lent.

[5] The organization of the rich designed to respond to the demonstrations of the workingmen. "To run a partridge" was to hold a footrace, the winner receiving a partridge.

[6] Civil wars between Protestants and Roman Catholics, 1562–1598.

communicating ideas. To understand what was going on, one must learn to read the language of festivity. Carnival language derived its vocabulary from the human body and its processes, which meant that the image of cannibalism, of eating another human being, helped express anger and encoded the desire for revenge. Understanding the syntax of the body as it was constructed in Carnival helps explain how a festival could dramatically shift from creating a sense of community to destroying it through violence. . . .

Among all the popular lay festivals Carnival presents the archetypical form against which others can be measured. It produced the richest symbolic imagery; had the greatest influence on European culture, especially on comic drama; and celebrated the materiality of everyday life, the realm of the body. Carnivals varied enormously from place to place and time to time, following local interests and traditions on the one hand and responding to changing political and economic circumstances on the other. Christian Carnival paralleled Jewish Purim,[7] and in areas where the two communities lived in close proximity to one another, such as Spain, Provence, or Rome, each influenced the other. Carnival proper was more popular in southern than in northern Europe, probably because in Sweden or Scotland February is not a pleasant time to frolic outside, but Carnival-like festivals were celebrated in the North during the spring and summer. No particular Carnival can represent all others, but certain themes reoccurred widely and frequently enough to be seen as characteristic.

Many Carnival rites concerning fertility, death, and the arrival of spring seem to echo agrarian rituals, but most of the information about Carnival comes from cities, especially German, French, Spanish, and Italian cities. In those cities the Carnival season began in January, sometimes in late December as an extension of the Christmas season, and gradually intensified until Fat Tuesday itself, the day before Ash Wednesday.[8] In many locales there were both official celebrations — such as processions or parades, competitions, and plays — and unofficial ones, such as neighborhood sports and private balls or banquets. Nuremberg, Rome, Florence, Naples, Montpellier, Seville, Barcelona, and many other cities had well-documented, highly popular Carnivals, but none were as famous as those of Venice, which by the seventeenth century attracted tourists from all over Europe.

The centerpiece of the official rituals of Carnival in Venice consisted of the ritualized chase and slaughter of twelve pigs and a bull in the small square next to the Palace of the Doges.[9] Although the butchering of pigs to make sausages and chitterlings was a seasonal chore attached to Carnival throughout much of Europe, in Venice it became ritualized into an elaborate allegory of justice and domination. The animals underwent a formal judicial sentencing procedure carried out in a

---

[7] A holiday commemorating the Jews' delivery from an evil advisor of the Persian king; characterized by raucous celebration.

[8] In the Christian calendar, the first day of Lent.

[9] Chief magistrates of Venice.

mock serious manner. After being herded into the courtroom and condemned to death, they were taken to a pen at the usual place of execution, where the "executioners" (who were actually blacksmiths) had to chase and capture them before they were beheaded. Later a group of octogenarian senators retired to their meeting hall to smash with cudgels miniature wooden castles, said to be reminders of Friulan fortresses destroyed by Venetian armies in the twelfth century. After a visiting bishop laughed himself silly at what he thought was an absurd practice, the government tried to abolish the ritual, but the pig slaughter was so popular that it persisted despite the hostility of many high officials. The official embarrassment, which intensified during the sixteenth century, provides a useful indicator of the ways in which the upper classes in sophisticated Venice began to separate themselves from the kinds of mass amusements that only a century before they had enjoyed with the same evident pleasure as youthful carpenters and fishermen. The interest of the Venetian Carnival ritual lies in the way in which the peculiarly carnivalesque preoccupation with eating and violence, presented by the public execution of pigs and bulls, came to be interpreted in ways useful to the regime.

Other entertainments proliferated around the pig slaughter: fireworks displays, acrobatic shows, and daredevil high-wire acts. In the neighborhoods there were bull chases and boat races, balls and pageants, which consisted of mimed shows on themes such as the battle between civilization and wildness, the temptations of the Goddess of Love, the fall of Troy, and the pursuit of nymphs by giants. During the early sixteenth century, festival clubs for aristocratic youths, called Companies of the Hose from the distinctively colored tights they wore, organized the production of comedies. At first they resurrected the classical comedies of Plautus[10] and Terence,[11] but during the 1520s several of the clubs commissioned plays by Ruzante,[12] a brilliant dramatist who employed peasant characters to satirize and sometimes bitterly criticize the pretensions of the upper classes. . . . [U]ntil his satire went too far and he disappeared from the Venetian stage, Ruzante explored more fully than anyone else the tense knot of social animosities at the core of Carnival culture. His depictions of the persistent hunger of the peasants, who would sell their bodies and their honor for a piece of bread, added a bitter taste to the gluttonous banquets that the upper classes enjoyed during Carnival. Later in the century the *commedia dell'arte*[13] introduced a repertoire of masked characters who appeared in plays and were widely imitated by casual maskers in the streets. The boastful Captain, pedantic Gratiano, and the clever servants Harlequin and Pulcinella turned up everywhere during Carnival. By the seventeenth century Venetian Carnival had become a major tourist attraction, trans-

---

[10] Roman playwright (ca. 254–ca. 184 B.C.).

[11] Roman writer of comedies (ca. 190–ca. 151 B.C.).

[12] Angelo Beolco Ruzante (1502–1542), Italian playwright and actor, reputed inventor of the masked comedy.

[13] A type of comedy developed in sixteenth-century Italy that was characterized by the portrayal of stock characters dressed in costumes and masks.

forming Venice into a city of pleasure and leisure, full of courtesans, gaming houses, and a vast range of theatrical entertainments. This was the environment that gave birth to grand opera, the ultimate blending of theater, music, ballet, and set-design. In the seventeenth and eighteenth centuries, at least 1,632 different operas were performed in Venice. Even though Venetian Carnival evolved into the centerpiece of the tourism and entertainment industries, it never seems to have lost its significance for the local people during the early modern period.

The word "Carnival" is apparently derived from *carne,* which means "flesh," and *levare,* which means "to take away"; hence Carnival literally means "the taking away of flesh," which could be understood in the double sense of giving up the meat of animals and abstaining from sexual intercourse. Lent required that Christians abstain from meat and sex during the forty-day fast, making Carnival in its most obvious form a final fling before a period of self denial. As the Venetian example conveys, however, Carnival could become far more than a moment of indulgence: it was a vast celebratory commentary on the material aspects of life.

Meat and sweets provided the symbolic framework for Carnival: in 1583 at Koenigsberg butchers carried a 440 lb. sausage in procession, in the renowned Nuremberg *Schembartlauf*[14] Carnival the butchers' guild played a central role in organizing festivities, and everywhere the King of Carnival looked something like the corpulent gourmand in Brueghel's[15] painting. Along with eating came excessive drinking. The people of Moscow were especially famous for their Carnival drunks, which made the city a very dangerous place during the holiday.

Not only did the symbolism of sexual indulgence pervade Carnival, but it appears that a great deal of it was going on during the season. . . . [I]n France the Carnival season produced more conceptions than any other period except the late spring period of May and June. Carnival was a preferred occasion for weddings, and in the early Middle Ages in Venice all weddings apparently were solemnized at that time. The prominent, long nose common on many masks was widely understood to represent the phallus, and bawdy jokes about sausages explicitly connected food and sex. . . . Sexual imagery during Carnival took many forms: in Germany unmarried girls and spinsters had to pull a plow through the streets while men cracked whips about their heads, in many Italian cities prostitutes held foot races (in Venice they had a regatta), in mock weddings men who cross-dressed as women formed the bridal party and the groom might be a dog or bear, and masked men and women in Italy and Spain enjoyed anonymity and considerable license in what they said and did.

In the processions, pantomimes, and plays that characterized Carnival in the big cities, the theme of the *world turned upside down* (variously called, the land of Cockaigne, *Die verkehrte Welt, le monde renversé, il mondo alla rovescia*), an ex-

---

[14] The bearded mask parade, so called because the participants in the parade wore masks with beards attached.

[15] Pieter Brueghel (ca. 1520–1569), Flemish painter of peasant life.

tremely widespread trope[16] in the later Middle Ages, unified Carnival festivity. The very battle between Carnival and Lent introduced the idea of a world in which the normal rules of social order and the pieties of Christian life were disputed and mocked. These Carnival inversions of normal life came in an extraordinary variety of forms — peasants imitating kings, artisans masquerading as bishops, servants giving orders to their masters, poor men offering alms to the rich, boys beating their fathers, and women parading about in armor. Carnival was an especially attractive venue for giving voice to subordinate groups. The ironic Christian text, the "Sermon of the Jews" from Carpentras, portrayed the reversal of fortunes for the Jews forced to live among Christians by depicting young David's victory over the giant Goliath. During the Protestant Reformation in Germany, *Fastnacht*[17] occasioned satirical attacks on the Catholics. In Zwickau in 1525, for example, a group of citizens and youths held a mock hunt of monks and nuns driving them through the streets into nets as in a hunt.

How are we to understand the great variety and paradoxical nature of Carnival? Obviously no single answer would be sufficient. Even those who witnessed and participated in Renaissance Carnivals did not agree about what was going on, its effects, or its meaning. There was often something to scandalize the prudish, such as the rectors of the University of Padua who in 1507 foolishly ordered that the usual Carnival vacation be suspended for the moral good of the students, who in turn rebelled by smashing the furniture in their classrooms and beating up professors who dared to continue lecturing. On the other hand, many otherwise pious individuals thought that Carnival helped make obedient subjects. Stephen of Bourbon observed that in Rome after Carnival all seven deadly sins evaporated making for peaceful relations between the pope and his flock.

During recent decades scholars from many disciplines and backgrounds have extensively investigated and theorized about Carnival. One common thesis sees Carnival as acting as a "safety valve" for the tensions that build up in any hierarchic, highly structured society. . . . From this point of view, Carnival is merely an interlude in normal life, a cyclic release of social pressures, or . . . rituals of rebellion. Such rituals allow subjects to express their resentment of authority but do not change anything and, in fact, strengthen the established government and social order. . . . The absurdity, paradox, extravagance, and illicit behavior of rituals of rebellion provide an emotional release, but since such behavior is set apart from everyday life by the ritual calendar, the ritual rebellion actually demonstrates the coherence of the social order as it is. A young Venetian artisan who parodied the doge, in fact, demonstrated the inevitability of the political inferiority of all artisans. . . .

The various versions of the "safety valve" thesis see Carnival as a kind of subplot to regular daily life. In contrast, the Russian literary theorist, Mikhail

---

[16] The figurative (metaphorical or ironical) use of a word or phrase.

[17] A Christian festival of Germanic origin held on the final day before Lent, a time of merrymaking before Lenten fasting.

Bakhtin,[18] argued that Carnival possesses a life and logic of its own; it is a kind of separate reality that is independent of the world of hierarchy and authority. Carnival offers alternatives to the normal world, even an experience of utopia. To Bakhtin Carnival liberated human consciousness and permitted a new outlook by allowing common people to organize themselves "in their own way" as a Carnival crowd.

According to Bakhtin, the basic mechanism by which Carnival achieved its liberating effects was through turning the world upside down, especially by privileging images from the earthly underworld and the lower body, what Bakhtin called the "material bodily lower stratum" represented through "grotesque realism." Carnival images of food, defecation, sex, and violence elaborate in a comic way processes associated with the lower body. Even fights, blows, curses, and insults bring the adversary down either literally to the ground or figuratively in public esteem. . . .

To Bakhtin and his followers, Carnival opens up the underworld of festive laughter and market-place language. This underworld has three characteristics: (1) *ambivalence,* the tendency to combine praise and abuse, as when a fat glutton is crowned King of Carnival; (2) *duality of the body,* the distinction between, on the one hand, the material bodily lower stratum of ingestion and secretions and, on the other, the ascetic upper stratum of reason and piety; and (3) *incompleteness,* the idea that nature is never finished and perpetually requires the old to die in order to make way for the new. In fact, the dominant participation of youth in the festivities, the positive emphasis on youthfulness in Carnival images, and the negative depictions of the old and authoritarian in Carnival lampoons conveyed the sense that the work of nature is always in the process of replacing the old with the young. Bakhtin's theory has been particularly useful for unraveling images in Carnival pageants, for analyzing the peculiar combinations of insult and laughter in masquerades, and for explicating the influences of Carnival on theater and literature, but it is less successful in explaining the complexity of crowd behavior in a wide variety of historical situations.

Social historians who have studied Carnival during the early modern period have tended to agree with Bakhtin's emphasis on the elements of popular culture in Carnival but have shown that the consequences of Carnival behavior for society and politics are not predictable. As Natalie Zemon Davis[19] puts it, "rather than being a mere 'safety valve,' deflecting attention from social reality, festive life can on the one hand perpetuate certain values of the community (even guarantee its survival), and on the other hand, criticize political order. Misrule can have its own rigor and can also decipher king and state." During the Protestant Reformation Carnival players who turned the values of the world upside down during a time of intense religious conflict saw themselves as liberating rather than de-

---

[18] Russian literary theorist and philosopher (1895–1975).

[19] Historian of early modern France and former president of the American Historical Association.

stroying. What religious conservatives and public authorities might see as criminal behavior was, in the eyes of Carnival revelers, an expression of deeply felt beliefs.

Carnival might best be understood in dramatic terms. The festival provided an occasion, the week or so before the beginning of Lent, and a stage, usually the market square and the streets of the town. It supplied some of the characters, mimed by average citizens who dressed in costumes as wild men, giants, kings, peasants, Turks, or peacocks, in short, something other than what they were in daily life. There was, however, a great deal of ambiguity about who was on stage and who was in the audience; in fact, the roles could be completely interchangeable. There was considerable ambiguity about what a particular Carnival character or motif meant; it may be futile to try to determine the meaning of performances that had the unpredictability of all forms of play. Finally, there was absolute ambiguity about the function of Carnival; what started out as mere satire could easily slip into violence, what one year brought neighbors together in collective laughter could the next divide them in a bloody confrontation. Something like that happened in Romans in 1580. In Carnivals the drama of representation and the experience of real life cannot be easily separated.

There can be no universal interpretation of Carnival that successfully explains all the variations. Carnival employed a set of images of its own that were independent of any particular social function they performed. By pulling down the established, the old, the authoritarian, turning the world upside down and making prominent the functions of the lower body, Carnival stimulated creativity, especially in theatrical productions, as well as music and dance, social commentary, and even rebellion. Through the inspiration of Carnival, numerous writers and artists created the forms of comedy that keep us amused to this day. Erasmus, Rabelais, Cervantes, and Shakespeare all employed motifs of grotesque realism to create comic effects in their work.

During the Renaissance in the great cities of Europe, Carnival came to be transformed from a truly universal festival with mass participation to one in which different forms of entertainment proliferated. In the fifteenth century street masquerades by average citizens presented gluttony, lust, and aggression as in Nuremberg where butchers organized dances and music in the streets. By the seventeenth century, however, many town dwellers had learned to enjoy theatrical comedies that employed the old Carnival themes and that were performed by actors, some of whom had become professionals. Now Carnival was not so much *presented* as *represented*. Commercial entertainment in the form of theatrical performances and spectator sports supplanted collective festive participation. . . .

Migrations of motifs from Carnival proper into other holidays "Carnivalized" much of Renaissance festivity, which in many places thrived on the mixings of sacred and profane images. Giants were especially popular in great public processions, notably in Iberia, Italy, the Low Countries, England, France, and Germany. The earliest reported festive giant comes from 1265 in a procession in Alenquer, Portugal, and by the fifteenth century, giants could be found in many Portuguese processions. The most popular subjects for these huge mannequins were

St. George and the dragon, which were paraded about in many towns on the patron saint's day. Even though these were sacred holidays, vital to civic pride and communal spirit, a carnivalesque atmosphere of licensed play permeated the celebrations. Giants such as Goliath and Gargantua appeared in many folk tales, which were suggested by the mere display of a gigantic statue in a procession. Such displays associated the townsfolk with the deeds of the giant, some of which were heroic but more often carnivalesque by virtue of the fact that giants had enormous bodies with enormous physical needs. Gargantua ate entire herds of cattle, drank barrels of wine, and pissed floods. Giants became one of the most translatable motifs of Carnival. . . .

During the Protestant Reformation in Germany and France, there were numerous occasions when carnivalesque travesty was employed to mock Catholicism. Some of the most famous examples of the world turned upside down occurred in Wittenberg at critical moments of Martin Luther's[20] defiance of the pope. On December 10, 1520, in the presence of the assembled university administration, Professor Luther burned both the papal bull condemning his writings and the university library's copies of the books of canon law. Even though it was outside the Carnival season, in the afternoon Luther's students staged a Carnival procession that included a float with a sail made out of a giant facsimile of the papal bull and a trumpeter with another bull affixed to his sword. As the satirical float passed through the streets, the citizens reacted with laughter and offered firewood to the students for another great bonfire. In the rekindled fire they burned the mock bulls and copies of the books of Professor Luther's academic enemies. One of the maskers dressed as the pope threw his tiara into the flames. Two months later during *Fastnacht* proper the Wittenberg students staged another Carnival travesty. After a sham pope paraded through the streets, he was pelted with dung in the market square; then he and a whole Curia[21] of cardinals and bishops were hunted through the streets. The Wittenbergers apparently found these satirical Carnival lampoons of the highest church authorities tremendously funny.

In June 1524 the bones of an eleventh-century bishop who had recently been canonized were disinterred for public veneration in Meissen. Later the same month miners from the rival town of Buchholz staged a parody of this heavily ritualized event. A satirical procession boasted banners made of rags and participants who wore bathing caps in place of the berets of cathedral canons and who sang while holding gaming boards instead of song books. A sham bishop had a fish basket on his head in place of a miter, wore vestments of straw, had a dirty cloth carried over his head as a canopy, used dung forks for candles, and aspersed unholy water from an old kettle. After marching out to an abandoned mine, the carnivalesque clerics raised a horse's head, the jawbone of a cow, and two horse legs out of the shaft to serve as relics, which were thrown on a manure cart. In his parody

---

[20] Martin Luther (1483–1546), initiator of the Protestant Reformation in Germany.

[21] The bureaucracy of the Roman Catholic Church.

sermon, the bishop identified the bones as coming from the ass of the good Meissen saint.

The ritual vocabulary of the carnivalesque had the powerful potential to be translated from the calendar of festivities to many other situations. Social satire, reform, and even rebellion were offshoots from carnivalesque rites, which provided a model for social creativity. The creativity of the carnivalesque required collective improvisations upon a theme using stock images more than individual acts of genius: carnivalesque scenes adapted the principle of grotesque realism to new applications, new objects of ridicule, new twists of meaning.

Practiced in various forms all across Europe — in England, Scotland, Portugal, Spain, France, Germany, Italy, Hungary, and Rumania — charivari was a ritual of popular judgment typically employed in cases involving some apparent violation of the community's standards for proper sexual or marital behavior. At its simplest it involved the defamation of a couple or individual in public by means of mocking songs and a noise made by beating pots and pans (rough music, *Katzenmusik,*[22] *mattinata*[23]). Usually the jesters formed a procession, sometimes in costume or masks, and subjected their victims to a dunking in water, a humiliating serenade, or a parade backwards on an ass. The mood was usually carnivalesque, full of laughter and rough parody, and if all went according to the typical ritual script, the charivari ended with a payoff from the victims, a round of drinks, and an evening of revelry. If the ritual took a different turn, it could end in quarrels, fist fights, even murder.

The kinds of people likely to find themselves victims of a charivari varied according to their reputation in the community and local views about what was proper. Anyone marrying for a second or third time produced an attractive target as did an old man marrying a young woman or vice versa. A girl who married a stranger or a boy who came courting from outside the village could be victimized; dominated husbands, adulterers, and childless couples were all potentially subject to the defamation of a charivari. For example, in Lyons in 1668 when the widow Florie Nallo, who had inherited a carting business from her husband and was the mother of a teenage daughter, married a younger man who may have been one of her employees, the couple suffered a "grand chirivary" outside their door on their wedding night. Unmarried journeymen, including three who worked in the saddle shop next door, organized the ridicule. In Geneva in 1669 a master craftsman of lace-trimming was paraded through the streets on an ass because he had been repeatedly beaten by his wife. In the late sixteenth century, the young peasant Martin Guerre, whose impotence and indifference to his wife Bertrande were widely known suffered a personally devastating charivari during which he was forced to dress up as a bear while his young neighbors beat him. Although

---

[22] Cat music, caterwauling.

[23] Literally, morning music.

charivaris were most commonly practiced among artisans and peasants, even the highborn were not exempt. When in 1502 the infamous Lucrezia Borgia,[24] who had considerable experience in the marriage bed, wedded her third husband, Alfonso d'Este,[25] who had also been married before, the couple called off the usual *mattinata*, which was to take place after they arose from their first night in bed, because they apparently dreaded the offensive derision they were likely to receive.

The ritual of the charivari might best be seen as an enforcement mechanism employed by the youth-abbeys,[26] which claimed jurisdiction over carnivalesque festivities and the behavior of marriageable girls, other youths, and aberrant married couples. The youth-abbeys included young male peasants or artisans who had passed the age of puberty but were not yet married. . . . [O]ne manifestation of the French youth-abbeys' sexual jurisdiction [was] through their collective rape of vulnerable young women who were then drawn into prostitution. In more benign situations, the youth-abbeys planted a smelly bush on May Day in front of the house of a girl whose morals were questionable and beat up strangers who attempted to court one of the girls in their village. At the very least, an outsider who wanted to see a local woman would be forced to pay a fine or treat the members of the youth-abbey to drinks. Even at normal weddings, they might try to obstruct the wedding procession or burst into the marital chamber in the middle of the night under some ridiculous pretext. Without wives of their own and jealously defensive of access to the pool of available mates, the young men attempted to regulate sexual access to the young women in their community through ritual and force. Although girls and unmarried women often had special ritual functions, especially on May Day, they did not have a parallel form of youth-abbey for themselves.

The charivari ritual extended the sexual jurisdiction of the youth-abbeys into the bedrooms of married couples. As in all carnivalesque rituals, charivari commented on the social realities of the community, serving to enforce proper behavior through mockery of the improper, but it also attempted to resolve dangerous tensions created by irregular marriages. In the case of second marriages, . . . charivari helped to placate the dead spouse whose spirit might be tempted to cause trouble. From this point of view, charivari was a form of prophylactic magic. Such a belief was indicated by the masks typically worn in French and Piedmontese charivaris, which besides representing animals and harlequins included demons and the souls of the dead, what were called *larvae*. In addition, there might be children from the first marriage who were threatened, both psychologically and economically, by the arrival of a step-parent. In such cases the perpe-

---

[24] Daughter of Pope Alexander VI and reputed poisoner (1480–1519).

[25] Alfonso I, ruler of Ferrara from 1505–1534; soldier and statesman.

[26] Muir defines these elsewhere as "urban gangs composed of young unmarried men who were led by an 'abbot' and who assumed authority over the streets of a town by organizing carnivalesque activities, conducting gang fights, performing charivari against married couples, and participating in gang rapes of vulnerable young women."

trators of a charivari enforced the claims of children on their parents. Male adolescents collectively exercised power on behalf of all children and youths who had not yet found a place in society.

Perhaps the most important problem with second marriages, however, was the resentment of the unmarried young men that a woman had been inappropriately removed from the marriage market by an older man who had already had a chance at nuptial joy. Marriages that included an older partner meant that the number of children to be produced from the union might be limited, a fact that threatened the survival of the entire community in an age of high mortality. . . .

In Italy charivari practices were closely associated with the *mattinata* tradition of lovers serenading their beloved, as Romeo serenaded Juliet outside her window in Shakespeare's famous play. An obligatory rite of courtship, serenading was often parodied in *cantilene,* which were songs full of obscene innuendoes and insulting words. Towns in northern and central Italy passed numerous laws against such songs, even absolving in advance any father who assaulted a man singing dirty songs to his daughter outside the house at night. In the seventeenth century a priest, Abramo Russo, composed a scandalous *cantilena* of some eighteen stanzas that questioned the honor of several of the city fathers of Carmiano in the south of Italy. Russo was brought to court by the offended parties on the charge of libel, and from the evidence presented it became clear how effectively a catchy song could smear someone: a witness stated that "When I went into the country to gather olives with my father I would hear, from near and far, a new song sung by the other women." In some situations a *mattinata* serenade would bring honor to a beautiful young girl and her family, but in others the same ritual form produced a *cantilena* of abuse that embarrassed and shamed the entire household, leading to court cases and violent retaliation.

Given the high charge of sexual matters in the closely packed atmosphere of villages and urban neighborhoods where everyone knew everyone else and where personal privacy was unknown, a charivari always played with danger. Like other aspects of the carnivalesque, charivari provided the occasion and a structure for violence when ridicule crossed the boundary to assault or the ridiculed attempted revenge. One of the most powerful symbolic devices of charivari consisted of the use of effigies, which were originally employed as stand-ins for the dead spouse in the case of second marriages. Charivari effigies were borrowed for other rites of abuse against tax-collectors, landlords, mayors, or members of an opposing religious group. Unpopular figures — Guy Fawkes,[27] the Turk, the Pope, Cardinal Mazarin[28] — were hanged or burned in effigy during popular demonstrations. Charivari became a school in which young men learned how to shame in a ritual fashion anyone they did not like.

---

[27] English Roman Catholic who conspired to blow up Parliament (1570–1606).

[28] Cardinal Jules Mazarin (1602–1661), French first minister.

The case of Florie Nallo, the Lyonnaise widow mentioned above who married one of her servants, illustrates how a charivari could turn dangerously sour. After parading around the newlyweds' house and raising a racket for about an hour, the journeymen performing the charivari broke in the door. Etienne Tisserand, the servant who had become a master by marrying his mistress, tried to bribe the revelers with a paltry sum that was insufficient to supply drinks for the several dozen men in the group. Dismissing the bribe with contempt, they promised to return the next evening. The following day Tisserand publicly insulted the master of the journeymen who had organized the charivari, and when a small group again showed up outside Tisserand's house that night, he met them armed with a stick and supported by some friends. The journeymen responded by arming themselves with tools and weapons, and in the ensuing exchange Tisserand was mortally wounded from a pistol shot. Although the ritual forms were initially observed, personal animosities and miscalculations allowed violence to take over.

Although the Tisserand murder seems exceptional, there may be no such thing as a normal non-violent charivari, but rather charivari provided a ritual form that could be employed for many different purposes and produced different levels of punishment. Moreover, charivari was a process with an open-ended outcome: it could be employed both to reintegrate a non-conformist couple into the community or to force them out; it could chide them or kill them; and the perpetrators may have neither known exactly what they wanted to achieve nor anticipated the outcome. Charivari constituted a ritual challenge to the honor of the victims, which could be answered in various ways: the victims could negotiate their way out by paying a fine that was sufficient to placate their tormentors, and having done so they might then be accepted back into the community; but they could refuse to pay the usual bribe and challenge the charivari revelers, who would then be obliged to defend their own honor. Charivari was a model for working out social and value conflicts through rituals of challenge and response, the course and results of which were unpredictable.

During periods of more widespread discord, as sometimes happened in the towns of France that had both Catholic and Protestant residents, charivari ritual went far beyond sexual and marital matters. In 1642 in the dominantly Catholic St.-Rambert-sur-Loire, the sole Calvinist family, the Peyretiers, suffered what on the surface appears to have been a traditional charivari. On the evening of the dinner to celebrate the signing of the marriage contract between Ysabeau Peyretier and Pierre de Montmain, a Protestant clock maker from Lyons, a crowd of young men surrounded the Peyretier house, beating drums, blowing trumpets, and parading about. After investigating the racket, the wedding party retreated into the house and bolted the door against the rowdy crowd that rapidly increased in size. Hurling blasphemous threats against the Huguenot faith and stones against the door, the crowd besieged the house. Assaults were repeated for several nights, while the magistrate coolly ignored the victims' complaints, and continued until the wedding couple were secreted out of town in the dead of night under the cover of decoys who were caught and beaten by the crowd. In the Peyretier case the traditional situation that might have called for a charivari — the marriage of a local woman to an outsider — was mixed up with religious animosities and the refusal of a Protestant family to recognize the legitimacy of the charivari, which they considered contrary to their faith.

Charivari provided ambivalent but powerful ritual forms not only for controlling marriage behavior but for ridiculing non-conformists of various kinds because it was basically a rite of intolerance employed in communities that were deeply threatened by any manifestation of difference. Charivari resolved conflict and furthered it, adapting to different functions depending on the situation and the position of the victims and participants in the community. In many ways, the ambivalent nature of charivari violence provided a bridge between the rowdy but usually peaceful carnivalesque and the rites of violence, which created a ritual frame around violent contests, feuding, punishments, and rebellions.

Most of the time in most places, Carnival, carnivalesque festivities, and charivari expressed the habitual social conflicts of normal life, provided outlets for those conflicts, and stimulated creative solutions to dangerous situations that were fraught with the potential for violence. These rituals typically contained discontent through play and ridicule, but they did not always function that way. The rituals of the lower body, which brought aggression into play, created the occasions for acts of violence. They also became associated with violence by virtue of the fact that the carnivalesque shared a common repertoire of bodily images with the rituals of vendetta and justice, exhibiting a continuum of behavior that makes it impossible to distinguish precisely between rituals that merely poked fun and those that led to killing.

The youth-abbeys that conducted charivaris also had jurisdiction over street fights among rival gangs. Daily life for young working-class men in many European towns was burdened with the constant potential for violent conflict, a situation similar to conditions today in the poorest sections of Los Angeles, Belfast, and Liverpool. Then and now, joining a gang provided some measure of security and solidarity in a dangerous, hostile world. In the seventeenth century in the Langhe region near Genoa, a son of one of the town's elite usually served as "abbot" of the youth-abbey and organized his fellows both for carnivalesque lampoons of authority and for fights with other gangs. In the big cities, gangs of youths roamed the streets at night, getting themselves into brawls and attacking defenseless bystanders. For example, in 1494 a fight between some young Venetian nobles, backed up by their artisan friends, on one side and the retainers of the ambassador of the Duke of Milan on the other left one man dead in the streets and created a major diplomatic incident.

The activities of the youth-abbeys might be seen as a manifestation of traditional ideals of masculinity, which the anthropologist David Gilmore has characterized as striving for "performance excellence." A man who was "good at being a man" followed a script that involved him in public displays of physical risk, which he met with decision and useful action. The "good" man was neither a saint nor a bully but someone who employed aggressiveness to deter challenges and was above all loyal to his own family and friends. Establishing a masculine identity, thus, required public performances of aggression that often took ritual forms.

The streets of daily life became the stage for proving manhood through "performative excellence." Ritual combats and dangerous sports provided the most obvious venue. These included the rough French and English versions of football, Spanish bull chases, and Sienese horse races (the *palio*). In Venice an elaborate culture evolved around "bridge battles," recurrent ritual combats held to gain possession of a bridge. Staged several times a year during the sixteenth and seventeenth centuries by fishermen, arsenal workers, and other laborers, the bridge battles consisted of several distinct phases: for several weeks in advance of the battle young boys, apprentices in violence, made forays into the neighborhoods of the rival faction, hurling insults and making challenges; on the day appointed for the battle individual champions first met on the designated bridge for individual fist fights; in the final phase general mayhem broke out between the two sides with combatants fighting with fists and sticks to drive their opponents off the bridge, some falling off the sides into the canal below, some retiring with serious injuries. There were frequent deaths. When a battle was staged for his entertainment in 1574, the future King of France, Henri III, observed that it was too small a combat to be a real war but too cruel an entertainment to be a game. The bridge battles serve as a useful example of how rites of violence often worked: they opened through a highly formalized series of rituals that gradually escalated the scale and intensity of the confrontation, moving from rule-laden boxing matches between individuals to a general disarray during which rules quickly changed or were abandoned. Rites of violence created an opening to disorder, the outcome of which could not be entirely contained by ritual or controlled by single leaders, characteristics shared by modern sports in which rules limit the nature of the competition but make it impossible to predict exactly the result.

The vast complex of behaviors associated with feuding shared with Carnival a ritual language of the body and of insult. Extremely widespread throughout the later Middle Ages, feuding persisted into the early modern period, especially in mountainous areas, regions distant from the political center of the country, and along borders between states, including such famous epicenters as Iceland, the Highlands of Scotland, Gévaudan in France, the island of Corsica, Liguria and Friuli in Italy, Albania and Montenegro in the Balkans. In many parts of the Mediterranean feuding constituted the principal framework for all social relationships.

The ritual nature of feuding is strikingly evident in the most famous Italian vendetta of the fifteenth and sixteenth centuries, the 200-year-long struggle between the Zambarlano and Strumiero factions in Friuli, which served as the historical prototype for the *Tragedy of Romeo and Juliet*, first penned by a participant named Alvise Da Porto, whose story was later adapted by William Shakespeare into a play.

Every year at Carnival time tensions between the two sides escalated, in part because the partisans of both factions gathered in the town of Udine to celebrate and in part because insulting enemies and contests of arms were appropriate to the occasion. The "Cruel Carnival" of 1511 was bloodiest of all. Late on the morning of February 27, which was Fat Thursday, a party of militiamen stumbled back through the gates of Udine after searching since dawn for a raiding party of German mercenaries rumored to be in the vicinity. The men were tired, hungry, and angry enough to blame the members of the town's aristocratic faction for their troubles. Instead of organizing the usual satirical pantomimes and drunken sports, the men became the nucleus of a huge crowd that looted and burned more than twenty great palaces. During three days of rioting they killed nearly fifty nobles and their retainers. The Carnival violence spread to the countryside where peasants attacked the castles of their feudal lords, resulting in the most extensive and most damaging popular revolt in Renaissance Italy.

Much of the violence toyed with the usual Carnival themes of social inversion and the butchering of animals. The leader of the victimized Strumieri, Alvise Della Torre, was forced to his knees to beg for his life in an inversion of the normal gesture of respect accorded a man of his rank. After the massacre the Zambarlani masqueraded in the clothing of their victims and reveled in wearing the hats of the dead aristocrats, the most obvious insignia of rank. The looters justified their actions by mimicking the customs of official justice. As one eyewitness observed, "I saw the goods taken in that sacking sold at the stands in the piazza of the city, as if such confiscations had been against rebels . . . and the property sold by commission of the [government]."

The Cruel Carnival rioters most graphically displayed the connection between carnivalesque mockery and vendetta vengeance through the disposal of the corpses of their victims. Some people were thrown into latrines or wells. Several of the corpses were purposely left in the street for days, and relatives were blocked from retrieving their dead so that the bodies would be eaten in a final degradation by roaming herds of pigs and packs of dogs. To make someone "dog meat" is not just a modern taunt but an ancient vendetta practice. Other victims were systematically dismembered in an imitation of the seasonal butchering of pigs that took place during the Carnival season. One witness described how "bloody butchers" carved up their victims "like cattle." Dismemberment deprived the victim of his body, the very source of masculine identity and social honor, just as a refusal to bury him denied salvation to his soul.

Dismemberment also had a broader significance as an act of rebellion. . . .

The leader of the faction of the Zambarlani, which did most of the killing at the Cruel Carnival, was a powerful if controversial aristocrat named Antonio Savorgnan. Despite the successes of his partisans in Udine, some six months later events turned against him and he was forced into exile, across the border in Villach, Austria. His assassination by the relatives of his Cruel Carnival victims included a moment of supreme carnivalesque degradation, described here by a brother of one of the assassins.

It was by divine miracle that Antonio Savorgnan was wounded: his head opened, he fell down, and he never spoke another word. But before he died, a giant dog came there and ate all his brains, and one cannot possibly deny that his brains were eaten. His servant did nothing about it. . . . Since I am a priest . . . I did not want to participate in that homicide, so I stayed at home.

The macabre detail of a dog eating Antonio's brains became for contemporaries the most revealing point of the whole assassination, one that most subsequent accounts included or embellished. Vendetta murders shared with Carnival and hunting practices a ritual language that established the forms for killing prey, both animals and men. During the Curel Carnival of Udine human victims were strung up and slaughtered as if they were Carnival pigs or cattle, and Antonio Savorgnan had his head fed to a dog in an inversion of hunting rituals, which prescribed that the least valued parts of the prey would go to the hunting hounds. By such means Antonio's head, which had masterminded the Cruel Carnival slaughter, was symbolically lowered and compared to the guts of a boar or deer killed in the hunt. Vendetta ritual inverted the upper and lower bodies in a decidedly dramatic fashion. . . .

The great repertoire of rituals employed in carnivalesque festivities, charivari, and rites of violence presented the human body as an image of society itself, to be fed, reproduced, dismembered, and devoured. A pervasive ambiguity of meaning and incompleteness of function characterized these rituals, making them extremely fertile sources for creative protest.

NUNS, WIVES, AND MOTHERS: WOMEN AND THE REFORMATION IN GERMANY

Merry Wiesner

In a famous essay, a historian argues persuasively that there was no Italian Renaissance for women, that the cultural flowering in the fourteenth and fifteenth centuries scarcely affected women's lives. According to this perspective, humanism, artistic innovations, and political experimentation did not improve the status of women in law, in the home, or in the workplace. In fact, the condition of women may even have worsened during the Renaissance. Merry Wiesner, professor of history at the University of Wisconsin at Milwaukee, finds that — unlike the Italian Renaissance — the sixteenth-century German Reformation made an appreciable difference to women, improving the lot of some while adversely affecting that of others. She bases her conclusions principally on the writings of the Protestant reformers as well as of women themselves, and on laws.

On the eve of and during the Protestant Reformation, German society placed social and political restrictions on women. What impediments closed possible avenues of advancement to women? Moving beyond these hindrances, Wiesner sketches neatly the impact of religious change on women according to their status in three categories: as members of female religious orders, as single or married, and as workers. Within these broad categories, different groups existed. It is important to understand how the religious transformation from Catholic to Protestant marked the lives of these various groups.

The Protestants closed convents, forcing nuns and lay sisters to fend for themselves or marry. The Reformation altered the lives of other women as well, whether single or married. How did the reformers view marriage and the relationship between wife and husband? Were women any less subordinate in the Protestant denominations than in Catholicism? Society regarded religious toleration as an evil and so reformers discussed marriages in which each spouse be-

Merry Wiesner, "Nuns, Wives, and Mothers: Women and the Reformation in Germany," in *Women in Reformation and Counter-Reformation Europe: Private and Public Worlds*, ed. Sherrin Marshall (Bloomington: Indiana University Press, 1989), 8–26.

longed to a different religion. What, then, was a Protestant wife to do when her husband, to whom she owed obedience, was Catholic?

There is a difference, to be sure, between the ideas of Protestant theologians on the nature of women, their proper place, and their duties, on the one hand, and the translation of those ideas into actual practice, on the other hand. Protestant states passed laws modifying the behavior of women in marriage and in religion. Wiesner rightly stresses that women reacted to the Reformation; they were not just acted upon. How did women — both aristocrats and commoners — contribute to the religious developments sweeping Germany? Overall, did the Reformation improve the status or situation of any groups of women?

It is in many ways anachronistic even to use the word "Germany" when discussing the sixteenth century. At that time, modern-day East and West Germany were politically part of the Holy Roman Empire, a loose confederation of several hundred states, ranging from tiny knightships through free imperial cities to large territorial states. These states theoretically owed obedience to an elected emperor, but in reality they were quite independent and often pursued policies in opposition to the emperor. Indeed, the political diversity and lack of a strong central authority were extremely important to the early success of the Protestant Reformation[1] in Germany. Had Luther[2] been a Frenchman or a Spaniard, his voice would probably have been quickly silenced by the powerful monarchs in those countries.

Because of this diversity, studies of the Reformation in Germany are often limited to one particular area or one particular type of government, such as the free imperial cities. This limited focus is useful when looking at the impact of the Reformation on men, for male participation and leadership in religious change varied depending on whether a territory was ruled by a city council, a nobleman, or a bishop. Male leadership in the Reformation often came from university teachers, so the presence or absence of a university in an area was also an important factor.

When exploring the impact of religious change on women, however, these political and institutional factors are not as important. Except for a few noblewomen who ruled territories while their sons were still minors, women had no formal political voice in any territory of the empire. They did not vote or serve on city councils, and even abbesses were under the direct control of a male church official. Women could not attend universities, and thus did not come into contact with religious ideas through formal theological training. Their role in the Refor-

---

[1] The sixteenth-century split in western Christianity between the Roman Catholic Church and a variety of Protestant denominations.

[2] Martin Luther (1483–1546), initiator of the Protestant Reformation in Germany.

mation was not so determined by what may be called "public" factors — political structures, educational institutions — as was that of men.

Women's role in the Reformation and the impact of religious change on them did vary throughout Germany, but that variation was largely determined by what might be termed "personal" factors — a woman's status as a nun or laywoman, her marital status, her social and economic class, her occupation. Many of these factors, particularly social and economic class, were also important in determining men's responses to religious change, but they were often secondary to political factors whereas for women they were of prime importance.

The Protestant and Catholic reformers recognized this. Although they generally spoke about and to women as an undifferentiated group and proposed the same ideals of behavior for all women, when the reformers did address distinct groups of women they distinguished them by marital or clerical status. Nuns, single women, mothers, wives, and widows all got special attention in the same way that special treatises were directed to male princes and members of city councils — men set apart from others by their public, political role.

It is important to keep in mind that although a woman's religious actions were largely determined by her personal status, they were not regarded as a private matter, even if they took place within the confines of her own household. No one in the sixteenth century regarded religion or the family as private, as that term is used today. One's inner relationship with God was perhaps a private matter (though even that is arguable), but one's outward religious practices were a matter of great concern for political authorities. Both Protestants and Catholics saw the family as the cornerstone of society, the cornerstone on which all other institutions were constructed, and every political authority meddled in family and domestic concerns. Thus a woman's choice to serve her family meat on Friday or attend the funeral of a friend whose religion was unacceptable was not to be overlooked or regarded as trivial.

Although "personal" is not the same as "private" in Reformation Germany, grouping women by their personal status is still the best way to analyze their role in religious change. This essay thus follows "personal" lines of division and begins with an exploration of the impact of the Reformation on nuns, Beguines,[3] and other female religious. It then looks at single and married women, including a special group of married women, the wives of the Protestant reformers. Although the reformers did not have a special message for noblewomen, the situation of these women warrants separate consideration because their religious choices had the greatest effect on the course of the Reformation. The essay concludes with a discussion of several groups of working women whose labor was directly or indirectly affected by religious change.

Women in convents, both cloistered nuns[4] and lay sisters, and other female religious, were the first to confront the Protestant Reformation. In areas becom-

---

[3] Roman Catholic lay sisterhoods.

[4] Confined to a convent and therefore secluded from the world.

ing Protestant religious change meant both the closing of their houses and a negation of the value and worth of the life they had been living. The Protestant reformers encouraged nuns and sisters to leave their houses and marry, with harsh
words concerning the level of morality in the convents, comparing it to that in
brothels. Some convents accepted the Protestant message and willingly gave up
their houses and land to city and territorial authorities. The nuns renounced their
vows, and those who were able to find husbands married, while the others returned to their families or found ways to support themselves on their own. Others did not accept the new religion but recognized the realities of political power
and gave up their holdings; these women often continued living together after the
Reformation, trying to remain as a religious community, though they often had to
rely on their families for support. In some cases the nuns were given a pension.
There is no record, however, of what happened to most of these women. Former
priests and monks could become pastors in the new Protestant churches, but former nuns had no place in the new church structure.

Many convents, particularly those with high standards of learning and morality and whose members were noblewomen or women from wealthy patrician
families, fought the religious change. A good example of this is the St. Clara convent in Nuremberg, whose nuns were all from wealthy Nuremberg families and
whose reputation for learning had spread throughout Germany. The abbess at the
time of the Reformation was Charitas Pirckheimer, a sister of the humanist
Willibald Pirckheimer and herself an accomplished Latinist. In 1525, the Nuremberg city council ordered all the cloisters to close; four of the six male houses in
the city dissolved themselves immediately, but both female houses refused. The
council first sent official representatives to try to persuade the nuns and then
began a program of intimidation. The women, denied confessors and Catholic
communion, were forced to hear Protestant sermons four times a week; their servants had difficulty buying food; people threatened to burn the convent, threw
stones over the walls, and sang profane songs when they heard the nuns singing.
Charitas noted in her memoirs that women often led the attacks and were the
most bitter opponents of the nuns. Three families physically dragged their daughters out of the convent, a scene of crying and wailing witnessed by many Nurem-
bergers. The council questioned each nun separately to see if she had any complaints, hoping to find some who would leave voluntarily, and finally confiscated
all of the convent's land. None of these measures was successful, and the council
eventually left the convent alone, although it forbade the taking in of new novices.
The last nun died in 1590.

Charitas' firmness and the loyalty of the nuns to her were perhaps extraordinary, but other abbesses also publicly defended their faith. Elizabeth Gottgabs, the
abbess of Oberwesel convent, published a tract against the Lutherans in 1550. Although she denigrated her own work as that of a "poor woman," she hardly held
back in her language when evaluating the reformers: "The new evangelical preachers have tried to plug our ears with their abominable uproar . . . our gracious God
will not tolerate their foolishness any longer." . . .

Nuns who chose to leave convents occasionally published works explaining
their actions as well. Martha Elizabeth Zitterin published her letters to her mother

explaining why she had left the convent at Erfurt; these were republished five times by Protestant authorities in Jena, who never mentioned that the author herself later decided to return to the convent. Even if the former nuns did not publish their stories, these accounts often became part of Protestant hagiography, particularly if the women had left the convent surreptitiously or had been threatened. Katherine von Bora and eight other nuns were smuggled out of their convent at night after they had secretly made contact with Luther. The fact that this occurred on Easter and that they left in a wagon of herring barrels added drama to the story, and Katherine's later marriage to Luther assured that it would be retold many times.

The Jesuits[5] and other leaders of the Catholic Reformation[6] took the opposite position from the Protestants on the value of celibacy, encouraging young women to disobey their parents and enter convents to escape arranged marriages. Although they did not encourage married women to leave their husbands, the Jesuits followed the pre-Reformation tradition in urging husbands to let their wives enter convents if they wished.

The Counter-Reformation church wanted all female religious strictly cloistered, however, and provided no orders for women who wanted to carry out an active apostolate; there was no female equivalent of the Jesuits. The church also pressured Beguines, Franciscan tertiaries,[7] and other sisters who had always moved about somewhat freely or worked out in the community to adopt strict rules of cloister and place themselves under the direct control of a bishop. The women concerned did not always submit meekly, however. The Beguines in Münster, for example, refused to follow the advice of their confessors, who wanted to reform the beguinage and turn it into a cloistered house of Poor Clares.[8] The women, most of whom were members of the city's elite families, appealed to the city council for help in defending their civil rights and traditional liberties. The council appealed to the archbishop of Cologne, the cardinals, and eventually the pope, and, though the women were eventually cloistered, they were allowed to retain certain of their traditional practices. In some ways, the women were caught in the middle of a power struggle between the archbishop and the city council, but they were still able to appeal to the city's pride in its traditional privileges to argue for their own liberties and privileges. Perhaps the fact that they had not been cloistered kept them aware of the realities and symbols of political power.

Of course most of the women in sixteenth-century Germany were not nuns or other female religious but laywomen who lived in families. Their first contact with the Reformation was often shared with the male members of their families.

---

[5] Members of the Society of Jesus, a Roman Catholic religious order established in 1540.

[6] The Roman Catholic Church's reform movement and resurgence in reaction to the Protestant Reformation during the late sixteenth century.

[7] A group of laywomen attached to the Franciscan order, a Roman Catholic religious order founded in 1209.

[8] An order of Franciscan nuns.

They heard the new teachings proclaimed from a city pulpit, read or looked at broadsides attacking the pope, and listened to traveling preachers attacking celibacy and the monasteries.

The reformers communicated their ideas to women in a variety of ways. Women who could read German might have read Luther's two marriage treatises or any number of Protestant marriage manuals, the first of which was published in Augsburg in 1522. They could have read tracts against celibacy by many reformers, which varied widely in their level of vituperation and criticism of convent life. Both Protestant and Catholic authors wrote books of commonplaces and examples, which contained numerous references to proper and improper female conduct attributed to classical authors, the church fathers, and more recent commentators.

The vast majority of women could not read but received the message orally and visually. Sermons, particularly marriage sermons but also regular Sunday sermons, emphasized the benefits of marriage and the proper roles of husband and wife. Sermons at women's funerals stressed their piety, devotion to family, and trust in God through great trials and tribulations and set up models for other women to follow. Vernacular dramas about marriage replaced pre-Reformation plays about virgin martyrs suffering death rather than losing their virginity. Woodcuts depicted pious married women (their marital status was clear because married women wore their hair covered) listening to sermons or reading the Bible. Protestant pamphlets portrayed the pope with the whore of Babylon, which communicated a message about both the pope and about women. Catholic pamphlets showed Luther as a lustful glutton, driven only by his sexual and bodily needs. Popular stories about Luther's home life and harsh attitudes toward female virginity circulated by word of mouth. . . .

The Protestant reformers did not break sharply with tradition in their ideas about women. For both Luther and Calvin, women were created by God and could be saved through faith; spiritually women and men were equal. In every other respect, however, women were to be subordinate to men. Women's subjection was inherent in their very being and was present from creation — in this the reformers agreed with Aristotle[9] and the classical tradition. It was made more brutal and harsh, however, because of Eve's responsibility for the Fall — in this Luther and Calvin[10] agreed with patristic[11] tradition and with their scholastic and humanist predecessors.

There appears to be some novelty in their rejection of Catholic teachings on the merits of celibacy and championing of marriage as the proper state for all individuals. Though they disagreed on so much else, all Protestant reformers agreed

---

[9] Greek philosopher (384–322 B.C.).

[10] John Calvin (1509–1564), French Protestant theologian, founder of Calvinism and religious leader of Geneva.

[11] Referring to the fathers, or theologians, of the early Christian Church.

on this point; the clauses discussing marriage in the various Protestant confessions show more similarities than do any other main articles of doctrine or discipline. Even this emphasis on marriage was not that new, however. Civic and Christian humanists also thought that "God had established marriage and family life as the best means for providing spiritual and moral discipline in this world," and they "emphasized marriage and the family as the basic social and economic unit which provided the paradigm for all social relations."

The Protestant exhortation to marry was directed to both sexes, but particularly to women, for whom marriage and motherhood were a vocation as well as a living arrangement. Marriage was a woman's highest calling, the way she could fulfill God's will: in Luther's harsh words, "Let them bear children to death; they are created for that." Unmarried women were suspect, both because they were fighting their natural sex drive, which everyone in the sixteenth century believed to be much stronger than men's, and because they were upsetting the divinely imposed order, which made woman subject to man. Even a woman as prominent and respected as Margaretha Blarer, the sister of Ambrosius Blarer, a reformer in Constance, was criticized for her decision to remain unmarried. Martin Bucer[12] accused her of being "masterless." Her brother defended her decision by pointing out that she was very close to his family and took care of the poor and plague victims "as a mother."

The combination of women's spiritual equality, female subordination, and the idealization of marriage proved problematic for the reformers, for they were faced with the issue of women who converted while their husbands did not. What was to take precedence, the woman's religious convictions or her duty of obedience? Luther and Calvin were clear on this. Wives were to obey their husbands, even if they were not Christians; in Calvin's words, a woman "should not desert the partner who is hostile." Marriage was a woman's "calling," her natural state, and she was to serve God through this calling.

Wives received a particularly ambiguous message from the radical reformers. . . . Some radical groups allowed believers to leave their unbelieving spouses, but women who did so were expected to remarry quickly and thus come under the control of a male believer. The most radical Anabaptists were fascinated by Old Testament polygamy and accepted the statement in Revelations that the Last Judgment would only come if there were 144,000 "saints" in the world; they actually enforced polygamy for a short time at Münster, though the required number of saints were never born. In practical terms, Anabaptist women were equal only in martyrdom.

Although the leaders of the Counter Reformation continued to view celibacy as a state preferable to matrimony, they realized that most women in Germany would marry and began to publish their own marriage manual to counter those published by Protestants. The ideal wives and mothers they described were, how-

---

[12] German Protestant reformer (1491–1551).

ever, no different than those of the Protestants; both wanted women to be "chaste, silent, and obedient."

The ideas of the reformers did not stay simply within the realm of theory but led to political and institutional changes. Some of these changes were the direct results of Protestant doctrine, and some of them had unintended, though not unforeseeable, consequences. . . .

Every Protestant territory passed a marriage ordinance that stressed wifely obedience and proper Christian virtues and set up a new court or broadened the jurisdiction of an existing court to handle marriage and morals cases which had previously been handled by church courts. They also passed sumptuary laws that regulated weddings and baptisms, thereby trying to make these ceremonies more purely Christian by limiting the number of guests and prohibiting profane activities such as dancing and singing. Though such laws were never completely successful, the tone of these two ceremonies, which marked the two perhaps most important events in a woman's life, became much less exuberant. Religious processions, such as Corpus Christi[13] parades, which had included both men and women, and in which even a city's prostitutes took part, were prohibited. The public processions that remained were generally those of guild masters and journeymen, at which women were onlookers only. Women's participation in rituals such as funerals was limited, for Protestant leaders wanted neither professional mourners nor relatives to take part in extravagant wailing and crying. Lay female confraternities, which had provided emotional and economic assistance for their members and charity for the needy, were also forbidden, and no similar all-female groups replaced them.

The Protestant reformers attempted to do away with the veneration of Mary and the saints. This affected both men and women, because some of the strongest adherents of the cult of the Virgin had been men. For women, the loss of St. Anne, Mary's mother, was particularly hard, for she was a patron saint of pregnant women; now they were instructed to pray during labor and childbirth to Christ, a celibate male, rather than to a woman who had also been a mother. The Protestant martyrs replaced the saints to some degree, at least as models worthy of emulation, but they were not to be prayed to and they did not give their names to any days of the year. The Protestant Reformation not only downplayed women's public ceremonial role; it also stripped the calendar of celebrations honoring women and ended the power female saints and their relics were believed to have over people's lives. Women who remained Catholic still had female saints to pray to, but the number of new female saints during the Counter Reformation was far fewer than the number of new male saints, for two important avenues to sanctity, missionary and pastoral work, were closed to women.

Because of the importance Protestant reformers placed on Bible-reading in the vernacular, many of them advocated opening schools for girls as well as boys. The

---

[13] A Roman Catholic festival instituted in the thirteenth century to honor the Blessed Sacrament (the body of Jesus).

number of such schools which opened was far fewer than the reformers had orig- inally hoped, and Luther in particular also muted his call for mass education after the turmoil of the Peasants' War.[14] The girls' schools that were opened stressed morality and decorum; in the words of the Memmingen school ordi- nance from 1587, the best female pupil was one noted for her "great diligence and application in learning her catechism, modesty, obedience, and excellent pen- manship." These schools taught sewing as well as reading and singing, and reli- gious instruction was often limited to memorizing the catechism.

Along with these changes that related directly to Protestant doctrine, the Re- formation brought with it an extended period of war and destruction in which in- dividuals and families were forced to move frequently from one place to another. Women whose husbands were exiled for religious reasons might also have been forced to leave. Their houses and goods were usually confiscated whether they left town or not. If allowed to stay, they often had to support a family and were still held suspect by neighbors and authorities. A woman whose husband was away fighting could go years without hearing from him and never be allowed to marry again if there was some suspicion he might still be alive.

Women were not simply passive recipients of the Reformation and the ideas and changes it brought but indeed responded to them actively. Swept up by the enthusiasm of the first years of the Reformation, single and married women often stepped beyond what were considered acceptable roles for women. Taking liter- ally Luther's idea of a priesthood of all believers, women as well as uneducated men began to preach and challenge religious authorities. In 1524 in Nuremberg, the city council took action against a certain Frau Voglin, who had set herself up in the hospital church and was preaching. In a discussion after a Sunday sermon by a Lutheran-leaning prior, a woman in Augsburg spoke to a bishop's represen- tative who had been sent to hear the sermon and called the bishop a brothel manager because he had a large annual income from concubinage fees. Several women in Zwickau, inspired by the preaching of Thomas Müntzer,[15] also began to preach in 1521.

All of these actions were viewed with alarm by civic authorities, who even ob- jected to women's getting together to discuss religion. In their view, female preach- ers clearly disobeyed the Pauline injunction[16] against women speaking in church and moved perilously close to claiming an official religious role. In 1529, the Zwickau city council banished several of the women who had gathered together and preached. In the same year, the Memmingen city council forbade maids to discuss religion while drawing water at neighborhood wells. No German gov-

---

[14] Uprisings in central and southwest Germany, 1524–1525, inspired by the Reformation lead- ers' defiance of authority.

[15] Radical religious leader who led a peasant rebellion in 1524–1525.

[16] "[W]omen should keep silence in the churches. For they are not permitted to speak, but they should be subordinate. . . . [I]is shameful for a woman to speak in church" (1 Corinthians 14, 34 ff).

ernment forbade women outright to read the Bible, as Henry VIII[17] of England did in 1543, but the authorities did attempt to prevent them from discussing it publicly.

After 1530, women's public witnessing of faith was more likely to be prophesying than preaching. In many ways, female prophets were much less threatening than female preachers, for the former had biblical parallels, clear biblical justification, and no permanent official function. Ursula Jost and Barbara Rebstock in Strasbourg began to have visions and revelations concerning the end of the world. When Melchior Hoffman, the Spiritualist, came to Strasbourg, they convinced him he was the prophet Elijah born again and thus one of the signs of the impending Apocalypse. He published seventy-two of Ursula's revelations, advising all Christians to read them. They were written in the style of Old Testament prophecy and became popular in the Rhineland and Netherlands. Several other female Anabaptists also had visions that were spread by word of mouth and as broadsides or small pamphlets. Though these women were illiterate, their visions were full of biblical references, which indicates that, like Lollard[18] women in England, they had memorized much of the Bible. Female prophecy was accepted in most radical sects, for they emphasized direct revelation and downplayed theological training. That these sects were small and loosely structured was also important for the continued acceptance of female revelation; in Münster, the one place where Anabaptism became the state religion, female prophecy was suppressed.

Not all female visionaries were radicals, however. Mysticism and ecstatic visions remained an acceptable path to God for Catholic women and increased in popularity in Germany after the works of Saint Theresa[19] were translated and her ideas became known. Even Lutheran women reported miracles and visions. Catherine Binder, for example, asserted that her speech had been restored after seven years when a pastor gave her a copy of the Lutheran Catechism. The Lutheran clergy were suspicious of such events, but did not reject them out of hand.

With the advent of the religious wars, female prophets began to see visions of war and destruction and to make political, as well as religious and eschatological,[20] predictions. Susanna Rugerin had been driven far from her home by imperial armies and began to see an angel who revealed visions of Gustavus Adolphus.[21] The visions of Juliana von Duchnik were even more dramatic. In 1628 she

---

[17] King from 1509 to 1547.

[18] Lollard was originally a name given to followers of the fourteenth-century English reformer John Wycliffe. Later the name was applied to any English religious dissenter in the fifteenth century.

[19] Spanish nun and mystic (1515–1582).

[20] Having to do with death, final destiny, the end of the world.

[21] Protestant king of Sweden from 1611 to 1632; defeated the Catholic imperial forces in Germany during the Thirty Years' War (1618–1648).

brought a warning from God to Duke Wallenstein, a commander of imperial troops, telling him to leave his estate because God would no longer protect him. Though Wallenstein's wife was very upset, his supporters joked about it, commenting that the emperor got letters from only the pope, while Wallenstein got them directly from God. Von Duchnik published this and other of her visions the following year and in 1634 returned to Wallenstein's camp warning him that she had seen a vision of him trying to climb a ladder into heaven; the ladder collapsed, and he fell to earth with blood and poison pouring out of his heart. Though Wallenstein himself continued to dismiss her predictions, others around him took her seriously. Her visions in this case proved accurate, for Wallenstein was assassinated less than a month later. In general, female prophets were taken no less seriously than their male counterparts.

The most dramatic public affirmation of faith a woman could make was martyrdom. Most of the female martyrs in Germany were Anabaptists, and the law granted women no special treatment, except for occasionally delaying execution if they were pregnant. Women were more likely to be drowned than beheaded, for it was thought they would faint at the sight of the executioner's sword and make his job more difficult. Some of them were aware that this reduced the impact of their deaths and wanted a more public form of execution. A good indication of the high degree of religious understanding among many Anabaptist women comes from their interrogations. They could easily discuss the nature of Christ, the doctrine of the Real Presence,[22] and baptism, quoting extensively from the Bible. As a woman known simply as Claesken put it, "Although I am a simple person before men, I am not unwise in the knowledge of the Lord." Her interrogators were particularly upset because she had converted many people: they commented, "Your condemnation will be greater than your husband's because you can read and have misled him."

Although most of the women who published religious works during the Reformation were either nuns or noblewomen, a few middle-class women wrote hymns, religious poetry, and some polemics. Ursula Weide published a pamphlet against the abbot of Pegau, denouncing his support of celibacy. The earliest Protestant hymnals include several works by women, often verse renditions of the Psalms or Gospels. Justitia Sanger, a blind woman from Braunschweig, published a commentary on ninety-six Psalms in 1593, dedicating it to King Frederick II of Denmark. Female hymn-writing became even more common in the seventeenth century when the language of hymns shifted from aggressive and martial to emotional and pious; it was more acceptable for a woman to write of being washed in the blood of the Lamb than of strapping on the armor of God. Not all female religious poetry from the seventeenth century was meekly pious, however. Anna Oven Hoyer was driven from place to place during the Thirty Years' War, finally

---

[22] That the body and blood of Jesus is actually present in the sacrament of communion (the Eucharist).

finding refuge in Sweden. She praised David Joris[23] and Caspar von Schwenkfeld[24] in her writings, which she published without submitting them for clerical approval. Some of them, including her "Spiritual Conversation between a Mother and Child about True Christianity," were later burned as heretical. In this dialogue she attacked the Lutheran clergy for laxness, greed, pride, and trust in worldly learning and largely blamed them for the horrors of the Thirty Years' War.

Seventeenth-century women often wrote religious poems, hymns, and prose meditations for private purposes as well as for publication. They wrote to celebrate weddings, baptisms, and birthdays, to console friends, to praise deceased relatives, to instruct and provide examples for their children. If a woman's works were published while she was still alive, they included profuse apologies about her unworthiness and presumption. Many such works were published posthumously by husbands or fathers and include a note from these men that writing never distracted the author from her domestic tasks but was done only in her spare time. Unfortunately, similar works by sixteenth-century German women are rare. Thus, to examine the religious convictions of the majority of women who did not preach, prophesy, publish, or become martyrs, we must look at their actions within the context of their domestic and community life.

Married women whose religious convictions matched those of their husbands often shared equally in the results of those convictions. If these convictions conflicted with local authorities and the men were banished for religious reasons, their wives were expected to follow them. Because house and goods were generally confiscated, the wives had no choice in the matter anyway. Women whose husbands were in hiding, fighting religious wars, or assisting Protestant churches elsewhere supported the family and covered for their husbands, often sending them supplies as well. Wealthy women set up endowments for pastors and teachers and provided scholarships for students at Protestant, and later Jesuit, universities.

Many married women also responded to the Protestant call to make the home, in the words of the humanist Urbanus Rhegius, "a seminary for the church." They carried out what might best be called domestic missionary activity, praying and reciting the catechism with their children and servants. Those who were literate might read some vernacular religious literature, and, because reading was done aloud in the sixteenth century, this was also a group activity. What they could read was limited by the level of their reading ability, the money available to buy books, and the effectiveness of the city censors at keeping out unwanted or questionable material. Women overcame some of the limitations on their reading material by paying for translations, thus continuing a tradition begun before the invention of the printing press. The frequency of widowhood in the sixteenth century meant that women often carried religious ideas, and the pamphlets and books that contained them, to new households when they remarried,

---

[23] A Dutch leader of the passive wing of the Anabaptists (ca. 1501–1556).

[24] German mystic and radical Protestant reformer (1489–1561).

and a few men actually admitted to having been converted by their wives. The role of women as domestic missionaries was recognized more clearly by Catholics and English Protestants than it was by continental Protestants, who were obsessed with wifely obedience. Richard Hooker,[25] a theorist for the Anglican church, commented that the Puritans made special efforts to convert women because they were "diligent in drawing away their husbands, children, servants, friends, and allies the same way." Jesuits encouraged the students at their seminaries to urge their mothers to return to confession and begin Catholic practices in the home; in this way, an indifferent or even Lutheran father might be brought back into the fold.

There are several spectacular examples among noble families of women whose quiet pressure eventually led to their husbands' conversions and certainly many among common people that are not recorded. But what about a married woman whose efforts failed? What could a woman do whose religious convictions differed from those of her husband? In some areas, the couple simply lived together as adherents of different religions. The records for Bamberg, for example, show that in 1595 about 25 percent of the households were mixed marriages, with one spouse Catholic and the other Lutheran. Among the members of the city council the proportion was even higher — 43 percent had spouses of a different religion, so this was not something which simply went unnoticed by authorities. Bamberg was one of the few cities in Germany which allowed two religions to worship freely; therefore, mixed marriages may have been only a local phenomenon. This, however, has not yet been investigated in other areas.

Continued cohabitation was more acceptable if the husband was of a religion considered acceptable in the area. In 1631, for example, the Strasbourg city council considered whether citizens should lose their citizenship if they married Calvinists. It decided that a man would not "because he can probably draw his spouse away from her false religion, and bring her on to the correct path." He would have to pay a fine, though, for "bringing an unacceptable person into the city." A woman who married a Calvinist would lose her citizenship, however, "because she would let herself easily be led into error in religion by her husband, and led astray."

As a final resort, a married woman could leave her husband (and perhaps family) and move to an area where the religion agreed with her own. This was extremely difficult for women who were not wealthy, and most of the recorded cases involve noblewomen with independent incomes and sympathetic fathers. Even if a woman might gather enough resources to support herself, she was not always welcome, despite the strength of her religious convictions, for she had violated that most basic of norms, wifely obedience. Protestant city councils were suspicious of any woman who asked to be admitted to citizenship independently and questioned her intensely about her marital status. Catholic cities such as Mu-

---

[25] Author (1554–1600) of the *Laws of Ecclesiastical Polity* (1594).

nich were more concerned about whether the woman who wanted to immigrate had always been a good Catholic than whether or not she was married, particularly if she wished to enter a convent.

Exceptions were always made for wives of Anabaptists. A tailor's wife in Nuremberg was allowed to stay in the city and keep her house as long as she recanted her Anabaptist beliefs and stayed away from all other Anabaptists, including her husband, who had been banished. After the siege of Münster, Anabaptist women and children began to drift back into the city and were allowed to reside there if they abjured Anabaptism and swore an oath of allegiance to the bishop. Both Protestant and Catholic authorities viewed Anabaptism as a heresy and a crime so horrible it broke the most essential human bonds.

It was somewhat easier for unmarried women and widows to leave a territory for religious reasons, and in many cases persecution or war forced them out. A widow wrote to the Nuremberg city council after the city had turned Lutheran that she wanted to move there "because of the respect and love she has for the word of God, which is preached here [that is, Nuremberg] truly and purely"; after a long discussion, the council allowed her to move into the city. But women still had greater difficulties than men being accepted as residents in any city. Wealthier widows had to pay the normal citizenship fee and find male sponsors, both of which were difficult for women, who generally did not command as many financial resources or have as many contacts as men of their class. Because of this, and because innkeepers were forbidden to take in any woman traveling alone, no matter what her age or class, women's cities of refuge were often limited to those in which they had relatives.

Women who worked to support themselves generally had to make special supplications to city councils to be allowed to stay and work. Since they had not been trained in a guild in the city, the council often overrode guild objections in permitting them to make or sell small items to support themselves and was more likely to grant a woman's request if she was seen as particularly needy or if her story was especially pathetic. A woman whose husband had been killed in the Thirty Years' War asked permission in 1632 to live in Strasbourg and bake pretzels; this was granted to her and several others despite the objections of the bakers because, in the council's words, "all of the supplicants are poor people, that are particularly hard-pressed in these difficult times." Another woman was allowed to make tonic and elixirs in Strasbourg after a city pastor assured the council that "she is a pious and godly woman who left everything to follow the true word of God."

One of the most dramatic changes brought about by the Protestant Reformation was the replacement of celibate priests by married pastors with wives and families. Many of the wives of the early reformers had themselves been nuns, and they were crossing one of society's most rigid borders by marrying, becoming brides of men rather than brides of Christ. During the first few years of the Reformation, they were still likened to priests' concubines in the public mind and had to create a respectable role for themselves. They were often living demonstrations of their husbands' convictions and were expected to be models of wifely obedience and Christian charity; the reformers had particularly harsh words for pastors who could not control their wives. Pastors' wives were frequently asked to be godmothers and thereby could be "important agents in the diffusion of evangelical domesticity from the household of the clergy to the rest of the population." But they also had to bring the child a gift appropriate to its social standing from the meager pastoral treasury. The demands on pastors' wives were often exacerbated by their husbands' lack of concern for material matters. Often former priests or monks, these men had never before worried about an income and continued to leave such things in God's (or actually their wives') hands.

Pastors' wives opened up their homes to students and refugees, providing them with food, shelter and medical care. This meant buying provisions, brewing beer, hiring servants, growing fruits and vegetables, and gathering herbs for a household that could expand overnight from ten to eighty. Katherine von Bora purchased and ran an orchard, personally overseeing the care of apple and pear trees and selling the fruit to provide income for the household. She occasionally took part in the theological discussions that went on after dinner in the Luther household and was teased by her husband for her intellectual interests; he called her "Professor Katie." . . .

Other pastors' wives assisted in running city hospitals, orphanages, and infirmaries, sometimes at the suggestion of their husbands and sometimes on their own initiative. Katherine Zell, the wife of Matthias Zell[26] and a tireless worker for the Reformation in Strasbourg, inspected the local hospital and was appalled by what she found there. She demanded the hospital master be replaced because he served the patients putrid, fatty meat, "does not know the name of Christ," and mumbled the table grace "so you can't tell if it's a prayer or a fart." Wealthy women set up endowments for pastors and teachers and provided scholarships for students at Protestant, and later Jesuit, universities.

Neither the Protestant nor the Catholic reformers differentiated between noblewomen and commoners in their public advice to women; noblewomen, too, were to be "chaste, silent, and obedient." Privately, however, they recognized that such women often held a great deal of power and made special attempts to win them over. Luther corresponded regularly with a number of prominent noblewomen, and Calvin was even more assiduous at "courting ladies in high places."

Noblewomen, both married and unmarried, religious and lay, had the most opportunity to express their religious convictions, and the consequences of their actions were more far-reaching than those of most women. Prominent noblewomen who left convents could create quite a sensation, particularly if, like Ursula of Münsterberg, they wrote a justification of why they had left and if their actions put them in opposition to their families. Disagreements between husband and wife over matters of religion could lead to the wife being exiled, as in the case of Elisabeth of Brandenburg. They could also lead to mutual toleration, however,

---

[26] Katherine (ca. 1497–1562) and Matthias Zell (1477–1548) were Protestant reformers at Strasbourg.

as they did for Elisabeth's daughter, also named Elisabeth, who married Eric, the duke of Brunswick-Calenburg. She became a Lutheran while her husband remained a Catholic, to which his comment was: "My wife does not interfere with and molest us in our faith, and therefore we will leave her undisturbed and unmolested in hers." After his death, she became regent and introduced the Reformation into Brunswick. . . . Several other female rulers also promoted independently the Reformation in their territories, while others convinced their husbands to do so. Later in the century noble wives and widows were also influential in opening up territories to the Jesuits.

Most of these women were following paths of action that had been laid out by male rulers and had little consciousness of themselves as women carrying out a reformation. Others as well judged their actions on the basis of their inherited status and power, for, despite John Knox's[27] bitter fulminations against "the monstrous regiment of women," female rulers were not regarded as unusual in the sixteenth century. Only if a noblewoman ventured beyond summoning and protecting a male reformer or signing church ordinances to commenting publicly on matters of theology was she open to criticism as a woman going beyond what was acceptable.

The best known example of such a noblewoman was Argula von Grumbach, who wrote to the faculty of the University of Ingolstadt in 1523 protesting the university's treatment of a young teacher accused of Lutheran leanings. She explained her reasons: "I am not unacquainted with the word of Paul that women should be silent in Church [1 Tim. 1:2] but, when no man will or can speak, I am driven by the word of the Lord when he said, 'He who confesses me on earth, him will I confess, and he who denies me, him will I deny' [Matt. 10, Luke 9] and I take comfort in the words of the prophet Isaiah [3:12, but not exact], I will send you children to be your princes and women to be your rulers."

She also wrote to the duke of Bavaria, her overlord, about the matter. Neither the university nor the duke bothered to reply but instead ordered her husband or male relatives to control her and deprived her husband of an official position and its income as a show of displeasure. Instead of having the desired effect, these actions led her to write to the city council at Ingolstadt and to both Luther and Frederick the Wise of Saxony to request a hearing at the upcoming imperial diet at Nuremberg. Her letters were published without her knowledge, provoking a student at Ingolstadt to write an anonymous satirical poem telling her to stick to spinning and hinting that she was interested in the young teacher because she was sexually frustrated. She answered with a long poem that was both satirical and serious, calling the student a coward for writing anonymously and giving numerous biblical examples of women called on to give witness. This ended her public career. . . . Though she died in obscurity, her story was widely known and frequently reprinted as part of Lutheran books of witnesses and martyrs.

---

[27] Leader (ca. 1505–1572) of the Protestant Reformation in Scotland.

In the case of Argula von Grumbach, her sex was clearly more important than her noble status. Political authorities would not have ignored a man of similar status who was in contact with major reformers. Grumbach exhibited a strong sense of herself as a woman in her writings, even before her detractors dwelled on that point alone. Despite the extraordinary nature of her actions, she did not see herself as in any way unusual, commenting in her letter to the Ingolstadt city council that "if I die, a hundred women will write to you, for there are many who are more learned and adept than I am." She recognized that her religious training, which began with the German Bible her father gave her when she was ten, was shared by many other literate women and expected them to respond in the same way she did, proclaiming "the word of God as a member of the Christian church."

Like noblewomen, women engaged in various occupations did not receive any special message from the reformers. Even Luther's harsh diatribe against the prostitutes of Wittenberg was addressed to the university students who used their services. This is because in the sixteenth century, women who carried out a certain occupation were rarely thought of as a group. A woman's work identity was generally tied to her family identity.

This can best be explained with an example. For a man to become a baker, he apprenticed himself to a master baker for a certain number of years, then spent several more years as a journeyman, and finally might be allowed to make his masterpiece — a loaf of bread or a fancy cake — open his own shop, marry, and hire his own apprentices and journeymen. He was then a full-fledged member of the bakers' guild, took part in parades, festivals, and celebrations with his guild brothers, lit candles at the guild altar in Catholic cities, and perhaps participated in city government as a guild representative. He was thus a baker his entire life and had a strong sense of work identity.

For a woman to become a baker, she had to marry a baker. She was not allowed to participate in the apprenticeship system, though she could do everything in the shop her husband could. If he died, she might carry on the shop a short time as a widow, but, if she was young enough, she generally married again and took on whatever her new husband's occupation was. She had no voice in guild decisionmaking and took no part in guild festivals, though she may have actually baked more than her husband. Changes in her status were not determined by her own level of training but by changes in her marital or family status. Thus, although in terms of actual work she was as much a baker as her husband, she, and her society, viewed her as a baker's wife. Her status as wife was what was important in the eyes of sixteenth-century society, and, as we have seen, many treatises and laws were directed to wives.

Although female occupations were not directly singled out in religious theory, several were directly affected by changes in religious practices. The demand for votive candles, which were often made and sold by women, dropped dramatically, and these women were forced to find other means of support. The demand for fish declined somewhat, creating difficulties for female fishmongers, although traditional eating habits did not change immediately when fast days were no longer required. Municipal brothels were closed in the sixteenth century, a change often linked with the Protestant Reformation. This occurred in Catholic cities as well, however, and may be more closely linked with general concerns for public order and morality and obsession with women's sexuality than with any specific religion.

Charitable institutions were secularized and centralized, a process which had begun before the Reformation and was speeded up in the sixteenth century in both Protestant and Catholic territories. Many of the smaller charities were houses set up for elderly indigent women who lived off the original endowment and small fees they received for mourning or preparing bodies for burial. They had in many cases elected one of their number as head of the house but were now moved into large hospitals under the direction of a city official. The women who worked in these hospitals as cooks, nurses, maids, and cleaning women now became city, rather than church, employees. Outwardly their conditions of employment changed little, but the Protestant deemphasis on good works may have changed their conception of the value of their work, particularly given their minimal salaries and abysmal working conditions.

Midwives had long performed emergency baptisms if they or the parents believed the child would not live. This created few problems before the Reformation because Catholic doctrine taught that if there was some question about the regularity of this baptism and the child lived, the infant could be rebaptized "on the condition" it had not been baptized properly the first time; conditional baptism was also performed on foundlings. This assured the parents that their child had been baptized correctly while avoiding the snare of rebaptism, which was a crime in the Holy Roman Empire. In 1531, however, Luther rejected all baptisms "on condition" if it was known any baptism had already been carried out and called for a normal baptism in the case of foundlings. By 1540, most Lutheran areas were no longer baptizing "on condition," and those persons who still supported the practice were occasionally branded Anabaptists. This made it extremely important that midwives and other laypeople knew how to conduct correctly an emergency baptism.

Midwives were thus examined, along with pastors, church workers, and teachers, in the visitations conducted by pastors and city leaders in many cities, and "shocking irregularities" in baptismal practice were occasionally discovered. In one story, perhaps apocryphal, a pastor found one midwife confident in her reply that, yes, she certainly baptized infants in the name of the Holy Trinity — Caspar, Melchior, Balthazar! During the course of the sixteenth century, most Protestant cities included a long section on emergency baptisms in their general baptismal ordinance and even gave copies of this special section to the city's midwives. They also began to require midwives to report all illegitimate children and asked them to question any unmarried mother about who the father of the child was. If she refused to reveal his identity, midwives were to question her "when the pains of labor are greatest," for her resistance would probably be lowest at that point.

In areas of Germany where Anabaptism flourished, Anabaptist midwives were charged with claiming they had baptized babies when they really had not, so that a regular church baptism would not be required. In other areas the opposite seems to have been the case. Baptism was an important social occasion and a chance for the flaunting of wealth and social position, and parents paid the midwife to conveniently forget she had baptized a child so that the normal church ceremony could be carried out.

Despite the tremendous diversity of female experience in Germany during the Reformation, two factors are constant. First, a woman's ability to respond to the Reformation and the avenues her responses could take were determined more by her gender than by any other factor. The reformers — Catholic and Protestant, magisterial and radical — all agreed on the proper avenues for female response to their ideas. The responses judged acceptable were domestic, personal, and familial — prayer, meditation, teaching the catechism to children, singing or writing hymns, entering or leaving a convent. Public responses, either those presented publicly or those which concerned dogma or the church as a public institution, shocked and outraged authorities, even if they agreed with the ideas being expressed. A woman who backed the "wrong" religion was never as harshly criticized as a man; this was seen as simply evidence of her irrational and weak nature. One who supported the "right" religion too vigorously and vocally, however, might be censured by her male compatriots for "too much enthusiasm" and overstepping the bounds of proper female decorum. Thus, whatever a woman's status or class, her responses were judged according to both religious and sexual ideology. Since women of all classes heard this message from pamphlet and pulpit and felt its implications in laws and ordinances, it is not at all surprising that most of them accepted it.

Second, most women experienced the Reformation as individuals. Other than nuns in convents women were not a distinct social class, economic category, or occupational group; thus, they had no opportunity for group action. They passed religious ideas along the networks of their family, friends, and neighbors, but these networks had no official voice in a society that was divided according to male groups. A woman who challenged her husband or other male authorities in matters of religion was challenging basic assumptions about gender roles, and doing this alone, with no official group to support her. Even women who reformed territories did so as individual rulers. Men, on the other hand, were preached to as members of groups and responded collectively. They combined with other men in city councils, guilds, consistories, cathedral chapters, university faculties, and many other bodies to effect or halt religious change. Their own individual religious ideas were affirmed by others, whether or not they were ultimately successful in establishing the religious system they desired.

The strongest female protest against the Reformation in Germany came from the convents, where women were used to expressing themselves on religious matters and thinking of themselves as members of a spiritual group. Thus, although the Protestant reformers did champion a woman's role as wife and mother by closing the convents and forbidding female lay confraternities, they cut off women's opportunities for expressing their spirituality in an all-female context. Catholic women could still enter convents, but those convents were increasingly cut off from society. By the mid-seventeenth century, religion for all women in Germany, whether lay or clerical, had become much more closely tied to a household.

MAKING CONNECTIONS:
WOMEN AND THE FAMILY

1. Historians have long debated the relationship of the Renaissance to the Reformation. Some historians see links between the two, in humanism, for example, or in the questioning of authority. Other scholars view the Reformation as a totally different development because of its emphasis on spirituality and its efforts to remake the personalities of individual Christians. Merry Wiesner discusses the impact that the Reformation made on women in various groups. Compare the ways in which the Reformation both affected and was influenced by women with David Herlihy's analysis of women's abilities to shape the culture of Renaissance Italy. To what extent did German women benefit from the Protestant Reformation? How does this compare to the experience of women during the Italian Renaissance? How have women influenced and been affected by recent religious or cultural developments, such as the growth of religious fundamentalism or changes in the family? Do you think women today would perceive their Renaissance and Reformation counterparts with any nostalgia? Why or why not?

2. Do you think Reformation families were stronger as a result of the split in western Christianity? How would you measure a family's strength or happiness? Which family members do you think benefited from the social changes of the Reformation? Explain whether or not family life was more satisfying for husbands, wives, and children during the Reformation than it had been in ancient Mesopotamia, Egypt, and Rome.

3. If you were writing a history of the family based on the articles you have read, what would you say were the most significant differences between the families in the various historical periods? What features of family life have not deviated much throughout the history of Western civilization?

THE BODY, APPEARANCE, AND SEXUALITY
Sara F. Matthews Grieco

One of the most dynamic areas of recent scholarship is the history of the body. Not only have people changed physically over time, but representations of the body have varied in the cultures that make up Western civilization. The body has symbolized different meanings — such as social rebellion or protest (as at Carnival) — and has allowed the individual to present him- or herself to society in many ways. Professor of history at Syracuse University (Florence), Sara F. Matthews Grieco specializes in the ideology of gender, the representation of women, and sexual roles in sixteenth-century Italy and France. Art, diaries, medical and theological writings, and literature lead Grieco to discern two conflicting attitudes toward the body: basic mistrust for its weaknesses and sexuality, and veneration of its physical beauty and opportunity for perfection.

The sixteenth- and seventeenth-century elite were hygienic, but their notion of cleanliness differed from ours today. How did early modern Europeans maintain their waterless cleanliness, and why was a faultless appearance so important?

What constituted a beautiful and feminine body, and how did women attempt to improve their appearances? Beauty was, of course, linked to love and sexuality. What was the "renaissance of prudery," and how did it affect women's status and condition? What types of sexuality did religious and political authorities consider proper and improper?

Grieco sees the eighteenth century as a watershed in the history of the body. What changes occurred in the eighteenth century with respect to marriage, sexuality, and the proper care of one's body?

Two conflicting attitudes toward the body characterize the early modern period. On the one hand, the Renaissance inherited from the Middle Ages a basic mistrust

Sara F. Matthews Grieco, "The Body, Appearance, and Sexuality," in *A History of Women in the West,* ed. Natalie Z. Davis and Arlette Farge, vol. 3 of *Renaissance and Enlightenment Paradoxes* (Cambridge: Belknap Press of Harvard University Press, 1993), 46–73, 76–84.

of the body, its ephemeral nature, its dangerous appetites, and its many weaknesses. This heritage of suspicion and diffidence carried over into the Protestant Reform[1] and the Catholic Counter-Reformation;[2] accordingly, sixteenth- and seventeenth-century Europeans were encouraged in prudery with respect to the body, its appearance, and its sexuality. On the other hand, the Renaissance also brought the rediscovery of the nude and a rehabilitation of physical beauty. The artists and humanists of the Italian peninsula disseminated throughout Europe classical ideals of physical and spiritual perfection as well as Neoplatonic[3] justifications for earthly love and beauty that were to form the basis for the aesthetic canons and elite mores of the early modern period. But it was also from Italy that the dual scourges of plague and syphilis reached the rest of Europe, causing the closure of most public baths and brothels, the rejection of water for bodily hygiene, and the promotion of marital sexuality at the expense of all other sexual practices. Attitudes toward the body and sexuality were thus marked by an unceasing dialectic between the obsession with erotic love and the obligations of social and religious duty. This same paradoxical dialectic was to define women's bodies and their sexuality for almost three hundred years.

Women's social identity has long been conditioned by their culture's perception of their bodies. Whether they be considered "imperfect males" or "walking wombs," earthly reflections of divine beauty or lascivious lures in the service of Satan, their lives are dominated as much by their society's attitudes toward the body in general as by its more specific definitions of gender. In order to understand both the social and imaginary dimensions of women's lives from the sixteenth through the eighteenth centuries, it is therefore essential to understand how the body was perceived and treated. What was considered necessary for its protection, hygiene, and maintenance? Above all, what were the criteria according to which women constructed their appearance, and what purposes did this appearance serve? Canons of feminine beauty and norms of physical hygiene underwent a series of significant changes between the end of the Middle Ages and the end of the early modern period. These evolutions in practice and taste reflected, however, more than just changes in the concept of the body and the appearance of women. In a period of chronic social instability and political and religious conflict, they also expressed a constant and overwhelming concern for order and clearly defined social boundaries in which the concept of gender played a ubiquitous and determining role.

Cleanliness and personal hygiene are relative concepts that underwent a radical transformation from the early Renaissance through the eighteenth century. Formerly dependent on regular baths and the luxury of the steam room, bodily

---

[1] The Protestant Reformation, the sixteenth-century split in western Christianity between the Roman Catholic Church and a variety of Protestant denominations.

[2] The Roman Catholic Church's reform movement and resurgence in reaction to the Protestant Reformation during the late sixteenth century.

[3] Relating to the third-century pagan philosophy that emphasized spiritual purity.

hygiene in the sixteenth and seventeenth centuries became a waterless affair. Clean linen replaced clean skin. A new fear of water gave rise to substitutes such as powder and perfume, which in turn created a new basis for social distinction. More than ever before, cleanliness became the prerogative of the wealthy.

During the sixteenth and seventeenth centuries the custom of bathing, either in public establishments or in the privacy of the home, virtually disappeared. Fear of contagion (plague and syphilis) and more stringent attitudes toward prostitution (a sideline of many baths) accounted for the closure of most public bathing establishments. In private homes, growing distrust of water and the development of new, "dry," and elitist techniques of personal hygiene brought about the disappearance of the bathing tub.

The deliberate elimination of public baths constituted an act of social and moral hygiene. Far from being devoted solely to personal cleanliness, these establishments also offered services that civil authorities regarded as a threat to the moral tenor of the cities. Wine and meals were served to bathers in or out of the water, and beds were available for those who wished to rest after their ablutions, to meet their lovers, or to be entertained by a prostitute. Although many bathing facilities allocated different rooms or separate bathing pools to men and women (some even alternated men's and women's days or served one sex only), most public baths were places of pleasure, associated with brothels and taverns in the minds of contemporaries. Preachers thus inveighed against the evil habits of young men who wasted their time and their patrimony in visiting "brothels, baths and taverns." Similarly, Albrecht Dürer's[4] careful accounts of travel expenses list his baths (often taken with friends) among the costs of other pastimes such as gambling and drinking.

Moral depravity was not, however, the only ill associated with those naked or scantily clad bodies that mingled in the intimacy of the steam room, partaking of the often boisterous pleasures of the collective tub. Like taverns and brothels, baths were among the first establishments to be closed in times of plague, in accordance with the prevailing belief that any gathering of people would facilitate the spread of the dread disease. Doctors and public health officials also discouraged bathing of any sort during epidemics for fear that the naked skin, its pores dilated by hot vapors, would become more vulnerable to the pestiferous "miasmas"[5] that were credited with carrying sickness. Throughout the sixteenth and seventeenth centuries, belief in the permeability of the skin and the threat that bathing presented for health in general continued to furnish medical texts with a variety of arguments against the evils of public baths and the dangers of water. In the sixteenth century, fear of syphilis joined that of other contagious diseases in the stock arguments against promiscuous baths, along with other, more fanciful but equally important fears such as that of "bath pregnancies," whereby women

---

[4] German painter and engraver (1471–1528).

[5] Bad-smelling vapors.

were supposedly inseminated by adventurous sperm wandering about in warm waters. . . .

Slowly baths became a medical rather than a pleasurable or hygienic practice, accompanied by the use of cupping-glasses[6] to draw off harmful humors and inevitably surrounded by a series of precautionary measures. The body was considered "open" and vulnerable when wet, "closed" and protected when dry; whence the development of new, waterless techniques to ensure the niceties of personal hygiene and presentability.

Scholars long believed that the disappearance of water from daily ablutions in the early modern period constituted a lapse into a universal state of grease and grime. This was not entirely true. Although the filth of the lower social orders remained, in this period, as much a characteristic of their inferior status as the dingy homespun garments on their back, those who could afford to do so tended to pay increasing attention to the care and appearance of their person, or at least to those parts visible to the public eye.

Where water disappeared, wiping and rubbing, powdering and perfuming took over. Courtesy books[7] such as Erasmus'[8] influential *De civilitate morum puerilium*[9] (1530) not only described the proper way to blow one's nose or to sit at table but also mandated the cleansing of the body and its orifices, thus emphasizing new social imperatives that distinguished the elite from the "vulgar." . . .

In accordance with the new norms of civility, more attention was paid to the parts of the body that were not covered: the face and the hands. But whereas in the sixteenth century water was still used for morning ablutions on these two parts of the body, by the seventeenth it was considered fit only for rinsing the mouth and the hands — and only on condition that its potentially harmful effects be tempered by the addition of vinegar or wine. Courtesy books especially discouraged the use of water on the face because it was believed to harm eyesight, cause toothache and catarrh,[10] and make the skin overly pale in winter or excessively brown in summer. The head was to be vigorously rubbed with a scented towel or sponge, the hair combed, the ears wiped out, and the mouth rinsed. Powder made its initial appearance as a kind of dry shampoo. Left on the head overnight, it was combed out in the morning along with grease and other impurities. By the end of the sixteenth century, however, perfumed and tinted powders had become an integral part of the daily toilet of the well-to-do, men and women alike. This visible and olfactory accessory not only proclaimed the privilege of cleanliness enjoyed by its wearer but also his or her social standing, for fashion was also a privilege of the wealthy. By the seventeenth century, powder had so conquered the

---

[6] Small glasses used to draw blood from the body.

[7] Works explaining proper manners and behavior.

[8] Desiderius Erasmus (ca. 1466–1536), Dutch humanist.

[9] *On Civility in Children.*

[10] Inflammation of the nose or throat.

upper classes of Europe that no self-respecting aristocrat would be seen in public without it, and by the eighteenth century young and old sported white heads of hair, either wigs or their own silvered locks. An absence of powder came to signal not only a dual impropriety (hygienic and social) but also social inferiority: it was the bourgeois[11] and their inferiors who had "black and greasy hair."

Perfume was likewise credited with a number of virtues, the most important of which were the aesthetic elimination or concealment of unpleasant odors and the hygienic functions of disinfection or purification. Scented towels were used for rubbing the face and the torso, especially the armpits. Long used by the rich to disinfect houses, furniture, and textiles in times of plague, incense and exotic scents were also used in clothing chests to "cleanse" their contents. . . . Like powder, perfumes became a sign of social standing, and the distance between "good" and "bad" odors increased to the extent that in 1709 the French chemist Nicolas Lémery[12] proposed three categories of scent: *parfum royal, parfum pour les bourgeois,* and a *parfum des pauvres*[13] made of oil and soot, whose sole purpose was to disinfect the air. Whence another class privilege, for perfume not only protected the body but also ensured good health. . . .

The new rules of propriety, which dictated that the visible parts of the body be inoffensive to the eye and pleasing to the nose, were more concerned with appearance than with hygiene. A clean appearance was a guarantee of moral probity and social standing; whence the importance of white linen, whose candid surface was identified with the purity of the skin below. Body linen, this "outer envelope" or second skin, also served as a protection for the "inner envelope" or epidermis, and in this respect it progressively came to act as a substitute for all other cleansing functions. White cloth was especially valued, not only because it absorbed perspiration but also because it was supposed to attract impurities and thus preserve the health of the wearer. As of the early seventeenth century a change of shirt or chemise[14] was an essential element of daily hygiene for both the bourgeoisie and the aristocracy — so much so that Savot,[15] in his 1626 treatise on the construction of châteaus and townhouses, pointed out that bathing facilities were no longer necessary "because we now use linen, which helps us keep our bodies clean better than the tubs and steam baths of the ancients, who were deprived of the use and convenience of undergarments."

In the late fifteenth century, shirts and chemises began to peek more and more boldly out from under the garments of men and women. By the end of the sixteenth century, touches of lace or a ruffle at neck and wrist had expanded into fanciful collars and ruffs, spreading into elegantly embroidered expanses that flowed

---

[11] Middle class.

[12] French physician and chemist (1645–1715).

[13] Literally, royal perfume, perfume for the middle class, and perfume of the poor.

[14] A woman's shirt-like, loose-fitting undergarment.

[15] Louis Savot (1579–1640), French physician and author of *French Architecture.*

over shoulder, breast, and forearm in the seventeenth, and turning into cascades of lace and transparent finery in the eighteenth. Throughout the Renaissance, the use of body linen thus increased significantly, in inverse proportion to the use of water and baths. . . .

Body linen and undergarments did not become widely used until the eighteenth century, when the standards set by the ruling classes not only filtered down to servants, salaried workers, and artisans but also inspired a proliferation and diversification of undergarments in which feminine fashion played a decisive role. . . .

Drawers[16] are reputed to have been an Italian invention, introduced to France by Catherine de Médicis[17] in order to ride a horse *à l'amazone* (sidesaddle) without transgressing the rules of decorum. Many contemporaries approved of this feminine adaptation of a male garment insofar as it both preserved "those parts that are not for male eyes" in case of a fall from a horse and protected women from "dissolute young men, who put their hands under women's skirts." The preservation of feminine modesty was not, however, the only function of this unusual garment. Noblewomen had their *caleçons* or *calzoni*[18] made from rich materials, thus adding yet another weapon to their intimate arsenal of suggestion and seduction. That drawers were considered a rather daring addition to the panoply of feminine lingerie is further attested by the fact that courtesans[19] were repeatedly condemned for wearing similar "masculine" articles of dress. Though popular with these ladies' admirers, pantalettes[20] not only transgressed ecclesiastical rulings against cross-dressing but also were suspected of constituting a concession to male homosexuality in that they made their wearers look like boys. Even in the eighteenth century only actresses, window-washers, prostitutes, and aristocrats wore drawers, whose primary functions remained, paradoxically, the protection of modesty and stimulation of the erotic imagination. It would take the hygienic revolution of the nineteenth century to impose underpants as a basic element of the feminine wardrobe.

Although water continued to be credited with many harmful powers and regarded with much suspicion throughout the early modern period, the bath made a comeback in the eighteenth century, both as a luxurious pastime and as a means of a therapeutic exercise. In the 1740s aristocrats began to construct luxurious bathrooms in their palaces and townhouses; some were embellished with fountains and exotic plants. Although most immersions were still surrounded by precautionary measures (a purge beforehand, bedrest and a meal afterward), the practice began to catch on. . . .

---

[16] Underpants.

[17] (1519–1589), queen of France and regent.

[18] Women's underpants.

[19] Prostitutes who have wealthy clients.

[20] Long underpants with a frill at the bottom of each leg.

It was the location and the temperature of the water, however, that deter-mined both the purpose of a bath and its impact on the body. Hot baths in pri-vate homes were voluptuous events practiced by indolent women (and men), often in preparation for an amorous encounter. Elsewhere, hot baths could serve a curative function. In 1761 a bathing establishment was built on the banks of the Seine where the wealthy (a bath there cost the equivalent of a week's salary for an artisan) could be "cured" close to home by the virtues of river water. Cold baths became increasingly popular after 1750, following a rash of monographs and medical studies on the value of bathing in maintaining health: a properly taken bath was believed to help the humors circulate, tone up the muscles, and stimu-late the functioning of the organs. A new generation of physicians waxed enthu-siastic about the tonic qualities of cold water, which contracted the body and in-creased its vigor. Cold baths were therefore considered useful, not because they cleansed the body, but because they strengthened it. On the whole, those who took cold baths did so as much out of a kind of ascetic morality as for health rea-sons. Favored by a rising bourgeoisie whose energy disdained aristocratic languor, the cold bath became the symbol of a new, "virile" class in opposition to an old, "effeminate" aristocracy whose delicacy was the proof of its decadance.

Beauty has always been just as relative a concept as personal cleanliness. From the end of the Middle Ages to the end of the early modern period the canons of feminine beauty and the ideal womanly form underwent a series of rad-ical transformations. From svelte to plump and from fresh to painted, the female silhouette and complexion responded to changing conditions of diet, status, and fortune, creating new standards of appearance and taste, new ideals of the beau-tiful and the erotic.

The medieval ideal of the graceful, narrow-hipped, and small-breasted aris-tocratic lady gave way in the sixteenth century to a plumper, wide-hipped, and full-breasted model of feminine beauty that was to remain valid until the late eighteenth century. This change in body aesthetics corresponded with a signifi-cant evolution in the alimentary habits of the elite. Cookbooks of the fourteenth and fifteenth centuries show a marked preference for sour and acid sauces, con-taining neither sugar nor fats, whereas those of the sixteenth and seventeenth cen-turies abound in butter, cream, and sweets. Were women of the ruling classes fat-ter than their medieval forebears, and did fashion thus adapt itself to a changing physical reality? Or did Renaissance women deliberately develop a rounded sil-houette to emulate the current ideal of beauty? In any case a "healthy" plumpness, like cleanliness, was generally reserved for the wealthy; thinness was considered ugly, unhealthy, and a sign of poverty. After all, the majority of women — peas-ants, servants, and artisans — ate less well than their menfolk, the best and the most food being reserved for the male members of the family, the children, and the women, in that order. European women also grew smaller as a result of an eco-nomic and agricultural crisis that persisted from the fourteenth through the eigh-teenth centuries. Another consequence of female undernourishment was a sig-nificant change in the age of puberty, which fluctuates as a function of the ratio between age and body weight. In the Middle Ages girls matured between twelve and fifteen. In the seventeenth and eighteenth centuries, however, the average age at puberty moved up to sixteen, being slightly lower for city dwellers and slightly higher for the peasantry.

Rickets, scurvy, and a variety of unsightly ills followed in the path of chronic undernourishment. No wonder that women of the upper classes took care to distinguish themselves from their less fortunate sisters, cultivating vast expanses of milky flesh in contrast to the haggard, brown, and emaciated physiques of those whose hard lives made them not only ugly in the eyes of contemporaries, but also prematurely old. . . .

The Renaissance was not only a period in which women of the ruling classes distinguished themselves from their social inferiors by means of their well-fed physique and the pristine whiteness of their body linen; it was also a period in which it became more important that women be "different" from men in all aspects of dress, appearance, and behavior. The vestiary[21] revolution of the late Middle Ages consisted in the differentiation of male and female clothing. Men's robes were shortened to reveal their legs, and the codpiece[22] was invented, destined to become increasingly prominent and beribboned in the sixteenth and seventeenth centuries. Women, on the other hand, tended to remain more chastely dressed. Their long and voluminous robes revealed a waist made even more slender by the use of a busk[23] and, more liberal mores permitting, might even disclose a pair of milky breasts, suitably powdered and rouged. Every movement, every gesture had to reflect the delicacy and tenderness now expected of women as opposed to the energetic virility of men. . . .

From the fifteenth century on, treatises on the family, courtesy books, and even medical literature all insisted upon the fragility of the female sex and the duty of men to protect women from their own innate weaknesses by ruling them with a gentle, if firm, hand. Gone were the courtly models of gender relations according to which the knight obeyed his mistress and served her as his sovereign. The Renaissance brought with it a desire for clearly defined social boundaries and immutable hierarchies (including gender hierarchies), a desire that became all the more important as the reality of economic and political life confused class distinctions and created new elites to challenge the old. Sumptuary laws[24] also reflected a chronic concern for issues of social status, sexual identity, and dress. Cross-dressing, for example, was universally condemned — a fact that did not prevent women from repeatedly affecting articles of male costume, much to the horror of their contemporaries. Vestiary legislation also denounced the "mad expenditure" of vain women and accused them of being the cause of a spectrum of

---

[21] Relating to clothing.

[22] A stuffed, penis-shaped bag attached to the front of men's tight-fitting breeches.

[23] Stiffening for corsets.

[24] Laws regulating the style and quality of clothing.

ills, from the ruin of the national economy to demographic crisis and their husbands' homosexuality. . . .

Although clerical culture throughout the early modern period tended to fear
feminine charms and the power they gave women over men, Renaissance Neo-
platonism specifically rehabilitated beauty by declaring it to be the outward and
visible sign of an inward and invisible goodness. Beauty was no longer considered
a dangerous asset, but rather a necessary attribute of moral character and social
position. It became an obligation to be beautiful, for ugliness was associated not
only with social inferiority but also with vice. Were not prostitutes rendered unsightly by syphilitic sores, and the degenerate poor monstrous by skin afflictions
and mange? The body's outer envelope became a window through which the
inner self was visible to all.

Feminine beauty was not only extolled as being a guarantee of moral probity
and an inspiration for those who had the privilege of gazing upon a pretty coun-
tenance; it was also codified by a massive production of love poems, courtesy
books, and collections of recipes for cosmetics. Beauty followed a formula, and
women went to a great deal of trouble and expense to make their appearance conform to standards that remained virtually unaltered throughout the early modern
period. In Italy, France, Spain, Germany, and England the basic aesthetic was the
same: white skin, blond hair, red lips and cheeks, black eyebrows. The neck and
hands had to be long and slender, the feet small, the waist supple. Breasts were
to be firm, round, and white, with rosy nipples. The color of the eyes might vary
(the French were fond of green; the Italians preferred black or brown), and occasional concessions might be made to dark hair; but the canon of feminine appearance remained essentially the same for some three hundred years. . . .

How did women achieve the perfection required of them? With the invention
of printing in the mid-fifteenth century, books of "secrets" and recipes for perfumes and cosmetics (some of which had already circulated in manuscripts in the
Middle Ages) began to appear throughout Europe, reinforcing and enriching an
oral tradition handed down from mother to daughter, from apothecary to son.
Written mostly by men, whose criteria of beauty were thus implicitly imposed on
their feminine readers, these collections were rarely restricted to beauty secrets.
Their contents were eclectic, often gathering medical information, kitchen recipes,
natural magic, astrological tables, and various other arts (such as physiognomy)
all between the covers of one book. Who read these books? Women (and men)
of a certain social standing, of course, who were educated enough to know how
to read. Not all, however, were necessarily members of the ruling classes. . . . Outside certain elite circles, where cosmetics were as essential an accessory as powder, perfume, and body linen, paints and creams were considered to be a sign of
vanity and an incitation to lust. Yet women of all social classes persevered in "improving" their appearance by means of cosmetic concoctions, some of which
ended up doing more harm than good. . . . A sixteenth-century *Tracte Containing
the Artes of Curious Paintinge, Carvinge & Buildinge* dedicates an entire section to
the nature of certain cosmetics then in daily use, since women were supposedly
unaware of their ingredients and the ill effects they had on their users. The sec-

tion begins with a gruesome description of the harmful effects of sublimate of mercury, which may have been partially responsible for the fast fading of youth and beauty bewailed by the ladies of Queen Elizabeth's[25] court. . . .

Warnings about the long-term effects of cosmetics were not the only argument used against makeup. Women who painted themselves were also accused of "altering the face of God" (was not humanity made in the image of the Lord?). In *A Treatise against Painting and Tincturing of Men and Women* (1616), Thomas Tuke[26] wondered how ladies were able to pray to God "with a face, which he doth not owne? How can they begge pardon, when their sinne cleaves onto their faces?" Beneath many criticisms of paint also lay a masculine fear of deception. Was the youthful beauty they desired not perhaps an old hag or a disease-ridden body, artfully camouflaged? Besides which, those who made cosmetics were often suspected of dabbling in the magic arts, for many recipes contained incantations to be recited during preparation and ingredients such as earthworms, nettles, and blood.

Despite repeated cautions, masculine accusations of adultery and deception, and daily examples of the untoward effects of cosmetics, women persevered in "improving" their appearance with the help of powders, creams, and paints. In sixteenth-century Italy it was said that all women in cities used makeup, "even the dish-washers." . . .

Most books on cosmetics and feminine beauty focused on the hair, the face, the neck, the breasts, and the hands — all parts of the body visible to the public eye. The recipes that filled these books generally fulfilled one of two functions: to correct existing faults or to improve upon nature. Hair, for example, was better if blond, thick, wavy, and long, whence the long hours Italian women spent bleaching their hair in the sun (their snowy complexions protected by the *solana,* a wide-brimmed sunhat without a crown), washing it in the juice of lemon or rhubarb, or applying other, more elaborate concoctions made with sulfur or saffron. . . . After the hair was bleached, the hairline was carefully plucked or treated with a depilatory cream in order to create the high, domed foreheads that were still fashionable in the sixteenth century. The eyebrows were also plucked, sometimes entirely, and sometimes just enough to make two thin, wide-spaced arcs that were then blackened to contrast with the hair and make a frame for the eyes. Eyelashes, on the other hand, were considered unaesthetic and were either left unadorned or entirely pulled out. . . .

The face, neck, breasts, and hands were supposed to be creamy white, enlivened by rosy hues in strategic places. White was the color associated with purity, chastity, and femininity. It was the color of the "female" heavenly body, the moon, as distinct from the more vibrant hues of the "masculine" sun. A white complexion was also the privilege of the leisured city dweller as distinct from the

---

[25] Queen of England from 1558 to 1603.

[26] Royalist theologian (d. 1657).

sunburnt skin of the peasant. . . . The ivory complexion so prized by women was not, however, a uniform white. The cheeks, ears, chin, nipples (when displayed), and fingertips were touched with rouge to give an impression of health and attract the eye. . . .

Over and above the role played by cosmetics in the social and moral obligation women felt to look beautiful, makeup was a necessary signifier of social rank. Paint was the "clothing" of the visible parts of the body, distinguishing its wearer as much as rich materials, fine linens, and expensive ornaments revealed the wealth and status of their owner. Cosmetics were the ultimate accessory, without which an elegant woman did not feel herself dressed. . . .

If early modern hygienic and cosmetic practices were motivated by a variety of beliefs and concerns, ranging from an acute interest in health to the social imperatives of physical appearance, perhaps the most universal purpose to which these practices were applied was the service of Eros. In seventeenth-century Europe, the few remaining public baths still served two main purposes, and he who did not bathe for reasons of health was most probably preparing for an amorous encounter. Similarly, feminine cosmetics were universally decried for their uncanny powers of seduction, which, according to moralists and theologians alike, lured men to their perdition in the sweet throes of lust. Ever present, and increasingly policed, sexuality became one of the bugbears of both secular and religious authorities. Authorized only in the context of marriage, and then solely in the function of procreation, sex was subject to a wave of control and repression that strove to mold the mores of urban and rural populations along lines strictly defined by both church and state.

Whereas the Middle Ages had witnessed the formulation of a sexual ethic based on the refusal of pleasure and the obligation of procreation, it was not until the sixteenth century that a coherent campaign was launched against all forms of nudity and extraconjugal sexuality. Between 1500 and 1700, new attitudes toward the body and new rules of behavior gave rise to a radical promotion of chastity and modesty in all areas of daily life. Brothels were closed, bathers were obliged to retain their shirts, and the nightgown replaced the birthday suit as approved sleeping apparel. The lower half of the body became a world apart, a forbidden territory that the seventeenth-century Précieuses[27] refused to name. Under the dual influence of the Protestant Reformation and the Catholic Counter-Reformation, artists relinquished their hard-won battle to display the human form, and a multitude of accidental draperies, leaves, and fortuitous shrubs once again veiled the nude. Nudity became vulgar, something only apprentices inflicted upon the public eye as they sported in the river on a hot summer's day; and even then they might find themselves in trouble, as did eight young men in Frankfurt in 1541, who ended up being condemned to a month in prison on

---

[27] "Precious Women," women who led a literary and linguistic movement to purify the French language in the mid-seventeenth century.

bread and water. In the seventeenth and eighteenth centuries refined Parisian ladies fainted at the sight of naked male bodies on the banks of the Seine, while even their occasional private bath was clouded with milk or a handful of bran in order to preserve their nudity from their servants' eyes. Modesty became a sign of social and moral distinction, especially dear to the middle ranks of society, who condemned both the uncouth physicality of the lower orders and the libertine nonchalance of the aristocracy.

The first victims of the new wave in social morality were women. Long decried by misogynist theologians and sexually frustrated clergy as the daughters of Eve, women were represented as insidious temptresses whose primary object in life was to seduce unsuspecting men and deliver them to Satan. Medical science reinforced this voracious vision of female sexuality by declaring erotic fulfillment to be a biological necessity for women. Not only did their "hungry" wombs ever clamor to be filled, but dire disorders would attend upon those who ignored the "natural" imperative of reproduction. Hysteria, a malady whose origin lay in the uterus, was accounted responsible for delusions of diabolic possession and other forms of mental illness. Another factor that strengthened the equation between women, sex, and sin was the appearance and rapid spread of syphilis in the late fifteenth century. Although the most virulent epidemics had abated by the 1550s, the disease had come to stay, indelibly imprinted on the contemporary imagination as a terrestrial punishment for the sin of lust and, above all, as a consequence of frequenting houses of ill repute.

Municipally owned or authorized brothels were a common feature of late medieval European towns and cities. Prostitution was encouraged and protected not only in order to meet the needs of growing numbers of sexually mature adolescents, unattached apprentices, and men who were marrying at a later and later age, but also to combat male homosexuality, considered to be one of the greater social ills of the time and responsible for various manifestations of divine wrath such as plague, famine, and war. In the sixteenth century, however, the same municipalities that had encouraged prostitution closed their official brothels. Accused of spreading lechery and disease, fomenting brawls and other forms of civil disturbance, leading young men astray, facilitating adultery, and ruining family fortunes, prostitutes became one of the "criminal" populations (along with vagabonds and witches) destined for elimination by both secular and religious authorities. . . .

In the eyes of both religious and secular authorities, there existed two basic types of sexual behavior, one acceptable and the other reprehensible. The first was marital and was practiced in the service of procreation. The second was governed by amorous passion and sensual pleasure, its outcome malformed or illegitimate, its logic that of sterility. Guilty outside of wedlock, sensual passion became all the more blamable within the bounds of matrimony, where it threatened not only the controlled, contractual concept of conjugal affections and the health of offspring conceived in the heat of amorous excess, but also the couple's ability to love God, contaminated as they were by terrestrial rather than spiritual love.

Despite the normative prescriptions of theologians, physicians, and civil officials, young people did not always wait for marriage to experiment with erotic pleasures. Since men and women married at an increasingly late age throughout the early modern period (an average of twenty-five to twenty-eight years), they were sexually mature for a good decade before being able to experience sex legitimately. Historians differ as to the extent of sexual activity in these years: was Europe swept by a wave of chastity, or did erotic needs find alternative outlets? The closure of the vast majority of brothels and a record low birthrate of illegitimate children from the sixteenth to the mid-eighteenth centuries have led some historians to postulate a mass internalization resulting in widespread sexual continence. Other scholars have asserted important changes in sexual behavior, ranging from an increase in masturbation to the spread of rudimentary contraception. Scholars do agree, however, on the existence of one well-documented sexual practice. Under circumstances subject to various controls, young men and women of the lower social orders could indulge in a certain amount of sexual experimentation as well as "try out" potential marriage partners without suffering moral censure.

Known as "bundling" in England, . . . various forms of parentally authorized premarital flirtation, sexual experimentation, and even cohabitation were practiced throughout Europe. Bundling generally involved paying court to a girl at night, in a room apart from the rest of the family, in bed, in the dark, and half-naked. However, although it involved two young people spending the night together, talking and petting, bundling did not lead to much pregnancy. In the Vendée in France, . . . couples of lovers [stayed] in the same room or even in the same bed, where they could control any one of their number who threatened to get carried away. In Savoy, the boy had to swear to respect the girl's virginity before bedding with her. In Scotland, the girl's thighs were symbolically tied together. What bundling did lead to were marriages based on affection and sexual attraction. It provided an opportunity for the two parties to explore each other's minds and characters in some depth as well as to obtain sexual satisfaction in the decade between maturity and matrimony without running the risk of an unwanted pregnancy or an ill-fated marriage. . . .

Neither Protestant nor Catholic authorities regarded such carryings-on with an indulgent eye. In the sixteenth century, and especially after the Council of Trent[28] (1563), the Roman church began to wage a systematic struggle against all forms of prenuptial sexual relations. Episcopal ordinances mark the progress of this battle in France. Young people in Savoy lost their right to albergement[29] in 1609. In the Pyrenean dioceses of Bayonne and Alet, intercourse during the period of *fiançailles*[30] remained customary until 1640, when it suddenly became grounds for excommunication. In Champagne boy-girl encounters in the *es-*

---

[28] Council (1545–1563) that clarified doctrines and reformed the Roman Catholic Church.

[29] Bundling.

[30] Betrothal, engagement.

craignes[31] became liable to the same penalty in 1680. Similarly, nocturnal visits were still being attacked in the Protestant county of Montbéliard by the civil magistrate, the Duke of Württemberg, in 1772.

Despite numerous and repeated attempts to suppress premarital sex and cohabitation, rural areas long resisted the "approved" model of marriage, according to which all matches were to be arranged by parents. . . . In the cities, however, where wealth weighed more heavily in the balance, parental influence in the choice of marriage partner became absolute. Sixteenth- and seventeenth-century Europe saw a rash of rulings against marriage without parental consent progressively deprive young people of the right to choose their helpmate, even if they had previously exchanged vows, given each other rings, or had sexual relations. Particularly efficient in urban areas, where marriage strategies played a key role in the social, economic, and political ambitions of the middle and upper ranks of society, the paternalist model of marriage remained unchallenged until the eighteenth century. . . .

There are several features of sexual behavior peculiar to early modern Europe. The first is the average interval of ten or more years between puberty and marriage. This gap, which tended to be larger among the lower social orders than among their betters, continued to widen throughout the seventeenth and eighteenth centuries. Moreover, a significant number of people never married at all, ranging from about 10 percent among the peasantry and urban poor to as much as 25 percent among the elites. A second unique feature is the superimposition of the notion of romantic love on the biological constant of sexual drive. Beginning as a purely extramarital ideology in troubadour literature[32] of the twelfth century, the concept of romantic love spread via the printing press and the increase in literacy in the sixteenth and seventeenth centuries, inspiring poetry, plays, and novels until it finally found its way into real life in the mid-eighteenth century. The third and last feature is the predominance of Christian ideology in the legitimation and practice of sexuality. Though somewhat mitigated by humanist and Protestant efforts to replace the medieval ideal of virginity by that of holy matrimony, the dominant attitude toward sexuality remained one of suspicion and hostility. . . .

Religious authorities considered any sexual act committed outside marriage to be a mortal sin, as well as any conjugal act not performed in the interest of reproduction. Saint Jerome[33] had declared the husband who embraced his wife overly passionately to be an "adulterer" because he loved her for his pleasure only, as he would a mistress. Restated by Saint Thomas Aquinas[34] and echoed end-

---

[31] Cottages.

[32] Lyric poetry written in the vernacular of southern France.

[33] Scholar and Bible translator (ca. 340–420).

[34] Saint and theologian (ca. 1225–1274).

lessly by authors of confession manuals throughout the sixteenth and seventeenth centuries, the denunciation of passion in marriage condemned the amorous wife as much as the libidinous husband. Even the positions adopted by the couple were subject to strict controls. The *retro* or *more canino*[35] position (not to be confused with sodomy) was declared to be contrary to human nature because it imitated the coupling of animals. *Mulier super virum*[36] was equally "unnatural" insofar as it placed the woman in an active and superior position, contrary to her passive and subordinate social role. All erotic acrobatics other than the approved formula — the woman supine and the man above her — were considered suspect in that they privileged pleasure at the expense of procreation. The only position that favored the planting of the male seed was the one metaphorically associated with the plowing of the earth by the laborer.

Medical texts supported theological rulings with respect to the optimum conditions for creating offspring in terms of both the moderation of passion and the most favorable position, threatening that any deviation from the norm might well result in deformed or deficient progeny. Both groups of authorities also stipulated a variety of days on which sexual intercourse was to be avoided. For the pious, fast days were also chaste days, as well as all religious holidays such as Sundays, Christmas, Good Friday, and Easter. Continence was also recommended throughout Lent, although early modern theologians no longer expected the faithful to be capable of total abstinence. Over and above the 120 to 140 days of religious observance during which sex was discouraged if not expressly forbidden, couples were urged to avoid intercourse during the hot summer months and during the wife's various periods of indisposition. Not only was intimacy during the monthly cycle or during the 40 days of "impurity" after childbirth considered potentially hazardous to the husband's health, but sexual relations during pregnancy and nursing were believed to threaten the child's chances for survival. A growing concern for the well-being of infants, whose mortality rate was extremely high in the first two years of life, led a number of physicians and religious authorities to forbid intercourse throughout the breast-feeding period. . . .

No doubt many women, worn out by numerous pregnancies and the care of many children, would willingly have availed themselves of the medieval right to refusal of the *debitum conjugale*,[37] especially as marital chastity was considered desirable once a good-sized family had been created. Theologians in the sixteenth, seventeenth, and eighteenth centuries, however, were not so quick to permit either partner to neglect the other's sexual needs. No longer seen solely in the light of reproduction or as a second-rate solution for concupiscence, conjugal sexuality was increasingly considered to be a legitimate remedy for a natural physical

---

[35] Having sex dog-style.

[36] Having sex with the woman on top.

[37] The marital obligation to have sex.

drive, the refusal of which might drive the frustrated partner into the greater sins of adultery or "pollution" (masturbation).

The crime of Onan (who was struck down by God for having spilled his seed upon the ground) became one of the major obsessions of early modern religious and medical authorities. . . . Along with *coitus interruptus*,[38] homosexuality, and bestiality, masturbation was one of the four sexual sins that defied nature's reproductive imperative in the name of "perverse" pleasures. Although this solitary practice was too widespread to merit the exemplary punishments reserved for sodomy and bestiality, it caused a great deal of anxiety on the grounds that bad habits acquired in youth might continue into adulthood, either polluting the marriage bed or even replacing marriage altogether. . . .

. . . Whatever pre- or extramarital behavior patterns may have been, it is likely that fear of the dangers of childbirth and the economic burdens of a growing brood of children also motivated many married couples to limit the size of their families through these prohibited practices. Of course the practice of *coitus interruptus* requires a considerable amount of control on the part of the man and affords little pleasure to the woman, who is often left sexually aroused but frustrated. But even within the context of procreational sex, the male tendency to hasty ejaculation would also have left many female partners unsatisfied. If one adds to this tendency the experience of some ten years' self-manipulation and the loveless matches that characterized both the aristocracy and the bourgeoisie, the chances for mutually satisfying sexual relations within the framework of marriage must have been very low indeed.

The only form of masturbation authorized by both physicians and Catholic confessors was feminine self-manipulation, either in preparation for intercourse (to facilitate penetration) or, after the husband had prematurely ejaculated and withdrawn, in order to reach orgasm, "open" the mouth of the womb, and release the female "seed," which, according to seventeenth-century medical authorities, was as useful to the act of procreation as that released by the male. Although the feminine "right to orgasm" continued to be debated in confession manuals well into the eighteenth century, the majority of theologians accepted Galenist medical theory[39] with respect to the desirability of female satisfaction: would God have given women this source of pleasure without a purpose? A snag in this logic was the fact that women could conceive passively and without pleasure, in which case their "semen" would be wanting. Never at a loss, medical science came to the aid of doctrine and declared the function of feminine seed to be auxiliary to that of its masculine counterpart. If emitted at the same moment as the man's, it would create more beautiful offspring. . . .

Outside marriage, there was no licit sexuality. The ascending scale of sexual crimes was defined in terms of the number of infractions committed against the

---

[38] In sexual intercourse, withdrawal before ejaculation.

[39] Medical theory based on the writings of the Greek physician Galen (ca. 130–ca. 201).

three basic justifications for authorized physical relations, namely, the obligation to procreate, conformity to "natural" laws, and a sacramental concept of marriage. A "first-degree" infraction would be simple fornication between unmarried individuals who had not taken vows of chastity. The crime could be judged more or less severe according to the age and social station of the two parties. The rape of a virgin, for example, was generally considered worse than that of a widow. Similarly, the threat of violence or a promise of marriage by the man would constitute a mitigating circumstance in the woman's favor. The "second degree" of sexual sin was adultery. Simple adultery implied only one married person; double adultery involved two. Incest was also considered a form of adultery, as was the seduction of a nun, "bride" of Christ.

The third and worst type of sexual infraction involved crimes "against nature," which surpassed the former two insofar as they precluded reproduction. Masturbation, homosexuality, and bestiality haunted churchmen, civil magistrates, and medical doctors throughout the early modern period. . . . Sodomy was "complete" if it entailed homoerotic relations, and "incomplete" if it described extravaginal heterosexual relations. Bestiality, on the other hand, was the sin "without a name." Always mentioned in Latin, even in the least prudish texts or manuals of confession, it not only reduced men to the level of animals but also was suspected of resulting in hybrid monsters.

Our knowledge of extraconjugal relations is based largely on historical records related to their fruit, although the actual birthrate of illegitimate children is hardly an indicator of the frequency or the quality of unauthorized sexuality. Extramarital pregnancy was, more often than not, an undesired complication, and studies of illicit relations in an age that knew neither effective contraception nor antibiotics have shown that various forms of sexual play could be preferred to coitus. Fear of venereal disease, pregnancy, and even emotional or legal entanglement was the cause of a great deal of fondling, groping, and mutual masturbation. And because a single act of intercourse had little chance of resulting in pregnancy, even relationships that did not rely upon some form of birth control (generally withdrawal; the prophylactic sheath was a rarity until the eighteenth century) stood an equally good chance of remaining undetected. The major source of information on illicit fornication during the ancien régime[40] is formal complaints, to civil or religious authorities, made by women who had been impregnated by men who would not or could not marry them. Known in France as the *déclaration de grossesse,*[41] these documents contain precious information on the mother and purported father of the child as well as on the circumstances of their relationship.

Three distinct patterns of illicit relationships can be discerned in the déclarations de grossesse. The first is the relationship between unequals, in which the man was generally the social and economic superior of the woman. Sometimes the

---

[40] Old Régime, the centuries before the French Revolution of 1789.

[41] Statement about the circumstances of pregnancy.

seducer was the employer of his sexual partner, and in some cases he offered her a job, money, or food in exchange for her favors. Lower-class women were especially vulnerable to this sort of exploitation, not only because they earned less than men in whatever calling they practiced, but also because masters had a lingering traditional right to the bodies of the women they employed. Servants were doubly vulnerable in this respect insofar as they not only depended upon the head of the household for their livelihood but also lived in daily proximity with a number of men: masters, sons, and other male servants. Women who took part in relations of inequality tended to be under twenty-five years of age, and ten to thirty years younger than the men they accused. This fact may indicate that women in their late teens or early twenties were more naive, and therefore more easily seduced. It may also indicate a preference among older men for girls. Not all of these women were innocent victims, however; calculating gold-diggers appear in all places at all times. Nor were all of the seducers heartless satyrs, but sometimes lovers or common-law husbands of long standing who promised to "take care" of their child. The keynote in relations of inequality, however, is the very different consequences they had for men and women. For men, there seems to have been little social opprobrium associated with paternity suits. For women, the consequences of an illicit affair were usually disastrous. Publicly disgraced, discharged from their job, and in some cases even sent to a house of correction, they would often be forced to choose between abandoning their child or turning to prostitution to support the two of them.

The second type of relationship that appears in official declarations of pregnancy is one of equality. Most women who appeared before the courts had had relationships with men of equal social standing whom they accused of having promised them marriage. Whereas women who were involved in relationships of inequality could hardly have hoped for legitimation of them, those who had relationships with their social equals generally believed (or pretended to believe) that theirs was a prebridal pregnancy gone wrong. The pattern seems to have been one of promise of marriage (often accompanied by a betrothal present), ritual rape, sexual relations approved by the woman's family, followed by desertion. Every step but the last was probably fairly typical of prenuptial behavior in the lower social orders in both city and country up through the eighteenth century. This situation would explain why the women's versions of the relationships tended to insist upon marriage promises and presents, whereas the men's focused on the sexual promiscuity of their partners and denied any serious intentions on their own part.

The third and last type of illegitimate relationship is the short-term, chance encounter. In this case the pregnancy was attributed either to an alleged rape or to the promiscuous behavior (or even prostitution) of the woman. The rapists were usually "unknown" men, identified from their clothing as soldiers or itinerant farm hands who had taken advantage of peasant girls or servants sent alone on errands. Inn servants and part-time prostitutes also had a hard time identifying the father of their child, given their tendency to have single encounters with different men. . . .

To what extend did women take pleasure in these encounters? Even with allowances made for the voluntary censorship and manipulation of information that undoubtedly characterize such autobiographical recitals, there is little evidence of a search for sexual fulfillment in the *déclarations de grossesse*. It would seem that most sexual relations were short and frequently brutal. Men apparently made little attempt to ensure the enjoyment of their partner, and foreplay was so rare as to be practically nonexistent. The stock description, "he threw me on the ground, stuck a handkerchief in my mouth, and lifted my skirts," is a constant of both legitimate and illegitimate relations, and even if force was not used, the threat of violence was always present. For most women, it would seem that sexual relations were instrumental and manipulative rather than affective. They were a means to an end — marriage, money, or simply survival — rather than an end in themselves.

The repression of concubinage[42] and all forms of nonmarital sex in the sixteenth and seventeenth centuries had a decisive influence on the birthrate of illegitimate children, which was under 3 percent of all births until the mid-eighteenth century. This low figure almost certainly reflects, over and above a stricter observance of premarital chastity, a significant rise in contraceptive practices, abortion, and infanticide. With the decline of medieval tolerance of bastard children and concubinage, there remained only the déclaration de grossesse and the paternity suit to protect unmarried women and preserve the lives of their babies. After all, the greater the social opprobrium attached to a fault, the greater the temptation to suppress the evidence; whence the proliferation of laws against infanticide, the creation of new foundling homes, and the new obligation of pregnancy declarations by single women, which automatically assumed that the unwed mother of a stillborn child was a murderess unless she had previously declared her pregnancy. . . .

The history of adultery is the history of a double standard: the extraconjugal affairs of men were tolerated, whereas those of women were not. One explanation for this disparity lies in the value attached to female chastity in the marriage market of a patriarchal and propertied society. Virginity was expected of a bride on her wedding night, and marital fidelity ever after, so as to ensure her husband of legitimate heirs. . . .

The view that masculine fornication and adultery were but venial sins to be overlooked by the wife was reinforced by the fact that before the eighteenth century, most middle- and upper-class marriages were arranged by parents in the interests of family economic or political strategies. Not only did neither bride nor groom have much opportunity before the wedding to get to know each other, but emotional attachment after marriage was considered inconvenient, indeed almost indecent. Male adultery with servants and lower-class women was therefore seen as normal, although some women protested the double standard and the wounds

---

[42] The cohabitation of a man and a woman not married to each other.

a husband's infidelity could inflict on feminine feelings. By the early seventeenth century, however, both Counter-Reformation and Puritan[43] sexual standards imposed greater secrecy on adulterous liaisons. Concubines and mistresses were not flaunted as openly as in the past, nor was the fruit of such relationships systematically provided for in wills.

A second explanation for the prevalence of the double standard lies in the fact that women were considered the sexual property of men, and their value would be diminished if they were used by anyone other than the legal owner. From this point of view, masculine honor became dependent upon female chastity. The cuckold was not only someone whose virility was in question because he was unable to "maintain" his property adequately (that is, sexually satisfy his wife), but he was also incapable of ruling his own household. In many countries, uxoricide[44] was pardonable if committed in *delictum flagrans*[45] and very lightly punished if motivated by adulterous conduct. This is all the more understandable if one remembers that an unfaithful wife was often considered a disqualifying factor for public office and other honors. In rural areas, village communities took matters into their own hands by subjecting cuckolded husbands[46] and their wayward wives to public shame rituals in churches and raucous skimmington[47] rides.

Only among the aristocracy did the otherwise universal double standard not prevail. Attractive court ladies were practically pushed into their sovereign's bed in order to advance their husbands' ambitions, while others felt at liberty to take lovers once they had performed their conjugal duty by providing their husbands with a legitimate male heir. Furthermore, few men of wealth and fashion were willing to risk their lives in a duel to avenge a wife's compromised honor. . . . Moreover, not all the ladies courted by aristocratic men were either married or noble. The end of the early modern period saw improved education of bourgeois daughters, together with a lack of career opportunities for genteel women suddenly impoverished by the economic uncertainties of their families' professional or mercantile fortunes. The result was a pool of good-looking and well-mannered mistresses who could be shown in public to the credit of their current lovers. . . .

For most women, however, illegitimate love remained an area in which the price to be paid for disposing of their own bodies and affections was much heavier than that paid by men. Less and less protected against the consequences of seduction and concubinage, women were equally discriminated against in the long-lived double standard for adultery. . . .

---

[43] Relating to English religious reformers of the late sixteenth and early seventeenth centuries who wanted to purify Christianity of any beliefs and practices not contained in the Bible.

[44] The murder of a wife by her husband.

[45] In the very act of committing a crime.

[46] Husbands whose wives have been unfaithful.

[47] The English equivalent of a *charivari* — a ceremony, especially in peasant societies, in which a community attempts to impose its values on deviant members by means of raucous music, public humiliation, and crowd intimidation.

In the sixteenth and seventeenth centuries two stereotypes of sexual conduct predominated: temperate, and often loveless, conjugal intercourse aimed at producing a male heir, whereas extramarital relations provided an arena for both sentimental love and sexual pleasure. In the lower classes, mutual affection, sexual compatibility, and marriage were more easily reconciled thanks to courtship practices that permitted couples to get to know each other intimately before betrothal. In the eighteenth century, however, the rise of illegitimate births in this same social bracket would seem to indicate a widening gap between love and marriage, with the penalty for aspiring to a union based on mutual inclination heavily visited upon mothers who remained unwed. The pattern was just the opposite in the middle and upper classes. Although the double standard with respect to premarital chastity and conjugal fidelity persisted throughout the early modern period, the eighteenth century saw the rise of a more affective model of conjugal relations based on compatibility of sentiment and mutual sexual attraction. This change, as well as the greater autonomy accorded to young men and women in their choice of marriage partner, encouraged the reshaping of the ideal model for wifely behavior to include carnal and emotional functions previously performed by the mistress. In the realm of extramarital sensuality, more tolerant mores also encouraged the proliferation of adulterous liaisons, prostitution, and homosexuality as well as the development of a number of sexual devices and diversions such as dildoes and pornography. In terms of sexual attitudes, however, the most radical change lay in an elite reconciliation of love, sex, and marriage that was to form the basis for our concept of marriage today.

MAKING CONNECTIONS:
SEXUALITY AND THE BODY

1. Compare the sixteenth- and seventeenth-century attitudes toward sexuality that Sara Grieco describes to those common in classical Greece and in fifteenth-century Dijon. How did these cultures link love to sex? What different attitudes did they have about the female body? How important was beauty in these societies? What made a person beautiful?

2. Grieco writes of a renaissance of prudery in early modern Europe. Does Dover reveal any prudery in ancient Greece or Rossiaud in late medieval Dijon? Explain.

3. All cultures proscribe certain types of sexual behavior. Describe legitimate and unauthorized sexuality in classical Greece, fifteenth-century Dijon, and early modern Europe. How similar are contemporary laws about sexual practices to those in the societies that Dover, Rossiaud, and Grieco profile?

THE WITCH-FIGURE AND THE SABBAT
Robin Briggs

During the age of the witch-hunts, which lasted from approximately 1450 to 1650 in western Europe and into the eighteenth century in eastern Europe, European courts condemned to death between forty thousand and fifty-three thousand people by burning, strangulation, or hanging. One-half of those died in Germany alone. Courts exiled or sentenced to prison countless others, many of whom had been tortured brutally. Some accused witches lucky enough to earn acquittal returned to their community only to be treated as outcasts.

In the last thirty years, a number of historians have researched witch-hunts, adding greatly to our knowledge of the alleged witches and those who persecuted them. But much about the period of the witch-hunts is still unclear. For example, historians disagree about why the hunts began during the Renaissance and the scientific revolution, supposed periods of intellectual advance. Certainly the belief in witches was not new, yet the so-called medieval Dark Ages witnessed no hunts for witches. Some scholars locate the origins of the hunts in folklore, theology, heresy, and changes in the law. Others look to the practice of ceremonial magic among socially prominent individuals, or to the development of a fictitious stereotype of a small, secret sect of night-flying witches who strove to destroy Christian society and who met regularly with the aid of the devil to engage in ritual murder, cannibalism, incest, and other antihuman activities.

Robin Briggs, a lecturer in modern history and a senior research fellow at All Souls College in Oxford, takes a different approach to European witchcraft. Briggs questions why some areas of Europe escaped witch-hunting and, if there was such fear of diabolical witches, why courts did not condemn hundreds of thousands of alleged witches. Briggs consults contemporary writings about witchcraft and exploits trial records in Lorraine (now an eastern province of France) to show that witchcraft was, above all, a village crime: Neighbors knew well those whom they accused. How did an accusation of witchcraft come about, and what was the profile of the average witch?

Briggs is especially interested in understanding the European belief system. What motivated the witches who signed pacts with Satan? The sabbat, an

Robin Briggs, *Witches and Neighbors: The Social and Cultural Context of European Witchcraft* (New York: Viking, 1996), 17–26, 28, 31–32, 34–35, 38, 40–41, 49, 51–59.

organized gathering of witches, was central to the idea of diabolical witchcraft. How did belief in the sabbat encourage witch panics, and how did the sabbat vary across Europe? What does Briggs mean when he refers to the sabbat as "the ultimate anti-world"? What was the role of torture in witch trials, and why did some accused witches freely confess without having been tortured?

In July 1596 the *prévôt* (the local administrator and law enforcement officer) of the small Lorraine town of Charmes reported the arrest of Barbe, wife of Jean Mallebarbe. This old woman of about sixty had fled Charmes some months earlier after being called witch in public, just as legal proceedings were being started against her. She evidently hoped that feelings would have calmed down in her absence, particularly since the old *prévôt* who had been very hostile to her had just died. When she found this was not the case, Barbe plainly wanted to get the inevitable over as quickly as possible — she even tried in vain to hang herself in prison, then asked to be put to death without being tortured. Few of the thousands of people executed as witches can have been more eager to please, or to confirm the beliefs of their persecutors. Her original confession had been simple and to a degree self-exculpatory. She and her husband of some twenty-seven years had always been day-labourers; more recently they had been forced to sell some small plots of land and, being left with only a house and garden, were increasingly dependent on charity (the husband was said to be old and crippled). Six months earlier Barbe, angry after a beating from her husband, had been seduced by "master Percy," as the Devil was often named in Lorraine, who promised her "money in abundance." The Devil gave her two sacks of powder, but she threw these in a stream, and had done no-one any harm. The judges were unimpressed, for they knew there were plenty of witnesses who thought they had suffered very real harm at her hands. They threatened Barbe with torture, beginning a process which over the next two weeks (ending with a session when she was lightly racked) would see her story become steadily more elaborate. Although to our eyes this was a parody of justice, with relentless pressure applied to a defenceless old woman, it was also, in its way, a negotiation. The questions indicated the kind of answers required, but the details were supplied by the accused, drawing on a common stock of stereotypes.

Barbe's culpability grew, until she was admitting to at least twenty years in the Devil's service. Early admissions to killing the cows of men against whom she had grievances, and a horse at each of three houses where she was refused alms, did not satisfy the court. The accused was pressed to admit that she had harmed people, responding with a story about how she had killed her neighbour Claudon Basle, with whom she had quarrelled, and who had called her an "old bigot and witch." Barbe's revenge was to throw powder down her neck, inflicting an illness which killed Basle 18 months later; Barbe had not wished to cure Claudon, who had never asked her to do so anyway. The imminent prospect of torture drew out a new series of confessions to crimes against those who had offended her. Some had been given lingering illnesses, so that their limbs were twisted and they became permanently crippled, while others were killed. Among these was a servant she met in the woods with a cart and horses; after he refused her some bread she heard the crows by the track calling to her "kill him, and break the necks of his horses," advice she duly followed. She had been changed into the form of a cat by her master, so that she could try to strangle the wife of Claude Hullon, after he had accused her of causing a fog on the lake. When she found she did not have the power to carry out this plan she still terrified the victim by speaking to her, then attacking her in her cat-form. After Laurent Rouille called her "old witch" and accused her of stealing wood from his barn she wanted to kill him too, but a wind had come in her ear telling her she had no power over him, so she had to be content with killing an ox and two cows. The torture produced a final batch of admissions of using her powder to kill men, women and children after she was refused alms. Barbe knew she must name accomplices she had seen at the sabbat,[1] where witches met, so identified three other women, two of whom were quickly arrested and tried after she maintained her accusations against them to the last.

Like many other witches, Barbe claimed she had simply been unable to escape the clutches of the Devil once she took the fatal decision to enter his service. On the other hand, she was not completely subservient to him. When the *receveur*[2] of Charmes, meeting her by chance on the road, called her an old witch, Percy urged her to avenge herself — but she remembered that he was often charitable to her and would not harm him despite beatings from her angry master. She suffered similar attacks at the sabbat, when she resisted plans to harm the crops, because of the prospect of death and hardship for the poor. When one male witch (recently executed nearby) wanted to cause a hailstorm, she accused him of hoping to raise the price of the grain he had in store, only to be kicked in the backside by Percy and propelled an incredible distance. Asked if the Devil spoke to them gently, she replied "ho, what gentleness, seeing that when he commanded us to cause harm and we did not want to obey his wishes, he would beat us thoroughly." With no more than the minimum of suggestion from her judges, whose questions are carefully recorded, Barbe was able to produce an extensive confession that included just about every stereotypical feature of general beliefs about witches. Unlike most other accused, she had not heard the specific charges against her because she had started to confess before the witnesses had been summoned. Her widespread anger and malevolence was something she either recalled or invented without specific prompting. Witnesses only entered the proceedings at the final stage, to confirm some of the quarrels and deaths she had already reported.

"La Mallebarbe" cannot be regarded as "typical," any more than any other individual witch. As we shall see, many different types of people were accused,

---

[1] An organized gathering of witches, presided over by the devil.

[2] Tax collector.

while the charges might vary widely. Nevertheless, her pathetic story of deprivation, insults and resentment was a familiar one across most of Europe during the hard decades of the late sixteenth and early seventeenth centuries. These, rather than grand theories about diabolical conspiracies, were the common currency of witchcraft as it was actually experienced and punished. They were stories anyone could tell, drawing on a great reservoir of shared beliefs and fantasies, endlessly recycled as part of everyday experience. Those who accused their neighbours could easily become suspects in their own turn, caught up in the same remorseless machinery of local conflicts and rumours. Even when reading the actual documents, it can be hard to believe that such trials really happened, that real people, flesh, blood and bone, were subjected to appalling cruelties in order to convict them of an impossible crime. If torture was barely used in this case it was only because the accused was already so frightened that she confessed without direct coercion. On 6 August 1596 Barbe was bound to the stake at Charmes, allowed to feel the fire, then strangled before her body was burned to ashes. The two other old women with whom she used to go begging and whom she had denounced as accomplices, Claudon la Romaine and Chesnon la Triffatte, followed her to the stake on 3 September of the same year. The sceptical English gentleman Reginald Scot[3] had written angrily a decade earlier, with reference to a scabrous passage in the early witch-hunting manual the *Malleus Maleficarum,*[4] "These are no jests, for they be written by them that were and are judges upon the lives and deaths of those persons." Elsewhere he had asked "whether the evidence be not frivolous, and whether the proofs brought against them [the witches] be not incredible, consisting of guesses, presumptions, and impossibilities contrary to reason, scripture, and nature." Indeed they were, but we have to go beyond indignation and horror to understand why just about everyone believed in witches and their power and why, within their own thought systems, it was neither irrational nor absurd for them to do so.

Modern ideas of the witch have been simplified to the point of caricature. It is easy to depict a witch with a few strokes of the pen or a crude silhouette; the least talented mime needs no more than a hat. A fascinating collection of descriptions from modern Newfoundland includes the following quite typical portrait of the witch as

> a creature with long, straight hair, a very sharp nose, and long slender fingers. She has a big mouth with pointed teeth. She dresses in black. Her dress is black and she wears a pointed black felt hat on her head. A witch usually sails through the air on a long broom and is always accompanied by a fierce-looking cat.

---

[3] Author (1538–1599) of *The Discoverie of Witchcraft* (1584), which ridiculed the belief in diabolical witchcraft and denounced the persecution of witches.

[4] *The Hammer of Witches* (1486), a demonology that two inquisitors wrote to serve as a handbook for witch-hunters.

The crude woodcuts which accompanied early witchcraft pamphlets are very similar, although contemporaries would have seen nothing odd about the dress or the hat, which were the normal attire of older women. In 1584 Reginald Scot described the Kentish suspects he knew as "women which be commonly old, lame, blear-eyed, pale, foul, and full of wrinkles"; they were also "lean and deformed, showing melancholy in their faces to the horror of all that see them." . . . Around 1600, therefore, this image was already in existence in most essentials. . . . This familiar portrait is nevertheless highly misleading as a guide to the people persecutors thought they had to deal with. It was the small group of sceptical writers on witchcraft, notably Johann Weyer[5] and Scot, who picked on the fact that many of the accused were pathetic old women whom their neighbours found obnoxious. Their aim was to ridicule the extravagant claims made for this secret resistance movement recruited by the Devil, whose chief accomplishment was apparently to kill a few cows and impede the making of butter or beer. There is good reason to think that this line of argument proved very effective among their educated contemporaries but believers in witchcraft saw the matter differently.

Those writers who pleaded for greater severity were usually careful to avoid any suggestion that witches could be typecast in such a facile manner. . . . The typical approach was to stress the seriousness of the diabolical fifth column, the secrecy with which it operated and its closeness to the centres of political and social power. Even those such as Jean Bodin,[6] who asserted (quite wrongly) that almost all witches were women, still made much of the minority of powerful male figures among them. The Catholic zealots of the Holy League,[7] who sought to overthrow King Henri III[8] of France, circulated pamphlets claiming to have found evidence that he was a witch himself. It was easier to argue that the Devil was successful up to the highest level because a number of early trials had been political set-ups directed at powerful individuals. The demonologists,[9] who openly plagiarized one another, made repeated reference to these cases. Fantasies about satanic conspiracies on a national or international scale could gather around the occasional elite victim, like Louis Gaufridy (a priest from Aix-en-Provence burned in 1611). Two years later the exorcists who had "unmasked" him had moved on to extract tales from possessed nuns in the Spanish Netherlands who described how Gaufridy presided as prince at great sabbats.

Early pictures of witches convey the same message. Old hags are usually present among them, but they mix with nubile young women, men and children.

---

[5] A German physician (1515–1588) who argued in his book *On Magic* (1563) that most accused witches were mentally disturbed.

[6] French political philosopher and demonologist (1530–1596). His *Demonomania of Witches* (1580) advocated the prosecution of alleged diabolical witches.

[7] The Catholic League, an uncompromisingly anti-Protestant faction during the French Wars of Religion (1562–1598).

[8] King of France from 1574 to 1589.

[9] Theologians and lawyers who specialized in the study of the diabolical.

Witchcraft was neither gender nor age specific for these artists, any more than it was confined to one social class. In reality members of the elite were rarely brought to trial, outside such exceptional pandemics as afflicted the German prince-bishoprics of Bamberg, Trier, and Würzburg. Nevertheless, there were enough scattered cases and, no doubt, more extensive rumours, to keep the notion of hidden satanists in high places alive well into the seventeenth century. A high proportion of those concerned were men, with clerics prominent among them. The exceptional rarity of men among those accused in England, coupled with misogynistic statements by various demonologists, has encouraged an uncritical belief that nearly all the accused were women. In many parts of Europe men comprised 20 or 25 per cent of those charged; in some, including large areas of France, they actually formed a majority. There does seem to have been a widespread conviction that women were specially vulnerable to the wiles of the Devil, so that most confessing witches said they were more numerous at the sabbat; however, a fair number insisted there was parity of the sexes, or even a preponderance of men.

For persecutors and general populace alike then, the stereotype of the old woman as witch had no more than a marginal purchase on their minds. Some old women who found themselves accused complained of their special vulnerability, and where statistics are available they bear this out to an extent, in that older women and widows are heavily over-represented among the sample. One of these, Marion le Masson, gave another woman some money to buy medicine from the apothecary, then said "poor old women, like herself, no longer dared to provide remedies, since when they did so for an illness, immediately people said they were evil people, so there was no need for her to reveal what she had told her." Despite this poignant evidence, the statistics need careful handling; we have to remember that many of those who came to court had been suspected for ten, fifteen or twenty years. Therefore their reputations very often went back to middle life or earlier, while relatively few first attracted suspicion as elderly crones. . . .

The popular image of the witch was that of a person motivated by ill-will and spite who lacked the proper sense of neighbourhood and community. Suspects were often alleged to have shown themselves resentful in their dealings with others and unwilling to accept delays or excuses in small matters. There seems little doubt that some of them were notoriously quarrelsome, although it is less clear whether this carried any *necessary* imputation of witchcraft. Indeed, to some extent such behaviour must have been as much the result as the cause of reputations, for there could hardly have been a more effective way of damaging communal or personal relationships than calling a neighbour a witch. There is a strong impression when studying larger groups of trials that such personal characteristics were commonly brought into play to reinforce suspicions which began for other reasons. Those who conciliated others were liable to find themselves described, like Marguitte Laurent, as "fine and crafty, careful not to quarrel with people or threaten them," while a failure to react was readily interpreted as betraying vengefulness. A particularly damaging charge was that the accused had talked of concealing anger until the moment for revenge had come. Jehenne la Moictresse was alleged to have told another woman that she should imitate her practice of giving no sign when angry, while Mengeotte Lausson claimed that when she had been angered she remembered it seven years later, without giving any sign. . . . The commonest of all remarks attributed to witches were those on the lines of "you will repent" or "you had better watch out," much of whose meaning depended on the context in which they were made. In many cases it was also said that the accused had taken no notice or pretended not to hear, when called a witch in public. In theory the proper response was to seek damages for slander, but suspects must have been very reluctant to embitter relationships further by such action.

Popular descriptions of witches do not therefore give any very certain guide to the reasons why they were identified; they are simply too flexible and circumstantial. Close analysis of the trials reveals why this was bound to be the case. There was no single or dominant reason why individuals fell under suspicion, while reputations were built up piecemeal over time and could incorporate very disparate elements. In consequence, supposed witches were a very heterogeneous group, even in the broadest terms. They were more often poor than rich, old rather than young and female rather than male, but there were quite numerous exceptions to all these tendencies. At any one time a particular community probably had a small group of strong suspects, with a much looser periphery of marginal ones; the latter were probably only known to individual families or close neighbours, and were not yet the subject of general village gossip. . . . For other members of the community, the witch appears to have alternated between being a terrifying enemy who could bring ruin or death and a pathetic figure to be despised and insulted.

One very powerful link did unite many of the accused; that of family and heredity. The idea that a "race" was either sound or tainted was much employed, both in self-defence and in accusations. To be the child of a convicted or reputed witch was inherently dangerous; in one pathetic case in Lorraine a young couple were both accused, and it emerged that they had decided to marry after attending the execution at the stake of their respective parents, "so that they would have nothing to reproach one another with." There are signs that as persecution became established in some areas this element was progressively strengthened, with a growing proportion of victims having such antecedents. How far this was just a natural statistical outcome of the situation is harder to determine; here we still lack good comparative information for different regions. The possibility remains open that in areas of endemic persecution this tended to concentrate increasingly on a self-defining group of "witchcraft families." It is also unclear how far the popular ideas on the subject implied some kind of congenital weakness, as opposed to the notion that parents might deliberately initiate their children as witches. Judges certainly showed considerable interest in the latter possibility, but it is less obvious in the testimony of witnesses. Confessing second-generation witches, who quite often blamed their parents for their initial seduction, are probably best seen as trying to displace responsibility rather than as expressing general beliefs.

Everyone seems to have known how the Devil carried out his seductions. Once witches decided to confess they told similar stories, with very little prompt-

ing, which rarely changed much over time. The Devil normally appeared unbid-
den to someone who was in a receptive psychological state. This might involve
anger against relatives or neighbours, despair caused by poverty or hunger, or anxiety at being called a witch. He offered consoling words, a gift of money and as-
surances that his followers would not want for anything. He might also promise
that they would have power to avenge their wrongs, often providing a powder
with which such revenge could be effected. Once the prospective recruit agreed
to renounce God and take the Devil for master, the latter gave symbolic force to
the change of allegiance. This normally meant touching the new witch to impose
the mark, leaving either a visible blemish on the skin or an insensible place. At
the same time the chrism[10] given at baptism was supposedly removed. With
women the Devil then took possession of them sexually, an experience they often
described in vivid terms as a virtual rape, made more unpleasant by the glacial
coldness of his penis. Any remaining illusions were shattered when the money
turned out to be leaves or horse-dung, at which point the witches knew they had
been cheated. Men occasionally produced their own version of the sexual element,
with the Devil taking female form, but this got the symbolism so obviously wrong
that it never became general. . . .

    . . . Once the witch had been lured into this disastrous error there was thought
to be no way back. A handful of the accused claimed they had made some attempt
to reintegrate themselves within the church, but all had apparently found this impossible. Catherine Charpentier tried to take advantage of the special terms available to penitents during the Jubilee[11] of 1602 by confessing her apostasy to a friar
at St. Nicolas. He made her promise to abandon the Devil, then absolved her, after
which she felt the Devil leave her. She was also to carry holy bread and candle wax
with her, then make a full confession to her own *curé*[12] the following Easter, with
three-monthly confessions thereafter. Unfortunately, although at the outset she
was determined to comply, "once she was at home and the time arrived to make
her confession to the *curé,* the shame of revealing herself to him, together with her
fear that he would expose and defame her, overcame her to such an extent that
she did not say a word to the *curé.*" The Devil saw his opportunity, duly appearing to reclaim her allegiance. . . .

    . . . The diabolical pact was a very ancient story that all concerned were read-
ily able to manipulate. The narratives combined elements of folklore and official
demonology, which were fitted around social and psychological determinants.
The Devil stood for the temptation to reject the normal constraints and obligations
which regulated personal relations. In a society where communal norms were so
coercive and privacy so elusive, the related stresses must have been peculiarly in-

---

[10] Holy oil used in Christian ceremonies.

[11] In Roman Catholic practice, a year, coming once every quarter century, during which believers
gain full remission of the punishment of their sins.

[12] Chief parish priest.

tense. The fantasy of the pact brought together an inner drama experienced by individuals with the judges' requirements for clear cut offences. As the ultimate treason against God and man it could be held to justify an automatic death sentence, even the bending of normal rules of procedure. . . .

In many accounts the pact was followed by the sabbat; either immediately after the seduction or within a few days, the Devil would lead the new witch to a meeting with others. This too was a notably malleable set of ideas, which formed part of the same narrative and overlapped with other elements in it. . . . It is impossible to determine how far these confessions sprang from an exceptionally rich local folklore and how far they were generated by a very active group of clerical and lay persecutors. Certainly the witchcraft panic in both French and Spanish Navarre in 1609–11 produced some of the most sensational testimony about the sabbat, whose influence has been remarkably durable. The French judge Pierre de Lancre[13] was largely responsible for this, for he wrote the statements up in a suitably lurid fashion. In a famous purple passage he described the purposes of those attending the sabbat as being

> to dance indecently, to banquet filthily, to couple diabolically, to sodomize execrably, to blaspheme scandalously, to pursue brutally every horrible, dirty and unnatural desire, to hold as precious toads, vipers, lizards and all sorts of poisons; to love a vile-smelling goat, to caress him lovingly, to press against and copulate with him horribly and shamelessly.

The idea of secret meetings where orgies take place and evil is planned must be one of the oldest and most basic human fantasies. Charges of nocturnal conspiracy, black magic, child murder, orgiastic sexuality and perverted ritual were nothing new in Europe when they were applied to witches. They had been used against early Christians and then against heretics, Jews and lepers. In the fourteenth century they were made against popes, bishops and the great Crusading order of the Knights Templar.[14] The stereotype is obvious; it consisted of inverting all the positive values of society, adding a lot of lurid detail (often borrowed from earlier allegations), then throwing the resulting bucket of filth over the selected victims. A kind of scholarly pornography was generated, while the use of torture secured the required confessions. It was also in the fourteenth century that humble people started to be convicted for witchcraft, at first in very small numbers; initially they were simply charged with causing harm to their neighbours by occult means, with no mention of devil-worship. This was quickly added to, however, drawing on a range of popular beliefs about nocturnal activities, mostly ascribed to women. Some were negative; stories of cannibalistic women who flew by night, killing and eating children in particular. Others were positive, concerning various forms of guardian spirits who were dangerous if not treated with

---

[13] A demonologist and judge (1553–1631) who was responsible for the execution of more than eighty accused witches.

[14] A religious order of knights, founded to protect Jerusalem from the Turks.

respect, but essentially acted as protectors of people, animals and crops. The stories of the sabbat represented a fusion between the persecuting stereotypes elaborated by clerics and judges and the various older folkloric traditions of the peasantry. . . .

. . . The belief in witchcraft was plainly widespread in Europe, leaving the way open for persecution to feed on itself. Each witch who came to trial might be tortured, then denounce several others seen at the sabbat, in a kind of infernal, elaborate domino effect. Although there does seem to have been a small peak of trials in the 1480s, it was not until the late sixteenth century that denunciations came to function widely in this way. In fact it looks as if the idea of the sabbat was slow to spread from its Alpine origins. The great early witch-hunter's manual of 1486, the *Malleus Maleficarum,* hardly mentions the sabbat; although the authors are evidently quite well aware of the idea that witches meet in assemblies, the rigid scholastic format of the work somehow prevents them putting any emphasis on this. When Bodin wrote his *Démonomanie des Sorciers*[15] in 1580 he felt it necessary to offer extensive proofs that witches really were transported to the sabbat, while commenting angrily on the way some judges and others ridiculed the whole notion. It can in fact be argued that the idea of the sabbat discouraged the elites from taking witchcraft seriously, because it was thought too implausible and too much tainted by popular credulity. In other words, for the better part of a century the destructive potential of the belief in groups of night witches failed to operate as might have been expected. Furthermore, even in the peak decades of persecution the role of the sabbat remains very ambiguous.

When trials did multiply, notably from the 1580s, there were numerous areas of Europe where the full-blown version of the sabbat was very slow to emerge from the trials or indeed never did so. Around this time the early critics of witch-hunting, such as Weyer and Scot, were already raising the question of whether such confessions did not merely demonstrate that their makers must be deluded. This was simply a more vigorous expression of long-standing uncertainties, for, in what may well have been the first formal discussion of the new crime of diabolical witchcraft, John Nider[16] seemed to imply that the sabbat was some kind of diabolical illusion. . . . Another idea shared by intellectuals and ordinary suspects was that some kind of substitution took place when the witch went to the sabbat; either their body stayed behind in bed, or a diabolical illusion took its place. Evasive reasoning of this kind, all too common, was really a sign of weakness faced with the implausibilities of the standard myth. . . .

Like other myths of its type, the sabbat worked on the basic principle of inversion; it presented a mirror image of the Christian world in which people actually lived. Familiar practices and relationships remained quite recognizable, but in distorted or parodic forms. . . .

---

[15] *Demonomania of Witches.*

[16] A theologian (ca. 1380–1438) and author of a demonology, *The Anthill* (1455).

The norm itself is very clear. Witches went to the sabbat under orders, often carried by their master or on a broom, even when it was so close that these methods of transport were gratuitous. Sometimes they returned on foot, which emphasized how the outward journey by air was a detail intended to stress the abnormality of the whole affair. Symbolically it expressed the extraordinary character and difficulty of transfer between the normal world and another opposed anti-world. Night flying could also explain large meetings of witches coming from long distances, but such big gatherings were rare events which appeared in few confessions. In a parody of a village festival the witches danced back to back, consumed horrible food and made hail, frosts or caterpillars which damaged their own crops. Sexuality and cannibalism were only mentioned in a handful of cases. This was an anti-fertility rite conducted on the familiar principle of inversion. Many accounts had the participants concealing their identity by wearing masks, aided by the fact it was night. . . . Nearly all the standard features of the sabbat could be reinverted — in the odd aberrant confession the witches even enjoyed a good meal or went by day. These symbolic constituents were apparently not very firmly grasped by a significant minority of those who confessed. Although the idea that witches held secret meetings was well established in popular folklore, the formal structures of inversion seem to have been rather insecurely attached to this central theme.

The really constant element in the confessions is harming the crops, occasionally omitted but never reversed. Just as the main purpose of most communal Christian rites was to protect the crops and encourage fertility, so the diabolical festivals sought to destroy them. This fundamental inversion was never misunderstood. That this was the primary meaning of the sabbat is emphasized by the numerous accounts of disputes between rich and poor witches over such plans. Catherine Charpentier claimed that the rich "who said that they still had enough grain in store, wished and suggested that they should make hail and destroy the grain and the other fruits of the earth. As for her, she had never wished to agree, because of her fear of being in want, knowing as she did the poverty of her husband, also, she had several times been beaten by her said master Persin, who supported the wishes of the others." This is a very common theme recounted by the witches, one which plainly expressed the basic social divisions of the local community. High prices meant desperate times for the poor but profits for those with a surplus of grain to sell, who were also likely to take advantage to increase their land holdings. Here inversion normally stopped in the fantasies, for only in a few cases did the rich not get their way at the sabbat as they did in the real world. Occasionally the poor won the argument; more often they managed to sabotage the hail-making in some way — perhaps by upsetting the pot being used — at the price of a beating from the Devil. . . .

. . . Like so much else in the concept of witchcraft, the sabbat was primarily concerned with power. Such visions were of course fundamentally deceptive. They could only be fulfilled in negative terms, through the destruction of the basic assets of rural society, the reverse of bringing any improvement to the lives of participants. A curious logic is evident, whereby the Devil needs the witches in order to produce corporeal effects and so uses a mixture of false promises, threats and compulsion to obtain their presence at his disgusting ceremonies. The betrayal which begins with the seduction and the pact is completed at the sabbat, where nothing is quite what it seems. The food, instead of being merely repellent might be entirely illusory, as for Hellenix Horrin, who reported that Persin "had promised to give her a meal, but did no such thing, and those who had already eaten said that when they left they were dying of hunger." The basis for virtual enslavement to this deplorable master was never really explained, except as a result of the witches' own pathetic gullibility and the pact they made. As for the proceedings at the sabbat, these appear to prefigure Hell itself, in which respect at least we may fairly see the sabbat as the gateway to the land of the dead. For those who made the confessions death loomed in a very real sense, although many seem to have felt that by making a clean breast of their sinful relations with the lord of the underworld they ensured ending up in the other place. Fortunately the historian is not called upon to decide whether this amounted to more than the exchange of one fantasy for another. . . .

   If the sabbat myth appeared in some form virtually everywhere witches were detected, it was still very far from presenting a uniform pattern. . . . It was mostly in German cities that the juridical, political and social peculiarities of virtually independent urban communities interacted to generate terrifying outbreaks of persecution. The cities involved had populations of only a few thousand, and functioned as market, legal and clerical centres for the surrounding countryside. Surviving examples suggest a rather claustrophobic environment, with narrow houses packed tightly within the medieval walls to make an ideal setting for a satanic thriller. Small Catholic cities ruled by bishops also had abnormally large clerical populations, and would have been filled with the sounds and symbols of belief, yet also with petty rivalries and jealousies. While the dramatic episodes that took place against such a background only made up a relatively small proportion of known European trials, they have inevitably dominated most later thinking about witchcraft. The unrestrained use of torture to extract confessions and denunciations horrified many contemporary observers. In fact these persecutions turned out to be self-limiting, for they created such social instability and general fear that finally the ruling groups brought them to an end. It should be added that major cities and centres of government were never involved; the places concerned were always relative backwaters, where small groups of zealots could have disproportionate influence. The most spectacular cases of all were in some prince-bishoprics — Trier in the 1590s, Bamberg and Würzburg around 1628–31, Cologne in the 1630s — but Protestant towns were also affected. There are striking similarities with earlier persecutions of Jews on charges of the ritual murder[17] of children and both types of outbreak brought efforts by the Emperor and his jurists to enforce higher judicial standards.

---

   [17] The belief, held by Christians, that Jews sacrificed Christian children during the Passover holiday.

These intense persecutions were necessarily built around the sabbat, for it was only through the identification of numerous accomplices that the panic could spread as it did. It is also noticeable that as accusations spread to clerics and other members of the elites the confessions became more elaborate, with much emphasis on complex diabolical rituals at the sabbat. The poor might go on brooms or pitchforks, but the rich allegedly travelled in silver coaches or other luxury conveyances. A particularly unpleasant feature of these outbreaks was the way in which children became involved in large numbers as both accusers and victims. This . . . was to be a major factor in the Swedish witch-hunt of 1668–76. In this last instance the confessions made much of the legend of Blåkulla (the blue mountain), a Swedish equivalent of the German peak known as the Brocken, which shared the reputation of the latter as a meeting place for witches. The children elaborated this into stories of a great hall where devils and angels alternated amidst a series of bizarre and often playful inversions, intermixed with devil-worship and scenes of punishment. Here the meshing together of demonology and local tradition is particularly obvious, alongside the fertile qualities and danger of juvenile fantasy. The children were grouped together in special houses, supposedly for their protection from the witches, and this encouraged them further in their role as mouthpieces for local opinion. Although there was considerable elite scepticism from the start, the local clergy and community leaders took up the hunt with enthusiasm; the persecution was only stopped after it spread to Stockholm. Only at this point did the government itself come to appreciate the dangers properly. Under hostile questioning the whole great edifice of fantasy collapsed as the children admitted their stories were lies from beginning to end. Over the previous years they had brought terror and panic to large areas of northern Sweden. Yet because there were dissenting voices and there was no systematic use of torture, less than 15 per cent of those accused were put to death, with the total number of executions being around 200.

In Sweden it was only during this late outbreak that ideas of the sabbat contributed much to witchcraft persecution. There were many other regions in Europe where the sabbat played a marginal role at best, appearing in small minorities of trials in other parts of Scandinavia or in Aragon and Hungary, for example. It is no surprise to find that it made only fleeting appearances in connection with Dutch witchcraft, while its absence from most English cases is often noted. In this context England seems much less exceptional than was once thought, and indeed the sabbat did creep gradually on to the English scene albeit in a rather tame and homely form. It surfaced hesitantly in the Lancashire trials of 1612 and 1634; these were unusually large group trials for England, and particularly good evidence has survived from the first, when nineteen persons were tried and most of them convicted and hanged. In 1634 an even larger group was tried, with seventeen known convictions, but intervention by king and council first stopped the executions, then finally exposed the main accuser, a boy named Edmund Robinson, as a fraud. There is an obvious natural association between these group trials and stories about secret meetings of the accused, and after this there are a few, more scattered references to witches' meetings in English trials. . . .

In north-western Europe the sabbat appears to have enjoyed greatest prominence in Denmark and Scotland, where there is a rather odd relationship. Danish witches often confessed to meetings with the Devil in their local churches and this has been plausibly linked with the wall-paintings in the churches, where scenes of temptation were commonplace. When King James VI[18] of Scotland married Anne of Denmark in 1590 the storms which troubled the return voyage were ascribed to witchcraft in both countries. In Scotland around a hundred individuals, supposedly led by the Earl of Bothwell,[19] were accused of high treason through meetings with the Devil in the kirk[20] at North Berwick. This bizarre affair took the sabbat into Scottish witchcraft trials, where it subsequently cropped up in numerous confessions. . . . Scottish witches were rather well behaved and in fact inversion played rather a limited role in most stories. In a society where almost all forms of spontaneous festivity were banned, the idea of disorderly gatherings was perhaps sufficient evidence of depravity on its own. In the coastal villages where many trials took place it was the sinking of ships, rather than the spoiling of crops, which exemplified the treason to the community. . . .

Such links between different countries crop up in various contexts. The account of the Swedish trials in Glanvill's *Sadducismus Triumphatus*[21] evidently influenced the New England clergyman Cotton Mather,[22] and may have had some indirect bearing on events in Salem Village.[23] The behaviour of the possessed girls during this famous episode has obvious parallels with that of the children in Sweden, although there is no sign of direct imitation. The sudden appearance of the sabbat in New England in 1692 remains mysterious; the children's stories have too much in common with European accounts not to have some literary or folkloric source whose exact nature is now impossible to recover. In comparison with their counterparts in the Old World, the authorities in the New came out remarkably well. Not only did they bring the trials to a close much more quickly and with a modest number of executions, they also sponsored public penitence for the wrongs committed, and ultimately rehabilitated both the accused and the dead. Whereas the Swedes executed four of the accusers, including a boy of thirteen, in Massachusetts the girls were left to wrestle with their own consciences. Another who engaged in painful self-examination was Cotton Mather, much troubled by his failure to intervene earlier and stop the persecution yet still fascinated by what he called "the wonders of the invisible world." For men like Mather,

---

[18] James VI was king of Scotland from 1567 to 1625 and, as James I, king of England from 1603 to 1625.

[19] James Hepburn, Earl of Bothwell (ca. 1536–1578), third husband of Mary, Queen of Scots.

[20] In Scotland, the parish church.

[21] Joseph Glanvill (1636–1680) confirmed the reality of witchcraft in *Sadducismus Triumphatus, or full and plain evidence concerning witches and apparitions* (1681).

[22] New England Puritan preacher and demonologist (1663–1728), author of *Wonders of the Invisible World* (1693).

[23] A town in Massachusetts, site of witchcraft trials in 1692.

the Devil's anti-world remained a vital part of their cosmology, even when they saw how easily the great enemy could lead them astray.

In a very different context, the Inquisitors[24] in the extreme north-east of Italy were confronted by a strange nocturnal world in the beliefs of the *benendanti*[25] of Friuli, peasants with a peculiar folklore of their own. These belonged to at least one widespread belief system, for they were allegedly marked out by an accident of birth, having been covered by the caul (or amniotic membrane) at the moment of delivery. Various similar chances — birth at a particular time or at a particular place in the family — were supposed to confer special powers of insight or healing elsewhere in Europe. In Friuli the *benendanti* went out in dreams to fight the witches and ensure the fertility of the crops; some of them also claimed the power to identify witches and treat their victims. The Inquisitors tried with some success to assimilate these local traditions to orthodox demonology, turning the dream meetings of the anti-witch cult into versions of the sabbat. However by the time they had achieved this, around 1650, the sceptical attitudes of both the Roman authorities and the Venetian secular administration averted the danger of an ensuing persecution. While male *benendanti* allegedly fought witches, women seem to have been more concerned to make contact with the souls of those recently dead, bringing back reports of their condition and their needs. There are hints of similar beliefs elsewhere, but nothing remotely as complex or systematic as this strange corpus of folklore. If most scholars have seen the *benendanti* as an exceptional local case rather than the tip of a submerged iceberg, this must of necessity remain a matter of opinion. Where there is certainly no problem is in linking them to the role of the sabbat as an anti-fertility rite, for their stories exemplify this in a particularly vivid fashion. . . .

We must also suppose that a wide range of local folklore was caught up in the judicial machinery, through whose distorting lens it is preserved. The complex process of interaction . . . provides a general model within which these beliefs can to some extent be reintegrated; it seems unlikely we shall ever be able to reconstruct them fully. What we do not need is any pseudo-empirical explanation, whether in the form of . . . pagan covens or . . . early drug cults. . . . It was often claimed in the course of trials that witches smeared themselves or the objects on which they flew with ointments, while there was quite widespread knowledge of various medical plants, including some hallucinogens. Dream experience is likely to have played a significant part in validating personal stories; it is even possible that some of it was drug-induced, perhaps by fungi with psychotropic qualities. When one looks in detail at the stories about ointments however, it becomes plain that the ingredients were usually magical in a quite different sense, for they only acquired their virtue by being placed in a symbolic system, through preparation at particular times and so forth. Powerful magical qualities were frequently

---

[24] Members of the Inquisition, a tribunal engaged in combating beliefs opposed to those of the Roman Catholic Church.

[25] Do-gooders.

accorded to human grease, simply because it carried such a charge of the forbidden. Wherever there is clear evidence about the alleged ointments they turn out to be harmless substances, identified or even deliberately manufactured to support confessions. It is hardly credible in any case that drugs could have produced specific visions of goats sitting on thrones or of perverted rituals; at most they could be linked to general sensations like that of flying through the air. To give them more importance requires us to homogenize the confessions in disregard of the endless local variations. This would be to repeat the error of demonologists like the Jesuit Martin Del Rio, whose enormous compendium on magic and witchcraft argued that the similarity of the confessions showed the sabbat was no illusion. As a notorious library-bound pedant, he was predictably confusing scholarly syncretism with reality, for the confessions were anything but uniform when taken one by one.

While confessions were normally extracted under thumbscrews, rack, strappado or other refinements of the torturer's art, a certain proportion of the accused made "free" confessions, which in some cases did not reflect even the implicit threat of torture. This led such a sceptical observer as Thomas Hobbes[26] to remark that "though he could not rationally believe there were witches, yet he could not be fully satisfied to believe there were none, by reason that they would themselves confess it, if strictly examined." Such confessions no longer seem as puzzling as they once did; some recent cases of alleged satanic abuse have provided yet more evidence of the way individuals placed under extreme stress will manufacture preposterous stories, apparently coming, at least for a while, to believe that they must be true. They mingle themes from their cultural milieu with elements derived from dream and fantasy, to generate self-incriminating narratives which have their own psychological significance. . . . Those witches who made a clean breast of such imaginary turpitudes were engaging in a form of self-purification, just as they should have done when they confessed to the priest, if they were Catholics. In the face of a terrifying situation, which saw them excluded and vilified by their own community, the confession represented an appeal for forgiveness and reintegration. The judges frequently emphasized the importance of a complete account, including all separate acts of witchcraft, as the condition for being received back into the church and rendered eligible for salvation. In practice they were very careless about enforcing this, but such exhortations produced statements such as that made by Claudatte Jean, who

> prayed for the honour of God that she should be put to death as soon as possible for the salvation of her soul, and wished that there might be no more witches in the world, but that she might be the last, so that the fruits of the earth might be more abundant than they had been, because so much and so long as there were witches it would be a great evil for the poor people. She then prayed she

---

[26] English political philosopher (1588–1679).

might have a good confessor to secure the salvation of her soul, and begged all those she had offended to pardon her.

. . . [O]thers were better aware of the fictitious nature of their accounts, to the extent that they could explain how they had concocted them. We should also remember such terrible stories as that of mayor Junius of Bamberg,[27] who wrote to his daughter explaining how the executioner — either very sly or unusually merciful — begged him to confess, rather than oblige him to inflict endless torment. These German witch-hunts were very different in some respects; since the accusations were spread by denunciations made under torture, the arbitrary nature of the process was far clearer to the accused and they were rarely suspected until the last moment. Those with long-standing village reputations were more likely to make a "sincere" confession, as part of a psychological *folie à deux*[28] with their interrogator, although one may wonder how long they continued to believe in it. . . .

The detailed accounts of the pact and the sabbat evidently reflect the everyday cultural and social concerns of their tellers, however fanciful the imaginary packaging may appear. They also reaffirm the creativity and significance of human fantasy, through which the juxtaposition of real and imaginary worlds took place. For their neighbours and the judges it was the witches who bridged the gap between the worlds, with the sabbats as the ultimate anti-world, hovering uneasily between diabolical illusion and some kind of perverted reality. Stories that the Devil incited those present to do wrong, then distributed the necessary powders or other poisons, sought to link the secret nocturnal meetings back to the *maleficium*[29] the witches operated in the ordinary sphere of village life. The weakness or absence of this element in most accounts of the sabbat suggests how imperfectly this element was ever integrated into popular thinking. One must add examples, such as that of England, which demonstrate how persecution and witch beliefs could function perfectly well without the sabbat at all. It is not a case of there being a "classic" type of European witchcraft built around the pact and the sabbat, with a few deviant types in peripheral regions; the picture is much more varied and the sabbat was only the central basis for persecution in a small number of extreme cases. What this complex superstructure does do is to give us enormously helpful insights into the minds of those concerned. Only so long as it is placed firmly in the mind, and allowed its full range of local variants, will its great symbolic richness help rather than hinder our understanding.

---

[27] Johannes Junius, famous for his tearful letter to his daughter after a court unjustly sentenced him to death as a witch in 1628.

[28] A psychological disorder in which the same delusions occur simultaneously in two persons who share a close relationship.

[29] Harmful or evil magic.

THE RITES OF VIOLENCE: RELIGIOUS RIOT IN SIXTEENTH-CENTURY FRANCE

Natalie Z. Davis

Eight religious wars rocked the kingdom of France from 1562 to 1598. Spurred by the grandiose ambitions of the leading aristocratic families and fueled by the religious fervor so characteristic of the Protestant and Catholic Reformations, these civil wars became international wars as Spain sought to dismember its northern neighbor — and nearly succeeded. The devastation was enormous, as Huguenot (French Protestant) and Catholic armies crisscrossed France. Indeed, by the late 1580s, there were three competing factions: Protestant, ultra-Catholic (receiving support from Spain), and the French who placed the state above religion. No wonder, then, that during these ungodly four decades of turmoil, violence and brutality were endemic.

Natalie Z. Davis, a historian of early modern France and former president of the American Historical Association, is professor emeritus from Princeton University. Here she explores one aspect of violent behavior in late-sixteenth-century France — the religious riot — and analyzes the patterns of riot behavior. Her sources include memoirs, journals, correspondence, sermons, contemporary books and pamphlets, and literary works. Davis does not see the riots as class warfare; they drew legitimacy from religious rituals and beliefs. Most notorious of the riots was the St. Bartholomew's Day Massacre of 23–24 August 1572, when Catholics killed perhaps two thousand Huguenots in Paris and, later, approximately three thousand in other parts of France. Davis goes beyond this well-known event to the dynamics of religious riots, and in so doing she raises important questions. What claims to legality did the rioters have? We are often tempted to dismiss rioters out of hand as lawbreakers, but sixteenth-century participants in crowd violence had other perspectives. Were the participants the very poor, hoping to profit from the occasion, or better placed social groups, sin-

Natalie Zemon Davis, "The Rites of Violence: Religious Riot in Sixteenth-Century France," *Past and Present: A Journal of Historical Studies* 59 (May 1973): 51–91.

cerely committed to specific goals? Did the rioters simply lash out at random, or were they organized, planning their acts of desecration, brutality, and death?

Davis's examination of the idea of pollution places us in the midst of the religious crowd. Sixteenth-century Catholics were certain that Protestants profaned god and the community by their actions and even by their very existence. Protestants believed the same about Catholics. The French felt an obligation, a duty to society and to god, to remove the uncleanliness and profanation. Sincere Christians in the sixteenth century could not permit defilement by others who threatened to overturn society, to rupture what should be, according to both Catholics and Protestants, a society unified by the one faith and only one faith. French people did not believe in the virtue of religious tolerance. In fact, they considered religious tolerance injurious to god and to god's plan. What were the differences between Catholic and Protestant riots, and how did the belief system of each religion affect the types of violence practiced by its adherents? Do you think religious violence was extraordinary or usual in Reformation France?

> These are the statutes and judgements, which ye shall observe to do in the land, which the Lord God of thy fathers giveth thee. . . . Ye shall utterly destroy all the places wherein the nations which he shall possess served their gods, upon the high mountains, and upon the hills, and under every green tree:
>
> And ye shall overthrow their altars, and break their pillars and burn their groves with fire; and ye shall hew down the graven images of their gods, and destroy the names of them out of that place [Deuteronomy xii. 1–3].

Thus a Calvinist pastor to his flock in 1562.

> If thy brother, the son of thy mother, or thy son, or thy daughter, or thy wife of thy bosom, or thy friend, which is as thine own soul, entice thee secretly, saying Let us go serve other gods, which thou hast not known, thou, nor thy fathers . . . Thou shalt not consent unto him, nor hearken unto him . . . But thou shalt surely kill him; thine hand shall be first upon him to put him to death, and afterwards the hand of all the people. . . .
>
> If thou shalt hear say in one of thy cities, which the Lord thy God hath given thee to dwell there, saying, Certain men, the children of Belial are gone out from among you, and have withdrawn the inhabitants of their city, saying Let us go and serve other gods, which ye have not known . . . Thou shalt surely smite the inhabitants of that city with the edge of the sword, destroying it utterly and all that is therein [Deuteronomy xiii. 6, 8–9, 12–13, 15].
>
> And [Jehu] lifted up his face to the window and said, Who is on my side? Who? And there looked out to him two or three eunuchs.[1] And he said, Throw

---

[1] Castrated men.

her down. So they threw [Jezebel] down: and some of her blood was sprinkled
on the wall, and on the horses: and he trode her under foot. . . . And they went
to bury her: but they found no more of her than the skull and the feet and the
palms of her hands. . . . And [Jehu] said, This is the word of the Lord, which he
spake by his servant Elijah . . . saying, In the portion of Jezreel shall dogs eat the
flesh of Jezebel: and the carcase of Jezebel shall be as dung upon the face of the
field [II Kings ix. 32–3, 35–7].

Thus in 1568 Parisian preachers held up to their Catholic parishioners the end of
a wicked idolater. Whatever the intentions of pastors and priests, such words
were among the many spurs to religious riot in sixteenth-century France. By religious riot I mean, as a preliminary definition, any violent action, with words or
weapons, undertaken against religious targets by people who are not acting *officially and formally* as agents of political and ecclesiastical authority. As food rioters bring their moral indignation to bear upon the state of the grain market, so religious rioters bring their zeal to bear upon the state of men's relations to the
sacred. The violence of the religious riot is distinguished, at least in principle, from
the action of political authorities, who can legally silence, humiliate, demolish,
punish, torture and execute; and also from the action of soldiers, who at certain
times and places can legally kill and destroy. In mid sixteenth-century France, all
these sources of violence were busily producing, and it is sometimes hard to tell
a militia officer from a murderer and a soldier from a statue-smasher. Nevertheless, there are occasions when we can separate out for examination a violent
crowd set on religious goals. . . .

. . . We may see these crowds as prompted by political and moral traditions
which legitimize and even prescribe their violence. We may see urban rioters not
as miserable, uprooted, unstable masses, but as men and women who often have
some stake in their community; who may be craftsmen or better; and who, even
when poor and unskilled, may appear respectable to their everyday neighbours.
Finally, we may see their violence, however cruel, not as random and limitless, but
as aimed at defined targets and selected from a repertory of traditional punishments and forms of destruction. . . .

. . . My first purpose is to describe the shape and structure of the religious riot
in French cities and towns, especially in the 1560s and early 1570s. We will look
at the goals, legitimation and occasions for riots; at the kinds of action undertaken
by the crowds and the targets for their violence; and briefly at the participants in
the riots and their organization. We will consider differences between Protestant
and Catholic styles of crowd behaviour, but will also indicate the many ways in
which they are alike. . . .

What then can we learn of the goals of popular religious violence? What
were the crowds intending to do and why did they think they must do it? Their
behaviour suggests, first of all, a goal akin to preaching: the defence of true doctrine and the refutation of false doctrine through dramatic challenges and tests.
"You blaspheme," shouts a woman to a Catholic preacher in Montpellier in 1558
and, having broken the decorum of the service, leads part of the congregation out
of the church. "You lie," shouts a sheathmaker in the midst of the Franciscan's

Easter sermon in Lyon, and his words are underscored by the gunshots of Huguenots waiting in the square. "Look," cries a weaver in Tournai, as he seizes the elevated host from the priest, "deceived people, do you believe this is the King, Jesus Christ, the true God and Saviour? Look!" And he crumbles the wafer and escapes. "Look," says a crowd of image-breakers to the people of Albiac in 1561, showing them the relics they have seized from the Carmelite monastery, "look, they are only animal bones." And the slogan of the Reformed crowds as they rush through the streets of Paris, of Toulouse, of La Rochelle, of Angoulême is "The Gospel! The Gospel! Long live the Gospel!"

Catholic crowds answer this kind of claim to truth in Angers by taking the French Bible, well-bound and gilded, seized in the home of a rich merchant, and parading it through the streets on the end of a halberd. "There's the truth hung. There's the truth of the Huguenots, the truth of all the devils." Then, throwing it into the river, "There's the truth of all the devils drowned." And if the Huguenot doctrine was true, why didn't the Lord come and save them from their killers? So a crowd of Orléans Catholic taunted its victims in 1572: "Where is your God? Where are your prayers and Psalms? Let him save you if he can." Even the dead were made to speak in Normandy and Provence, where leaves of the Protestant Bible were stuffed into the mouths and wounds of corpses. "They preached the truth of their God. Let them call him to their aid."

The same refutation was, of course, open to Protestants. A Protestant crowd corners a baker guarding the holy-wafer box in Saint Médard's Church in Paris in 1561. "Messieurs," he pleads, "do not touch it for the honour of Him who dwells here." "Does your God of paste protect you now from the pains of death?" was the Protestant answer before they killed him. True doctrine can be defended in sermon or speech, backed up by the magistrate's sword against the heretic. Here it is defended by dramatic demonstration, backed up by the violence of the crowd.

A more frequent goal of these riots, however, is that of ridding the community of dreaded pollution. The word "pollution" is often on the lips of the violent, and the concept serves well to sum up the dangers which rioters saw in the dirty and diabolic enemy. A priest brings ornaments and objects for singing the Mass into a Bordeaux jail. The Protestant prisoner smashes them all. "Do you want to blaspheme the Lord's name everywhere? Isn't it enough that the temples are defiled? Must you also profane prisons so nothing is unpolluted?" "The Calvinists have polluted their hands with every kind of sacrilege men can think of," writes a Doctor of Theology in 1562. Not long after at the Sainte Chapelle,[2] a man seizes the elevated host with his "polluted hands" and crushes it under foot. The worshippers beat him up and deliver him to the agents of Parlement.[3] . . .

One does not have to listen very long to sixteenth-century voices to hear the evidence for the uncleanliness and profanation of either side. As for the Protes-

---

[2] A Gothic church in Paris, built in the thirteenth century to house relics.

[3] The Parlement of Paris, a sovereign judicial court with jurisdiction over approximately one-half of France.

tants, Catholics knew that, in the style of earlier heretics, they snuffed out the candles and had sexual intercourse after the voluptuous Psalmsinging of their nocturnal conventicles.[4] . . . But it was not just the fleshly licence with which they lived which was unclean, but the things they said in their "pestilential" books and the things they did in hatred of the Mass, the sacraments and whole Catholic religion. As the representative of the clergy said at the Estates[5] of Orléans, the heretics intended to leave "no place in the Kingdom which was dedicated, holy and sacred to the Lord, but would only profane churches, demolish altars and break images."

The Protestants' sense of Catholic pollution also stemmed to some extent from their sexual uncleanness, here specifically of the clergy. Protestant polemic never tired of pointing to the lewdness of the clergy with their "concubines."[6] It was rumoured that the Church of Lyon had an organization of hundreds of women, sort of temple prostitutes, at the disposition of priests and canons; and an observer pointed out with disgust how, after the First Religious War,[7] the Mass and the brothel re-entered Rouen together. One minister even claimed that the clergy were for the most part Sodomites. But more serious than the sexual abominations of the clergy was the defilement of the sacred by Catholic ritual life, from the diabolic magic of the Mass to the idolatrous worship of images. The Mass is "vile filth"; "no people pollute the House of the Lord in every way more than the clergy." Protestant converts talked of their own past lives as a time of befoulment and dreaded present "contamination" from Catholic churches and rites.

Pollution was a dangerous thing to suffer in a community, from either a Protestant or a Catholic point of view, for it would surely provoke the wrath of God. Terrible wind storms and floods were sometimes taken as signs of His impatience on this count. Catholics, moreover, had also to worry about offending Mary and the saints; and though the anxious, expiatory processions organized in the wake of Protestant sacrilege might temporarily appease them, the heretics were sure to strike again. It is not surprising, then, that so many of the acts of violence performed by Catholic and Protestant crowds have . . . the character either of rites of purification or of a paradoxical desecration, intended to cut down on uncleanness by placing profane things, like chrism,[8] back in the profane world where they belonged. . . .

For Catholic zealots, the extermination of the heretical "vermin" promised the restoration of unity to the body social and the guarantee of its traditional boundaries:

---

[4] Secret religious meetings.

[5] The Estates in French provinces were assemblies that maintained relations with the central government and dealt with provincial affairs.

[6] A concubine is a woman who cohabits with a man to whom she is not married.

[7] 1562–1563.

[8] Holy oil used in Christian ceremonies.

And let us all say in unison:
Long live the Catholic religion
Long live the King and good parishioners,
Long live faithful Parisians,
And may it always come to pass
That every person goes to Mass,
One God, one Faith, one King.

For Protestant zealots, the purging of the priestly "vermin" promised the creation of a new kind of unity within the body social, all the tighter because false gods and monkish sects would no longer divide it. Relations within the social order would be purer, too, for lewdness and love of gain would be limited. As was said of Lyon after its "deliverance" in 1562:

. . . When this town so vain
Was filled
With idolatry and dealings
Of usury and lewdness,
It had clerics and merchants aplenty.

But once it was purged
And changed
By the Word of God,
That brood of vipers
Could hope no more
To live in so holy a place.

Crowds might defend truth, and crowds might purify, but there was also a third aspect to the religious riot — a political one. . . .

. . . When the magistrate had not used his sword to defend the faith and the true church and to punish the idolators, then the crowd would do it for him. Thus, many religious disturbances begin with the ringing of the tocsin,[9] as in a time of civic assembly or emergency. Some riots end with the marching of the religious "wrongdoers" on the other side to jail. In 1561, for instance, Parisian Calvinists, fearing that the priests and worshippers in Saint Médard's Church were organizing an assault on their services . . . , first rioted in Saint Médard and then seized some fifteen Catholics as "mutinous" and led them off, "bound like galley-slaves," to the Châtelet prison.

If the Catholic killing of Huguenots has in some ways the form of a rite of purification, it also sometimes has the form of imitating the magistrate. The mass executions of Protestants at Merindol and Cabrières in Provence and at Meaux in the 1540s, duly ordered by the Parlements of Aix and of Paris as punishment for heresy and high treason, anticipate crowd massacres of later decades. The Protestants themselves sensed this: the devil, unable to extinguish the light of the Gospel through the sentences of judges, now tried to obscure it through furious war and

---

[9] Bell used to sound an alarm.

a murderous populace. Whereas before they were made martyrs by one executioner, now it is at the hands of "infinite numbers of them, and the swords of private persons have become the litigants, witnesses, judges, decrees and executors of the strangest cruelties."

Similarly, *official* acts of torture and *official* acts of desecration of the corpses of certain criminals anticipate some of the acts performed by riotous crowds. The public execution was, of course, a dramatic and well-attended event in the sixteenth century, and the wood-cut and engraving documented the scene far and wide. There the crowd might see the offending tongue of the blasphemer pierced or slit, the offending hands of the desecrator cut off. There the crowd could watch the traitor decapitated and disemboweled, his corpse quartered and the parts borne off for public display in different sections of the town. The body of an especially heinous criminal was dragged through the streets, attached to a horse's tail. The image of exemplary royal punishment lived on for weeks, even years, as the corpses of murderers were exposed on gallows or wheels and the heads of rebels on posts. . . . [C]rowds often took their victims to places of official execution, as in Paris in 1562, when the Protestant printer, Roc Le Frere, was dragged for burning to the Marché aux Pourceaux,[10] and in Toulouse the same year, when a merchant, slain in front of a church, was dragged for burning to the town hall. "The King salutes you," said a Catholic crowd in Orléans to a Protestant trader, then put a cord around his neck as official agents might do, and led him off to be killed.

Riots also occurred in connection with judicial cases, either to hurry the judgement along, or when verdicts in religious cases were considered too severe or too lenient by "the voice of the people." Thus in 1569 in Montpellier, a Catholic crowd forced the judge to condemn an important Huguenot prisoner to death in a hasty "trial," then seized him and hanged him in front of his house. . . . And in 1561 in Marsillargues, when prisoners for heresy were released by royal decree, a Catholic crowd "rearrested" them, and executed and burned them in the streets. . . .

The seizure of religious buildings and the destruction of images by Calvinist crowds were also accomplished with the conviction that they were taking on the rôle of the authorities. When Protestants in Montpellier occupied a church in 1561, they argued that the building belonged to them already, since its clergy had been wholly supported by merchants and burghers in the past and the property belonged to the town. . . .

To be sure, the relation of a French Calvinist crowd to the magisterial model is different from that of a French Catholic crowd. The king had not yet chastised the clergy and "put all ydolatry to ruyne and confusyon," as Protestants had been urging him since the early 1530s. Calvinist crowds were using his sword as the king *ought* to have been using it and as some princes and city councils outside of

---

[10] Pig market.

France had already used it. Within the kingdom before 1560 city councils had only *indicated* the right path, as they set up municipal schools, lay-controlled welfare systems or otherwise limited the sphere of action of the clergy. During the next years, as revolution and conversion created Reformed city councils and governors (such as the Queen of Navarre) within France, Calvinist crowds finally had local magistrates whose actions they could prompt or imitate.

In general, then, the crowds in religious riots in sixteenth-century France can be seen as sometimes acting out clerical rôles — defending true doctrine or ridding the community of defilement in a violent version of priest or prophet — and as sometimes acting out magisterial rôles. Clearly some riotous behaviour, such as the extensive pillaging done by both Protestants and Catholics, cannot be subsumed under these heads; but just as the prevalence of pillaging in a war does not prevent us from typing it as a holy war, so the prevalence of pillaging in a riot should not prevent us from seeing it as essentially religious. . . .

So long as rioters maintained a given religious commitment, they rarely displayed guilt or shame for their violence. By every sign, the crowds believed their actions legitimate.

One reason for this conviction is that in some, though by no means all, religious riots, clerics and political officers were active members of the crowd, though not precisely in their official capacity. In Lyon in 1562, Pastor Jean Ruffy took part in the sack of the Cathedral of Saint Jean with a sword in his hand. Catholic priests seem to have been in quite a few disturbances, as in Rouen in 1560, when priests and parishioners in a Corpus Christi[11] parade broke into the houses of Protestants who had refused to do the procession honour. . . .

On the other hand, not all religious riots could boast of officers or clergy in the crowd, and other sources of legitimation must be sought. Here we must recognize what mixed cues were given out by priests and pastors in their sermons on heresy or idolatry. . . . However much Calvin[12] and other pastors opposed such disturbances (preferring that all images and altars be removed soberly by the authorities), they nevertheless were always more ready to understand and excuse this violence than, say, that of a peasant revolt or of a journeymen's march. Perhaps, after all, the popular idol-smashing was due to "an extraordinary power (*vertu*) from God." . . .

The rôle of Catholic preachers in legitimating popular violence was even more direct. If we don't know whether to believe the Protestant claim that Catholic preachers at Paris were telling their congregations in 1557 that Protestants ate babies, it is surely significant that . . . Catholic preachers did blame the loss of the battle of Saint Quentin[13] on God's wrath at the presence of heretics in France. . . .

---

[11] A Roman Catholic festival instituted in the thirteenth century to honor the Blessed Sacrament (the body of Jesus).

[12] John Calvin (1509–1564), French Protestant theologian, founder of Calvinism and religious leader of Geneva.

[13] Spanish victory over the French in 1557.

And if Protestant pastors could timidly wonder if divine power were not behind the extraordinary force of the iconoclasts, priests had no doubts that certain miraculous occurrences in the wake of Catholic riots were a sign of divine approval, such as a copper cross in Troyes that began to change colour and cure people in 1561, the year of a riot in which Catholics bested Protestants. . . .

In all likelihood, however, there are sources for the legitimation of popular religious riot that come directly out of the experience of the local groups which often formed the nucleus of a crowd — the men and women who had worshipped together in the dangerous days of the night conventicles, the men in confraternities, in festive groups, in youth gangs and militia units. It should be remembered how often conditions in sixteenth-century cities required groups of "little people" to take the law into their own hands. Royal edicts themselves enjoined any person who saw a murder, theft or other misdeed to ring the tocsin and chase after the criminal. Canon law allowed certain priestly rôles to laymen in times of emergency, such as the midwife's responsibility to baptize a baby in danger of dying, while the rôle of preaching the Gospel was often assumed by Protestant laymen in the decades before the Reformed Church was set up. . . .

. . . [T]he occasion for most religious violence was during the time of religious worship or ritual and in the space which one or both groups were using for sacred purposes. . . .

Almost every type of public religious event has a disturbance associated with it. The sight of a statue of the Virgin at a crossroad or in a wall-niche provokes a Protestant group to mockery of those who reverence her. A fight ensues. Catholics hide in a house to entrap Huguenots who refuse to doff their hats to a Virgin nearby, and then rush out and beat the heretics up. Baptism: in Nemours, a Protestant family has its baby baptized on All Souls' Day[14] according to the new Reformed rite. With the help of an aunt, a group of Catholics steals it away for rebaptism. A drunkard sees the father and the godfather and other Protestants discussing the event in the streets, claps his sabots[15] and shouts, "Here are the Huguenots who have come to massacre us." A crowd assembles, the tocsin is rung, and a three-hour battle takes place. Funeral: in Toulouse, at Easter-time, a Protestant carpenter tries to bury his Catholic wife by the new Reformed rite. A Catholic crowd seizes the corpse and buries it. The Protestants dig it up and try to rebury her. The bells are rung, and with a great noise a Catholic crowd assembles with stones and sticks. Fighting and sacking ensue.

Religious services: a Catholic Mass is the occasion for an attack on the Host or the interruption of a sermon, which then leads to a riot. Protestant preaching in a home attracts large Catholic crowds at the door, who stone the house or otherwise threaten the worshippers. . . .

---

[14] Commemoration of the souls of the departed, celebrated on 2 November.

[15] Cheap wooden shoes worn by peasants and workers.

But these encounters are as nothing compared to the disturbances that cluster around processional life. Corpus Christi Day, with its crowds, coloured banners and great crosses, was the chance for Protestants *not* to put rugs in front of their doors; for Protestant women to sit ostentatiously in their windows spinning; for heroic individuals, like the painter Denis de Vallois in Lyon, to throw themselves on the "God of paste" so as "to destroy him in every parish in the world." Corpus Christi Day was the chance for a procession to turn into an assault on and slaughter of those who had so offended the Catholic faith, its participants shouting, as in Lyon in 1561, "For the flesh of God, we must kill all the Huguenots." A Protestant procession was a parade of armed men and women in their dark clothes, going off to services at their temple or outside the city gates, singing Psalms and spiritual songs that to Catholic ears sounded like insults against the Church and her sacraments. It was an occasion for children to throw stones, for an exchange of scandalous words — "idolaters," "devils from the Pope's purgatory," "Huguenot heretics, living like dogs" — and then finally for fighting. . . .

The occasions which express most concisely the contrast between the two religious groups, however, are those in which a popular festive Catholicism took over the streets with dancing, masks, banners, costumes and music — "lascivious abominations," according to the Protestants. . . .

As with liturgical rites, there were some differences between the rites of violence of Catholic and Protestant crowds. . . .

. . . [T]he iconoclastic Calvinist crowds . . . come out as the champions in the destruction of religious property ("with more than Turkish cruelty," said a priest). This was not only because the Catholics had more physical accessories to their rite, but also because the Protestants sensed much more danger and defilement in the *wrongful use of material objects*. . . .

In bloodshed the Catholics are the champions (remember we are talking of the actions of Catholic and Protestant crowds, not of their armies). I think this is due not only to their being in the long run the strongest party numerically in most cities, but also to their stronger sense of *the persons of heretics* as sources of danger and defilement. Thus, injury and murder were a preferred mode of purifying the body social.

Furthermore, the preferred targets for physical attack differ in the Protestant and Catholic cases. As befitting a movement intending to overthrow a thousand years of clerical "tyranny" and "pollution," the Protestants' targets were primarily priests, monks and friars. That their ecclesiastical victims were usually unarmed (as Catholic critics hastened to point out) did not make them any less harmful in Protestant eyes, or any more immune from the wrath of God. Lay people were sometimes attacked by Protestant crowds, too, such as the festive dancers who were stoned at Pamiers and Lyon, and the worshippers who were killed at Saint Médard's Church. But there is nothing that quite resembles the style and extent of the slaughter of the 1572 massacres. The Catholic crowds were, of course, happy to catch a pastor when they could, but the death of any heretic would help

in the cause of cleansing France of these perfidious sowers of disorder and dis-
union. . . .

. . . [T]he overall picture in these urban religious riots is not one of the "people" slaying the rich. Protestant crowds expressed no preference for killing or assaulting powerful prelates over simple priests. As for Catholic crowds, contemporary listings of their victims in the 1572 massacres show that artisans, the "little
people," are represented in significant numbers. . . .

. . . Let us look a little further at what I have called their rites of violence. Is
there any way we can order the terrible, concrete details of filth, shame and torture that are reported from both Protestant and Catholic riots? I would suggest
that they can be reduced to a repertory of actions, derived from the Bible, from
the liturgy, from the action of political authority, or from the traditions of popular folk justice, intended to purify the religious community and humiliate the
enemy and thus make him less harmful.

The religious significance of destruction by water or fire is clear enough. The
rivers which receive so many Protestant corpses are not merely convenient mass
graves, they are temporarily a kind of holy water, an essential feature of Catholic
rites of exorcism. . . .

Let us take a more difficult case, the troubling case of the desecration of
corpses. This is primarily an action of Catholic crowds in the sixteenth century.
Protestant crowds could be very cruel indeed in torturing living priests, but paid
little attention to them when they were dead. (Perhaps this is related to the Protestant rejection of Purgatory and prayers for the dead: the souls of the dead experience immediately Christ's presence or the torments of the damned, and thus the
dead body is no longer so dangerous or important an object to the living.) What
interested Protestants was digging up bones that were being treated as sacred
objects by Catholics and perhaps burning them, after the fashion of Josiah in
I Kings. The Catholics, however, were not content with burning or drowning
heretical corpses. That was not cleansing enough. The bodies had to be weakened
and humiliated further. To an eerie chorus of "strange whistles and hoots," they
were thrown to the dogs like Jezebel, they were dragged through the streets, they
had their genitalia and internal organs cut away, which were then hawked through
the city in a ghoulish commerce.

Let us also take the embarrassing case of the desecration of religious objects by
filthy and disgusting means. It is the Protestants . . . who are concerned about objects, who are trying to show that Catholic objects of worship have no magical
power. It is not enough to cleanse by swift and energetic demolition, not enough to
purify by a great public burning of the images, as in Albiac, with the children of the
town ceremonially reciting the Ten Commandments around the fire. The line between the sacred and the profane was also re-drawn by throwing the sacred host to
the dogs, by roasting the crucifix upon a spit, by using holy oil to grease one's boots,
and by leaving human excrement on holy-water basins and other religious objects.

And what of the living victims? Catholics and Protestants humiliated them by
techniques borrowed from the repertory of folk justice. Catholic crowds lead
Protestant women through the streets with muzzles on — a popular punishment

for the shrew — or with a crown of thorns. A form of charivari[16] is used, where the noisy throng humiliates its victim by making him ride backward on an ass. . . . In Montauban, a priest was ridden backward on an ass, his chalice in one hand, his host in the other, and his missal at an end of a halberd.[17] At the end of his ride, he must crush his host and burn his own vestments. . . .

These episodes disclose to us the underlying function of the rites of violence. As with the "games" of Christ's tormentors, which hide from them the full knowledge of what they do, so these charades and ceremonies hide from sixteenth-century rioters a full knowledge of what they are doing. Like the legitimation for religious riot . . . , they are part of the "conditions for guilt-free massacre." . . . The crucial fact that the killers must forget is that their victims are human beings. These harmful people in the community — the evil priest or hateful heretic — have already been transformed for the crowd into "vermin" or "devils." The rites of religious violence complete the process of dehumanization. So in Meaux, where Protestants were being slaughtered with butchers' cleavers, a living victim was trundled to his death in a wheelbarrow, while the crowd cried "vinegar, mustard." And the vicar of the parish of Fouquebrune in the Angoumois was attached with the oxen to a plough and died from Protestant blows as he pulled.

What kinds of people made up the crowds that performed the range of acts we have examined in this paper? First, they were not by and large the alienated rootless poor. . . . A large percentage of men in Protestant iconoclastic riots and in the crowds of Catholic killers in 1572 were characterized as artisans. Sometimes the crowds included other men from the lower orders. . . . More often, the social composition of the crowds extended upward to encompass merchants, notaries and lawyers, as well as clerics. . . .

In addition, there was significant participation by two other groups of people who, though not rootless and alienated, had a more marginal relationship to political power than did lawyers, merchants or even male artisans — namely, city women and teenaged boys. . . .

Finally, as this study has already suggested, the crowds of Catholics and Protestants, including those bent on deadly tasks, were not an inchoate mass, but showed many signs of organization. Even with riots that had little or no planning behind them, the event was given some structure by the situation of worship or the procession that was the occasion for many disturbances. In other cases, planning in advance led to lists of targets, and ways of identifying friends or fellow rioters. . . .

That such splendor and order should be put to violent uses is a disturbing fact. Disturbing, too, is the whole subject of religious violence. How does an historian talk about a massacre of the magnitude of St. Bartholomew's Day? One approach is to view extreme religious violence as an extraordinary event, the product of frenzy, of the frustrated and paranoic primitive mind of the people.

---

[16] Davis defines this elsewhere as "a noisy, masked demonstration to humiliate some wrongdoer in the community."

[17] A combined spear and battleaxe.

A second approach sees such violence as a more usual part of social behaviour, but explains it as a somewhat pathological product of certain kinds of child-rearing, economic deprivation or status loss. This paper has assumed that conflict is perennial in social life, though the forms and strength of the accompanying violence vary; and that religious violence is intense because it connects intimately with the fundamental values and self-definition of a community. The violence is explained not in terms of how crazy, hungry or sexually frustrated the violent people are (though they may sometimes have such characteristics), but in terms of the goals of their actions and in terms of the rôles and patterns of behaviour allowed by their culture. Religious violence is related here less to the pathological than to the normal.

Thus, in sixteenth-century France, we have seen crowds taking on the rôle of priest, pastor or magistrate to defend doctrine or purify the religious community, either to maintain its Catholic boundaries and structure, or to re-form relations within it. We have seen that popular religious violence could receive legitimation from different features of political and religious life, as well as from the group identity of the people in the crowds. The targets and character of crowd violence differed somewhat between Catholics and Protestants, depending on their perception of the source of danger and on their religious sensibility. But in both cases, religious violence had a connection in time, place and form with the life of worship, and the violent actions themselves were drawn from a store of punitive or purificatory traditions current in sixteenth-century France.

In this context, the cruelty of crowd action in the 1572 massacres was not an exceptional occurrence. St. Bartholomew was certainly a bigger affair than, say, the Saint Médard's riot, it had more explicit sanction from political authority, it had elaborate networks of communication at the top level throughout France, and it took a more terrible toll in deaths. Perhaps its most unusual feature was that the Protestants did not fight back. But on the whole, it still fits into a whole pattern of sixteenth-century religious disturbance.

This inquiry also points to a more general conclusion. Even in the extreme case of religious violence, crowds do not act in a mindless way. They will to some degree have a sense that what they are doing is legitimate, the occasions will relate somehow to the defence of their cause, and their violent behaviour will have some structure to it — here dramatic and ritual. But the rites of violence are not the rights of violence in any *absolute* sense. They simply remind us that if we try to increase safety and trust within a community, try to guarantee that the violence it generates will take less destructive and less cruel forms, then we must think less about pacifying "deviants" and more about changing the central values.

MAKING CONNECTIONS:
RELIGION AND RITUAL

1. We have seen that Western religions have often fought among themselves and within their own faiths. Pagels brings to light the conflict between Gnostic and orthodox Christians, whereas Hsia documents Christian persecution of Jews. These are, of

course, only two examples of innumerable religious hostilities in Western civilization that involved not only Christianity and Judaism but Islam as well. Natalie Davis describes one aspect of the horrendous religious wars that racked Reformation Europe in the late sixteenth and early seventeenth centuries. In detailing the nature of the religious riot during the wars of religion in France, Davis uncovers its ritualized violence, sense of legitimacy, goals, and its preoccupation with the concept of pollution. She applies the notion of pollution to Christian fears that different denominations sullied society and Christianity, thereby offending god and so proving that the legitimate religion could — in fact must — purge the polluters from society. Apply Davis's idea of pollution to Soler's discussion of Jewish concerns about proper diet, to Pagels's depiction of the hostility between orthodox and Gnostic Christians, and to Hsia's analysis of the ritual murder trial of Jews. What other examples of fears in Western civilization might fit Davis's idea of pollution? To what degree can we use pollution as a category of analysis to understand social as well as religious history? Provide instances of cultures' fear of social pollution in European history. Here you might consider the attitudes of various social groups toward one another and to those they considered marginal or deviant.

2. Was the religion of the sixteenth-century French people more a matter of belief or of behavior? What was the difference between religious and social behavior among the French people Davis describes? Compare the extent to which religion permeated the lives of the following groups: ancient Hebrews, early Christians, late medieval Germans, and the French during the late sixteenth century. Do you think religion affects the lives of people in contemporary society as much as it did in earlier periods? Why or why not? Are there areas of life today that religion does not seem to affect? Is religious ritual as important today as it was in earlier societies? Explain.

WEDDING CELEBRATIONS IN TUDOR AND STUART ENGLAND
David Cressy

The ritual performance of marriage was an important rite of passage in six-teenth- and seventeenth-century England, and wedding festivities were funda-mental to the event, as they are today. David Cressy, professor of history at Cal-ifornia State University at Long Beach, refers to social commentaries, popular literary works, church court records, diaries, and personal letters in order to re-create wedding celebrations and their ritual activities. The early modern English had differing attitudes toward them, and Cressy describes the conflicts that emerged over the celebration of marriage, a fundamental life-cycle event. It was precisely the significance of wedding rituals, which marked a new social status for bride and groom, that led to both great festivities and acrimonious debate about proper ritual and behavior.

What features of weddings did some theologians revile? What matrimonial rituals did English society follow? Were nuptial celebrations normally tranquil, or did they customarily involve excessive eating and drinking as well as eroti-cism? What do the wedding clothes, flowers, gifts, and food and drink reveal about society and popular beliefs in early modern England? What were the cus-toms concerning the consummation of the marriage?

Marriages were festive as well as sacred occasions. Indeed, the English popu-lation at large appears to have invested more cultural energy in the social than in the religious aspects of weddings. Whereas the ecclesiastical solemnization took place in a matter of minutes, the nuptial cheer could go on for hours or even days. Even the most scrupulously austere religious authors accepted some secular re-joicing at weddings, while being careful to criticize festive excess. Had not Christ himself graced the wedding at Cana and contributed to the revels by turning the

---

David Cressy, *Birth, Marriage, and Death: Ritual, Religion, and the Life-Cycle in Tudor and Stuart England* (Oxford: Oxford University Press, 1997), 350–376.

water into wine? It was impossible to gainsay this example, which was remembered in each reading of "the form of solemnization of matrimony."[1]

Since wedding festivity lay outside the area of ecclesiastical cognizance and rarely concerned the ecclesiastical courts, our reconstruction of this aspect of the life cycle depends on diaries, correspondence, and commentaries, and on popular literary texts. This . . . [essay] examines "Hymen's revels"[2] and the rituals of "nuptial cheer" that brought the "concomitants" of marriage to a conclusion.

For their own polemical purposes, sixteenth-century reformers exaggerated the wantonness, excess, and irreligion that commonly prevailed at weddings. "The devil hath crept in here also," wrote Miles Coverdale[3] (adapting Heinrich Bullinger),[4] "and though he cannot make the ordinance of going to the church to be utterly committed and despised, yet is he thus mighty, and can bring it to pass that the ordinance is nothing regarded but blemished with all matter of lightness." This complaint, of course, was a hostile caricature by an early protestant reformer of manners, but many of its features could be found in later and more sympathetic accounts of weddings. Eating, drinking, dancing, music, jesting, and sexual innuendo remained standard accompaniments to the rituals of holy matrimony, despite godly disapproval of these "unmannerly and froward[5] customs."

According to Coverdale, the wedding day began with "superfluous eating and drinking." The ritual would be celebrated with food, dress, and noise. Even before going to church "the wedding people" became mildly intoxicated. Many consented to go to church "only because of custom," and were "half drunk, some altogether," before the preaching and prayer.

> Such folks also do come unto the church with all manner of pomp and pride, and gorgeousness of raiment and jewels. They come with a great noise of basins and drums, wherewith they trouble the whole church and hinder them in particulars pertaining to God. They come into the lord's house as if it were into an house of merchandize, to lay forth their wares, and offer to sell themselves unto vice and wickedness. And even as they come to the church, so go they from the church again light, nice, in shameful pomp and vain wantonness.

With their church duty done, the wedding party accelerated their irreverent abandon.

> After the banquet and feast there beginneth a vain, mad and unmannerly fashion. For the bride must be brought into an open dancing place. Then is there such a running, leaping and flinging among them, then is there such a lifting up

---

[1] The official title of the Anglican marriage ceremony.

[2] Hymen is the Greek god of marriage.

[3] English Bible translator (ca. 1488–1569).

[4] Swiss Protestant religious reformer (1504–1575).

[5] Wayward, obstinate.

and discovering of the damsels' clothes and of other women's apparel, that a man might think all these dancers had cast all shame behind them, and were become stark mad and out of their wits, and that they were sworn to the devil's dance. . . . As for supper, look how much shameless and drunken the evening is more than the morning, so much the more vice, excess, and misnurture is used at the supper. After supper must they begin to pipe and dance again of anew. And though the young persons, being weary of the babbling noise and inconvenience, come once toward their rest, yet can they have no quietness. For a man shall find unmannerly and restless people that will go to their chamber door, and there sing vicious and naughty ballads, that the devil may have his whole triumph now to the uttermost.

The Elizabethan puritan[6] *Admonition to the Parliament*[7] expressed similar outrage at the disorderly mingling of the sacred and the secular at weddings. The authors complained "that women contrary to the rule of the apostles, come and are suffered to come bare headed, with bagpipes and fiddlers before them, to disturb the congregation, and that they must come in at the great door of the church, or else all is marred." And in their second edition they added that, "with divers other heathenish toys in sundry countries, as carrying of wheat sheaves on their heads, and casting of corn, with a number of such like . . . they make rather a May game[8] of marriage than a holy institution of God." The polemical point of these observations was to associate the half-reformed Book of Common Prayer[9] with the excesses of popish traditionalism and rustic superstition. Protestant zealots implied that the festive delights of the wedding day were incompatible with devout solemnization, whereas ordinary folk saw wedding cheer as the natural joyful accompaniment to the priestly business in church.

A chorus of Elizabethan and Jacobean divines[10] criticized the "gluttony and drunkenness, and strife, and envy, and chambering, and wantonness" at otherwise laudable festive occasions, though that did not stop them attending. . . . Even God's ministers were known to loosen their collars.

More moderate voices, even those of Jacobean[11] puritans, acknowledged a positive role for "nuptial cheer," and went so far as to say that the festive celebration of marriage added to the honour and distinction of the occasion. Under this heading William Gouge[12] included "all those lawful customs that are used for the setting forth of the outward solemnity thereof, as meeting of friends, accompa-

---

[6] The Puritans were English religious reformers of the late sixteenth and early seventeenth centuries who wanted to purify Christianity of any beliefs and practices not contained in the Bible.

[7] Puritan manifesto (1572) demanding that Queen Elizabeth I restore the "purity" of New Testament worship in the Church of England.

[8] The merrymaking and sports associated with the first of May.

[9] The official book of religious worship of the Church of England.

[10] English theologians active during the reign of King James I, from 1603 to 1625.

[11] Relating to England during the reign of King James I.

[12] English Puritan writer (1578–1653).

nying the bridegroom and bride both to and from the church, putting on best apparel, feasting, with other tokens of joy, for which we have express warrant out of God's word." In Gouge's view there was no reason for godly families to forswear the customary festivities of weddings, so long as they were not "unlawfully abused." The problem was not custom but excess. Moderate and decent enjoyment was encouraged, disorderly abuse condemned. Cakes and ale would be relished, "gluttony and drunkenness" abhorred. The "mirth and joy" of the occasion would be marked by "witty questions" rather than "unchaste songs." Outside the church as well as within, the ideal wedding celebration would demonstrate cheerful sobriety, Christian edification, neighbourly affection, and remembrance of the poor. . . .

Church court records occasionally permit glimpses of the rowdier side of popular behaviour. Charged with allowing dancing in his house during service time in 1572, Robert Browne of Leyton, Essex, explained "that it was a wedding day, and that he could not rule the youth." Overcome by the permissive licentiousness of social ritual, the householder's patriarchal authority was temporarily set aside. Henry Gray of Southweald, Essex, was cited for practising his dancing during sermon time and for "dancing the morris[13] home" with the bridegroom after a wedding service in 1604. He was, indeed, making "rather a May game of marriage than a holy institution of God." Remarkably, when John Wilkins, the parish clerk of Whitstable, Kent, was cited in 1599 "for going about the street in women's apparel" he excused himself by saying "that at a marriage in a merriment he did disguise himself in his wife's apparel to make some mirth to the company."

Thomas Moulder, his wife (formerly widow Burnell), and friends, of Ealing, Middlesex, were cited "for keeping disorder and disturbing the parish in time of divine service on the sabbath day" in October 1613. Moulder's explanation throws unusual light on social and festive practices among the poor. He told the court "that on a sabbath day about three weeks ago he was married, and divers of his friends and others of his acquaintance came to solemnize the same; who in the afternoon at service time made orders as is usual at marriages, which was to tipple[14] at the aforesaid widow Burnell's house." Moulder acknowledged that the drinking went on all afternoon, following the ecclesiastical solemnization, but promised that he would "take warning by this to avoid the like fault hereafter."

Alcohol was frequently responsible for turning reputable good cheer into disorderly excess. In 1635 a wedding celebration among the clergy and gentry of Durham — those models of sobriety and good order — degenerated into a violent brawl as wine and ill-humour did their work. After John Falder, clerk,[15] and Jane Forster were married the guests retired to a tavern in Alnwick to drink wine and take tobacco. The bride's kinsman Thomas Forster, esquire, and the groom's

---

[13] An English folk dance associated with the Robin Hood legends.

[14] Drink to excess.

[15] A clergyman of the Church of England.

friend, Robert Stephenson, clerk, were drinking together, when Forster allegedly blew smoke in Stephenson's face. Goodwill rapidly turned to recrimination, and angry words led to bloody faces. Another wedding in 1635 descended into disorder even before the bridal party had left the church. Edward Cumberland of Rayleigh, Essex, was cited "for offering violence unto John Riggs, pulling off his garters and behaving . . . in a very irreverent and uncivil manner in the church of Rayleigh, at the communion table, upon the 12th of September." Cumberland acknowledged his fault, "that he did pull the bridegroom's garter off at the communion table," but suggested that it was simply a lark, the sort of thing one did at weddings. Disciplined ceremonialists and puritan reformers alike would be offended by this raucous irreverence in the midst of solemn ceremonies, at the sacred heart of the church. Neither would have much sympathy for Richard Peacock, the vicar[16] of Swaffham Prior, Cambridgeshire, who allegedly got so drunk at one wedding in 1641 that he could not recite evening prayers.

Compared with the records of ecclesiastical courts and the misgivings of religious reformers, literary sources offer a much more benign, indulgent, and approving view of nuptial festivity. Though prone to sentimental idealization and often self-consciously archaic, imaginative representations shed valuable light on social and cultural processes. The following section contributes to the reconstruction of matrimonial ritual by reference to Thomas Deloney's[17] account of Jack of Newbury, the popular "Ballad of Arthur of Bradley," the ballad of "The Winchester Wedding," and the wedding poetry of Robert Herrick[18] and Sir John Suckling.[19] It makes no claim to literary criticism, but rather intends to harness this material for the purpose of historical analysis.

Writing in the 1590s for an audience of gentlefolk, citizens, and literate artisans, Thomas Deloney immortalized the exploits of the early Tudor[20] tycoon Jack of Newbury. Little is said about the conduct of Jack's first wedding to a wealthy widow, but his second wedding, to a former servant, is lovingly described. "The marriage day being appointed, all things were prepared meet for the wedding, and royal cheer ordained." Jack, as bridegroom, wore his finest clothes and wedding shoes, but the focus of attention was his bride, her "head attired with a biliment[21] of gold." Jack of Newbury's bride was led to church

> according to the manner in those days . . . between two sweet boys, with bride laces and rosemary tied about their silken sleeves. . . . There was a fair bride cup of silver and gilt carried before her, wherein was a goodly branch of rosemary

---

[16] Chief parish priest; paid a stipend.

[17] English poet and novelist (ca. 1543–ca. 1600).

[18] English poet (1591–1674).

[19] English poet (1609–1642).

[20] England under the House of Tudor, 1485–1603.

[21] The front of a woman's headdress.

gilded very fair, hung about with silken ribbons of all colours; next was a great noise of musicians that played all the way before her; after her came all the chiefest maidens of the country, some bearing bride cakes, and some garlands of wheat finely gilded, and so she passed into the church.

Deloney skips over the religious service, as is usual in this kind of account, to dwell on the social comcomitants of the ceremony. "The marriage being solemnized," he continues, "home they came in order as before, and to dinner they went, where was no want of good cheer, no lack of melody." Jack's nuptial festivities, in Deloney's account, did not end on the wedding night, for "this wedding endured ten days, to the great relief of the poor; and in the end the bride's father and mother came to pay their daughter's portion;[22] which when the bridegroom had received, he gave them great thanks" and gifts in exchange. Finally, "the bride kneeled down and did her duty to her parents; who weeping for very joy, departed."

This, of course, is a nostalgic and idyllic account, extolling the virtues of harmony, hospitality, and largesse. Many would have considered these virtues in short supply in the stressed economy of the late Elizabethan era when Deloney's *Pleasant History* was first published. . . .

"The Ballad of Arthur of Bradley," a traditional entertainment collected in *An Antidote Against Melancholy* in 1661, cheerfully sets forth the principal festive elements of a traditional country wedding. Replete with jollity, plenty, music, dance, and the promise of sexual fulfilment, the nuptial festivity became the epitome of merry England. Ignoring the religious ceremony, the energy of the ballad is entirely invested in the secular activities of movement, noise, food, and licentiousness.

The wedding party is piped to church by "Peirce the piper, / His cheeks as big as a mitre, / Piping among the swains / That danced on yonder plains." A vibrant turnout of young people escorts the bridal pair.

> *The chief youths of the parish*
> *Came dancing of the morris,*
> *With country lasses trouncing,*
> *And lusty lads bouncing,*
> *Dancing with music pride*
> *And every one his wench by his side.*

Returned from church, the revellers tackled their feast of beef and mustard, furmity,[23] mince pies, and custard. "But when that dinner was ended / The Maidens they were befriended." Now it was time for the serious business of promiscuous kissing and sexual jesting, with music, dancing, and "mirth and merry

---

[22] Dowry.

[23] Hulled wheat boiled in milk, sweetened and flavored with cinnamon.

glee." Samuel Pepys[24] and the king[25] himself would surely have enjoyed themselves if invited.

> *Then 'gan the sun decline,*
> *And everyone thought it time*
> *To go unto his home,*
> *And leave the bridegroom alone.*
> *To 't, to 't quoth lusty Ned,*
> *We'll see them both in bed;*
> *For I will jeopard[26] a joint[27]*
> *But I will get his codpiece[28] point. . . .*

Another ballad in this style, "The Winchester Wedding," first printed in 1670, similarly celebrates the pleasures of nuptial celebrations. Here too were processions of lads and lasses, attended by fiddlers, escorting the couple home. Here too was abundant food, memorable good cheer, and the sexual frisson of games with garters and stockings. As in the ballad of Arthur of Bradley, the religious solemnization is taken for granted and the focus moves at once to the secular festivities. Larger than life, the event at Winchester was "a wedding, the like was never seen," though many of its features were conventional. There were musicians galore in attendance, "for all the whole country came in." . . .

The Winchester wedding supper, like Arthur of Bradley's, concluded with health-drinking, dancing, and games involving intimate items of costume. It was not only the bridal couple who were encouraged towards erotic arousal, for the young wedding guests too were sexually charged. One imagines the crowd, slightly tipsy, pulling at points[29] and laces and loosening each other's clothes. Of fifty maids in attendance, the ballad suggests, scarce five were still maids at the evening's end.

> *And now for throwing the stocking,*
> *The bride away was led;*
> *The bridegroom, got drunk, was knocking*
> *For candles to light them to bed. . . .*
>
> *And now the warm game begins,*
> *The critical minute was come,*
> *And chatting, and billing[30] and kissing,*
> *Went merrily round the room. . . .*

---

[24] Diarist (1633–1703).

[25] Charles II, who reigned from 1660 to 1685 and who was known for his love of pleasure.

[26] Bet.

[27] A place where clothing is laced together.

[28] A stuffed, penis-shaped bag attached to the front of men's tight-fitting breeches.

[29] Decorative lace.

[30] Caressing.

Sukey that danc'd with the cushion
An hour from the room had been gone,
And Barnaby knew by her blushing
That some other dance had been done.

These ballads, of course, were artful creations, saturated with nostalgia; they contributed to a vision of bucolic harmony, and were more intended to amuse than to inform. We might think of them as the verse equivalent of the social sketches made famous by Hogarth[31] in the eighteenth century, or certain modern cinema productions, mingling affectionate comedy and gentle social criticism. Some of these verses may even have been recited at weddings, both to entertain the company and to prepare them for the festive routines that would follow. Despite their caricature quality, these accounts reveal a range of rituals that are but hinted at in many other sources. Even if the depictions of Jack of Newbury, Arthur of Bradley, and his ilk are archaic, exaggerated, or mildly satiric, their performances and accessories would have been immediately recognizable to Elizabethan and Stuart[32] audiences.

The cavalier[33] poet Sir John Suckling drew on this tradition when he composed his "Ballad upon a Wedding" in 1638. Written to honour the marriage of Lord John Lovelace and Lady Anne Wentworth, it construes these conventional aristocratic nuptials as "the rarest things . . . without compare." The procession to the church, "forty at least, in pairs," supported the young man who was "going to make an end of all his wooing." Relishing her role, the blushing bride appeared to say to her lover, "I will do what I list today, And you shall do 't at night." Even the parson was stirred by her beauty. "Just in the nick the cook knocked thrice," and thoughts of the bedroom gave way to "the business of the kitchen." The party sat to dinner, with a hurried grace, before round after round of health-drinking. "Now hats fly off, and youths carouse," and the feasting, dancing, and drinking continued until late in the day. The bridal pair enjoyed centre-stage. "O' th' sudden up they rise and dance; / Then sit again and sigh, and glance; / Then dance again and kiss." Eventually, it was time to withdraw. "By this time all were stol'n aside / To counsel and undress the bride." The couple were readied for bed, with lively assistance from the guests. "But just as Heav'ns would have to cross it, / In came the bridesmaids with the posset."[34] Heartened and stimulated by this traditional drink, husband and wife were finally left to each other. "At length, the candle's out; and now / All that they had not done they do." The entire poem, like the nuptial festivity itself, builds to this sexual consummation.

---

[31] William Hogarth (1697–1764), English painter known for satirical pictures of eighteenth-century lowlife.

[32] English royal dynasty, 1603–1714.

[33] Supporter of King Charles I in the Civil War.

[34] A drink of hot spiced milk curdled with ale or wine.

Robert Herrick's wedding verses, slightly earlier than Suckling's, also dwell on the social and sexual elements of "Hymen's revels." Though written by a minister of the church, they focus on dressing, feasting, and bedding rather than the religious solemnization of matrimony. Herrick's "Nuptial verse to Mistress Elizabeth Lee, now Lady Tracy," captures the erotic elements in a single couplet, "Despatch your dressing then; and quickly wed: / Then feast, and coy't a little; then to bed." Another Herrick epithalamium,[35] . . . has the refrain, "Then away, come Hymen guide / To the bed the bashful Bride." . . .

Herrick's "Nuptial Song, or Epithalamie, on Sir Clipseby Crew and his Lady" has as its central motif the adornment, disrobing, and defloration of the bride. At the beginning the bride appears like "emergent Venus," finely attired and richly perfumed, her head "with marjoram crowned." Virgin bridesmaids shower flowers and sprinkle the bridal pair with wheat as they proceed from the church ("the shrine of holy saints") to the wedding feast. By the middle of the poem the couple are in bed, after a semi-public ceremonial disrobing. The young men and women of the wedding party crowd around to catch the ribbons and laces that held the couple's clothes together. . . .

The bride has "green hopes," signifying freshness but also alluding to the "green" condition of newly delivered motherhood. Her marriage bed is an erotically encoded bower, ideal for defloration.

> *Strip her of spring-time, tender-whimpring maids,*
> *Now autumn's come, when all those flowery aids*
> *Of her delays must end; dispose*
> *That* lady-smock, *that* pansy, *and that* rose
> *Neatly apart;*
> *But for* prick-madam, *and for* gentle-heart;
> *And soft* maidens-blush, *the Bride*
> *Makes holy these, all others lay aside:*
> *Then strip her, or unto her*
> *Let come, who dares undo her.*

Lady-smocks were a kind of wild watercress, prick-madam was a house leek used in salads, gentle-heart may have been heart's-ease, a kind of pansy, and maidens-blush may have been a rose. Herrick appears to have chosen these plants for their suggestive names rather than their floral or pharmacological virtues. . . .

The literary depiction of wedding festivity tended to be deeply conservative, self-consciously antique, and mildly lascivious. But many of the elements of "Hymen's revels" described in the poems and ballads can also be traced in more conventional historical sources. Diaries, letters, court records, and sermons allude to the clothing, ornaments, entertainments, feasting and sexual titillation customarily associated with weddings. . . .

---

[35] A poem in honor of a bride, bridegroom, or marriage.

There is hardly an account of a Tudor or Stuart wedding that does not draw attention to the bride's or bridegroom's costume, or to the wedding guests who were tricked out in nuptial knots and ribbons. Even today published reports of weddings tend to focus on what the participants wore rather than how they behaved. Wealthy couples spent lavishly on their nuptial attire, and even the poorest attempted to look their best. New shoes and fresh clothes were considered appropriate wear for a ceremony of new beginnings. The Elizabethan puritan Henry Smith[36] attempted to turn this custom to godly use observing that "Christ showeth that before parties married they were wont to put on fair and new garments, which were called wedding garments, a warning unto all which put on wedding garments to put on truth and holiness too." "For when a man putteth on fair clothes," said Smith, "he maketh himself fair too." The Stuart preacher John Gauden[37] wrote similarly on behalf of "comely adornings," arguing against the austerity of the 1650s that "it would seem very grievous to bridegrooms and brides, to be denied the use of their best clothes, their richest ornaments and jewels, which God permits and scripture alludes to."

Not only the bridal couple but their friends and attendants favoured wedding clothes, new gowns or fresh costumes. As soon as the parties had named the day, according to the Yorkshireman Henry Best in 1641, "they get made the wedding clothes, and make provision against the wedding dinner." Following this custom, as soon as he had finalized the terms for his marriage in 1657, the Derbyshire yeoman, Leonard Wheatcroft, "took notice for wedding apparel." Wheatcroft and his love "went to a market not far distant, where we did provide ourselves of apparel both linen and wool," so that they would look their best. . . .

Elizabethan and Stuart reports concur in associating marriages with bride-knots,[38] gloves, and favours. Trinkets and ornaments of the kind that courting couples gave each other to cement their affection were also worn at weddings and distributed to friends and kinsfolk as tokens of affinity or mementoes of the occasion. According to Henry Best[39] it was customary for marriage partners

> to buy gloves to give to each of their friends a pair on that day; the man should be at cost for them; but sometimes the man gives gloves to the men, and the women to the women, or else he to her friends and she to his; they give them that morning when they are almost ready to go to church to be married.

Custom preferred the bride herself to go bare-handed; only widows and married women were expected to wear gloves. Guests at gentle weddings came to expect a gift of gloves, and even associates who had not attended the ceremony might receive a pair as a token, a symbolic extension of the hand of friendship. . . .

---

[36] Puritan theologian, known as "silver-tongued Smith" (ca. 1550–1591).

[37] Bishop of Worcester (1605–1662).

[38] Wedding favors.

[39] Landowner (ca. 1592–1645) who wrote for his son an account of farming methods and other country matters.

A later seventeenth-century observer, Henri Misson, commented that the custom of wedding guests accepting bridal ribbons "to be worn by the guests upon their arms" was followed by all social classes in England, even nobles, whereas in the France of Louis XIV[40] it was confined to peasants. Similar ribbons were given as favours to friends and relations who did not attend the wedding, along with buttons and gloves, according to purse and fashion. . . .

Depending on their seasonal availability, fresh flowers served as wedding ornaments and nosegays, as sprigs and bouquets to be worn or carried, and as decorations for the church, the table, and the bed. They brought colour and delight to the nuptial ceremony, and further emphasized the marriage as a special festive occasion. Floral garlands, according to early Tudor commentary, betokened "the gladness and the dignity of the sacrament." . . .

Among gentry collections the Verney[41] family papers evoke the gaity of a young aristocratic bride dancing her way through a flower-filled house in 1657, as "servants waited on her and the music followed her" to her wedding. Along the way the party was greeted by "women with garlands." "This is a day for roses and violets," announced the preacher at a London wedding in June 1655. Other commentators describe the wedding table strewn with floral "rose cake . . . bone-lace, and Coventry blue," the bride adorned with "ginger, rosemary and ribbons," and the groom with "a sprig of willow in his hat." . . . Evergreen rosemary and myrtle would substitute in colder months for spring and summer blossoms.

According to early modern lore, the myrtle was "dedicated by the poets to Venus, and consecrated to wedlock." The rose too, a symbol of secrecy and silence, was thought to be especially suitable for brides. Elizabethan observers knew as well as twentieth-century theorists that floral arrangements at weddings united nature and culture to promote the liminal *communitas*[42] of the rite of passage. "At bride-ales the house and chambers were wont to be strewed with these odiferous and sweet herbs, to signify that in wedlock all pensive wrangling strife, jarring variance and discord ought to be utterly excluded and abandoned, and that in place thereof all mirth, pleasantness, cheerfulness, mildness, quietness and love should be maintained." Nor was the church neglectful when it came to construing meanings. The Jacobean preacher Roger Hacket,[43] rector[44] of North Crawley, Buckinghamshire, saluted the "ancient and laudable custom . . . to grace the married couple with divers presents." His own "marriage present," in the form of a sermon, invoked the properties of flowers in the wedding bouquet — primroses, maiden's blush, violets, and rosemary — to recommend obedience, mild patience,

---

[40] King of France from 1643 to 1715.

[41] Prominent family of country gentlemen.

[42] The threshold of the community.

[43] Famous preacher (1559–1621).

[44] A clergyman in charge of a parish.

and faithfulness to the wife, and wisdom, love, and loyalty to the husband. Who is to say that the bridal nosegay was not an instrument of patriarchal domination?

William Vaughan[45] described the practice among literate Elizabethans of sending written invitations to a wedding. "In some shires, when the marriage day approacheth, the parents of the betrothed couple do certain days before the wedding write letters to invite all their friends to the marriage, whom they desire to have present." In most cases the publication of banns[46] would serve as notice, to be supplemented by word of mouth among neighbours. The Derbyshire yeoman Leonard Wheatcroft spread news of his impending marriage in 1657 through a network of markets, inns, and relations, and "did invite many to our wedding, who did promise to come in their own person." Others were "bid" through intermediaries to join in this "nuptial feast." Close family members would be expected to attend, along with neighbours and friends. Only in the case of clandestine weddings, where speed and secrecy were of the essence, would broad attendance be curtailed.

Though the bridal couple or their kinsfolk were expected to provide hospitality, they were also accustomed to receive wedding presents. Weddings were occasions of reciprocal giving and receiving, in a culture that calibrated the honour as well as the intrinsic worth of a gift. Presents could be financial, material, consumable, or symbolic. Parents or guardians might present the bride's dowry, or some representation of it, in the course of the wedding service or at the reception. Wealthy relations might give money or silverware. Neighbours might bring food or drink for the feast. Guests at a Surrey gentry wedding in 1567 contributed swans, capons, partridges, woodcocks, and other birds, hares, does, hinds, and other game, fish, sweetmeats, puddings, cheeses, spices, and wine, to keep the party going. In recognition of their relationship to a seigneurial[47] family, when Lord Desmond's daughter married Lady Gawdy's son in 1657, "all the country sent her in presents, she had four brace of bucks and fish and fruits and all good things," as subfeudal tokens of esteem and respect. . . . Samuel Pepys "bespake three or four dozen bottles of wine" for a cousin's marriage in 1660, and never went to a wedding without taking a gift.

A minister might contribute his fee or offer the gift of a sermon before taking his place at the wedding banquet, as did Giles Moore, the Restoration-era rector of Horsted Keynes, Sussex. As an act of charity to his parishioners, Moore sometimes forgave them their wedding fees, or returned the money to them twofold. To help those "newly married to begin the world" — a telling phrase — Moore would sometimes give a few shillings to a newly married couple. Sometimes he

---

[45] Poet and colonial pioneer (1577–1641).

[46] The announcement of an intended marriage, made in the parish church on three successive Sundays.

[47] Pertaining to the lord of a manor.

would treat the fiddlers at a wedding and pay for the cost of a sugar loaf. On special occasions he might offer a silver spoon. One such wedding spoon cost him 9s. 6d.[48] in 1658, another cost 3s. 6d. in 1670. When two of his former servants "married away" in 1676, Giles Moore not only performed the ceremony "gratis," but also covered their wedding expenses. His largesse included "fiddlers . . . a large cake, all their fuel and free use of my house and stables for two days, with a quart of white wine with recipes, being in all not less than 40s. or one year's wages." . . .

Traditional sixteenth-century bride-ales raised funds by brewing and baking to supply the needs of the wedding. Parish accounts sometimes record such payments as 6d. "for bread and wine for three weddings" at Tallaton, Devon, in 1595, or 2d. "for bread and wine against a wedding" at the same place in 1601. These refreshments allowed the parish clerk and bell-ringers to join in the festivity. Bid-ales invited neighbours to drink in honour of the wedding, "and then for all guests to contribute to the house-keepers." Far from preventing indigents from getting married, parishioners at Hackney, Middlesex, organized collections at the church door in 1663 to help the poorest newly weds to set up their households. . . .

Traditionally, a public wedding, like a public funeral, was an occasion for the central participants to distribute doles to the poor. At weddings, in particular, the bridal party was expected to share its goodwill. Documented reports of this practice are rare, but the substantial amount of £3 was distributed to the poor at a wedding at All Hallows, Barking, Essex, in 1654. A gentleman who was married in the same church on Easter Tuesday, 1661, gave 6s. to the poor. The late seventeenth-century *Ladies Dictionary* depicts newly weds passing from the church through "the congratulating crowd" bestowing charitable largesse on the poor. . . .

Literary accounts of traditional grand weddings describe the festive procession that escorted the couple to and from the church. A cavalcade of dancers, prancers, and musicians added to the honour of the participants and to the delight of the occasion, and singled out the ceremony as a significant rite of passage. By the later seventeenth century, however, the great bridal processions of the kind that supported Jack of Newbury and Arthur of Bradley were increasingly rare. As the *Ladies Dictionary* of 1694 observed, after describing some ancient processional traditions, "we find that custom is laid aside, and the matter is managed with less ceremony and more decency; the good natured bride not expecting such fantastical attendance." The new-found taste for privacy and decorum worked against festive processions. The post-Restoration[49] urban élite would go to their nuptials by coach, "environed with a throng of starers and gapers," and might even "sneak to church by themselves [and] sneak to a taven by themselves," to avoid all "pomp and public ceremony." For the rest of the population, on most occasions, the wedding party and guests simply turned up for the ser-

---

[48] Shillings and pence; English coins.

[49] After the restoration of the monarchy in 1660.

vice; in many villages, where weddings were attached to routine worship, the congregation was already assembled in church. . . .

No doubt there continued to be celebrated weddings with large and formal turnouts. But the later Stuart gentry preferred equestrian escorts or lines of coaches to the bouncing lads and lasses of the ballad tradition. "Six score horse of the gentlemen and yeomen" escorted the aristocratic Gawdy-Desmond wedding party on the final three miles of their ride home to Debenham in 1657. Twelve riders on horseback accompanied the bridegroom at a Northamptonshire gentry wedding in 1672. After Ralph Thoresby married Anna Sykes in February 1685, in what was supposed to be a quiet ceremony, Thoresby writes, "notwithstanding our designed privacy, we were met at our return to Leeds by about 300 horses." This large equestrian attendance was an appropriate honour for the son-in-law and daughter of the lord of the manor.[50] . . .

Ever attentive to deviance and disorder, church court records reveal that weddings could be targets for derision as well as good cheer. Thomas Bred of Coddington, Oxfordshire, confessed in 1599 "that at such time as Thomas Paxton was to be married he was set on by Mrs. Boskyn and Mrs. Jackson to carry a garland to the church and to blow a horn in the middle of the street." The noise and display drew attention to the wedding, though not in the manner that respectable families would have wished. Mocking the usual floral accoutrements of the bridal procession, William Gilchrist of West Ham, Essex, allegedly spoilt a wedding in the summer of 1602 by taunting gestures. "He the said Gilchrist, in derision of holy matrimony, got a bough hanged with ropes ends and beset with nettles and other weeds, and carried the same in the street and churchyard before the bride, to the great offence of the congregation." Unfortunately the evidence is insufficient to gauge whether Gilchrist was drunk or simple-minded, whether he was driven by anger as a suitor spurned, or whether his bouquet of nettles was intended to comment on the chastity or character of the bride. Another possibility is that Gilchrist's obstacle belonged to a tradition of jesting, pranking, and barring the way, comparable to the modern Anglo-American practice of tying tin cans or shoes to the rear of a newly married couple's car.

Edward Row's behaviour at the marriage of Thomas Brock and Rebecca Foster at Thorrock Parva, Essex, in 1605, is easier to understand. Row "did fasten a pair of horns upon the churchyard gate . . . and being rebuked for the same afterwards did avow that he did it, and if it were to do again he would do it." Horns were the standard symbol for cuckoldry[51] and incontinence, and their display announced that the bride was notorious for her sexual misconduct. Robert Brooke of Arlington, Sussex, was similarly charged with disorderly behaviour in 1639 "for wearing a great pair of horns upon his head in the churchyard when Henry Hall and his wife were going to be married, showing thereby that the said Hall was like

---

[50] The chief landholder and magistrate.

[51] A cuckold is a husband whose wife has been unfaithful.

to be a cuckold." Often used to comment on discordant relationships *within* marriage, the charivari[52] tradition was here used to publicize irregularities at its beginning.

Wedding feasts were ideally occasions of amity and *communitas,* appropriate to rituals of separation and incorporation. No nuptial festivity would be complete without convivial distribution of food and drink, as the business with the ring gave way to "the business of the kitchen." It would not do to start married life hungry, or to fail to offer hospitality to guests. Clandestine weddings, by their nature, were low-key and discreet, but they too were usually followed by dining and drinking at an inn. Participants in public weddings, the minister often included, retired to the table or the tavern. If the wedding was performed within canonical hours, between eight and twelve of the forenoon, the rest of the day could be spent in feasting. The quality and range of refreshments varied with the ability of families to provide them, and the menu also varied with seasonal conditions. Late summer weddings could turn harvest abundance into spreads of breads and pastries. Autumn weddings would find more fresh-killed livestock for serving of meats — roast, baked, or boiled.

Traditionalists might insist on the preparation of such delicacies as a "bride cake." The antiquarian John Aubrey[53] recalled seeing "the bride and bridegroom kiss over the bride cakes at the table; it was about the latter end of dinner; and the cakes were laid one upon another, like the picture of the sew-bread[54] in the old Bible." This custom may have faded by the time Aubrey wrote in the later seventeenth century, for he locates it "before the civil wars . . . according to the custom then." Other sources refer to the continuation of "confarreation . . . a ceremony used at the solemnization of a marriage, in token of most firm conjunction between man and wife, with a cake of wheat or barley; this ceremony is still retained in part with us, by that which we call the bride cake, used at weddings." It was customary at wedding dinners for the bridegroom to serve the bride, an inversion of the household etiquette that would prevail for the rest of their married career. In a Civil-War era[55] pamphlet mocking "the new fashion of marriage" among artisan-class conventiclers,[56] "our young holy sister waited at the table on her bridegroom," in ostentatious violation of the former fashion.

Diaries and letters permit glimpses of wedding festivity, mostly among the middling and upper classes. The London diarist Henry Machyn[57] observed a citizen's wedding in 1559 which offered "a bride cup and wafers and hippocras

---

[52] A ceremony, especially in peasant societies, in which a community attempts to impose its values on deviant members by means of raucous music, public humiliation, and crowd intimidation.

[53] English antiquarian and writer (1626–1697).

[54] Loaves of unleavened bread placed at the altar of the Jewish god each sabbath.

[55] England between 1642 and 1649.

[56] People who attended religious services other than those of the Church of England.

[57] English diarist (1498–1563).

[spiced wine] and muscadel plenty to everybody," before proceeding "unto Mr. Blackwell's place to breakfast, and after a great dinner." At Sir Philip Herbert's wedding at court in 1604, "there was none of our accustomed forms omitted, of bride-cakes, sops in wine, giving of gloves, laces and points . . . and at night there was sewing into the sheet, casting of the bride's left hose, and twenty other petty sorceries." Dudley Carleton, who provides this account, seemed both satisfied and amused that the check-list of customary actions had been accomplished. . . .

Puritan discipline would not stand in the way of wedding festivities, even under the exigiencies of war or during the allegedly austere days of the Cromwellian protectorate.[58] Most good Christians knew the difference between festivity and excess. Of his marriage in London in 1643 John Greene writes,

> the wedding was kept at my father's house in the Old Jewry[59] very privately, none but brothers and sisters and a friend or two more were at it. My wife expected an ague upon Sunday and Tuesday, and for that reason it was done on Monday, the Wednesday after being fast day. On Tuesday, the day after my wedding, we went to the Mermaid in Bread Street to dance and to be merry, where music met us.

When the godly Oliver Heywood married the devout Elizabeth Angier in April 1655 they were joined by "a numerous congregation in the chapel . . . and then feasted above an hundred persons of several ranks, ages and sexes." . . .

Restoration-era weddings perpetuated many of the traditional customs, adapted as needed to the conventions of polite society. It is no surprise to find the "Ballad of Arthur of Bradley" and "The Winchester Wedding" printed at this time. The dissenting preacher[60] Oliver Heywood described a North-Country wedding in 1678 where "all at the marriage give the 2d. a piece to the music, then the pipers go with the bridegroom and bride to invite guests for the second day." The wedding feast for a London alderman's son at Drapers' Hall in 1675 went on for three days. After a long afternoon of festivities at a naval purveyor's wedding in 1666, Samuel Pepys wrote appreciatively of "a good dinner, and what was best, good music. After dinner the young women went to dance." . . .

The French visitor Henri Misson, whose observations of late seventeenth-century England are so valuable, recognized many of the social, regional, and religious variables in marriage customs. Weddings, he commented, "generally vary according to the several customs of the countries, the rank or quality of the persons, and their different religions. The Presbyterians profess so great a strictness, and such a mighty reservedness, that their weddings are commonly very plain and very quiet." At weddings of the middling sort, unless held quietly in private,

---

[58] England during the rule of Oliver Cromwell, from 1642 to 1658.

[59] A street in London.

[60] The leader of a religious group that rejected the worship of the Church of England.

they invite a number of friends and relations; every one puts on new clothes, and dresses finer than ordinary; the men lead the women, they get into coaches, and so go in procession, and are married in full day at church. After feasting and dancing, and having made merry that day and the next, they take a trip into the country, and there divert themselves very pleasantly.

Nonconformist[61] weddings were not necessarily as austere as Misson imagined. Though Oliver Heywood's remarriage in 1667 was, reportedly, "a very solemn business," conducted at Salford chapel "in a decent manner" in the presence of "under twenty persons of the nearest relations," his guests would not be denied good eating. Heywood was by this time a prominent dissenter and a model to Lancashire nonconformists. A few years later Heywood was disturbed, though not so upset as some brother dissenters, at the worldly excess of a "marriage dinner" in 1678. The couple, though nonconformists, "made such a public business of it, inviting twenty mess [i.e. eighty dinner guests], keeping two days of feasting, had fiddlers" and pipers, and made "a sad compliance with the vain corrupt customs of the world." What especially disgusted the staunch nonconformists was that Mr. Ashburn, the Anglican minister who "refused to marry them," none the less invited himself to the feast.

Misson marked what he took to be a new feature of the later seventeenth century, the fashion among "persons of quality and many others who imitate them" of marrying quietly, privately, or clandestinely, away from the public gaze. The Frenchman's observation accords with other developments at this time, like the taste for private christenings and night-time funerals. Many of the élite were detaching themselves from the culture of neighbourliness and display, preferring quiet, private, and select solemnities to the public extravaganzas of the sort that Leonard Wheatcroft praised for their "mirth and melody." John Verney's wedding in London in May 1680 was described as "private," for example, but only to indicate that attendance was limited to close family members. There was certainly nothing clandestine about it, although the celebration was modest by gentry standards. Having concluded the religious formalities in church, the party adjourned to the Rummer in Queen Street for a dinner costing £3. 17s. . . .

No marriage was complete without consummation. Bridal couples and wedding guests alike knew that the time was rapidly approaching for the completion of "the act." In reality, of course, a large proportion of brides may already have lost their virginity, and some 20 per cent were already pregnant; but the fiction was maintained that the wedding night was the time for defloration. Given the double standard, it seems reasonable to assume that a higher proportion of bridegrooms were already sexually initiated, though not necessarily competent or experienced. Bulstrode Whitelock's[62] wedding night in 1630 was a disaster for bride

---

[61] Member of a religious group that rejected the worship of the Church of England.

[62] Member of Parliament and ambassador to Sweden (1605–1675).

and groom when "expecting marriage joys" they "met with strange discomforts." By contrast, a note of triumph appears in the Sussex merchant Samuel Jeake's entry in his diary for his wedding night in 1681, "devirgination."

To help them to their happiness, and to help establish plausible evidence of their consummation, wedding parties conventionally escorted the bridal couple to bed. Notoriously, the air was filled with sexual jokes and commendations. The bed itself might be flower-strewn, "decked with ribbons and scented with violets and essence of jasmine," if anyone had taken the trouble, and in older times under Roman Catholicism the bed itself would have been blessed or sprinkled with holy water.

By custom, at this point, the couple consumed a specially prepared drink, like the strengthening caudle[63] given to newly delivered mothers. The "sack posset," made of fortified wine and spices, was supposed to relax the woman and embolden the man. According to Samuel Pepys, the sack was to make him lusty, the sugar to make him kind. . . . When Oliver Cromwell threw sack posset over the women's dresses at his daughter's wedding in 1646, his action was interpreted as a ribald jest.

An associated tradition was "throwing the stocking," which was a prelude to the sight of four bare legs in a bed. If the wedding party followed custom, when they crowded into the bridal chamber, they played a rowdy game with the bride's and bridegroom's hose. Such was the practice at some courtly and gentry weddings, as well as in popular ballads. Unlike the modern divination practice, in which the woman who catches the bridal bouquet is thought next in line for the altar, the stockings were thrown at, not by, the married couple. "And after it comes the bride-groom who when he was in bed, the stocking being mentioned, the bride must sit up to have it thrown at her nose, that the bachelors may know by him that first hits it, who is to be married next."

When it came to the bedding of the bride, the traveller Henri Misson so out-did himself as an ethnographic reporter that his late Stuart description deserves to be given at length.

> When bed-time is come the bride-men pull off the bride's garters, which she had before untied that they might hang down and so prevent a curious hand coming too near her knee. This done, and the garters being fastened to the hats of the gallants, the bride-maids carry the bride into the bed chamber, where they undress her and lay her in bed. The bridegroom, who by the help of his friends is undressed in some other room, comes in his night-gown as soon as possible to his spouse, who is surrounded by mother, aunt, sisters, and friends, and without any further ceremony gets into bed. Some of the women run away, others remain, and the moment afterwards they are all got together again. The bride-men take the bride's stockings, and the bride-maids the bridegroom's; both sit down at the bed's feet and fling the stockings over their heads, endeavouring to direct them so as that they may fall upon the married couple. If the man's stockings,

---

[63] A warm, spiced and sugared gruel with wine or ale added.

thrown by the maids, fall upon the bride-groom's head, it is a sign she will quickly be married herself; and the same prognostic holds good of the woman's stockings thrown by the man. Oftentimes these young people engage with one another upon the success of the stockings, though they themselves look upon it to be nothing but sport. While some amuse themselves agreeably with these little follies, others are preparing a good posset, which is a kind of caudle, a potion made up of milk, wine, yolks of eggs, sugar, cinnamon, nutmeg, etc.. This they present to the young couple, who swallow it down as fast as they can to get rid of so troublesome company; the bridegroom prays, scolds, entreats them to be gone, and the bride says ne'er a word, but thinks the more. If they obstinately continue to retard the accomplishment of their wishes, the bridegroom jumps up in his shirt, which frightens the women and puts them to flight. The men follow them, and the bridegroom returns to the bride.

Not until these rituals were accomplished would the couple be left in peace. And even then they might be interrupted by drums and fiddles, and the noise of drunken laughter, which might greet them again in the morning. Leonard Wheatcroft's wedding guests put the couple to bed "with no small ado," and had to be chased from the room, the bridegroom writes, "so that none might seem to hinder or molest us from our nearer unitings." Next morning, awakened by music from "our bed of pleasure," the dutiful Leonard sought a blessing from Elizabeth's father, "who was then made my father-in-law, for I had lain with his daughter." Noting the omission of this ritual at a "private" wedding in 1667, Samuel Pepys commented, "there was no music in the morning to call up our new-married people, which is very mean methinks, and is as if they had married like dog and bitch." As Pepys's observation suggests, Hymen's revels were loosely scripted, with nothing to enforce them but the tyrannies, sanctions, and vagaries of custom.

ACKNOWLEDGMENTS

Vern L. Bullough, Brenda Shelton, and Sarah Slavin, "Formation of Western Attitudes Toward Women" from *The Subordinate Sex: A History of Attitudes Toward Women.* Copyright © 1988 by The University of Georgia Press. Reprinted with the permission of the publishers.

Isaac Mendelsohn, "Slavery in the Near East" from *Biblical Archaeologist* 9 (December 1946). Reprinted with the permission of *Biblical Archaeologist.*

Jean Soler, "Why the Hebrews Kept Kosher" [Editor's title. Originally titled "The Semiotics of Food in the Bible"] from Robert Forster and Orest Ranum (eds.), *Food and Drink in History.* Copyright © 1979 by The Johns Hopkins University Press. Reprinted with the permission of the publishers.

K. A. Kitchen, "Workaday Life under Ramesses the Great" from *Pharaoh Triumphant: The Life and Times of Ramesses II, King of Egypt.* Reprinted by permission.

William J. Baker, "Organized Greek Games" from *Sports in the Western World.* Copyright © 1982. Reprinted with the permission of Rowman and Littlefield Publishers.

K. J. Dover, "Classical Greek Attitudes to Sexual Behavior" from John Peradotto and J. P. Sullivan (eds.), *The Arethusa Papers, Volume 6: Women in the Ancient World.* Copyright © 1984 by the State University of New York. Reprinted with the permission of the State University of New York Press. All rights reserved.

Suzanne Dixon, "Roman Marriage" from *The Roman Family.* Copyright © 1992 by The Johns Hopkins University Press. Reprinted with the permission of the publishers.

Paul Veyne, "Pleasures and Excesses in the Roman Empire" from Philippe Ariès and Georges Duby (eds.), *A History of Private Life, Volume I: From Pagan Rome to Byzantium.* Copyright © 1987 by the President and Fellows of Harvard College. Reprinted with the permission of Harvard University Press.

Alex Scobie, "Slums, Sanitation, and Mortality in the Roman World" from *Klio,* 68 (1986): 399–433. Reprinted with the permission of the publishers.

Elaine Pagels, "God the Father/God the Mother: The Gnostic Gospels and the Suppression of Early Christian Feminism" from *The Gnostic Gospels.* Copyright © 1979 by Elaine Pagels. Reprinted with the permission of Random House, Inc.

Georges Duby, "Rural Economy and Country Life in the Medieval West," translated by Cynthia Postan. Copyright © 1968. Reprinted with the permission of the University of South Carolina Press and Hodder Headline PLC.

David Herlihy, "Medieval Children" from Bede Karl Lackner and Kenneth Roy Phillip, eds., *Essays on Medieval Civilization.* Copyright © 1978 by the University of Texas at Arlington. Reprinted with the permission of the Walter Prescott Webb Memorial Lecture Committee at the University of Texas at Arlington.

Jacques Rossiaud, "Sexual Order and the Subversion of Youth" from *Medieval Prostitution,* translated by Lydia Cochrane. Copyright © 1988. Reprinted with the permission of Blackwell Publishers, Ltd.

David Herlihy, "The Family in Renaissance Italy" from *The Family in Renaissance Italy.* Copyright © 1974 by The Forum Press, Inc. Reprinted with the permission of Harlan Davidson Inc.

John Keegan, "The Face of Battle: Agincourt, October 25th, 1415" from *The Face of Battle: A Study of Agincourt, Waterloo and the Somme.* Copyright © 1976 by John Keegan. Reprinted with the permission of Viking, a division of Penguin Putnam Inc.

Norbert Elias, "The Development of Manners" from *The Civilizing Process: The History of Manners, Volume 1: Sociogenetic and Psychogenetic Investigations.* Translation copyright © 1978 by Urizen Books, Inc. Reprinted by permission.

R. Po-Chia Hsia, "A Ritual Murder Trial of Jews in Germany" from *The Myth of Ritual Murder: Jews and Magic in Reformation Germany.* Copyright © 1988 by Yale University. Reprinted with the permission of Yale University Press.

William H. McNeill, "Transoceanic Disease Exchanges, 1500–1700" from *Plagues and Peoples.* Copyright © 1976 by William H. McNeill. Reprinted with the permission of Doubleday, a division of the Bantam Doubleday Dell Publishing Group, Inc.

Edward Muir, "Carnival, Charivari, and Rites of Violence" from *Ritual in Early Modern Europe*. Reprinted with the permission of Cambridge University Press.

Merry Wiesner, "Nuns, Wives, and Mothers: Women and the Reformation in Germany" from Sherrin Marshall, ed., *Women in Reformation and Counter-Reformation Europe: Public and Private Worlds*. Copyright © 1989 by Indiana University Press. Reprinted with the permission of the publishers.

Sara F. Matthews Grieco, "The Body, Appearance, and Sexuality" from Natalie Zemon Davis and Arlette Farge (eds.), *Renaissance and Enlightenment Paradoxes, Volume III: A History of Women in the West*. Copyright © 1993 by the President and Fellows of Harvard College. Reprinted with the permission of The Belknap Press of Harvard University Press.

Robin Briggs, "The Witch-Figure and the Sabbat" from *Witches and Neighbors: The Social and Cultural Context of European Witchcraft*. Copyright © 1996 by Robin Briggs. Reprinted with the permission of Viking, a division of Penguin Putnam, Inc.

Natalie Z. Davis, "The Rites of Violence: Religious Riot in Sixteenth-Century France" from *Past and Present: A Journal of Historical Studies* 29 (May 1973). Reprinted with the permission of the Past and Present Society and the author.

David Cressy, "Wedding Celebrations in Tudor and Stuart England" from *Birth, Marriage and Death: Ritual, Religion and the Life-Cycle in Tudor and Stuart England*. Reprinted with the permission of Oxford University Press, Ltd.